MANAGERIAL ACCOUNTING

Fifth Edition

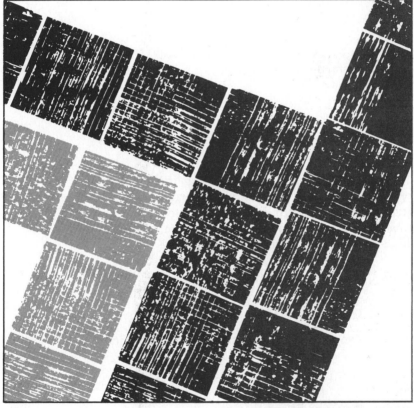

CARL L. MOORE, MA, CPA
Professor of Accounting
Lehigh University

ROBERT K. JAEDICKE, PhD
William R. Kimball Professor of Accounting
Stanford University

914 738-3600

Published by

A94 **SOUTH-WESTERN PUBLISHING CO.**

CINCINNATI   WEST CHICAGO, ILL.   DALLAS   PELHAM MANOR, N.Y.   PALO ALTO, CALIF.

ISBN: 0-538-01940-9

Library of Congress Catalog Card Number: 78-63605

1 2 3 4 5 6 7 8 9 K 8 7 6 5 4 3 2 1 0

Printed in the United States of America

PREFACE

The objective of this edition of *Managerial Accounting*, as it was in the earlier editions, is to explain how accounting data can be interpreted and applied by management in planning and controlling business activities. The major purpose of this book is to show how accounting can help to solve the problems that confront those who are directly responsible for the management of an enterprise. Attention is also given to the use of accounting data by investors and potential investors whenever appropriate.

In this edition, the basic structure has been changed to give the students a foundation in the fundamentals of managerial accounting at the beginning of the course. Many textbooks are now available that deal with the fundamentals of financial accounting in one semester. Hence, the authors believe that preliminary chapters, such as Chapters 1, 2, and 3 of the fourth edition, that deal with problems more peculiar to financial accounting are no longer necessary. These chapters have been eliminated from this edition. Material has been drawn from these chapters, as needed, and combined with a review for the students given in Appendix A at the end of the book.

The chapters have been rearranged and revised extensively in an effort to concentrate more completely on the problems of managerial accounting. The book has two parts: Part I, Planning and Control, (Chapters 1 through 7) and Part II, Analysis and Decision Making, (Chapters 8 through 15).

The budget concept is introduced in the first chapter in a simple form to show the student that a budget plan comes first and permeates all aspects of the managerial function. In Chapter 2, attention is directed to costs and how they can be used for planning and control. Chapter 3 deals with how costs are estimated and used for control. The chapters that follow discuss profit planning, product costs, and standard costs to complete Part I.

In Part II, the more specialized managerial decisions are discussed along with topics such as price level, analysis of financial statements, and net working capital and cash flows that are important to both financial and managerial accounting. The overall managerial theme is brought together in the final chapter on the master budget plan.

At the end of each chapter, as in earlier editions, are questions, exercises, and problems. Present value tables are given at the back of the book for use in working some of the problems for Chapter 10. The questions may be used as a basis for classroom discussion, or they may be used by the student to review the chapter. Essential points are included in the questions in the order in which they are presented in the chapters. The exercises are simple problem situations to help the student apply the concepts discussed in the chapters. The problems are more rigorous than the exercises and are usually listed in order of difficulty or according to the amount of time required for solutions. All exercises and problems retained from earlier editions have been revised. In this edition, exercises and problems have been added, with special attention being given to shorter exercises and problems that should provide more flexibility and a variety of situations for assignment.

The book is intended for a one-semester or a one-quarter course for students who expect to use accounting data in their future occupations. We believe that accounting majors will benefit from this material as much as those students who are studying other fields of business and economics but who are not going to be professional accountants. After all, professional accountants must be as familiar with the use of data as they are with its collection and presentation. It is important for professional accountants to know the *why* as well as the *how*. Students should use this book after having had a one-semester or two-quarter course in the introductory principles of accounting. Students who need a review of introductory accounting are referred to Appendixes A and B, which deal concisely with the accounting cycle. Also, students who are not familiar with the present value concept should study Appendix C before Chapter 10 is covered.

The chapters may be assigned in sequence, or they may be assigned in a different order, depending upon the background of the class and the objectives of the course. With students who need a review of basic accounting, it may be helpful to start with Appendixes A and B. Some instructors may prefer to start with Chapter 2 and take up budgets at the end of the course by combining the material from

Chapters 1 and 15. Inasmuch as the price-level problem has recently received much attention, some instructors may want to give it emphasis by starting with Chapter 12 and continuing with statement analysis in Chapter 13 and the flow of net working capital and cash in Chapter 14 before going to Chapter 1.

The authors acknowledge with gratitude the many helpful comments received from instructors and students who have used the fourth edition. Particular recognition is given for the help received from Professors F. B. Flores, University of Texas at El Paso; Robert Graham, Baldwin-Wallace; and James Wallis, Wayne State University.

In addition, we are grateful to the Literary Executor of the late Sir Ronald A. Fisher, F.R.S., to Dr. Frank Yates, F.R.S., and to Longman Group Ltd., London, for permission to reprint a segment of Table III from their book *Statistical Tables for Biological, Agricultural and Medical Research* (6th edition, 1974).

We are indebted for the use of materials included in the publications of the American Institute of Certified Public Accountants, the Financial Accounting Standards Board, and the National Association of Accountants.

Carl L. Moore
Robert K. Jaedicke

CONTENTS

**MANAGERIAL ACCOUNTING: DEFINITION
AND FRAMEWORK**   **1**

Scope of Managerial Accounting, 1/ The Objective of Management, 2/ The
Method of Management, 3/ Planning and control Decisions, 3/ Classification
of Decisions by Function and Time Element, 5/ The Contribution of the Accountant, 5/ Planning, 6/ Control, 8/ The Use of Accounting Data, 9.

PART ONE • PLANNING AND CONTROL

1 THE BUDGETING PROCESS   **10**

The Advantages of Budgets, 10/ The Scope of Budgeting, 11: Flexible Budget,
12; Project or Product Budget, 12; Responsibility Budget, 13; Capital Investment Budget, 13/ **Personal Attitudes, 13/ Master Budget Plan, 14/ The Budget
Period, 15/ The Timing Concept, 15/ Preparation of the Budgets, 16/ Budget
Illustration, 17/ Sensitivity to Changes, 21.**

2 COSTS FOR PLANNING AND CONTROL   **30**

Costs, 30: Fixed and Variable Costs, 31; The Troublesome Fixed Costs, 32/
Costs and Control, 33: Direct and Indirect Costs, 34; Cost Allocations, 35; Con-
trollable and Noncontrollable Costs, 37/ **Responsibility Accounting, 38**: Cost
Reports, 39; Some Difficulties with Responsibility Accounting, 41; Control Fea-
tures, 42/ **Costs and Planning, 43**: Differential Costs, 44; Irrelevant Costs, 45;
Sunk Costs, 46; Opportunity Costs, 47; An Illustration of Decision-Making
Costs, 47.

3 COST ESTIMATION AND CONTROL   **61**

The Cost Estimation Problem, 61: Significance of Cost Estimation, 62; Cost Segregation, 62; The Visual Fit, 63; The High-Low Point Method, 64; The Line of Regression Method, 64/ **Control Limits, 66**: Normal Distribution, 67; Checking Some Inferences, 69/ **Correlation, 70**: The r^2 Test, 72; The t-Value, 73; Other Considerations, 75; Multiple Regression, 75.

4 PROFIT PLANNING   **87**

Break-Even Analysis, 88: The Break-Even Chart, 89; Cost Detail on the Break-Even Chart, 90; Curvature of Revenue and Cost Lines, 90; An Alternative Form of Break-Even Analysis, 92/ **The Profit-Volume Graph, 93**: Sales Volume, 94; Variable Costs, 95; Price Policy, 97; Fixed Costs, 99; Changes in the Sales Mix, 101/ **Short-Term and Long-Term Plans, 104.**

5 PRODUCT OR PROJECT COSTS   **116**

Costs, 116: Cost Transitions, 117; Period Cost, 117; Product Cost, 118; Cost Accounting Beyond the Manufacturing Area, 118; The Cost Elements, 119; The Costing Procedure, 120/ **The Job Order Cost System, 120**: Costing Direct Materials and Direct Labor, 120; Costing the Factory Overhead, 122; Control of Factory Overhead, 125; Disposition of the Overhead Variance, 126; Normal Capacity, 127/ **A Job Order Cost Illustration, 128/ The Process Cost System, 131**: The Departmental Production Report, 131; A Process Cost Flow, 132; The Equivalent Unit Concept, 134; The Cost Elements, 135/ **Process Cost Accounting Problems, 136**: Joint Product Costing, 136; The Product Mix Decision, 137; Time Constraints, 139.

6 MATERIALS AND LABOR CONTROL   **154**

The Use of Standards, 154/ Advantages of Standard Cost Accounting, 155/ The Quality of Standards, 157/ Revising the Standards, 159/ Materials Standards and Control, 159: Materials Price Variance, 160; Materials Quantity Variance, 161; Materials Acquisition, 163; The Inventory Level, 164; Balancing Order and Storage Costs, 165; Shipping Routes, 167/ **Labor Standards and Control, 169:** Labor Rate Variance, 169; Labor Efficiency Variance, 170; Additions to Labor Cost, 171; Incentives, 172; The Learning Curve, 173/ **Summary of Variances, 175.**

7 FACTORY OVERHEAD CONTROL   **189**

A Flexible Budget and Variances, 189: Overhead Variances, 191; The Spending Variance, 191; The Efficiency Variance, 192; The Controllable Variance, 192; Capacity or Volume Variance, 193; Plant Capacity and Control, 194/ **Summary of Overhead Variances, 196/ A Standard Cost Illustration, 197/ Nonmanufacturing Costs, 200.**

PART TWO • ANALYSIS AND DECISION MAKING

8 VARIABLE COSTING   **216**

Absorption Costing, 216/ Variable Costing, 218/Absorption and Variable Costing Compared, 218/ A Balance of Sales and Production, 220/ Sales and Production Out of Balance, 222/ Profits and Inventory, 225/ Emphasis on Production or Sales, 226/ The Advantages of Variable Costing, 226/ The Disadvantages of Variable Costing, 227/ Variable Costing in Planning and Decision Making, 228/ Variable Costing and Budget Variances, 229.

9 ACCOUNTING DATA FOR MANAGERIAL DECISIONS   **245**

Relevant Cost Data for Decision Making, 245: Costs and Decisions — An Illustration, 246; Opportunity Cost, 247/ **Combination Decisions, 247:** Process or Sell, 248; Product Combinations, 248; Two Products, No Constraints, 249; Two Products, One Constraint, 249; Two Products, Many Constraints, 251; Make or Buy, 253; The Elimination of a Product Line, 254/ **The Pricing Decision, 255:** Price Based on Full Cost, 256; Variable Cost Pricing, 259; Outside Influences on Price, 262.

10 THE CAPITAL INVESTMENT DECISION   **275**

The Investment Problem, 276/ Factors in the Investment Decision, 276: The Net Investment, 277; The Net Returns, 277; The Lowest Acceptable Rate of Return, 278/ **Rating Investment Alternatives, 278:** The Payback Method, 279; The Discounted Rate-of-Return Method, 279; The Net Present Value Method, 281/ **Refining the Investment, 282:** Avoidable Costs, 282; Additional Investment in Current Assets, 283; Net Proceeds from the Sale of Other Properties, 284/ **Depreciation and Income Tax, 285/ Accelerated Depreciation, 287/ Incremental Returns, 290/ A Graphic Solution, 291/ The Evaluation Process, 292/ Anticipation of Change, 292/ The Post Audit, 293.**

11 MANAGERIAL CONTROL AND DECISION MAKING IN
DECENTRALIZED OPERATIONS   **302**

The Criteria Needed for a Control System, 303/ The Profit Index, 305: Division Net Profit, 306; Division Direct Profit, 306; Division Controllable Profit, 307; Division Contribution Margin, 307/ **Some Problems in Using Division Controllable Profit as an Evaluation Index, 308/ Determining Division Investment, 309/ The Intracompany or Transfer Pricing Problem, 312:** Market Price, 312; Negotiated or Bargained Market Price, 314; Transfer Price Based on Cost, 315; Dual Transfer Prices, 316/ **Transfer Prices for Decision Making — A System of Information and Communication, 318:** The Intermediate Market Case, 319; The No Intermediate Market Case, 322/ **The Evaluation Criterion or Standard, 323.**

12 THE PRICE-LEVEL PROBLEM   **338**

General and Specific Prices, 339/ Matching Current Cost Against Revenue, 340: Lifo vs Fifo, 341; Accelerated Depreciation, 342/ **Replacement Costs, 343/ Price Level — Index Adjustments, 346/ The Character of Assets and Equities, 347:** Monetary Items, 347; Nonmonetary Items, 347/ **Financial Statements and Index Conversions, 348/ Current Value and the Price Index, 355/ Dividend Policy, 357/ The Price Level and Management Policy, 358.**

13 ANALYSIS OF FINANCIAL STATEMENTS   **373**

Rate-of-Return Concept, 374: Rate of Return — Assets, 374; Net Income, 374; The Asset Base, 375; Asset Turnover and Rate of Return, 376/ **The Management of Assets, 377:** The Combination of Assets, 377; Direct Materials, 377; Direct Labor, 378; Factory Overhead, 378; Rate of Return by Segment, 378; Depreciable Assets, 379/ **Leverage, 380/ Earnings and Market Value of Stock, 383/ Comprehensive Analysis, 384/ Some Hazards of Analysis, 385:** A Mixture of Valuations, 385; Differences Between Companies, 385; Variations in Accounting Methods and Estimates, 385; An Average Concept, 386/ **Illustration of Analysis, 386/ A Review of Earning Power, 387/ The Management of Working Capital, 389:** Current Asset Turnover, 390; Current and Acid-Test Ratios, 390; Accounts Receivable Turnover, 391; Inventory Turnovers, 392/ **The Equity Relationships, 393/ Net Income and Fixed Charges, 393/ An Evaluation of the Company, 394.**

14 TRACING THE FLOW OF NET WORKING CAPITAL AND CASH   **411**

Description and Evaluation of the Statements, 411/ The Significance of Net Working Capital Flows, 412/ Net Working Capital Flows 413: Sources of Net Working Capital, 414; Uses of Net Working Capital, 416/ **A Comprehensive Illustration — Sources and Uses of Net Working Capital, 417/ Schedule of Changes in Net Working Capital, 418:** Net Working Capital from Operations, 419; Analysis of Noncurrent Items, 420; Statement of Sources and Uses of Net Working Capital, 421; Statement of Changes in Financial Position, 422/ **The Demand for Net Working Capital, 422/ Cash Flow, 423:** Cash and Operations, 424; Analysis of Other Current Items, 428; A Statement of Cash Flow, 429; Simplified Cash Flow from Operations, 429.

15 A MASTER BUDGET PLAN   **452**

Budget Limitations, 452: Budget Relationships, 453/ **Sales Forecasting and the Sales Budget, 455/ Sales and Production, 457/ Inventories and Production, 458/ The Production Budget Illustrated, 459/ The Manufacturing Cost Budget, 460:** The Direct Materials Budget, 460; The Purchases Budget, 461; The Direct Labor Budget, 462; The Factory Overhead Budget, 464/ **The Selling Expense Budget, 465/ The General and Administrative Expense Budget, 466/ The Capital Budget, 467/ The Cash Receipts Budget, 468/ The Cash Payments Budget, 470/ Financial Planning, 471/ The Estimated Income Statement, 473/ The Estimated Balance Sheet, 476/ Work Sheet, 477/ The Use of Budgets, 479.**

APPENDIX A/AN OVERVIEW OF THE ACCOUNTING PROCESS   **496**

APPENDIX B/THE ACCOUNTING CYCLE PRACTICE PROBLEMS   **535**

APPENDIX C/THE PRESENT VALUE CONCEPT   **542**

Table I — Present Value of $1, 551
Table II — Present Value of $1 Received Annually for N Years, 552

INTRODUCTION
Managerial Accounting: Definition and Framework

Managerial accounting or *management accounting* is a segment of accounting that deals specifically with how accounting data and other financial information can be used in the management of business, governmental, or not-for-profit entities. Because managerial accounting is designed to assist internal management, it is relatively free from the restrictions imposed by regulatory bodies that prescribe how accounting information should be presented to the public.

Although managerial accounting is to a large extent free from restrictions, it does rely upon broad general concepts and certain applications that are most useful to management. Specific applications in given situations, however, depend upon the needs and preferences of the individual managers who are to receive the information.

SCOPE OF MANAGERIAL ACCOUNTING

Often it is thought that managerial accounting is a variation of cost accounting and that it deals exclusively with costs and prices. Cost and price data are very important, but management cannot afford to limit itself to this area.

Management wants to consider the total situation. For example, if management decides to finance business growth with long-term debt, it may question: What effect will this decision have upon the earnings

1

per share of stock? Will debt in the equity structure become too large in relation to the stockholders' equity? In still other situations, management may want to consider how it can guard against losses in purchasing power from rising prices or how it can plan a flow of cash receipts from operations that will be sufficient for the payment of current obligations.

Managerial accounting makes use of information that is drawn from financial accounting and may extend beyond the boundaries of accounting to draw upon economics, finance, statistics, operations research, or other disciplines as necessary.

THE OBJECTIVE OF MANAGEMENT

If managerial accounting is expected to serve management, it is necessary to consider the goals of management. It may seem that management is striving only to increase business volume or to maximize profit, but this may not be so.

Many enterprises do not even attempt to produce profit. A governmental agency may be primarily concerned with giving a needed service to the public. Individuals may also form an association for the purpose of promoting some common idea. The success of the enterprise is measured by the realization of an established common goal rather than in economic terms. However, the economic realities cannot be ignored. In any type of enterprise, management must use its resources in such a way that the desired goals will be attained in an efficient manner.

A *governmental unit*, for example, may make use of the profit concept in measuring whether or not resources have been used effectively and efficiently. Plans may be made with profit goals included and with activity conducted accordingly. Performance may then be rated by comparing the results with the resources and effort dedicated to the achievement of the objectives.

A *commercial enterprise*, of course, is normally interested in profit; management is judged according to its ability to earn profit from the resources entrusted to its care.

Modern management recognizes that business enterprise is also responsible to many persons who belong to diverse groups. For example, the general public expects to receive dependable products at a fair cost, and the employees depend upon the business for a means of livelihood. In addition, the business is expected to be a good neighbor in the community in which it operates. Various groups must be given recognition along with the owners and the creditors who have invested tangible resources in the enterprise. It is now generally understood that the interests of each group are best served by the harmonious reconciliation of all interests. Hence, the objective of maximizing the rate of profit must be accomplished within socially and legally accepted bounds.

THE METHOD OF MANAGEMENT

Management accomplishes its objectives by working with people. The efforts of many individuals are combined in an organization. The top-level management, as it is called, assumes responsibility for overall planning and policy formation. Decisions that affect the business as a whole are made in a corporate form of organization by the president, the vice-presidents, and other officers. The work of the organization is divided so that each officer has authority to act in a given area of activity. For example, one vice-president may be in charge of production, while another is in charge of sales.

Managers at the top level are unable to make all of the decisions. They are assisted by lower levels of management who make specific decisions in prescribed areas. A vice-president in charge of production may delegate the authority for plant operation to superintendents, each of whom assumes responsibility for the operation of a given plant. Part of the plant superintendent's authority may be delegated to section superintendents, who in turn depend upon departmental supervisors who are responsible for operations at the department level. Company policy is thus established and carried out with a hierarchy of managerial personnel extending from the president to the department supervisors. This division of work throughout the organization applies not only to production but to other functional areas as well.

PLANNING AND CONTROL DECISIONS

The decisions of management may be classified as planning and control decisions. In any type of enterprise, plans must be made to guide future operations. An enterprise must have its course charted and must be given direction in light of future expectations. A coordinated and detailed plan for the future is a *budget*. The various interrelated budgets of the operation are brought together and synchronized in a master or comprehensive budget. Included in the budget but extending beyond the current fiscal period are plans for the selection of new product lines, investments in new facilities or equipment, and ways of financing new investments.

Plans, of course, are not enough. There must be a follow-through. Steps must be taken to put the plans into operation and to see that they are being carried out as intended. Actual operations have to be directed and controlled if the plans are to be realized. Sometimes as operations progress it becomes necessary to revise the plans and to direct activities along a different course from that originally plotted. The decisions that pertain to the direction of actual business activity may be looked upon as decisions of control.

Both planning and control decisions are made at all levels of management. Top-level management, for example, may investigate new investment opportunities and may plan for the future by accepting or rejecting certain proposals. When a course of action has been decided upon, the results should be measured and compared with the original plan. Operations should be directed so that unfavorable tendencies are eliminated or at least minimized. Whenever necessary, the initial plan should be altered to fit a change in circumstances.

Supervisors may likewise make planning and control decisions within their own jurisdictions. It may be up to them to plan the work within their departments, to assign people to different tasks, and to guide operations in accordance with established plans.

A firm does not have complete freedom of choice in making decisions. Limitations are imposed by conditions in the marketplace and by other outside influences. A company may find it necessary to adjust to the demand for its products, the relative scarcity of productive factors, their cost, and other conditions that prevail. Basic managerial decisions of a business enterprise have often been classified under three general headings as decisions with respect to:

1. The methods of operation.
2. The size or scale of the operation and prices to be charged.
3. The combination of products or services to be offered.

Under the methods of operation, management considers the services to be rendered or products to be sold. In operating a motel, for example, will a restaurant be included and will limousine service to the airport be furnished? Should products be manufactured or should they be purchased in completed form for resale?

Management must also consider the size of the operation. How much service will be rendered or what quantity of products will be available for sale? In order to handle a given volume of business, the firm must have adequate resources. These resources must be in balance so that there will be sufficient cash to pay creditors, an adequate quantity of goods to deliver to customers, and satisfactory facilities to support the operation. Prices and costs are examined in relation to the volume of business conducted, and decisions are made that tend to maximize the rate of return on the resources invested.

If there is more than one product line or service to be considered, management has to select the combination that appears to be the most profitable. Prices and costs are identifiable with each product or service. In a combination situation, it may be better to concentrate attention on the product or service that yields the greatest profit. Further analysis may show, however, that profit can be improved by selling a combination that does not necessarily maximize the sale of the most profitable item.

These decisional classifications are mentioned for the sake of convenience. In practice, one type of decision cannot be isolated from another; they tend to blend together. A combination decision, for example, may very well influence methods of operation and the size of the operation.

CLASSIFICATION OF DECISIONS BY FUNCTION AND TIME ELEMENT

Managerial decisions may sometimes be classified under given functions such as sales, production, and finance. A decision may be spoken of as a sales decision or as a production decision. A decision to concentrate sales effort in a given area would be primarily a sales decision, whereas a decision to use a certain method in manufacturing would be primarily a production decision. The breakdown of decisions according to function and activity is possible in many cases.

However, there is some risk in the classification of decisions by function. Not all decisions can be classified. In some instances, decisions that appear to fall within a functional area will have a widespread effect upon the entire operation. It would seem, for example, that the decision to manufacture a part instead of buying it would be a production decision. Yet, the effect may extend beyond the production area. By producing parts, the company may be competing with its former suppliers. This in turn may have an effect upon sales, particularly if excess parts produced are sold on the market. It is also possible that the costs of administering the business will increase if parts are manufactured. Before going ahead with its plans, management should make certain that it has considered the total effect of these plans upon the enterprise as a unit.

It is also possible to classify decisions according to time element. Certain decisions have an effect for only a relatively short period of time, while others are so long-range as to have an impact extending many years into the future. A budget for the coming year would be a short-range plan. Likewise, an estimate of expected cash collections during the next three months would be a plan of short duration. On the other hand, a plan to construct a new plant or to lease properties would probably commit the enterprise to a course of action extending several years into the future. Decisions having an influence over a relatively long period of time are spoken of as long-range decisions.

THE CONTRIBUTION OF THE ACCOUNTANT

Management depends upon information in making decisions. Much of this information is provided within the framework of the managerial organization itself. Policies and instructions are transmitted to subordinates, who in return report to their superiors showing how well they have discharged the tasks assigned to them. Without these channels of communication, effective business management would be impossible.

The accountant is expected to furnish financial information. It is also the accountant's responsibility to maintain the financial records and to prepare the statements that present the financial position of the business, the changes in the financial position, and the results of operations. In addition, the accountant combines financial data in various ways in the preparation of reports that serve as a guide to management.

The accountant is not only a service arm to management but is a part of management. The controller of a company, for example, is responsible for the management of the accounting function, thus selecting ways to process accounting data and methods of presentation. In the accounting area itself, the principles of management are applied. What combination and quantity of reports should be prepared, how should they be prepared, and what is the best method of collecting data? By the nature of the work, the accountant is drawn into the management of the business and often assists in the decision-making process.

PLANNING

Planning through the use of budgets has already been pointed out as a highly significant management function. The accountant helps to bring together budget estimates and the results of various decisions to form a comprehensive plan for the future. Throughout this text, attention is given to the decision-making process. As mentioned earlier, management may question: Should the firm continue processing a product to its finished form or sell it partially processed, and should the firm make or buy the parts used in production? These individual decisions have ramifications throughout the firm and must be considered in the preparation of a comprehensive budget for the year. After all separate decisions have been made, the results can be brought together to form a coordinated budget of total sales revenue, total cost of operation, and a projection of the financial position.

Accounting data can be used selectively to fit special situations. Learning to use accounting data properly is very important in the process of mastering managerial accounting. Accounting data are like tools, and one must carefully select the appropriate accounting information to fit the specified requirement.

A plant manager, for example, may plan to introduce a new product line that can be sold for $15 per unit and has collected the following cost information:

Cost for each unit manufactured:

Materials	$ 5
Labor	3
Other costs	2
Increased cost per unit	$10

Plant facilities must be used; and the cost of rent, heat, light, insurance, and taxes assigned to this portion of the plant each year has been estimated at $6,000. To simplify the illustration, assume that there are no selling and administrative expenses for this product line.

The plant manager believes that 6,000 units of product can normally be manufactured and sold each year. On this basis the full cost to manufacture the product must be determined. The *full cost* is the total cost to produce the product including the apportioned cost of facilities used.

Full production cost:

	TOTAL COST (6,000 UNITS)	UNIT COST
Materials (6,000 × $5)	$30,000	$ 5
Labor (6,000 × $3)	18,000	3
Other costs (6,000 × $2)	12,000	2
Plant facility cost (unit cost: $6,000 ÷ 6,000)	6,000	1
Total	$66,000	$11

The total profit, after income tax at a 40 percent tax rate, has been estimated at $14,400.

Estimated total revenue (6,000 × $15)	$90,000
Estimated total cost (6,000 × $11)	66,000
Profit estimated before income tax	$24,000
Income tax (40%)	9,600
Profit estimated after income tax	$14,400

This estimate is good only if 6,000 units are manufactured and sold.

By using full cost, however, the manager knows that the product line can bear its share of the cost of facilities when 6,000 units are made and sold. The profit in relation to the investment made can also be evaluated. At this point, however, it is not known how much each unit sold contributes to profit nor is there a basis for comparing this line of product with a competing line that can be produced with the same facilities.

In selecting from alternative courses of action, the manager should consider only the *differential revenue* and *costs* (the revenue and costs that will be changed by the decision). Suppose that the facilities can also be used to manufacture a line of product that can be sold for $25 per unit and that the increased cost to produce each unit has been estimated at $17. However, the company can only manufacture and sell 5,000 of these units each year.

The additional revenue expected from the alternate product line when compared with the original is $35,000.

Revenue from alternative line (5,000 × $25)	$125,000
Revenue from original line (6,000 × $15)	90,000
Additional revenue expected	$ 35,000
Increased cost, alternative line (5,000 × $17)	$ 85,000
Increased cost, original line (6,000 × $10)	60,000
Additional cost expected	$ 25,000
Net advantage, alternative line	$ 10,000

With the information given, the alternative line is better. The cost of $6,000 to use the facilities each year may be disregarded in making the decision. It will be the same in either case.

In planning, both full costs and differential revenue and costs are relevant when used for given purposes. When a decision is to be made between alternatives, the differential revenue and costs should be used, not the full costs.

CONTROL

Strictly speaking, cost control is not so much a control over costs as it is a control over the people who incur the costs. No one likes to be controlled; however, any type of control, if it is to be successful, depends upon the willingness of people to accept certain objectives and the means by which the objectives may be attained. In the control area, the relevant costs are the costs that can be identified with the individual who authorizes the costs. This approach to accountability — cost identification with the responsible person — is called *responsibility accounting*.

To illustrate, assume that Lisa DeBrosse has prepared a budget of costs that she expects to incur in operating her department for the month of June, 1980. Actual results for the month are compared with the budget, as shown below.

Department 5
Manager — Lisa DeBrosse
Operations Report
For the Month of June, 1980

	Budget	Actual	Actual Over	Actual Under
Materials used	$18,400	$18,350		$ 50
Labor	14,600	14,800	$200	
Indirect materials and supplies	3,200	3,350	150	
Travel and entertainment	600	800	200	
Heat and light	150	450	300	
Repairs and maintenance	850	750		100
Miscellaneous	100	150	50	
Total	$37,900	$38,650	$900	$150

Assuming that the budget fits the level of operations with which it is compared, attention is immediately called to heat and light. What has caused the relatively large variance? With a knowledge of the department costs, DeBrosse can determine the reason for the variance and can use this information to prepare a more realistic budget and to exert tighter control over the operation. In many instances a monthly report is not sufficient. Sometimes a report of weekly or even daily costs may be required so that the costs can be brought under control more quickly.

THE USE OF ACCOUNTING DATA

The focus in this discussion of the framework of managerial accounting has been on the idea that management needs data in making decisions. The remainder of this text is devoted to showing how accounting data can be used in decision making, budget preparation, and control. Accounting data are useful to both the insider and the outsider; hence, the use of data by both types of users will be considered. For the most part, however, the problems of business management will receive attention. Problems that arise in the collection and the processing of data are not of primary concern. The important problem is the use of data by management, and this use will be emphasized.

1

THE BUDGETING PROCESS

One of the most important functions of management is planning. In this chapter, attention is directed primarily to that part of planning that relates to the preparation of a comprehensive budget for a fiscal period. Usually a budget covers a period of one year, defined as a fiscal year, and is broken down as desired by months or quarters of a year.

A *budget* is a plan showing how resources are to be acquired and used over a specified time interval. While operations are in progress, the budget serves as a basis for comparison and facilitates the control process. The use of a budget as a means for controlling activity is called *budgetary control*. Also, information derived from operations is used in forming better budgets for the future.

Budgeting and budgetary control operate together as essential features of a total management system. The system is set forth in the diagram on the following page. If investigation reveals that the plan is satisfactory but that performance can be improved, steps are taken to bring future performance into line with the plan. If investigation reveals that the plan is unsatisfactory, the plan is corrected. These corrective actions are shown on the diagram as the feedback loops.

THE ADVANTAGES OF BUDGETS

Budgets are tools that are made and used by management. Benefits can be derived from the budgeting process, although budgeting is

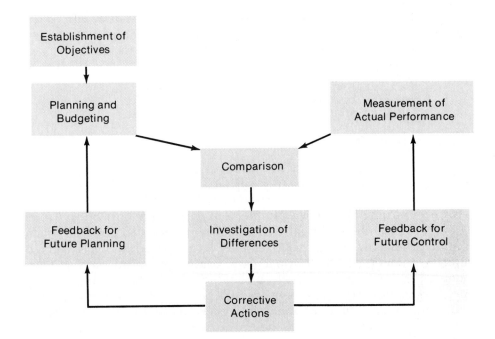

not an end in itself. By preparing a budget, management is forced to look ahead and to consider how the various functions of a business fit together. Some of the more significant advantages of budgets and budget preparation are as follows:

1. Budgeting is a means of coordinating activities with the cooperation of those who seek to achieve a common goal.
2. Budgeting helps to make the various members of management aware of the problems faced by others and the factors that interlock in running a business organization.
3. A budget is more than speculation; it is a workable pattern to be followed.
4. A budget places an obligation upon the enterprise to maintain adequate financial records that can be tied in with the budget.
5. With a budget, all people in the organization become conscious of the need to conserve business resources.
6. Efficient or inefficient use of resources is revealed by budgets intended for that purpose.
7. A budget gives management a means for self-evaluation and can be used to measure progress.

THE SCOPE OF BUDGETING

Budgeting and budgetary control are at the heart of the managerial planning and control process. Therefore, in studying managerial accounting it is appropriate to start with the concepts that underlie the overall budgeting process. In subsequent chapters, attention is directed to specialized budgets that are prepared for particular purposes. These budgets, however, also fit within the framework of the comprehensive budget for the company or entity. Examples of specialized budgets are listed below and discussed briefly at this point.

1. A flexible budget.
2. A project or product budget.
3. A responsibility cost budget.
4. A capital investment budget.

Flexible Budget

A *flexible budget* is in reality a series of cost budgets, each prepared for a different level of operating activity. Activity levels may be expressed as units of output, direct-labor hours, machine hours, or any other appropriate base. For example, a departmental cost budget may be prepared for the practical number of hours used to obtain a given volume of output. Another budget may be prepared for the expected number of hours used to obtain a given volume of output. Still another budget may be prepared for the amount of output that should be produced if the department is used at 100 percent of its rated capacity. Additional budgets may be made for other hours of operation. Collectively, the budget for various hours of operation is called a flexible budget.

A summarized flexible budget is given below for Department B of Hadden Company for four different estimates of hours of operation.

Hours of operation	15,000	20,000	25,000	30,000
Indirect materials and supplies	$ 45,000	$ 60,000	$ 75,000	$ 90,000
Lubrication	37,500	50,000	62,500	75,000
Power	20,000	25,000	30,000	35,000
Heat and light	16,000	21,000	26,000	31,000
Maintenance and repairs	13,000	16,000	19,000	22,000
Depreciation	5,000	5,000	5,000	5,000
Total	$136,500	$177,000	$217,500	$258,000

Project or Product Budget

A budget for a particular segment of a business such as a project or a product line, serves as a general guideline to the probable results of that particular activity. For example, total cost to remodel a portion of a building can be budgeted and then actual cost can be compared with the budget. Similarly, revenue and costs can be budgeted for various product lines. Fixed costs may be allocated, as a separate item, to determine whether or not the activity or product line can bear its share of total fixed cost. Budgets prepared in this way provide an overall picture of various functions and projects. However, an overall picture may not be suitable as a means of personalized control. Various persons may be responsible for individual costs of a function or project with no one person being responsible for the total operation.

Responsibility Budget

A budget that identifies revenue and costs with the individual responsible for their incurrence, a *responsibility* or *control budget*, is more suitable for control purposes. In this type of budget, revenue and costs are not allocated but are identified directly with the responsible individual. A departmental supervisor, for example, has a budget for the department which includes only revenue and costs that are subject to the supervisor's control. Actual data from operations are then accumulated, and a comparison with the budget shows whether or not the supervisor achieved what was expected. A budget of this type localizes differences between the budget and actual operations, making it possible to measure individual performance. In responsibility accounting, the manager budgets the costs that he or she controls and thus has a valuable tool for evaluating his or her own performance.

Capital Investment Budget

In many cases a *capital investment budget* is a long-range plan for the acquisition of facilities or equipment or for an investment in an intangible item such as a patent that yields benefits for a relatively long period of time. A *capital investment* is an investment that is expected to yield benefits over a relatively long life. Capital investment planning may extend five, ten, or more years into the future with each annual segment of the plan being brought into the appropriate comprehensive budget.

PERSONAL ATTITUDES

The term "budget," like the terms "restriction" or "rationing," evokes negative emotions. A budget imposes restraint and, hence, is not favorably received by many individuals. The discipline of a budget, however, is necessary and is accepted reluctantly as a means to attain a desired goal.

The negative aspects of budgeting may be minimized, if not eliminated entirely, by an enlightened management. If top management does not judge a subordinate manager too closely by demanding strict adherence to a budget, the budget tends to be more realistic and as a result is more valuable to the company. The person to whom the budget applies is more likely to cooperate if some latitude has been permitted in the preparation of the budget and in any subsequent revision. A top management that is aware of how persons tend to react in certain situations formulates budget policy to motivate individuals to cooperate in achieving desired goals.

An authoritarian type of manager who overemphasizes conformity with a budget may encourage tacit compliance. Yet operations may not in fact be controlled as strictly as it would appear. Lower levels of management armed with a detailed knowledge of a particular function or operation tend to overstate cost budgets or understate revenue budgets, that is, incorporate budget slack.[1] During periods of reasonably good business, for example, a manager may budget costs higher than necessary and with a minimum of control may meet the budget. When business conditions are less favorable, cost saving programs may be introduced. The manager with slack in the budget may then give up some of the slack to receive credit for cost savings, savings that could have been obtained before.

Sometimes, particularly with governmental entities, an unexpended appropriation for a given purpose expires at the end of a fiscal year. The manager, knowing that the unexpended balance cannot be carried over to another year, is encouraged to spend the balance before the end of the year and as a result may not spend it wisely. If the balance is not spent, the manager fears that the budget request for the next year will be reduced. A better practice would be to encourage thrift and to permit a carryover of unexpended balances to future budgets if a need for later expenditure can be justified.

A preoccupation with the budget as a means of rewarding or penalizing managers can have a backlash effect. Managers tend to view the budget negatively and consider the budgeting operation a game to be played against higher levels of management. The result may be that operations are not controlled realistically, and the company is not making the best use of budgeting and budgetary control.

MASTER BUDGET PLAN

The types of budgets discussed earlier in the chapter are not separate in the sense that they are unrelated. Costs that are budgeted by project or product line can also be budgeted according to the individual responsible for incurring the costs. The costs may be collected and reported in various ways, but they are brought together in one coordinated master budget for the firm. The master budget plan will be discussed in greater detail in Chapter 15.

The computer has made it possible to rearrange costs and other data in many different ways with relatively little clerical effort. If basic information is entered on a punched card, magnetic tape, or other input media, it can be processed to serve different purposes. For example, actual and budgeted costs can be classified by product line, by territory, or by any other relevant basis and can be brought together in a total budget report for the firm. The realignment of costs for different cost reports would be a formidable task if it were carried out manually, but the task is relatively easy for a computer. Furthermore, the costs can be reconciled with little risk of error.

---

[1]Mohamed Onsi, "Factor Analysis of Behavioral Variables Affecting Budgetary Slack," *The Accounting Review*, Vol. XLVIII, No. 3 (July, 1973), pp. 535–548.

THE BUDGET PERIOD

The length of the budget period may be a week, a month, a quarter of a year, a year, or even more than a year. There is no set interval of time. The duration depends upon how the budget is to be used. Normally, a budget is made for a year and is divided into months or quarters of a year. In any case it should be complete, tracing an activity or a project from the time it starts until it ends. The comprehensive operating budget, for example, should cover at least one cycle of operations. The cycle that begins with plans to purchase merchandise extends to a sales budget, a cash collection budget, and plans to repay any debt incurred to finance the purchase of the merchandise.

A budget for the acquisition of capital investments may be made for five or more years into the future. The plans for later years will probably be somewhat indefinite, because they are based upon long-term prospects. With the passage of time, the plans should be revised to reflect current conditions.

Generally, some provision is made for revising the budget and bringing it up to date. After a few months have elapsed, it may be quite evident that the budget for the year no longer applies. Usually at the end of the first quarter or at some other designated time, the budget is reviewed and corrections are made as necessary.

Sometimes a *rolling* or *progressive budget* is used. When a month goes by, the budget is extended one more month into the future. At the end of February, for example, a budget for the following February is added; and at the end of March, a budget for the following March is added, and so forth. Budgeting is then a continual process. There is always a budget for a year in advance; and as time passes, the budgets for future months are adjusted as circumstances warrant.

Often it is desirable to compare one month with another; but the comparison may be distorted merely because of the variations in the lengths of months. Perhaps more business may be transacted in January than in February because there are more days in January. On a comparable time basis, the business volume may be constant. Some companies eliminate these arbitrary differences by dividing their fiscal year into 13 periods of four weeks each, thereby making it possible to compare one period of the year with another.

THE TIMING CONCEPT

In business planning, however, time is not looked upon only as a means for measuring intervals such as months or years. Allowance must also be made for the sequential flow of events and the time required for events to unfold and influence different parts of the total operation. Activities and transactions are not translated into results right away in many instances, but instead they develop and reach fruition at some later date.

Timing the logical progression of events is also important in non-business situations. Heavy mountain snowfalls, for example, may result in spring floods for downstream areas; but the conditions leading to the floods precede them by several weeks. Steps may be taken to prepare for the floods, or, if possible, to prevent them.

Similarly, in business, plans are formulated so that all activities are synchronized. If a new plant is to be built, weeks or months may elapse before products can be manufactured and sold. When a new product line is to be added, it may take several months or years to develop its profit-making potential. Even in the normal course of operations, there is a natural sequence of events. If large purchases are made in certain months, some arrangement has to be made to pay the suppliers. Cash may be borrowed from the bank, or presently held cash reserves may be reduced. As cash is realized from subsequent sales, it may be applied to reduce loan balances, it may be retained, or it may be used in various ways.

PREPARATION OF THE BUDGETS

In budgeting, all functions and activities of the business are carefully interlocked. The plans for the manufacturing division must be tied in with the plans for the sales division. If large shipments are to be made to customers during particular months, the manufacturing division should have the products ready at that time. At a still earlier date, the materials to be used in production have to be ordered, allowing enough time for their receipt from suppliers and their conversion into finished products. This concept of timing and coordinating activities applies in all areas of budgeting.

A budget is prepared by combining the efforts of many individuals. Those who are in charge of a particular function or activity make up the budget estimates. The estimates for separate departments or divisions that perform a similar function are adjusted as necessary and are summarized in one budget for that function. For instance, sales estimates may be made by regional sales managers, with the approved estimates being combined into one sales estimate for the company. At the same time, the functions such as sales, production, product engineering, purchasing, and so forth, are coordinated so that all of the budgets fit together properly.

Ordinarily individuals prepare their own budgets or, at the very least, are consulted before any budget is assigned to them. This is particularly true if the budget is to be used in controlling their activities. The self-imposed budget has certain distinct advantages, as follows:

1. A person who is in immediate contact with an activity should be able to make reliable estimates.
2. The person tends to feel recognized as a member of the team.
3. Most likely the person makes every effort to fulfill a self-imposed budget.

4. The self-imposed budget has its own peculiar control. The individual is forced to assume the blame if unable to operate within the limits.

The self-imposed budget, however, is not necessarily accepted as it stands. If too much freedom is allowed, there is a possibility that the budgets will be too easy and that they will offer no challenge. Undeserved credit may be taken for favorable budget comparisons. Before the budgets are accepted, they are reviewed by higher levels of management. If changes are to be made, they can be discussed and compromises can be reached that are acceptable to all concerned.

The person in immediate contact with any activity is in a good position to make budget estimates but is also apt to have a narrow viewpoint. An individual whose energy is devoted to one thing is very likely to exaggerate its importance, forgetting that it is only a part of a bigger activity. For instance, a regional salesperson may wonder why a product line that has sold successfully has been discontinued. The company, however, may have discovered that the sales in total were not sufficient to justify further production.

Top management and the lower levels of management work together to produce the budget. As a general rule, those who are in higher positions are not familiar with the details of any activity and depend upon their subordinates for underlying information. On the other hand, the top executives of the firm know more about the business as a whole, are better informed with respect to the general business outlook, and take a broader point of view. Each member of the management group, acting as an individual and cooperating with others, makes a contribution to the budget.

BUDGET ILLUSTRATION

An illustration of a complete budget operation is given for Midland Farm Stores, Inc. Plans are made for the purchase of merchandise, sales, the collections on sales, the payments for merchandise purchased, and various operating and other costs. The budget covers the first two fiscal quarters of 1981 and is greatly condensed for purposes of simplicity.

A sales revenue budget has been prepared for Midland Farm Stores, Inc., as shown below:

3d quarter, 1980 (actual)	$320,000
4th quarter, 1980 (actual)	180,000
1st quarter, 1981 (estimated)	220,000
2d quarter, 1981 (estimated)	450,000
3d quarter, 1981 (estimated)	240,000

All sales are made on a credit basis. Other budget information follows:
(1) The cost of goods sold is equal to 60% of sales revenue.
(2) Merchandise is purchased to cover half of the sales requirement for the next quarter.
(3) All merchandise purchases are paid for in the quarter following the purchase quarter.

(4) Operating and other expenses are estimated at 10% of sales revenue for the quarter plus $40,000. Included in the $40,000 each quarter is interest on the long-term notes and depreciation amounting to $9,000.

(5) The operating and other expenses and the income tax estimated at 40% of income before income tax are paid during the following quarter. (No payment is made for the $9,000 depreciation each quarter. Depreciation is an estimate of the deterioration of the equipment and does not involve a cash payment.)

(6) Cash collections are estimated as follows:

    20% of the sales are collected during the quarter of the sale.

    80% of the sales are collected during the following quarter.

Provisions for returns, allowances, and uncollectible accounts are excluded to simplify the illustration.

The balance sheet as of December 31, 1980, is given below.

Midland Farm Stores, Inc.
Balance Sheet
December 31, 1980

Assets

Cash	$ 62,000
Accounts receivable	144,000
Inventory	66,000
Equipment, net of accumulated depreciation	140,000
Total assets	$412,000

Equities

Accounts payable (merchandise)	$120,000
Other current liabilities	55,000
Notes payable, due March 1, 1983	45,000
Capital stock, $10 par value	100,000
Retained earnings	92,000
Total equities	$412,000

An estimated income statement for each of the next two quarters has been prepared from the budget information. Note that the cost of goods sold is equal to 60 percent of the sales revenue and that the operating and other expenses are equal to 10 percent of the sales reve-

Midland Farm Stores, Inc.
Estimated Income Statement
For Six Months Ending June 30, 1981

	First Quarter	Second Quarter	Total
Sales	$220,000	$450,000	$670,000
Cost of goods sold	$132,000	$270,000	$402,000
Operating and other expenses	62,000	85,000	147,000
Total	$194,000	$355,000	$549,000
Income before income tax	$ 26,000	$ 95,000	$121,000
Income tax, 40%	10,000	38,000	48,000
Net income	$ 16,000	$ 57,000	$ 73,000

nue plus $40,000 each quarter. All computations have been rounded to the nearest thousand.

Purchases must be made to meet the sales requirements, and the merchandise must be available when needed. A budget of purchases is given below:

PURCHASES BUDGET

	(Actual) Fourth Quarter	First Quarter	Second Quarter	Total
50% of the requirement for current quarter[1]	$ 54,000	$ 66,000	$135,000	$255,000
50% of the requirement for next quarter[2]	66,000	135,000	72,000	273,000
Total	$120,000	$201,000	$207,000	$528,000

[1]Cost of goods sold is computed at 60% of sales. Amount equals 50% of cost of goods sold for the current quarter.
[2]Amount equals 50% of cost of goods sold for the next quarter.

Cash disbursements must be planned for discharging debt, paying income tax and dividends, acquiring new machinery, and covering operating expenses. A budget of cash payments follows:

CASH PAYMENTS BUDGET

	First Quarter	Second Quarter	Total
Payments for purchases of preceding quarter	$120,000	$201,000	$321,000
Payments for operating expenses of preceding quarter[1]	49,000	53,000	102,000
Payment of estimated income tax of preceding quarter[2]	6,000	10,000	16,000
Total	$175,000	$264,000	$439,000

[1]10% of sales of preceding quarter plus $31,000 ($40,000 − depreciation of $9,000).
[2]Income tax, 4th quarter, 1980: [($180,000 − $108,000 − $18,000 − $40,000) × .4].

In this illustration, all cash receipts are from sales activity. In practice, a company may receive cash from the sale of plant property, from a loan, or from other various sources. The cash receipts budget for Midland Farm Store, Inc., is given below.

CASH RECEIPTS BUDGET

	First Quarter	Second Quarter	Total
Cash collections on accounts receivable:			
20% of sales for quarter of sale	$ 44,000	$ 90,000	$134,000
80% of sales for preceding quarter	144,000	176,000	320,000
Total	$188,000	$266,000	$454,000

The cash receipts and cash payments budgets are combined to form the following cash budget:

CASH BUDGET

	First Quarter	Second Quarter	Total
Cash balance, beginning of quarter	$ 62,000	$ 75,000	$ 62,000
Cash receipts	188,000	266,000	454,000
	$250,000	$341,000	$516,000
Cash payments	175,000	264,000	439,000
Cash balance, end of quarter	$ 75,000	$ 77,000	$ 77,000

From the information developed, it is possible to obtain account balances that can be used in the preparation of an estimated balance sheet for June 30, 1981, which is shown on the following page.

	ACCOUNTS RECEIVABLE	INVENTORY	EQUIPMENT, NET
Beginning balance	$144,000	$ 66,000	$140,000
Add:			
Sales	670,000		
Purchases (exclude fourth quarter)		408,000	
	$814,000	$474,000	$140,000
Less:			
Collections	454,000		
Cost of sales		402,000	
Depreciation			18,000
Ending balance	$360,000	$ 72,000	$122,000

	ACCOUNTS PAYABLE	OTHER CURRENT LIABILITIES	RETAINED EARNINGS
Beginning balance	$120,000	$ 55,000	$ 92,000
Add:			
Purchases	408,000		
Expenses[1]		177,000	
Net income			73,000
	$528,000	$232,000	$165,000
Less:			
Payments	321,000	118,000	—
Ending balance	$207,000	$114,000	$165,000

[1]Operating expenses of $147,000 plus income tax of $48,000 minus depreciation of $18,000.

In this illustration, it can be seen that many factors must be estimated and brought together to form a comprehensive budget. The budgeting process involves the cooperation of many persons who share the responsibility for planning and controlling the direction of the enterprise.

Midland Farm Stores, Inc.
Estimated Balance Sheet
June 30, 1981

Assets

Cash	$ 77,000
Accounts receivable	360,000
Inventory	72,000
Equipment, net of accumulated depreciation	122,000
Total assets	$631,000

Equities

Accounts payable (merchandise)	$207,000
Other current liabilities	114,000
Notes payable	45,000
Capital stock, $10 par value	100,000
Retained earnings	165,000
Total equities	$631,000

SENSITIVITY TO CHANGES

As time passes, it may become evident that original estimates need to be revised. Errors in forecasting or changes not anticipated may make it necessary to revise the budget. A small revision in one area alone will have an effect on other areas of the operation. A computer may be utilized to test various budget models by deriving information that predicts the impact of a change in one area on the other areas and on the total budget. A series of questions are asked, and a budget model will show results based on a possible change.

In the illustration just given, assume that the president of the company questions the timing of cash receipts and anticipates that cash collections may follow the pattern given below:

20% of sales collected during the quarter.
50% of sales collected during the next quarter.
30% of sales collected during the second following quarter.

All sales from the third quarter of 1980 were collected by the end of the last quarter of 1980. The new pattern of collections will begin in 1981.

This type of change, while it does not affect profits, does result in a lower cash balance and a higher balance of accounts receivable. On June 30, the end of the second quarter, according to the original estimate, the cash balance would be relatively low after completing a quarter of heavy sales activity. With a slowdown in collections, it may even be necessary to borrow funds on a short-term basis to meet payment demands.

A revised cash receipts budget is given on page 22 along with a summary cash budget.

CASH RECEIPTS BUDGET (REVISED)

	First Quarter	Second Quarter	Total
Cash collections on accounts receivable:			
20% of sales for the quarter	$ 44,000	$ 90,000	$134,000
50% of sales for the preceding quarter..	90,000	110,000	200,000
30% of sales for the second preceding quarter	—	54,000	54,000
Total	$134,000	$254,000	$388,000

CASH BUDGET (REVISED)

	First Quarter	Second Quarter	Total
Cash balance, beginning of quarter	$ 62,000	$ 21,000	$ 62,000
Cash receipts	134,000	254,000	388,000
	$196,000	$275,000	$450,000
Cash payments................................	175,000	264,000	439,000
Cash balance, end of quarter	$ 21,000	$ 11,000	$ 11,000

With a slowdown in cash collections, the accounts receivable balance will be higher by $66,000 for a total of $426,000 by the end of the second quarter under the revised plan ($360,000 + $66,000). The cash balance will be $66,000 less at the end of the second quarter than originally planned because of the decrease in collections on accounts receivable ($77,000 − $11,000).

The revised cash budget shows that, with a slowdown in the collectibility of accounts receivable, the cash balance at June 30 may be too low to meet various contingencies. Hence, the company should plan to borrow funds on a short-term basis.

The change illustrated affects cash and accounts receivable only. A change in the sales estimate, however, would affect the cost of goods sold, operating expenses, income tax, and net income. In addition, there would be changes in accounts receivable, inventory, accounts payable, other current liabilities, and retained earnings. Even relatively minor changes can have an impact on many areas of the operation. Recognizing this fact, management plans the budget most carefully and controls operations to stay within the guidelines of the budget.

QUESTIONS

1. What is a budget?
2. What is budgetary control?

3. Explain how budgeting and budgetary control operate together in a total management system.

4. What is a flexible budget?

5. How does a project or product budget differ from a responsibility budget?

6. What is a capital investment budget?

7. How can top management administer a budget to obtain more cooperation from subordinates?

8. Explain what is meant by budget slack.

9. What is likely to happen if a manager is not permitted to carry over an unexpended portion of a budget to a subsequent year?

10. What is a budget period? Is a budget prepared for a month, for a year, or for some other interval of time? Explain.

11. What is the minimum period of time to be covered by a comprehensive operating budget?

12. What is a rolling or progressive budget?

13. How does the concept of timing enter into budgeting?

14. What are the advantages that can be derived from a self-imposed budget? disadvantages?

15. How can a company prepare budget models that will show the effect of changes in the original budget estimate?

16. Indicate the income statement or balance sheet accounts that will be affected by a slowdown in cash collections from customers.

17. How will a reduction in the estimate of sales volume affect the income statement or balance sheet accounts?

EXERCISES

1. Budget Policy. The plant superintendent at the Tupelo plant of Sereno Fixtures, Inc., watches budget performance closely and evaluates departmental managers almost exclusively on their ability to stay within the budgets.

Recently the company started a cost reduction campaign. One of the department managers who always had a good budget record found a way to save $16,000 on a certain operation for the year and was rewarded with a bonus equal to 20% of the amount saved.

Required: Comment briefly on the advantages and disadvantages of the plant superintendent's policy. Explain how this policy may have made it possible for the department manager to receive an undeserved bonus.

2. Budget Policy. Melvin Granger retired after many years of service as plant manager at Wilson Processing Company. He gained a reputation for being an astute cost-conscious manager and tolerated no budget overruns. Angela Moyer, a department manager who had been with the company many years retired soon after Granger. She was always able to meet her budget of about $26,000 a month for labor, supplies, repairs, maintenance, and other costs over which she had control. Sometimes she operated very close to the budget but never exceeded it. Granger was very pleased with this department manager.

The new plant manager took a more liberal point of view and permitted department managers to take an active part in budget preparation. Furthermore, the budget was only one of several criteria used to evaluate them. The new department manager prepared a budget of $19,000 for the month and in the first month of operation was $1,500 over budget.

Required:

(1) Comment briefly on the budget policies of the two plant managers.
(2) Should the new department manager be censured for being over budget? Explain.
(3) Calculate the possible minimum slack in the retired department manager's budget.

3. Budget Timing. Cotter Metals Company has been awarded a contract to manufacture 200 castings at a unit price of $650 per casting. The castings are to be delivered on May 1. The customer agrees to pay 50% of the contract price in May and the other 50% in June.

Estimates indicate that a full month will be needed for production and a month will be required for inspection, rework, and shipment of the finished castings. Materials for the contract estimated to cost $65,000 are to be delivered and paid for in the month preceding the month of production. Other costs of completing the contract estimated at $41,000 will be incurred during the month of production. These costs include depreciation of plant and equipment at $1,500. The other costs that are to be paid will be paid during the month of production.

Required:

(1) Determine the income before tax to be earned on the contract.
(2) For each relevant month, determine the cash receipts and disbursements relating to the contract. (No cash payment is to be made for depreciation charges.)

4. Estimated Income Statement. Melendez Stores, Inc., is in the process of planning a budget for the next fiscal year. Sales revenue has been estimated at $1,500,000. The cost of goods sold has been estimated at 70% of sales revenue. Depreciation of the building and fixtures is budgeted at 5% of the cost of $800,000 that is subject to depreciation. Salaries and wages should amount to 5% of sales revenue. Advertising has been budgeted at $25,000. Heat and light should amount to $8,000. Other operating costs are expected to amount to $17,000. Income tax is estimated at 40% of income before income tax.

Required: Prepare an estimated income statement for the next fiscal year.

5. Cash Payments Budget. A budget of cash payments is to be prepared for six months for Woodburne Products Company. Cost of goods sold has been estimated at 70% of sales, and payments on merchandise are to be made during the month preceding the month of sale. Wages are estimated at 10% of sales and are paid during the month of sale. Other operating costs amounting to 5% of sales are to be paid in the month following the month of sale. A payment of $12,000 is to be made on a loan in the month of June. Sales revenue has been budgeted as follows:

March — $240,000	July	— $140,000
April — 220,000	August	— 150,000
May — 180,000	September — 230,000
June — 160,000	October	— 250,000

Required: Prepare a budget of cash payments for each month from April to September, inclusive.

6. Simple Cash Budget. June Wagner is planning a cash budget for the next three months for Darnley Products, Inc. Estimated sales revenue has been budgeted as follows:

| March — $180,000 |
| April — 140,000 |
| May — 125,000 |
| June — 130,000 |

All sales are made on credit terms. Forty percent of the sales are collected during the month of sale, and 60% are collected during the next month.

Cost of goods sold is equal to 70% of sales. Payments for merchandise sold are made in the month following the month of sale. Operating expenses to be paid amount to $35,000 each month and are paid during the month incurred.

Required: Prepare a cash budget for each month: April, May, and June.

7. A Cash Budget. On January 1, Cordova Company had a cash balance of $142,000. The president of the company would like to receive a budget of cash receipts and payments for each of the six months extending from January to June, inclusive. Sales revenue has been estimated as follows:

November — $120,000	March — $ 70,000
December — 140,000	April — 90,000
January — 80,000	May — 110,000
February — 70,000	June — 120,000

All sales are on credit terms, and 70% of the sales are to be collected during the month of sale, 20% of the sales are to be collected during the next month, and 10% are to be collected during the second month following the month of sale.

Cost of goods sold is expected to amount to 60% of sales revenue. One half of the merchandise is acquired during the month preceding the month of sale and is paid for during the month of sale. The other half of the merchandise is acquired during the month of sale and is paid for during the next month.

Various costs of operation have been estimated at $20,000 each month and are paid for during the month incurred.

Required: Prepare a cash budget for each of the six months extending from January to June, inclusive.

8. Budget of Collections on Accounts Receivable. The Wye Company is planning a budget of cash receipts expected from the collection of accounts receivable for the next fiscal year. The budget is to be broken down by quarters of a year.

Sales activity has been budgeted as follows:

4th quarter (current year)	$650,000
1st quarter (budget year)	380,000
2d quarter	260,000

3d quarter $320,000
4th quarter 730,000

There are no cash sales. It has been estimated that 30% of the sales will be collected during the quarter of the sale and that the balance will be collected during the following quarter.

Required: Prepare a budget of cash collections from accounts receivable by quarter for the next fiscal year.

9. Estimated Cash Accounts Receivable. The Forks Valley Fabric Company is planning the cash inflow expected from sales activity over the next six months. Also, the accounts receivable balance is to be estimated inasmuch as it represents a potential source of cash for the future. The company expects to collect 30% of sales during the month of sale, 50% during the following month, and the remaining 20% during the second month following month of sale. The accounts receivable balance at July 1 was $446,000. Actual and budgeted sales are given below:

May	— $550,000 (actual)	September —	$460,000
June	— 480,000 (actual)	October —	520,000
July	— 420,000	November —	570,000
August —	360,000	December —	630,000

Required: Prepare a cash collections budget for each month from July to December inclusive. Determine the estimated balance of accounts receivable at the end of each month.

10. Estimated Cash and Accounts Receivable. Tangiers Fixtures Company is in the process of estimating cash receipts from sales activity for the next six months. The accounts receivable balance is to be estimated at the end of each month also. Cash sales are estimated at 10% of the sales for the month. The balance of sales should be collected as follows:

40% during the month of sale.
40% during the following month.
20% during the second month following month of sale.

The accounts receivable balance at October 1 was $109,800 actual, and budgeted sales are given below.

August	— $230,000 (actual)	December —	$150,000
September —	190,000 (actual)	January —	180,000
October	— 170,000	February —	210,000
November —	160,000	March —	240,000

Required: Prepare a cash collections budget for each month from October to March, inclusive. Determine the estimated balance of accounts receivable at the end of each month.

PROBLEMS

1-1. An Estimated Income Statement and Cash Budget. The board of directors of Hilley Stores, Inc., requests budget information for the fiscal quarter ending June 30. Sales volume has been forecast as follows:

	Units of product
February	15,000
March	19,000
April	21,000
May	22,000
June	24,000

Each unit of product is sold for $5.

Cash sales are equal to 20% of the total sales. The balance of sales is to be collected as follows: 60% during the month of sale and 40% during the following month.

Cost of goods sold is equal to 60% of sales. All merchandise for resale is purchased during the month preceding the month of sale, and payment is made in the following month.

Operating expenses amount to $12,000 a month and are all paid for during the next month.

Income tax is at the rate of 40% of income before tax. A payment of $35,000 is to be made on estimated income tax in June.

Required:
(1) Prepare a budgeted income statement for the quarter ended June 30 with detail shown for each month.
(2) Prepare a cash budget for the quarter ended June 30 with detail shown for each month. The cash balance at April 1 was $123,000.

1-2. Budgeted Financial Statements. Argus Supply Company is preparing a budget for the first and second fiscal quarters of the next year. The balance sheet as of December 31, 1980, is given below.

Argus Supply Company
Balance Sheet
December 31, 1980

Assets

Cash	$ 91,200
Accounts receivable	120,000
Inventory	28,800
Total assets	$240,000

Equities

Accounts payable (merchandise)	$124,800
Operating expenses payable	30,000
Income tax payable	18,000
Capital stock	15,000
Retained earnings	52,200
Total equities	$240,000

The company has planned sales revenue as follows:

3d quarter, 1980 (actual)	$180,000
4th quarter, 1980 (actual)	200,000
1st quarter, 1981 (estimated)	240,000
2d quarter, 1981 (estimated)	250,000
3d quarter, 1981 (estimated)	260,000

Forty percent of the sales revenue is collected during the quarter of sale with the balance collected during the following quarter.

Cost of goods sold is equal to 60% of sales revenue. An inventory equal to 20% of the sales requirement for the next quarter is to be maintained during each quarter. All merchandise purchased for resale is paid for in the quarter following the quarter of purchase.

Operating expenses for each quarter are estimated at 5% of sales revenue plus $20,000. All operating expenses are paid during the following quarter.

Income tax has been estimated at 40% of income before tax. The income tax liability at December 31, 1980, is to be paid during the first quarter of 1981.

Required: From the budget data given, prepare a budgeted income statement for each of the first two fiscal quarters of 1981 and a budgeted balance sheet at June 30, 1981.

1-3. Budgeted Financial Statements. A budget is being prepared for the third and fourth fiscal quarters of 1981 for College Stores, Inc. The balance sheet as of June 30, 1981, is given below.

College Stores Inc.
Balance Sheet
June 30, 1981

Assets

Cash	$ 83,000
Accounts receivable	48,000
Inventory	54,000
Store equipment, net of accumulated depreciation	92,000
Total assets	$277,000

Equities

Accounts payable*	$ 96,800
Income tax payable	26,000
Capital stock	80,000
Retained earnings	74,200
Total equities	$277,000

*Includes obligations for merchandise and operating expenses.

Actual and budgeted sales revenue are given below.

1st quarter, 1981 (actual)	$120,000
2d quarter, 1981 (actual	160,000
3d quarter, 1981 (estimated)	240,000
4th quarter, 1981 (estimated)	150,000
1st quarter, 1982 (estimated)	100,000

Thirty percent of the sales revenue is collected during the quarter of sale with the balance collected during the next quarter.

Cost of goods sold is equal to 75% of sales revenue. Inventory is to be equal to 30% of the sales requirement for the next quarter. Payments are made for 40% of the merchandise purchased during the quarter of purchase. The balance is paid during the following quarter.

Certain operating expenses, including depreciation of $2,000, amount to $8,000 each quarter. Certain other operating expenses are equal to 5% of the sales revenue for the quarter. All operating expenses that are to be paid are paid in the following quarter.

Income tax is equal to 40% of income before tax. No payments are to be made on income tax during the third or fourth quarter.

Required: Prepare an estimated income statement for the third and fourth quarters of 1981, and prepare an estimated balance sheet at December 31, 1981.

1-4. Revision of Budget Estimates. Holly Reinland speculates on the effect of a change in sales revenue estimates on the budgeted financial statements for Reinland Products Company for the fourth quarter of 1981.

Original sales revenue estimates are given below:

3d quarter, 1981	$760,000
4th quarter, 1981	950,000
1st quarter, 1982	820,000

Cost of goods sold is estimated at 70% of sales revenue. Inventory is to be maintained at 20% of the sales requirement for the next quarter. Payments for merchandise purchased are to be made in the quarter following the quarter of purchase. Operating expenses amount to $156,000 each quarter and are paid during the quarter that the expenses are incurred. Income tax is to be computed at 40% of income before tax and is not to be paid until the following quarter. SCREWED up

Holly Reinland believes that the sales revenue estimated for the fourth quarter is too optimistic. She believes that sales revenue is more likely to amount to $880,000.

Cash sales are to be 10% of sales revenue. Forty percent of the credit sales are to be collected during the quarter of sale with the balance being collected during the following quarter.

A balance sheet at September 30, 1981, is given below:

Reinland Products Company
Balance Sheet
September 30, 1981

Assets

Cash	$406,300
Accounts receivable	410,400
Inventory	133,000
Total assets	$949,700

Equities

Accounts payable	$558,600
Capital stock	150,000
Retained earnings	241,100
Total equities	$949,700

Required:

(1) Prepare a budgeted income statement for the fourth quarter of 1981 and a balance sheet at the end of the quarter based upon the original estimates.

(2) Prepare a budgeted income statement for the fourth quarter of 1981 and a balance sheet at the end of the quarter based upon the prediction of reduced sales for the quarter.

(3) What effect does the revision of the sales estimate have on net income, cash, accounts receivable, inventory, and accounts payable?

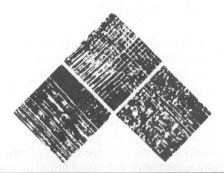

2
COSTS FOR
PLANNING AND CONTROL

In the previous chapter, attention was directed to the overall planning operation as reflected in a summary budget. The budget, when broken down into sufficient detail, serves as a basis for the comparison of actual results with the plan. With this information management can detect disparities and take control measures to correct any undesirable deviations. Also, the comparison may reveal errors in planning that can be corrected during the next round of budget planning.

Both revenue and costs are important factors in planning and control and are given attention in this chapter and in later chapters. Revenue is a function of the volume of business and the price of the service or product. In many cases, because they are often established by forces in the general market, the selling prices may not be subject to mangement control. Also, a not-for-profit entity may furnish a service at a nominal price. However, every entity must be concerned with cost, and cost can generally be controlled to some degree by management.

COSTS

A *cost* may be very broadly defined as being the sacrifice required to obtain a given object or objective. There are many different kinds of costs, however, and it is important to understand how one conception of cost may be suitable for a given purpose while another conception is entirely unsuitable. It is tempting to ask for the cost of a good or service, not recognizing that there may be more than one cost. The problem of working with costs can be simplified if one considers carefully how the costs are to be used and selectively chooses cost data that serve that purpose. Costs can be useful tools when used properly. A hammer is a useful tool for driving nails but is not a very satisfactory instrument for smoothing wood surfaces. Similarly, costs must be selected carefully to fit the need.

Management, stockholders, employees, and other groups are interested in summarized cost data. Management, however, requires more detailed information. For example, to manage an enterprise effectively, it is necessary to know how much it costs to operate a given segment of the business such as a division or a department, how much it costs to produce and sell a given quantity of a certain product line, and how much it costs to produce and sell each unit of the various lines handled. Detailed cost information is furnished by a system of cost accounting and can be used to control business activities, plan operations, and make decisions.

Fixed and Variable Costs

If costs are to be identified with some relevant unit, such as a department, product line, or given amount of service, it is necessary to determine how costs can be expected to behave under different conditions. For example, which costs can be expected to remain constant when there are increases or decreases in the amount of work done? Also, which costs increase as more work is performed and decrease when less work is performed? If costs are to be estimated and controlled properly, it is necessary to know whether or not the cost can be expected to change under given conditions and, if so, by what amount.

In accounting, *fixed costs* refer to the costs that do not change in total amount with changes in volume of output or activity over an established or relevant range. Such items as salary of a plant superintendent, depreciation, insurance, taxes, and rent usually remain the same regardless of whether the plant is above or below its normal operating capacity. However, a fixed cost, like any cost, is subject to certain variations. Rent may increase or insurance rates go up, but these changes are caused by factors independent of the firm's operating level.

Fixed costs are sometimes classified as being either *committed costs* or *programmed costs*. Management, in making long-range decisions, may commit a company to a cost pattern that extends several years into the future. For example, when a building is acquired, future years have to absorb the depreciation cost and the related property tax, insurance, repairs, and maintenance. These fixed costs are committed costs. Programmed costs, also referred to as *managed costs* or *discretionary costs*, are determined as a part of general management policy. A budget for product research and development, for example, may be established each year; or supervisory salaries are set each year by management decision. These costs are established at a certain fixed amount, but the amount is determined by management.

Variable costs, in the strict sense, are costs that vary in direct proportion, or in a one-to-one relationship, to changes in productive output or activity. For example, direct materials cost is usually a variable cost with each unit manufactured requiring a certain quantity of material. Thus, the materials cost changes in direct proportion to the number of units manufactured.

Many costs are *semivariable*; they may change, but not in direct proportion to the changes in output. Often semivariable costs, which have the attributes of both variable and fixed costs, are falsely designated as variable costs. Repairs, for example, are not fixed in amount but probably increase as hours of activity increase. Among costs that are semivariable are indirect materials, supplies, indirect labor, fuel, and payroll taxes. Semivariable costs may be broken down into fixed and variable components, thus making it easier to budget and control costs and to apply cost data for decision-making purposes.

The Troublesome Fixed Costs. Fixed costs are often responsible for difficulties in accounting for costs. By definition, the total fixed cost remains constant over a specified range of activity or output, which means that the fixed cost per unit of product will vary. When a greater number of units are produced, the fixed cost per unit decreases. Conversely, when a smaller number of units are produced, the fixed cost per unit increases. This variability with respect to unit costs creates problems in product costing. The cost per unit depends upon the number of units being manufactured.

This problem of product costing is illustrated by assuming that variable factory overhead costs vary at a rate of $8 per unit of product manufactured and that the total fixed factory overhead amounts to $600,000 for the year. Cost budgets show the following:

Number of units of product manufactured	30,000	40,000	50,000
Variable factory overhead	$240,000	$320,000	$ 400,000
Fixed factory overhead	600,000	600,000	600,000
Total factory overhead	$840,000	$920,000	$1,000,000
Unit factory overhead cost:			
Variable	$ 8	$ 8	$ 8
Fixed	20	15	12
Total	$28	$23	$20

Note that the total variable cost increases with increases in the number of units produced but remains the same per unit of product. On the other hand, the total fixed cost, by definition, does not change with changes in output; it remains at $600,000. As more units are manufactured, however, the cost per unit decreases. For example, the fixed cost per unit is $20 when 30,000 units are produced but is only $12 when 50,000 units are produced.

Thus, the fixed costs create a problem in cost accounting. The unit cost of a manufactured product depends upon the number of units produced during the year. However, the products must be assigned a cost before the number of units produced during the year is determined. Ordinarily this problem is resolved by assigning a fixed factory overhead cost to each unit of product from a budget of costs and units to be manufactured at a defined normal level of operation.

For example, assume that the company in the illustration is normally expected to manufacture and sell 40,000 units a year with its present facilities. In this case, each unit of product would bear $15 of fixed factory overhead. At the end of the year, it may be found that only 30,000 units were actually manufactured. Therefore, only $450,000 of the total fixed factory overhead of $600,000 has been costed to the products by using a rate of $15 per unit (30,000 units × $15). The remaining $150,000 that was *unabsorbed* can be measured in the accounts as a capacity variance. It is the *variance*, or in other words the difference, that was caused by not using the manufacturing facilities according to the plan incorporated in the normal budget of operations. This type of problem is quite common in cost accounting and is discussed at greater length in later chapters.

COSTS AND CONTROL

Management, in carrying out its control over operations, must rely heavily on cost data. However, the costs that are useful for control purposes are not necessarily the costs that are reported on conventional accounting statements. Much of the disagreement about how costs should be accounted for arises because of a misunderstanding of how the cost data will be used. One concept of cost will not serve all purposes.

For example, cost to operate a given plant for a year totaled $870,000, and the costs to operate the two departments in the plant were $450,000 and $420,000 respectively. This information may not be satisfactory, however, if management wants to know how much cost is specifically incurred for the operation of a particular department. Suppose that depreciation of the plant, the plant superintendent's salary, and other costs of operating the plant as a unit have been included in the departmental cost totals. Assume further that these costs of overall plant operation amounted to $360,000 and that they have been allocated equally to both departments; that is, $180,000 to each department. On this basis, the costs specifically incurred to operate each department were $270,000 for the first department and $240,000 for the second department.

	DEPT. 1	DEPT. 2	TOTAL
Total cost	$450,000	$420,000	$870,000
Less allocated cost	180,000	180,000	360,000
Specific department cost	$270,000	$240,000	$510,000

Further assume that management wants to know how much cost can be controlled by each departmental supervisor. The salary of each departmental supervisor is included as a specific cost incurred for operation of the department, but the departmental supervisor does not set or control this salary. Also, depreciation of equipment used exclusively within a department is not controlled by the supervisor if the supervisor does not acquire the equipment; but it is included as a specific cost of the department. Assume that costs of $200,000 and $80,000 for each of the respective departments are included as specific costs of the departments but cannot be controlled by the departmental supervisors. The costs controllable at the departmental level are computed below.

	DEPT. 1	DEPT. 2	TOTAL
Specific departmental cost	$270,000	$240,000	$510,000
Less costs not controllable at departmental level............................	200,000	80,000	280,000
Costs controllable at departmental level..	$ 70,000	$160,000	$230,000

Note that the supervisor of Department 2 has control over a large proportion of the cost of this department while the supervisor of Department 1 controls a smaller proportion of the departmental cost. The information was not revealed by the previous cost reports.

An allocation of costs does serve a purpose in that it shows the full cost of operating a unit. But cost allocation tends to blur areas of responsibility. In the evaluation of departmental supervisors, it would be more useful to charge them with only the costs for which they are responsible. Their particular areas can be controlled more effectively by comparing the costs over which they have jurisdiction with budgets or standards prepared on the same basis.

In arriving at a decision as to whether or not operations have been conducted efficiently, management depends upon some basis of measurement, such as a budget or a *cost standard*. The budget or the standard serves as a point of reference. Differences between the actual costs incurred and the budgeted or standard costs can be calculated and put to use in evaluating performance. If further investigation reveals that budget differences were caused by unsatisfactory conditions, positive steps can be taken to correct the situation. In other words, budget comparisons produce information that can be used to control the business at various levels of operation.

Direct and Indirect Costs

Costs are sometimes spoken of as being direct or indirect with respect to an activity, a department, or a product. The distinction depends upon whether or not the cost can be identified with the activity or other relevant unit without allocation. A cost such as the plant superintendent's salary can be readily identified with the plant and hence is a direct cost of the plant. However, it is an indirect cost of any department within the plant or of any line of product manufactured. The plant superintendent's salary cannot be identified with any unit within the plant except by allocation. With respect to product lines, the materials and labor that are easily identified as a part of the product cost are the direct materials and the direct labor cost of the product. The factory overhead costs are not directly identifiable with any particular product and are thus indirect costs with respect to the product. The cost of supplies used, for example, may be identified directly as a cost of a particular department yet not be a direct cost of the products manufactured. If a cost can be directly attached to the unit under consideration, it is a *direct cost* of that unit. If it is a cost of a unit only through allocation, it is an *indirect cost*.

There is a dangerous tendency to oversimplify and to look upon direct costs as being variable costs and indirect costs as being fixed costs. This is not necessarily true. For example, a plant superintendent's salary is a fixed cost. It does not increase or decrease automatically with changes in activity or production. However, as stated earlier, it is a direct cost of the plant. It is also an indirect cost with respect to departments within the plant or with respect to the products. Supplies used may vary with the number of hours of production and be a variable cost. The cost of the supplies used may be a direct cost of a given department but an indirect cost of any particular product manufactured within that department. One must be careful not to confuse the direct and indirect distinction with the fixed and variable distinction. There is no established relationship between the two concepts.

Cost Allocations

The indirect costs, the costs that cannot be directly identified with a department or division of the company, may be allocated to the departments or divisions as indicated earlier in the chapter. The allocation is made on a judgmental basis by using a factor that can be identified with both the department or division and the cost in question. The allocation, while based on logical assumptions, cannot be viewed as a precise cost measurement for the department.

For example, assume that a building is used for four different operating departments. The costs of building occupancy such as taxes, insurance, repairs, and depreciation are allocated to the departments. The space in the building that is occupied by each department can be measured and can be reasonably identified with the cost of occupancy.

Craig Products Company, for example, has four operating departments in one building. Data relative to occupied space are given on the following page.

	SQUARE METERS OF SPACE	PERCENTAGE OF TOTAL SPACE
Department 1	45 000	30%
Department 2	60 000	40
Department 3	15 000	10
Department 4	30 000	20
Total	150 000	100%

The total cost of building occupancy has been estimated at $120,000 for the year. The cost is allocated to the departments on the basis of the percentage of the building occupied.

	DEPARTMENTS				
	1	*2*	*3*	*4*	*Total*
Building occupancy	$36,000	$48,000	$12,000	$24,000	$120,000

As stated earlier, cost allocation is misleading if the intention is to determine the direct costs of operating a department with no support from the rest of the organization. However, cost allocation does indicate whether or not a department is producing enough revenue not only to cover its direct costs but also its share of the total costs of the organization. Some departments, for example, may cover all of their direct costs but not all of the allocated costs. Still other departments may cover all of their direct costs, their entire share of allocated costs, and show a final profit.

In the planning and control operation, it is most important to distinguish between the direct costs of a department and the allocated costs. Under normal circumstances, the cost to be allocated will not be reduced by the elimination of any one department; that is, the amount of insurance, taxes, and depreciation will continue at the same amount whether or not all building space is utilized. Therefore, the allocated cost may not be relevant in deciding whether or not to retain a department.

In the last example, assume that Department 4 is to be eliminated. The cost of building occupancy would still remain at $120,000 and could be reallocated to the other three departments as shown below.

	DEPARTMENTS			
	1	*2*	*3*	*Total*
Revised space occupancy (square meters).........................	45 000	60 000	15 000	120 000
Revised percentages	37.5%	50%	12.5%	100%
Revised cost allocation................	$45,000	$60,000	$15,000	$120,000

If the cost was not reallocated, the portion of cost previously assigned to Department 4 may be unassigned as a form of *capacity variance*, a cost of the unused space. Or, if the space assigned to Department 4 was used for another purpose, the allocated cost would be assigned to the new use.

The key point is that the cost is not reduced by $24,000 if Department 4 is eliminated. The total cost remains at $120,000. The elimination of a department or function does not eliminate the allocated portion of a fixed cost.

Controllable and Noncontrollable Costs

Another important aspect of cost to be considered is the distinction between costs that can be controlled by a given person and those that cannot be controlled by that person.

This cost classification also depends upon a point of reference. Costs are incurred upon the authorization of some member of the management group. If a manager is responsible for a given cost, that cost is said to be *controllable* with respect to that person. If the manager does not authorize that cost, the cost is *uncontrollable* with respect to that manager. Almost all costs are controllable at some level of management. Top management has broad authority over costs and directly or indirectly controls most of the costs of the entity. For example, top management can increase or decrease executive salaries and can initiate or abandon major projects. At intermediate or at lower management levels, such costs are beyond their authority and are uncontrollable. Costs that can be authorized at a certain managerial level are said to be controllable at that level. A departmental supervisor, for example, may have control over the supplies used by the department but have no control over the plant asset acquisitions that result in the depreciation allocated to the department.

Direct costs and controllable costs are not necessarily the same. A cost may be a direct cost of a given department but may not be controlled by the departmental supervisor. For example, the salary of a departmental supervisor, which is a direct cost of the department, is controlled at a higher level of management rather than by the supervisor.

In addition, a cost cannot be looked upon as being uncontrollable because it is a fixed cost. Often there is a tendency to view a cost as either controllable or uncontrollable because it is either variable or fixed. It is as incorrect, however, to confuse cost behavior characteristics with controllability as it is to confuse cost behavior characteristics with the direct and indirect concept. While a fixed cost such as property insurance may be uncontrollable at a given managerial level, it is nevertheless subject to control by a manager who has the authority to obtain insurance coverage for the firm.

Time also plays a part in controllability. A cost that can be controlled in the long run may not be controllable over a short period of time. For example, a sales manager may have committed the company to a contract for advertising and may have no control over the cost while the contract is in force. However, when the contract has expired,

...nager is free to renegotiate and thus has control over the
...ng run.

RESPONSIBILITY ACCOUNTING

A system of *responsibility accounting* relies heavily upon the distinction between controllable and noncontrollable costs and is designed to fit the requirements of the persons within the firm. It is a people-oriented system of accounting. In responsibility accounting, costs are identified with the persons responsible for their incurrence. With responsibility localized, it is possible to rate individual managers on a cost basis by comparing the controllable costs of the department or division with a budget prepared on the same basis.

Managers are expected to prepare budgets of the costs that they control, and they are expected to operate within the limits of their budgets. Periodic cost reports prepared on this basis of cost responsibility are compared with the budgets and are used by each manager as a basis for self-evaluation. Managers at higher levels may rate subordinate managers by using this information.

The frequency of reporting, the type of information reported, and the detail depend upon the attitudes of the recipients. The success of responsibility accounting depends in large part upon the sensitivity of top-level management and the accountants to the needs and preferences of the individuals within the organization. The accountant is a supplier of financial and other business data. The information must be presented so that it can be understood by the recipient and must be communicated in a way that best helps users carry out their functions.

Some individuals want reports at frequent intervals so that they can control an operation while it is in progress. Others, who may feel that frequent reporting is not necessary and that it may even become a nuisance, prefer that reports be furnished over longer intervals of time.

The kind of information required also varies according to the type of operation and the desires of the recipient. Some managers, for example, are responsible for several projects and may tend to favor a form of cost report that shows the controllable costs for each project, the direct costs, and the allocated costs. Other managers may have no projects but may have continuous functions. For them reports on controllable costs broken down by natural classification, such as telephone, rent, and insurance, may be sufficient.

By nature, some individuals like to receive a large amount of statistical detail, and these individuals want detailed reports. On the other hand, there are those who are annoyed with detail and want condensed reports that give them a summary of the areas requiring attention. The accountant working with management seeks the form of report that best serves the purposes of the responsible manager and the firm.

Cost Reports

Costs that have been authorized by Joan Leddon, the plant manager of the Bremerton Plant of Kuchar Fabrics, Inc., for the administration of her own office are reported below. The costs that have been incurred by her subordinates, the departmental supervisors, are not included on this report.

Kuchar Fabrics, Inc.
Cost Report — Plant Administration
Plant Manager — Bremerton Plant
For the Month of June, 1981

	Year to Date			June, 1981		
	Budget	Actual	Variance Over (Under)	Budget	Actual	Variance Over (Under)
Materials and supplies..............	$10,870	$10,880	$ 10	$ 1,760	$ 1,710	$ (50)
Wages and payroll taxes...................	47,550	49,320	1,770	7,830	8,460	630
Labor fringe benefits..............	8,450	10,100	1,650	1,410	1,700	290
Travel and entertainment.....	2,680	2,290	(390)	430	320	(110)
Insurance..............	1,500	1,500	—0—	250	250	—0—
Telephone.............	1,140	1,110	(30)	170	180	10
Miscellaneous........	570	590	20	100	—0—	(100)
Total...................	$72,760	$75,790	$3,030	$11,950	$12,620	$ 670

This report can help Leddon to control the costs that she is responsible for in the administration of the plant. Costs that are substantially over budget may be given closer attention. In this report, for example, both labor and fringe benefit costs are well over the budgeted amounts. Perhaps this increased cost has become necessary because of changes in the type or volume of work done since the budget was prepared. The information derived from the report may be useful both as a tool for control and as a basis for budget revision or for the preparation of future budgets.

If more detail is needed, supplemental reports may be issued. For example, a report may be furnished to show the voucher numbers and the names of payees for individual items of cost under each natural cost classification. Before computers were commonly used, management hesitated to request detailed information since the cost of the information in both hours of work and in dollars might well have exceeded its value. Detailed reports in many cases would have taken too long to prepare and could have taken office personnel away from regularly assigned duties. Now management must be careful to select what is necessary or run the risk of being confused by unnecessary detail. If information is included in coded form on input media, it is relatively easy to design computer programs that reclassify and accumulate information in various ways to serve the needs of management. In this example, suppose that the plant manager wants to know the composition of the wages and payroll taxes for the month of June. A report prepared by computer can show the payroll detail for the month and provide basic information on charges to this classification.

The plant manager, in addition to being responsible for the administration of her own office, is also responsible for the activities of subordinates. Hence, she receives a report showing in summary form the costs incurred by her and by the departmental supervisors. A report for the month of June is given below.

Kuchar Fabrics, Inc.
Cost Report — Departmental Costs
Bremerton Plant
For the Month of June, 1981

	Year to Date			June, 1981		
	Budget	Actual	Variance Over (Under)	Budget	Actual	Variance Over (Under)
Plant administration....	$ 72,760	$ 75,790	$ 3,030	$ 11,950	$ 12,620	$ 670
Department 1.........	386,420	385,280	(1,140)	68,210	68,970	760
Department 2.........	263,140	278,230	15,090	46,300	49,500	3,200
Department 3.........	143,810	143,670	(140)	23,970	23,920	(50)
Total....................	$866,130	$882,970	$16,840	$150,430	$155,010	$4,580

Supervisors receive cost reports on their own operation like the one prepared for the plant manager and also receive a detailed report showing individual vouchers charged in each cost classification.

All costs that are controllable at the plant level may also be reported to the plant manager by natural classification, as shown below.

Kuchar Fabrics, Inc.
Cost Report — Natural Classification
Bremerton Plant
For the Month of June, 1981

	Year to Date			June, 1981		
	Budget	Actual	Variance Over (Under)	Budget	Actual	Variance Over (Under)
Materials and supplies..............	$391,650	$393,890	$ 2,240	$ 70,600	$ 72,000	$1,400
Wages and payroll taxes	380,180	390,660	10,480	64,520	67,060	2,540
Labor fringe benefits..............	76,220	80,320	4,100	12,380	13,180	800
Travel and entertainment.....	4,970	5,110	140	750	680	(70)
Insurance...............	6,000	6,000	—0—	1,000	1,000	—0—
Telephone..............	4,280	4,340	60	670	710	40
Miscellaneous........	2,830	2,650	(180)	510	380	(130)
Total....................	$866,130	$882,970	$16,840	$150,430	$155,010	$4,580

In general a manager expects to receive a report on the costs that he or she personally incurs, a summary report on the controllable costs for each subordinate manager, and a report of these controllable costs broken down by natural classification. A network of reports showing a comparision of controllable costs with budgets extends all the way from the president's office to the lowest level of management.

Some Difficulties with Responsibility Accounting

It may seem that costs can be budgeted and reported quite easily on the basis of controllability, but such is not the case. Costs may be authorized by one responsible individual, and in that sense are controlled by that person; but other persons within the organization may influence the amount of the cost. Thus, control by one individual is not absolute.

For example, it may be more economical to have one service contract for repair and maintenance for the entire plant than to have several separate contracts negotiated by each of the departmental supervisors. One of the departmental supervisors may be given the authority to obtain the contract for all departments. This is similar to a personal situation in which one person plans a dinner party at a restaurant for several persons. The person who has the authority to execute the plans has control in one sense but in another sense does not. The participants will probably demand some exceptions, and a compromise may increase costs. As a result, the budget may be exceeded; and the fault cannot be placed entirely with the person making the plans. On the other hand, an allocation of the costs is a violation of the responsibility accounting concept because individuals are being held accountable for costs that they did not personally incur.

Service departments can also create problems in a responsibility accounting system. For example, a plant engineering department may prepare blueprints and templates for the production departments. The supervisor of the plant engineering department is responsible for the costs incurred, but these costs in turn are influenced by the actions of other departments. If one department requests rush service, the service department may incur overtime and go over the budget. While other departments may have no direct control over the costs of the service department, they influence the costs and in that sense are responsible.

Sometimes the problem is solved by allocating the service department costs to other departments on the basis of (1) the investment in machinery and equipment in other departments or (2) hours of service given. In making allocations, however, the basic principle of responsibility accounting is violated; that is, an individual should only be held accountable for the costs that are personally incurred. The allocation procedure may also be unsatisfactory because the service department may not control its costs properly and may pass these higher costs to other departments by allocation. Also, an increase in the service department costs because of a request by one department for rush service should not be considered a responsibility of the service department nor should it be allocated to other departments.

One solution is to establish for the service department an hourly billing rate based on a normal service department budget. Each department is billed as if it were an outside customer, thus absorbing the penalty cost for rush work. Charging the managers only for the costs that they control directly may cause them to operate more efficiently and may also minimize friction over cost responsibility between the service department and the other departments of the company.

In some cases it is believed that costs should be allocated even though they are not controlled directly by the departments receiving the service. The argument for cost allocation is that all managers should be conscious of the full cost of operating their departments and as a result will be more careful in requesting services. This is a departure from pure responsibility accounting. Whether or not it produces results depends upon the attitudes of the individuals within the organization. Responsibility accounting, at the very least, is an attempt to identify costs with individuals and in some circumstances may have to be modified to receive acceptance by the various individuals that comprise management.

Control Features

The responsibility cost reports provide a basis for control. They identify specific responsibility centers and costs within the centers that may require further attention. An identification of trouble areas, however, is only the beginning of the control process. Questions must be asked. Is the difference between the budgeted cost and the actual cost material enough to justify further investigation? What caused the variation? Is it likely that a variation from the budget will be repeated in the future if action isn't taken? It may be found that measures can be taken that reduce variations in the future or that the variation was a normal variation from the average and didn't warrant investigation. In some cases it is found that the budget was unrealistic and should be revised. The responsibility reports are somewhat like switchboards that flash warning lights when there is trouble. They furnish the initial information that serves as a basis for corrections.

A responsibility cost system can be a subtle means of enforcing company policy. Decisions are made at the top management level which compel cost control at the lower management levels. At all levels of management, supervisory personnel are especially careful when costs are charged against them. Top management does not have to spell out policy in a directive; lower levels of management will be guided according to how the costs are charged to their responsibility areas.

Costs that would normally be included in the reports of subordinates may be excluded if top management believes that the company will benefit from a more liberal policy. On the other hand, costs that are to be controlled more rigorously are given more attention if they are authorized by and charged to the area manager.

For example, a company may provide a copying service to expedite the duplication of forms and reports. The services may be given to all departments with no charge, thus encouraging the departmental supervisors to make use of this service with no cost appearing on their cost reports. However, if top management believes that the service is being drawn upon too freely, a charge may be made to the departments for this service. Managers, knowing that they will be charged for the service, tend to use the service more sparingly.

The successful operation of a responsibility accounting system depends to a large extent upon the attitudes of company personnel. Some research has been done in the area of human behavior within organizations, but there is still much to be done. The central objective is to assign cost responsibility in such a way that the individuals affected are motivated to act in the best interests of the company to achieve the established goals. A policy that may work in one organization may not necessarily work in another because of the differences in the attitudes and behavior of the personnel.

Often it is believed that the only goal of business enterprise is to maximize profits. This is not necessarily true. Ordinarily there is a combination of goals. In addition to profits, the company may seek to provide a superior product or service and may be concerned with the welfare of the employees and community at large.

The various goals of the organization should be coordinated. If one goal is inconsistent with another, management will be confused and will need direction as to how much attention is to be given to one objective as compared with another. For example, a company may seek to train employees on the job in an effort to develop skilled personnel. However, this can interfere with efficient performance and may reduce profits. Guidelines should be established that spell out how much cost and supervisory effort is to be expended on job training, and a balance must be struck that is clearly understood by the personnel affected.

COSTS AND PLANNING

Budgets have already been discussed to some extent in relation to responsibility accounting, but this is only one application of the budget principle. In cost accounting, for example, budgets and standards are used in determining how much it costs to operate a department or to manufacture a certain line of product or even to manufacture one unit of a product line. In budgeting, a thorough study of operations is combined with past experience and estimates of future possibilities. Individual budgets prepared for each function, department, and product line are related to each other and are interlocked in a master budget plan. For example, the estimated production for the next fiscal year is broken down by product line. From this figure it is possible to estimate the activity level and draw up cost budgets for the manufacturing departments. In turn, the budgets of costs for the departments, when related to the number of units of various product lines to be manufactured, yield budgeted costs per unit for each line of product. Budgets are prepared in the same way for other functions of the business, such as sales and administration.

Cost data can be combined and analyzed in the process of either budgeting or reporting costs. Some costs, such as past or historical costs, may serve as a basis for estimating what costs will be in the future; yet these costs are not accounted for in a conventional manner in decisional analysis. The costs measured in the accounting records are not necessarily costs used in decision making. If past performance is to be measured, historical costs are relevant; but if plans are to be made for the future, estimated changes in costs and revenue are more significant.

Various cost concepts are appropriate (1) for controlling operations, (2) for conventional product costing, or (3) for planning future operations. Some of the cost concepts that have particular value in planning are identified and discussed in the following paragraphs.

Differential Costs

Management is expected to make decisions and in doing so compares alternatives. Perhaps a choice must be made between two types of equipment that can be used to perform the same work, or the choice may involve the selection of a plant location. There are various business situations in which alternatives must be compared with one alternative being accepted to the exclusion of the others.

In making a decision, management compares the costs of the alternatives. The costs that remain the same in any case can be disregarded but the difference in cost between alternatives is relevant to decision making. A difference in cost between one course of action and another is a *differential cost*. If a decision results in an increased cost, the differential cost may be more specifically referred to as an *incremental cost*. If the cost is decreased, the differential cost may be referred to as a *decremental cost*.

Differential cost is a broad concept. For example, it may cost $6 to produce one unit of product and $11 to produce two units. The differential cost is $5. Often the additional cost to produce one more unit of product is spoken of as the *marginal cost* of producing that unit. But it is also the differential cost or the incremental cost. The additional cost of producing a unit of product over a given range of productive output is ordinarily spoken of as the *variable cost per unit*. (Within a given range of production, the marginal cost per unit is equal to the variable cost per unit.) The variable cost can also be designated as the differential cost or the incremental cost of producing and selling one more unit. In the situations mentioned on the preceding page, the cost differentials are usually designated specifically as marginal costs or as variable costs, as the case might be.

A decision may result in changes in costs that are ordinarily fixed. As stated before, costs are said to be fixed if they are not altered by changes in output or activity. But a fixed cost may be changed by a management decision. Assume that plans are being made to change a certain production process. Some of the costs will be higher, and some will be lower. Costs that are ordinarily considered to be variable costs may change in the rate of variability, and fixed costs may be increased or decreased if the new production process is accepted. Costs of the present process and the new process are listed below.

	PRESENT PROCESS	NEW PROCESS	DIFFERENTIAL COST (DECREMENTAL)
Materials and labor.......	$ 90,000	$ 93,000	$ 3,000
Supervision....................	49,000	31,000	(18,000)
Insurance.......................	5,000	4,000	(1,000)
Property tax	11,000	11,000	—0—
Depreciation	6,500	6,500	—0—
Total...........................	$161,500	$145,500	$(16,000)

In the example, the costs of materials and labor, supervision, and insurance are changed. They are differential costs with respect to the decision and in this case are net decremental costs, decreasing by a net amount of $16,000, thus favoring the new process. The differential cost is the difference in cost from operating under one alternative as compared with another.

Irrelevant Costs

An *irrelevant cost* is a cost that will not be changed by a decision. Because an irrelevant cost will not be affected, it may be disregarded in the decision-making process. The cost may be a variable cost or a fixed cost. The important point is that the cost is not changed by the decision. If the decision involves the production of more units of product, variable costs are increased and are not irrelevant costs. On the other hand, if no change in productive output or hours of activity is involved in the decision, the variable costs may not be affected, in which case they are disregarded with respect to the decision.

In the prior example, the production costs are expected to decrease by $16,000 a year if the new production process is used. The property tax and depreciation are not expected to change and are irrelevant costs with respect to this decision. Because these costs are unaffected by the decision, they may be excluded in the decisional analysis. The costs relevant to the decision are listed at the top of the next page.

	PRESENT PROCESS	NEW PROCESS	DIFFERENTIAL COST (DECREMENTAL)
Materials and labor	$ 90,000	$ 93,000	$ 3,000
Supervision	49,000	31,000	(18,000)
Insurance	5,000	4,000	(1,000)
Total	$144,000	$128,000	$(16,000)

The differential cost in favor of the new decision is $16,000, and this is the significant factor in the decision.

Sunk Costs

A *sunk cost* is a cost that has already been incurred. Therefore, a sunk cost cannot be changed by any decision made at the present time or in the future. An individual may regret having made a purchase but, after the purchase has been made, cannot avoid the cost by taking subsequent action. Perhaps the property can be sold, in which case the cost of the property is matched against the proceeds from the sale in the determination of gain or loss. Or the person may decide to keep the property, in which case the cost is matched against revenue over the time that it is used in operations. In any event, the cost has been incurred and cannot be avoided. It is a sunk cost with respect to present and future decisions.

To illustrate, assume that Lafayette Products Company purchased a hydraulic hoist for $26,000. The hoist can be used in operations for five years and is not expected to have any residual salvage value. Shortly after making the purchase, the management of the company recognizes that the investment should not have been made. The hoist cannot yield the operating advantages originally contemplated but can probably yield cost savings of $14,000 over the five years. However, the company is committed to the purchase and cannot avoid the $26,000 cost. The company is considering whether to use the hoist or to sell it.

	USE	SELL
Saving in cost over 5 years by using the hoist	$ 14,000	
Proceeds from immediate sale of the hoist		$ 18,000
Less cost of the hoist:		
Depreciation over 5 years	26,000	
Cost of the hoist		26,000
Net loss over 5 years	$(12,000)	
Net loss on the sale		$ (8,000)

The relevant amounts for decision making are the $14,000 in cost saving over five years as compared with the $18,000 that can be received from the sale of the property. The $26,000 invested in the property is not relevant; it is the same in both cases. Lafayette Products Company should sell the property for $18,000. The decision is obvious in this situation. Ordinarily future dollar amounts should be reduced to present values when a comparision is to be made. (The present value concept is discussed in Appendix C.)

Opportunity Costs

Costs are generally looked upon as being outlays or expenditures that must be made either in the present or in the future to obtain goods and services. But the concept of cost can be extended to include sacrifices that are made when incoming benefits or returns are refused. In choosing between alternatives, management tries to select the best alternative but in doing so has to give up the returns that could have been derived from the rejected alternatives. The sacrifice of a return or benefit from a rejected alternative is spoken of as being the *opportunity cost* of the alternative accepted. Opportunity costs are not entered in the accounting records, of course, but they are used in decision making.

Often management is confronted with alternatives, each having its advantages. For example, there may be an opportunity to make one of two different product lines, but both product lines cannot be manufactured with the present facilities. It may be estimated that Product A will contribute $16,000 a year to profits and that Product B will contribute $21,000 a year to profits. Product B should be selected, and the opportunity cost of selecting Product B is the sacrifice of the $16,000 that could be earned by Product A.

Estimated increase in annual profits from Product B	$21,000
Less opportunity cost (sacrifice of estimated annual profits from Product A)	16,000
Advantage of Product B	$ 5,000

An Illustration of Decision-Making Costs

The distinctions that have been made between direct and indirect costs, controllable and noncontrollable costs, and fixed and variable costs are important in product costing and are important in the control of operations. In costing products and in controlling operations, management needs to know which costs can be identified directly with a function or operation and which costs can be controlled at a certain management level. In addition, cost behavior is important. A distinction must be made between costs that are expected to vary with changes in activity or output and costs that remain fixed over a given range of changes in activity or output. These cost distinctions are important in product costing and in controlling operations and, when used properly, are most helpful in planning and in decision making.

Differential costs and opportunity costs have little or no value in costing products or in controlling costs, but these cost concepts are most valuable in decision making. Decisions influence the future course of events, and the emphasis is on what lies ahead and not on what has already taken place.

Assume that Damon and Kell, Inc., are presently using a unit of equipment to manufacture a certain line of product. The results of operation are shown below.

Revenue from product sales	$170,000
Cost of products sold and operating expense excluding depreciation..	$110,000
Depreciation of equipment	21,000
	$131,000
Net income	$ 39,000

The present operation can be continued, or the company can use the equipment to manufacture another line of product that should produce revenue of $210,000 each year. The cost to manufacture this product and the operating expenses excluding depreciation of the equipment are estimated at $130,000.

The new product line adds $40,000 to revenue, and the incremental cost is $20,000. Hence, there is an advantage of $20,000 in accepting the new product line. The depreciation of the equipment is a sunk cost and can be ignored in making the decision. Perhaps sunk costs are included in the cost of the products sold and in the operating costs; but if they are included in both of the alternatives, they do not affect the analysis. The differentials are the relevant factors in making the decision.

Additional revenue from new product line ($210,000 − $170,000)	$40,000
Additional costs of new product line ($130,000 − $110,000)	20,000
Net advantage of new product line	$20,000

The problem can be examined in still another way. The present operation provides $60,000 each year, as determined by adding depreciation, a sunk cost, to the net income ($21,000 + $39,000 = $60,000). Any alternative use of the equipment must provide at least $60,000 if it is to be equally acceptable. Stated in another way, the opportunity cost of any other alternative is the $60,000 that must be sacrificed if another alternative is selected.

The new product line is expected to contribute $80,000 each year: the $210,000 revenue minus the cost of goods sold and operating expenses of $130,000.

Expected contribution from new product line each year....	$80,000
Less opportunity cost (the sacrifice of the contribution of the present product line each year)	60,000
Net advantage of new product line each year	$20,000

QUESTIONS

1. Why is it necessary for management to have detailed cost information?

2. Distinguish between fixed costs and variable costs.

3. Why are fixed costs considered to be troublesome?

4. Distinguish between direct and indirect costs.

5. Are direct costs always variable costs? Explain.

6. Describe the logic that is used in making cost allocations.

7. Explain how cost allocation can help management to decide whether or not a department is able to carry its share of total supporting costs.

8. Will an allocated cost be reduced by the elimination of a department? Explain.

9. If a department is eliminated, how is the cost that was previously allocated to that department handled?

10. A plant superintendent's salary has been established at $80,000 a year and is allocated to departments on the basis of the number of employees in the departments. A department to which $10,000 of the salary was allocated has been eliminated. Does this mean that the salary cost of $80,000 will be reduced? Explain.

11. Referring to Question 10, are there circumstances under which the salary of $80,000 could be reduced by elimination of a department? Explain.

12. Distinguish between controllable and noncontrollable costs.

13. Are fixed costs uncontrollable? Explain.

14. Does time have any effect upon the controllability of cost? Explain.

15. What is responsibility accounting?

16. How does a responsibility accounting system serve as a subtle means of enforcing company policy?

17. Why might some managers prefer to have costs reported to them by project while others prefer costs reported to them on a time basis?

18. How may service department costs be handled in responsibility accounting systems?

19. What are differential costs?

20. Why are sunk costs not relevant in decision making?

21. What are opportunity costs? Are opportunity costs important in decision making? Explain.

EXERCISES

1. Fixed and Variable Costs. A flexible budget of costs for Division A has been prepared for the next year showing costs at different hours of operation.

Hours of operation	120,000	130,000	140,000
Materials	$ 72,000	$ 78,000	$ 84,000
Labor	96,000	104,000	112,000
Heat and light	30,000	30,000	30,000
Maintenance and repairs	25,000	25,000	25,000
Supplies used	60,000	65,000	70,000
Taxes and insurance	18,000	18,000	18,000
Other labor costs	48,000	52,000	56,000
Depreciation	11,000	11,000	11,000
Total	$360,000	$383,000	$406,000

Required:
(1) Identify the variable costs and the fixed costs.
(2) From the information given, determine the rate of variability per hour for each of the variable costs.

2. Unit Fixed Costs. Slocum Supply Company has budgeted fixed costs for the year at $75,000. It is anticipated that no less than 10,000 units of product are to be manufactured next year. Even in a poor year, probably 15,000 units will be made. If the company operates at an average or normal level, 20,000 units should be made. With good conditions, even 25,000 units may be made.

Required:
(1) Determine the fixed cost per unit under each of the assumptions stated.
(2) Which unit cost would you be inclined to use in determining product cost in the long run? Explain.

3. Unit Product Cost. You have been told that materials costing $17 for each unit of product are needed to produce a certain product line. Two units of product can be manufactured in each hour with labor cost of $12 per hour. Total fixed costs of manufacturing amount to $180,000 per year. No other costs are incurred in manufacturing.

Required:
(1) Determine the total unit cost to manufacture the product. Why are you unable to answer this requirement?
(2) If 20,000 units are to be manufactured each year, what would the unit product cost be?

4. Direct and Indirect Cost. Catamount Outfitters, Inc., operates with three divisions, A, B, and C. Division A produces revenue of $1,200,000 for the year; Division B produces revenue of $700,000; and Division C produces $600,000. The total costs for the year for each division are given below.

	Divisions			
	A	B	C	Total
Materials, labor, and other direct costs	$680,000	$720,000	$480,000	$1,880,000
Allocated company costs	200,000	200,000	200,000	600,000
Total costs	$880,000	$920,000	$680,000	$2,480,000

Required:
(1) List the costs by division that can be directly attributed to that division.

(2) Do all three divisions provide an amount over their direct costs to the total operation? Identify any division that does not.

(3) Is there any division that covers direct costs but does not bear its full share of costs of the total operation? Identify that division, if any.

(4) Which division(s) can bear all of its share of the allocated cost?

5. Full Cost of Departmental Operation. The superintendent of a division of Blyer Controls, Inc., is responsible for the operation of three departments that are located in one building. Department A occupies 60% of the space, and the remaining two departments share the rest of the space equally. Total building occupancy cost amounts to $75,000 for the year. The superintendent's salary for the year is $50,000. There are 50 employees in Department A, 40 employees in Department B, and 10 employees in Department C.

The direct costs of departmental operation for the year are given below.

| | Departments | | | |
	1	2	3	Total
Direct costs	$63,000	$52,000	$46,000	$161,000

The superintendent wants to know the total cost to operate each department including each department's share of total divisional costs.

Required: Prepare a report showing the total costs to operate each department.

6. Elimination of a Department. The president of Grunewald Appliance Company notes that Department 3 has been operating at a loss. The president reasons that profits will be increased by $9,000 by elimination of this department inasmuch as costs of this department are in excess of revenue by this amount.

| | Departments | | | | |
	1	2	3	4	Total
Revenue................................	$132,000	$168,000	$125,000	$ 98,000	$523,000
Direct costs of department	$ 82,000	$108,000	$104,000	$ 61,000	$355,000
Allocated company costs...	30,000	36,000	30,000	25,000	121,000
Total costs	$112,000	$144,000	$134,000	$ 86,000	$476,000
Net income (loss)................	$ 20,000	$ 24,000	$(9,000)	$ 12,000	$ 47,000

Required: Is the president correct? Prepare an analysis to indicate what the results would be if Department 3 were eliminated.

7. Controllable and Noncontrollable Costs. Sandra Nash buys materials for her department and is responsible for hiring personnel and setting wage rates. She also incurs telephone, postage, and supply costs for the department. Heat and light, rent on the building, and taxes and insurance are allocated on the basis of space occupied. Home office costs are apportioned to the departments on the basis of the number of employees in the departments.

A budget report for Sandra Nash's department for the month of June, 1981, is given on the following page.

Required:

(1) Which of the costs are controllable by Nash?

(2) Prepare a cost report that shows only the costs controlled by Nash.

	Budget	Actual	Variance Over (Under) Budget
Materials...	$ 8,400	$ 8,200	$(200)
Wages...	7,400	7,400	—
Telephone	300	320	20
Postage...	65	50	(15)
Supplies..	440	450	10
Heat and light.................................	600	740	140
Rent	700	700	—
Taxes and insurance.........................	250	300	50
Home office costs.............................	850	1,200	350
Total costs	$19,005	$19,360	$ 355

8. Cost Classifications. The supervisor of Department 10 purchases supplies, authorizes repairs and maintenance service, and hires labor for the department. Various costs for the month of October, 1980, are given below.

Sales salaries and commissions...	$ 9,850
Salary, supervisor of Dept. 10...	1,800
Factory heat and light...	650
General office salaries..	14,200
Depreciation, factory	750
Supplies, Dept. 10..	1,430
Repairs and maintenance, Dept. 10...	820
Factory insurance	460
Labor cost, Dept. 10...	17,220
Salary of factory superintendent	2,400
Total..	$49,580

Required:

(1) List the costs that can be controlled by the supervisor of Department 10.
(2) List the costs that can be directly identified with Department 10.
(3) List the costs that will have to be allocated to the factory departments.
(4) List the costs that do not pertain to factory operation.

9. Cost Decision. Blaine Cramer plans to use a specialized machine for work on a product line that will add $9,000 to total profits. This machine may also be used for work on a contract that is expected to contribute $17,000 to total profits. The cost of $1,500 to operate the machine will be the same under either alternative and has not been deducted in either case in determining the expected addition to profits. If the machine is used for one alternative, it cannot be used for the other.

Required:

(1) Identify the sunk cost in this decisional situation.
(2) What is the opportunity cost?
(3) Compute the profit advantage from the better alternative.

10. Cost Decision. Ten Mile Construction Company has just purchased a derrick for use in the construction of high-rise buildings at a cost of $68,000. The derrick has not been entirely satisfactory and has broken down at various critical times. Lou Goldman, the superintendent, believes that the equipment can be used for four years and after four years will have little, if any, value.

Kathleen Smith, the office manager, tells Goldman that it would be best to sell the equipment now and purchase a new derrick that would be more appropriate for their needs. According to estimates made, she has computed net returns for the entire four years at $18,000.

Goldman concedes that the derrick is not strong enough for the required work but feels that it can be used if due care is taken. He knows that he cannot get more than $30,000 if he sells the equipment now, and he believes that the company cannot afford that kind of loss. He states that since the company has invested $68,000 in the derrick, they should keep it and recover the investment over the next four years.

Required: Comment on the positions taken by Smith and by Goldman. Give a simple analysis to support your recommendation.

11. Opportunity Cost and Sunk Cost. Marvin Skubik has retired from business and plans to operate a bait shop at St. John's Pass. He has always been interested in fishing and boating and sees this as an opportunity to live and work in this environment.

He has prepared estimates of anticipated revenue and costs for a year as follows:

Revenue	$38,000
Cost of materials and supplies	$11,000
Wages for helpers	9,800
Rent	4,200
Utilities	600
Miscellaneous	400
	$26,000
Net income	$12,000

While considering this opportunity, he receives an offer to act as a business consultant on a part-time basis for $18,000 a year. This would mean that he could not operate the bait shop. However, he could still rent the shop and use the office portion for record storage and rent out the remaining space for $3,800.

Required:
(1) If Skubik rejects consulting in favor of operating the bait shop, what is the minimum value that he places on the pursuit of his hobby?
(2) If Skubik decides to consult, what is the opportunity cost of this decision?
(3) What is the sunk cost in this decisional situation?

12. Product Line Decision. Any one of three different product lines can be produced by Steiner Mills, Inc., with the present equipment in one of the divisions. The annual depreciation of the equipment is $6,400; and the annual cost to operate the equipment, regardless of product line manufactured, is $4,600.

Product A is expected to yield sales revenue of $71,000 a year with increased costs of production amounting to $42,000. Product B should yield sales revenue of $46,000 a year with increased costs of $15,000. Product C should yield sales revenue of $117,000 with increased costs of $96,000.

Required:
(1) Which of the three product lines seems to offer the best profit potential based on the information given? Show computations.

(2) Identify the sunk costs.

(3) What is the opportunity cost of selecting only the best product line?

PROBLEMS

2-1. Cost Classification. Various costs of production are listed below for the Bellevue Plant.

Materials — used only for the manufacture of Product 17 in Department 8
Production wages in Department 8
Plant taxes and insurance
Lubrication of equipment, Department 8
Supplies used, Department 8
Plant heat and light
Plant supervision
Depreciation of equipment, Department 8
Salary, supervisor of Department 8
Plant depreciation

Required:

(1) Identify the costs that are direct or indirect with respect to Department 8.

(2) Identify the costs that are controllable by the supervisor of Department 8. (Give your reason for classification in situations that are uncertain.)

(3) Identify the costs that are fixed or variable. (Give your reason for classification in situations that are uncertain.)

2-2. Cost allocations. Sheriden Public Library operates with four divisions classified by type of books and reading materials. The four divisions are Technical, Historical, General, and Children. Direct costs of operation of each division for the year are given below.

	Technical	Historical	General	Children
Salaries	$55,000	$28,000	$32,000	$27,000
Books	8,800	7,600	11,200	2,700
Periodicals	3,700	3,400	2,300	1,400
Supplies	3,200	4,100	2,500	2,800

Other data with respect to library operation are given below.

	Space Occupied	Number of Employees	Number of Orders Processed
Technical	30	50	40
Historical	20	10	20
General	40	20	20
Children	10	20	20
Total	100	100	100

The costs of operating the library as a total entity follow.

Building occupancy and utilities	$35,000
Library administration	80,000
Order department	45,000

Required: Prepare a cost report showing the total direct costs for each library division, the total allocated costs, and the total costs for each division.

2-3. Identification of Controllable Costs. The departmental supervisors at Reed-McAlister, Inc., are authorized to purchase the materals needed in production, hire and assign the production workers, and incur various costs for their departments. The equipment used in the department is acquired at a higher management level, but supervisors are responsible for proper care and maintenance. The salaries of the supervisors are shown under the cost of supervision.

Sometimes labor is loaned to another department. Company policy is to charge the supervisor who loans the workers with the labor cost. However, the cost of this labor is not included as a cost of the products of the lending department.

During the year, Department 7 manufactured 40,000 units as budgeted. Budgeted and actual costs for Department 7 are given below.

	Budget	Actual
Materials	$210,000	$208,600
Labor	119,000	121,300
Labor loaned to Department 11	17,000	16,500
Department costs:		
Supervision	21,000	21,000
Indirect materials	14,300	14,700
Repairs and maintenance	2,100	2,200
Equipment operating cost	3,400	3,300
Depreciation, equipment	4,000	4,000
Allocated plant costs:		
Superintendence	19,500	21,000
Heat, light, and power	3,700	3,900
Taxes and insurance	5,400	6,100
Other plant occupancy cost	5,000	6,700
Depreciation, plant	7,000	7,000
Total cost	$431,400	$436,300

Required:

(1) Compute the budgeted unit cost of the product and the actual unit cost following the established company policy.
(2) Prepare a cost report that will show only the costs that can be controlled by the supervisor. Show cost variations from the budget.
(3) Does it appear that the supervisor was responsible for a large part of the variation between budgeted and actual costs?
(4) Why should a supervisor be held accountable for the labor cost of workers loaned to other departments?

2-4. Product Costs and Control. A small metal cabinet is manufactured by Cardiff Metals, Inc. The materials for each cabinet cost $8.80; the labor cost per cabinet is $6.20. Various supplies cost $1.50 per cabinet.

The cost to operate the department in which the cabinets are produced are fixed and have been estimated for the year as follows:

Supervision	$47,000
Equipment operating costs	4,200
Repairs and maintenance of equipment	2,800
Depreciation of equipment	2,000
Total	$56,000

The supervisor of this department can control all of these costs with the exception of depreciation of equipment at $2,000 and the salary of the department supervisor of $26,000 that is included in the total cost of supervision.

Costs for the overall plant have been estimated for the year as follows:

Plant superintendence	$ 53,000
Indirect labor	29,000
Plant occupancy cost	22,000
Depreciation, factory	6,000
Total	$110,000

Factory overhead is allocated to the various departments on the basis of a factor that combines space occupied with the number of employees. The department in which the cabinets are produced is expected to absorb 20% of the total plant cost of $110,000, and this department produces cabinets exclusively.

Required:

(1) What is the variable cost per cabinet? Does your answer depend upon the number of cabinets produced?

(2) Identify the indirect costs of the department. Identify the costs that can be controlled by the departmental supervision. Assume production of 90,000 cabinets.

(3) What is the total cost per cabinet when 80,000 cabinets are manufactured? When 90,000 cabinets are manufactured?

2-5. Responsibility Cost Report. Charles Sidener is responsible for the operation of the welding shop at Lieberman Metals Company. A budget for the shop for the month of July is given below.

Materials and supplies	$ 8,180
Labor	6,430
Supervision	2,000
Fuel	1,340
Telephone	350
Postage	170
Taxes and insurance	1,480
Heat and light	1,630
Repairs and maintenance	1,460
Depreciation, equipment	500
Other allocated plant costs	2,100
Total	$25,640

The cost of materials and supplies for the month was $8,210, fuel, $1,480. Postage amounted to $190. Repairs and maintenance cost was $1,350. Heat and light costs were $2,170, and the other allocated plant costs were $3,200. All other costs were in agreement with the budget.

The taxes and insurance, heat and light, depreciation of equipment, and other allocated plant costs are controlled by upper levels of management. All other costs with the exception of supervision are approved by Sidener.

Required:

(1) Prepare a responsibility cost report showing a comparision of the budget and actual costs for July.

(2) Compare total costs for the department with the total budget. Does it appear that Sidener was responsible for a large part of the unfavorable cost variation?

2-6. Responsibility Cost Report. A cost report for the month of April is given for the assembly department of Taveras Engines, Inc.

	Budget	Actual	Variance (Under) Over
Materials and supplies............................	$16,230	$16,260	$ 30
Wages...	17,500	17,500	—
Payroll taxes...	1,200	1,200	—
Employee benefits..................................	3,200	3,200	—
Taxes and insurance..............................	1,500	2,200	700
Travel expense.......................................	300	530	230
Postage..	180	160	(20)
Heat and light..	1,000	1,140	140
Repairs	1,200	1,400	200
Lubrication of equipment......................	150	180	30
Fuel..	600	750	150
Department supervision.........................	2,200	2,200	—
Plant supervision...................................	1,400	1,400	—
Depreciation, equipment	300	300	—
Other plant costs allocated..................	2,500	3,800	1,300
Total..	$49,460	$52,220	$2,760

The departmental supervisor states that the budget for repairs was based on 150 hours of service expected to be requested from the company's plant maintenance department at the internal billed rate of $8 per hour. At the beginning of the month, the billing rate was increased to $10 per hour. Only 140 hours of service were requested; hence, the supervisor disclaims responsibility for this variance.

The travel expense was higher than expected because of an emergency trip to obtain a replacement part for a machine that suddenly broke down in operation.

The supervisor has no authority over taxes and insurance, heat and light, department supervision, plant supervision, or other plant costs allocated.

Required:
(1) Prepare a revised cost report showing only the costs controlled by the supervisor.
(2) Do you accept the reasoning given for the relatively large variances in repairs and in travel expense? Comment.

2-7. Preparation of Responsibility Cost Budget. Andrew Judd has just been appointed as the supervisor of a production department of Warden Industries, Inc. This department manufactures small parts used by other departments. To a large extent, costs are influenced by the demand of the other departments.

In preparing the budget, Judd goes over the production budgets of the other departments that have requested hours of service from his department, as shown at the top of the following page. He discussed the budget estimates with his superior, Clara Kolkoski. She advises him that the supervisor of Department 15 is inclined to overestimate requirements and that a budget of 7,000 hours is more likely. Conversely, the supervisor of Department 26 is likely

Requesting Department	Hours Requested
15	8,400 7,000
17	4,300
23	6,400
26	5,400 6,300

to underestimate and come in with a last minute request for additional hours. It is quite likely that Department 26 will eventually request a total of 6,300 hours.

All workers in the department are to receive a wage rate of $9 per hour, and each will be expected to work 1,600 hours per year. Judd has the authority to hire an assistant at a salary of $19,000 per year, and his own salary has been established by Kolkoski at $27,000.

Materials required for the year are estimated to cost $263,000. Other costs related to departmental operation have been budgeted as follows:

Supplies	$32,000
Fuel	6,000
Repairs and maintenance	3,500
Plant occupancy cost allocated	12,000
Total	$53,500

Kolkoski states that top management does not like to see much overtime but recognizes that some of it may be unavoidable. She advises that 600 hours of overtime pay at time and a half be added to the budget.

Required: From the information given, prepare a responsibility cost budget for Judd's department. Estimate the number of employees needed for production.

2-8. New Product Line Decision. The superintendent of Hathaway Plains Company has been using equipment in one area of the plant to manufacture a product line that yields a net income of $20,700 each year after deducting both direct costs and allocated plant costs. The superintendent is not satisfied with the results and believes that the equipment could be used more productively to manufacture a new product line. The new product line should yield the following results each year:

Net sales	$160,700
Materials, new product	$ 81,600
Labor, new product	28,700
Additional cost of supervision, new product	5,000
Allocated plant costs:	
Factory heat and light	5,700
Factory repairs and maintenance	3,800
Factory taxes and insurance	1,700
Factory superintendence	8,600
Factory depreciation	2,200
Depreciation, equipment	1,100
	$138,400
Net income	$ 22,300

Required:

(1) How much will the new product line contribute to the total operation? (Exclude allocated costs.)

(2) How much does the present product line contribute to the total operation?

(3) Identify the sunk costs in this decision.

(4) Should Hathaway Plains Company produce the new product line? Identify the opportunity cost in this decision.

2-9. Cost Decision. Huntsville Stove Company plans to shut down one division of the plant which has been contributing $80,000 a year to the total company operation. This division contributes but does not carry its full share of the allocated company cost.

The president of the company plans to use the space occupied by this division for the production of a portable wood stove that has recently become popular with campers. The stove can be sold for $150 per unit, and it is estimated that the variable cost to make each stove would be $125. Also, there would be additional fixed costs of $40,000 a year if the portable stove is made. Conservative estimates indicate that 6,000 units should be sold each year.

The superintendent of this division is trying to persuade the president that the space is still not being used to its full potential. The company costs allocated to the division under examination amount to $120,000 per year. The superintendent argues that there is a market for the sale of 5,000 additional mobile home heating units each year at a selling price of $120 per unit. These units cannot be manufactured without the release of space from this division for this purpose exclusively. The variable cost per unit amounts to $80. However, fixed costs related to this operation would have to be increased by $60,000 a year.

Required:

(1) Which alternative is better?

(2) Determine the opportunity cost of any alternative competing for the space released by the discontinued line.

(3) Determine the opportunity cost of the better alternative.

(4) Can either alternative absorb all of the allocated company cost?

2-10. Cost Decision. Weir and Manning, Inc., operates as a building contractor. Three contracts are available for bids, but the company can only handle one of the contracts because of the time constraints. Bidding will be competitive, but management believes that any one of the three contracts can be obtained at the bid prices indicated.

The accountant has prepared estimate sheets for each of the contracts as shown on the following page.

The supervision cost consists of the salary of the construction supervisor who will supervise whichever job is undertaken. If none of the contracts is accepted, the supervisor will be reassigned to other work. The same equipment can be used for any of the jobs. The costs of the division have been allocated to the contracts at 60% of the labor cost. All of the other costs are additional costs that are associated with the contracts.

The equipment to be used on these contracts can be rented to other contractors for $40,000 if none of the contracts is accepted. Depreciation on the equipment would remain the same; and taxes, licenses, and insurance in the amount of $8,500 would be incurred.

Required:

(1) What is the opportunity cost of selecting any one of the three contracts?

	Contracts		
	1	2	3
Bid price..	$2,350,000	$1,900,000	$2,500,000
Materials	$1,422,000	$1,242,000	$1,570,000
Labor..	514,000	372,000	480,000
Supplies	47,000	31,000	66,000
Power and lubrication	8,200	7,100	9,200
Repairs and maintenance................	6,300	5,200	6,800
Taxes and insurance........................	9,400	8,600	9,700
Licenses and permits.......................	1,200	1,200	1,200
Supervision.......................................	30,000	30,000	30,000
Depreciation, equipment.................	25,000	25,000	25,000
Allocated costs................................	308,400	223,200	288,000
Total cost......................................	$2,371,500	$1,945,300	$2,485,900
Estimated profit (loss).....................	$(21,500)	$(45,300)	$ 14,100

(2) Identify the sunk costs.
(3) Which alternative should be selected? Show computations. Explain why certain costs are not included in your computation.

3
COST ESTIMATION AND CONTROL

Effective budgeting and control depend upon the ability of management to estimate costs accurately under different circumstances. Costs behave in various ways, even within a company, depending upon how particular services or materials are used in the departments.

THE COST ESTIMATION PROBLEM

Cost studies are made continuously inasmuch as cost behavior may change over time as conditions change. Management is constantly examining cost behavior in an effort to prepare better budgets through accurate cost prediction. Cost estimation is a very serious business. The firm that has a thorough knowledge of its costs has a distinct advantage over less knowledgeable competitors.

The costs of projects or departments may be estimated or predicted by a combination of two approaches:

1. Engineering estimates of materials and work requirements.
2. An examination of past cost behavior.

Engineers who are familiar with the technical requirements estimate the quantities of materials that are needed for production and the labor or machine hours required for various operations. Prices and rates are applied to the physical measurements to obtain cost estimates. In the preparation of budgets, the effect of changes in critical factors, such as materials prices, labor rates, or machine hours of operation, must be considered in the prediction process and controlled to the extent possible in actual operations.

Past cost behavior is also studied as a guide in predicting costs. The future is seldom a duplication of the past, yet a study of past cost behavior can be effectively utilized in predicting cost.

It may appear that costs that have already been incurred can be determined precisely. This is not always true. For example, the cost of repairs may have been $1,200 at a time when a department operated at 800 hours and may have been $1,500 in another period of similar length. The rate of cost variability per hour may not be determinable at a precise amount, but an estimate should be made of the average rate of cost variability.

Significance of Cost Estimation

Cost estimation is extremely important. In order to manage effectively, management must be able to estimate costs under different conditions and at different levels of volume. This is essential in the preparation of budgets and in the subsequent control of the costs. Cost estimation is fundamental to the task of setting prices, bidding on contracts, and planning profits.

Costs, as stated in the previous chapter, do not always behave in the same manner. Certain costs that increase or decrease with changes in the amount of activity or volume of products or services are the variable costs. Other costs that remain constant over a wide range of activity or volume are the fixed costs. However, many costs are neither entirely variable or fixed. These semivariable costs must be examined closely to determine the variable portion and the fixed portion.

It is very unlikely that costs can be segregated precisely into variable and fixed components. Various factors influence cost behavior, and conditions existing at different levels of activity are dissimilar. Hence, the cost at a given level cannot be expected to be at an exact amount. Even when controlled carefully, it tends to fall within a range. Nevertheless, the segregation process must be undertaken to obtain the best cost data possible.

Cost Segregation

Costs are segregated to determine the portion that is variable and the portion that is fixed. A segregation of past costs into variable and fixed components provides a foundation for the prediction of future cost behavior. To gain an understanding of the cost estimation problem and the limitations imposed upon exactitude, it is necessary to have some knowledge of the technical procedures. There are certain mechanical and routine procedures that cannot be avoided in trying to arrive at the best possible estimate of costs.

Three general methods are often employed in cost segregation:

1. The visual fit.
2. The high-low point.
3. The line of regression.

The Visual Fit. Costs for various hours of operation may be plotted on a graph, and a line of average may be drawn on the graph by visual approximation. The line is drawn, insofar as it is possible by visual judgment, so that the distances of the observations above the line are equal to the distances of the observations below the line. The line represents the data as a line of conditional expected values and is called the *line of regression*. The variable cost per hour is indicated by the slope of the line, and the fixed cost is measured where the line begins at zero hours of activity.

For purposes of illustration, it is assumed that a record of maintenance cost has been kept for various hours of operation as follows:

Hours X	Maintenance Cost Y
50	$120
30	110
10	60
50	150
40	100
30	80
20	70
60	150
40	110
20	50

The maintenance costs have been plotted on the graph shown below, and a line of regression has been fitted to the data. The line is drawn so that the sum of the distances from the line to all points above the line is equal to the sum of the distances from the line to all

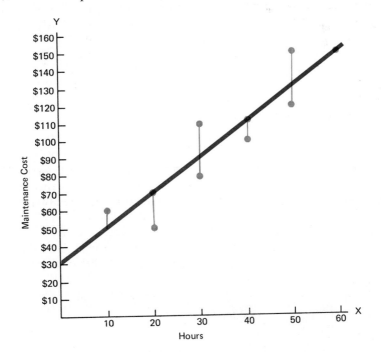

points below it. The average (defined as an arithmetic mean) is the point at which the sum of the deviations above that point is equal to the sum of the deviations below that point. The line of regression represents a continuous series of average points and thus is a line of averages.

The line of regression illustrated begins at $30 and rises $20 for each increase of 10 hours. Therefore the estimated fixed cost is $30, and the variable cost is an average rate of $2 per hour ($20 ÷ 10 hours).

The High-Low Point Method. In the high-low point method, the observed costs for various hours of activity are listed in order from the highest number of hours in the range to the lowest. The difference in hours between the highest level and the lowest is divided into the difference in cost for the corresponding hours to arrive at a rate of variable cost per hour. For example, the costs of a certain supply for various hours of operation have been incurred in the past as follows:

	HOURS OF ACTIVITY	SUPPLIES COST
High	95,000	$397,000
	90,000	377,000
	87,000	365,000
	82,000	345,000
	78,000	329,000
	75,000	317,000
	66,000	281,000
	58,000	239,000
Low	50,000	217,000

The difference in hours is 45,000 (**95,000 − 50,000**), and the difference in cost is $180,000 (**$397,000 − $217,000**). The variable supplies cost is computed below:

$$\frac{\textbf{Difference in cost}}{\textbf{Difference in hours}} = \frac{\$180,000}{45,000} = \frac{\$4 \textbf{ variable cost}}{\textbf{per hour}}$$

The fixed cost can be estimated at any level (assuming a uniform or constant variable cost) by subtracting the variable cost portion from the total cost. At 95,000 hours, for example, the total cost is $397,000; and the total variable cost is $380,000 (95,000 hours × $4 variable cost per hour). Hence, the fixed cost is $17,000 ($397,000 − $380,000). In this example, it is assumed that uniform variability applies over the entire range. In some cases, however, the rate of variability may change, and this must be considered in cost analysis.

The Line of Regression Method. A line of regression can be fitted to a large quantity of data more precisely by the *least squares method*. Basically, the line is determined so that the algebraic sum of the squared deviations from that line is at a minimum. The line of regression is derived by solving two simultaneous equations which are based on the condition that the sum of deviations above the line equals the sum of deviations below the line.

The equation for the determination of a straight line is given below:

$$Y = a + bX$$

This equation states that the value of Y is equal to a point (*a*) plus a percentage of variability applied to X. In the last example, *a* was the $30 of fixed cost. The percentage (*b*) was the change in Y in relation to the change in X. In the example, Y increased by $20 for each increase of 10 hours. Hence, the percentage of change was 200 percent (20/10).

$$Y = \$30 + 200\%X$$

If X is assigned a value of 10, Y is equal to 50.

$$Y = \$30 + 2(10)$$
$$Y = \$50$$

By substituting various values for X, a line is formed on a graph.

As another illustration, assume that supplies costs for various hours of operation have been recorded and that computations have been made as shown below:

HOURS X	SUPPLIES COST Y	X²	XY
30	$ 500	900	$ 15,000
50	650	2,500	32,500
20	300	400	6,000
10	300	100	3,000
60	900	3,600	54,000
50	750	2,500	37,500
40	650	1,600	26,000
60	700	3,600	42,000
30	450	900	13,500
10	350	100	3,500
40	600	1,600	24,000
20	450	400	9,000
ΣX = 420	ΣY = $6,600	ΣX² = 18,200	ΣXY = $266,000

The first step in obtaining a line of regression is to set up an equation for a line that will represent all of the data.

Equation (1) $\Sigma Y = Na + b\Sigma X$

Another equation [Equation (2)] is formed by multiplying each point that constitutes Equation (1) by ΣX. Note that Equation (1) is not merely multiplied by ΣX. Instead, each point (Y = a + bX) is multiplied by ΣX.

Equation (2) $\Sigma XY = \Sigma Xa + b\Sigma X^2$

Referring to the data listed above, substitute values and by simultaneous equations solve for either *a* or *b*.

Equation (1) $\$6,600 = 12a + 420b$
Equation (2) $\$266,000 = 420a + 18,200b$

To solve for b, multiply Equation (1) by 35 (420 ÷ 12):

Equation (3) $231,000 = 420a + 14,700b$

Subtract Equation (3) from Equation (2); the a values will cancel out to yield:

$35,000 = 3,500b$
$b = \$10$ the rate of variable supply cost per hour

Substitute the value of b in Equation (1) and solve for a.

$6,600 = 12a + 4,200$
$12a = \$2,400$
$a = \$200$ estimated fixed supply cost

A line of regression for the data given is shown on the graph below.

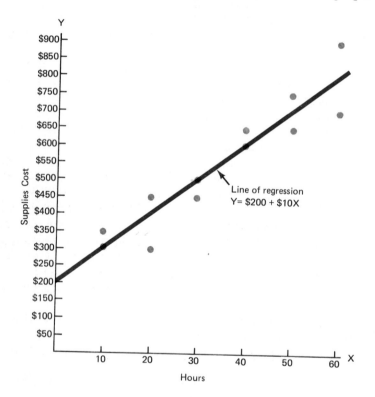

CONTROL LIMITS

From the data given in the preceding example, it has been estimated that the fixed supply cost should amount to $200 and that the variable supply cost should vary at the rate of $10 per hour. For 30 hours of operation the total cost is estimated to be approximately

$500. This is an average cost, however, and it is unlikely that the actual cost will be precisely $500.

Because some variation in cost can be expected, management should establish an acceptable range of tolerance. Costs that lie within the limits of variation can be accepted. Costs beyond the limits, however, are identified and may be investigated.

Normal Distribution

In dealing with cost variances, or variances in any type of data, it is necessary to consider the way that the data are distributed. Statistical data may form a pattern of distribution designated as a normal distribution. In a *normal distribution*, data can be plotted on a smooth, continuous, symmetrical bell-shaped curve with a single peak in the center of distribution. Surveys have revealed, for example, that the height of persons in a given society or the length of steel bars manufactured in a production process can be described by a normal distribution.

Management may find that cost data are normally distributed for a given level of operation and, in deciding upon an acceptable range of cost variability, may employ the concept of standard deviation that is commonly used in statistics. The *standard deviation* measures the extent of variation that may be expected in a distribution of data, and in this chapter it will be assumed that cost data are normally distributed for each relevant level of operation. Published tables show what proportion of the data may be expected to lie within plus and minus a given number of standard deviations from the mean (average).

In the example, an estimated conditional standard deviation is computed. It is conditional because it is dependent upon the number of hours of operation. Also, it is an estimated conditional standard deviation inasmuch as it has been derived from a sample. The estimated conditional standard deviation is conceptually the same as the standard deviation, except that it is based upon a sample rather than upon the universe of data. Also, it is subject to changes in hours of operation or some other independent variable. In this illustration, the sample size has been kept small in order to simplify the computations. Ordinarily in practical applications many more cost observations would be included.

The equation for the computation of an estimated conditional standard deviation is given below:

$$\text{Estimated conditional standard deviation} = \sqrt{\frac{\Sigma(Y - \overline{Y})^2}{N - 2}}$$

Y = actual supplies cost
$\overline{Y}$ = line of regression supplies cost
N = number of items of data

Expressed in words, the estimated conditional standard deviation is equal to the square root of the sum of the squares of the deviations from the line of regression, divided by the number of items reduced by two. The sample size (N) is reduced by two because both the fixed cost and the variability by hours had to be estimated from the sample.

An estimated conditional standard deviation is computed from the twelve items of data given in the supplies cost illustration. This computation is as follows:

HOURS	ACTUAL COST Y	*CONDITIONAL EXPECTED AVERAGE COST $\overline{Y}$	DEVIATIONS $(Y - \overline{Y})$	DEVIATIONS SQUARED $(Y - \overline{Y})^2$
30	$500	$500	—0—	—0—
50	650	700	$ 50	$ 2,500
20	300	400	100	10,000
10	300	300	—0—	—0—
60	900	800	100	10,000
50	750	700	50	2,500
40	650	600	50	2,500
60	700	800	100	10,000
30	450	500	50	2,500
10	350	300	50	2,500
40	600	600	—0—	—0—
20	450	400	50	2,500
			$\Sigma(Y - \overline{Y})^2 =$	$45,000

*Line of regression values (hours multiplied by $10 plus $200).

The estimated conditional standard deviation is calculated as follows:

$$\text{Estimated conditional standard deviation} = \sqrt{\frac{\$45,000}{12 - 2}} = \$67.08$$

A table of probabilities for a normal distribution shows that approximately two thirds of the data (more precisely, 68.27%) lie within plus and minus one standard deviation from the mean. In this example, then, approximately two thirds of the cost observations should lie within plus and minus one estimated conditional standard deviation from the line of regression, or lie between $67.08 above the line of regression and $67.08 below it.

At 40 hours of operation, for example, the cost can be expected to lie between $532.92 and $667.08 about two thirds of the time.

	ESTIMATED CONDITIONAL STANDARD DEVIATION	
	Plus One	Minus One
Line of regression cost.............................	$600.00	$600.00
Estimated conditional standard deviation	+67.08	−67.08
	$667.08	$532.92

If more confidence is desired in the prediction that a cost is within the limits of tolerance, the limit of variation may be extended. For example, there is a 95 percent probability that a cost in a normal distribution will lie within plus and minus 1.96 standard deviations. From the data given, there is a 95 percent probability that the cost will be between $468.52 and $731.48 at 40 hours of operation ($600 plus and minus $131.48 [1.96 × $67.08]). Management must make a decision by balancing two alternatives:

1. A relatively narrow range of cost variation with a relatively low probability of a cost being within the zone.
2. A relatively wide range of cost variation with a relatively high probability of a cost being within the zone.

Checking Some Inferences

Before making use of a sample of cost data for cost estimation and control, one must have assurance that inferences with respect to cost behavior are correct. Otherwise the cost data may be misleading.

In this chapter, the illustrations show that the cost data are represented by a straight line (line of regression) and not by a curve. In some situations, the linear relationship may not be appropriate. Costs, for example, may not increase at a constant rate but instead increase at an increasing or a decreasing rate with increases in the independent variable. Hence, the cost data would be represented by a curve rather than a straight line. The shape of the line can be revealed by plotting a sufficient amount of data for various hours of operation.

Also, the data may not be uniformly dispersed along the line of regression. At the extremes, for example, the data may be more widely dispersed than at the middle portion of the range. As a result, lines drawn for plus and minus one estimated conditional standard deviation may not be parallel. This is illustrated on the graph given below.

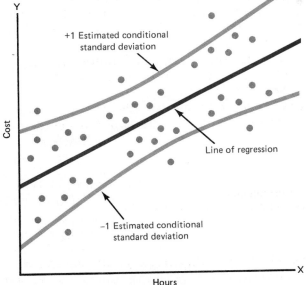

Wide Dispersion at Extremes

In each situation, the data should be plotted and inspected as a part of the total evaluation. As more data are collected, the cost estimation process can be refined. In general, there is more risk in making predictions at the extremes of the range, that is, when the costs are further from the average (total cost divided by the total hours).

In the graph shown below, it is assumed that the lines for the estimated conditional standard deviation are parallel to the line of regression over the relevant range depicted. A value for the estimated conditional standard deviation may then be helpful in the identification of costs that should be investigated over this range of activity. In situations where the degree of dispersion varies over the range, it will be necessary to determine the estimated conditional standard deviation for each position in the range.

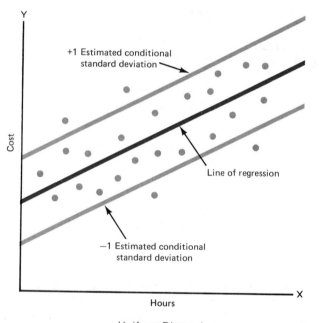

Uniform Dispersion

CORRELATION

In the process of estimating and controlling costs, management must determine whether or not the factor selected for estimating cost behavior is suitable for that purpose. Costs may or may not vary with changes in hours of operation or with changes in the factor selected for cost analysis. In making a study of cost behavior, management is constantly looking for relationships between costs and various factors in the operation, such as pounds of materials used, hours of operation, or labor cost.

Sometimes it may be found that the costs are randomly distributed and are not at all related to the factor selected, as illustrated below:

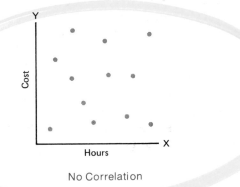

No Correlation

At the other extreme, the relationship may be so close that the data can almost be plotted on a line, as shown below:

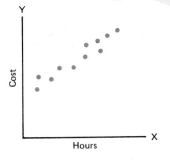

Positive Correlation

Between these extremes the correlation may not be so evident. A high degree of correlation exists when the estimated conditional standard deviation from the line of regression is relatively small when compared with the standard deviation from the average determined without respect to changes in the factor selected.

Assume, for example, a situation with all data lying relatively close to a line of regression for costs related to hours of operation. Cost data are plotted on the graph shown at the top of the next page.

The average is computed in the conventional way by adding the costs and dividing by the number of items. In this case, the average is $225. Any variance between the line of regression and the average can be explained by hours of operation. The unexplained variances are the variances between the actual costs and the line of regression. In the example given, a large part of the variance from the average can be explained by hours of operation; only a small amount is unexplained. Hence, there is a good correlation between cost and hours.

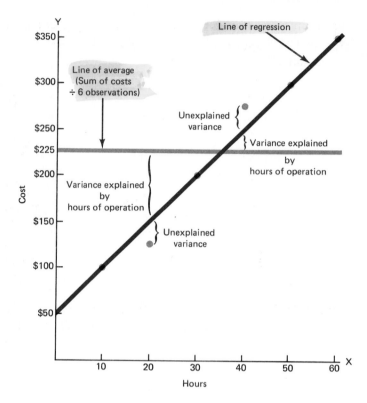

The r² Test

The degree of correlation is measured by the *coefficient of determination*, most frequently designated as r^2. The equation is given below:

$$r^2 = 1 - \frac{\text{(Estimated conditional standard deviation measured from the line of regression)}^2}{\text{(Standard deviation measured from the average of all data)}^2}$$

If the squared estimated conditional standard deviation from the line of regression is small in proportion to the squared standard deviation measured from the average, the value of the fraction in the equation will be small. When this fraction is subtracted from one, the value of r^2 expressed as a percentage will be relatively large and the correlation will be good. On the other hand, a large squared estimated conditional standard deviation from the line of regression in relation to the squared standard deviation from the average results in a low r^2. Hence, the costs do not closely follow the factor selected and the correlation is poor.

A value for r^2 is computed using data from the earlier supplies cost example. The estimated conditional standard deviation from the line of regression has already been computed at $67.08. The average for the data is computed by dividing the sum of costs by the number of items ($6,600 ÷ 12). The average is $550. The variations from this average are computed, squared, and totaled.

SUPPLIES COST	AVERAGE	VARIATIONS	VARIATIONS SQUARED
$ 500	$550	$ 50	$ 2,500
650	550	100	10,000
300	550	250	62,500
300	550	250	62,500
900	550	350	122,500
750	550	200	40,000
650	550	100	10,000
700	550	150	22,500
450	550	100	10,000
350	550	200	40,000
600	550	50	2,500
450	550	100	10,000
$6,600			$395,000

The standard deviation to be used in the r^2 application is equal to the square root of the sum of the squared variations divided by 10 (N − 2, or 12 − 2).

$$\text{Standard deviation} = \sqrt{\frac{\$395,000}{10}} = \$198.75$$

The r^2 is computed by substituting values in the equation:

$$r^2 = 1 - \frac{(\$67.08)^2}{(\$198.75)^2}$$
$$r^2 = 1 - \frac{\$4,500}{\$39,502}$$
$$r^2 = 1 - .1139$$
$$r^2 = .8861 \text{ or } 88.61\%$$

In the illustration given, there is apparently a high degree of correlation between hours of operation and supplies cost.

The t-Value

The correlation of 88.61 percent is quite high, but it must be remembered that the r^2 was derived from a relatively small sample. Perhaps the r^2 for the universe would be much smaller or even larger. With more extensive sampling, it is possible to obtain an r^2 value that is more truly representative of the r^2 for the universe.

Is there any justification for further sampling? The r^2 of 88.61 percent from the sample may be a peculiarity of the sample, and there may be no correlation at all. Before sampling further, a test may be made to determine whether or not a sample would give an r^2 of this magnitude if in fact there was no correlation.

A *null hypothesis* may be established; that is, an assumption that there is no correlation between the variables in the population from which the sample was drawn. If the null hypothesis is true, no further sampling to determine a relationship is warranted. On the other hand, if a relationship is established by disproving the null hypothesis, a larger sample may be drawn for additional study to determine whether or not the relationship may be useful in estimating and controlling costs.

The test may be based upon the probability that a value of r would occur in random sampling from a population in which there is no correlation. A value designated as t is computed, and the t-value is compared with values of t in a table of distributions of t. The table shows the probabilities of t-values if the real r is equal to zero. There should be a small probability that such a value of t would be obtained when there is no correlation.

$$t = r \sqrt{\frac{N - 2}{1 - r^2}}$$

$$t = {}^*.9413 \sqrt{\frac{10}{1 - .8861}}$$

$$t = 8.820$$

$${}^* \sqrt{r^2} \quad \text{or} \quad \sqrt{.8861} = .9413$$

In this example, a t-value of 8.820 is beyond the value given in a table of t-distributions. The row for 10 degrees of freedom ($N - 2$) is given below.[1]

DEGREES OF FREEDOM	PROBABILITY						
	.50	*.30*	*.20*	*.10*	*.05*	*.02*	*.01*
10	.700	1.093	1.372	1.812	2.228	2.764	3.169

The table shows that if t has a value of 3.169 there is only one chance in a hundred (one percent) that a t-value of this magnitude would be obtained if there was no correlation. No probability is given for a value as high as 8.820. Hence, there is a very slight probability that there is no correlation when a sample of 12 items gives an r^2 of 88.61 percent. Accordingly, the sampling process should be continued. The t-distribution is useful in that it can help in deciding between discontinuing the investigation or extending it by selecting even larger samples. In this sample, with such a high r^2 from a small sample, it is

---

[1]Segment of table is taken from Table III of Fisher and Yates: *Statistical Tables for Biological, Argicultural and Medical Research*, published by Longman Group Ltd., London (previously published by Oliver and Boyd, Edinburgh), and by permission of the authors and publishers.

quite evident that further sampling is warranted; but with smaller r^2 values, the decision may not be so evident.

Other Considerations

In making regression studies, the manager, from a knowledge of the operation, must decide first of all whether or not the relationship seems to be reasonable. If it appears reasonable, an r^2 may be computed from a sample. With a high value for r^2, a t-value may be computed to determine whether or not the correlation relationship warrants further study.

Other basic assumptions should be tested to avoid errors that may lead to unwarranted conclusions based upon a spurious correlation. For example, it may be demonstrated that beer consumption increases as the salaries of college professors increase. Offhand this would seem to indicate that college professors spend their salary increases for beer. However, in reality, salaries and wages throughout the economy may have increased; and the consumption of various products may also have increased.

There may also be a tendency to predict Y from values of X beyond the range of X values used in the sample. Predictions beyond the range of the sample values are extremely risky.

Various errors can be made quite easily. In general, an astute manager with an intuitive grasp of cost relationships can benefit by teaming up with a statistician who can test the various relationships for their validity.

Multiple Regression

Usually it will be found that more than one factor will be related to cost behavior. Hours of operation, for example, may not be the only factor to be considered. A certain cost may vary not only with changes in the hours of operation but also with the weight of product produced, temperature changes, or other factors. In simple regression only one factor is considered, but in *multiple regression* several factors are considered in combination. Insofar as possible, all factors that are related to cost behavior should be brought into the analysis. With a penetrating analysis, costs can be predicted and controlled more effectively.

The equation for simple regression can be expanded to include more than one variable factor. Two variable factors are given in the equation below:

$$Y = a + bX + cZ$$

The b is the average change in Y resulting from a one unit change in X, and c is the average change in Y resulting from a one unit change in Z. The cost relationship can no longer be depicted on a two-dimensional graph. The value of Y (cost), however, can be determined by using simultaneous equations. The arithmetic computations become more complex as other factors are introduced, but the principle is the same as it is in simple regression. However, with the use of computer library programs, the complexity of the computations is reduced insofar as the numerical manipulations are concerned.

QUESTIONS

1. Why is cost estimation so important?

2. When costs are plotted on a graph, it is possible to draw a line to represent the variability of costs with hours of operation. What is this line called?

3. How can the average rate of cost variability be determined from the line?

4. Describe the high-low point method of cost segregation.

5. How can a standard deviation measurement be used in cost control?

6. In a normal distribution of data, what proportion of the data should lie within plus and minus one standard deviation?

7. Assume that an average cost was $3,000 and that the actual cost was $5,000. With a standard deviation of $2,000, determine the number of standard deviations above the mean for $5,000. What is the probability of a cost being this number of standard deviations from the average?

8. Costs may tend to vary with hours of operation. How can the degree of correlation between costs and hours of operation be measured?

9. Should all cost variations from an average or standard be investigated? Why or why not?

10. What is the purpose of a t-value?

11. Is it possible to predict costs beyond the range of X values used in the sample? Explain.

EXERCISES

1. Cost Segregation by High-Low Point Method. The maintenance costs of Department 6 have been recorded for various hours of operation as follows:

Hours	Cost
21,600	$141,600
19,800	130,800
24,200	157,200
23,700	154,200
20,600	135,600
21,500	141,000
19,200	127,200
21,900	143,400
23,300	151,800
22,400	146,400

Required: Determine the average rate of cost variability per hour and the fixed cost.

2. Cost Segregation by High-Low Point Method. The costs to lubricate equipment in Department 4 have been recorded for various hours of operation as follows:

Hours	Cost	Hours	Cost
6,720	$36,160	6,560	$35,680
7,140	37,420	7,220	37,660
5,860	33,580	8,460	41,380
7,190	37,570	8,210	40,630
8,070	40,210	5,930	33,790

Required: Determine the average rate of cost variability per hour and the fixed cost.

3. Cost Segregation by Least Squares Method. Barbara Pierson wants to estimate the variability of the cost of supplies used with hours of operation. With this information, she hopes to be able to prepare a more accurate budget and have better control over costs for which she is responsible.

Cost data for various hours of operation are given below.

Hours	Cost	Hours	Cost
600	$7,400	1,000	$9,000
500	7,000	800	8,200
600	7,300	700	7,800
700	7,900	900	8,400
900	8,800	500	6,900

Sum of hours (ΣX)	7,200
Sum of the cost (ΣY)	$ 78,700
Sum of hours multiplied by costs (ΣXY)	$57,800,000
Sum of hours squared (ΣX^2)	5,460,000

Required: Compute the estimated variable cost per hour and the amount of the fixed cost. (Round answers to third decimal place.)

4. Cost Segregation by Least Squares Method. The cost of repairs in the drill department of Schumaker Machine Company is partly variable and partly fixed. In order to estimate costs more accurately for budgeting and control purposes, management wants an estimate of cost variability per hour and fixed costs. Cost data for various hours of operation are given below.

Hours	Cost	Hours	Cost
280	$3,300	300	$3,500
310	3,550	310	3,600
360	3,820	280	3,200
430	4,100	430	4,200
360	3,800	360	3,780

Sum of the hours (ΣX)	3,420
Sum of the costs (ΣY)	$ 36,850
Sum of the hours multiplied by the costs (ΣXY)	$12,759,500
Sum of hours squared (ΣX^2)	1,197,600

Required: Compute the estimated variable cost per hour and the amount of the fixed cost. (Round answers to third decimal place.)

5. The r^2 Test. The cost of packaging and crating a unit of product averages $40 per unit of product plus a fixed cost of $2,200 per month. This information has been derived from cost data collected at various times. An estimated conditional standard deviation for these data has been computed at $90. The standard deviation from the general average (mean) has been computed at $120.

Required:

(1) Compute the r^2.
(2) Does there appear to be a high correlation between cost and the number of products packaged and crated?

6. The r^2 Test. The cost of a material used in a chemical process is to be estimated at various hours of operation. Management wants to know whether or not there appears to be a good correlation between the cost and hours of operation. A sample of 10 items has been selected, and you have determined that the sum of the deviations from the line of regression values squared is equal to $7,200. You have also determined that the sum of the deviations from the general average squared is equal to $64,000. The general average has been computed without regard to hours of operation.

Required:

(1) Compute the r^2.
(2) Is there a high correlation between the cost of materials and hours of operation?

7. Control Limits. Studies of cost behavior show that there is a valid correlation between the cost of fuel consumed and the weight of metal charged in a furnace at Harmony Metals, Inc. A line of regression has been computed for various weights of materials, and an estimated conditional standard deviation has been computed at $150. Weights and costs from the line of regression are given for the range of input weights.

Weights (kilograms)	Cost
800	$10,200
900	11,400
1 000	12,600
1 200	15,000
1 300	16,200
1 400	17,400
1 500	18,600
1 600	19,800

Required:

(1) From the information given, what is the rate of cost variability for each kilogram of metal heated?
(2) Determine the cost for each weight at plus and minus one estimated conditional standard deviation from the line of regression.
(3) Assume that a rule has been established to investigate any variation in cost that is in excess of or below one estimated conditional standard deviation from the line of regression. On one occasion the cost for 1 300 kilograms was $16,550. According to the rule, should this cost be investigated?
(4) Assume that the rule has been relaxed so that only costs outside of the limits of plus and minus 1.96 estimated conditional standard deviations are to be investigated. About 95 percent of the data should lie within these limits. Would a cost of $16,550 at 1 300 kilograms be investigated according to this rule?

8. Control Limits. The controller of Missouri Products, Inc., has established a general guide that a variation from a budgeted cost of more than one estimated conditional standard deviation from the line of regression should be investigated. For the cost of an indirect material, one estimated conditional standard deviation has been computed at $60. Hours and costs from the line of regression are given for a typical range.

Hours	Cost	Hours	Cost
80	$620	120	$780
90	660	130	820
100	700	140	860
110	740		

Required:

(1) For each of the observations given, determine the acceptable range of cost variance according to the established rule.
(2) Assume that the acceptable limit is defined at 1.96 estimated conditional standard deviations so that approximately 95 percent of the data should be within the range. Determine the range under this assumption.
(3) Which of the above, (1) or (2), will probably require more cost investigations? What is the risk when there are fewer investigations?

9. The r^2 Test and the t-Value. The manager of Cummins Supply Company questions whether or not the cost of a material used in a processing operation tends to increase with a decrease in the quality of material used. A sample of 12 items is selected to test the effect. An estimated conditional standard deviation from the line of regression is $20, and an estimated standard deviation measured from the average is $25.

Required:

(1) Compute the r^2. Does the r^2 seem to indicate a good correlation?
(2) Determine a value for t. Does the value of t show that a larger sample size should be drawn and that the relationship should be studied further? (Use t-values given on page 74).

10. Estimating Costs from a Sample. Data with respect to the cost of a certain polishing material have been collected for various hours of operation and are given below.

Hours	Cost	Hours	Cost
2,400	$17,400	3,100	$21,500
2,100	15,600	2,400	17,500
2,000	15,000	2,500	18,000
2,100	15,800	2,100	15,700
2,600	18,500	2,800	19,900
3,300	22,800	2,600	18,600

The plant controller notes that the costs have followed a certain pattern and that they should be relatively easy to estimate. Plans have been made to increase the hours of operation to 3,600 next month.

Required:

(1) By the high-low point method, estimate the variable cost per hour and the fixed cost.
(2) Estimate the cost of the polishing material at 3,600 hours.
(3) Explain why the cost estimates may not be reliable beyond the range of sampled data.

PROBLEMS

3-1. Least Squares Method of Cost Segregation. The cost of labor for a manufacturing operation has been found to be partly fixed and partly variable with units of product manufactured. Virginia Grayson supervises this operation and has kept cost records for various production levels as shown below.

Units	Cost	Units	Cost
800	$1,650	300	$ 700
600	1,300	400	900
500	1,100	600	1,250
400	900	700	1,500
500	1,150	300	650

Sum of the units (ΣX)	5,100
Sum of the costs (ΣY)	$ 11,100
Sum of units multiplied by costs (ΣXY)	$6,150,000
Sum of units squared (ΣX^2)	2,850,000

Required: Compute the estimated variable cost per hour and the amount of the fixed cost. (Round answers to nearest cent.)

3-2. Cost Segregation by Two Methods. The plant controller at Germain Equipment Company is searching for a way to estimate the maintenance cost. It has been noted that the cost varies with hours of operation, but the cost does not vary in direct proportion to the hours of operation. In fact, the cost may be different even when the department is operating for the same number of hours.

Up to this point, rough approximations have been made of the cost for budgeted hours of operation. Often the approximations are off by two or three thousand dollars. The controller would like to narrow the variations in the estimates and has collected data as follows:

Hours	Cost	Hours	Cost
3,000	$33,000	9,000	$ 86,000
3,000	32,500	9,000	86,200
3,000	32,400	9,000	87,000
3,000	33,200	9,000	87,500
3,000	33,800	9,000	87,000
6,000	60,000	12,000	112,110
6,000	59,200	12,000	114,000
6,000	60,800	12,000	113,700
6,000	61,000	12,000	114,300
6,000	59,700	12,000	113,700

Sum of the hours (ΣX)	150,000
Sum of the costs (ΣY)	$ 1,467,100
Sum of hours multiplied by costs (ΣXY)	$13,015,800,000
Sum of hours squared (ΣX^2)	1,350,000,000

Required:

(1) Use the high-low point method to compute average rate of variability per hour and the fixed portion of the cost.

(2) Use the least squares method to compute the average rate of variability per hour and the fixed portion of the cost.

(3) Which of the two methods should give better results?

(4) What other steps might you take before relying on the data?

3-3. Least Squares Method of Cost: Correlation. Paul Yauss is trying to determine whether or not there is a good correlation between hours of machine operation and the maintenance cost. Cost data have been collected from 40 observations used as a sample. The deviations of the cost from the line of regression have been squared and totaled at 950. The sum of the squared deviations of the cost from the average computed without respect to hours of operation has been computed at 15,200.

Required:

(1) Compute the estimated conditional standard deviation.
(2) Compute the standard deviation measured from the average of all data.
(3) Determine the r^2. Does there appear to be a good correlation between the hours of operation and the cost?

3-4. Correlation. In processing a pharmaceutical item used in the treatment of minor cuts and abrasions, Cole Laboratories, Inc., wants to test the validity of the relationship between hours of processing and the cost of mixing the basic ingredients. If a significant relationship is found, estimated hours of processing may serve as a guide in the prediction of costs.

The estimated conditional standard deviation based on data from past years amounts to $120. The standard deviation from the average of the data has been computed at $130.

Required:

(1) Determine the r^2. Does it appear that there is a good correlation between hours of processing and the cost of mixing?
(2) When cost is related to several factors, how can the control problem be approached?

3-5. Cost Estimation and Correlation. Wilson Leinbach handles summer conferences for business executives. He is looking for a general guide to help him estimate the cost of conducting a conference. Advance reservations, he believes, may be useful in making predictions.

He has kept records of advance reservations and the corresponding costs. Computations are given below.

Sum of advance reservations (ΣX)	4,000
Sum of conference costs (ΣY)	$ 46,000
Number of conferences (N)	20
Sum of advance reservations multiplied by costs (ΣXY)	$17,200,000
Sum of advance reservations squared (ΣX^2)	2,800,000
Average cost ($\Sigma Y/N$)	$ 2,300
Standard deviation from the average	$ 100
Estimated conditional standard deviation from the line of regression	$ 20

Wilson wants to know if there is a reasonably good correlation between advance reservations and cost of the conference. At the present time he would like to have an estimate of the range of expected cost for 500 advance registrations so that he will have a probability of being correct approximately two times out of three.

Required:

(1) Determine the variable and fixed portions of the conference cost. (Round answers to the nearest cent.)

(2) Compute the r^2. Does there appear to be a good correlation between advance reservations and conference cost?

(3) With 500 advance reservations, what is the expected range of conference cost that will give him a probability of being correct about two times out of three?

3-6. Correlation and Cost Estimation. The management of Lanark Instruments, Inc., has had some difficulty in estimating the cost of a material used to manufacture a certain product line made in conformity with various specifications of the customer. One of the engineers has a theory that cost tends to increase with the complexity of the specifications. To test this theory, a classification of product specifications has been prepared in ascending order from Type 1 to Type 10 for a standard quantity to be produced for each order. A record of materials cost has been kept for each classification. For example, the type 4 specification may show a cost of $1,200 on one observation. Computations are given below.

Sum of product type classification (ΣX)	600
Sum of the materials costs (ΣY)	$ 75,000
Number of observations (N)	30
Average cost ($\Sigma Y/N$)	$ 2,500
Sum of product type classifications multiplied by materials cost (ΣXY)	$1,410,000
Sum of product type classifications squared (ΣX^2)	9,000
Standard deviation from the average	$ 900
Estimated conditional standard deviation from the line of regression	$ 400

It is hoped that fixed costs and variable costs can be estimated by product type as a guide in pricing orders.

Required:

(1) Determine the variable and fixed portions of the materials cost.

(2) Compute the r^2. Does there appear to be a good correlation between the classifications by product specifications and the materials cost?

3-7. Correlation and Cost Estimation. The plant controller of Chieco Machine Company would like to find a way to estimate the cost of a cooling fluid used in the machine operation based upon the hours of machine running time.

A sample of 12 observations has been made as a preliminary to a possible full-scale study of the data. Information from the sample is given below.

Sum of the hours (ΣX)	96
Sum of the costs (ΣY)	$ 5,000
Sum of the hours multiplied by the costs (ΣXY)	$39,300
Sum of hours squared (ΣX^2)	668

From the sample, an estimated conditional standard deviation when squared has been computed at $25. The standard deviation from the average of the data when squared has been computed at $300.

Required:

(1) Compute the estimated variable cost per hour and the fixed cost.

(2) Determine the r^2. From the value for r^2, does it appear that other factors aside from hours may be related to cost?

(3) Compute a t-value. (The probabilities for distribution of t for 10 degrees of freedom are given on page 74.)

(4) Does the *t*-value indicate that the relationship may be studied further by drawing a larger sample?

3-8. Control Limits. For several years, Castor and Pollock, Inc., has used the least squares method in the segregation of semivariable costs into variable and fixed components. Also, correlation studies have been made to determine whether or not the relationship established between the independent variable and the dependent variable (hours and cost in this case) appears to be valid.

The two principal owners, however, are not in agreement as to the criterion used for cost control. Harriet Castor believes that all costs should be investigated if they lie outside of the zone bounded by plus and minus one estimated conditional standard deviation from the line of regression. Georgia Pollock, however, is of the opinion that this would involve needless cost investigation and prefers to investigate only if the cost is more than plus or minus 1.96 estimated conditional standard deviations from the line of regression. She states that only about two thirds of the data can be expected to lie within plus and minus one estimated conditional standard deviation from the line of regression but that 95% of the data can be expected to lie within plus and minus 1.96 estimated conditional standard deviations from the line of regression.

The company incurs an equipment maintenance cost that has been estimated at $20 per hour of operation with a fixed cost of $6,000. The estimated conditional standard deviation from the line of regression is $450.

Required:
(1) Evaluate the position taken by each of the principal owners. Which position is better?
(2) What should the equipment maintenance cost be at 1,200 hours of operation?
(3) What is the range of tolerance before the cost is investigated at 1,200 hours with limits set at plus and minus one estimated conditional standard deviation from the line of regression?
(4) What is the range of tolerance before the cost is investigated at 900 hours with limits set at plus and minus 1.96 estimated conditional standard deviations from the line of regression?

3-9. Control Limits. Wesley Donahue has recently acquired a new type of equipment to be used in testing the precision of small parts manufactured by Kuhnsman Medical Products, Inc. By observation he notes that the cost to operate this equipment amounts to $20 an hour and that there is $8,000 fixed cost per month. This observation seems to be verified by the least squares method that was used for cost data from the past year. Further study of the cost behavior will be made. In the meantime, Donahue plans to use the data for cost control purposes.

Data on costs and hours are given for the first six months of the current year.

Hours	Cost	Average Cost
760	$22,900	$23,200
850	24,500	25,000
940	27,000	26,800
740	23,700	22,800
680	21,800	21,600
880	25,800	25,600

Additional costs and hours for the past year are given below.

Hours	Cost	Average Cost
740	$23,000	$22,800
920	25,900	26,400
860	25,300	25,200
980	27,600	27,600
820	24,800	24,400
680	21,200	21,600
740	22,600	22,800
650	21,300	21,000
820	24,400	24,400
980	27,700	27,600
600	20,300	20,000
650	21,000	21,000

Required:

(1) Compute the estimated conditional standard deviation, using only the data from the past year. (Round your answer to the nearest hundred dollars.)

(2) Donahue plans to investigate any cost variance that is more or less than one estimated conditional standard deviation from the mean. Identify the costs that should be investigated during the current year, following this criterion.

3-10. Comparison of Cost Segregation Methods. The Van Sickle Processing Company is trying to predict production costs at a new plant. Some data from past experience have been collected, and cost data for equipment mainte- nance in one of the departments are given below.

Hours of Operation	Cost	Hours of Operation	Cost
500	$5,500	660	$6,080
550	5,800	650	6,000
720	6,560	820	6,460
850	6,350	550	5,700
450	5,200	900	6,700
650	5,950	840	6,400
580	5,640	750	6,250
		550	5,500

The department supervisor suggests that the variable and fixed portions of the cost be estimated by the high-low point method.

One of the persons in the plant controller's office objects to this method, stating that it is not accurate. As an alternative, it has been suggested that costs be segregated by the least squares method and the above information has been processed as follows:

Sum of the hours (ΣX)	10,020
Sum of the costs (ΣY)	$ 90,090
Sum of the hours multiplied by the costs (ΣXY)	$60,902,900
Sum of the hours squared (ΣX^2)	6,968,400

Required:

(1) Determine the variable cost and the fixed cost by the high-low method. (Round to the nearest cent.)

(2) Determine the variable cost and the fixed cost by the least squares method. (Round to the nearest cent.)

(3) Comment as to why the results differ between the two methods and whether one method is better than the other.

3-11. **Control Limits.** Heat and light costs for Santa Cruz Patterns, Inc., are given below for various hours of operation during the past year. Conditional expected average costs are also given. Lester Friedman has found that the costs to investigate a variance from the expected average cost is relatively high, and he is reluctant to investigate unless there is a strong probability that the cost variance is not attributable to random factors. Hence, he has determined that the cost must be more than 1.96 estimated conditional standard deviations from the line of regression before it will be investigated. There is a 95% probability that a cost will lie within plus and minus 1.96 estimated conditional standard deviations from the line of regression.

Hours of Operation	Conditional Expected Average Cost	Actual Cost
1,500	$16,000	$16,500
1,800	18,400	18,300
2,200	21,600	21,600
2,400	23,200	23,000
1,600	16,800	16,800
1,500	16,000	16,300
2,900	27,200	26,700
3,300	30,400	30,400
3,700	33,600	34,000
2,800	26,400	26,000
2,400	23,200	23,000
1,600	16,800	16,900

Required:

(1) Compute the estimated conditional standard deviation from the line of regression. (Use high-low point method to segregate costs. Round answer to the nearest dollar.)

(2) During the next month, the heat and light cost for 2,800 hours of operation was $27,000. According to the rule established, should the cost be investigated?

(3) Comment on the control limit established by Friedman.

3-12. Control Limits. The manager of Machine Shop #10 believes that a cost of $1,720 for equipment maintenance is high for 250 hours of operation in a month. Past studies of cost behavior indicate that equipment maintenance cost should vary at a rate of $5 per hour with a fixed cost of $300 for the month.

Cost data for the past 20 months are given on the following page along with the conditional expected average cost.

Required:

(1) From the data given, compute the estimated conditional standard deviation.

(2) Inasmuch as 95% of data in a normal distribution are randomly distributed within plus and minus 1.96 standard deviations of the mean, does

Hours of Operation	Actual Cost	Conditional Expected Average cost
280	$1,750	$1,700
300	1,700	1,800
250	1,600	1,550
300	1,820	1,800
220	1,360	1,400
220	1,420	1,400
250	1,600	1,550
200	1,350	1,300
350	2,000	2,050
400	2,200	2,300
350	2,100	2,050
400	2,400	2,300
200	1,250	1,300
300	1,600	1,800
250	1,600	1,550
220	1,300	1,400
200	1,200	1,300
400	2,400	2,300
300	1,700	1,800
280	1,650	1,700

it appear that there is a relatively small probability of maintenance cost being $1,720 for 250 hours of operation? (For purposes of the problem, assume that the operation has not changed significantly and that a variable cost averaging $5 per hour with a fixed cost of $300 per month is reasonable.)

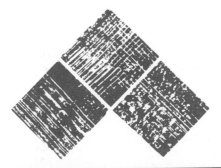

4
PROFIT PLANNING

Profit planning is fundamental to the overall management function of a business. The profit plan is an essential part of the total budgeting process. Before a detailed budget can be prepared for the various segments of the total operation, there must be a profit plan. Management establishes profit goals and prepares budget plans that will lead to the realization of these goals.

In order to plan profit, management must have knowledge of cost behavior. Under given conditions, does a cost vary and if so by how much? Also what costs can be expected to remain fixed over a range of different amounts of activity or volume of production? In the preceding chapter, much attention was paid to the important problem of segregating costs into variable and fixed components. In this chapter, discussion will focus on the application of the differences in cost behavior to the specific problems of planning future profits.

The difference between sales revenue and the variable cost is called the *contribution margin*. Stated in another way, the contribution margin is the balance remaining after deducting total variable cost from revenue. This balance contributes to the recovery of the fixed cost and to the realization of profit. The concept of the contribution margin is essential to the process of planning profit.

Several factors affect profit. They are:

(1) Selling prices.
(2) Volume of sales.

(3) Unit variable cost.
(4) Total fixed cost.
(5) Combinations in which the various product lines are sold.

All of these factors must be considered in profit planning. Fundamental to profit planning is the relationship of the contribution margin per unit of product, the volume of sales, the mix of product lines in sales, and the total fixed cost.

BREAK-EVEN ANALYSIS

Break-even analysis, sometimes called *cost-volume-profit analysis*, stresses the relationship of the factors affecting profit. The *break-even point*, the point at which there is no profit or loss, serves as a base indicating how many units of product must be sold if a company is to operate without a loss.

Each unit of product sold is expected to yield revenue in excess of its variable cost and thus contribute to fixed cost and profit. At the break-even point, the profit is zero; that is, the contribution margin is equal to the fixed cost. If the actual volume of sales is higher than the break-even volume, there will be profit.

Assume that a company manufactures and sells a single product line as follows:

Unit selling price	$	20
Unit variable cost		10
Unit contribution margin	$	10
Total fixed cost		$100,000

Each unit of product sold contributes $10 to cover fixed cost and profit. Based on these data, the company must sell 10,000 units of product to break even. The break-even volume is calculated by dividing the total fixed cost by the contribution per unit as shown below:

$$\frac{\$100,000 \text{ fixed cost}}{\$10 \text{ unit contribution margin}} = 10,000 \text{ units break-even volume}$$

If the company can sell more than 10,000 units, it earns a profit. If less than 10,000 units are sold, a loss is incurred. The profit is equal to the number of units sold in excess of 10,000 multiplied by the unit contribution margin. For example, if 22,000 units are sold, the company is operating at 12,000 units above its break-even point and can earn a profit of $120,000 (12,000 units over break-even point × $10 unit contribution margin).

Sales (22,000 units @ $20)	$440,000
Less variable cost (22,000 units @ $10)	220,000
Contribution margin	$220,000
Less fixed cost	100,000
Income before income tax	$120,000

The Break-Even Chart

Total revenue and total cost at different sales volumes can be estimated and plotted on a *break-even chart*. The information shown on the break-even chart can also be given in conventional reports, but it is sometimes easier to grasp the fundamental facts when they are presented in graphic or pictorial form. Dollars are shown on the vertical scale of the chart, and the units of product sold (or produced) are shown on the horizontal scale. The total costs are plotted for the various quantities to be sold and are connected by a line. Total revenues are similarly entered on the chart. The break-even point lies at the intersection of the total revenue and the total cost line. Losses are measured to the left of the break-even point, the amount of the loss at any point being equal to the dollar difference between the total cost line and the total revenue line. Profit is measured to the right of the break-even point and at any point are equal to the dollar difference between the total revenue line and the total cost line.

The data from the last example are presented on the following break-even chart:

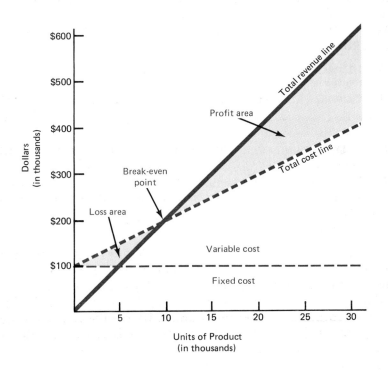

The data provided from an analysis of the chart is presented in tabular form at the top of the following page.

It is assumed, of course, that the selling price remains at $20 and that the variable cost per unit remains at $10 over the range of units

Units of product sold	5,000	10,000	15,000	20,000	25,000	30,000
Total revenue	$100,000	$200,000	$300,000	$400,000	$500,000	$600,000
Total cost:						
Variable	$ 50,000	$100,000	$150,000	$200,000	$250,000	$300,000
Fixed	100,000	100,000	100,000	100,000	100,000	100,000
Total cost	$150,000	$200,000	$250,000	$300,000	$350,000	$400,000
Profit (loss)	$(50,000)	—0—	$ 50,000	$100,000	$150,000	$200,000

sold. With only one product, there is no problem of sales mix. The sales mix or product combination problem will be discussed later.

Cost Detail on the Break-Even Chart

Additional information is sometimes shown on the break-even chart by drawing separate lines for the different cost classifications. A desired profit before tax can also be added as if it were a fixed cost. Then, both the break-even point and the point of desired profit are revealed on the chart. Using the same data as before, assume that the costs are broken down as follows:

Unit variable costs:		
Direct materials	$	4
Direct labor		2
Variable factory overhead		2
Variable selling and administrative expense		2
Total unit variable cost	$	10
Fixed factory overhead		$ 80,000
Fixed selling and administrative expense		20,000
Total fixed expense		$100,000

The desired profit before income tax is $100,000. The company must sell 10,000 units to recover the $100,000 in fixed cost (to break even) and must sell another 10,000 units to earn a $100,000 profit before tax. In other words, the company must sell 20,000 units if it expects to earn a profit of $100,000 before income tax. The break-even chart at the top of the next page shows cost and profit details.

Curvature of Revenue and Cost Lines

In some cases, revenue and cost cannot be represented by straight lines. If more units are to be sold, selling prices may have to be reduced. Under these conditions, the revenue function may be a curve rather than a line. Cost on the other hand, may also be nonlinear. The curve may rise slowly at the start but may rise more steeply as volume is expanded. As more units are manufactured, the variable cost per unit may become higher. Therefore, it may be possible to have two break-even points as shown at the bottom of the next page.

In many cases, however, revenue and cost can be represented by straight lines. Any given company probably operates within certain

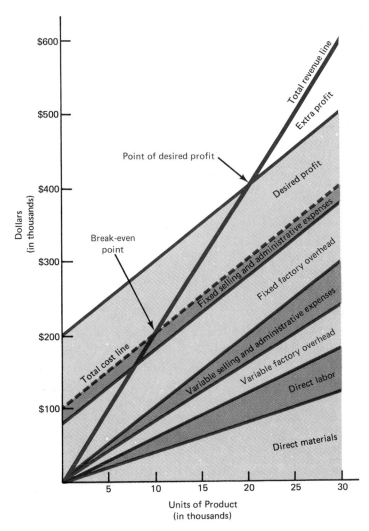

volume ranges where revenue and cost can usually be plotted without any noticeable curvature. If the revenue and the cost curves begin to converge, the company is not maximizing its profit. Total cost is increasing faster than total revenue; that is, each unit sold is adding more to cost than to revenue.

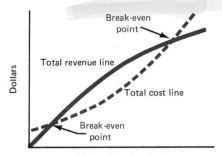

An Alternative Form of Break-Even Analysis

Frequently a break-even point is calculated in terms of the sales revenue that must be realized in order to break even. A break-even point is not necessarily expressed in units of product. The variable cost may be stated as a percentage of sales revenue and subtracted from 100 percent to arrive at the percentage of the contribution margin to sales revenue. For example, a company may sell one line of product for $15 a unit with unit variable cost of $9 and total fixed cost for a year of $60,000.

		PERCENTAGE
Unit selling price	$15	100%
Unit variable cost	9	60
Unit contribution margin	$ 6	40%

The break-even point can be calculated at 10,000 units by dividing the total fixed cost of $60,000 by the unit contribution margin of $6. But the break-even point can also be computed in dollars of sales. As shown above, 60 percent of the revenue is needed to cover the variable cost. This means that 40 percent of the sales revenue remains for the recovery of the fixed cost and for profit. When 40 percent of the sales revenue is equal to the fixed cost of $60,000, the company will break even. Therefore, divide $60,000 by 40 percent to arrive at a break-even revenue of $150,000. Hence, a break-even point in terms of sales dollars can be computed by using the equation given below:

$$\frac{\text{Fixed cost}}{\substack{\text{Contribution margin expressed} \\ \text{as a percentage of sales} \\ \text{revenue}}} = \text{Sales revenue required to break even}$$

$$\frac{\$60,000}{40\%} = \$150,000 \text{ sales revenue required to break even}$$

	AMOUNT	PERCENTAGE
Sales revenue	$150,000	100%
Variable cost	90,000	60
Contribution margin	$ 60,000	40%
Fixed cost	60,000	
Profit or (loss)	—0—	

By extending the break-even concept further, it is possible to set a profit goal and to calculate the required sales revenue necessary to produce a given or desired profit.

$$\frac{\text{Fixed cost} + \text{Desired profit}}{\substack{\text{Contribution margin expressed as} \\ \text{a percentage of sales revenue}}} = \substack{\text{Sales revenue required to earn} \\ \text{a desired profit}}$$

Using the data from the last example, assume that an income before income tax of $72,000 is budgeted. The sales revenue must then be $330,000 as computed below:

$$\frac{\$60,000 + \$72,000}{40\%} = \$330,000 \text{ sales revenue required to earn a profit of } \$72,000$$

In many cases, the profit objective may be stated as a net income after income tax, in which case an additional computation must be made to solve for the income before income tax. Assume that the company wants a net income after income tax of $60,000 and that the income tax rate is 40 percent. If the income tax is 40 percent of the income before tax, then the net income after tax is 60 percent of the income before tax.

Income before income tax..	100%
Less income tax..	40
Net income after income tax......................................	60%

To compute the income before tax, divide the after-tax net income by 60 percent; that is, by the complement of the tax rate or, in other words, by (1 − tax rate). The break-even equation is given below:

$$\frac{\text{Fixed cost} + \dfrac{\text{Desired after-tax profit}}{1 - \text{Tax rate}}}{\text{Contribution margin percentage}} = \begin{array}{c}\text{Sales revenue required to earn} \\ \text{a desired profit after tax}\end{array}$$

$$\frac{\$60,000 + \dfrac{\$60,000}{1 - 40\%}}{40\%} = \frac{\$60,000 + \$100,000}{40\%}$$

$$= \$400,000$$

A proof of the computation follows:

Sales revenue...	$400,000
Variable cost (60% of revenue).............................	240,000
Contribution margin (40% of revenue).................	$160,000
Fixed cost...	60,000
Income before income tax.....................................	$100,000
Income tax (40%)...	40,000
Net income after income tax.................................	$ 60,000

THE PROFIT-VOLUME GRAPH

A *profit-volume graph*, or P/V graph, is sometimes used in place of or along with a break-even chart. Profit and loss are given on the vertical scale; and units of product, sales revenue, or percentages of activity are given on the horizontal scale. A horizontal line is drawn on the graph to separate profit from loss. The profit and loss at various sales levels are plotted and connected by the profit line. The break-even point is measured at the point where the profit line intersects the horizontal line. Dollars of profit are measured on a vertical scale above the line, and dollars of loss are measured below the line. The P/V graph may be preferred to the break-even chart because profit and loss at any point can be read directly from the vertical scale; but the P/V graph does not clearly show how cost varies with activity. Break-even charts and P/V graphs are often used together, thus obtaining the advantages that can be derived from each form of presentation.

Data used in the earlier illustration of a break-even chart given on pages 88 to 90 have also been used in preparing the P/V graph given below:

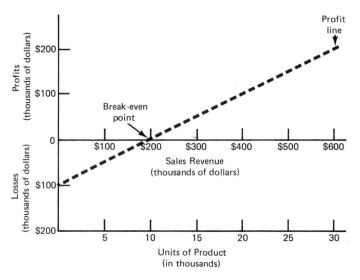

The profit-volume graph is a convenient device to show how profit is affected by changes in the factors that affect profit. For example, if unit selling price, unit variable cost, and total fixed cost remain constant, how many more units must be sold in order to realize a greater profit? Or if the unit variable cost can be reduced, what additional profit can be expected at any given volume of sales? The effect of changes in sales volume, unit variable cost, unit selling price, total fixed cost, and sales mix are discussed in the following paragraphs.

Sales Volume

In some industries profit depends upon high sales volume. If each unit of product is sold at a relatively low contribution margin, profit can be made only by selling in large quantities. This will be all the more true when the fixed cost is high. For instance, a company may handle one product line that sells for $1 a unit. Assume that the variable cost per unit is 70 cents and that the fixed cost per year amounts to $180,000. Each unit sold contributes 30 cents in excess of its variable cost to fixed cost and profit. Before any profit can be made, enough units must be sold at a 30-cent contribution per unit to recover the fixed cost. Therefore, 600,000 units must be sold just to break even. For every unit sold in excess of 600,000, there will be a 30-cent profit before tax. In such a situation, the company must be certain that it can sell substantially more than 600,000 units to earn a reasonable profit on the investment.

When the products sell for relatively high prices, the contribution margin per unit is often higher even though the rate of contribution may be fairly small. The fixed cost is recaptured with the sale of fewer units, and a profit can be made on a relatively low sales volume. Suppose that each unit of product sells for $1,000 and that the variable cost per unit is $900. The fixed cost for the year is $180,000. The percentage of contribution margin is only 10 percent, but the company receives a contribution of $100 from each unit sold for fixed cost and profit. Break-even point will be reached when 1,800 units are sold. The physical quantity handled is much lower than it was in the preceding example, but the same principle applies. More than 1,800 units must be sold if the company is to produce a profit.

Variable Costs

The relationship between the selling price of a product and its variable cost is important in any line of business. Even small savings in the variable cost can add significantly to profit. A reduction of a fraction of a dollar in the unit cost becomes a contribution to fixed cost and profit. If 50,000 units are sold in a year, a 10-cent decrease in the unit cost becomes a $5,000 increase in profit. Conversely, a 10-cent increase in unit cost decreases profit by $5,000.

Management is continuously searching for opportunities to make even small cost savings. What appears to be a trivial saving may turn out to be the difference between profit or loss for the year. In manufacturing, it may be possible to save on materials cost by using a cheaper material that is just as satisfactory. Savings can also come from buying more economically or by using materials more effectively. With improved methods of production, labor and overhead costs per unit can be decreased.

A small saving in unit cost can give a company a competitive advantage. If prices must be reduced, the low-cost producer will usually suffer less. At any given price and fixed cost structure, the low-cost producer will become profitable faster as sales volume increases.

The comparison of the operating results of three companies given at the top of the next page shows how profit is influenced by changes in the variable cost pattern. Each of the three companies sells 100,000 units of one product line at a price of $5 per unit and has an annual fixed cost of $150,000. Company A can manufacture and sell each unit at a variable cost of $2.50. Company B has found ways to save cost and can produce each unit for a variable cost of $2, while Company C has allowed its unit variable cost to rise to $3.

	COMPANY A	COMPANY B	COMPANY C
Number of units sold	100,000	100,000	100,000
Unit selling price..............................	$5.00	$5.00	$5.00
Unit variable cost............................	$2.50	$2.00	$3.00
Unit contribution margin..............	$2.50	$3.00	$2.00
Percent of contribution margin	50%	60%	40%
Total sales revenue.........................	$500,000	$500,000	$500,000
Total variable cost	250,000	200,000	300,000
Total contribution margin	$250,000	$300,000	$200,000
Fixed cost......................................	150,000	150,000	150,000
Income before income tax	$100,000	$150,000	$ 50,000

A difference of 50 cents in unit variable cost between Company A and Company B or between Company A and Company C adds up to a $50,000 difference in profit when 100,000 units are sold. The low-cost producer has a $1 per unit profit advantage over the high-cost producer. If sales volume should fall to 60,000 units per company, Company B would have a profit of $30,000, Company A would break even, and Company C would suffer a loss of $30,000.

The profit picture at different operating levels for the three companies is shown on the P/V graph below.

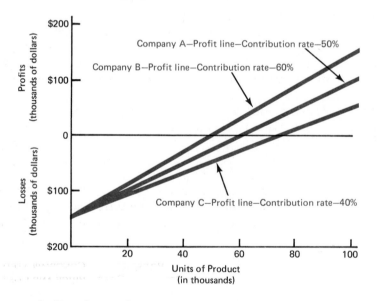

The profit line for each company starts at $150,000, the amount of the fixed cost. When 40,000 units are sold, there is a difference of $20,000 between each profit line. The lines diverge as greater quantities are sold, and at the 100,000-unit level the difference is $50,000. Company B can make a profit by selling any quantity in excess of 50,000 units, but Company C must sell 75,000 units to break even. With its present cost structure, Company C will have to sell in greater volume if it is to earn a profit equal to those earned by Company A or Company B. Company C is the inefficient producer in the group and as such operates at a disadvantage. When there is enough business for everyone, Company C will earn a profit but will most likely earn less than the others. When business conditions are poor, Company C will be more vulnerable.

Price Policy

One of the ways to improve profit is to get more sales volume; and to stimulate sales volume, management may decide to reduce prices. But results may not work out as anticipated. It does not necessarily follow that sales volume will be increased by reducing prices. If the demand for the product is perfectly inelastic, volume will not respond to change in price. The price reduction will result only in lower profits.

Suppose, however, that greater quantities can be sold at a lower price. The advantage, if there is one, is soon eliminated if competitors retaliate by lowering their prices also. Eventually the market will be shared as it was before, and possibly with lower profits for all. Even assuming that competitors will not react to price reductions, there is still no guarantee that profit can be increased by increasing sales. In fact, profit may decline in the face of increased sales. It may turn out that more effort is being put forth to get a smaller return.

While sales volume may increase with reductions in price, it may not increase enough to overcome the handicap of selling at a lower price. This point is often overlooked by the optimistic business person who believes that a small increase in volume can compensate for a slight decrease in price.

Price cuts, like an increase in the variable unit cost, decrease the contribution margin. On a unit basis, price decreases may appear to be insignificant; but when the unit differential is multiplied by thousands of units, the total effect may be tremendous. Perhaps many more units must be sold to make up for the difference.

Company A, for example, hopes to increase profit by selling more units; and to sell more, it plans to reduce the unit price by 10 percent. The present price and cost structure and one contemplated are given below:

	PRESENT PRICE AND COST	CONTEMPLATED PRICE AND COST
Selling price.....................................	$5.00	$4.50
Variable cost.....................................	2.50	2.50
Contribution margin.......................	$2.50	$2.00
Percentage of contribution margin...	50%	44.4%

At present, one half of each dollar in revenue can be applied to fixed cost and profit. When sales are twice the fixed cost, Company A will break even. This means that 60,000 units yielding a revenue of $300,000 must be sold if fixed cost is $150,000. But when the price is reduced, less than half of each dollar can be applied to fixed cost and profit. To recover $150,000 in fixed cost, sales revenue must amount to $337,500. Not only must the revenue be higher but, with a lower price per unit, more units must be sold to obtain that revenue. It will no longer be possible to get $337,500 in revenue by selling 67,500 units ($337,500 ÷ $5). Instead, 75,000 units must be sold just to break even.

To overcome the effect of the cut in price, sales volume in physical units must be increased by 25 percent:

$$\underline{\begin{array}{l} 75{,}000 \quad \text{units to be sold at lower price to break even} \\ 60{,}000 \quad \text{units to be sold at present price to break even} \end{array}}$$
$$\underline{15{,}000} \quad \text{increase in number of units}$$

$$\frac{15{,}000}{60{,}000} = \text{¼ or 25\%}$$

Sales revenue must be increased by 12½ percent:

$$\underline{\begin{array}{l} \$337{,}500 \quad \text{sales revenue at new break-even point} \\ 300{,}000 \quad \text{sales revenue at present break-even point} \end{array}}$$
$$\underline{\$\ \ 37{,}500} \quad \text{increase in sales revenue}$$

$$\frac{\$37{,}500}{\$300{,}000} = \text{⅛ or 12½\%}$$

The present income before income tax of $100,000 can still be earned by selling 125,000 units for a total revenue of $562,500, as shown below:

	PRESENT OPERATION	CONTEMPLATED OPERATION
Number of units sold......................	100,000	125,000
Sales...	$500,000	$562,500
Cost of goods sold	250,000	312,500
Contribution margin	$250,000	$250,000
Fixed cost	150,000	150,000
Income before income tax...............	$100,000	$100,000

After 125,000 units are sold, the company can improve its profit, but at a slower rate than when it operated with a price of $5. For every $4,500 increase in revenue, profit increases by $2,000. At present, a $4,500 increase in revenue beyond the break-even point yields $2,250 in profit.

The effect of the price reduction on profit can be depicted on a P/V graph as shown on the next page.

The increase in sales volume required to overcome the effect of a price reduction is proportionately greater when the rate of contribution margin is relatively low at the start. If each unit of product makes

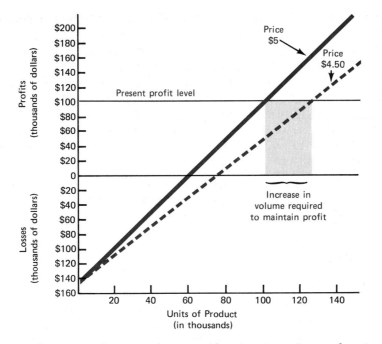

only a modest contribution, then a reduction in price makes it all the more difficult to recover the fixed cost and to earn profit.

Seemingly, the price should not be reduced. The handicap imposed by the decrease in price appears to be overwhelming; yet, in many circumstances, profit can be increased by lowering prices. A saving in variable cost, for example, can be passed along to the customer. The contribution margin remains the same; and if more units can be sold, profit can be increased. Even with no change in variable cost, increased profit may be realized by lowering prices, provided that sales volume can be increased by more than enough to make up for the effect of the decrease in price.

The policy with respect to price will depend upon the long-range and short-range objectives of management. In any event, it is important to know what will probably happen if a certain course of action is adopted. Prices may be cut with full knowledge that immediate profit will be reduced. The company accepts this disadvantage in the hope that it will be able to establish itself as a volume producer in the market. Another company, whose management is not informed with respect to cost-volume relationships, may cut prices in an attempt to gain immediate profit; then when the profit does not materialize, the management will be unpleasantly surprised. Price policy will be discussed more fully in Chapter 9.

Fixed Costs

A change in fixed cost has no effect on the contribution margin. Each unit yields the same margin as before. Increases in fixed cost are recovered when the contribution margin from additional units sold is equal to the increase in fixed cost. On a P/V graph, the slope of the profit line is unaffected by changes in fixed cost. The new profit line is drawn parallel to the original line, and the distance between the two lines at any point on the horizontal scale is equal to the increase or the decrease in cost.

In the P/V graph below, fixed cost has increased from $600,000 to $700,000. The product sells for $5 per unit, variable cost is $3 per unit, and the contribution per unit to fixed cost and profit is $2. Under the new fixed cost structure, the profit line has shifted to the right and at any point is $100,000 lower than it was originally. To maintain the same profit as before, 50,000 more units must be sold.

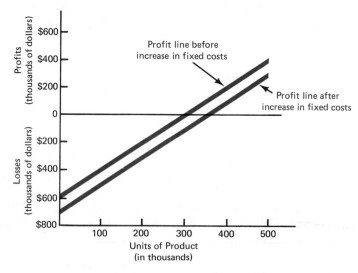

Increases in planned profit have the same effect as increases in fixed cost. For example, suppose that the fixed cost is to remain at $600,000 but that profit is to be increased from $200,000 to $300,000. Once again, 50,000 more units would have to be sold to provide $100,000, which in this case would be applied to increase profit.

Decreases in fixed cost will cause the profit line to shift to the left. The contribution to fixed cost and profit can be reduced by the amount of the decrease in cost without affecting profit. The decrease in sales volume can be calculated by dividing the unit contribution into the decrease in fixed cost. The new profit line is parallel to the original line at a distance equal to the decrease in fixed cost.

The fixed cost, like variable cost, is reduced whenever possible. Often it is necessary to handle a large volume of business merely to recover fixed cost. In some industries, fixed cost is relatively high. When expensive machinery and equipment are used in manufacturing, the fixed cost, of necessity, is large. This makes it all the more impera-tive to look for ways of keeping the cost down. Fixed cost has a habit of creeping upward; and before long a company is confronted with a high fixed cost structure, the result being that a large volume must be sold even though the contribution margin per unit is adequate.

Changes in the Sales Mix

Usually more than one type of product is sold. Several different product lines may be handled, each of which makes a different contribution to fixed cost recovery and profit. The total profit depends to some extent upon the proportions in which the products are sold. If the more profitable products make up a relatively large part of the sales mix, the profit is greater than they would be if more of the low-margin contributors were sold instead.

For any assumed mix of product sales, a break-even point can be computed. For example, assume that unit sales budget data are as shown below. In addition, the fixed cost for the year has been estimated at $500,000.

PRODUCT LINE	SALES VOLUME (UNITS)	UNIT SELLING PRICE	UNIT VARIABLE COST	UNIT CONTRIBUTION MARGIN
A	20,000	$50	$20	$30
B	10,000	50	30	20
C	10,000	50	40	10

The weighted contribution margin is $90 as computed below. Each combined unit consisting of 2 units of Product A and 1 unit each of Products B and C will contribute $90 to the recovery of fixed cost and profit. The company will break even when 5,555 combined units are sold. The combined units are converted to product-line units by multiplying the combined units by the sales mix proportions.

PRODUCT LINE	SALES MIX PROPORTIONS	UNIT CONTRIBUTION MARGIN	WEIGHTED CONTRIBUTION MARGIN
A	2	$30	$60
B	1	20	20
C	1	10	10
	Total weighted contribution margin........		$90

$$\frac{\$500,000 \text{ fixed cost}}{\$90 \quad \text{weighted contribution margin}} = 5,555 \text{ combined units}$$

PRODUCT LINE	SALES MIX PROPORTIONS	COMBINED UNITS	BUDGETED UNITS EACH LINE	UNIT CONTRIBUTION MARGIN	TOTAL CONTRIBUTION MARGIN
A	2	5,555	11,110	$30	$333,300
B	1	5,555	5,555	20	111,100
C	1	5,555	5,555	10	55,550
		Budgeted contribution margin..............			$499,950*

*Approximately equal to fixed cost of $500,000. Difference is due to rounding.

The total sales revenue at the break-even point is computed below.

PRODUCT LINE	SALES VOLUME (UNITS)	UNIT SELLING PRICE	SALES REVENUE
A	11,110	$50	$ 555,500
B	5,555	50	277,750
C	5,555	50	277,750
	Total sales revenue		$1,111,000

Sometimes management concentrates on total sales volume, unit selling prices, unit variable cost, and total fixed cost but overlooks the importance of the sales mix. The total revenue, unit selling prices, unit variable cost, and total fixed cost may be in agreement with the budget; but the profit may be lower. A lower profit can result from a shift in the sales mix. For example, larger quantities of the less profitable product lines may be sold with a corresponding decrease in the sales of the more profitable product lines.

The effect of a change in the sales mix is illustrated by assuming a budget plan for sales of the three product lines in a ratio of 2:1:1.

PRODUCT LINE	QUANTITY	UNIT SELLING PRICE	UNIT VARIABLE COST	UNIT CONTRIBUTION MARGIN	TOTAL CONTRIBUTION MARGIN	SALES REVENUE	CONTRIBUTION MARGIN PERCENTAGE
A	20,000	$50	$20	$30	$600,000	$1,000,000	60%
B	10,000	50	30	20	200,000	500,000	40
C	10,000	50	40	10	100,000	500,000	20
	Total				$900,000	$2,000,000	
	Less fixed cost				500,000		
	Budgeted income before income tax				**$400,000**		

During the next year, the company operated at the capacity budgeted with fixed cost of $500,000. The unit selling prices and unit variable cost were in agreement with the budget. The results were as follows:

PRODUCT LINE	QUANTITY SOLD	UNIT CONTRIBUTION MARGIN	TOTAL CONTRIBUTION MARGIN	SALES REVENUE
A	5,000	$30	$150,000	$ 250,000
B	20,000	20	400,000	1,000,000
C	15,000	10	150,000	750,000
	Total		$700,000	$2,000,000
	Less fixed cost		500,000	
	Actual income before income tax ..		**$200,000**	

Instead of earning $400,000 before income tax, the company earned only $200,000. Sales of Products B and C, the less profitable lines, were much better than expected. At the same time, sales of the best product line, Product A, were less than expected.

When more than one product line is handled, profit data for all products combined may be shown on one line of a P/V graph, the sales mix being assumed; or a separate graph may be made for each product line. Sometimes the effect of each product as well as total products on profit is depicted by plotting several lines on one P/V graph. A solid line is drawn to represent the net income or loss for total products. Next a broken line is drawn to the point of net income or loss contributed by one product, and then the line is extended to the point of net income or loss contribution of two products combined and continued until all of the products and the net income or loss are accounted for. The broken line is drawn so that the most profitable product is depicted first and so on until all of the products are included. The products sell in a fixed proportion, and the broken line does not indicate that the most profitable product is sold first with a certain profit or loss and that the total profit or loss is increased or decreased by a certain amount as other product lines are sold. Instead, the broken line shows the sales volume for each product in the mix; and the relative profitability of each product is revealed by the changes in the slope of the profit line. The total company profit for any combined sales volume must be read from the solid line. To illustrate, the budget data from the preceding example are entered on the P/V graph below, and the actual results are entered on the graph on page 104.

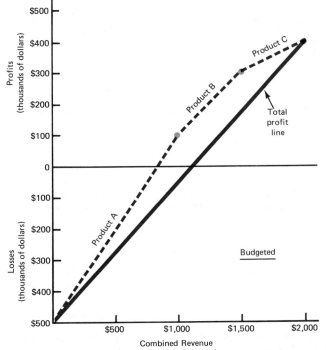

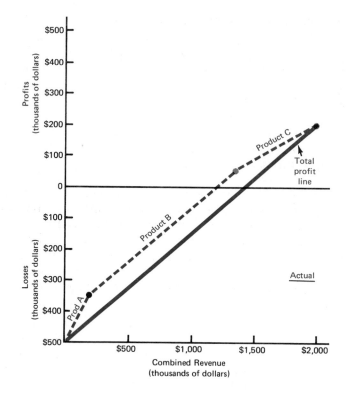

SHORT-TERM AND LONG-TERM PLANS

It is possible to earn additional profit by reducing the selling price of a product below the total unit cost, provided that the selling price is in excess of the unit variable cost. A policy of price cutting to increase sales volume and to increase profit, however, may be shortsighted. The company is expected to earn an adequate return on invested resources and may be overlooking the best use of resources in the long run by paying too much attention to short-run advantages. The contribution to profit in itself is not enough. The company should strive to obtain the best return possible on invested resources.

With existing facilities and productive resources, management should seek the best contribution margin per unit of the limiting or scarce factor. The scarce factor, in some cases, may be hours of labor time; or it may be space used for production. For example, assume that three product lines can be produced and sold as follows:

PRODUCT LINE	UNIT CONTRIBUTION MARGIN	÷	PRODUCTION HOURS PER UNIT OF PRODUCT*	=	CONTRIBUTION MARGIN PER HOUR
A	$10		5		$2
B	6		2		3
C	4		1		4

*Fixed cost of $6,000 for the year is allocated on the basis of hours of production.

A profit budget for the year is given below.

PRODUCT LINE	NUMBER OF UNITS	UNIT CONTRIBUTION MARGIN	TOTAL CONTRIBUTION MARGIN
A	1,000	$10	$10,000
B	1,000	6	6,000
C	1,000	4	4,000
Total			$20,000
Less fixed cost...			6,000
Estimated profit			$14,000

The company has 2,500 hours of idle capacity. Further study reveals that a government contract can be obtained for the sale of 500 additional units of Product A if the price is reduced by $5 per unit. This will reduce the contribution margin per unit on the contract to $5. At a production rate of five hours per unit, 500 units of Product A can be manufactured in the 2,500 additional hours available. Total profit for the firm will be increased by $2,500 (500 units × $5) as shown below.

PRODUCT LINE	NUMBER OF UNITS	UNIT CONTRIBUTION MARGIN	TOTAL CONTRIBUTION MARGIN
A	1,000	$10	$10,000
	500	5	2,500
B	1,000	6	6,000
C	1,000	4	4,000
Total			$22,500
Less fixed cost..			6,000
*Estimated profit			$16,500

*Increased profit: $16,500 with contract − $14,000 without contract = $2,500.

While profit is increased by accepting the government contract, it can be even better if the 2,500 hours are used to manufacture 2,500 additional units of Product C. Product C can be manufactured at the rate of one unit of product per hour. It is assumed that a market can be developed for the sale of a total of 3,500 units of Product C.

Additional contribution margin from sale of 2,500 more units of Product C (2,500 × $4 unit contribution margin)...	$10,000
Less contribution margin from sale of 500 units of Product A on contract	2,500
Additional contribution margin, net..................................	$ 7,500

In making plans, the short-term expediency of obtaining more sales volume by price cutting may not be the best in the long run. The objective is to obtain the best possible return from resources used. The problem of optimizing the profit from available resources is discussed more fully and in a somewhat different manner in a later chapter.

QUESTIONS

1. What is meant by the term contribution margin?

2. What factors are interrelated in profit planning?

3. What is meant by break-even point?

4. When the total contribution margin is equal to the total fixed cost, is the company operating at a profit or at a loss?

5. If the total fixed cost and the contribution margin per unit of product are given, is it possible to compute the number of units that must be sold in order to break even? Explain.

6. How is a break-even chart prepared?

7. If the total fixed cost and the percentage of the contribution margin to sales revenue are given, is it possible to compute the sales revenue at the break-even point? Explain.

8. If the total fixed cost and the percentage of the variable cost to sales revenue are given, is it possible to compute the sales revenue at the break-even point? Explain.

9. Can there be two break-even points? If there are two break-even points, how would the revenue and cost lines be drawn on the break-even chart?

10. In conventional practice, there is only one break-even point. Why?

11. Is it possible to compute the number of units that must be sold to earn a certain amount of income *before* income tax? Explain.

12. Is it possible to compute the number of units that must be sold to earn a certain amount of income *after* income tax? Explain.

13. (a) How does a P/V graph differ from a break-even chart?
    (b) Which form of presentation is superior?

14. When the contribution margin is high in relation to sales revenue, is the slope of the profit line on the P/V graph relatively steep or flat?

15. If there is an increase in the variable cost per unit of product, is there any effect on the profit line on the P/V graph? Explain the effect.

16. If there is a decrease in the selling price per unit of product, is there any effect on the profit line on the P/V graph? Explain the effect.

17. A 10% decrease in the selling price of a product has the same effect on profits as a 10% increase in the unit variable cost of the product. Is this true? Explain.

18. Does the slope of the profit line on the P/V graph change when the total fixed cost is increased or decreased? How is the profit line affected by changes in the total fixed cost?

19. What is meant by sales mix?

20. If more than one line of product is sold, can a P/V graph be prepared for the combined operation? How?

21. How can a contribution margin be computed so that it will include factors other than the physical number of units to be sold?

22. Is it possible to earn a profit while selling a product at a price that is less than the total unit cost? Explain.

23. In planning profit, the important point is to maximize the sales volume of the product lines with the highest contribution margin per unit of product. Is this entirely true? Explain.

24. Point out differences between short-term and long-term planning.

EXERCISES

1. Contribution Margin. Helen Rayburn has a franchise to sell small tools and appliances. An electric grass trimmer that sells for $28.50 is a very popular item, and she tells you that this item by itself can contribute enough sales volume to cover the entire fixed cost of her operation amounting to $45,500. The trimmer is purchased by Helen Rayburn at a cost of $15.50 per unit. Last year 4,600 of these trimmers were purchased and sold.

   Required:
   (1) What was the total contribution margin from the sale of 4,600 trimmers?
   (2) Did Rayburn cover the fixed cost with the sale of the trimmers?
   (3) What was the amount of the excess or the deficiency of the contribution margin when compared with the fixed cost?

2. Break-Even Point. Greggs Company incurs fixed manufacturing cost of $370,000 each year. The variable cost to manufacture the product amounts to $7 per unit. Each unit of product is sold for $11.

   Required: Determine the number of units that must be sold in order to break even.

3. Break-Even Revenue. Cogwell Company sells a product line at a unit price of $30. The contribution margin amounts to $10 per unit. Fixed manufacturing cost for the year amounts to $270,000.

   Required: How much revenue must be obtained from the sale of this product line in order to break even?

4. Break-Even Computations. Compute the number of units of product that must be sold if the company is to break even in each of the independent situations described below.

(1) The fixed cost is $312,000 a year. Each unit sold contributes $6 to the recovery of fixed cost and to profit.
(2) The variable cost is equal to 70% of sales revenue. Each unit of product is sold for $20. The fixed cost amounts to $420,000 for the year.
(3) Contribution margin is equal to 28% of the revenue. Each unit of product sells for $50. The fixed cost is $210,000 for the year.
(4) A variable cost of $9 per unit of product is equal to 60% of the selling price. The fixed cost for the year amounts to $390,000.
(5) Each unit of product sold contributes 30% of its revenue to the recovery of fixed cost and to profit. The fixed cost is $420,000 for the year, and each product is sold at a price of $10.

5. Effect of Variable Cost Changes. The manager of a department of Conwell Springs, Inc., is searching for ways to improve the profit margin of a product line selling for $30 per unit. The materials required for each unit of product cost $14, and this is the lowest possible cost at which the materials can be obtained. Labor and other variable costs to produce the product amount to $15 per hour. Under current operating conditions, 3 units of product can be manufactured each hour. The manager has found a way to produce 5 units per hour. The fixed cost for the year has been budgeted at $440,000.

Required:

(1) Compute the number of units that must be sold under the current operating conditions in order to break even.
(2) Compute the number of units that must be sold under the manager's plan in order to break even.

6. Effect of Price Change. Bidwell Supply Company has an established price of $36 per unit for a certain product line. The variable cost per unit is $27. The fixed cost for the year amounts to $216,000. Next year the selling price is to be increased to $39 per unit.

Required:

(1) How many units had to be sold at the old established price each year in order to break even?
(2) How many units would have to be sold at the new price each year in order to break even?

7. Planning for a Profit Goal. Kenneth McNeil has set a profit objective of $240,000 before income tax for a product line he handles. This product sells for $32 per unit. The variable cost to produce and sell the line amounts to $20 per unit. The fixed cost of this operation amounts to $420,000.

Required: How many units of product must be sold in order to achieve the profit objective?

8. Solving for Sales Revenue. Gary Waliczek, Inc., earned an income before income tax last year of $235,000. The fixed cost of operation amounts to $315,000 for the year. The average contribution margin on sales was equal to 25% of the sales revenue.

Required: Compute the sales revenue last year.

9. Planning Profit After Taxes. The manager of a department of Frostline Products, Inc., has estimated that the department should yield an income after income tax of $432,000. The fixed cost of operation amounts to $210,000 each year. The variable cost of the product line sold is equal to 70% of the selling price per unit of $50. Income tax is computed at 40% of income before income tax.

Required: How many units of product must be sold in order to achieve the profit objective?

10. Profit and Variable Cost Changes. Ravenna Metals and Dealtry Models, Inc., are in competition with a line of product selling for $140 per unit. Both companies can produce and sell this product at a variable cost of $120 per unit. Ravenna Metals has found a way to reduce the variable cost to $110 per unit and shares a portion of the cost saving with the customers by reducing the selling price to $135 per unit. Dealtry Models, Inc., is unable to reduce its variable cost but must meet the selling price of Ravenna Metals to remain competitive. Each company sells 45,000 units of product each year.

Required:

(1) What effect does this change have on the profit of Ravenna Metals?

(2) What effect does this change have on the profit of Dealtry Models, Inc.?

11. Profits and Price Change. The president of Phoenix Implements, Inc., notes that the income before income tax last year was $460,000. This income was earned by selling 148,000 units of a product at a price of $15 per unit. By reducing the selling price to $12 per unit, the president believes that sales volume can be increased to 250,000 units next year and that profit will be increased as a result. The fixed cost for the year is $428,000.

Required:

(1) Will income before income tax be increased by the reduction in the selling price and the expected increase in sales volume? Show computations.

(2) With a selling price of $12 per unit, how much sales volume is needed to earn no less than $460,000 before income tax?

12. Effect of Fixed Cost Reductions. Rocky Mountain Supplies, Inc., sells a type of quilted jacket at a price of $50 per jacket. The variable cost to manufacture and sell each jacket is $35. The fixed cost amounts to $195,000 for the year. A weaker market is anticipated by management, and efforts have been made to reduce fixed cost. It has been estimated that the annual fixed cost can be reduced to $172,500.

Required:

(1) How many units must be sold at the original fixed cost structure in order to break even?

(2) How many units will have to be sold at the reduced fixed cost structure in order to break even?

13. Sales Mix. In past years, Scott Parts, Inc., has sold 3 units of Product A for every unit of Product B that is sold. The fixed cost per year has remained at $140,000. The contribution margin per unit for Product A is $6 and for Product B is $10. The sales mix is expected to change so that 2 units of Product A will be sold for every unit of Product B that is sold.

Required:

(1) In order to break even, how many units of Products A and B must be sold when 3 units of A are sold for every unit of B?

(2) In order to break even, how many units of Product A and B must be sold when 2 units of A are sold for every unit of B?

14. Graphic Representations. A television set is manufactured and sold by Boston Manufacturing Company at a price of $150 per unit. The variable cost amounts to $120 per unit. The fixed cost is $300,000 for the year.

Required:

(1) Prepare a break-even chart for this operation in intervals of 5,000 units from 5,000 units to 25,000 units.

(2) Prepare a profit-volume graph showing a profit line with intervals of 5,000 units from 5,000 units to 25,000 units.

15. Graphic Representations. Vinson and Madden, Inc., produce and sell electric heating units. Each unit sells for $20. The variable cost to manufacture and sell each unit amounts to $15. The fixed cost is $100,000 each year.

With improved production methods, the variable cost can be reduced to $12 per unit. Also the fixed cost can be reduced to $80,000 each year.

Required: Prepare a profit-volume graph showing a profit line to reflect conditions before the improved production methods. Draw another profit line on the same chart to reflect conditions after the improved production methods become operational. Show intervals of 5,000 units from 5,000 units to 25,000 units.

PROBLEMS

4-1. Product Pricing and Break Even. Jim Sotzing plans to introduce a new product line for Vallejo Parts Company. His plan is to price the product at $160 per unit. As an alternative, he may price the product at $145 per unit. The variable cost of producing and selling each unit is estimated at $120. The fixed cost is expected to amount to $625,000 for the year.

Required:

(1) How many units must be sold in order to break even at a price of $160 per unit?
(2) How many units must be sold in order to break even at a price of $145 per unit?

4-2. Sales Volume and Profit. The management of Perryville Stores, Inc., has established a profit objective of $480,000 after income tax for the year on one of its product lines. The profit objective was determined by considering the rate of return that the company should earn on its investment. Income tax is estimated at 40% of the income before income tax.

The product line is expected to sell for $220 per unit with a unit variable cost of $145. The fixed cost for the year has been estimated at $550,000.

Required:

(1) How many units of product must be sold in order to earn the desired profit after tax?
(2) How many units must be sold merely to break even?

4-3. Sales Promotion and Profits. The manager of Bay Area Furnishings at Pine Creek Mall has a plan to increase sales volume at the store. The average operating results for each week are given below.

Sales revenue..	$60,000
Variable cost	45,000
Fixed cost for the week..	10,000

The manager plans to bring shoppers into the store by having a weekly drawing for a prize of $1,000. For each dollar of merchandise purchased, the shopper will receive a numbered ticket for the drawing. The variable cost to print and distribute the tickets has been estimated at five cents per ticket. Promotion and other fixed costs in connection with the drawing have been estimated at $500 per week.

The manager estimates that sales can be doubled with the weekly drawing. The regional manager is skeptical and believes that the cost of this promotion will be very high although it may increase sales slightly to $65,000 a week.

Required:

(1) Compute the sales revenue required to break even without the drawing.
(2) Compute the sales revenue required to break even with the drawing.

(3) If the drawing can increase sales to $65,000, how much will be added to profit?

(4) If the sales can be increased to $120,000 per week, how much will be added to profit?

(5) Should the drawings be held?

4-4. Additional Sales at Lower Price. Last year Omar Fittings, Inc., sold two lines of product with the following selling prices and variable cost.

Product Line	Unit Selling Price	Unit Variable Cost
A	$60	$40
B	50	35

The sales revenue was $1,200,000 from Product A and $500,000 from Product B. The fixed cost for the year of $300,000 was allocated to each product line on the basis of the number of units sold.

Next year the president of the company plans to sell 2,000 additional units of Product B on the export market at a price of $40 per unit. Sales volume in the regular market will be the same as it was last year.

The vice-president of the firm states that if Product B is to be sold on a special contract at a price of $40 per unit, it will be sold below the total unit cost of $45. Hence, the additional units should not be sold on the export contract.

Required:

(1) Compute the contribution margin per unit for each product line.

(2) Prepare an income statement for the past year that shows the contribution margin for each product line and the income before income tax for each product line after the deduction of the fixed cost.

(3) Prepare an estimated income statement for the next year that shows the contribution margin for each product line and the income before income tax for each product line after the deduction of the fixed cost. Assume that the export contract is accepted.

(4) Evaluate the position of the vice-president. Consider both the positive and negative aspects of the argument.

4-5. Additional Sales at Lower Price. Last year Bettis Machine Company sold 12,000 small motors at a price of $120 per motor. An income statement is given below in summary form.

	Unit	Total
Sales	$120	$1,440,000
Cost of goods sold:		
Variable	$ 80	$ 960,000
*Fixed	15	180,000
Selling and administrative expense (variable)	2	24,000
	$ 97	$1,164,000
Income before income tax	$ 23	$ 276,000

*Unit fixed cost was calculated by dividing $180,000 by 12,000 units produced and sold.

Only one line of product is manufactured and sold.

The company has the capacity to produce and sell 15,000 units each year. Next year the company can sell 12,000 units in the regular market and has the opportunity to sell an additional 3,000 units in the export market for $95 per unit. There would be no effect on the selling and administrative expenses. The president of the company recommends that the order be rejected because the cost to make each unit is more than the price.

Required:

(1) Assume that the order is accepted. Prepare an income statement for the year that will show the contribution margin for each type of sale.

(2) Explain why the income before income tax is higher or lower with the export order.

4-6. Increased Sales at Lower Price. In the year before last, Ray Armour, as sales manager for Britton Products, Inc., sold 80,000 units of a product for $30 per unit. The unit variable cost was $20, and the fixed cost for the year was $350,000. Income tax was at the rate of 40% of income before tax.

Last year the selling price was reduced to $27, and 120,000 units of product were sold. The variable cost remained at $20 per unit, and fixed cost and the income tax rate were the same.

Armour believes that profit can be increased further by reducing the selling price to $25 per unit in the coming year. He anticipates that 160,000 units can be sold at this price. Variable cost is estimated at $20 per unit, and the fixed cost and the income tax rate are expected to remain the same.

Required:

(1) Determine the net income for the year before last, last year, and the estimated net income for the coming year.

(2) Was profit increased by a reduction of the selling price and an increase in sales volume? Will it be increased further by the sales manager's plan?

(3) How many units must be sold in the coming year to earn the same net income as was earned in the best profit year?

4-7. Increased Sales at Lower Price. Sales demand for a certain consumer product is very sensitive to changes in price. As prices increase, sales demand falls sharply; but reductions in price increase sales demand by a large amount.

Minton Industries sold 200,000 units of this product line at a unit price of $15 last year. The variable cost per unit was $10. The fixed cost was $400,000 for the year.

Next year it is estimated that 400,000 units of the product can be sold at a price of $13 per unit. The variable cost per unit is expected to remain at $10, and fixed cost for the year should remain at $400,000.

Required: Can the company increase profit at the lower price with increased sales volume? Show computations.

4-8. Profit Advantage of Cost Reductions. Celia McKay, as president of Morning Star Products, has been looking for ways to reduce costs. Some of the cost savings are passed along to customers, and the company has been able to gain a competitive advantage and to increase profit.

In 1978, for example, a product line that is sold by one of the divisions was priced at $140 per unit with a unit variable cost of $125. The fixed cost for the year was $270,000. During that year 40,000 units were sold.

In 1979, the variable cost per unit was reduced to $120. The selling price was cut to $136 per unit, and fixed cost was reduced to $240,000 for the year. The company sold 40,000 units of product.

In 1980, variable cost was reduced further to $115 per unit. The selling price was reduced to $132 per unit. Unfortunately, fixed cost increased to $255,000 for the year. The company sold 40,000 units of product.

Required:

(1) Determine the contribution margin and the income before income tax for each of the three years.
(2) How many units would have to be sold in each of the years under the conditions stated in order to break even?

4-9. Sales Volume and Capacity Limits. The sales manager of Piedmont Machine Company is confident that sales volume for a certain piece of equipment can be increased by 200% next year if the price is reduced from $2,000 to $1,800 per unit. Present sales volume is 5,000 units. The variable cost per unit amounts to $1,200 and is expected to be at that amount next year. The fixed cost of $1,600,000 for the year will likely be the same for the next year.

The production manager states that only 10,000 units of this equipment can be manufactured with the present facilities. Hence, it will not be possible to obtain the sales volume anticipated by the sales manager. The manager recommends that no price concessions be given to the customers to increase sales volume.

Required: Which person is correct, the sales manager or the production manager, assuming that the basic facts are stated correctly? Show contribution margins and income before income tax to support your position.

4-10. Sales Mix and Profit Planning. Darlington Industries produces three lines of product. Data with respect to these lines are as follows:

Product	Unit Contribution Margin	Percentage of total Sales Volume
A	$20	50
B	50	20
C	10	30
		100

The total fixed cost for the year has been budgeted at $920,000. Management is planning to earn a profit after income tax of $828,000. Income tax is at the rate of 40% of income before tax.

Required:

(1) How many units of each product line must be sold merely to break even at the sales mix given?
(2) How many units of each product line must be sold to earn the desired profit at the sales mix given?

4-11. Sales Mix and Profit Planning. Pappas Products, Inc., manufactures and sells four product lines. Normally, the lines sell in the following proportions:

Product	Percentage	Time Required to Make Each Unit
A	15	20 minutes
B	25	30 minutes
C	30	60 minutes
D	30	10 minutes

The contribution margin for each unit sold for each of the four product lines is given below.

Product	Unit Contribution Margin
A	$ 6.00
B	15.00
C	20.00
D	8.00

The fixed cost for the year has been budgeted at $391,500.

Required:

(1) Determine how many units of each product line must be sold in order to break even.

(2) If it were possible to change the product mix, which product line should be favored if there is a limitation on production time? Show calculations.

(3) Assume that products sell in the mix given. How many units of each line must be sold in order to earn an income before tax of $783,000?

4-12. Sales Mix and Time Limitations. A small manufacturing plant produces three lines of product. Management has become concerned with fixed cost that has steadily been creeping upwards and reducing the desired profit. A profit goal has been established at a minimum of $320,000 before income tax on the manufacturing operation for the year.

Data with respect to the three lines of product are given below.

	Product Lines		
	1	2	3
Unit selling price	$20	$30	$32
Number of units sold	50,000	90,000	60,000
Labor time required to manufacture each unit	30 minutes	10 minutes	40 minutes
Materials cost per unit	$ 6	$24	$15

Labor is paid at the rate of $9 per hour, and variable overhead cost varies with labor hours. The total variable overhead cost at 80,000 labor hours is estimated at $480,000.

Required:

(1) With sales volume distributed among the product lines as shown above, determine the maximum level of fixed manufacturing cost if the plant is to earn an income before income tax of $320,000 on manufacturing.

(2) How many labor hours are used to produce the sales mix and volume given?

(3) Determine the contribution margin per labor hour. If there is a limit on labor hours, which product line should be favored?

(4)   Product #1 — 50,000 units
          Product #2 — 50,000 units
          Product #3 — 100,000 units

With this mix, determine the level of fixed manufacturing cost to earn an income before income tax of $320,000 on manufacturing.

(5) How many labor hours must be used to yield the sales mix and volume given in part (4)?

(6) What factors may make it impossible for the company to attain the revised sales mix and volume given in part (4)?

4-13. Selling Price to Break Even. Four students from Roseberry College have had experience in making various decorative items and plan to make and sell attractive window planters including the small flowering plants.

A local garden center offers them space for a working area at $100 rent for the late winter and early spring working season.

A national commercial company sells a similar item for $8.95 plus shipping and handling charges of $1.

Estimates of the cost to make and sell the planters are given below.

Container materials	$ .90 per container
Plants...	.60 per container
Compost (100 planters per bale)	10.00 per bale
Wrapping and shipping...	1.00 per container

The students plan to do their own work and hope to earn a salary of $900 each for the time that they are engaged in this activity.

They plan extensive advertising by radio, newspaper, and direct mail in the general area at a cost of $6,000.

One of the students estimates that 4,000 units can be made and sold. Each unit can be priced below the national company's price so that they will break even, that is, earn their salaries with no profit on the operation.

One of the others believes that it is more realistic to estimate sales of 2,000 units and that the price can still be competitive without running as much risk of loss with a lower price.

Required:

(1) Determine a selling price to break even if 4,000 units are made and sold.
(2) Determine a selling price to break even if 2,000 units are made and sold.
(3) Assume that a selling price was established to break even at 4,000 units. Determine the loss if only 2,000 units are sold.
(4) How many units must be sold in order to break even if the price is equal to the competitor's with the additional charge made to the customer for wrapping and shipping costs?

4-14. Selling Price and Profit Planning. Cheryl Kress purchases old kerosene lamps and converts them to decorative electric lamps. This business started as a hobby and has developed into a full-time activity with several employees.

An ornate lamp is sold for $40 a unit, and a plain model is sold for $20 a unit. According to estimates made, 30,000 units of the ornate lamp should be sold next year; and 10,000 units of the plain model should be sold.

The fixed cost of the operation has been budgeted at $190,000 for the year. Income before income tax of at least $50,000 is desired.

The contribution margin from each unit of each product line is to be equal. Kress tells you that the variable cost to produce an ornate lamp is $8 and that the variable cost to produce a plain lamp is $3. She wants to know how much she can afford to pay for each type of kerosene lamp if she is to realize her profit objective under the terms stated.

Required: Determine the maximum price that can be paid for each type of kerosene lamp to meet the conditions.

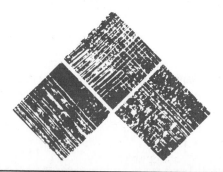

5
PRODUCT OR PROJECT COSTS

In many cases, management wants to know how much it costs to manufacture a batch of products or a unit or product or how much it costs to render a given service or to complete a certain project. This type of information is furnished by a system of cost accounting.

Product cost as determined in cost accounting may or may not be helpful in managerial planning and control. In making decisions and in controlling operations, management uses cost selectively; and the cost used may not necessarily be the cost of the products. These applications are discussed in later chapters. In certain cases, however, the person responsible for cost control tends to view the operation in terms of projects, production orders, or batches of products. Product cost is then applied, at least to some extent, in planning and control.

COSTS

The use of the term "cost accounting" implies that cost accounting is an entirely different system of accountability, but it is really only an extension of general accounting. Cost is accounted for in any event. In general financial accounting, the costs are reported in aggregate; in cost accounting, they are broken down on a unit basis. The unit may be a plant, department, product line, function, or other item to which costs can be assigned.

Cost Transitions

Cost accounting is based upon the premise that assets which are acquired are transformed within the enterprise and ultimately become a part of the inventory of products to be sold. An asset may lose its original identity in the transformation process, but its status as an asset is retained until the products are sold. When the products are sold, the cost of the various assets that have been transformed into product cost is released as expense.

The transformation process is illustrated by using a simple example. Gasoline is purchased to give power to a saw used in Operation 3 to trim lumber. The saw is employed to make the products. The table below shows the process of transformation.

TRANSACTION	ASSET CONVERSION	ACCOUNT	TYPE OF ACCOUNT
1. Purchase of gasoline	Acquisition of potential energy	Gasoline Inventory	Asset
2. Consumption of fuel by saw in Operation 3	Potential energy becomes active energy	Manufacturing Cost in Operation 3	Asset
3. Cost of Operation 3 applied to products	Active energy identified with products	Work in Process	Asset
4. Products completed and transferred to finished stock	Products are completely manufactured	Finished Goods	Asset
5. Products removed from finished stock and sold	Products sold	Cost of Goods Sold	Expense

The use of the gasoline does not constitute expense. The gasoline has merely changed form and has been converted to energy. The cost of the energy used (gasoline used) becomes a part of the cost of the products that have been manufactured. The fuel cost becomes expense when the products leave the business as a result of sales transactions. Gasoline cost, along with other costs, then becomes a part of the cost of goods sold.

Period Cost

The cost that is referred to as *period cost* is identified with measured time intervals and not with goods or services. Insurance protection, for example, may be furnished at a cost of $1,200 per year or at a rate of $100 a month. Each month the insurance cost is $100 regardless of the amount of business transacted. The cost is matched against revenue as expense according to the time interval that has elapsed. An income statement for the year will show insurance expense of $1,200.

Cost is usually recorded by *natural classification* to identify the type of service received, such as telephone, electric, repairs, and rent. A designation such as wages is a natural classification for the cost of labor service. Cost may also be classified by *function*, that is, according to the type of work performed — manufacturing, selling, or administrative. The cost of labor service, for example, is under the natural classification of wages and if used to manufacture products, is classified by function as a manufacturing cost.

Product Cost

Cost cannot always be properly matched against revenue on a period-of-time basis. In the income determination process, costs incurred to produce revenue should be offset as expenses against the resulting revenue. The period in which the benefit is received is the period in which the cost should be deducted as expenses. For example, insurance on a factory building for a certain year should not be charged to insurance expense for that year if the products that were manufactured are not sold until the next year. The insurance cost should follow the products and should be matched against the revenue from their sale as expense. The cost incurred to manufacture products should become a part of the product cost and should become expense only when the products to which they are attached are sold. Usually manufacturing cost is treated as a product cost and not as a period cost. Factory insurance accrues on a time basis, but even so it is not treated as a period cost. Instead it is a manufacturing cost and is generally considered to be a part of the cost of the goods produced. If the goods produced during a year are the only goods sold in that year with no inventory remaining at the end of the year, the resulting net income will be the same under either a time basis or a product basis of accountability. But if completed or partially completed goods are on hand at the end of the fiscal year, some of the insurance cost will be inventoried.

Cost Accounting Beyond the Manufacturing Area

The principles of cost accounting do not have to be restricted to manufacturing operations. In recent years, much attention has been given to the determination of costs by units in service industries. For example, automobile insurance companies have calculated the cost of servicing customers by age classification, marital status, accident record, location, etc. Banks also make use of cost analysis in arriving at service charges and amounts to be charged for handling special checking accounts.

Even in a manufacturing enterprise, the principles of cost accounting can be extended to include the selling and administrative areas.

Usually the formal accounting records show selling and administrative cost as a period cost and not as a part of product cost. But for managerial purposes, supplemental analysis may be made to show what it costs to serve certain customers, or what it costs to sell certain product lines, or the cost to sell in particular geographical areas. This breakdown of cost provides a means for control over sales and administration in much the same way as manufacturing cost accounting provides a means for control over production.

The Cost Elements

The manufactured cost of any product consists of three elements:

(1) **Direct materials.**
(2) **Direct labor.**
(3) **Factory overhead.**

Direct materials cost is the cost of materials incorporated in the product and measurable as such. For example, the steel used in manufacturing socket wrenches would be a part of the product, and its cost could be measured as direct materials cost. A galvanizing solution used to coat the tools, while a part of the product, may not be easy to measure as a cost of any particular unit processed. The cost per unit may be too insignificant to measure as direct materials cost and may be classified under factory overhead as an indirect materials cost. Similarly, the cost of other materials that are not even a part of the product, such as abrasives and polishes, are classified as indirect materials.

Direct labor cost is the labor cost directly traceable to the creation of the products. Some workers, frequently designated as production workers, spend most of their time in turning out products. The labor cost attached to this time is called the direct labor cost. The idle time of the production workers, which is not related to any group of products under production, may be wasted, or may be used in cleaning the factory and repairing the equipment, or may be put to use in some other way. Labor cost that cannot be traced to the products is included as a part of factory overhead under the general heading of indirect labor. The wages or salaries of the factory supervisors, engineers, maintenance crew, and others who do not work on the product itself but who assist in the manufacturing operation are likewise classified as indirect labor.

Factory overhead cost consists of all manufacturing costs with the exception of direct materials and direct labor. Included under the heading of factory overhead are the costs of indirect materials, supplies used, indirect labor, repairs and maintenance, heat and light, taxes, insurance, depreciation, and other costs to operate the manufacturing division. The factory overhead cost cannot be readily identified with individual products and thus is allocated to the products by a procedure discussed later in this chapter.

The Costing Procedure

The costs of manufacturing, regardless of their various characteristics, are accumulated by cost element and are recorded in an inventory account designated as Work in Process. This asset account is a focal account into which all product costs are funneled. After the products have been completed and placed in finished stock, the cost is transferred to another asset account, Finished Goods. When the products are sold, the cost is transferred from Finished Goods to Cost of Goods Sold.

Two basic systems of cost accounting are employed in the assignment of cost to products or service units:

(1) The job order cost system.
(2) The process cost system.

The system used depends upon the type of manufacturing operation.

THE JOB ORDER COST SYSTEM

The *job order cost system* is used when the products are manufactured in identifiable lots or groups or when the products are manufactured according to customer specifications. A printer, for example, may receive an order to print 5,000 copies of a summer school bulletin. This bulletin is prepared as directed by the school, and it differs in form and content from the printing work done for other customers. The printer's cost is accumulated by customer order. Manufacturers and contractors, like the printer, may work on a project or order basis and identify cost by project or order.

In a job order cost system the cost is assigned to the jobs passing through the plant and accumulated on forms referred to as job or production orders. Each order is usually divided into three basic sections — materials, labor, and overhead; thus, the three cost elements can be accounted for separately. A section is usually provided in which a summary of the cost is shown and a unit cost determined. This section is completed when the job is finished.

A separate production order is kept for each job going through the plant, and the file of production orders in process constitutes a subsidiary ledger in support of the work in process account in the general ledger. A production order is shown on page 129.

Costing Direct Materials and Direct Labor

Direct materials and direct labor cost can usually be charged to the products by measuring the cost of materials and labor that have been used for particular orders. When materials are purchased, an entry is made to debit Materials and to credit Accounts Payable as shown at the top of the next page.

Materials..	75,000	
Accounts Payable		75,000
Purchase of materials to be used in production.		

As direct materials are used in production, requisition tickets are prepared showing the cost of materials used on specific production orders. If requisition tickets indicate that direct materials costing $60,000 have been transferred from the materials inventory to production, the journal entry appears as follows:

Work in Process	60,000	
Materials...		60,000
Direct materials requisitioned for production.		

Assume that included in the total is $20,000 for Order #1018. Entries are also made on the individual production orders supporting the work in process account.

Factory payroll is recorded by a debit to Payroll with offsetting credits to Employees Income Tax Payable, FICA Tax Payable, other liability accounts for payroll deductions, and Wages Payable as follows:

Payroll	50,000	
Employees Income Tax Payable...		10,000
FICA Tax Payable...		3,000
Union Dues Payable		1,000
Wages Payable...		36,000
To record factory payroll for the month.		

Assume that all labor is direct labor.

The entry for distribution of the above direct labor payroll to the various production orders assuming that direct labor time tickets show 10,000 hours of labor at $5 an hour were used in producing various orders is:

Work in Process	50,000	
Payroll..		50,000
Direct labor costed to production.		

Assume that $10,000 applies to Order #1018. Entries are also made on the individual production orders supporting the work in process account.

Production supervisors, in planning their operations, may estimate the direct materials and direct labor cost for each of the orders for which they are responsible. They subsequently measure the actual cost and compare it with the estimates, taking into account the stage of completion for each order.

For example, the production schedule may be prepared as follows:

DIRECT MATERIALS

Order Number	Estimate	Actual	Dollar Variance	Percentage of Completion
1017	$22,000	$21,000	$(1,000)	100%
1018	19,500	20,000	500	100
*1019	10,000	14,000	4,000	50
*1020	5,000	5,000	—0—	25
Total	$56,500	$60,000	$ 3,500	

*Estimates adjusted to percentage of completion basis.

DIRECT LABOR HOURS

Order Number*	Estimate	Actual	Variance	Dollar Variance	Percentage of Completion
1017	4,450	4,000	(450)	$(2,250)	80%
1018	1,800	2,000	200	1,000	50
1019	3,300	3,500	200	1,000	50
1020	450	500	50	250	10
Total	10,000	10,000	—0—	—0—	

*Estimates adjusted to percentage of completion basis.

In the case of direct materials, the percentage of completion refers to the percentage of materials used at the point of measurement in relation to the total materials requirement for the order. Similarly, the percentage of completion with respect to labor measures the percentage of labor used to date in relation to the total labor requirement for the order.

Supervisors are able to use such cost information as they follow each order from its inception to completion. As a *cost overrun* (unfavorable variation from estimate) develops, they can take corrective measures. The preceding example shows that Order Number 1019 is 50 percent completed with respect to both materials and labor and that more materials and more hours were used than anticipated. Knowing what caused the overrun may enable the supervisor to find ways to reduce cost. Or, it may be found that the estimate was unrealistically low; in which case, budgets are revised.

Costing the Factory Overhead

Factory overhead, unlike direct materials and direct labor, cannot be requisitioned or measured directly as a cost of any particular production order. Factory overhead consists of a variety of costs such as indirect materials, indirect labor, insurance, and taxes, all of which are indirectly related to the products.

Factory overhead is attached to the products indirectly by means of a factor that can be directly related to thé products. This factor serves as a bridge between factory overhead and the products. Often the factor chosen for overhead allocation is direct labor hours, machine hours, or direct labor cost. Factory overhead is budgeted for the year, and the factor selected is also budgeted. The budgeted factor is then divided into the budgeted overhead to obtain an *overhead rate*. Products then are assigned overhead cost by multiplying the actual quantities of the factor by the rate calculated.

The factor chosen as a basis for overhead allocation should be related logically to both the overhead and the product. If machinery plays an important role in the manufacturing operation, the overhead cost likely consists largely of power cost, lubrication, maintenance, repairs, depreciation, and other costs closely related to machine operation. This cost is necessary in the manufacturing process and assists in the creation of the products. The benefits received by the products can probably be best measured by the machine hours used in their production. Therefore, overhead cost should be allocated to the products on a machine hour basis. For other departments in the plant that are more "labor intensive" than "capital intensive," direct labor cost, direct labor hours, or some other basis may be more appropriate for overhead allocation.

The calculation of an overhead rate is illustrated by assuming that several factory overhead budgets have been prepared for various levels of operating activity. A series of budgets for various levels of operating activity, as discussed in Chapter 1, is called a flexible budget.

A flexible budget is given below.

Budgeted direct labor hours	6,000	8,000	10,000*	12,000
Budgeted factory overhead:				
Variable:				
Indirect materials.............................	$ 7,500	$10,000	$12,500	$15,000
Repairs and maintenance................	5,700	7,600	9,500	11,400
Power and light.................................	4,800	6,400	8,000	9,600
Total	$18,000	$24,000	$30,000	$36,000
Fixed:				
Indirect labor and supervision........	$18,000	$18,000	$18,000	$18,000
Repairs and maintenance................	6,500	6,500	6,500	6,500
Power and light.................................	5,500	5,500	5,500	5,500
Factory rent..	8,000	8,000	8,000	8,000
Depreciation of equipment..............	12,000	12,000	12,000	12,000
Total	$50,000	$50,000	$50,000	$50,000
Total budgeted overhead	$68,000	$74,000	$80,000	$86,000
Rate per direct labor hour:				
Variable...	$ 3.000	$ 3.000	$ 3.000	$ 3.000
Fixed	8.333	6.250	5.000	4.167
Total	$11.333	$ 9.250	$ 8.000	$ 7.167

*Level selected for rate to cost the products.

In this example, direct labor hours have been selected as the factor for obtaining a product costing rate. Note that the variable cost is $3 per hour at any level of operation, whereas the fixed rate depends upon the number of direct labor hours used in the computation. The total rate of $8 per hour used for this illustration has been computed at 10,000 direct labor hours.

$$\frac{\text{Budgeted factory overhead}}{\text{Budgeted direct labor hours}} = \frac{\$80,000}{10,000} = \$8 \text{ per direct labor hour}$$

During the year, the products passing through the plant were charged with budgeted factory overhead. Assume that 10,000 hours of direct labor were used during the year. While the manufacturing operation was going on, various entries were made to cost the products. In aggregate, it would be as if one summary entry were made as follows:

Work in Process	80,000	
Applied Factory Overhead		80,000
Allocation of factory overhead cost to the orders, 10,000 hours at $8 each.		

Each order is charged with a portion of the overhead as it goes through production at the rate of $8 for each direct labor hour charged to the order.

The cost shown for Order Number 1018 may now be summarized at this stage of its production as follows:

Direct materials	$20,000
Direct labor (2,000 hours at $5 each)	10,000
Factory overhead (2,000 hours at $8 each)	16,000
Total cost	$46,000

Cost for direct labor and overhead is accumulated for orders until they are completed. At completion, the cost of the orders is transferred out of work in process and into finished goods.

Why does the accountant go to so much trouble in assigning factory overhead cost to the products, instead of waiting until the end of the year when all of the actual factory overhead has been collected, the actual direct labor hours of operation have been determined, an actual overhead rate has been calculated, and actual cost has been allocated to the orders that were manufactured during the year? Why bother with a budget and a budget rate?

When a budget rate is used, product costs can be determined quickly. There is no need to wait until the end of a month or other fiscal period to determine the cost of making a certain order or batch of product units. The cost is available while production is in process, thus making it easier to control operations as they occur.

Also, product cost does not fluctuate as it would if actual overhead rates were used in computing monthly cost. Seasonal variations throughout the year would cause the overhead cost per unit to be higher or lower depending upon the volume produced. Interim financial reports might show various unit product cost, total cost, and profit depending upon seasonal operations. These variations can be leveled out by using a budget rate.

Control of Factory Overhead

Returning to the illustration, assume that the actual factory overhead for the year amounted to $81,500. The total of $81,500 is recorded as a debit to the control account, Factory Overhead. Supporting the control account is a subsidiary ledger in which the detailed costs of factory overhead are accumulated.

The actual factory overhead cost is compared with the budgeted cost as shown below.

COMPARISON — BUDGET WITH ACTUAL FACTORY OVERHEAD

	Budget	Actual	Variance Over (Under)
Variable:			
Indirect materials	$12,500	$13,400	$ 900
Repairs and maintenance...................	9,500	9,300	(200)
Power and light	8,000	8,800	800
Total..	$30,000	$31,500	$1,500
Fixed:			
Indirect labor and supervision............	$18,000	$18,000	—0—
Repairs and maintenance...................	6,500	6,500	—0—
Power and light	5,500	5,500	—0—
Factory rent	8,000	8,000	—0—
Depreciation of equipment.................	12,000	12,000	—0—
Total..	$50,000	$50,000	—0—
Total factory overhead	$80,000	$81,500	$1,500

Each of the overhead classifications, such as indirect materials and repairs and maintenance, is controlled by management. In this example, questions may arise as to why indirect materials cost $900 more than budgeted. If the $900 variation is within a tolerable limit of variation, then no further action is necessary.

Overhead by its very nature is not directly related to production orders or projects. Hence, control is exercised to a large extent over each individual overhead classification. However, the aggregate variable overhead can be controlled to an extent on a production order basis if the overhead varies with a factor that can be brought under control.

If variable overhead, for example, varies with direct labor hours, the supervisor should recognize that the variable overhead will be higher if more direct labor hours are used on an order than budgeted. Both the direct labor cost and the variable overhead cost will depend upon the efficient use of production hours.

In the example, variable overhead varies at the rate of $3 per hour. An estimate of the difference in variable overhead cost attributable to a difference between the actual and estimated hours is shown at the top of the next page.

ORDER NUMBER	VARIANCE IN HOURS*	VARIABLE OVERHEAD DIFFERENCE (VARIANCE × $3)
1017	(450)	$(1,350)
1018	200	600
1019	200	600
1020	50	150

*This is the same as the variance for direct labor hours.

All of the costs of production cannot be controlled on a project or production order basis. Direct materials and direct labor cost, however, may be budgeted and controlled by specific order. Variable overhead, to an extent, may be controlled by controlling the factor related to the job.

The fixed overhead cannot be controlled by job or project. The fixed overhead does not increase or decrease with changes in the hours of operation. It is allocated to the orders by the use of hourly costing rate. In this example, all of the fixed costs were apportioned to the orders because the actual hours of operation were in agreement with the budgeted hours used for costing purposes. Suppose, however, that there were only 8,000 hours of operation. Then, only $40,000 of the fixed overhead would be costed to the products by using the fixed overhead rate of $5.00 an hour established for 10,000 hours.

$$8,000 \text{ actual hours} \times \begin{array}{c} \$5 \text{ fixed overhead} \\ \text{rate per hour} \end{array} = \begin{array}{c} \$40,000 \text{ of the fixed over-} \\ \text{head costed to products} \end{array}$$

Budgeted fixed overhead	$50,000
Fixed overhead costed to products..	40,000
Capacity variance	$10,000

The difference between the budgeted fixed overhead and the fixed overhead costed to products by the use of the predetermined fixed overhead rate is designated as a *capacity variance* or as a *volume variance*. Capacity variance is discussed further in Chapter 7.

Disposition of the Overhead Variance

While the products were being costed with budgeted factory overhead, actual factory overhead costs were being incurred and recorded as debits to Factory Overhead. At the end of the year, after all adjusting entries have been made, the factory overhead accounts would have balances as follows:

	Debit	Credit
Factory Overhead...	$81,500	
Applied Factory Overhead...		$80,000

Not all of the actual factory overhead was charged to products by means of the budget. There was a difference or variance of $1,500. This difference can be closed to Cost of Goods Sold at the end of the year or, if desired, can be allocated to Cost of Goods Sold, Finished Goods, and Work in Process on the basis of relative cost. If too little overhead has been costed to the products, the variance is called an *underapplied, unabsorbed,* or *unfavorable variance.* On the other hand, if too much overhead has been costed to the products, the variance is called an *overapplied, overabsorbed,* or *favorable variance.* The entry to close out the actual overhead, the applied overhead, and the variance is given below:

UNDERAPPLIED

Applied Factory Overhead	80,000	
Cost of Goods Sold	1,500	
Factory Overhead		81,500
To close out applied and actual overhead accounts, with the variance being charged to Cost of Goods Sold.		

If the overhead had been overabsorbed in the example given, the variance would have been credited to Cost of Goods Sold.

Normal Capacity

Products are usually costed by using an overhead rate calculated at the level of normal capacity or normal activity. The reason for having to choose a certain level of capacity is that the fixed cost per unit depends on the number of units produced. This practice of assigning fixed overhead cost to units is necessary as long as full cost is to be used in the income determination process. Hence, the prime emphasis on the costing procedure comes from the need for data to calculate profit.

Normal capacity is not easy to define. The term has been used in many different ways, partly because there is no real agreement as to what is meant by "normal." In a good many cases, *normal capacity* is looked upon as an average use of facilities over a sufficiently long period of time so that minor variations in production cost due to seasonal and cyclical influences can be evened out. Sometimes plant capacity is considered to be a theoretical maximum capacity without regard for sales demand and for delays and inefficiencies in production. This concept of maximum output may be useful in evaluating what the plant could conceivably produce, but it cannot be considered a normal condition. Practical capacity may be a more useful concept in costing products for profit determination. Certain interruptions and inefficiencies in production can be expected. Perfection cannot be achieved. For example, production may be slowed down or stopped at times because of breakdowns, shortages of labor and materials, or retooling. These possibilities should be taken into account in arriving at practical plant capacity. Sales demand is also a factor. If there is insufficient demand for the product, then there is little point in striving to produce at practical plant capacity. Normal capacity is often a compromise between practical plant capacity and sales demand over the long run.

Seemingly, a normal overhead rate should not be used if the company does not plan to operate at normal capacity during the next year. For profit reporting, if all the overhead is to be attached to the products, it would appear that the costing rate should be calculated from a budget at the expected level of operation. However, if this were done, the product cost would increase or decrease each year because of differences in the volume of production. Also, management would not have a measurement of the extent of plant utilization. The capacity variance is a measurement of the underutilization or overutilization of the plant and should be brought to the attention of management.

A JOB ORDER COST ILLUSTRATION

Summarized cost data for the year ended April 30, 1980, are presented below and on the following page for Gable Machine Company to illustrate job order cost procedures using historical cost.

Historical cost is the actual cost that has been incurred, and in this chapter it will be assumed that the actual or historical cost is to be assigned to the products to the extent that this is possible. In Chapters 6 and 7, a standard cost accounting system will be discussed. Standards of cost and performance will be established, and standard cost will be identified with the products. Actual cost is measured and compared with the standard. The difference is identified and serves as a basis for better control and for better planning.

It should be borne in mind that the entries given are in composite form and that in practice there are many repetitious entries to record individual transactions that take place during the fiscal year.

The sequential order of the cost transactions should also be understood. For example, the budget of factory overhead and the overhead rate calculation were made before the beginning of the fiscal year. The overhead rate must be calculated from a budget of factory overhead so that the products being manufactured during the year can be assigned the proper overhead cost, as nearly as it can be determined. Only at the end of the year did the company know that 220,000 direct labor hours were used and that the actual factory overhead cost was $1,336,200. Throughout the year, the manufacturer purchased materials and incurred labor and factory overhead costs as products were continually being worked on, completed, and sold. At the same time, costs were being attached to the products and released as expenses when deliveries were made against sales.

Gable Machine Company
Transactional Data
For the Year Ended April 30, 1980

(1) Materials were purchased during the fiscal year at a cost of $840,000.
(2) Direct materials requisitioned for production cost $631,400. Included in this amount are the materials costs for Job 216 of $3,480. Indirect materials costing $47,200 were also requisitioned.

(3) Factory payrolls in total amounted to $1,874,000. The income taxes withheld from the employees' wages totaled $393,400, and the deduction for FICA taxes withheld amounted to $106,600.

(4) A distribution of the factory labor cost of $1,874,000 shows that $1,760,000 was direct labor while the remaining $114,000 was indirect labor. The portion of the direct labor cost that pertained to Job 216 was $1,600.

(5) Factory overhead at the normal operating level of 250,000 direct labor hours has been calculated at $6 an hour. During the year, 220,000 direct labor hours were used.

(6) The factory overhead, in addition to the indirect materials and the indirect labor referred to above, amounted to $1,175,000. Included in this amount was depreciation of $120,000. The balance of the overhead was acquired through accounts payable. Job 216 was completed with 200 direct labor hours. The production order for Job 216 is shown below.

PRODUCTION ORDER

Customer: Del Ray Supply Co.   Job Order: 216

Description: Welded Parts Code #735   Date Started: 1/19/80

Quantity: 1,000   Date Completed: 1/27/80

Materials			Labor			Overhead	
Date	Code	Amount	Date	Hours	Amount	Direct Labor Hours	200
Jan. 19	52	$3,130	Jan. 19 to 23	140	$1,120	Overhead Rate	$6.00
						Applied Overhead	$1,200
23	68	350	Jan. 26 to 27	60	480		
						Summary	
						Direct Materials	$3,480
						Direct Labor	1,600
						Factory Overhead	1,200
						Total Cost	$6,280
						Unit Cost	$6.28
Total		$3,480	Total	200	$1,600		

(7) Jobs costing $2,945,200 were completed and transferred to stock during the year.

(8) The cost of orders sold during the year was $2,320,000.

(9) Applied Factory Overhead and Factory Overhead were closed out at the end of the fiscal year with the variance being closed to Cost of Goods Sold.

The transactions were entered in the accounts as follows:

(1) Materials purchased:

Materials 840,000

Accounts Payable 840,000

Purchase of materials.

(The cost of each type of material was also entered on the appropriate materials inventory ledger cards.)

(2) Materials requisitioned:

Work in Process	631,400	
Factory Overhead...	47,200	
Materials...		678,600

Materials issued to production.

(Requisition forms were the basis for entries reducing the materials inventory ledger cards and for posting direct materials costs to each job order and the indirect materials costs to the factory overhead subsidiary ledger.)

(3) Factory payrolls:

Payroll	1,874,000	
Employee's Income Tax Payable......................		393,400
FICA Tax Payable...		106,600
Wages Payable..		1,374,000

Aggregate factory payrolls.

(4) Distribution of labor cost:

Work in Process	1,760,000	
Factory Overhead...	114,000	
Payroll...		1,874,000

Payroll distribution for the year.

(A classification of labor time by jobs as shown by labor time tickets was a basis for distribution of direct labor cost to individual job orders and for posting indirect labor cost to the factory overhead subsidiary ledger..)

(5) Factory overhead applied:

Work in Process	1,320,000	
Applied Factory Overhead		1,320,000

Factory overhead applied to products on direct labor hour basis. 220,000 hours × $6 rate = $1,320,000.

(6) Actual factory overhead (in addition to indirect materials and indirect labor):

Factory Overhead...	1,175,000	
Accumulated Depreciation		120,000
Accounts Payable..		1,055,000

Actual factory overhead recorded.

(Entries were made to record costs in the factory overhead ledger.)

(7) Work completed during the year and transferred to stock:

Finished Goods	2,945,200	
Work in Process...		2,945,200

Transfer of cost of completed orders to Finished Goods.

(Completed job orders were removed from the file of job orders in process and held as a subsidiary ledger supporting the finished goods inventory. Separate ledger cards may be kept for the finished goods inventory if sales are not made on a strict order basis.)

(8) The cost of products sold:

Cost of Goods Sold...	2,320,000	
Finished Goods...		2,320,000

To record the cost of products sold to the customers.

(Deductions were recorded in the finished goods inventory ledger cards. Entries were also made to bill the customers for the sales.)

(9) Applied Factory Overhead and Factory Overhead closed:

Applied Factory Overhead....................................	1,320,000	
Cost of Goods Sold...	16,200	
Factory Overhead		1,336,200

To close factory overhead accounts.

(Actual overhead not absorbed during the year as a part of the product cost is closed to Cost of Goods Sold.)

THE PROCESS COST SYSTEM

In many cases cost cannot be identified readily with any particular batch of products. For example, in the candy industry all chocolate of a given type will be the same. When all of the units of product are similar, a *process cost system* can be used. The cost is directly or indirectly assigned for an interval of time to the departments in which the products are made, rather than identified by product groups or orders. Unit cost is computed by dividing the number of units completed in the department into the corresponding departmental cost.

The unit cost is applied to the number of units transferred in the manufacturing process and ultimately identified with the units completed and sold. Before a product is completed, it may be transferred from one department to another in a series of processing operations. Each unit of product carries the cost that has been charged to it from the various departments in which it is processed.

The Departmental Production Report

Both the number of units manufactured and the cost are accounted for on a departmental basis. Monthly production reports are prepared for each producing department showing the quantities of product, the total cost, and the unit cost. The production report is the focal point in process cost accounting, whereas in job order costing it is the production order. The production report may provide departmental cost and quantity data either separately or combined in one report with each section showing (1) what responsibility is charged to the department, and (2) how that responsibility is discharged.

The number of units accounted for is always equal to the number of units charged to the department. Lost units must be accounted for as such. Cost is similarly charged to a department and must be accounted for.

A production report for both quantities and costs is given below:

Departmental Production Report
Department I
For the Month of August, 1976

Quantities:

Charged to the department:

In process, beginning	*20000*	2,000 units
Transferred in	*158000*	20,000
Total units charged to department	*178000*	22,000

Units accounted for:

Transferred out	*148000*	22,000 units
In process, ending	*30000*	—0—
Total units accounted for	*170000*	22,000

Costs:

Charged to the department:

In process, beginning	*70000*	$ 3,000
During the period	*586,000*	41,000
Total cost charged to department	*656,000*	$44,000

Cost accounted for:

Transferred out		$44,000
In process, ending		—0—
Total cost accounted for		$44,000

A Process Cost Flow

Often the units of product go through several manufacturing operations (departments) before they are completed. In the first operation, for example, impurities may be removed from the basic raw materials. In subsequent operations, the materials may be refined and treated in various ways before the product units are completed.

A flow of cost through two departments is illustrated using the cost data given below. Work in process in Department I at the beginning of the month amounted to $3,000, but there was no work in process in either department at the end of the month. All units of product were sold during the month.

	DEPARTMENTS	
	I	*II*
Work in process, beginning of month	$ 3,000	—0—
Materials	18,000	—0—
Labor	14,000	$ 8,000
Factory overhead	9,000	3,000
Total cost	$44,000	$11,000
Number of units produced	22,000	22,000
Unit cost (department)	$2.00	$.50

Accumulated unit cost:

Dept. I	$2.00
Dept. II	.50
Total unit cost	$2.50

The 22,000 units completed with respect to Department I each had a unit cost in that department of $2. These units were transferred to Department II and accumulated an additional unit cost of 50 cents. The total unit cost was $2.50.

The cost elements for each department were entered in the respective work in process accounts. As the units moved through the departments, the related cost was transferred to the next departmental work in process account and was combined with the cost of that department. Eventually the goods were completed and transferred to the finished goods inventory. When the units were sold, the cost was transferred to the cost of goods sold account and the customers were billed for the sales.

A diagram of the cost flow is given below:

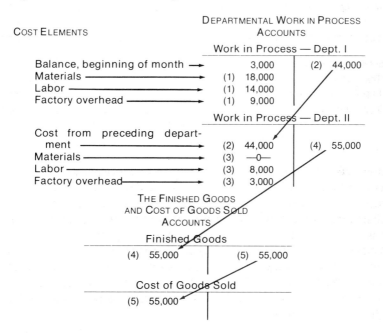

Journal entries to record the flow of costs follow:

(1)

Work in Process — Department I	41,000	
Materials		18,000
Payroll		14,000
Applied Factory Overhead		9,000
Cost of manufacturing during the current month for Department I.		

(2)

Work in Process — Department II	44,000	
Work in Process — Department I		44,000
Transfer of cost from Department I to Department II.		

(3)

Work in Process — Department II	11,000	
Factory Labor		8,000
Applied Factory Overhead		3,000
Manufacturing cost of Department II.		

(4)

Finished Goods	55,000	
Work in Process — Department II		55,000
Transfer of cost from Department II to Finished Goods (20,000 × $2.75).		

(5)

Cost of Goods Sold	55,000	
Finished Goods		55,000
Cost of goods sold during the month.		

The Equivalent Unit Concept

In the preceding illustration all of the work was completed in each department, and the entire production for the month was sold. In most cases, however, not all of the work is completed and sold within the month. Usually there are units and cost remaining in process and in finished goods at the end of the month. Cost is attached to the units transferred out of a department and to the remaining work in process by means of a unit cost.

In process cost accounting, the problem of determining unit cost is resolved by using equivalent units. *Equivalent units*, as defined under the average cost method, are units completed during the month, regardless of when the work was begun, plus the equivalent units of work done on the ending work in process inventory. The objective of this computation of equivalent units is to obtain an average cost by adding the cost of work done in previous months to the cost of work done during the current month.

Assume that equivalent units and unit cost are to be computed for Department A. Quantity and cost data follow:

	NUMBER OF PRODUCT UNITS	TOTAL COST
Charged to department:		
Inventory in process at the beginning of the month	2,000	$ 3,000
Placed in production during the month	26,000	37,000
Total units and cost charged to department	28,000	$40,000

	NUMBER OF PRODUCT UNITS	TOTAL COST
Accountability:		
Completed and transferred to Department B...	16,000	?
Inventory in process at the end of the month (1/3 completed)	12,000	?
Total units accounted for.................................	28,000	

At this point, the costs to be assigned to the units transferred to Department B and to the ending inventory of work in process have not been determined. However, they can be computed as follows:

EQUIVALENT UNITS COMPUTATION

Units completed during the month	16,000
Equivalent units of work done on the ending work in process (12,000 units × 1/3)..	4,000
Equivalent units...	20,000

AVERAGE UNIT COST COMPUTATION

$$\text{Average unit cost} = \frac{\text{Costs of Dept. A}}{\text{Equivalent units}} = \frac{\$40,000}{20,000} = \$2$$

ACCOUNTABILITY — COSTS OF DEPARTMENT A

Cost of units completed and transferred to Department B (16,000 units × $2 average unit cost)	$32,000
Cost of work in process at the end of the month (4,000 units × $2)..	8,000
Total costs accounted for	$40,000

The Cost Elements

In a process cost accounting system, no distinction is made between direct materials and indirect materials with respect to the product. The materials are not requisitioned for particular orders. Instead, both the direct materials and the indirect materials are identified only with the department in which they are used. A measurement is taken of the materials consumption in a department over a stated interval of time, but the requisition forms do not show how much material was used in the manufacture of any particular group of products.

Labor cost is also accumulated by department with no distinction being made between direct and indirect labor. The wages of the workers are identified by department rather than by order.

The various factory overhead costs are assigned to departments directly or by allocation. If factory overhead cost is evenly distributed throughout the year and production is at a fairly uniform level, this method may result in reasonably accurate product cost. However, if production is seasonal or if overhead cost is unequally distributed throughout the year, a more accurate product cost can be obtained by using a predetermined annual overhead rate calculated from a budget. Departmental overhead rates can be computed in the same way as they are in job order cost accounting. When a predetermined overhead rate is used, all products processed during the year bear their share of the overhead cost.

PROCESS COST ACCOUNTING PROBLEMS

Two important problems that are often encountered in a process type of manufacturing operation are:

(1) Joint product costing.
(2) The product mix decision.

These problems arise because several product lines may be produced in combination. How should cost be allocated to the individual product lines, and what cost is relevant in making decisions as to what quantities of the various lines should be produced?

Joint Product Costing

Often more than one line of a product is derived from some basic material. The cost of the basic material and the costs of processing it to a point where the end products can be identified are usually allocated to the end products for income determination purposes. This cost, which is common to all of the resulting products, is called a *joint cost*; and the products are called *joint products*. Joint products often result from processing some basic material found in nature. For example, timber may be converted into various grades of lumber. Coal may be broken down into coke, gas, tar, etc.; or crude oil when refined becomes gasoline, kerosene, burning oil, asphalt, etc.; or a meat packer may get various cuts of meat from one animal.

If the resulting products have approximately equal relative sales values, they are often referred to as *coproducts*. If each of the coproducts is to share the joint cost, it is not always easy to decide how the cost should be allocated. Cost may be apportioned according to weight, the assumption being that the weight of the basic material is distributed over the end products. Other characteristics, such as chemical content, specific gravity, or energy potential, may be selected as a basis for allocation. Sometimes joint cost is apportioned according to the relative market values of the end products or according to the cost that must be incurred to process the products after the point of split-off from the basic material. The cost determined for the coproducts may serve as a basis for the transfer of cost to other company divisions; or if the allocation appears to be too arbitrary, transfers may be made at market values.

In a manufacturing process, incidental products may be produced which are not necessarily desired but result automatically from the operation. These products are known as *by-products*. Usually the by-products are not assigned any original cost but bear only the cost required to process them after the split-off point. The proceeds that can be derived from the sale of by-products reveal whether or not additional processing cost is justified. Initially it may seem better to scrap the by-product; however, a by-product may grow in importance until it becomes a main product.

The Product Mix Decision

Assume, for example, that a basic chemical substance is put through a manufacturing process which will yield three product lines designated as Product A, Product B, and Product C. Joint costs of $500,000 are incurred in processing the basic material into 1,000,000 pounds of finished products during the year. This cost is allocated to the product lines on a relative weight basis. An allocation of a joint cost must be made if the full cost is to be attached to the products and used in income determination and in reporting inventory cost. This allocation is shown in the following table.

| | PRODUCT LINES | | | |
	A	*B*	*C*	*Total*
Pounds produced..........	500,000	300,000	200,000	1,000,000
Joint costs:				
Direct materials.......				$200,000
Direct labor..............				180,000
Factory overhead.....				120,000
Total	$250,000	$150,000	$100,000	$500,000
Costs after split-off:				
Direct labor..............	100,000	55,000	70,000	
Factory overhead.....	50,000	20,000	30,000	
Total cost..................	$400,000	$225,000	$200,000	
Total cost per pound...	$ .80	$ .75	$1.00	
Unit selling price.........	1.20	.70	1.50	

The cost after split-off can be easily identified with the product lines and is combined with the allocated joint cost in the computation of the total cost for each line of product.

According to the selling prices given, it would seem that Product B should not be manufactured. For each pound sold there is a loss of 5 cents. In this manufacturing process, however, Product B may be involuntarily produced along with Products A and C. To get 500,000 pounds of Product A and 200,000 pounds of Product C, there may be an automatic production of 300,000 pounds of Product B.

Even so, why should the company incur a cost of 75 cents a pound to get a return of 70 cents a pound? It would appear that the product should be disposed of and that the additional processing cost of $75,000 should not be incurred. Yet by incurring the additional cost, the company will have a better total profit than it would have otherwise. By selling 300,000 pounds at a unit price of 70 cents, there is additional revenue of $210,000. This covers the additional processing cost and provides $135,000 toward the recovery of the joint cost.

Additional revenue from the sale of 300,000 pounds of Product B	$210,000
Additional cost to obtain Product B	75,000
Contribution to joint cost	$135,000

The additional cost to process Product B after point of split-off and the revenue to be derived from Product B are compared in making the decision. The joint cost, however, is ignored in decision making. It is a sunk cost with respect to Product B and cannot be changed or eliminated by any decision with respect to Product B. The joint cost of $500,000 is incurred for the total operation, and $150,000 of this cost has been allocated to Product B. But the joint cost will not be affected by decisions as to what should be done with Product B.

Using the same data as before, assume that it is possible to continue processing Product C to get a new product called Product D that will sell for $2.40 a pound. From 200,000 pounds of Product C, 150,000 pounds of Product D can be derived at an additional processing cost of $75,000. The $100,000 in cost to process Product C after split-off must still be incurred to obtain Product D. Neither the cost of $100,000 after split-off nor the joint cost is relevant to the decision. This cost will be incurred in any event and is a sunk cost with respect to the decision of producing or not producing Product D. But the changes in cost and revenue, that is, the differential cost and revenue, are important. From the information given, it appears that the company should not process and sell Product D.

Revenue to be derived from the sale of Product D (150,000 pounds × $2.40)	$360,000
Less:	
Additional processing cost to obtain 150,000 pounds of Product D	$ 75,000
Opportunity cost (the loss of revenue that could be obtained by selling 200,000 pounds of Product C at $1.50 a pound)	300,000
Total incremental cost	$375,000
Net disadvantage in processing and selling Product D	$(15,000)

The loss of revenue from the sale of Product C is not an incurred cost, but it represents a sacrifice and is an opportunity cost attached to the production and sale of Product D. The sacrifice of a benefit to be derived from some course of action is designated as the opportunity cost of any other action under consideration. This cost is not an incurred cost to be entered in the accounting records, but it has significance in decision making. The opportunity cost attached to the decision to make Product D is the sacrifice of the $300,000 in revenue that can be obtained from the sale of Product C.

Time Constraints

In the preceding illustration the choice was between processing the various product lines to final completion or discarding them. Assume, however, that each product line in its uncompleted state can be sold immediately after split-off or can be processed further. Also assume that the time required to process each line to completion is unequal and can be applied to one line or the other as desired. Additional data are given below:

	PRODUCT LINES		
	A	*B*	*C*
Pounds produced	500,000	300,000	200,000
Rate of production per hour	10 lbs. per hr.	100 lbs. per hr.	5 lbs. per hr.
Unit selling price of finished product	$1.20	$ .70	$1.50
*Unit cost of further processing	$ .30	$ .25	$ .50
Opportunity cost of further processing (unit selling price after split-off)...	.40	.30	.60
Total unit cost of finished product.....	$ .70	$ .55	$1.10
Advantage per pound, further processing...	$ .50	$ .15	$ .40
**Advantage per hour, further processing..	$5.00	$15.00	$2.00

*Additional processing cost after split-off divided by pounds processed.
**Advantage per pound multiplied by production per hour.

If there is no constraint on production time for additional processing and if only 1,000,000 pounds can be put through the basic operation to yield the product mix given, then each product line should be completed and sold in its finished form. Note that in making the decision, the sacrifice of the revenue that can be obtained by selling the product in its unfinished state is the opportunity cost of further processing.

When 93,000 hours are available for additional processing, all three lines should be processed completely.

PRODUCT LINE	POUNDS	POUNDS PER HOUR	HOURS REQUIRED
A	500,000	10 lbs.	50,000
B	300,000	100 lbs.	3,000
C	200,000	5 lbs.	40,000
Total hours			93,000

Suppose, however, that only 50,000 hours are available. The first 3,000 hours should be used to finish Product B to earn an advantage of

$15 an hour. The next 47,000 hours should be used to finish Product A, thus earning an advantage of $5 per hour. All other products should be sold in the unfinished form.

In making decisions, it is not necessarily the profit advantage per unit of product that will govern. It is the profit per unit of the scarce or limiting factor; in this case, time. In more complicated situations, optimal combination decisions are solved by a technique known as *linear programming*. More complicated decisions of this type are discussed in Chapter 9.

QUESTIONS

1. Explain how product cost may sometimes be used in controlling cost.

2. How does a period cost differ from a product cost?

3. Explain how a bank would make use of cost accounting analysis.

4. Name the three cost elements. Can all three cost elements be identified directly with the product? Explain.

5. What are the characteristics of a manufacturing operation when a job order cost system is used? When a process cost system is used?

6. In a job order cost system, how is the cost of direct materials and direct labor identified with the production orders?

7. Why is it difficult to identify factory overhead with the products manufactured?

8. Explain why a budget is used in costing factory overhead and why actual overhead cost is not assigned to the products after the end of the year.

9. What is the basis for selecting a factor to be used in costing factory overhead?

10. Explain how factory overhead may be controlled in part by the time spent in manufacturing various orders.

11. What account is credited when factory overhead cost is assigned to work in process?

12. How is the difference between the actual factory overhead and the overhead assigned to the products handled at the end of the year?

13. What is normal capacity?

14. If the company does not expect to operate at normal capacity during the next year, why should the products be costed by using an overhead rate determined at normal capacity?

15. Identify the two basic sections of the production report used in process cost accounting. Explain how the data are presented in each of these two sections.

16. Give a brief explanation of how cost flows through various departments in the processing operation.

17. Explain how equivalent units are computed by an average cost method.

18. Are the equivalent units the equivalent units of work done in a given month under the average cost method, or are they the number of units completed during the month plus the equivalent units of work in process at the end of the month? Explain.

19. Explain how a predetermined overhead rate can be helpful in costing products in a process cost system.

20. What is a joint cost? How can the joint cost be allocated to the products?

21. What are by-products?

22. Why is a joint cost ignored in decision making?

23. Is the cost that is incurred after the split-off point relevant in decision making?

24. Can the loss of revenue from a decision alternative be looked upon as being a cost? Explain.

25. Is the most profitable product line always the one that yields the largest profit advantage per unit when selling price is compared with the cost of finishing and the opportunity cost of selling the unit in an unfinished state? Explain.

26. If limitations are imposed in a processing cost situation with a combination of products, what is the relevant factor in selecting the product combinations?

EXERCISES

1. Cost Transitions. A clay used in making ceramic figures was purchased by Historic Figures, Inc., during September at a cost of $3,200. There were no inventories of any kind on September 1. Clay costing $200 was withdrawn during the month and used by the sales department for promotional purposes. Other clay costing $2,400 was withdrawn for use in manufacturing. Eighty percent of the products that required the use of this clay were completed and transferred to finished stock. Two thirds of these products were sold in September.

Required: Estimate the cost of the clay included in the following accounts on September 30:
   (1) Materials
   (2) Work in Process
   (3) Finished Goods
   (4) Cost of Goods Sold
   (5) Selling Expense

2. Cost Control of Project. Arthur Benjamin is responsible for the completion of a project that has been estimated to require a total of $135,000 in direct materials and 4,000 direct labor hours to be paid at a rate of $9 per hour. Variable overhead generally varies at the rate of $6 per direct labor hour. He estimates that 60 percent of the direct materials cost has been incurred, and the cost was $83,500. The labor work is 50% complete, and 2,140 hours were used at the rate per hour indicated. Variable overhead amounted to $12,500.

Required: Compare the actual cost with the estimates and determine the variances. How would the labor hour variance affect variable overhead?

3. Cost Control of Orders. Blanton Machine Company started work on two production orders in November, Order 85 and Order 86. The total materials cost for both orders has been estimated at $48,000 with 75% of the cost applying to Order 85 and the balance for Order 86. At the end of November, two thirds of the total materials to be used cost $51,000 and were placed in process in the proportions indicated. Total direct labor hours were estimated at 500 for Order 85 and 200 for Order 86. The labor rate amounts to $8 per hour. Variable overhead varies at the rate of $3 per hour. By the end of November, each order was 50% complete with respect to labor and overhead. Labor hours were charged as follows during November: 230 hours to Order 85 and 95 to Order 86. Variable overhead was $720 on Order 85 and $260 on Order 86.

Required: Compare the actual cost with the estimate and determine variances. What effect would the labor hour variance have on variable overhead?

4. Journal Entries for Flow of Job Order Cost. During 1980, Venable Tube Company purchased materials at a cost of $212,000. Direct materials costing $171,000 were requisitioned for the various job orders. Factory payrolls for the year amounted to $335,000. Income tax of $68,000, FICA tax of $21,000, and union dues of $6,000 were withheld from wages. Assume that all of the factory payroll was direct labor for the job orders. Factory overhead was applied to production at the rate of $6 per machine hour. During the year, the company operated at 42,000 machine hours. Actual factory overhead for the year was $261,000. Credit the actual factory overhead to Accounts Payable.

Required: Prepare journal entries to record the information given. Close the factory overhead variance to Cost of Goods Sold.

5. Journal Entries for Flow of Job Order Cost. The Porterfield Equipment Company purchased materials in 1980 at a cost of $143,000. Direct materials costing $86,000 were requisitioned for various job orders. Other indirect materials costing $47,000 were withdrawn for general factory use (charge Factory Overhead.) The factory payroll for the year amounted to $218,000. Income taxes of $43,000 and FICA taxes of $14,000 were withheld from wages. The direct labor portion of the payroll amounting to $181,000 has been identified with the job orders. The balance of the factory payroll consisting of indirect labor should be charged to Factory Overhead. Factory overhead is applied to the job orders at the rate of $4 per machine hour. During the year, the company operated at 30,000 machine hours. Actual factory overhead in addition to the indirect materials and indirect labor already referred to amounted to $31,000. This portion of the overhead should be credited to Accounts Payable.

Required: Prepare journal entries to record the information given. Close the factory overhead variance to Cost of Goods Sold.

6. Factory Overhead Rate. Magill Timers, Inc., normally operates at 150,000 direct labor hours a year. Factory overhead cost budgeted at this level of operation is shown at the top of the next page.

Required:
(1) Compute the total factory overhead rate per hour at normal capacity.
(2) Determine the variable portion of the overhead rate at normal capacity. Would this rate be different if normal capacity had been established at 120,000 direct labor hours? Explain.

Variable:

Indirect materials and supplies	$ 75,000
Power and light	30,000
Repair and maintenance	15,000
Total variable overhead	$120,000

Fixed:

Indirect labor	$161,000
Power and light	38,000
Repair and maintenance	53,000
Property tax and insurance	26,000
Depreciation	22,000
Total fixed overhead	$300,000
Total overhead	$420,000

(3) Determine the fixed portion of the overhead rate at normal capacity. Would this rate be different if normal capacity had been established at 120,000 direct labor hours? Explain.

7. Factory Overhead Rates. Ramirez Fixtures Company has prepared a flexible budget of factory overhead for the year. This budget is summarized below.

Budgeted machine hours	60,000	80,000	100,000
Variable overhead	$300,000	$400,000	$500,000
Fixed overhead	300,000	300,000	300,000
Total overhead	$600,000	$700,000	$800,000

Required:

(1) If 80,000 machine hours are considered to be a normal level of operation, determine the factory overhead costing rate. Give the variable and fixed portions of the rate.

(2) Assume that the company operated at an actual level of 60,000 machine hours. How much of the variable overhead would be apportioned to the products by using the rate determined at 80,000 machine hours? Would all of the variable overhead budgeted for 60,000 machine hours be absorbed?

(3) Assuming again that the company operated at 60,000 machine hours, how much of the fixed overhead would be apportioned to the products by using the rate determined at 80,000 machine hours.

(4) Explain why all of the budgeted fixed overhead would not be absorbed at 60,000 machine hours. What name is given to the difference between the budgeted fixed overhead and the fixed overhead absorbed by the products?

8. Factory Overhead Costing. The Arbor Windings Company has estimated that variable factory overhead varies at the rate of $4 per machine hour. Fixed factory overhead has been budgeted at $750,000 for the year.

Normal capacity has been determined to be 50,000 machine hours for the year. Actual factory overhead for the year was in agreement with the budget established for 40,000 machine hours of actual operation.

Required:

(1) Compute the factory overhead costing rate breaking it into a variable and a fixed rate.

(2) Determine the balance of actual overhead in the factory overhead control account before closing.

(3) Determine the balance of Applied Factory Overhead before closing.

(4) Was there a factory overhead variance for the year? Explain why there was a variance and determine the amount of the variance.

9. Factory Overhead Costing. A summary flexible budget of factory overhead for the year is given below for Hartzell Machine Company.

Budgeted direct labor hours	80,000	90,000	100,000
Variable overhead..................................	$480,000	$540,000	$600,000
Fixed overhead	250,000	250,000	250,000
Total overhead	$730,000	$790,000	$850,000

The factory overhead rate has been computed at a normal operating capacity of 100,000 direct labor hours for the year.

During the next year, the company operated at 90,000 direct labor hours. The actual variable overhead amounted to $552,000, and the actual fixed overhead was $250,000.

Required:

(1) Prepare a journal entry to record the application of factory overhead to the job orders.

(2) Record by journal entry the actual factory overhead for the year. (Credit Accounts Payable.)

(3) Close the actual and applied factory overhead, closing the variance directly to Cost of Goods Sold.

(4) How much of the total variance was caused by operating at below normal capacity?

10. Journal Entries for Flow of Process Cost. A new type of hair spray sold under the trade name of Fast is made by Tanner Products, Inc., in three processing operations. In November, the company made 350,000 packages of this product. Materials costing $28,000 were started in Process 1. Labor and overhead cost of that process amounted to $35,000. Other costs for the month of November are given below:

	Process 2	Process 3
Materials..	—0—	$20,000
Labor and overhead	$8,000	9,500

Required:

(1) Prepare journal entries to trace the manufacturing cost through the three processes and into finished goods. (There were no inventories of work in process at the beginning or at the end of the month.)

(2) Compute the cost of each package.

11. Equivalent Units in Process Cost Accounting. Paula Drug Company uses a process cost accounting system and traces cost through the records on average cost basis. Compute the number of equivalent units manufactured in the following situations. Each situation is independent of the others.

(1) On May 1, Department 10 had 6,000 units in process. During the month, 45,000 units were received from Department 9. Department 10 transferred 51,000 units to Department 11 in May.

(2) Department 3 had an inventory of 16,000 units in process on July 1, half completed in that department. During the month, the department finished

the units in process at the beginning of the month and started and completed 72,000 units. Work was started on 15,000 units still in process at July
31, 60% completed.

(3) Department 1 started 340,000 units in production in February. At the end of
the month 50,000 units were in process, 40% completed. There was no
work in process at the beginning of the month.

(4) On June 1, Department C had an inventory of 18,000 units, 1/6 complete
with respect to operations in Department C. During the month, 146,000
units were received from Department B. Department C transferred 152,000
units to Department D. The work in process in Department C on June 30
was 25% complete with respect to that department.

12. Process Cost and Unit Cost. During the month of May, Department C received 120,000 units of product from Department B. During the month 100,000
of these units were completed in the department and transferred to Department D. There were no units in process at the beginning of the month, and the
units in process on May 31 were 75% complete with respect to work in Department C. Costs of production for Department C in the month of May were
$276,000.

Required:

(1) Determine the equivalent units by the average cost method.
(2) Compute the cost per unit for Department C in the month of May.

13. Joint Product Cost. Dodds Blending Company incurs a cost of $350,000 to
process a basic material into 30,000 units of Product A, 10,000 units of Product
B, and 10,000 units of Product C. The joint cost is allocated to the product
lines on the basis of the relative market values of the final products produced.

Additional cost to refine the products after the point of split-off is given
below.

> Product A — $240,000
> Product B —   42,000
> Product C —   130,000

The unit selling prices for the refined products are given below.

> Product A — $10.00
> Product B —   20.00
> Product C —   50.00

Required:

(1) Compute the total unit cost to process each product line to its finished
state.
(2) According to the data given, should Product A be refined and sold?
Explain.

14. Product Mix Decision. Data with respect to the processing of four distinct
product lines from a basic material are given at the top of the next page.

The cost of the basic processing operation is $240,000 and is apportioned
to the final products on the basis of the relative number of units produced.

Required:

(1) Compute the total unit cost to process each product line to its finished
state. Is this cost relevant in deciding upon which lines should be sold
at point of split-off and which lines should be sold in a refined state?
Explain.

Product Line	Number Units Produced	Unit Selling Price at Point of Split-off	Unit Selling Price Refined Product	Total Cost to Refine Products
1	40,000	$5.00	$ 8.00	$160,000
2	20,000	7.00	14.00	100,000
3	20,000	3.00	9.00	80,000
4	40,000	2.00	3.00	60,000

(2) Which product lines should be sold at point of split-off? Which product lines should be sold in finished form? Show computations.

(3) Should Product 4 be produced and sold? Explain.

15. Product Mix and Time Constraint. Cost and price data for Guderau Mills, Inc., are given below.

	Product Lines		
	1	*2*	*3*
Units produced from basic process.............	60,000	60,000	100,000
Basic process cost allocated to products...	$180,000	$180,000	$300,000
Additional processing cost..........................	$ 18,000	$ 42,000	$ 60,000
Time required for additional processing in hours...	30,000	15,000	25,000
Unit selling price, finished product..............	$ 7.00	$ 7.50	$ 4.50
Unit selling price, unfinished product	$ 4.50	$ 4.00	$ 2.60

The total time available for additional processing is limited to 50,000 hours, and the market can absorb all units of any product line that can be finished or sold in unfinished form.

Required: How should the 50,000 hours be applied to gain the maximum profit advantage? Show computations.

PROBLEMS

5-1. Job Order Cost Transactions. A summary of manufacturing cost transactions for Weldon Products, Inc., for 1980 follows:

(1) Materials costing $827,000 were purchased from suppliers on account.

(2) Materials were requisitioned during the year as follows:

Direct materials	$712,000
Indirect materials (factory overhead)...	86,000

Included among the requisitions were requisitions for $9,500 of direct materials for Order 163.

(3) The factory payroll for the year amounted to $274,000. FICA taxes withheld amounted to $17,300. Income taxes withheld amounted to $53,900, and the net amount paid to the employees amounted to $202,800.

(4) The factory labor was utilized as follows:

Direct labor	$192,000
Indirect labor (factory overhead)	82,000

Direct labor costing $3,800 included in the total direct labor cost, was identified by labor time tickets with Order 163.

(5) Factory overhead was applied to production at 150 percent of the direct labor cost.

(6) Factory overhead costs during the year, in addition to the cost of indirect materials and indirect labor referred to above, amount to $126,000. Included in the $126,000 is depreciation of $34,000. Credit the balance of the cost to Accounts Payable.

(7) Orders costing $933,000 were completed during the year. Order 163 is included among the completed orders.

(8) Goods costing $803,000 were sold to customers on credit terms for $1,224,000.

Required:

(1) Journalize the transactions and close the factory overhead variance to Cost of Goods Sold.

(2) Compute the cost of Order 163 and the cost per unit of product assuming that 3,800 units were produced on that order.

5-2. Factory Overhead Rates. Starke Products Company apportions factory overhead to products on a machine hour basis. The machine hour rate is computed from a budget of factory overhead at normal operating capacity. The company operated at 140,000 machine hours in 1980.

Budgeted factory overhead at a normal capacity of 150,000 machine hours a year is given below.

Variable overhead:

Indirect materials	$ 328,200
Supplies	204,500
Power	33,600
Repairs and maintenance	87,100
Lubrication	21,600
Total variable overhead	$ 675,000

Fixed overhead:

Supervision	$ 254,000
Indirect labor	168,400
Repairs and maintenance	117,300
Rent	84,000
Heat and light	46,600
Taxes and insurance	38,700
Depreciation	41,000
Total fixed overhead	$ 750,000
Total overhead	$1,425,000

In 1980 the fixed factory overhead cost was in agreement with the budget. Variable factory overhead in 1980 was recorded as follows:

Indirect materials	$302,700
Supplies	198,700
Power	32,100
Repairs and maintenance	85,400
Lubrication	22,900
Total variable overhead	$641,800

Required:

(1) Determine the machine hour rate for costing variable overhead and the machine hour rate for costing fixed overhead.

(2) Compute the overabsorbed or unabsorbed factory overhead.

(continued)

(3) How much of the total variance was caused by operating at below the normal operating capacity?

5-3. Factory Overhead Rates. Under normal operating conditions, Ponds Bearings, Inc., uses 200,000 machine hours in production. One type of product is manufactured with direct materials of $2 per unit of product and direct labor cost of $1 per unit of product.

A budget of factory overhead in summary form for 200,000 machine hours is given below.

Variable overhead	$176,000
Fixed overhead	280,000
Total budgeted overhead	$456,000

The product is priced at 140% of full cost. Two units of product are manufactured in each machine hour.

Next year the company anticipates a sharp drop in sales and expects to operate at only 125,000 machine hours.

The plant superintendent suggests that the overhead rate be recomputed at the 125,000 expected machine hours of operation and that the product be priced at 140% of the revised cost.

The president of the company disagrees with the plant superintendent, stating that the product will be overpriced on the market if the price is based on a cost for the expected machine hours of operation. Furthermore, the president believes that the failure to operate at normal capacity should be revealed as a capacity variance and not buried in product cost.

Required:

(1) Compute the variable and the fixed overhead rate at normal operating capacity.
(2) Determine the selling price of the product by using the cost determined for 200,000 machine hours.
(3) Determine the selling price of the product by using the cost determined for 125,000 machine hours.
(4) Evaluate the arguments of the plant superintendent and the president.

5-4. Factory Overhead Rates. Aspen Hills Company manufactures a product line that has a direct materials cost of $8 per unit and a direct labor cost of $3 per unit. The factory overhead cost is applied to production on the basis of machine hours. Under normal conditions, the company operates at 250,000 machine hours each year.

A summarized flexible overhead budget is given below.

Machine hours	200,000	250,000	300,000
Variable overhead	$400,000	$500,000	$600,000
Fixed overhead	300,000	300,000	300,000
Total overhead	$700,000	$800,000	$900,000

Required:

(1) Compute the overhead rate at the normal operating capacity. $3.20
(2) If 200,000 machine hours were considered to be normal capacity, what would the overhead rate be?   3.50
(3) Determine the total unit cost of the product at a normal operating capacity of 250,000 machine hours.

(4) If the company operated at 300,000 machine hours during the year, what would the capacity variance be? Would the fixed overhead be overapplied or underapplied to the products? (Use 250,000 machine hours as normal.)

5-5. Factory Overhead Cost Control. A flexible budget of factory overhead for the year in summary form is given below for the Southern Division of Quinones Industries, Inc.

Machine hours	130,000	140,000	150,000	160,000
Variable overhead	$ 780,000	$ 840,000	$ 900,000	$ 960,000
Fixed overhead	420,000	420,000	420,000	420,000
Total overhead	$1,200,000	$1,260,000	$1,320,000	$1,380,000

The total overhead cost is assigned to the products at a rate of $9 per machine hour. This rate was computed at normal operating capacity.

The actual total overhead for the year was $1,238,000 for 130,000 machine hours of operation. The fixed overhead was in agreement with the budgeted overhead.

Required:
(1) How many machine hours are utilized at normal operating capacity?
(2) How much of the total overhead was applied to production at 130,000 machine hours of operation?
(3) Determine the total factory overhead variance.
(4) How much of the total variance was caused by a failure to operate at normal capacity?
(5) How much of the total variance can be attributed to a difference between actual and budgeted variable overhead cost?

5-6. Factory Overhead Cost Control. Linda Augsburger is the supervisor of Department 6 in the Columbia plant of Precision Instruments, Inc. She is responsible for the cost of direct materials, direct labor, and variable overhead costs incurred in this department. The fixed overhead cost is not under her jurisdiction.

During the month of March, factory overhead costs for Department 6 were as follows:

Variable overhead:

Indirect materials	$18,400
Supplies	12,200
Heat and light	8,600
Power	3,700
Repairs and maintenance	10,200
Total variable overhead	$53,100

Fixed overhead:

Indirect labor	$ 5,000
Supervision	16,000
Heat and light	11,000
Repairs and maintenance	5,000
Depreciation	3,000
Total fixed overhead	$40,000
Total overhead	$93,100

The department operated at 15,000 direct labor hours during the month of March.

A budget of factory overhead for 15,000 direct labor hours follows.

Variable overhead:

Indirect materials..	$18,750
Supplies...	12,000
Heat and light...	7,500
Power..	3,750
Repairs and maintenance..	10,500
Total variable overhead..	$52,500

Fixed overhead:

Indirect labor..	$ 5,000
Supervision	16,000
Heat and light...	11,000
Repairs and maintenance..	5,000
Depreciation...	3,000
Total fixed overhead...	$40,000
Total overhead	$92,500

SHOULD

Variable overhead is costed to the products at the rate of $3.50 per direct labor hour, and fixed overhead is costed to the products at the rate of $2 per direct labor hour.

Required:

(1) How much overhead was costed to the products in March? *82,500*
(2) Compute the total factory overhead variance for March. *10,600*
(3) How much of the total overhead variance can be attributed to operating below the normal level of capacity?
(4) Prepare a cost report for Augsburger that will compare the actual overhead cost with the budgeted overhead cost. Indicate variances over or under the budget for each item of overhead under her jurisdiction.
(5) Identify any item or items of overhead that are over the budgeted amount by more than 10 %.

5-7. Process Cost Transactions. A household cleaner is manufactured by Seaside Industries, Inc., in three processing operations. During the month of June, 80,000 units were started in process in Operation 1. There were no units in process at the beginning or at the end of the month in any operation. The materials are all added at the beginning of Operation 1, and the cost of the materials used in June was $272,000.

Labor and overhead cost for the three operations for the month of June is summarized below.

	Operations		
	1	*2*	*3*
Labor...	$48,000	$104,000	$88,000
Overhead	72,000	52,000	22,000

Required:

(1) Journalize the flow of cost to each of the three operations and to finished goods inventory.
(2) Determine the unit cost for each of the three operations and the total unit cost of the product.

5-8. Process Cost and Production Report. At the first of August, Ostrum Supply Company had 20,000 units of product in process in Department 1. These units were 70% complete with respect to work in Department 1.

During the month of August, 150,000 units of product were started in Department 1. At the end of August, 30,000 units remained in work in process that were 80% complete as to materials, labor, and overhead.

The cost of the 20,000 units in process at August 1 was $70,000. Production cost in Department 1 during August amounted to $586,000.

Required:

(1) Compute the equivalent units of production for the month of August and the unit cost.

(2) Prepare a production report for the month of August.

5-9. Process Cost and Production Report. A popular brand of hand lotion is manufactured by Padgett Manufacturing Company in two processing operations.

Data with respect to Operation 1 is given below for the month of April.

Units in process at the beginning of the month	15,000
Units started in production during April	190,000
Units transferred from Operation 1 to Operation 2 during April.....	175,000
Units in process at the end of the month	30,000
Cost of beginning work in process on April 1	$ 6,000
April production cost	$142,000

The work in process at the end of the month was 1/3 complete in Operation 1.

Required:

(1) Compute the number of equivalent units of production.

(2) Determine the unit cost for the month of April.

(3) Prepare a production report for the month of April.

5-10. Joint Product Cost and Decisions. Three identifiable product lines, Products A, B, and C, are obtained in fixed quantities from a basic processing operation. The cost of the basic operation is $320,000 for a yield of 5 000 metric tons of Product A, 2 000 metric tons of Product B, and 1 000 metric tons of Product C. The basic processing cost is allocated to the product lines in proportion to the relative weights produced.

Beltway Products Company does both the basic processing work and the further refinement of the three product lines. After the basic operation, the products can be sold at the following prices per metric ton.

Product A — $60
Product B — 53
Product C — 35

Costs to refine each of the three product lines are given below.

	Product Lines		
	A	*B*	*C*
Variable cost per metric ton	$8	$7	$4
Total fixed cost	$20,000	$16,000	$ 6,000

The fixed cost of the refining operation will not be incurred if the product line is not refined.

The refined products can be sold at the following prices per metric ton:

Product A — $75
Product B — 65
Product C — 40

Required:

(1) Determine the total unit cost of each product line in a refined state.
(2) Which of the three product lines, if any, should be refined and which should be sold after the basic processing operation? Show computations.
(3) Does any one of the three product lines sell at a price that is less than the unit cost assigned to it from the basic operation? If it sells below the basic processing cost, should the product be produced?
(4) What is the minimum number of metric tons of Product A that must be refined and sold at the refined price to justify the fixed cost to refine the product? In other words, determine the break-even point to refine Product A.

5-11. Product Mix Decision and Time Constraint. Donald Kaplan has been allowed only 40,000 machine hours to be used in refining four different product lines. The machine hours may be switched from one product line to another, and the problem is to decide upon the most profitable use of the time.

A basic material is processed at a cost of $65,000 to yield four unrefined products in the fixed quantities given:

Product A — 40,000
Product B — 40,000
Product C — 20,000
Product D — 50,000

The unrefined products can be sold as follows:

	Selling Price per Unit
Product A	$ 2.00
Product B	10.00
Product C	7.00
Product D	12.00

Data with respect to additional processing are given below.

	Product Lines			
	A	B	C	D
Machine hours per unit	½	2	1	¼
Selling price per unit of refined product	$7.00	$18.00	$16.00	$16.00
*Total additional cost:				
Materials	$40,000	$30,000	$15,000	$25,000
Labor and overhead	20,000	60,000	25,000	25,000
Total	$60,000	$90,000	$40,000	$50,000

*Based on the assumption that all of the product is refined. All of the costs are variable. Materials vary on a unit-of-product basis, and the labor and overhead vary on a machine-hour basis.

Required: How should the 40,000 machine hours be used to yield maximum profits? Show computations.

5-12. Product Mix Decision. A basic material is processed at the Concord plant of Jewel and Hansford, Inc., into 4 000 000 kilograms of three identifiable product lines with the weight distributed as follows:

> Product 1 —   800 000
> Product 2 — 2 000 000
> Product 3 — 1 200 000

The basic material used in processing, costs $1.50 per kilogram. Labor and overhead costs amount to $5,200,000 and are distributed to the product lines in relation to the weights produced.

Following the basic operation, each product line is put through an additional processing cycle. The costs of the additional operations are given below.

	Product Lines		
	1	*2*	*3*
Variable cost per kilogram......................	$.70	$.50	$.30
Fixed cost of the operation.....................	$400,000	$1,400,000	$1,200,000

If the additional processing operation is eliminated, the fixed cost of that operation, as well as the variable cost, can be eliminated.

Another company has offered to purchase the output of Product 1 after it has gone through the basic operation at a price of $2.20 per kilogram. The plant manager dismissed the offer as ridiculous, stating that it costs more than $2.20 per kilogram to obtain Product 1 from the basic operation.

Subsequent investigation reveals that the space devoted to the additional processing of Product 1 can be used to produce another product line designated as Product A. Market estimates show that the space used to refine Product 1 can be used to make and sell 150,000 units of Product A at a price of $8.50 per unit. The variable cost to make each unit would amount to $3.50, and the fixed cost would be the same as it would be if Product 1 were put through the additional processing operation.

At present, Product 1 when completely processed sells for $4.50 per kilogram, Product 2 sells for $6 per kilogram, and Product 3 sells for $5 per kilogram.

Required:

(1) Compute the profit in total and by product line with the present yield and structure.
(2) Should the company accept the offer for the sale of partially processed Product 1 and then use the released space for the production of the new product line? Show computations.

6
MATERIALS AND
LABOR CONTROL

In exercising control over any activity, there is usually some basis for comparison. When one states that a job was exceptionally well done, it means that the performance was better than usual or better than some *standard* established as acceptable. Likewise, control over costs can be exercised by comparing actual performance and costs with standards. *Variations* from the standards are a basis for either tighter control over the operation or a revision of the standards. During this process, efforts are made to protect the company from waste or loss and to determine the most economical way to acquire and use goods and services.

Inasmuch as the cost of materials and labor is often substantial, a great deal of effort is made to control their cost. Even a very small saving on a unit basis or on an operation performed can add many dollars to profit. Although this chapter will consider materials and labor as direct costs, many of the control measures apply to both direct and indirect materials and labor.

THE USE OF STANDARDS

A standard may be used as a basis for control by service industries, retailers, manufacturers, or governmental and not-for-profit entities. Wherever it is possible to establish a criterion for cost of a material or service and to set standards of performance, standards can be used as a basis for control. For example, the driver of a delivery truck is expected to handle a certain number of deliveries in a normal day. The number of expected or normal deliveries serves as a standard for the measurement of performance.

Standards such as budgets tend to be viewed by employees with suspicion. A standard has a restricting or inhibiting effect upon a person and in that sense interferes with individual expression. With increased automation and the demands of a large society, a person may feel lost in the crowd and merely an appendage of some gigantic production system.

While it is not possible to return to a simple craft economy, it may be possible to reduce some of the tedium of repetitive chores by permitting changes in assignments and by breaking down the work so that it can be handled by small closely knit groups. Some steps have already been taken in this direction by large companies.

Along with changes in work patterns, there may be more participation by workers and lower levels of management in the setting of standards. Values and attitudes of individuals differ, and this may be reflected in setting standards. Better results may be obtained by grouping together workers who share common values and attitudes and giving them a right to participate in setting reasonable standards of performance.

Work measurement techniques are usually employed in setting standards. A thorough study is made of plant operations, general economic conditions, and the effect of economic conditions on the cost that must be incurred for materials and services. Engineers measure the length of time required to complete various manufacturing operations and establish standards of performance. Cost standards are also set and, when related to performance standards, may be referred to as the standard costs of the operations to which they apply.

Often a standard cost is expressed on a unit basis. There is a standard price for a unit of materials and a standard quantity of materials to be used for a unit of product, and there is a standard labor rate and a standard length of time to perform a certain amount of work. The standards remain unchanged as long as there is no change in the method of operation or in the unit prices of materials or services.

ADVANTAGES OF STANDARD COST ACCOUNTING

Standards are particularly useful in accounting as a basis for evaluating various operations. Within a standard cost accounting system, there are checkpoints at which variations from the standards can be detected and brought under control. While operations are in progress, comparisons of actual results with the standards can be made and unfavorable conditions can be corrected before losses accumulate.

Standard cost accounting follows the principle of *management by exception.* Actual results that correspond with the standards require little attention. The exceptions, however, are emphasized. In actual or historical cost accounting, it is sometimes difficult to separate the exceptions from the flow of data being processed. Furthermore, many of the measurements may not be made until after it is too late to take corrective action.

The management by exception principle can be desirable in that it calls attention to weak areas that require control and saves management the task of going over data that require no attention. When applied to persons, however, the management by exception principle has some drawbacks. If a worker is ignored when operating according to the standard and is noticed only when something is wrong, the worker may become resentful and perform less satisfactorily. While it may be argued by some that the worker is being paid to operate at standard, the human factor cannot be ignored. Without recognition, the worker becomes discontented, and this discontent may spread throughout the organization with a loss of both morale and productivity.

When reasonable standards are used, there is normally a desirable secondary effect. Often employees become cost conscious, watching the standards and seeking ways to improve their work. This tendency can, of course, be encouraged by having an incentive system that is tied in with the standards.

For purposes of income determination as well, a standard cost system may be more economical and less complicated than a historical cost accounting system. Standard cost cards are set up for each job or process showing what quantities of materials, labor, and overhead should be used according to the standards. These cards are printed in advance, with the standard quantities and costs being listed. When a job is started in production, the standard cost card shows the complete costs that should apply to it. Materials, for example, are issued on a standard requisition according to the standard quantities required for the order. If more materials are needed than are called for by the standard, a supplemental requisition having a distinctive color may be prepared to call attention to a quantity variance on the order. Many of the transactions follow the preestablished standard pattern. Any variations from the standards receive extra attention.

When operations are automated, standard conditions can be built into the computer program that controls the manufacturing process. Any deviation from the standards can be detected immediately, and corrections can be made while the work is being performed. Losses can be reduced or eliminated entirely in a system that provides for an immediate reaction to any tendency to stray from a predetermined standard. Automatic control devices are used to redirect space vehicles in mid-flight when the vehicle strays off the prescribed course. Similarly, a manufacturing operation can be controlled automatically by an on-line, real-time system. An *on-line, real-time system* is a system that provides immediate feedback of actual conditions so that corrections can be made at the time the event itself is taking place.

In an automated production system, management is not as concerned with the problem of controlling the actual operations as it is with the planning of controls. Considerable attention should be given to the development of standards and to the development of programs that provide checkpoints to keep the operation in line with the standards. Variations from the standards may measure, in part, inadequacies of the program, unreliability of the equipment, or conditions that were not provided for in the program of instructions. Control by means of standards and a comparison of results with standards is employed in any case and is applied by management to fit the circumstances.

THE QUALITY OF STANDARDS

The term "standard" has no meaning unless it is known what type of standard is being used. A standard may be very strict, or it may be very loose. Standards may be broadly classified as follows:

(1) Strict or tight standards.
(2) Attainable standards.
(3) Loose or lax standards.

There is no easy solution to the problem of how standards should be set. The objective, of course, is to obtain the best possible results at the lowest possible cost. Often this problem involves human behavior. A very high standard may motivate the employees and may produce the best results. On the other hand, it may discourage them to such an extent that they will not even meet fairly modest standards of achievement. In setting a level of standards, management must consider the employees, their abilities, their aspirations, and their degree of control over the results of operations.

The *strict standards* are set at a maximum level of efficiency, representing conditions that can seldom if ever be attained. They ignore normal materials spoilage and idle labor time due to such factors as machine breakdowns. This type of standard is more a standard of perfection than a standard for the measurement of practical or attainable efficiency. Idealistically it would appear that high standards should be set. As a practical matter, however, a standard that is virtually unattainable will not necessarily motivate employees to do their best. An employee is more likely to put forth increased effort when feeling successful. Stated in another way, a person increases aspirations with success while the aspiration level is lowered with failure. In addition, with strict standards the variance accounts have little significance for control purposes. Large unfavorable variations from strict standards not only measure shortcomings from good performance but also measure expected variations from the ideal.

The *attainable standards* can be achieved with reasonable effort. Perhaps the standards should be somewhat lower than what can be achieved by earnest effort. With success the employees gain confidence and tend to be more productive. It is not easy to generalize. For a more experienced group of workers, an exacting standard may serve as a challenge and may be a strong motivating factor. With less experienced workers, standards may have to be set at a lower level at first. As learning takes place, the standards may be raised. Increases in standards should be made with caution and should be accepted by the employees as being fair.

Loose standards are not likely to motivate employees to perform at their best; also, if workers are paid bonuses for exceeding the standard, they may receive a bonus for performance that deserves no additional reward. If the standards are too loose, certain variations from efficiency are not revealed but, instead, are incorporated as a part of the standards. As a result, management does not receive the most useful information for the control of operations.

The variations from the standards will be relatively large or small depending upon how the standards are set. Suppose, for example, that the standard cost to manufacture a unit of a certain product has been calculated in three ways as shown below:

	TYPES OF STANDARDS		
Cost Elements	Strict	Attainable	Loose
Materials	$10.00	$10.00	$10.00
Labor	2.00	2.50	3.00
Overhead	1.00	1.25	1.50
Total unit cost	$13.00	$13.75	$14.50

During the year, this product was manufactured at a total unit cost of $14.30, as shown in the following comparative summary:

Cost Elements	Actual Cost	TYPES OF STANDARDS			ACTUAL OVER (UNDER)		
		Strict	Attainable	Loose	Strict	Attainable	Loose
Materials	$10.00	$10.00	$10.00	$10.00	–0–	–0–	–0–
Labor	2.80	2.00	2.50	3.00	$ .80	$.30	$(.20)
Overhead	1.50	1.00	1.25	1.50	.50	.25	–0–
Total	$14.30	$13.00	$13.75	$14.50	$1.30	$.55	$(.20)

Materials prices and quantities were in agreement with the standards, which provide in each case for a unit materials cost of $10. The labor and the overhead variances are relatively high when the ideal standard is used. But this total variance of $1.30 per unit is not necessarily a measurement of excessive costs or of poor performance. A portion of the variance may be looked upon as a normal deviation from perfection and hence not controllable. The more significant difference, which management has the ability to control, is not revealed but instead is buried within the total variation of $1.30. At the other extreme, when comparison is made with expected operations, it appears that the company has done very well in trimming 20 cents off the standard unit labor cost. This also may be misleading. The budget standards may be too lax. Assuming that the normal or attainable standards are reasonably tight and are realistic, the controllable variance of 55 cents will be more useful in evaluating costs and performance.

REVISING THE STANDARDS

Standards may be set with the intention that they will be retained over long periods of time, barring any substantial changes in the methods of production. Standards of this type are often called *bulletin standards*, *basic standards*, or *bogies*. When conditions change so that the standard is out of date, an adjustment is made by using index numbers in much the same way that index numbers are used in making adjustments for the effect of price-level changes. Often the standards are not entered in the accounting records but are used as statistical supplements in arriving at information for control purposes. On the other hand, both the actual data and the standard cost data may be entered in the accounts by dual recording.

In many cases standards are established for relatively short periods of time with revisions being made whenever necessary. For example, a standard price for a material may be relevant for a certain period of time but has no meaning after there has been an increase in the price level of that material. A variation of the actual price from the standard price does not measure purchasing department inefficiency if an outdated standard price is used for the measurement. Therefore, standards have to be changed from time to time so that they correspond to current conditions. Similarly, labor standards have to be revised if the rate structure is changed or if changes have been made in the methods of production.

MATERIALS STANDARDS AND CONTROL

Standards may be established for the cost of obtaining materials and for the quantities to be used in production. Actual costs can be compared against these standards, and variances can be measured. Basically there are two types of variances: (1) *price* and (2) *quantity*. Several different variances may be developed for specialized purposes, but they can always be classified as being variations in the price of materials, the quantities used, or a combination of price and quantity. If the actual cost is greater than the standard used in comparison, the variance is *unfavorable*; if actual is less than the standard, the variance is *favorable*.

Materials Price Variance

A standard price is set for each class of material to be purchased. If the purchasing function is being carried out properly, the standard price should be attainable. When lower prices are paid, a favorable materials price variance is recorded, indicating that the purchasing department was under the standard; whereas, higher prices are reflected in an unfavorable materials price variance, showing that the purchasing department did not meet the standard. Quality standards have to be watched, of course; otherwise the purchasing department in its zeal to surpass the standard may acquire poor quality materials that will be costly on the production floor.

A *materials price variance* measures the difference between the prices at which materials were purchased and the prices at which they should have been obtained according to the established standards. Production management is responsible for how materials are used, but it may have no control over the prices that are paid. A factory may be operated efficiently; but if materials are not purchased at reasonable prices, potential profits will be lost before the manufacturing operation begins.

Periodic reports show how actual prices compare with standard prices for the various types of materials purchased. The total cost effect is equal to the quantities purchased multiplied by the price differentials. Reports on price variances may be made monthly to the purchasing agent and to the executive who is responsible for the purchasing function. They reveal which materials, if any, are responsible for a large part of any total price variation and can help the purchasing department in its search for more economical sources of supply.

Standard costs are not always incorporated in the accounting records. The price variance, for example, can be measured even though both the materials and the liability to the supplier are accounted for on an actual cost basis. In this chapter, however, the operation of a standard cost system is illustrated by tracing the standard costs through the accounting records. At different points in the accounting operation, variations can be measured in the accounts quite easily; and a knowledge of the flow of actual and standard costs helps in understanding how the variances are determined.

A materials price variance can be isolated at the time materials are purchased. The actual quantity of materials purchased can be recorded in the materials inventory at standard prices, but the liability to the supplier must be recorded by using actual quantities and actual prices. The difference between the debit to Materials and the credit to Accounts Payable is caused by the difference in price and is recorded as a price variance.

To illustrate, it is assumed that the purchasing department did better than the standard by buying 1,000 units of a certain material at a price of 70 cents when the standard price was 80 cents. This is recorded by a journal entry as follows:

Materials		800	
Materials Price Variance			**100**
Accounts Payable			700

Purchases at below standard price, favorable variance.

The principle of isolating the materials price variance can be expressed in abbreviated form as shown below.

$$(1) \ \textbf{AQP} \times \textbf{AP} = \textbf{AC}$$
$$(2) \ \textbf{AQP} \times \textbf{SP} = \textbf{MC}$$
$$\textbf{AC} - \textbf{MC} = \textbf{PV}$$

AQP = actual quantity purchased
AP = actual price
AC = actual cost
SP = standard price
MC = mixed cost (actual quantity purchased multiplied by standard price)
PV = price variance (materials)

Note that the quantities (actual) are the same in Equations (1) and (2). Only the prices differ, and the variation is designated as a price variance. The variance can be computed more directly by multiplying the actual quantity by the difference in the prices.

$$\textbf{AQP} \times (\textbf{SP} - \textbf{AP}) = \textbf{PV}$$

The materials price variance for the previous example is computed as follows:

$$
\begin{aligned}
\text{AQP} \times (\text{SP} - \text{AP}) &= \text{PV} \\
1{,}000 \times (\$.80 - \$.70) &= \text{PV} \\
1{,}000 \times \$.10 &= \text{PV} \\
\$100 &= \text{PV (favorable)}
\end{aligned}
$$

The variance is favorable because the materials were purchased at a cost below the established standard.

Materials Quantity Variance

Materials are withdrawn and used in production, but more or less materials may be used than specified by the standards. The variations in the use of materials are called *materials quantity* or *materials usage variances*. The differences can be calculated by comparing the record of materials withdrawn with consumption standards, or the differences may be directly recorded in a materials quantity variance account at the time materials are transferred into production.

Reports on the quantities of materials used are made to responsible production personnel. A production supervisor, for example, may receive daily or weekly summaries showing how the quantities used in the department compared with the standards. At the operating level, the use of materials can be controlled directly. The supervisors should have daily or weekly reports on their operations so that corrections can be made before losses become too great. Summary reports of actual and standard materials consumption given in dollars, with variances and percentages of variances to the standards, can be presented to the general supervisor or to the plant superintendent on a monthly basis. If the variances in any department are too large, this is revealed so that the superintendent can localize the differences and take steps to reduce them in future months. During the month, of course, the operating supervisors are expected to watch materials use; and if they have been doing their jobs properly, the accumulated variances for the month should be relatively small.

Ordinarily, materials quantity variances are chargeable to the production departments. They often arise as a result of wasteful practices in working with materials, or they arise because of products that must be scrapped through faulty production. For example, it should be possible to get a certain number of stamped parts from a metal sheet of a given size. But if the stamping operation is not performed properly, more sheets will be used in getting the desired number of parts. Or some part may be machined improperly, with the result that the part has to be discarded.

Not all excessive materials consumption can be charged to inefficient factory operation. The purchasing department may have to share the blame. Perhaps poor quality materials were acquired in order to obtain a price saving. An inferior grade of material may contribute to losses that are detected in the factory. Any measured variance reveals a condition, but it does not tell why that condition exists. Management is given the basic information, which it can apply in looking for the underlying causes. For example, the purchase of an inferior grade of materials may be an acceptable condition if the anticipated favorable purchase price variance is expected to outweigh the unfavorable quantity variance resulting from the use of such materials.

Returning to the last example, assume that 600 units of materials are withdrawn from the inventory for use in the factory. The standard calls for only 500 units. The 100-unit difference between actual and standard use is multiplied by the standard unit cost of 80 cents to arrive at an unfavorable quantity variance of $80. If standard costs are recorded in the accounts, Work in Process is charged with standard quantities priced at standard unit costs. In other words, the work in process inventory is carried at standard cost. The materials inventory, however, is credited with actual quantities used as multiplied by the standard unit costs. The journal entry is shown below.

Work in Process	400	
Materials Quantity Variance	80	
Materials		480
Materials charged to production at standard cost.		

The materials quantity variance can also be computed from equations as shown at the top of the next page.

$$(1) \; \text{AQU} \times \text{SP} = \text{MC}$$
$$(2) \; \text{SQ} \;\; \times \text{SP} = \text{SC}$$
$$\text{MC} \; - \text{SC} = \text{QV}$$

AQU = actual quantity used
SP = standard price
MC = mixed cost (actual quantity used multiplied by standard price)
SQ = standard quantity
SC = standard cost
QV = quantity variance (materials)

In Equations (1) and (2) the prices are the same, standard. Only the quantities differ, and the variation is designated as a quantity variance. The variance can be computed more directly by multiplying the standard price by the difference in quantities:

$$\text{SP} \times (\text{AQU} - \text{SQ}) = \text{QV}$$

The materials quantity variance shown in the previous journal entry is unfavorable because the amount of materials used is greater than the amount called for by the standard. The amount of the variance is computed as follows:

$$\text{SP} \;\; \times (\text{AQU} - \;\; \text{SQ}) = \text{QV}$$
$$\$.80 \times (600 \;\; - \; 500) = \text{QV}$$
$$\$.80 \times \;\;\;\;\;\;\;\;\;\; 100 \;\; = \text{QV}$$
$$\$80 \;\; = \text{QV (unfavorable)}$$

When indirect materials are used, the actual quantities are recorded at standard prices as factory overhead. No variances are measured at this point. Assuming that 100 units of materials are transferred to the factory for use as indirect materials, the following entry is made:

Factory Overhead..	80	
Materials...		80

Withdrawal of 100 units of materials having a standard unit cost of 80 cents for indirect use in factory operations.

Materials Acquisition

Control over materials begins with procurement. The purchasing department will seek a reliable supplier whose materials meet the quality standard in the desired quantity at the lowest price. After receiving a purchase requisition from individual departments, the purchasing department places the order for the materials. When the materials are received, they are counted, inspected, and turned over to the storekeeper.

The storekeeper is the only person with access to the physical materials, which are stored in an enclosed area to prevent theft or loss. An accounting record of the quantities of materials received and withdrawn is maintained by a stores ledger clerk. Incoming items are entered from receiving reports on the inventory cards, which constitute the inventory subsidiary ledger. The requisition forms for materials to be withdrawn for production support the entries for inventory withdrawals. The physical inventory kept by the storekeeper should be in substantial agreement with the book record revealed by independent counts. The separation of the duties acts as a check on both the storekeeper, who realizes that a book record of the inventory is being maintained, and the stores ledger clerk, who has no access to the physical inventory and thus no reason to falsify the record. This separation of physical custodianship of a property and the responsibility for accountability follows a general principle of internal control: that one person should control the physical asset while another person maintains the accounting record. This is true not only in inventory accounting but also in accounting for cash, securities, and other business properties.

Invoices received for materials purchased are compared against purchase orders and receiving reports to determine whether or not the company was properly billed for materials ordered and received. Arithmetic computations on the invoices are checked, and the verified invoices are filed by the dates when payments must be made.

The Inventory Level

Included as a very important part of materials control is control over inventory balances. Excessive amounts should not be kept on hand, nor should the inventories be allowed to become dangerously low. With insufficient inventories, there is the risk that production may be disrupted by the depletion of some critical item and that a customer may not receive an order on time. The tendency may be to overstock rather than to risk a *stock out*. However, there is a cost of maintaining excessive inventory balances. Resources that should be used more productively may be needlessly tied up in inventory. The rate of return sacrificed by holding resources idle is an implicit cost to the business. Hence, if the company has too much invested in inventory, it has sacrificed a return that could be earned by an alternative employment of resources. This return is an opportunity cost attached to inventory investment. There is also the cost of storing inventories, the cost of insurance, and the risk of loss through spoilage or obsolescence.

Insofar as possible, the company should plan to hold a minimum balance that will take care of its needs during a *procurement period* (the time elapsed from when materials are ordered until they are received). There is no perfect solution to the problem, but it may be possible to develop guidelines from past experience.

Assume, for example, that a procurement period is defined as one month. Forecast use and actual use of units for past months are given in the table on the next page.

MONTH	FORECAST USE	ACTUAL USE	VARIATIONS	VARIATIONS SQUARED
January	510	520	10	100
February..............	500	500	–0–	–0–
March	480	490	10	100
April......................	520	515	5	25
May......................	540	530	10	100
June	540	535	5	25
July	520	525	5	25
August	500	520	20	400
September...........	500	480	20	400
October................	480	490	10	100
Total................				**1,275**

An estimated standard deviation is computed below.

$$\sqrt{\frac{1,275}{10-1}} = 11.9 \text{ estimated standard deviation, or 12 units}$$

Assume a forecast use for November of 500 units. If the company wants to guard against stock depletion with a 95 percent probability of being covered, it will order 524 units. The forecast is increased by two standard deviations or by 2×12. (There is roughly a 95 percent probability that data are plus or minus two standard deviations from the mean.) This is admittedly an approximate guide, but improvements can be made as more data are collected.

Balancing Order and Storage Costs

There is a cost to order materials, and there is a cost to store materials. As mentioned on the previous page, when materials are stored, the company has to use space that has a rental value, there may be higher insurance costs, and the funds that are invested in inventories are committed so that they are not available for other purposes. In some industries the cost to order may be trivial; hence, there is no problem of balancing order and storage costs.

However, in industries that deal with bulky materials, the costs of receiving and handling a shipment may be substantial. For example, it may be necessary sometimes to authorize overtime pay for persons who must be available when a shipment arrives. Also, by placing frequent orders, the company may be losing quantity discounts that could be obtained by purchasing in bulk. Perhaps the saving to be obtained from placing large orders more than compensates for the increased storage costs.

Various factors must be considered, and these factors should be quantified, if possible. The cost to order and store materials is minimized in many cases when the cost of storage is equal to the cost of ordering. Normally the cost of ordering increases as orders are placed more frequently, but the cost of storage decreases; the total cost may be at a minimum when the two costs are approximately equal.

The order and storage costs can be tabulated under different assumptions as to the number of orders placed and the inventory investment. Assume that a company predicts that 3,000 units of a certain material are needed next year. Each unit costs $6. Past experience indicates that the storage costs are approximately equal to 10 percent of the inventory investment. The cost to place an order amounts to $9. If only one order were placed for the year, it would be for 3,000 units, and the average number of units held in the inventory during the year would be 1,500 (3,000 ÷ 2) assuming a uniform rate of withdrawal. With two orders, 1,500 units would be purchased on each order, and the average inventory would be only 750 units. The cost to order and store the inventory is computed and set forth in the table at the top of the next page. It is computed under different assumptions as to the number of orders and the investment in inventory. The company should place ten orders each for 300 units. The storage cost of $90 is equal to the total ordering cost at this point, and the combined costs are at a minimum.

This same result can be computed by use of the following formula:[1]

$$Q = \sqrt{\frac{2\,DO}{S}}$$

When **Q** = optimum quantity per order (unknown)
    D = annual demand for materials expressed in units of material — 3,000 units
    O = cost per order placed — $9
    S = storage cost per unit — 60¢ (10% of material cost, $6)

---

[1]Formula was derived as follows:

$$\text{Cost to order} = \frac{\text{Annual demand}}{\text{Optimum quantity per order}} \times \text{Cost per order} \quad \text{or} \quad \frac{DO}{Q}$$

$$\text{Cost to store} = \frac{\text{Optimum quantity per order}}{2^*} \times \text{Storage cost} \quad \text{or} \quad \frac{QS}{2^*}$$

*Divide by 2 to get an average.

$$\frac{DO}{Q} = \frac{QS}{2}$$

$$DO = \frac{Q^2 S}{2}$$

$$Q^2 S = 2\,DO$$

$$Q^2 = \frac{2\,DO}{S}$$

$$Q = \sqrt{\frac{2\,DO}{S}}$$

		STORAGE COST			ORDER COST
Number of Orders	Number of Units per Order	Average Inventory	Cost of Average Inventory	10% Storage Cost	$9 Each Order
1	3,000	1,500	$9,000	$900	$ 9
2	1,500	750	4,500	450	18
3	1,000	500	3,000	300	27
4	750	375	2,250	225	36
5	600	300	1,800	180	45
6	500	250	1,500	150	54
7	429	215	1,290	129	63
8	375	188	1,128	113	72
9	333	167	1,002	100	81
10	**300**	**150**	**900**	**90**	**90**
11	273	137	822	82	99
12	250	125	750	75	108

The optimum order quantity can be computed directly from the formula by inserting the inventory data developed.

$$Q = \sqrt{\frac{2 \times 3,000 \times \$9}{.60}}$$

$$Q = \sqrt{\frac{54,000}{.6}}$$

$$Q = \sqrt{90,000}$$

$$Q = 300 \text{ units}$$

The annual requirement of 3,000 units purchased on the basis of 300 units per order would require the placing of ten (3,000 units ÷ 300 units) orders.

Shipping Routes

Often a problem arises when materials or merchandise can be obtained from various sources for shipment to various locations. With proper planning, a program can be designed that minimizes the total cost of shipping. Routes are chosen so that all units can be delivered as scheduled with the least total cost. For example, assume that 3 units of a material are required at Destination 1 and that 3 units of this material are also required at Destination 2. There are 2 units available at Warehouse I and 4 units available at Warehouse II. The cost to ship each unit from each warehouse to each destination is shown in the matrix given at the top of the following page.

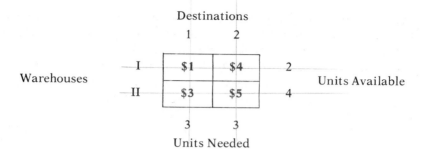

At present, the units are being shipped along the routes given below at a total cost of $21.

No. Units	From Warehouse	To Destination	Unit Cost	Total Cost
1	I	1	$1	$ 1
2	II	1	3	6
1	I	2	4	4
2	II	2	5	10
Total shipping cost				$21

By changing the route structure, the total shipping cost can be reduced to $20. Ship one more unit from Warehouse I to Destination 1 and one less unit from Warehouse II to Destination 1. The total effect on cost in this example is trivial; but in actual practice with many units and various shipping costs, the total cost may be substantial.

COST EFFECT OF ROUTE CHANGE FOR DESTINATION 1

Reduced cost: 1 less unit from Warehouse II $3
Added cost: 1 more unit from Warehouse I 1
Net advantage of this change.. $2

However, this route change makes it necessary to ship one less unit from Warehouse I to Destination 2 and to ship one more unit from Warehouse II to Destination 2.

COST EFFECT OF ROUTE CHANGE FOR DESTINATION 2

Added cost: 1 more unit from Warehouse II................................. $5
Reduced cost: 1 less unit from Warehouse I............................... 4
Net disadvantage of this change.. $1

The net effect of the entire change is a net reduction in total cost of $1 as shown on the revised route schedule.

No. Units	From Warehouse	To Destination	Unit Cost	Total Cost
2	I	1	$1	$ 2
1	II	1	3	3
3	II	2	5	15
Total shipping cost				$20

An optimum shipping schedule is obtained when no further cost reductions can be made by shifting the routes. The schedule given at the bottom of page 168 is the optimum schedule.

In linear programming, this type of problem is called the *transportation model*. With many points of origin and destination, the problem becomes more complicated; and a computer may be used in testing for route changes that result in the lowest possible cost. The principle, however, remains the same. Each change in the route structure is tested for its effect on the total cost. The opportunity cost of shipping by other routes is compared with the cost of the present plan, and the lowest cost routes are chosen until no further cost reductions can be made.

LABOR STANDARDS AND CONTROL

Standards are established for direct labor, and variances from the standards can be measured in much the same way as they were measured for materials. Following the same general principle used for materials, there are two types of variances: (1) price and (2) quantity. Often, in working with labor, the price variance is called a *rate variance*; and the quantity variance is called an *efficiency variance*.

Labor Rate Variance

The *labor rate variance* measures the difference between the actual hours worked multiplied by the actual labor rates (actual labor cost) and the actual hours worked multiplied by the standard labor rates. This can be expressed in an abbreviated form as follows:

$$(1)\ \mathbf{AH \times AR = AC}$$
$$(2)\ \mathbf{AH \times SR = MC}$$
$$\mathbf{AC - MC = RV}$$

AH = actual labor hours
AR = actual labor rate
AC = actual labor cost
SR = standard labor rate
MC = mixed cost (actual hours multiplied by standard rates)
RV = rate variance (labor)

The hours are the same in Equations (1) and (2), but the rates differ. Hence, the labor rate variance can be obtained directly by multiplying the actual labor hours by the difference in the rates:

$$\mathbf{AH \times (AR - SR) = RV}$$

Labor rate variances are often created by transferring workers with high pay rates to jobs that call for low standard rates or by authorizing overtime work at premium pay. These labor cost differences are caused by rate differences rather than by changes in performance. The cost effect of unfavorable transfers or of premium pay for overtime should be called to management's attention as a price variance.

Assume, for example, that a payroll for direct production workers shows a gross wage cost of $130,000 for a pay period. Workers were paid $5 an hour for 20,000 hours and $7.50 an hour for 4,000 hours. The standard labor rate is $5 an hour. In this example, 4,000 hours were paid at $2.50 per hour in excess of standard.

The labor rate variance is computed as follows:

$$
\begin{aligned}
\text{AH} \quad &\times (\text{AR} - \text{SR}) &&= \text{RV} \\
4{,}000 &\times (\$7.50 - \$5) &&= \text{RV} \\
4{,}000 &\times \$2.50 &&= \text{RV} \\
&\$10{,}000 &&= \text{RV (unfavorable)}
\end{aligned}
$$

In this case, the variance is unfavorable because the work was performed at a cost greater than the standard rate.

Labor Efficiency Variance

Labor productivity is also measured. When labor is used more efficiently, not only is the labor cost per unit of product lower, but the overhead per unit of product may also be lower. This is true if variable overhead varies with labor hours. However, if variable overhead varies on a unit-of-product basis or is related to some other factor, labor hours have no effect on the cost. Because overhead often varies on a labor hour basis, it is easy to understand why management tries to increase the productivity of its labor force by introducing better work methods and more modern equipment. There can be a double advantage in that both labor and overhead cost per unit can be reduced.

Labor performance, or labor efficiency as it is sometimes called, is compared by department and by job with established standards. Daily or weekly reports to the supervisor and the plant superintendent help to locate and solve difficulties on a particular job or in a department. The vice-president in charge of production or the plant superintendent receives a report relating labor efficiency to labor cost on a weekly or monthly basis. Differences between jobs and departments may show that a job cannot be handled at the standard labor cost or that a department is not being managed properly.

The labor efficiency variance can also be determined by equations.

$$
\begin{aligned}
(1)\ &\text{AH} \times \text{SR} = \text{MC} \\
(2)\ &\text{SH} \times \text{SR} = \text{SC} \\
&\text{MC} - \text{SC} = \text{EV}
\end{aligned}
$$

AH = actual hours
SR = standard rate
MC = mixed cost (actual hours multiplied by standard rates)
SH = standard hours
SC = standard cost
EV = efficiency variance (labor)

Because the rates are the same in Equations (1) and (2), standard, the variance can be computed as follows:

$$\text{SR} \times (\text{SH} - \text{AH}) = \text{EV}$$

Using the data from the preceding example, suppose that the 24,000 direct labor hours were used to complete work that should have been done in 25,000 hours. In this case, there is a favorable variance because the work was done in less than the standard time.

The labor efficiency variance is computed as follows:

$$\begin{array}{ll} SR \times (SH - AH) & = EV \\ \$5 \times (25{,}000 - 24{,}000) & = EV \\ \$5 \times 1{,}000 & = EV \\ \$5{,}000 & = EV \text{ (favorable)} \end{array}$$

In labor accounting, the payrolls are accounted for in the usual manner, with gross wages earned being recorded in a payroll account pending distribution to the production account. A journal entry to record the payroll follows:

Payroll	130,000	
Employees Income Tax Payable...		28,500
FICA Tax Payable...		7,500
Wages Payable...		94,000
To record direct labor payroll for the payroll period.		

When the payroll is distributed to product cost, an entry is made to charge Work in Process with the standard cost of $125,000 (25,000 × $5), obtained by multiplying standard hours by standard labor rates.

Work in Process	125,000	
Labor Rate Variance	10,000	
Labor Efficiency Variance..		5,000
Payroll...		130,000
Transfer of factory labor cost to the products.		

A payroll for indirect labor may be recorded directly in Factory Overhead. Even a direct labor payroll will likely include some indirect labor in the form of idle time, and this cost can be transferred out of Payroll to Factory Overhead when information is available for a distribution of the labor cost.

Additions to Labor Cost

There are additional related costs in connection with labor much the same as there are related costs in connection with materials. An employee, in addition to being paid a straight hourly rate, may receive bonuses, vacation payments, sick leave payments, supplemental unemployment benefits, pensions, overtime pay, and shift differential adjustments. The extras are often referred to as *fringe benefits*.

The proper accounting for these costs in the income determination process can be rather complicated. The estimated cost of providing pensions, for example, may be broken down by years and related to the active work force. A supplemental hourly rate can then be calculated and added to the regular hourly rate in attaching the cost to the products. Similarly, the vacation pay for the year can be reduced to an hourly rate basis for costing products. In many cases, however, the extra pay is charged to Factory Overhead and is apportioned to all jobs accordingly. If factory overhead is allocated on a direct labor hour basis, the results will be the same under either method. Additional or premium pay for overtime work or for work on a less desirable shift may be charged to Factory Overhead and allocated to all jobs. A job should not be penalized with extra cost because it happened to be worked on during an overtime period due to random production scheduling. On the other hand, a special job that causes overtime work should be charged with the additional cost.

Incentives

Additional pay may also be given for superior work performance. When employees produce more units of product in a given time period, the company gains advantages. There is increased revenue from the sale of the additional units produced, and there is an increase in the variable cost of production. But the increase in revenue should be greater than the increase in the variable cost of production resulting in increased profit.

To increase productivity, a company may install superior machinery and equipment, search for better work methods, and reward the employees for superior work performance. There are a variety of incentive pay plans that may be used to encourage employees to increase production. Employees may be given bonus pay for the time saved in production or may receive higher rates of pay when they exceed standard rates of production for sustained periods of time.

The advantage of increased labor productivity is illustrated by the following example:

(1) Arbuckle Company employs five persons, each working 1,800 hours per year at a standard labor rate of $8 per hour.

(2) The standard labor cost per unit of product is 80 cents. In short, each employee is expected to produce 10 units each hour.

(3) An employee who can exceed this standard receives a bonus equal to one half of the pay for the time saved.

(4) During the year, all employees produced at the constant rate of 15 units per hour per employee.

(5) Each unit of product was sold for $8. The direct materials cost per unit was $3, and the variable overhead cost per unit was $1. The fixed factory overhead for the year was $67,500.

Any worker who can increase productivity from 10 units an hour to 15 units an hour saves 30 minutes on the standard. The worker produces in 1 hour what would normally be produced in 1 hour and 30 minutes. The bonus is equal to 50 percent of the pay for 30 minutes or (50% of 1/2 hour × $8 hourly rate). The total pay per hour including the bonus is $10.

With five workers producing at a rate of 15 units per hour, a total of 135,000 units (15 units per hour × 5 workers × 1,800 hours per year) would be produced during the year instead of 90,000 units at the standard rate.

The comparative income statement given below shows the actual results and the standard results expected.

	Arbuckle Company Comparative Income Statement For the Year Ended December 31, 1981			
	STANDARD 90,000 UNITS		ACTUAL 135,000 UNITS	
	Per Unit	Total	Per Unit	Total
Sales...	$8.00	$720,000	$8.00	$1,080,000
Cost of goods sold:				
Direct materials..............................	$3.00	$270,000	$3.00	$ 405,000
Direct labor	.80	72,000	.67*	90,000
Variable overhead..........................	1.00	90,000	1.00	135,000
Fixed overhead	.75	67,500	.50	67,500
Total..	$5.55	$499,500	$5.17	$ 697,500
Manufacturing margin	$2.45	$220,500	$2.83	$ 382,500
*Rounded				

Note that the direct labor cost per unit is lower even with the bonus. The workers received pay for only 50 percent of the time saved. The increase in manufacturing margin is explained below.

Additional revenue from the sale of 45,000 more units of product (45,000 × $8)...	$360,000
Additional variable costs for the production of 45,000 more units of product:	
Direct materials (45,000 × $3)...................................	$135,000
*Direct labor bonus (45,000 × $.40)...........................	18,000
Variable overhead (45,000 × $1)...............................	45,000
	$198,000
Additional manufacturing margin......................................	$162,000
*Bonus per hour (50% of 1/2 hour × $8.00).......................	$ 2.00
Bonus for each additional unit ($2 ÷ 5 additional units per hour)...	$ .40

The Learning Curve

Management can obtain additional profit from increased productivity. With more units manufactured in a given time period, there is a greater manufacturing margin even after sharing the benefits of increased productivity with the employees. Efforts are constantly being made to upgrade the skills of employees and to increase their efficiency through education and motivation.

A study can be made of the rate of learning a new task with the resulting productivity plotted on a graph as a *learning curve*. As experience is gained in production, the average time to manufacture a unit will decrease. This condition is known as the *learning phase*. Assume, for example, that the first batch of 100 units to be manufactured is produced in 500 labor hours. After this experience, the workers can produce the next 100-unit batch in less time. Perhaps the second 100-unit batch can be produced in 300 hours. An additional batch of 200 units may be produced with an additional 480 hours. When an optimum point is reached at some stage, no further increases in productivity can be expected and productivity is known to be at the static phase.

The example just given illustrates what is called an 80 percent learning curve. It is so designated because when production doubles, the cumulative average time per unit decreases to 80 percent of the previous cumulative average time.

UNITS PER BATCH	CUMULATIVE NUMBER OF UNITS	HOURS PER BATCH	CUMULATIVE HOURS	CUMULATIVE AVERAGE HOURS PER UNIT*
100	100	500	500	5.0
100	200	300	800	4.0*
200	400	480	1,280	3.2*

*Cumulative average is 80 percent of previous cumulative average.

The learning rate may be such that when the production is doubled, the cumulative average time per unit is 70 percent, 60 percent, or any other percentage of the previous cumulative average time per unit. At some point, learning stage is completed and further increases in productivity cannot be expected. Experience with the learning rates for certain types of functions may be used in predicting expected results.

The data given for the 80 percent learning curve is plotted on a graph as follows:

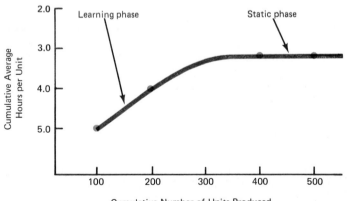

Sometimes data are plotted on log-log graph paper so that the learning curve will be a straight line and somewhat easier to read.

SUMMARY OF VARIANCES

In this chapter, a great deal of attention has been devoted to the concept of standards and the measurement of variances with respect to materials and labor. The variances provide information to guide management. Perhaps the prices paid for materials were excessive; or the employees were scheduled improperly, resulting in higher labor rates than required for certain productive functions; or the quantity of materials used or labor time was excessive for the amount of work performed.

The procedure used in isolating the price and quantity variances was described by journal entry presentations and by means of short equations. These variances can also be segregated quite easily by tracing the cost flows. This approach is summarized in the following diagram:

	ACCOUNTS USED	
	Materials	*Labor*
(1) Actual quantities at actual prices	Accounts Payable	Payroll
Difference is a price variance	Materials Price Variance	Labor Rate Variance
(2) Actual quantities at standard prices*	Materials	
Difference is a quantity variance	Materials Quantity Variance	Labor Efficiency Variance
(3) Standard quantities at standard prices	Work in Process	Work in Process

*The actual quantities of materials purchased during a fiscal period are not necessarily equal to the actual quantities withdrawn for use in production.

QUESTIONS

1. Why are budgets and standards generally considered to be unpleasant?

2. What is meant by management by exception?

3. Point out advantages and disadvantages of following the principle of management by exception.

4. What are some of the aspects of human behavior that must be considered in setting standards?

5. Explain why it may be necessary to revise standards from time to time.

6. During the month of April, Hess Products purchased 50,000 units of a material to be used in production at a price of 40 cents per unit. The standard price for this material was 36 cents per unit. What was the materials price variance?

7. During the month of May, Pasco Company used 30,000 units of a certain material in production. Standards indicate that only 27,000 units should have been used. The standard price per unit was $3.00. What was the materials quantity variance?

8. Explain how the purchase of materials at less than the standard price may have an adverse effect upon the use of materials in production.

9. An examination of the cost records of Judson Machine Company reveals that the materials price variance is favorable but that the materials quantity variance is unfavorable by a relatively large amount. What might this indicate?

10. What is meant by procurement period?

11. How can the concept of standard deviation be used in predicting order requirements?

12. The controller of Milford Castings, Inc., states that the inventories of materials are held at a high level to prevent the risk of production shutdown that would result if a supplier could not make deliveries. Furthermore, the materials are difficult to handle, and it is more convenient to purchase large lots infrequently. Comment on this policy.

13. What is the transportation model? How can opportunity costs be applied in selecting the least expensive shipping routes?

14. How are labor rate variances and labor efficiency variances computed?

15. The departmental supervisor assigned 3 persons with a labor rate per person of $6 an hour to a project with a standard labor rate of $5 an hour. Each person spent 70 hours on this project. What effect will this have on the labor rate variance?

16. A job calling for 350 hours of direct labor time was completed in 330 hours. The standard labor rate per hour is $5.50. What was the labor efficiency variance?

17. Does the increased productivity of labor have any relationship to factory overhead? Explain.

18. D'Ambrosio Products, Inc., incurs direct labor cost of $8 per unit to manufacture a unit of product that can be produced in one hour and fifteen minutes. Factory overhead varies at the rate of $12 an hour. If the labor time can be reduced to one hour, what will be the total expected cost saving per unit of product?

19. Is it possible to predict increases in productivity as employees gain more experience? Explain.

20. How can variances be used to control operations?

21. Describe briefly the way in which the variances are isolated in standard cost accounting.

EXERCISES

1. Materials Price Variance. On October 10, 6,000 clasps were purchased by Elton Metals, Inc., at a cost of $21,000. The standard cost for 6,000 of these clasps is $19,200.

Required: Determine the materials price variance.

2. Materials Price Variance. Three types of materials designated as K6, K8, and K10 are used in production by Bender Products Company. The standard cost per unit of K6 is $3, of K8, $4.50, and of K10, $7. The actual cost of units purchased during March is as follows:

Materials Code	Quantity	Total Cost
K6	3,000	$10,500
K8	7,000	30,800
K10	4,500	30,600

Required:

(1) Determine the total materials price variance for the month of March.
(2) Do you believe that sufficient information is provided by the total materials price variance? Explain.

3. Materials Quantity Variance. During the month of August, 16,000 units of materials having a standard cost of $.40 a unit were requisitioned for the production of 4,000 units of a product line. Standards reveal that 3 units of this material should be used for each unit of product manufactured.

Required: Prepare a journal entry to cost materials to production and to set up the materials quantity variance.

4. Materials Variances. A snow blower is manufactured and distributed by Northern Products, Inc. Standard quantities and costs of the parts used are as follows:

	Cost per Unit of Part
1 aluminum housing	$18.00
1 handle assembly	4.50
1 blower chute	2.30
1 motor	37.00
15 screws	.05
1 switch	.60
25 rivets	.05
4 wheels	.30
2 rubberized handle covers	.50

In 1981, the company assembled 30,000 snow blowers. No materials were on hand either at the beginning or at the end of the year. The quantities purchased and used in production are given at the top of the following page at actual costs.

30,000 aluminum housings	$ 570,000
30,200 handle assemblies	138,920
30,600 blower chutes	76,500
30,000 motors	1,200,000
453,000 screws	22,650
30,700 switches	24,560
752,000 rivets	37,600
120,000 wheels	36,000
61,000 rubberized handle covers	24,400

Required: Determine the total materials price variance and the total materials quantity variance.

5. Materials Control Features. Rodriguez Supply Company observes the following practices in purchasing materials and in processing claims for payment:

(1) Orders are placed for standard quantities of materials when the materials inventory records indicate the quantities are down to certain minimum levels.

(2) The orders are placed with established suppliers whenever possible. If the orders cannot be filled by established suppliers, bids are requested from competing suppliers. The bids are opened in the presence of two individuals, and the purchase order is awarded to the lowest responsible bidder.

(3) The materials are tested for purity when received with the quantity and results of the test entered on a receiving report.

(4) The purchase order, the receiving report, and the supplier's invoice are compared in the accounting department, and a voucher is prepared.

(5) The voucher is filed so that it will be paid within the discount period.

(6) The voucher is approved for payment, and a check is drawn. The check is signed by two individuals, each of whom examines the underlying voucher.

(7) The amount is recorded on the check in perforations by a check protector.

Required: Explain the control features behind each practice described.

6. Shipping Route Costs. Dwyer Products, Inc., has two plants: one located at Roanoke and the other at Odessa. Shipments are made from both plants to three regional warehouses. Next month the Roanoke plant is expected to produce 15 units. Eight of these units will be shipped to Warehouse A, and the remaining units will be shipped to Warehouse C. The Odessa plant is expected to produce 5 units and will ship all 5 units to Warehouse B. Unit shipping costs from each plant to each warehouse are given below:

	Warehouses		
Plants	*A*	*B*	*C*
Roanoke	$7	$10	$ 8
Odessa	4	8	11

Required:

(1) Compute the expected shipping costs next month under the existing plan.

(2) Prepare a shipping plan for the next month that will provide the required number of units per warehouse and will minimize the costs of shipment.

7. Labor Rate Variances. Standard labor rates per hour are given for three levels of employees, the levels depending upon degree of skill.

Level	Standard Rate per Hour
I...	$5.00
II..	6.00
III...	7.50

Production requiring 600 hours of Level I work were completed in 600 hours, but 80 hours of Level II work were included in the total.

Other production having a standard labor cost of $1,500 for 250 labor hours was completed with 190 hours of Level II labor and 60 hours of Level III labor.

Required: Prepare a journal entry to distribute factory payroll and to record the labor rate variance. Show computations.

8. Selection of Standards. A time and motion study shows that a very skilled operator can stamp 60 units of a certain part from sheet metal in an hour. The supervisor has established this rate as a standard for all employees. At the end of a 35-hour week, four workers stamped out 5,600 units. The labor rate is $6 per hour. Before the standard of 60 units per hour was put into effect, the workers produced at a rate of 50 units per hour. During the week that 5,600 units were produced, the materials scrap cost was $1,800. Furthermore, upon inspection it was found that 200 parts were imperfect and had to be rejected. The materials cost of the rejected parts was $600.

Required:

(1) If the new labor standard could be sustained without materials loss, what would be the expected production for the week and the labor cost per unit?

(2) Compare the unit labor cost under actual conditions with the expected labor cost with a standard of 50 units per hour.

(3) Comment on the new labor standard using solutions to (1) and (2) as a basis for your answer.

9. Labor Productivity. A product line manufactured by Eddystone Company sells for $3.30 per unit. The standard cost of direct materials per unit is $1.50. Direct production workers are paid at the rate of $8 per hour, and standards specify that 20 units should be manufactured in each direct labor hour. Variable overhead varies at the rate of $4 per direct labor hour.

Employees who exceed the standard time for production receive a bonus equal to pay for 50% of the time saved.

During one 40-hour week, one employee produced 880 units.

Required:

(1) Compute the manufacturing margin per unit and in total from the production and sale of 800 units.

(2) Compute the manufacturing margin per unit and in total from the production and sale of the 880 units produced by the one employee.

10. Labor Efficiency Variance. During the month of April, Hawkins Garden Shop repaired and serviced 90 power mowers. Two persons are assigned to this work and work together as a team. Each person is paid $4 per hour, and according to the standards, it should be possible to service one mower in two hours. By working a total of 320 hours a month, two persons (each at 160 hours) should service 80 mowers a month.

Required:

(1) What is the labor cost of servicing each mower according to the standard?
(2) What is the labor cost to service each unit when 90 units are serviced in a month?
(3) Determine the labor efficiency variance for the month of April on the basis of the increase in the number of mowers serviced.

11. Labor Efficiency Variance. Yost Products, Inc., has established a labor production standard of 3 units per hour for a certain product line. During the month of June, the company manufactured 11,400 units in 3,600 direct labor hours. The standard labor rate is $6 per hour.

Required:

(1) Prepare a journal entry to distribute the labor cost to work in process and to set up the labor efficiency variance.
(2) Determine the labor cost per unit at the standard rate of production.
(3) Determine the actual labor cost per unit for the month of June.

12. Labor Variances. The payroll for Jackson Products, Inc., for the month of September amounted to $230,000. Income taxes of $54,000 were withheld, FICA taxes of $14,000 were withheld, and union dues of $6,000 were deducted. The net amount paid to the employees was $156,000.

Included in the total payroll was indirect labor of $41,000.

The standard labor rate of $6 was paid for 27,000 hours of direct labor. The remaining 3,000 direct labor hours were paid at the rate of $9 per hour.

The company manufactured 115,000 units of product during the month. Standards show that 4 units of product should be manufactured each hour.

Required: Journalize the payroll for the month of September and prepare whatever other journal entries are needed to cost production and to isolate the labor rate and efficiency variances.

13. Labor Variances. During the month of November, the actual wages for 18,000 hours of direct labor were $119,000. According to standards established, half of the hours should have been paid at a standard rate of $7 per hour and the other half at standard rate of $6 per hour.

The standard rate of production has been set at 5 units of product per direct labor hour. In November, the company manufactured 81,000 units of product at a total standard labor cost of $105,300.

Required: Compute the labor rate variance and the labor efficiency variance for the month of November.

14. Labor Variances. In September, Dayton Fabrics, Inc., had direct labor payrolls with 8,000 hours at $6 an hour and 4,000 hours at $8 an hour. All work done during the month should have been at a standard labor rate of $6 an hour.

The company manufactured 5,800 units of product during the month. Standard production has been established at the rate of two hours per unit.

Required: Compute the labor rate variance and the labor efficiency variance for the month of September.

15. Variances and Incomplete Data. Information is given on materials and labor for five situations, each of which is independent from the other.

(1) The unfavorable materials price variance has been computed at $6,800. The standard price for materials is $4 per unit and the actual price was $4.40 per unit. Determine the actual quantity purchased.

(2) A favorable materials price variance was computed at $3,800. The company purchased 40,000 units of materials at an actual price of $.80 per unit. Determine the standard price for materials per unit.

(3) The materials quantity variance was favorable by $6,000. The standard unit price was $3, and the actual quantity used was 23,000 units. Determine the standard quantity to be used.

(4) The actual labor rate was $6 an hour for 8,000 actual labor hours. The unfavorable labor rate variance for these hours was computed at $4,000. Determine the standard labor rate.

(5) The company used 7,500 direct labor hours to manufacture products that should have been manufactured in 7,200 direct labor hours. The actual labor rate was $5 an hour, and the standard labor rate was $4.50 an hour. Compute both the labor rate variance and the labor efficiency variance.

PROBLEMS

6-1. Inventory Level. Carla Jenkins has been following a company policy of holding inventories to a minimum level in order to minimize the cost of storing inventories. Each month she has estimated consumption for the next month and has placed orders accordingly. The procurement period is one month. For example, if she estimates on May 1 that 500 units will be needed in June, she will order that quantity and will receive the order in time to make deliveries on June sales.

Last year she found that there were times when the inventory was insufficient to meet customer demand. If possible, she would like to improve the estimation technique and have 95% assurance that her decision will not result in stock depletion before the new order arrives. The company agrees that it would be better to have some extra inventory storage cost and minimize the risk of inventory shortages.

A record of estimates and consumption for the past year is given below.

Month	Forecast Use	Actual Use
January	180	200
February	170	180
March	200	180
April	230	220
May	220	240
June	250	250
July	240	250
August	240	250
September	210	200
October	200	180
November	180	170
December	160	170

The estimate for October of the current year is 200 units.

Required:

(1) From the record of past estimates and consumption, set up a plan that may help Jenkins avoid stock depletion and yet hold reasonably low inventory balances.

(2) How many units should she order in September for October sales?

6-2. Balancing Order and Storage Costs. At a recent meeting of purchasing executives, David Raub stated that in his line of business the economic order quantity has little significance. The cost to place an order is nominal, and the cost of receiving and handling the material is a fixed cost for the year. Hence, it did not matter whether or not he ordered at frequent intervals.

One of the other members, Jan Crawford, stated that her situation is different. In her company, basic raw materials are bulky and must be handled promptly with the use of heavy equipment. When a shipment arrives, all effort must be made to unload the cars so that they can be released to the carrier as soon as possible. Persons who do not ordinarily work in receiving are released from their regular assignments and are given extra pay for this work.

Ordering data are given below:

Estimated annual demand	3,000 units
Cost per unit	$50
Cost per order placed	$40

Storage costs are estimated at 20 percent of the inventory investment.

Required: How many orders should be placed to minimize the combined costs of placing orders and the costs of storage? Show computations and prove your answer by showing the combined costs for 10 orders, 20 orders, etc., until a maximum of 60 orders is reached.

6-3. Balancing Order and Storage Costs. A mixture of sand and gravel is acquired by Daly Contractors, Inc., and is stored on a large lot. The material is delivered by trucks and is moved on the lot by front-end loaders and bulldozers. The material costs $60 per unit as defined by the company, and it is estimated that 15,000 units will be required next year. The costs to process each order are estimated at $100. The costs of storage, including finance charges, are estimated at 20% of the cost of the materials.

Required: Determine the optimum number of orders that should be placed each year to minimize the total annual cost of placing orders and storage. Prove your answer by showing the combined costs for 20 orders, 25 orders, etc., until a maximum of 40 orders is reached.

6-4. Selection of Shipping Routes. Shipments are to be made from three regional plants of Armand Wire Company to a customer who wants deliveries made at three different locations. The number of units available at each plant and the customer demand schedule are given along with the unit costs of shipment from each plant to each location.

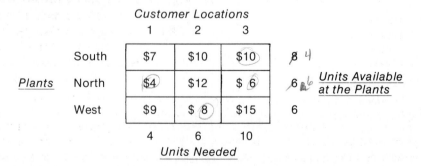

		Customer Locations			
		1	2	3	
	South	$7	$10	$10	8
Plants	North	$4	$12	$6	6
	West	$9	$8	$15	6
		4	6	10	

Units Available at the Plants

Units Needed

Required: Plan a shipping schedule that will minimize the total cost of delivery to the customer.

6-5. Materials Variances. Lukehart Processing Company has established a standard cost of $3 per unit for Material A and $7 per unit for Material B. In December, the company purchased 10,000 units of Material A and 5,000 units of Material B. With the exception of 800 units, all Material A was purchased at the standard unit cost. The 800 units had a unit cost of $3.50. The company purchased 4,500 units of Material B at standard cost and 500 units at a unit cost of $8.

According to the standards, two units of Material A and one unit of Material B should be used to manufacture each unit of Product 785. In January, 4,000 units of Product 785 were manufactured, and 8,600 units of Material A were used and 4,100 units of Material B were used.

Required:
(1) Compute the materials price variance and the materials quantity variance for each of the two types of materials.
(2) Prepare journal entries to record the acquisition of materials and their use of production. Isolate the variances in the entries.

6-6. Materials Variances. The purchasing department of Fanning Supplies, Inc., took pride in the fact that they purchased 50,000 units of a material at a price of $4.20 per unit. The standard price for this item is $5 per unit.

During the following month, 35,000 of these units were used to manufacture 5,000 units of product. The standard use is 5 units of this material per unit of product.

Required:
(1) Compute the materials price variance and the materials quantity variance.
(2) Assume that the materials quantity variance resulted from the purchase of inferior materials. Determine the net advantage or disadvantage of purchasing materials below the standard price.

6-7. Labor and Overhead Savings. Standard costs have been established for Rivera Plastics, Inc., for the production of a plastic part. The production workers are paid $7.20 an hour and are expected to make 8 units of this part each hour. The direct materials cost per unit of product is $5. Variable factory overhead, consisting of indirect materials, varies at the rate of $2.50 per unit of product. Other variable factory overhead varies at the rate of $4.80 per direct labor hour. By revising the production process slightly, management expects to increase output to a level of 10 units of product per hour.

Required:
(1) Determine the standard unit variable cost of the product at the present time.
(2) Determine the standard unit variable cost of the product under the revised production plan.

6-8. Labor Savings with a Labor Bonus. The labor standards at Orangeburg Refining Company specify that a certain product line should be manufactured at a rate of 20 units of product per direct labor hour. Workers receive a regular wage of $6.80 per hour. A bonus equal to 80% of the regular pay for the time saved in production is awarded for exceeding the standard rate of 20 units per hour. Variable factory overhead is estimated to vary at the rate of $5 per direct labor hour. Direct materials cost per unit is $1.50. During 1981, the company manufactured 1,500,000 units of product in 50,000 direct labor hours. The product is sold for $4 per unit. All costs in 1981 conformed with the standards with the exception of the differences caused by increased labor efficiency.

Required:
(1) Compute the manufacturing margin by unit and in total according to the standards. Assume standard production for 50,000 direct labor hours. (Show detail by cost elements.)
(2) Compute the manufacturing margin by unit and in total for the operation in 1981. (Show detail by cost elements.)

6-9. Materials and Labor Variances. Standard costs have been determined for the direct materials and direct labor used in the production of a small storage tank that is manufactured at the Bluefield plant of Cotter Industries, Inc. The standard costs per tank are given below.

Direct materials:

3 units of Material 133	$ 6.60
4 units of Material 146	20.00
6 units of Material 187	18.00
Standard materials cost	$44.60

Direct labor:

3 hours each at $6.20	18.60
Total standard materials and labor	$63.20

In November, 14,000 of these tanks were manufactured in 36,400 direct labor hours. All direct labor hours with the exception of 600 hours were at the standard rate. The 600 hours were at a rate of $7.50 per hour. The plant used 42,000 units of Material 133, 56,000 units of Material 146, and 86,000 units of Material 187.

During the month, all materials were purchased at standard prices with the following exceptions:

5,000 units of Material 133 at a price of $2.25 per unit of material.
8,000 units of Material 187 at a price of $3.50 per unit of material.

Required:
(1) Calculate the materials price variance, the materials quantity variance, the labor rate variance, and the labor efficiency variance.
(2) Identify the type of material that was primarily responsible for the materials quantity variance.
(3) Did the favorable labor efficiency variance compensate for the unfavorable labor rate variance?

6-10. Standards and Productivity. A review of standards is being conducted by the management of Toledo Mills, Inc. In one department unfavorable variances for the month were identified as follows:

Materials price variance	$55,000
Materials quantity variance	81,000
Labor rate variance	8,120
Labor efficiency variance	61,800

The variances appear to be quite large, indicating that drastic control measures are needed. Further information with respect to direct materials and direct labor cost per unit of product is given below.

Direct materials (4 units each at $3)	$12.00
Direct labor (1/2 hour, hourly rate $6)	3.00
Standard cost — materials and labor	$15.00

The materials used in production can no longer be obtained at the old price of $3 per unit. The price that must be paid for this material is now $4.50 per unit. Last month the company bought 85,000 units at the standard price before the price increased. A subsequent purchase of 30,000 units was made at $4.50 per unit. An additional emergency purchase of 5,000 units was made at a price of $5 per unit.

During the month, 20,000 units of product were started and completed. The department used 107,000 units of material. The original standards made no allowance for a shrinkage of materials in production. Under normal operating conditions, 5 units of materials are needed in the process to obtain the equivalent of 4 units of materials needed for each unit of finished product.

A new union wage scale provides for an hourly wage of $6.40. The old rate for production of 2 units per hour was established before the product was redesigned. With more complexities in the production process, it now takes an average of one hour to complete each product unit. Last month 20,300 labor hours were utilized and paid at the rate of $6.40 per hour.

Required:

(1) Show how the variances for the month were computed.
(2) Set up a more realistic schedule of standard unit costs for direct materials and direct labor.
(3) Recompute the variances measured from the revised standards.

6-11. Standard Cost Accounting Entries. A component sold to other manufacturers is produced at the McDowell plant of Harlow Industries, Inc. Last year the plant started 200,000 of these components in production. Cost data are summarized below.

(1) Materials were purchased for production at a total cost of $428,000. The standard cost of the materials was $416,000.
(2) During the year, the company used 311,000 units of material. The standards show that 300,000 units at a standard cost of $1.30 per unit of material should have been used.
(3) Direct labor payrolls are summarized below:

Gross wages	$153,000
Employees income tax payable	31,200
FICA tax payable	9,200
City wage tax payable	1,600

Wages consist of 23,000 hours at the standard rate of $6.50 per hour and 500 hours at $7.00 per hour.

(4) The standard rate of production is 8 units per hour.
(5) All of the components started in production were completed during the year and transferred to finished goods.

Required: Prepare journal entries to trace the costs through the records. Transfer the direct materials and factory labor costs of the completed units to Finished Goods. Isolate the price or rate and quantity or efficiency variances in the journal entries.

6-12. Standards and Productivity. The Marcel Processing Company is establishing standard costs for a new product line. This line may be produced with either of two different grades of a basic material. Also, a variation in the skill of the employees is possible.

Test runs show that Grade A material may be used with a cost of $15 per unit of product. There is no loss of materials in production with this grade of material. Grade B material, costing $9 per unit of product, may be used as a substitute for Grade A material. When this material is used, however, final output of product is only equal to 75% of the materials started in process.

A crew of five workers working a total of 500 hours (100 hours per worker) should produce 6,000 units of product. The direct labor cost per worker is $6 per hour.

As an alternative, a crew of five very highly skilled workers can produce 6,000 units of product in a total of 400 hours (80 hours per worker). These workers, however, are paid at the rate of $7.50 per hour.

Variable overhead varies at the rate of $3 per hour when the highly skilled labor is used and increases to $4.80 an hour when the less skilled labor is used.

Required:

(1) Calculate the standard variable cost per unit of product for each of the alternatives given.
(2) Which alternative should yield the lowest product cost?

6-13. Standards and the Learning Process. A new production technique has been put into operation by Croft Brothers, Inc. While this method is being learned, it is anticipated that the time required to make each unit of product will be relatively long. As experience is gained, the time should be reduced.

Estimates show that the first batch of 200 units will require 1,000 direct labor hours. The next batch of 200 units should be completed in 600 additional labor hours. It is expected that another 400 units can be produced in 960 additional labor hours.

No standards have been established for the first batch. If the second batch of 200 units can be produced as expected in 600 additional hours, a bonus equal to 50% of the time saved will be paid to any worker who can produce at a rate better than 3 hours per unit. The workers receive a regular wage of $5.40 an hour.

The second batch was produced as expected in 600 additional hours, and no bonus was paid. The workers at this point came up to the anticipated standard.

The workers produced an additional 400 units in 960 additional hours as estimated and were paid the stipulated bonus for hours saved in production.

Required:

(1) Compute the bonus paid for the third batch of 400 units.
(2) Determine the labor cost per unit on the first batch, on the second batch, and on the third batch with the bonus.
(3) From the information given, what is the predicted rate of learning? Show computations.

6-14. Standard Costs and Learning Curve. Over the years, Ellison Parts Company has established a reputation for producing quality parts that are purchased by industrial customers. During the past few months, the company has started production of a new part designated as SK432.

By the end of the month of March, 1,500 units of SK432 were produced in two batches of 750 units each. The results show that labor has followed an 80% learning curve. It is anticipated that the next 1,500 units (to be produced in April) will continue to follow the 80% learning curve pattern. Labor data with respect to the two batches of 750 units already produced are given at the top of the following page.

Units per Batch	Cumulative Number of Units	Hours per Batch	Cumulative Hours	Time per Unit
750	750	312.5	312.5	25 min.
750	1,500	187.5	500	20 min.

The standard labor cost per hour for this type of work is $6.60.

Two types of direct material are used in production of SK432, Material A and Material B. The standard price of Material A is $1.50 per unit of material, and three units of this material are required in the production of SK432. The standard price of Material B is $8, and one unit of this material is required in the production of SK432.

During April, the company purchased 4,000 units of Material A at a unit price of $1.50 and 1,200 units at a unit price of $1.80. All units of Material B were purchased at the standard unit price.

Standards have been defined on the basis of continuation of the learning curve in April.

During the month of April the company produced 1,500 units of SK432. Actual cost data are given below.

Direct materials

Material A — 4,650 units used
Material B — 1,540 units used

Direct labor

320 hours each at $6.60
55 hours each at $9.90

Required:

(1) Determine the standard unit materials and labor cost of SK432.
(2) Compute the materials price variance and the materials quantity variance for the month.
(3) Compute the labor rate variance and the labor efficiency variance for the month.
(4) Does it appear that the 80% learning curve is working according to the plan? Explain.

6-15. Bid Price and Learning Curve. The Bayeau Instrument Company manufactures various precision instruments and safety devices that are used for aircraft and space vehicles. Recently, 2,500 units of a more sophisticated directional guidance instrument were produced at the following cost:

Direct materials..	$ 37,500
Direct labor (10,000 hours @ $8)..	80,000
Variable overhead (10,000 hours @ $2)...............................	20,000
Fixed overhead	24,000
Patterns and designs...	15,000
Total cost...	$176,500
Unit cost..	$ 70.60

Previous studies show that an 80% learning curve can be used in estimating costs.

The company has an opportunity to bid on a contract for the production of 7,500 units of the new guidance instrument. The patterns and designs that were used for the 2,500 units already produced can be used again for this contract. With a larger quantity, the company can obtain the direct materials at a lower cost of $12 per unit of product. No change is expected in the hourly labor rate or the variable cost rate. Fixed overhead is estimated at $37,440 for the contract.

Ordinarily, the company plans for a profit margin of 40% on manufacturing cost. However, in this case, with the opportunity to develop a new line of product, a profit of 25% on manufacturing cost will be acceptable.

Required:

(1) Using an 80% learning curve, compute a total cost for the 7,500-unit contract. Also, compute a unit cost for each element of cost.
(2) Determine a bid price with a 25% profit on manufacturing cost.
(3) What would the price be if a 40% profit were allowed on manufacturing cost?
(4) Comment on the advantages and disadvantages of setting a lower price for a 25% profit on manufacturing cost instead of setting a price to obtain a 40% profit on manufacturing cost.

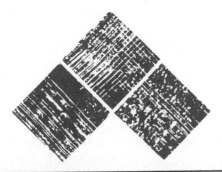

7
FACTORY OVERHEAD CONTROL

Factory overhead cost can also be controlled by making use of information developed through a standard cost accounting system. Overhead cost is accumulated by departments or other identifiable units of the company. The actual cost is then compared with a budget prepared for various levels of output. This comparison shows whether the price paid for and the quantity used of indirect materials, indirect labor, and other overhead were too high or too low in relation to the budget.

For example, Department 15 used supplies costing $3,200 for 5,000 hours of operation during the month of June. A budget for supplies at 5,000 hours of operation shows that the cost should have been $2,500. The unfavorable variance of $700 is used as a basis for investigating underlying causes. It may be found that supplies were used excessively or that the prices of the supplies were too high. Perhaps steps can be taken to correct this condition before cost becomes more excessive.

A FLEXIBLE BUDGET AND VARIANCES

As explained in Chapter 5, overhead is applied to the products by means of an overhead rate that is calculated by dividing a budgeted factor such as machine hours into budgeted overhead at normal capacity. As an aid in the control process, a series of budgets, known as a flexible budget, is prepared for different levels of activity.

Standards are established for the time required to make a given quantity of product as well as for the level of activity expected at normal capacity. Hence, the standard overhead cost per unit of product can be determined for the normal capacity level.

Assume that Ellis Parts Company has a normal operating capacity of 100,000 machine hours, and standards indicate that 4 units of product should be manufactured each hour. The total overhead at normal operating capacity has been budgeted at $600,000.

In 1981, it is assumed that the company (1) produced 280,000 units of product, (2) used 80,000 machine hours, and (3) incurred total overhead cost of $529,000. The fixed overhead included in the total amounted to $203,000. A flexible budget for the company is summarized below. Details with respect to individual items such as indirect materials, repairs, and heat and light are omitted in the interest of brevity.

Ellis Parts Company
Summarized Flexible Budget (Standard Cost)

	Overhead Budgets (at various hours of operation)				
Machine hours of operation....	110,000	100,000*	90,000	80,000	70,000
Standard production (product units)...	440,000	400,000	360,000	320,000	280,000
Variable overhead....................	$440,000	$400,000	$360,000	$320,000	$280,000
Fixed overhead.........................	200,000	200,000	200,000	200,000	200,000
Total overhead......................	$640,000	$600,000	$560,000	$520,000	$480,000

Overhead rate per hour:	
Variable..	$4.00
Fixed..	2.00
Total rate..	$6.00

Overhead rate per unit of product:	
Variable..	$1.00
Fixed..	.50
Total rate..	$1.50

*Normal operating capacity

Note that the overhead rate has been computed at the normal capacity and that it can be expressed either as a rate per hour or as a rate per unit of product. Cost computations can be made using either the hourly rate or the unit-of-product rate. To avoid error, it is necessary to be consistent; that is, use hours with the hourly rate and units of product with the unit-of-product rate.

Overhead Variances

Each unit of product has a standard overhead cost of $1.50. The standard overhead cost of the 280,000 units manufactured was $420,000 (280,000 units × $1.50 rate per unit of product).

The total overhead variance is the difference between the actual overhead and the standard overhead assigned to the products.

	VARIABLE	FIXED	TOTAL
Actual overhead..............................	$326,000	$203,000	$529,000
Standard overhead for 280,000 units produced...........................	280,000	140,000	420,000
Total unfavorable overhead variance......................................	**$ 46,000**	**$ 63,000**	**$109,000**

The total variance can be analyzed in three portions and used as a tool for planning and control. The three variances are:

1. Spending variance.
2. Efficiency variance.
3. Capacity (or volume) variance.

The first two of these variances, the spending variance and the efficiency variance, are often called the *controllable variance*. These two variances are called controllable because production management should be able to minimize any unfavorable variances of this type by economic and efficient operation.

The Spending Variance

The difference between the actual overhead cost and the budgeted cost for the actual hours of operation is called a *spending variance*. Note that this variance is to overhead what the price and quantity variances are to direct materials and direct labor. It is the combination of the price and quantity variances for overhead. The other variances developed for overhead do not pertain to overhead itself but rather to the relationship of overhead to the level of activity expressed as machine hours, direct labor hours, and direct labor cost.

To summarize the concept of a spending variance, note that actual overhead cost is $529,000 and that the budget for the level of machine hours operated is $520,000. The spending variance is computed as follows:

	VARIABLE	FIXED	TOTAL
Actual overhead..............................	$326,000	$203,000	$529,000
Budget of overhead for actual hours of operation (80,000 hours)..	320,000	200,000	520,000
Unfavorable spending variance....	**$ 6,000**	**$ 3,000**	**$ 9,000**

The company either used more overhead materials and services or paid higher prices than anticipated by the budget. The spending variance has been computed by comparing the actual overhead costs with a budget for the actual time used.

The Efficiency Variance

The efficiency variance reveals the difference in variable overhead cost as a result of using more or fewer hours than planned for the manufacture of the products. It does not result from the saving or improper use of overhead or favorable or unfavorable overhead prices. Instead, it measures the difference in variable overhead that arises by efficient or inefficient use of the factor used in costing overhead to the products.

The *efficiency variance*, in this illustration, is computed as the difference between the budget for the actual hours used and budget for the hours that should have been used to obtain the quantity of product produced. The efficiency variance is computed below.

	VARIABLE	FIXED	TOTAL
Budget of factory overhead for 80,000 machine hours (actual) ..	$320,000	$200,000	$520,000
Budget of factory overhead for 70,000 machine hours (standard hours allowed to manufacture 280,000 units)................	280,000	200,000	480,000
Unfavorable efficiency variance ...	**$ 40,000**	**—0—**	**$ 40,000**

The variance can also be computed simply by multiplying the difference between the actual hours used and the budgeted hours allowed by the variable overhead rate per hour: (80,000 actual hours − 70,000 standard hours) × $4 variable rate per hour = $40,000 unfavorable efficiency variance.

The efficiency variance includes only the variable cost. Fixed cost by definition remains the same over the relevant range of hours and is not affected by the efficient or inefficient use of machine time or labor time.

The Controllable Variance

As stated earlier, the spending variance and the efficiency variance together constitute the controllable variance. The earlier results are summarized at the top of the next page in a computation of the controllable variance which is unfavorable by $49,000. It is equal to the unfavorable spending variance of $9,000 plus the unfavorable efficiency variance of $40,000. It may also be computed as the difference between the actual overhead of $529,000 and the budget of $480,000 for the standard time allowed to complete 280,000 units.

Production management is expected to obtain overhead materials and services at the budgeted prices and to use such materials and services efficiently. There can be a spending variance for either variable

			VARIABLE	FIXED	TOTAL
		Actual overhead	$326,000	$203,000	$529,000
	Spending $9,000				
Controllable $49,000		Budget, actual time (80,000 hours)	320,000	200,000	520,000
	Efficiency $40,000				
		Budget, standard time allowed (70,000 hours)	280,000	200,000	480,000

or fixed overhead. For example, a budget for property insurance for the year (fixed cost) may have no allowance for an increase in the premium. Hence, there will be a difference between the actual insurance cost and the budgeted amount. Although the insurance cost in itself cannot be controlled on a day-to-day basis, management should be careful to revise budgets as necessary and to consider how much insurance service is required relative to its cost.

Production management is also expected to control the time used for production. As stated in the previous chapter, both labor cost and variable overhead are affected by the efficient or inefficient use of labor time. A saving in labor or machine time not only saves labor cost but also saves variable overhead cost.

Capacity or Volume Variance

The third variance developed in connection with overhead is the capacity or volume variance. Overhead is costed to the products using a rate computed at a defined normal capacity. If the company does not operate at normal capacity, the fixed overhead will be either overabsorbed or underabsorbed. The over- or underabsorption of fixed overhead reveals that the company did not operate at normal capacity. This is the capacity or volume variance. In this text, the term "capacity" variance will be used.

In the illustration given, the company operated at 70 percent of normal capacity. It produced an output of 280,000 units but was expected to produce 400,000 units at normal capacity. Hence, it produced at 70 percent of the normal capacity (280,000 ÷ 400,000 = 70%). This percentage can also be computed by using hours of operation. The output of 280,000 units should have been completed in 70,000 machine hours. Normal capacity is 100,000 machine hours. The company operated at 70 percent of normal capacity (70,000 ÷ 100,000 = 70%).

By operating at only 70 percent of normal capacity, only 70 percent of the fixed overhead was absorbed by the products. The absorbed fixed overhead was $140,000 (70% × $200,000). The balance of the fixed overhead amounting to $60,000 was unabsorbed ($200,000 −

$140,000). The capacity variance was an unfavorable $60,000, the amount of capacity available but unused.

The capacity variance can be computed in still another way as shown below:

	VARIABLE	FIXED	TOTAL
Budget of factory overhead for 280,000 units or 70,000 hours of standard time allowed	$280,000	$200,000	$480,000
Standard overhead costed to 280,000 units of product (280,000 units × $1.50 product rate or 70,000 hours × $6 hourly rate)	280,000	140,000	420,000
Unfavorable capacity variance	—0—	$ 60,000	$ 60,000

The variable overhead is not relevant in the computation of a capacity variance, because the variable overhead cost varies with the level of production. The computation could be simplified by considering only the fixed overhead.

	FIXED OVERHEAD
Budget of factory overhead for 280,000 units or 70,000 hours of standard time allowed	$200,000
Standard fixed overhead costed to products at rate of 50 cents for each of 280,000 units	140,000
Unfavorable capacity variance.......................................	$ 60,000

One may argue that the company used 80,000 machine hours and should have produced 320,000 units of product when manufacturing at the rate of 4 units per hour, reasoning that the company operated at 80 percent of normal capacity and that the capacity variance was only 20 percent or was equal to $40,000 (20% × $200,000). It is true that the company did use 80,000 machine hours, but 10,000 of these hours were wasted. The company produced 280,000 units, and these units should have been made in 70,000 machine hours. Hence, only 70 percent of the normal capacity was used effectively. It is also true that 320,000 units should have been made in 80,000 hours, but they were not. Standard overhead cost can only be applied to the tangible units that are available, the 280,000 units produced.

Plant Capacity and Control

In general, the capacity variance is not considered to be controllable by plant management. The plant produces what is needed to meet sales requirements, and plant management cannot be blamed if the sales demand is unable to absorb production at a normal level of plant operation. Moreover, factors such as excessive machine downtime, lack of rapidity in completing tasks due to unskilled workers, and inefficient production scheduling may all contribute to not producing at capacity.

In attempting to place responsibility for idle capacity, it is better to measure in terms of units of product rather than dollars. Also, different concepts of capacity should be considered.

In the preceding example, normal capacity was defined at 100,000 machine hours or 400,000 units of product. *Normal capacity*, as defined in Chapter 5, is an average concept representing the average level of plant operation over the years considering variations from year to year.

Practical plant capacity, on the other hand, is the level at which the plant can operate if all facilities are used to the full extent. Some allowance must be made for expected delays because of changes in machine setups, necessary maintenance time, and other interruptions. Hence, practical capacity is less than theoretical maximum capacity that could be obtained only under ideal conditions.

A comparison of the actual output with the output for practical plant capacity broadly measures the failure of the plant to operate at the level for which the plant was designed. Assume, for example, that Ellis Parts Company has a plant that can reasonably be expected to produce 500,000 units a year. Yet only 280,000 units were produced.

Practical capacity	500,000 units
Actual production	280,000
Total idle capacity	**220,000 units**

The idle capacity, as expressed in product units, can be analyzed further to determine why the plant was not used as intended. Assume that the sales budget shows that 400,000 units were to be sold during the year but that orders for only 350,000 units were received.

Practical capacity	500,000		
		100,000	(1)
Sales budget	400,000		
		50,000	(2)
Sales orders received	350,000		
		70,000	(3)
Actual production	280,000		

(1) Practical capacity minus sales budget

The difference between the practical plant capacity and the sales budget for the year requires further investigation. Perhaps the company was overly optimistic and provided too much plant capacity. Or the sales department may not be obtaining potential available sales. Additional analysis may reveal the true nature of the problem and provide a foundation for improvements.

(2) Sales budget minus sales orders received

The difference between the sales budget for the year and the sales orders received is a measurement of the inability of the sales department to meet the budget quota. Perhaps the sales quota was too high, or the sales department was not sufficiently aggressive.

(3) Sales orders received minus actual production

The difference between the sales orders received and actual production reflects a mixture of idle capacity and inefficiency. Ellis Parts Company used enough machine time to produce 320,000 units of product but only produced 280,000 units. Hence, 40,000 units included under idle capacity really indicate wastefulness rather than nonutilization. The difference between the sales orders received and the expected production for the time used (350,000 − 320,000) is a measurement of idle capacity. The idle capacity may be chargeable to poor production scheduling or to some other lapse in production management that caused production to fall below scheduled customer deliveries.

In the example given for Ellis Parts Company, no allowance was made for inventories at either the beginning or the end of the period in order to simplify the example. In practice, adjustments must be made for units carried over into the year as inventory or for units remaining on hand at the end of the year.

The significance of the variances may be emphasized by considering the dollar effect. If the sales department fails to meet the sales quota, there is an opportunity cost of lost profit that should be realized. For example, assume that 50,000 units of product may be expected to bring in $750,000 in revenue. Additional cost to manufacture and deliver these units is estimated at $500,000. The $500,000 consists of the direct materials, direct labor, and variable overhead costs as well as the cost to deliver the units. The opportunity cost of not meeting the sales budget (sales budget of 400,000 units minus sales orders received of 350,000 units = 50,000 units) is then estimated at $250,000. At best this is an approximation. Arguments can be made that the additional units could only be sold by reducing prices or that the cost estimates are not entirely accurate. Nevertheless, this approach to the problem can be helpful in that it points out how dollars of profit may be sacrificed by not using the facilities as intended.

SUMMARY OF OVERHEAD VARIANCES

The overhead variances that were discussed in this chapter are now summarized. The diagram given below indicates how the total overhead variance can be subdivided into three segments when the system is used for both product costing and control.

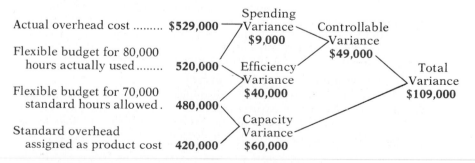

A STANDARD COST ILLUSTRATION

Cost transactions for Dantzer Mills, Inc., are traced through the records for the year in summary form. Only one product line is manufactured, with a standard unit cost shown on the standard cost card which appears below.

Dantzer Mills, Inc. Standard Cost — Product A	
Materials: 5 units of material × $2 standard price	$10
Labor: 6 hours × $6 standard labor rate	36
Overhead: 6 hours × $8 standard overhead rate	48
Standard production cost per unit	$94

The total factory overhead at normal operating capacity has been budgeted at $960,000, and 120,000 direct labor hours have been budgeted at normal capacity. The overhead rate per direct labor hour is $8.

Summary transactions and cost data pertaining to the year are as follows:

(1) Materials purchases, 100,000 units at a unit cost of $2.40.
(2) Direct materials issued to production, 93,000 units. The standards required only 90,000 units of materials.
(3) Factory payrolls, $814,000; employees income tax withheld, $178,000; FICA tax withheld, $48,000.
(4) Labor distribution:
    Direct labor, 90,000 hours @ $6
                 6,000 hours @ 9
    Indirect labor, $220,000
(5) Factory overhead other than indirect labor:

Indirect materials	$258,000
Reduction of prepaid insurance	4,000
Accrued expenses	219,000
Depreciation	172,000

(6) There were no units in process at either the beginning or the end of the year. During the year, 18,000 units of product were manufactured; and 17,000 units were sold on account for $200 apiece.
(7) A portion of the flexible factory overhead budget is given in summary form below:

	PERCENTAGE OF NORMAL OPERATING CAPACITY			
	70%	*80%*	*90%*	*100%*
Standard production in units of product...	14,000	16,000	18,000	20,000
Variable overhead	$350,000	$400,000	$450,000	$500,000
Fixed overhead	460,000	460,000	460,000	460,000
Total overhead	$810,000	$860,000	$910,000	$960,000
Budgeted direct labor hours	84,000	96,000	108,000	120,000
Overhead rate per hour				$8.00

The flow of the transactional data through the accounts is shown in summary journal entry form below and on pages 199–200.

(1) Materials purchased during the year:

Materials	200,000	
Materials Price Variance	40,000	
Accounts Payable		240,000

Acquisition of materials. (Standard: 100,000 units × $2 = $200,000; actual: 100,000 units × $2.40 = $240,000.)

(2) Direct materials issued to production at various times:

On standard requisitions:

Work in Process	180,000	
Materials		180,000

Standard quantities issued. (5 material units × 18,000 product units = 90,000 standard units of materials × $2 standard unit cost = $180,000.)

On supplemental requisition:

Materials Quantity Variance	6,000	
Materials		6,000

Requisition of 3,000 (93,000 issued minus 90,000 standard) units in excess of standard at $2 standard unit cost.

(3) Factory payrolls for the year:

Payroll	814,000	
Employees Income Tax Payable		178,000
FICA Tax Payable		48,000
Wages Payable		588,000

Summary of factory payrolls.

(4) Labor distribution for the year:

Work in Process	648,000	
Factory Overhead	220,000	
Labor Rate Variance	18,000	
Labor Efficiency Variance		72,000
Payroll		814,000

Distribution of payroll. Standard hours per unit of product of 6 × 18,000 product units = 108,000 standard hours × $6 standard rate = $648,000 product cost.

Rate variance = $3 per hour ($9 actual minus $6 standard) × 6,000 hours = $18,000. Efficiency variance = 12,000 hrs. (108,000 standard minus 96,000 actual) × $6 standard rate.

(5) Actual factory overhead for the year, excluding indirect labor:

Factory Overhead	653,000	
Accounts Payable		258,000
Prepaid Insurance		4,000
Accrued Expenses Payable		219,000
Accumulated Depreciation		172,000

Summary of factory overhead including result of adjusting entries made at end of year. (In this example, it is assumed that indirect materials have been expensed as acquired with no adjustment necessary.)

(6) Factory overhead applied to production during the year:

Work in Process	864,000	
Applied Factory Overhead		864,000

Standard hours allowed for production: 6 standard hours per unit × 18,000 units = 108,000 total standard hours. 108,000 standard hours × $8 rate = $864,000 standard overhead cost.

Completed units transferred to finished goods inventory:

Finished Goods..	1,692,000	
Work in Process...		1,692,000

Transfer of 18,000 units to stock at a standard cost of $94 apiece.

Total sales of 17,000 units:

Accounts Receivable......................................	3,400,000	
Sales...		3,400,000

Sale of 17,000 units at $200 per unit.

Cost of Goods Sold	1,598,000	
Finished Goods		1,598,000

The standard cost of 17,000 units is charged to Cost of Goods Sold (17,000 units × $94 per unit).

(7) Actual and applied factory overhead accounts closed and variance recorded:

Applied Factory Overhead	864,000	
Factory Overhead Variance....................................	9,000	
Factory Overhead		873,000

To close actual and applied overhead accounts. The unfavorable variance is recorded. (Indirect labor, $220,000 + other factory overhead, $653,000 = $873,000.)

Analysis of Factory Overhead Variance

Spending:

Actual overhead incurred	$873,000	
Flexible budget for 96,000 hours of operation	860,000	
Spending variance (unfavorable).....................		$13,000

Efficiency:

Flexible budget for 96,000 hours of operation	$860,000	
Flexible budget for 108,000 standard hours allowed...	910,000	
Efficiency variance (favorable).....................		(50,000)

Capacity variance:

Flexible budget for 108,000 standard hours allowed...	$910,000	
Standard overhead applied (108,000 standard hours × $8 rate).................................	864,000	
Capacity variance (unfavorable)		46,000
Total variance (unfavorable).............................		$ 9,000

Variances closed to Cost of Goods Sold at the end of the year:

Cost of Goods Sold	1,000	
Labor Efficiency Variance	72,000	
Materials Price Variance		40,000
Materials Quantity Variance		6,000
Labor Rate Variance		18,000
Factory Overhead Variance		9,000

To close out all variances for the year.

NONMANUFACTURING COSTS

The use of a standard cost as a basis for cost control is most frequently illustrated by a manufacturing operation. However, these same concepts can be adapted and applied to selling and administrative cost and to entities that do not manufacture and sell products but instead render services. Outside of the manufacturing area, standard costs and variances are usually not incorporated in the accounts but are determined by supplemental analysis.

Banks, insurance companies, finance companies, and other companies that sell services instead of products can determine how much it should cost to render their service under different conditions to various customer groups. Work measurement techniques can be used to measure the standard output expected in a unit of time from a given activity or function. The time standards are then combined with cost standards to establish a standard cost for a service.

Assume that 2 hours are required to process an insurance claim. The standard variable cost per hour is $5. The fixed cost of operating the claims division is budgeted at $4,000 a month; normally 400 claims are processed each month. The standard cost to process a claim is:

Variable cost (2 hours × $5)	$10.00
Fixed cost ($4,000 ÷ 400 claims)	10.00
Standard cost per claim	$20.00

In a given month, assume that 360 claims were processed in 750 hours with actual fixed cost as budgeted and actual variable cost of $3,840. Variations from the standards can be identified for control purposes by the following analysis:

Actual variable cost	$3,840	
Budget of variable cost for 750 actual hours (750 hours × $5 rate)	3,750	
Unfavorable spending variance		$ 90
Budget of variable cost for 750 actual hours	$3,750	
Budget of variable cost for 720 standard hours allowed (360 claims × 2 hours per claim = 720 standard hours × $5 rate)	3,600	
Unfavorable efficiency variance		150
Fixed overhead	$4,000	
Overhead absorbed (360 claims × $10 rate)	3,600	
Unfavorable capacity variance		400
Unfavorable total variance		$640

For any function or activity that can be performed in a measured unit of time, a standard cost can be developed. The general principles of variance analysis can be employed as an aid in cost control.

QUESTIONS

1. How can management use an overhead spending variance in controlling the cost of overhead?

2. Explain how an overhead spending variance is similar to price and quantity variances for direct materials and rate and efficiency variances for direct labor.

3. What is a flexible budget?

4. At what level of capacity is a factory overhead rate computed?

5. Explain how a standard overhead cost per unit of product can be determined.

6. With increases in production, variable cost in total will increase; but the variable cost per unit will tend to remain the same. Explain.

7. Explain why the fixed overhead cost per unit depends upon the level of production that is selected for computing the rate.

8. Name three factory overhead variances that are often developed in standard cost accounting.

9. Which two of the three variances are called the controllable variance?

10. How does an overhead efficiency variance help management in the control of overhead?

11. Is fixed overhead cost included in an overhead efficiency variance? Why or why not?

12. Does an overhead efficiency variance measure efficiency in the use of overhead? Explain.

13. What is a capacity or volume variance?

14. Should the standard overhead be applied to the products actually manufactured or to the products that should have been manufactured in the time used? Explain.

15. How can variances be used to control operations?

16. Can a capacity variance be controlled?

17. How are the variances handled at the end of the year?

18. Explain briefly how the total factory overhead variance can be analyzed into a spending variance, an efficiency variance, and a capacity variance.

19. Can the principles of standard cost accounting be applied by nonmanufacturing companies? Explain.

EXERCISES

1. **Spending Variance.** Last year High Ridge Company operated at 165,000 direct labor hours and incurred total factory overhead cost of $483,500. A bud-

get of overhead shows that variable overhead should vary at the rate of $2 per hour and that fixed overhead should amount to $150,000.

Required: Compute the total overhead spending variance.

2. Spending Variance. A department of Magden Supply Company incurred the following overhead costs during the month while operating at 30,000 direct labor hours:

Indirect materials	$18,000
Indirect labor	10,000
Heat and light	4,500
Repairs and maintenance	3,200
Taxes and insurance	2,800
Depreciation	4,000
Total	$42,500

A budget for 30,000 direct labor hours shows indirect materials cost of $16,500, heat and light of $4,800, and repairs and maintenance of $3,000. All other budgeted costs agreed with the actual costs.

Required:

(1) Compute the overhead spending variance.
(2) Which of the costs seems to warrant more attention?
(3) Were the variances caused by differences in price or use? What can management do to find out why the variances occurred?

3. Efficiency Variance. Posnacht, Inc., made 46,000 units of a product line in the time allowed for the manufacture of 50,000 units. Factory overhead varies at the rate of $3 per hour. Fixed overhead has been budgeted at $120,000 for the year. Standards show that 5 units of product should be manufactured each hour.

Required: Compute the factory overhead efficiency variance.

4. Efficiency Variance. The La Barre Company has established 300,000 machine hours as normal capacity. A unit of product is to be manufactured each 30 minutes according to the standards. The standard variable overhead rate is $5 per machine hour, and the fixed overhead rate is equal to $1 per hour. In 1981, the company manufactured 400,000 units of product in 220,000 machine hours. One of the production managers reasons that 400,000 units of product should have been made in 200,000 machine hours. Hence, the company was over the standard by 20,000 hours; and the overhead efficiency variance was $100,000 (20,000 hours × $5 rate per hour).

Required:

(1) Determine the correct overhead efficiency variance.
(2) Explain why the calculation made by one of the production managers was or was not in error.

5. Controllable Variance. One of the departments of Janis Machine Company operated at 45,000 machine hours and incurred overhead of $186,000 during the month of August. The department produced what should have been produced in 40,000 hours. The factory overhead budget for 45,000 hours was $185,000 and $170,000 for 40,000 hours.

Required:

(1) Compute the controllable overhead variance.
(2) Split the controllable variance into a spending variance and an efficiency variance.
(3) From the information given, determine the variable overhead rate per hour.

6. Capacity Variance. From the records of Saunders Supply Company, you have derived the following information:

Actual variable overhead for the year...	$345,000
Budget of fixed overhead for the year..	$250,000
Actual hours of operation during the year..	48,000
Standard hours allowed to manufacture the 230,000 units made during the year...	46,000
Normal hours of operation for a year...	50,000

Required: Compute the capacity variance for the year.

7. Flexible Budget. Overhead budget data for two manufacturing departments of Fyfe Instruments, Inc., are given below in summary form.

Dept. 1

Factory overhead varies at the rate of $5 for each machine hour, and the fixed factory overhead is budgeted for the year at $450,000. At normal capacity, the department should operate at 150,000 machine hours.

Dept. 2

The department is expected to incur variable overhead of $120,000 when operating at 80,000 direct labor hours and is expected to incur $135,000 in variable overhead at 90,000 direct labor hours. The fixed overhead rate is $2.50 at a normal capacity of 100,000 direct labor hours.

Required: Prepare in summary form a flexible budget for each department showing costs at normal capacity and at 90%, 80%, and 70% of normal capacity. Determine the overhead rate per hour at normal capacity for each department.

8. Standard Product Cost and Variances. A budget of factory overhead at normal capacity was estimated by Vasquez Enterprises, Inc., at $720,000. Normal capacity was defined as 120,000 machine hours with a standard production of 3 units of product per machine hour. The fixed overhead rate per machine hour was $2.40. During the year the company manufactured 240,000 units of product in 90,000 machine hours. Actual overhead for the year was $552,000. The plant superintendent stated that 270,000 units should have been manufactured and that the standard overhead applied to production should be $540,000 (90,000 hours × $6 machine hour rate).

Required:

(1) Explain why the plant superintendent is incorrect.
(2) Compute the spending variance, the efficiency variance, and the capacity variance.
(3) Determine the controllable variance.

9. Efficiency and Capacity Variance. A flexible budget prepared for a normal operation of 60,000 direct labor hours shows that Helms Pipe Company should incur variable overhead of $60,000 and fixed overhead of $30,000. Two direct labor hours are required to produce each unit of product.

The company operated at 40,000 direct labor hours and incurred overhead equal to the cost budgeted for 40,000 hours. During the 40,000 hours, 25,000 units of product were manufactured.

Required:

(1) Prepare flexible budgets for 60,000, 50,000, and 40,000 direct labor hours.
(2) Compute the overhead efficiency variance. Was any fixed overhead included in the variance? Why or why not?
(3) Compute the overhead capacity variance. Was any variable overhead included in the variance? Why or why not?

10. Standard Product Cost and Variances. Campbell Liners, Inc., has established a standard variable overhead cost per machine hour of $4. The fixed overhead cost computed at a normal capacity of 150,000 machine hours has been set at a standard of $2 per machine hour. Four units of product are to be manufactured in a machine hour. During the year the company operated at 130,000 machine hours and manufactured 500,000 units of product.

Required:

(1) Compute the standard overhead cost per unit of product. Would this standard unit cost be different if a different quantity of products were defined as being normal production? Explain.
(2) What is the total budgeted fixed overhead?
(3) How much of the fixed overhead was absorbed by the products during the year?
(4) Compute the capacity variance.
(5) Compute the efficiency variance. Is fixed overhead included in the efficiency variance? Explain.

11. Overhead Variances. The Reiner Company has prepared a flexible budget of factory overhead for the year. A summarized portion of the budget is given below.

	Percentages of Normal Capacity		
	80%	*90%*	*100%*
Variable overhead	$27,600	$31,050	$34,500
Fixed overhead	28,000	28,000	28,000
Total overhead	$55,600	$59,050	$62,500

The company has budgeted 10,000 machine hours at the normal capacity level. Five units of product should be manufactured each machine hour. The company actually produced 40,000 units of product during the year in 9,000 hours. Actual overhead for the year amounted to $60,150.

Required:

(1) Compute the overhead spending variance.
(2) Determine the overhead efficiency variance.
(3) How much fixed overhead was costed to the products?
(4) Compute the capacity variance.

12. Overhead Variances. A flexible budget of factory overhead for Coblentz Fixtures, Inc., is summarized on the next page.

	Percentage of Normal Capacity				
	70%	80%	90%	100%	110%
Variable overhead...............	$168,000	$192,000	$216,000	$240,000	$264,000
Fixed overhead	120,000	120,000	120,000	120,000	120,000
Total overhead	$288,000	$312,000	$336,000	$360,000	$384,000

Standard cost is used to measure managerial performance. According to the standards established, 2 hours are required to produce 1 unit of product. When operating at a normal capacity of 120,000 machine hours, 60,000 units of product should be manufactured. Last year the company produced 42,000 units of product in 96,000 machine hours. The total variable overhead for the year was $197,500, and the total fixed overhead amounted to $124,000.

Required: Compute the overhead variance for the year. Analyze the variance, determining a spending variance, an efficiency variance, and a capacity variance.

13. Variances in a Service Enterprise. City Delivery Service delivers packages in the city area and hires drivers to make deliveries. Variable cost has been budgeted, and an average standard time has been established to make a delivery. According to the standards, it should be possible to make a delivery in an hour. The office is located in the center of the city, and it takes as much time to deliver to one location as it does to another. Fixed cost has been budgeted at $72,000 for the year. Under normal conditions, the company expects to make 15,000 deliveries in a year. The variable cost has been budgeted at $10 per hour. Last year the company made 12,500 deliveries in 14,000 hours and incurred a total cost of $215,000 including the fixed cost as budgeted.

Required:
(1) Compute the standard cost of making a delivery.
(2) Determine the spending variance and the efficiency variance.
(3) How much of the total variance can be considered to be a capacity variance?

14. Variances in a Service Enterprise. Four Corners Typing Service types manuscripts for students, professors, and the general public. A standard of 4 pages an hour has been established for straight copy that involves no equations or tabulations. The variable cost of operation has been estimated at a standard rate of $7 an hour. The fixed cost to rent an office and to rent typewriters has been estimated at $600 per month. In a normal month, the manager estimates that the business should operate at 500 hours. During July, 2,250 pages were typed in 450 hours. Actual variable cost is $3,080, and the fixed cost is in agreement with the budget.

Required:
(1) Determine the total standard cost for the 2,250 pages typed in July.
(2) Compute the total variance from standard cost and analyze the variance into a spending variance, an efficiency variance, and a capacity variance.

15. Labor and Overhead Variances. At a normal operating capacity, Donahoe Parts Company operates at 300,000 direct labor hours with a standard labor rate of $7. Variable factory overhead is applied at the rate of $5 per direct labor hour, and fixed overhead is applied at the rate of $4 per direct labor hour. Two units of product should be manufactured in an hour. Last year 500,000 units of product were manufactured in 240,000 direct labor hours. All labor hours were paid at the standard rate. Actual factory overhead for the year was as follows:

Variable	$1,186,000
Fixed...	1,200,000

Required:

(1) How much labor cost was saved by producing at more than the standard rate?

(2) What was the saving in variable overhead cost by using less than the standard direct labor hours?

(3) Compute the overhead spending variance and the capacity variance.

PROBLEMS

7-1. All Standard Cost Variances. Summarized manufacturing cost data from the records of Tucker Parts Company are given below.

(1) <u>Direct materials</u> — Purchased 40,000 units of materials at an actual cost of $84,000. Standard cost is $2 per unit of materials. Used 38,000 units of direct materials in production. Only 35,000 units should have been used.

(2) <u>Direct labor</u> — The standard rate is $7 per hour. The company operated at 60,000 direct labor hours but produced a quantity of product that should have been produced in 50,000 direct labor hours. All but 1,000 of the direct labor hours were paid for at the standard rate, and the 1,000 hours were paid for at the rate of $10 per hour.

(3) <u>Overhead</u> — The factory overhead budget for a normal capacity of 80,000 direct labor hours was $160,000. Actual overhead was $138,000.

Budget — 60,000 hours — $140,000
Budget — 50,000 hours — 130,000

Required: Compute all the variances determinable from the data given.

7-2. Variances in a Service Enterprise. Blaine Paving, Inc., contracts to pave residential driveways. Management has established time and cost standards for this work in order to control cost more effectively and to have a basis for estimating bids for customers. Based on past experience, it is estimated that an asphalt drive of 300 square meters can be rolled and packed down in a period of 2 hours per person with a crew of three workers. Each worker is paid $6 per hour. Gasoline, oil, and other supplies used vary at a rate of $2 an hour of elapsed time (not labor time). Fixed overhead has been budgeted at $60,000 for the year with normal labor hours established at 6,000 (hours elapsed multiplied by number of workers.) Last year the company paved 240 000 square meters of drive and operated at 4,500 labor hours at the standard labor rate with total variable overhead cost of $3,100 and total fixed overhead of $60,000.

Required:

(1) What was the total standard labor and overhead cost of paving 240 000 square meters of drive?

(2) Compute a spending and efficiency variance for labor and for overhead.

(3) What was the capacity variance?

7-3. Capacity Variance Analysis. Van Cort Company has the practical plant capacity to make 3,000,000 units of a certain product line each year. Normal

, Normal

capacity, however, provides for the production of only 2,500,000 units per year. At normal capacity, the variable overhead is budgeted at $500,000, and the fixed overhead is budgeted at $750,000. During the last year, 2,000,000 units were produced in 450,000 machine hours, which is 90% of the machine hours budgeted for a normal capacity operation. The sales department budgeted for the sale of 2,250,000 units but received orders for only 2,100,000 units. Difficulties in production were such that only 2,000,000 units were produced and delivered to the customers. Actual variable overhead for the year was $448,000, and fixed overhead was in agreement with the budget.

Required:
(1) Determine the factory overhead spending variance and efficiency variance.
(2) Determine the capacity variance.
(3) Compute a supplemental capacity variance expressed in number of product units that may reveal:
  (a) Excess plant capacity.
  (b) Failure of sales department to meet budget quotas.
  (c) Poor production scheduling.

7-4. Journal Entries for Flow of Costs. Silva Plastics Company has established standard cost for a unit of product manufactured as follows:

Materials (3 kilograms @ $1.50)	$ 4.50
Labor (1 hour @ $7)	7.00
Variable overhead ($4 per labor hour)	4.00
Fixed overhead ($6 per labor hour)	6.00
Total standard unit cost	$21.50

At normal operating capacity, 100,000 units of product should be manufactured in a year.

Cost data pertaining to the operations for the year are summarized below:

Materials purchased (200 000 kilograms)	$318,000
Materials used in production	182 000 kilograms
Labor hours	57,000 hours
Labor rate	$8 per hour
Factory overhead:	
Variable	$230,000
Fixed	$600,000

During the year, 60,000 units of product were put into production and were completed. There were no units in process at the beginning or at the end of the year.

Required: Prepare journal entries to record the flow of cost data from the time the materials were purchased until the products were completed. (Ignore withholdings from the wages of employees and credit Accounts Payable for all factory overhead costs incurred). Variances from the standard costs are to be segregated in the accounts.

7-5. Overhead Variance Analysis with Cost Detail. Standard costs have been established for Gulf Coast Pump Company. At a normal operating capacity of 200,000 machine hours, the company should produce 600,000 units of product in a year. Standard costs have been established at this level of operation and rate of output. The factory overhead cost in 1980 is given along with standard factory overhead budgets for 200,000 and 180,000 machine hours of operation.

	Actual Cost	180,000- Hour Budget	200,000- Hour Budget
Variable overhead:			
Supplies..	$ 93,000	$117,000	$130,000
Indirect materials	61,000	81,000	90,000
Indirect labor..................................	152,000	198,000	220,000
Maintenance....................................	75,000	90,000	100,000
Repairs..	14,000	18,000	20,000
Total...	$395,000	$504,000	$560,000
Fixed overhead:			
Supervision.....................................	$150,000	$150,000	$150,000
Depreciation	180,000	180,000	180,000
Heat and light.................................	45,000	45,000	45,000
Taxes and insurance......................	65,000	65,000	65,000
Total...	$440,000	$440,000	$440,000
Total overhead	$835,000	$944,000	$1,000,000

In 1980, the company manufactured 450,000 units of product in 140,000 machine hours of operation.

Required:

(1) Prepare a report that will show the spending variance for each item of overhead.

(2) Prepare another report that will show the efficiency variance.

(3) Identify the costs with relatively large spending variances.

(4) Determine the capacity variance.

7-6. Variances from Incomplete Data. The Maguire Manufacturing Company is in the process of relocating some of the plant offices at the Knoxville plant. Much of the data with respect to standard cost and variances for the past month were sent by the planning office to Anchorage, Alaska, by mistake and were lost on the route.

However, you do have some information and hope that you can reconstruct data that will be helpful in cost control.

Standard costs for each unit of the product line produced at the Knoxville plant are:

Direct materials (4 units of materials for each product unit)	$28.80
Direct labor (1/2 hour, each unit)	4.00
Factory overhead:	
Variable	6.00
Fixed	12.50
Total standard cost, each unit	$51.30

The plant operates at a normal rate of 40,000 product units each month and applies factory overhead to the products on the basis of direct labor hours.

Last month 200,000 units of direct materials were purchased at a cost of $1,660,000. The inventories of direct materials increased by 55,000 units.

During the month, 37,000 units of product were produced.

The total direct labor payroll for the month consisted of 16,000 labor hours at a total cost of $152,000. The labor rate variance was unfavorable by $24,000.

The factory overhead spending variance was unfavorable by $19,000, and capacity (or volume) variance was unfavorable by $37,500.

Required:

(1) Determine the direct materials quantity variance.
(2) Determine the direct materials price variance on the basis of materials purchased.
(3) Determine the direct labor efficiency variance.
(4) What was the budgeted fixed factory overhead for the month?
(5) How much fixed factory overhead was costed to the products during the month?
(6) Determine the factory overhead efficiency variance.
(7) How many direct labor hours should have been used for the production for the month?

7-7. Variances from Incomplete Data. Stephen Roget, a financial analyst for Croton Industries, Inc., has been given information with respect to standard cost variances for one of the plants. These variances are given below.

Materials quantity variance	$ 7,000 (unfavorable)
Labor rate variance	4,000 (unfavorable)
Labor efficiency variance	12,000 (favorable)
Factory overhead spending variance	3,000 (unfavorable)
Factory overhead efficiency variance	6,000 (favorable)
Factory overhead capacity variance	50,000 (unfavorable)

He has determined that the company has manufactured 50,000 units of product with standard costs as follows:

Direct materials	$ 700,000
*Direct labor	300,000
Variable factory overhead	150,000
Fixed factory overhead	250,000
Total standard cost	$1,400,000

*Standard labor time per product unit is 45 minutes.

The fixed factory overhead was in agreement with the budgeted fixed factory overhead.

Roget would like to use the variances to develop some of the cost data for the fiscal period.

Required:

(1) How many units of product should be manufactured at normal operating capacity?
(2) Determine the total fixed factory overhead.
(3) How many direct labor hours should have been used to manufacture 50,000 units of product?
(4) How many direct labor hours were used?
(5) What was the actual variable factory overhead cost?
(6) What was the budget of variable factory overhead for the actual time used to manufacture the 50,000 units of product?
(7) What was the budget of variable factory overhead for the required time to manufacture the 50,000 units of product?
(8) What was the actual direct labor cost?
(9) What was the standard cost of the direct materials that were actually used in production?

(10) Determine the standard unit cost of the product by cost element, dividing the factory overhead into a variable portion and a fixed portion.

7-8. Variance Analysis. Last year Folkes, Inc., manufactured 1,800,000 spring assemblies at a unit cost of over $5.16 each. This cost was well over the standard unit cost of less than $5 per unit. The company operates in a highly competitive industry and must make every effort to keep costs down.

Actual manufacturing costs for last year are given below.

Direct materials used	$6,630,000
Direct labor	705,000
Factory overhead	1,959,375
Total actual cost	$9,294,375

The direct materials were all acquired at the standard cost of $.85 per unit of materials. Four units of materials are required for each unit of product.

All direct labor hours were at the standard rate of $8 per hour with the exception of 2,500 hours at a rate of $10 per hour. The standard rate of production is 20 units of product per direct labor hour.

Normal capacity has been established at 100,000 direct labor hours per year. Last year the company operated at 87,500 direct labor hours. The fixed overhead is applied to the products at the rate of $.75 per unit of product, and the fixed overhead for the year was in agreement with the budgeted fixed overhead. The variable overhead for the year was 5% over the standard variable overhead cost.

Required:

(1) Determine the standard cost per unit of product. Show separate costs for direct materials, direct labor, variable overhead, and fixed overhead.
(2) Determine variances from the total standard cost, showing price and quantity variances for direct materials and rate and efficiency variances for direct labor.
(3) Analyze the overhead variance into a spending variance, an efficiency variance, and a capacity variance.
(4) Identify the unfavorable variances that were primarily responsible for the actual cost being in excess of standard.

7-9. Variance Analysis. Teller Machine Company produced 70,000 units of product during the month of March, 1980.

Four units of materials, each having a standard cost of $3, are required for each unit of product. The company purchased 300,000 units of materials at a cost of $915,000. During the month, 283,000 units of materials were used to produce the 70,000 units of product.

According to the standards, 70,000 units of product should be manufactured in 14,000 labor hours at a standard labor rate of $7.50 per hour. The actual labor time was 13,200 hours, and 12,000 of these hours were paid at the standard rate. The remaining hours were paid at the rate of $9.25 per hour.

The company has a normal operating capacity of 20,000 labor hours per month. The variable overhead cost is budgeted at $5 per labor hour, and the fixed overhead is budgeted at $160,000 for the month.

Actual overhead for the month amounted to $228,000. The fixed overhead was in agreement with the budget.

Required: Calculate price and quantity variances for direct materials and rate and efficiency variances for direct labor. Divide the factory overhead variance into a spending variance, an efficiency variance, and a capacity variance.

7-10. Fixed Overhead Cost Budgets and Rates. With a decline in sales volume, the superintendent of Hogan Mills, Inc., has been searching for ways to reduce both variable and fixed overhead costs. At the present time, the company has been operating at a normal capacity of 900,000 machine hours each year with a fixed overhead budget as given below.

Plant superintendence	$ 850,000
Indirect labor	610,000
Taxes and insurance	135,000
Repairs and maintenance	80,000
Depreciation	125,000
Total fixed overhead	$1,800,000

The normal level of capacity is to be reduced to 600,000 machine hours next year. Plant superintendence cost is to be reduced to $620,000 a year, indirect labor is to be reduced to $480,000, and all other fixed costs are expected to remain the same.

Standards at the present time show that 4 units of product should be manufactured per hour. With improved production scheduling, it is estimated that 5 units of product should be made per hour next year.

Required:

(1) At the present time, what is the fixed overhead rate per machine hour? per unit of product?

(2) According to standards established for next year, what is the expected fixed overhead rate per machine hour? per unit of product?

7-11. Efficiency Variance and Capacity Variance. The Trecartin Electric Company produces various lines of electrical appliances. One of the divisions manufactures a line of products that is sold for $60 per unit.

A standard cost accounting system is used. The standard direct materials cost per unit of product is $24, and the standard direct labor cost per unit of product is $3.50. There are seldom any variances in direct materials cost, and the only direct labor variance is ordinarily a favorable efficiency variance inasmuch as the employees generally are highly skilled and are motivated to produce at better than the standard rate. The employees are paid a bonus equal to the time saved in production. As a result, the direct labor cost per unit of product remains at $3.50.

In 1980 the division operated at a normal capacity of 800,000 direct labor hours and produced 1,800,000 units of product. At a standard rate of production, 1,600,000 units should be produced in 800,000 direct labor hours.

Competition in the industry made it necessary to reduce the selling price to $55 per unit for 1981. Also sales volume and production for the year were budgeted at 1,400,000 units. There were no variations from standard cost other than the production of 1,400,000 units in 600,000 direct labor hours.

A summary budget for factory overhead for normal operating capacity is given below.

Variable overhead (varies with direct labor hours)	$ 5,600,000
Fixed overhead	6,800,000
Total budgeted factory overhead	$12,400,000

The president of the division believes that the favorable overhead efficiency variance will overcome to a large extent the effect of the unfavorable capacity variance.

Required:

(1) What is the standard unit cost for the product line?
(2) Compute the actual unit cost for 1980, including the variances in the computation.
(3) Compute the actual unit cost for 1981, including the variances in the computation.
(4) Show the extent by which the favorable overhead efficiency variance compensated for the unfavorable overhead capacity variance.

7-12. Capacity Variance and Net Income. Ann Longworth estimated that Davis Products Company would report a gross margin of $4,800,000 for the year if production standards were met and if 300,000 units of product were sold during the year. Standard costs per unit are given below:

Direct materials..	$12
Direct labor (1/2 hour at $8 per hour)...	4
Variable overhead (rate of $6 per hour)...	3
Fixed overhead (at normal capacity of 150,000 hours)........................	5
Standard unit cost	$24

During the year, the company manufactured and sold 250,000 units of product at the estimated selling price of $40 per unit. Direct materials cost amounted to $3,000,000. The actual labor rate was in agreement with the standard rate, and the company operated at 125,000 direct labor hours. Variable costs were in agreement with the amount budgeted for 125,000 hours. Fixed overhead was in agreement with the amount budgeted.

Required:

(1) Prepare a partial income statement for Davis Products Company according to Longworth's estimates.
(2) Prepare a partial income statement for the year according to actual operations.
(3) Explain why the expected results were not realized.

7-13. Manufacturing Income Statement with Variance Analysis. A standard cost accounting system is used by Strunk Parts Company in a plant where farm tractor parts are manufactured. At normal operating capacity, the plant should manufacture 800,000 units of a given part with fixed factory overhead of $1,920,000.

During 1980, the company purchased 850,000 units of materials at a price of 60 cents per unit. The standard price per unit has been established at 50 cents per unit, and one unit of materials is required for each unit of product. In 1980, the plant used 642,000 units of materials to manufacture 600,000 units of product.

The standard labor rate is $7 per hour, and 5 units of product should be manufactured each direct labor hour. During 1980, the company recorded 116,000 hours of direct labor. The standard rate was paid for 112,000 hours, and the balance of the hours were paid for at the rate of $9 per hour.

Variable factory overhead varies at the rate of $6 per direct labor hour. The variable factory overhead for the year amounted to $704,000, and the fixed overhead was in agreement with the budgeted amount.

At the beginning of the year, there were 40,000 units of product in finished goods inventory at standard cost. At the end of the year, there were 20,000 units of product in finished goods inventory at standard cost. Each unit of product was sold for $9.50.

Required: Prepare an income statement for the manufacturing division for 1980 using standard costs. Show variances at the end of the statement.

7-14. Change in the Standards. The general manager of Hibbard Engines, Inc., believes that some improvements in operation can be incorporated in the standards and are necessary if the company is to maintain its position in the market.

The existing standards for one of the major product lines are given below on a unit-of-product basis.

Direct materials..	$ 28
Direct labor (4 hours each at $8)...	32
Variable overhead:	
Per unit of product..	5
Per hour (4 hours each at $5)...	20
Fixed overhead (at a normal capacity of 60,000 units of product per year)..	15
Total unit standard cost...	$100

The company has followed the practice of selling this product at 140% of standard manufactured cost.

Improvements in production have reduced the direct labor time per unit of product from 4 hours to 3 hours. Furthermore, the variable cost per direct labor hour can be reduced to $3. The total fixed overhead can be reduced to $750,000 for the year.

The company has a market for all the units that can be produced provided the selling price is competitive at no more than $125 per unit.

Required:

(1) Compute the selling price per unit under existing conditions.
(2) Prepare a new standard cost schedule per unit of product.
(3) Determine the new selling price at 140% of standard manufactured cost.
(4) With the new standard, how much profit should be earned for a year from the production and sale of 60,000 units of product?

7-15. Comparison of Years. Barnaby Liner Company has established standard cost for the production of one of its product lines as follows:

	Cost per Unit
Direct materials...	$ 7.50
Direct labor (2 hours each at $7)...	14.00
Variable overhead (2 hours at $5)	10.00
Fixed overhead (normal production of 40,000 units of product each year)	6.00
Unit standard cost..	$37.50

During 1980, the company manufactured and sold 40,000 units of product at a price of $60 per unit. The standard cost of direct materials used in production was $315,000. The company used 83,000 direct labor hours. All of these hours were at the standard labor rate with the exception of 1,500 hours which were at the rate of $10 per hour. Fixed overhead was in agreement with the budget, and the variable overhead was $438,000.

During 1981, the company manufactured and sold 36,000 units of product at a price of $60 per unit. The standard cost of direct materials used in production was $268,500. The company used 69,000 direct labor hours, all paid for at the standard rate. Fixed overhead was in agreement with the budget, and the variable overhead was $332,000.

Required:

(1) Prepare a comparative income statement for the manufacturing operation for 1980 and 1981. Show the variances at the bottom of the statement after computing the income from operations with standard cost.
(2) In which year did the company operate more efficiently? Explain.

7-16. Variances and Decrease in Profits. The president of Eicher Plastic Company is disappointed to find that the profit for one division was lower than expected in 1981.

The product manufactured by this division sells for $80 per unit, and 150,000 units were produced and sold as anticipated. The standard unit cost of the product is given below.

Direct materials..	$18
Direct labor (15 minutes of labor at $8 per hour)	2
Variable overhead (15 minutes at $12 per hour)...	3
Fixed overhead (based on normal production of 150,000 units per year)	5
Unit standard cost..	$28

During the year, the actual use of materials at standard cost amounted to $2,808,000. To produce these products, the company operated at 55,000 direct labor hours. The variable overhead cost was $732,000. The fixed overhead was in agreement with the budgeted amount.

The president recognizes that the profit may deviate to some extent from the standard manufacturing profit expected of $7,800,000, but in this case, the deviation is too much.

Required:

(1) Compute the actual income from operations for 1981.
(2) Compute the variances.
(3) Explain to the president what caused the profit to be lower than expected.

7-17. Variances and Bonus Payments. The employees at Selma Container Company receive a bonus equal to pay for the time saved in production. The standard rate of production for plastic bottles produced in one division of the plant is 600 bottles per hour. Employees in that division are paid at the rate of $6 per hour. Variable overhead varies at the rate of $1.80 per hour.

Production is automated to a large extent, but savings in labor time are possible by improvements in the facility of handling the materials in the processing operation.

During the month of May, the division operated at 35,000 direct labor hours and manufactured 25,200,000 bottles. The total variable overhead amounted to $63,000.

The bonus is computed on the basis of production for one month with payment being made to the employees in the following month.

Required:

(1) Compute the labor bonus for the production in the month of May.

(2) How much did the company save by the increased labor efficiency?

7-18. Variances and Bonus Payments. Dresen Implements Company has established a standard rate of production of 20 units of product per hour in one department of the plant. Employees who exceed this rate of production for a sustained period of one week receive a bonus equal to 50% pay for the time saved. Bonus checks are issued in the week following the week in which the standards are exceeded. The standard pay per labor hour is $7.20. Factory overhead varies at the rate of $8.40 per hour.

During one week in August, the employees worked a total of 800 labor hours and manufactured 26,000 units of product. The variable overhead for the week was $7,870.

Required:

(1) Compute the labor and overhead efficiency variances for the week.

(2) Calculate the net saving to the company for the week after subtracting the bonus.

(3) How much of the saving was lost because of the unfavorable overhead spending variance?

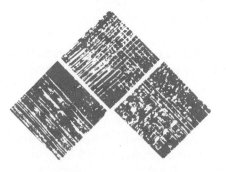

PART TWO
Analysis and Decision Making

8
VARIABLE COSTING

Fixed costs are troublesome in product costing because they tend to remain the same in total dollar amount within various ranges of productive output. This creates a problem in determining the cost to manufacture a unit of product. The unit cost depends upon how many units are manufactured in the same fiscal period.

ABSORPTION COSTING

According to generally accepted cost accounting theory underlying income determination, all manufacturing costs are allocated to the products either directly or indirectly. Accordingly, the cost of any manufactured article includes the cost of the direct materials, the cost of the direct labor, and an apportioned share of the other manufacturing costs. These other manufacturing costs, collectively referred to as factory overhead, differ greatly from each other. Some of the costs, such as the salary of the plant manager, depreciation, and insurance on the plant, tend to remain fixed within various ranges of output; other costs, such as the cost of supplies used, fuel, and electric power, may increase or decrease with changes in output. All of these costs, however, are to be identified with the manufactured products. This conventional theory of product costing is sometimes called an *absorption costing* or a *full costing method*, the terms being derived from the fact that the full or total manufacturing cost is to be absorbed by the products.

Each product line and each unit of product should bear its share of the total cost. However, some product lines may not be able to carry their full share of the total cost but may be able to contribute to the overall profitability of the firm. For example, a product line may be sold at a price which is sufficient to recover more than the variable cost required to produce it but which is not sufficient to recover all of its share of the fixed cost. By contrast, other product lines are able to bear their share of the total cost and produce a return on the total supporting investment. Management needs to know whether or not a product line can produce an adequate return on investment after absorbing its share of the overall cost. In the long run, both variable and fixed costs must be recovered with a remaining profit that is satisfactory in relation to the invested resources.

One of the more difficult problems in cost accounting centers around the allocation of cost to the various products. The cost that cannot be directly identified with any particular department, function, or product may be apportioned; but then there is always some doubt about the validity of the product cost. Because some costs cannot be directly identified with the product lines, they are apportioned on the basis of some measurable factor such as machine hours, labor hours, or the relative amount of space used in production. It is not easy to prove that costs should be traced to the products by some method of apportionment. In fact, it may even be said that the costs should not be apportioned at all.

The total fixed cost, for example, is not affected to any extent by differences in the volume of productive output that fall within an established range. Therefore, when only a few units of product are made, the fixed cost per unit is high. The unit cost decreases as more units are produced. This in turn means that the profit for the year is influenced not only by the volume of sales, the sales price, and the cost of production but also by the quantity of units manufactured during the year.

As explained in the earlier chapters, factory overhead is applied to the products by using a predetermined rate. The fixed factory overhead, for example, is budgeted along with the hours of operation at a normal level of production. The budgeted cost is divided by the budgeted hours to obtain a rate per hour that can be used in costing the products. The products then are assigned a normal or a standard charge for fixed overhead. Variable factory overhead cost is, of course, assigned to the products in the same way. If the plant operates above or below its normal capacity, the fixed overhead will be over- or underabsorbed. The over- or underabsorbed overhead is designated as the capacity variance and is written off to operations for the year.

VARIABLE COSTING

In cost accounting there will always be the problem of cost apportionment. The real issue is whether or not certain costs should be assigned to the products. According to the *variable costing concept*, only the variable manufacturing costs should be assigned to the products. The fixed manufacturing costs should be written off each year as period costs. An investment in facilities and other productive factors is required before any products can be manufactured. There are fixed costs, such as depreciation, insurance, taxes, heat and light, and salaries of plant management, that must be incurred each year. Hence, the fixed cost of manufacturing is not a product cost but is the annual cost incurred in operating a plant. The fixed manufacturing cost, like the selling and administrative cost, is too remotely related to the product to be assigned as a part of its cost. Following this theory, the fixed cost of manufacturing should be expensed each year and not included as a part of the cost of an inventory of product.

Variable costing is more widely known as *direct costing*. This is unfortunate. It is not correct to say that the direct cost is attached to the products; rather, the variable cost is assigned. A *direct cost* can be identified readily with a department, a function, a unit of product, or some other relevant unit. Factory overhead cost is an indirect cost with respect to the products, yet the variable factory overhead is included in product cost when the direct costing method is used. Direct costs can be either fixed or variable. For example, a machine operator's salary may be a direct cost and may be fixed under a guaranteed annual wage agreement. The salary is a fixed cost; and although it may be directly identified with a product line, it is not considered a part of the product cost in direct costing. A variable cost that may or may not be directly identified with the product becomes part of the product cost in direct costing; hence, direct costing is more appropriately called *variable costing*. Both terms should be recognized, but the term "variable costing" is a more accurate designation.

ABSORPTION AND VARIABLE
COSTING COMPARED

The differences between the two costing concepts can be emphasized by showing how an income statement prepared by the absorption costing method compares with an income statement prepared by the variable costing method. To illustrate, a comparative income statement is presented on page 219 for Platt Supply Company using the data that appear below and at the top of the next page.

	PER UNIT OF PRODUCT
Selling price	$80
Variable manufacturing cost	10
Variable selling and administrative expense	5

TOTAL COST

Fixed manufacturing cost for the year $2,000,000
Fixed selling and administrative expense for the year 500,000

When products are costed by the absorption costing method, the fixed manufacturing cost is allocated to the products. Assume that the company produced 50,000 units of product at its normal capacity. The fixed manufacturing cost per unit is $40 ($2,000,000 ÷ 50,000 units). The total manufacturing cost per unit of product is $50.

Variable manufacturing cost per unit $10
Fixed manufacturing cost per unit 40
Total manufacturing cost per unit $50

If the variable costing method is used, however, only the variable manufacturing cost of $10 a unit will be assigned to the products.

Assume that 50,000 units of product were manufactured and sold in 1980 and that there were no units in inventory at the beginning or at the end of the year. The income statement is illustrated using both the absorption costing method and the variable costing method.

Platt Supply Company
Comparative Income Statement
For the Year Ended December 31, 1980

	Absorption Costing	Variable Costing
Number of units manufactured and sold	50,000	50,000
Sales (50,000 units @ $80)	$4,000,000	$4,000,000
Cost of goods manufactured and sold:		
Variable manufacturing cost (50,000 units @ $10)	$ 500,000	$ 500,000
Fixed manufacturing cost (50,000 units @ $40)	2,000,000	—0—
Cost of goods manufactured and sold	$2,500,000	$ 500,000
Gross margin	$1,500,000	
Manufacturing margin		$3,500,000
Selling and administrative expenses:		
Variable selling and administrative expense (50,000 units @ $5)	$ 250,000	250,000
Fixed selling and administrative expense	500,000	—0—
Total selling and administrative expense	$ 750,000	
Contribution margin		$3,250,000
Fixed costs:		
Manufacturing		$2,000,000
Selling and administrative		500,000
Total fixed cost		$2,500,000
Income before income tax	$ 750,000	$ 750,000
Income tax (40%)	300,000	300,000
Net income	$ 450,000	$ 450,000

The net income, in this case, is the same under either costing method. All of the fixed cost for the year has been matched against revenue in both methods. Due to the absence of inventories, the fixed manufacturing cost has not been carried over from an earlier year as a part of beginning inventory cost, nor has it been included in inventory at the end of the year. In the absorption costing column, the fixed manufacturing cost is deducted as a part of the cost of goods sold. In the variable costing column, the fixed manufacturing cost is deducted as a period cost.

The excess of the revenue over the variable manufacturing cost of goods sold is designated as *manufacturing margin*. It is the amount contributed to the recovery of fixed manufacturing cost, operating expense, and profit. The difference between the revenue and all variable costs is the *contribution margin*. It is equal to the revenue minus all variable costs and is the net contribution to fixed cost and profit. The contribution margin concept is most important and can be applied by management in planning profit and in making certain types of decisions. The contribution margin concept and applications are discussed later in this chapter.

A BALANCE OF SALES AND PRODUCTION

When sales and production are in balance at any level of operation, the results tend to be the same under either absorption or variable costing. If standard costs are assigned to the products, each unit of product bears the same amount of cost. Therefore, when sales and production are in balance, the number of units in the beginning inventory is equal to the number of units in the ending inventory, and the costs of the beginning and ending inventories are the same. As a result, fixed manufacturing cost equal in amount to the fixed manufacturing cost for the year is deducted from revenue by either costing method. If the absorption costing method is used, the fixed manufacturing cost is deducted as cost of goods sold. If the variable costing method is used, the fixed manufacturing cost is deducted as an expense of the fiscal period.

For example, assume that Platt Supply Company had an inventory of 10,000 units of product on hand at the beginning of a certain year and that 50,000 units were manufactured and sold during the year. The selling price and cost data are the same for beginning inventory and current production. A partial income statement showing results of the manufacturing operation by the two costing methods is given at the top of the next page.

Fixed cost of $2,000,000 has been deducted in both columns. The cost of production (the cost of goods manufactured in this case) is equal to the cost of goods sold; and in the absorption costing column, the fixed cost of $2,000,000 has been deducted (included in $2,500,000) as cost of goods sold. In the variable costing column, the same amount has been deducted as a period cost.

Platt Supply Company
Partial Comparative Income Statement
(Manufacturing Operation)
For the Year Ended December 31, 19--

	Absorption Costing	Variable Costing
Number of units manufactured and sold...............................	50,000	50,000
Sales (50,000 units @ $80)..	$4,000,000	$4,000,000
Cost of goods sold:		
Inventory, beginning of year:		
[10,000 units @ ($10 + $40)]	$ 500,000	
(10,000 units @ $10)...		$ 100,000
Cost of production:		
[50,000 units @ ($10 + $40)]	2,500,000	
(50,000 units @ $10)...		500,000
Cost of merchandise available for sale	$3,000,000	$ 600,000
Less inventory, end of year:		
[10,000 units @ ($10 + $40)]	500,000	
(10,000 units @ $10)...		100,000
Cost of goods sold	$2,500,000	$ 500,000
Gross margin	$1,500,000	
Manufacturing margin		$3,500,000
Less fixed manufacturing cost.....................................		2,000,000
Income from manufacturing......................................	$1,500,000	$1,500,000

If the company operates above or below its normal operating capacity, part of the fixed manufacturing cost is deducted as product cost under the absorption costing method, and the balance of the fixed manufacturing cost is shown as a capacity variance. An amount equal to the fixed manufacturing cost for the year is deducted from revenue assuming a standard cost system and assuming that inventories are not increased or decreased during the year.

In another year, assume that Platt Supply Company began the year with no inventory, operated at 90 percent of its normal capacity, and manufactured and sold 45,000 units of product. There were no changes in the selling price or the cost. An income statement prepared by the absorption costing method and the variable costing method is illustrated at the top of page 222.

Again, note that the net income as reported by both costing methods is the same. This is true whether or not the company operates at normal capacity as long as there is a balance between sales and production.

Platt Supply Company
Comparative Income Statement
For the Year Ended December 31, 19--

	Absorption Costing	Variable Costing
Number of units manufactured and sold..............................	45,000	45,000
Sales (45,000 units @ $80)...	$3,600,000	$3,600,000
Cost of goods manufactured and sold:		
Variable manufacturing cost (45,000 units @$10)............	$ 450,000	$ 450,000
Fixed manufacturing cost (45,000 units @ $40)................	1,800,000	—0—
Cost of goods manufactured and sold (standard cost).........	$2,250,000	$ 450,000
Capacity variance (5,000 units @ $40)................................	200,000	
Total	$2,450,000	
Gross margin	$1,150,000	
Manufacturing margin		$3,150,000
Selling and administrative expenses:		
Variable selling and administrative expense (45,000 units @ $5)...	$ 225,000	225,000
Fixed selling and administrative expense..........................	500,000	—0—
Total selling and administrative expense	$ 725,000	
Contribution margin...		$2,925,000
Fixed costs:		
Manufacturing...		$2,000,000
Selling and administrative..		500,000
Total fixed cost		$2,500,000
Income before income tax	$ 425,000	$ 425,000
Income tax (40%)..	170,000	170,000
Net income..	$ 255,000	$ 255,000

SALES AND PRODUCTION OUT OF BALANCE

Differences in net income reported under the two costing methods appear when the sales for the year are more or less than the production. When absorption costing is employed, the fixed manufacturing cost is shifted from one year to another as a part of the inventory cost. If a company produces more than it sells in a given year, not all of the current fixed manufacturing cost is deducted against revenue; part of it is held as inventory. This fixed cost will be released as part of the cost of goods sold in a later year, perhaps in a year when sales are in excess of production.

Hence, profit does not necessarily increase with increases in sales revenue. In fact, profit decreases if the effect of shifting the fixed cost from one year to another as a part of inventory cost is more than the increased contribution margin to be derived from the increased sales.

Management may find it difficult to understand how profit can decrease with increased sales volume and no change in selling price and cost. Seemingly, profit should increase when sales revenue increases. The shift of fixed manufacturing cost from one year to another must be recognized when an absorption costing system is used.

The peculiarity in profit behavior is illustrated by income statement data for 1981 and 1982. The selling price and cost data remain the same. Sales and production data follow:

1981 —	Produced	50,000 units
	Sold	45,000 units
1982 —	Produced	45,000 units
	Sold	50,000 units

A comparative income statement prepared by the absorption costing method for 1981 and 1982 is illustrated below.

The income statement shows that Platt Supply Company earned less in 1982 than it did in 1981, and yet more units were sold in 1982 with no change in the selling price or the cost structure. Ordinarily profit is expected to increase with increases in sales volume.

Platt Supply Company
Comparative Income Statement
(Absorption Costing)
For the Years Ended December 31, 1982 and 1981

	1982	1981
Number of units manufactured	45,000	50,000
Number of units sold	50,000	45,000
Sales	$4,000,000	$3,600,000
Cost of goods sold:		
Inventory, beginning of year	$ 250,000	—0—
Current production costs:		
Variable cost	450,000	$ 500,000
Fixed cost	1,800,000	2,000,000
Cost of merchandise available for sale	$2,500,000	$2,500,000
Less inventory, end of year	—0—	250,000
Cost of goods sold (standard cost)	$2,500,000	$2,250,000
Capacity variance	200,000	—0—
Total	$2,700,000	$2,250,000
Gross margin	$1,300,000	$1,350,000
Selling and administrative expenses:		
Variable cost	$ 250,000	$ 225,000
Fixed cost	500,000	500,000
Total selling and administrative expense	$ 750,000	$ 725,000
Income before income tax	$ 550,000	$ 625,000
Income tax (40%)	220,000	250,000
Net income	$ 330,000	$ 375,000

The income statement prepared by the absorption costing method tends to conceal the fact that fixed manufacturing cost from 1981 in the amount of $200,000 (5,000 × $40) has been shifted to 1982 as a part of the inventory carry-over to 1982. The reduction in income before income tax of $75,000 can be explained as follows:

Increased revenue (5,000 more units @ $80)..		$400,000
Increased variable costs:		
Manufacturing (5,000 more units @ $10)....	$ 50,000	
Selling and administrative (5,000 more units @ $5)..	25,000	75,000
Increased contribution margin		$325,000
Less fixed cost included in inventory (5,000 units @ $40 = $200,000):		
Shift of fixed cost out of 1981 by inventory carry-over..	$200,000	
Shift of fixed cost into 1982 by inventory carry-over..	200,000	400,000
Decrease in income before income tax............		$ 75,000

An income statement on a variable costing basis shows that the final contribution margin has increased in 1982 as a result of selling 5,000 more units of product. The fixed manufacturing cost is not transferred from one year to another as part of the inventory cost. A comparative income statement on a variable costing basis for 1981 and 1982 is given below.

Platt Supply Company
Comparative Income Statement
(Variable Costing)
For the Years Ended December 31, 1982 and 1981

	1982	1981
Number of units manufactured	45,000	50,000
Number of units sold...	50,000	45,000
Sales	$4,000,000	$3,600,000
Cost of goods sold:		
Inventory, beginning of year	$ 50,000	—0—
Current production cost, variable	450,000	$ 500,000
Cost of merchandise available for sale	$ 500,000	$ 500,000
Less inventory, end of year	—0—	50,000
Cost of goods sold	$ 500,000	$ 450,000
Manufacturing margin	$3,500,000	$3,150,000
Less variable selling and administrative expense	250,000	225,000
Contribution margin..	$3,250,000	$2,925,000
Less fixed costs:		
Manufacturing...	$2,000,000	$2,000,000
Selling and administrative...	500,000	500,000
Total fixed cost	$2,500,000	$2,500,000
Income before income tax	$ 750,000	$ 425,000
Income tax (40%)	300,000	170,000
Net income...	$ 450,000	$ 255,000

The income statement as prepared by the variable costing method shows that the net income was greater in 1982 when more units were sold. The income before income tax in 1982 was $325,000 greater than it was in 1981. This would be expected, considering that 5,000 more units were sold with each unit making a contribution of $65 to fixed cost and profit (selling price of $80 minus variable unit manufacturing cost of $10 and variable selling and administrative expense of $5). The profit tends to vary with sales volume when the variable costing method is used. However, differences attributable to a lack of balance between sales and production are not revealed by variable costing. Sales may be overemphasized at the expense of production. In reality, profit depends upon both sales and production.

PROFITS AND INVENTORY

With a standard absorption costing system, profit can be shifted from one year to another with increases or decreases in inventory. Management should be aware of this effect in evaluating operations. For example, assume that Platt Supply Company, in preparing a budget for the next year, estimates sales of 40,000 units with price and cost data remaining the same. There is no inventory at the beginning of the year. With sales of 40,000 units expected, the company may plan to produce 40,000 units. However, the profit for the year can be increased by producing 50,000 units and selling 40,000 units, as shown in the table below.

	50,000 UNITS PRODUCED	40,000 UNITS PRODUCED
Sales (40,000 units @ $80)	$3,200,000	$3,200,000
Cost of goods sold:		
Cost of production:		
(40,000 units @ $50)		$2,000,000
(50,000 units @ $50)	$2,500,000	
Cost of merchandise available for sale	$2,500,000	$2,000,000
Less inventory, end of year	500,000	—0—
	$2,000,000	$2,000,000
*Capacity variance	—0—	400,000
Cost of goods sold	$2,000,000	$2,400,000
Income from manufacturing	$1,200,000	$ 800,000

*Production at 40,000 units is 80 percent of the normal capacity of 50,000 units. Hence, 20 percent of the fixed manufacturing cost of $2,000,000 was not absorbed by the products.

Income has been increased merely by building up the inventory. In both examples, the total fixed manufacturing cost for the year has been matched against revenue. With production at 80 percent of normal capacity, 80 percent of the fixed manufacturing cost is charged to the products produced and sold. The remaining 20 percent is deducted as a capacity variance. At normal capacity, the products bear all of the fixed manufacturing cost; but the portion of the fixed manufacturing cost attached to the ending inventory is not deducted as a part of the cost of goods sold but is carried over as a cost to the next year. As a result, the income is increased by the amount of fixed manufacturing cost included in the inventory at the end of the year.

EMPHASIS ON PRODUCTION OR SALES

In absorption costing, the effects of sales and production are combined. Particular emphasis is placed upon plant utilization. The cost of idle facilities either is added to product cost or is shown separately as a capacity variance.

In variable costing, the emphasis is placed on sales. The cost of each unit of product manufactured is not affected because of changes in the level of activity. Unit variable cost is assumed to remain the same over certain ranges of output. Of course, both unit variable cost and total fixed cost may change in certain production levels. However, the data used for variable costing apply to a range of output at which unit variable cost and total fixed cost are relatively constant. Variable costing serves a useful purpose in bringing out the relationships between prices, costs, and volume.

But if management relies too heavily on variable cost analysis, it may be deluded into thinking that the company can operate profitably at low contribution margin rates only to find that volume does not come up to expectations. Selling at less than normal prices may be helpful in short-term situations, but in the long run this policy may result in margins that are not adequate in relation to invested resources. Short-term expediency should be recognized for what it is and should not be allowed to become a part of long-term strategy. Both costing methods can be useful when applied in appropriate circumstances.

THE ADVANTAGES OF VARIABLE COSTING

Variable costing is particularly useful to management in applications where the relative profitability of product lines is to be determined or where the effect of changes in volume, prices, or costs is to be calculated. When fixed cost is allocated to the products, analysis by product line becomes more difficult.

The following advantages to be derived from variable costing are summarized in NA(C)A Bulletin, Research Series No. 23:

1. Cost-volume-profit relationship data wanted for profit planning purposes is readily obtained from the regular accounting statements.

Hence management does not have to work with two separate sets of data to relate one to the other.

2. The profit for a period is not affected by changes in absorption of fixed expenses resulting from building or reducing inventory. Other things remaining equal (e.g., selling prices, costs, sales mix), profits move in the same direction as sales when direct costing is in use.

3. Manufacturing cost and income statements in the direct cost form follow management's thinking more closely than does the absorption cost form for these statements. For this reason, management finds it easier to understand and to use direct cost reports.

4. The impact of fixed costs on profit is emphasized because the total amount of such cost for the period appears in the income statement.

5. Marginal income figures facilitate relative appraisal of products, territories, classes of customers, and other segments of the business without having the results obscured by allocation of joint fixed costs.

6. Direct costing ties in with such effective plans for cost control as standard costs and flexible budgets. In fact, the flexible budget is an aspect of direct costing and many companies thus use direct costing methods for this purpose without recognizing them as such.

7. Direct cost constitutes a concept of inventory cost which corresponds closely with the current out-of-pocket expenditure necessary to manufacture the goods.[1]

The data produced by variable costing are easily understood by management. By considering the troublesome fixed costs as period costs rather than product costs, sales revenue can be directly related to the variable costs. The difference between the sales revenue and the variable cost is the contribution of the products to the recovery of fixed cost and to profit.

THE DISADVANTAGES OF VARIABLE COSTING

Variable costing may encourage a shortsighted approach to profit planning at the expense of the long-run situation. Over a short period of time, there may be an advantage in selling products at prices that are below the total unit cost. Profit is made so long as the fixed cost is covered by the sales from regular operations and so long as the selling price is in excess of the unit variable cost. Or in other cases, the fixed cost that would not be covered otherwise may be recovered through making sales at a price below the total unit cost. Products may also be sold in another market at less than the full cost to absorb idle plant capacity. This approach should be recognized, however, for what it is, a short-term expediency.

In the final analysis, all costs must be recovered along with an adequate return on investment. The product lines that cannot carry their share of the fixed cost are reducing the overall profit. A low-profit line may be carried to round out the other product lines or as a cus-

---

[1]*NA(C)A Bulletin, Research Series No. 23,* "Direct Costing" (New York: National Association of Cost Accountants, 1953), p. 1127.

tomer service. But unless there is some compelling reason for continuing with low-profit products, these products should be replaced with more profitable items.

Variable costing tends to give the impression that variable cost is recovered first, that fixed cost is recovered later, and that finally profit is realized. Actually the revenue from the sale of each unit of product contains a portion of variable cost, fixed cost, and profit. No one cost has priority over another, and each unit of product earns a share of the profit.

The nonacceptability of variable costing for general reporting purposes and for income tax is not a valid argument against the use of the method in reporting to management. There are various cost concepts and techniques like variable costing that are useful to management but that are not acceptable in reporting to outsiders. If they can be utilized by management, they should not be discarded.

VARIABLE COSTING IN PLANNING AND DECISION MAKING

The concept of variable costing may be applied in the measurement of income, but it is most important in planning and decision making. For example, a certain line of product selling for $10 a unit with a variable cost of $7 contributes $3 per unit to the fixed cost and profit. If the fixed cost amounts to $300,000 a year, the company must sell 100,000 units to break even ($300,000 fixed cost ÷ $3 unit contribution margin). As defined in Chapter 4, the *break-even point* is the point at which there is neither profit nor loss.

In this example, management knows that at least 100,000 units must be sold if there is to be no loss. In addition, management plans profit on the basis of the expected contribution margin. Suppose that income before income tax is budgeted at $120,000. The contribution margin must then be equal to the fixed cost of $300,000 plus the budgeted profit of $120,000, or $420,000. The company must sell 140,000 units of a product yielding a $3 contribution margin a unit to cover the fixed cost of $300,000 and to earn income before income tax of $120,000.

Management may also plan to sell a product at a regular price in one market and to sell the same product at a reduced price in another market. It is presumed, of course, that the additional sales can be made without disturbing the regular market or without violating any price discrimination laws. The fixed cost does not have to be considered. The additional profit that can be obtained from selling at a lower price in another market can be calculated easily from variable cost information.

Kelly Forms, Inc., manufactures and sells 150,000 units of a product that sells for $20 a unit. The variable manufacturing cost amounts to $12 per unit, and the fixed manufacturing cost amounts to $600,000. The results of the manufacturing operation appear as follows:

Sales (150,000 units @ $20)..	$3,000,000
Cost of goods sold (150,000 units @ $12 unit variable cost)...	1,800,000
Contribution margin..	$1,200,000
Fixed cost	600,000
Income from manufacturing...	$ 600,000

An opportunity presents itself to sell 50,000 additional units at a price of $14 per unit. Apparently the opportunity should be rejected because the manufacturing cost is $16 per unit according to conventional or absorption costing with normal capacity defined at 150,000 units of product. There is a unit variable cost of $12 and a unit fixed cost of $4 ($600,000 ÷ 150,000 units). Even when 200,000 units are produced, the unit fixed cost would still seem too high at $3 a unit ($600,000 ÷ 200,000 units) to permit the sale of products at $14 per unit. Yet variable costing shows that Kelly Forms, Inc., can earn an additional profit of $100,000 by accepting this opportunity. The profit computation is shown below:

	TOTAL	REGULAR OPERATIONS	ADDITIONAL SALES
Sales..	$3,700,000	$3,000,000	$700,000
Cost of goods sold.................	2,400,000	1,800,000	600,000
Contribution margin.............	$1,300,000	$1,200,000	$100,000
Fixed cost..............................	600,000		
Income from manufacturing.......................................	$ 700,000		

The sale of the additional units has no effect upon the fixed cost. In making this type of decision, only the additional revenue and the additional cost are important.

The distinction between the variable cost and the fixed cost can be helpful in planning profit and in making decisions with respect to the pricing and sale of the various product lines. For managerial purposes, it is not essential that variable costing be used for income measurement. But the data processing system should furnish information on variable cost and fixed cost for use in planning operations and in making decisions.

VARIABLE COSTING AND BUDGET VARIANCES

For cost control purposes, however, a distinction between variable and fixed costs may not be too important; nor will it make much difference whether products are costed with the variable manufacturing cost or total manufacturing cost when the objective is to control the total cost of the manufacturing operation.

For example, assume that Maguire Tool Company budgeted sales and manufacturing costs for 1981 as follows:

Estimated production		200,000 product units
Estimated sales		180,000 product units

	PER UNIT OF PRODUCT	TOTAL
Sales revenue (180,000 units sold)	$5	$900,000
Variable cost (200,000 units produced)	2	400,000
Fixed cost (normal production of 200,000 product units)	1	200,000

There was no inventory on hand at the beginning of the year.

During the year, the company sold 180,000 units at $5 apiece and incurred a variable manufacturing cost of $412,000 and a fixed manufacturing cost of $208,000. The actual variable cost was $12,000 more than budgeted for the production of 200,000 units, and the actual fixed cost was $8,000 more than budgeted resulting in a total unfavorable variance for the year of $20,000.

It must be remembered that fixed costs are fixed only in the sense that they do not vary with changes in productive output or activity. They are not fixed in the sense that they cannot be changed. An outside influence, such as an increase in property tax rates or a change in management policy with respect to discretionary cost, can result in a change in the fixed cost.

A comparison of the budgeted income statement with the actual income statement is given on a variable costing basis, below, and on an absorption costing basis, on the following page.

Maguire Tool Company
Income Statement (Variable Costing)
Budget and Actual Comparison
For the Year Ended December 31, 1981

	Budget	Actual	Variance Over (Under) Budget
Sales	$900,000	$900,000	—0—
Cost of goods sold:			
Variable manufacturing cost	$400,000	$412,000	$12,000
Less inventory, end of year (20,000 units @ $2)	40,000	40,000	—0—
Cost of goods sold	$360,000	$372,000	$12,000
Manufacturing margin	$540,000	$528,000	$(12,000)
Less fixed manufacturing cost	200,000	208,000	8,000
Income from manufacturing	$340,000	$320,000	$(20,000)

Maguire Tool Company
Income Statement (Absorption Costing)
Budget and Actual Comparison
For the Year Ended December 31, 1981

	Budget	Actual	Variance Over (Under) Budget
Sales..	$900,000	$900,000	—0—
Cost of goods sold:			
Variable manufacturing cost...........................	$400,000	$412,000	$12,000
Fixed manufacturing cost................................	200,000	208,000	8,000
Total manufacturing cost	$600,000	$620,000	$20,000
Less inventory, end of year (20,000 units @			
$3 standard unit cost)...................................	60,000	60,000	—0—
Cost of goods sold...	$540,000	$560,000	$20,000
Income from manufacturing..............................	$360,000	$340,000	$(20,000)

A review of the statements shows that the income reported by absorption costing is $20,000 more than the income reported by variable costing. The budgeted statements show the same difference. This difference arises because the fixed cost of $20,000 is included in the ending inventory and will be carried over to 1982 under the absorption costing method, whereas it is expensed as a period cost under the variable costing method. The budget variance is $20,000 in both cases.

The budgeted and actual cost comparison is not affected by the costing method selected. The cost comparison is based on the total cost that is incurred and used in production. The method used to match costs against revenue is important in measuring income but is of little importance when the objective is to control costs.

QUESTIONS

1. Why do fixed costs create difficulties in product costing?

2. In conventional cost accounting practice, how is the fixed factory overhead cost applied to the products?

3. How is a fixed manufacturing cost shifted from one year to another in absorpotion costing?

4. When the variable costing concept is employed, how is the fixed factory overhead cost applied to the products?

5. How does absorption costing differ from variable costing?

6. The fixed manufacturing cost should be treated as a period cost. Give arguments to support this statement. Give arguments against it.

7. Why is there no capacity variance under variable costing?

8. What is the contribution margin?

9. Why is the concept of a contribution margin important to management?

10. When a company sells the same number of units that it produces, the profit as reported by absorption costing and by variable costing tends to be the same. Explain.

11. If a company sells more units than it produces, would the profit reported by absorption costing tend to be higher or lower than the profit reported by variable costing? Why?

12. Explain why profit may be higher with a standard absorption cost system when production volume exceeds sales volume.

13. Assume that a company is operating at a profit. Can the profit be increased by selling additional units at a price that is only slightly higher than the variable cost per unit?

14. Why might variable costing be looked upon as a shortsighted approach to profit planning?

15. Should management make use of techniques that may not be accepted for use in the preparation of financial statements for the public? Explain.

EXERCISES

1. Contribution Margin. Higgins Stores, Inc., reported sales of $1,640,000 during 1980. The variable cost of the operation amounted to 60% of sales revenue. The fixed cost was $280,000 for 1980.

Required: Prepare a summary income statement that shows contribution margin and income before income tax.

2. Contribution Margin. Colby Manufacturing company sold 80,000 units of a product line at a price of $50 per unit in 1980. The variable manufacturing cost for the year was $2,800,000. The fixed manufacturing cost was $300,000. Selling and administrative costs were $3 per unit sold. The fixed selling and administrative expenses were $260,000.

Required: Prepare a summary income statement showing the manufacturing margin, the contribution margin, and the income before income tax.

3. Variable and Absorption Costing. Hector Equipment Company operated at 70% of normal capacity in 1980 and manufactured 140,000 units of product. There was no inventory at the beginning of the year. The company sold 120,000 units during the year at a price of $20 per unit. The variable manufacturing cost was $14 per unit, and the actual and budgeted fixed manufacturing cost was $400,000 in total.

Required: Prepare a summary income statement for the manufacturing operation:
   (1) Using the variable costing method.
   (2) Using the absorption costing method.

4. Variable and Absorption Costing. During 1980, Ressler Forms, Inc., operated at normal capacity and made 400,000 units of product. The variable manufacturing cost for 400,000 units was equal to 70% of the sales revenue of

$2,080,000 derived from the sale of 320,000 units. The total fixed manufacturing cost for the year was $440,000. There was no inventory at the beginning of the year.

Required:

(1) Prepare a summary income statement for the manufacturing operation using the absorption costing method.

(2) Prepare a summary income statement for the manufacturing operation using the variable costing method.

5. Sales and Production Out of Balance. Production and cost data are given below for Pratt Motors, Inc.

	1981	1980
Number of units manufactured	32,000	40,000
Number of units sold	40,000	32,000
Unit selling price	$20	$20
Unit variable manufacturing cost	$ 4	$ 4
Total fixed manufacturing cost	$480,000	$480,000

In 1980, the company operated at a normal level of capacity. There was no inventory on hand at the beginning of 1980.

Required:

(1) Prepare a comparative income statement for the manufacturing operation for the two years on a standard absorption costing basis.

(2) Explain the difference in income from the manufacturing operation, pointing out why the income for 1981 was higher or lower than it was in 1980.

6. Sales and Production Out of Balance. Production and cost data are given for Todd Fabric Company.

	1981	1980
Number of units manufactured	80,000	50,000
Number of units sold	40,000	45,000
Unit selling price	$100	$100
Unit variable manufacturing cost	$25	$25
Unit fixed manufacturing cost	$50	$50

There was no inventory of finished product on hand at the beginning of 1980, and the company manufactures 80,000 units of product at normal operating capacity.

Required:

(1) Prepare a comparative income statement for the manufacturing operation for the two years on a standard absorption costing basis.

(2) Explain the difference in income from the manufacturing operation, pointing out why the income for 1981 was higher or lower than it was in 1980.

7. Variable Costing and Income Differences. The president of Santa Rosa Mills, Inc., has been examining past income statement data in an attempt to estimate income expected for the next year. Past data are given in the table which appears at the top of the following page.

The fixed cost per unit was computed at a normal operating level of 4,000 units to be produced each year. Actual fixed cost has remained at the same

Years	Number of Units Sold	Selling Price per Unit	Variable Cost per Unit	Fixed Cost
1978	3,000	$600	$300	$150
1979	3,500	600	300	150
1980	4,000	600	300	150

level over the years. The president estimates that 5,000 units will be sold in 1981 with no other changes expected.

Required:

(1) Compute the contribution margin for 1978, 1979, and 1980 and the income from manufacturing by the variable costing method.
(2) Estimate the contribution margin for 1981 and the income from manufacturing by the variable costing method.

8. Variable Costing and Price Revisions. During 1979, Ashland Products, Inc., sold 120,000 units of a product at a price of $15 per unit. In 1980, the company sold 150,000 units at the same price. The variable cost for both years was $10 per unit, and the fixed cost for each year was $150,000.

The company plans to sell 150,000 units in 1981, but the selling price must be reduced to $12 per unit. With a great deal of effort, ways have been found to reduce the variable cost to $9 per unit. The fixed cost is expected to remain at $150,000 for the year.

Required: Determine the income from manufacturing by the variable costing method for 1979 and 1980. Compute the estimated income for 1981 by the same method.

9. Variable Costing and Pricing Policy. Michael O'Riley has found that variable costing concepts have helped him in pricing products. He knows that he can reduce prices to a point where his store will recover more than the variable cost and that profit will increase when he gets more sales volume as a result of underselling the competitors. Data for 1979 and 1980 are given below.

Years	Sales Volume	Selling Price per Unit	Variable Cost per Unit	Total Fixed Cost
1979	80,000 units	$15	$7	$450,000
1980	150,000 units	12	7	450,000

In 1981, he plans to sell 200,000 units for $10 per unit. The cost structure is not expected to change.

Required:

(1) How much income before income tax was realized in 1979 and 1980?
(2) How much income before income tax can be expected in 1981?
(3) Comment on the policy established by O'Riley.

10. Production and Profit. Reed Hefner notes that sales volume in 1981 will probably be down from 50,000 units in 1980 to 35,000 units. To prevent profit from decreasing, he decides to build up inventories at the end of the year by producing 70,000 units. Some of the fixed cost will then be held over as part of the ending inventory. The normal capacity is 50,000 units per year with a fixed overhead cost per unit of $20. By producing 70,000 units, a favorable capacity variance will be credited to 1981.

In 1980, the company had an inventory of 5,000 units at both the beginning and at the end of the year. The company made and sold 50,000 units at a price of $40 per unit. The variable cost per unit was $10. The selling price and the cost structure are expected to be the same in 1981.

Required:

(1) Prepare a comparative income statement for the manufacturing operation for both 1980 and 1981 by the absorption costing method.
(2) Comment upon the position taken by Hefner.

11. Unexplained Profit Decrease. The board of directors of Red Star Fixtures, Inc., is disappointed to find that increased sales volume in 1981 did not result in increased profits.

The fixed manufacturing cost for 1980 and 1981 amounted to $800,000 for the year. The variable manufacturing cost per unit of product in both years was $12. Operating at a normal capacity, 100,000 units should be manufactured each year.

In 1980, the company produced 100,000 units and sold 70,000 units at a price of $40 per unit. Income from manufacturing was reported at $1,160,000. There was no inventory at the beginning of 1980.

In 1981, the company made 70,000 units and sold 100,000 units at a price of $40 per unit. The variable cost per unit remained at $12, and total fixed cost was $800,000. The directors anticipated a manufacturing profit of $2,000,000.

Required:

(1) Prepare an income statement for manufacturing for 1981 by the absorption costing method.
(2) Prepare an income statement for manufacturing for 1981 by the variable costing method.
(3) Explain to the board of directors why the profit was less than expected for 1981.

12. Fixed Costs and Inventories. Madeline Jung, the president of Waverly Appliances, Inc., asks you to show how fixed manufacturing cost was shifted from one year to another as a part of inventory cost. The fixed manufacturing cost for each year was $300,000. At normal capacity, 50,000 units of product should be manufactured. Capacity variances are charged or credited to the year in which the company operated over or below normal capacity. There was no inventory at the beginning of 1978.

Years	Production in Units	Sales in Units	Inventory in Units, End of Year
1978	50,000	40,000	10,000
1979	50,000	35,000	25,000
1980	40,000	60,000	5,000

Required: For each year determine the following data:

(1) Fixed cost included in cost of goods sold.
(2) Fixed cost included in inventory at the end of the year.
(3) Capacity variance for the year.

PROBLEMS

8-1. Profit Effect of Inventory Reduction. The Wisser Milling Company reported a record profit in the previous year. It appears, however, that profit will be lower this year even with a higher volume of sales. The inventory at the beginning of the year consisted of 35,000 units. Cost data for this inventory are given below:

Variable cost	$210,000
Fixed cost	525,000
Total inventory cost	$735,000

In the current year, the company made 100,000 units and operated at normal capacity. Fixed cost is applied at a normal capacity rate, and variable cost per unit and total fixed cost are the same as they were in the previous year.

The company sold 130,000 units of product this year at a price of $35 per unit.

Required:

(1) Prepare a partial income statement for the current year by the absorption costing method.

(2) Explain why the net income may be lower than it was last year.

8-2. Profit Effect of Inventory Increase. Owens Supply Company has increased inventory in anticipation of future increases in sales volume. The inventory at the beginning of 1980 consisted of 10,000 units at a unit variable cost of $2 and a unit fixed cost of $15. The unit fixed cost is computed at a normal operating capacity of 60,000 units per year.

During 1980, the company made 60,000 units and sold 40,000 units at a price of $30 per unit. There were no changes in the cost structure during 1980.

Required:

(1) Prepare an income statement for the manufacturing operation for 1980 by the absorption costing method.

(2) Would your answer have been different if the company had made and sold 40,000 units during 1980? Explain.

8-3. Income Determination by Variable Costing. Data from the records of Dawn Products Company are given below.

Years	Units Produced	Units Sold	Unit Variable Cost	Total Fixed Cost
1977	80,000	70,000	$8	$120,000
1978	90,000	80,000	8	120,000
1979	60,000	80,000	8	120,000
1980	70,000	70,000	8	120,000

Each unit of product was sold for $15 in each year.

Required:

(1) For each year, compute the income from manufacturing by the variable costing method.

(2) With the variable costing method, is there a capacity variance for any year in which production is above or below the normal level? Explain.

(3) With variable costing, explain why profit tends to increase or decrease with increases or decreases in the contribution margin.

8-4. Income Determination by Variable Costing. The Ettlinger Parts Company had no inventory of finished goods at July 1, 1980, the beginning of the fiscal year. Several estimates have been made of sales volume and production for the fiscal year ending June 30, 1981. These estimates appear on the next page.

Alternatives	Units of Sales	Units of Production
1	65,000	70,000
2	60,000	70,000
3	75,000	80,000
4	90,000	100,000

The selling price per unit is $12, and the variable manufacturing cost per unit is $7. Fixed manufacturing cost for the fiscal year has been estimated at $160,000, or $2 per unit, at a normal operating level of 80,000 units per year.

The president of the company requests an estimate of income from manufacturing for each of the four alternatives. Variable costing concepts are to be used in making the computations.

The production superintendent states that the production level must be considered inasmuch as the fixed cost will be carried over from one year to another as a part of inventory cost.

Required:

(1) Provide the information requested by the president.
(2) Explain why the production superintendent is correct or incorrect in being concerned about the effect of production level on the income from manufacturing.

8-5. Variable Costing Statements. For the past three years, King and Grayson, Inc., has had wide fluctuation in production and sales. Sales volume has increased, and the variable cost of production has also increased with no compensating increase in the selling price for the product. Unit cost data follow:

	1980	1979	1978
Direct materials	$2.50	$2.00	$1.50
Direct labor	3.00	2.00	2.00
Variable factory overhead	2.00	1.00	.50

In each of the three years, the product was sold at $12 per unit.

The fixed manufacturing cost amounted to $250,000 each year. Each year the selling and administrative expense amounted to 60 cents for each unit sold, and the fixed selling and administrative expense amounted to $80,000 a year. Income tax is estimated at 40% of income before tax.

Production and sales data for the three years follow:

Inventory on hand, January 1, 1978	20,000 units

Number of units produced:
1978	150,000
1979	160,000
1980	160,000

Number of units sold:
1978	140,000
1979	150,000
1980	180,000

Required: Prepare a comparative income statement for the three years by the variable costing method. (Use the fifo method of inventory costing and assume that the inventory on January 1, 1978, is stated at 1978 costs.)

8-6. Comparison of Absorption and Variable Costing. Lorraine Hufford, the president of Capstone Products, Inc., would like to see a comparison of the absorption costing method with the variable costing method. Operations for the past three years are to be used as a basis for comparison. Sales and production data are given below.

	1980	1979	1978
Number of units manufactured	80,000	100,000	100,000
Number of units sold	100,000	70,000	80,000
Unit selling price	$10	$10	$10
Standard variable cost of goods produced	$320,000	$400,000	$400,000
Total fixed cost (manufacturing)	$200,000	$250,000	$250,000

Production was at normal operating capacity in 1978 and 1979, and there was no inventory on hand at January 1, 1978. Inventories are maintained on a first-in, first-out basis.

Selling and administrative expense varied at the rate of 50 cents per unit sold. The fixed selling and administrative expense for each year amounted to $75,000. Income tax is estimated at 40% of income before tax.

Required:

(1) Prepare a comparative income statement for the three years by the absorption costing method.

(2) Prepare a comparative income statement for the three years by the variable costing method.

8-7. Explanation of Profit Decline. Edgar Jamison supervises the production of a specialized part made in the Toledo plant of Mason Patterns, Inc. During April 1980, the department made 1,000 units, and 700 units were sold at a price of $100 per unit. In May 1980, the department made 700 units and sold 1,000 units at a price of $100 per unit. The variable manufacturing cost per unit was $10 in each month, and the fixed manufacturing cost was $50,000 in each month. The fixed cost is applied at the rate of $50 for each unit manufactured.

Jamison believes that an error has been made in reporting the operation of his department for April and May. The summarized income statement shows a $3,000 reduction of income from April to May. If sales volume increased from 700 to 1,000 units and selling prices and cost remained at the April levels, he states that he will bet you $100 that the summarized income statement is incorrect. The statement is given below.

	May	April
Number of units sold	1,000	700
Number of units manufactured	700	1,000
Sales	$100,000	$ 70,000
Cost of goods sold at standard	60,000	42,000
Gross margin (standard)	$ 40,000	$ 28,000
Capacity variance (unfavorable)	15,000	—0—
Gross margin (actual)	$ 25,000	$ 28,000

There was no inventory on hand at April 1, 1980.

Required:

(1) Prepare a summary income statement for Jamison on a variable costing basis.

(2) Show why the profit decreased by $3,000 and pick up an easy $100 on your bet with Jamison.

8-8. Explanation of Profit Decline. An income statement for the first and second quarters of 1981 is given below for Bridgeport Products, Inc.

Bridgeport Products, Inc.
Comparative Income Statement
For the First Two Quarters of 1981

	First Quarter	Second Quarter
Number of units sold	15,000	20,000
Sales	$300,000	$400,000
Cost of goods sold:		
Inventory, beginning of quarter	$ 14,000	$ 84,000
Current production cost	280,000	210,000
Cost of merchandise available for sale	$294,000	$294,000
Less inventory, end of quarter	84,000	14,000
Cost of goods sold	$210,000	$280,000
Capacity variance	—0—	50,000
Total	$210,000	$330,000
Gross margin	$ 90,000	$ 70,000
Selling and administrative expense	25,000	25,000
Income before income tax	$ 65,000	$ 45,000
Income tax (40%)	26,000	18,000
Net income	$ 39,000	$ 27,000

In the first quarter, Ana Perez, the president of the company, planned to increase inventory in anticipation of increased sales volume in the second quarter. The sales volume increased as expected, but Perez was surprised to find that, instead of having increased profit, the profit was lower than it was for the first quarter. Inasmuch as selling price and costs did not change, she believes that the income statement is incorrect.

The company operated at normal capacity and manufactured 20,000 units during the first quarter. Total manufacturing cost per unit amounts to $14 at normal capacity with the fixed cost per unit at $10. During the second quarter, 15,000 units were manufactured. All selling and administrative expense is fixed.

Required:

(1) How would you explain the profit difference to Perez? Show why the income before income tax decreased from $65,000 in the first quarter to $45,000 in the second quarter.

(2) Revise the statement for the two quarters to show the operating results on a variable costing basis.

8-9. Absorption and Variable Costing Statements. Geraldine Herrick, the president of Council Bluffs Metals Company, notes that one of the divisions reported a substantial increase in net earnings for 1980. She does not see how this can be possible considering that the sales volume did not increase and selling prices and costs remained about the same.

You have been given a summary of the operations of this division for 1980 as shown on the next page.

Units of product manufactured	300,000
Units of product sold	200,000
Units of inventory, beginning of year	40,000
Sales revenue	$1,600,000
Variable manufacturing cost per unit	$1.50
Total fixed manufacturing cost (applied to each unit at a normal capacity rate of $2.50 per unit.)	$750,000

Required:

(1) Prepare an income statement for manufacturing for the division by the standard absorption costing method.

(2) Prepare an income statement for manufacturing by the standard absorption costing method, assuming that 200,000 units were manufactured and sold.

(3) Explain to the president why the profit increased in 1980.

(4) Prepare an income statement for manufacturing for 1980 on a variable costing basis.

8-10 Profits and Sales Volume. Gilbert Krogh finds it difficult to predict how profit will be affected by changes in sales volume. As vice-president for Verity Machine Company, he would like to have some direct way of measuring the effect of sales volume increases and decreases on the net income.

The income statement for the past three years is given below. Krogh shakes his head and says that he cannot understand this statement even though all costs are stated on a standard basis with no changes in the standards during the three years.

Verity Machine Company
Comparative Income Statement
For the Years Ended June 30, 1980, 1979, and 1978

	1980	1979	1978
Sales	$800,000	$720,000	$640,000
Cost of goods sold:			
Inventory, beginning of year	$200,000	$100,000	$ 50,000
Current production cost:			
Variable	70,000	110,000	90,000
Fixed	280,000	440,000	360,000
Cost of products available	$550,000	$650,000	$500,000
Less inventory, end of year	50,000	200,000	100,000
Cost of goods sold (standard)	$500,000	$450,000	$400,000
Capacity variance	120,000	40,000*	40,000
Cost of goods sold (actual)	$620,000	$410,000	$440,000
Gross margin	$180,000	$310,000	$200,000
Selling and administrative expenses:			
Variable	$ 20,000	$ 18,000	$ 16,000
Fixed	60,000	60,000	60,000
Total	$ 80,000	$ 78,000	$ 76,000
Income before income tax	$100,000	$232,000	$124,000
Income tax (40%)	40,000	92,800	49,600
Net income	$ 60,000	$139,200	$ 74,400

*Favorable capacity variance

Sales volume, Krogh explains, has increased moderately from 80,000 units in 1978 to 90,000 units in 1979 and to 100,000 units in 1980. Yet, the income before income tax in 1980 was somewhat lower than it was in 1978. The variable manufacturing cost was $1 per unit.

Required: Prepare a revised income statement for the three years that will give Krogh a better picture of how profits are related to sales volume.

8-11. Inventory Increase and Profits. Noonan Supplies, Inc., manufactured and sold 25,000 units of product during the first quarter of 1980. Each unit of product was sold for $15. The variable cost per unit was $2, and the total fixed cost was $200,000. An absorption costing system is used with 25,000 units defined as normal capacity. There was no inventory on hand at the beginning of the quarter.

It appears that sales volume will decrease to 20,000 units for the second quarter. The vice-president of sales expresses concern to the vice-president of manufacturing, stating that profit will be lower for the second quarter because of the lower sales volume. The vice-president of manufacturing states that there is a way to improve the profit picture, and this will be accomplished in the second quarter by producing 30,000 units of product. Increases in inventory will increase profit from $125,000, as reported in the first quarter, to $140,000 for the second quarter.

Required:

(1) Prepare a comparative income statement for the manufacturing operation for the two quarters using the absorption costing method.
(2) Explain how profit can be increased with the reduced sales volume and no changes in selling prices or in the cost structure.
(3) Prepare a comparative income statement for the manufacturing operation for the two quarters using the variable costing method to show a better relationship between sales volume and profits.

8-12. Conversion of Variable Costing to Absorption Costing. A summary income statement for 1980 on a variable costing basis is given below for Gully Parts Company.

Gully Parts Company
Income Statement — Manufacturing
For the Year Ended December 31, 1980

| | Product Lines | | | |
	G-226	G-348	G-714	Total
Number of units sold (in thousands)	650	280	120	—
Sales revenue..	$7,800	$2,240	$1,920	$11,960
Cost of goods sold	5,200	840	480	6,520
Manufacturing margin	$2,600	$1,400	$1,440	$ 5,440
Fixed overhead...				3,600
Income from manufacturing.........................				$ 1,840

Inventories of finished stock were increased during the year in anticipation of increases in sales volume in the current year. Inventories in units of product are given on the next page for the beginning and end of the year.

	Beginning Inventory	Ending Inventory
G-226	20,000	90,000
G-348	50,000	90,000
G-714	20,000	50,000

The normal operating level defined for the assignment of fixed overhead to production has been established at 1,800,000 machine hours. According to the standards, one-half hour is required to produce a unit of G-226; two hours are required for a unit of G-348; and four hours are required for a unit of G-714. Assume that all standards have been maintained; cost inventories at standard costs.

Required:

(1) Recast the income statement on an absorption costing basis. Include cost of inventory in the computation of the cost of goods sold.

(2) Explain why the income from manufacturing on the absorption costing statement differs from income from manufacturing on the variable costing statement. Show computations.

8-13. Conversion to Variable Costing. Vincent Kim has gone over the financial statements for Kim Parts, Inc. The income statement has been prepared on an absorption costing basis, and Kim would like to have the statement revised on a variable costing basis.

Kim Parts, Inc.
Income Statement — Manufacturing
For the Year Ended December 31, 1979

Sales			$20,700,000
Cost of goods sold:			
Inventory, first of year		$ 1,980,000	
Current production		13,200,000	
Cost of products available for sale		$15,180,000	
Less inventory, end of year		1,380,000	13,800,000
Gross margin			$ 6,900,000
Factory overhead capacity variance			500,000
Income from manufacturing			$ 6,400,000

The company has a normal productive capacity of 1,200,000 units of product each year. Only one line of product is manufactured, and the inventory is accounted for on a fifo basis. In 1979 the fixed factory overhead was $6,000,000. During the year, Kim Parts, Inc., manufactured 1,100,000 units of product.

For the current year 1980, plans have been made to manufacture 1,400,000 units of product and to sell 1,450,000 units. The unit variable cost and the selling price are expected to be the same as they were last year. The normal capacity level will remain unchanged, but fixed factory overhead can be reduced to $5,400,000 for the year.

Required:

(1) Recast the income statement for 1979 to place it on a variable costing basis. (In your solution, show beginning inventory at variable cost.)

(2) Prepare an estimated income statement for 1980 on an absorption costing basis.

(3) Prepare another estimated income statement for 1980 on a variable costing basis.

8-14. Conversion to Variable Costing. Henry and Livingston, Inc., manufactures three product lines that are sold to industrial suppliers. An income statement for the fiscal year ended June 30, 1980, is given below.

Henry and Livingston, Inc.
Income Statement
For the Year Ended June 30, 1980

		Product Lines		
	A	B	C	Total
Net sales...	$5,250,000	$ 940,000	$1,650,000	$7,840,000
Cost of goods sold	3,450,000	775,500	957,000	5,182,500
Gross profit..	$1,800,000	$ 164,500	$ 693,000	$2,657,500
Unabsorbed fixed overhead (capacity variance)..				$ 440,000
Selling and administrative expense (fixed)...				720,000
				$1,160,000
Income before income tax				$1,497,500

The president of the company would like to see the income statement revised to show the total contribution margin from each product line and the total fixed cost deducted from the total revenue.

Details with respect to the cost of goods sold are given below.

			Product Lines			
	A		B		C	
	Units	Cost	Units	Cost	Units	Cost
Inventory, July 1, 1979 ..	5,000	$ 230,000	3,000	$ 49,500	7,000	$ 101,500
Current production	80,000	3,680,000	45,000	742,500	75,000	1,087,500
Total............................	85,000	$3,910,000	48,000	$792,000	82,000	$1,189,000
Less inventory, June 30, 1980	10,000	460,000	1,000	16,500	16,000	232,000
Cost of goods sold........	75,000	$3,450,000	47,000	$775,500	66,000	$ 957,000

The materials cost per unit and labor and overhead data are given below.

	Product Lines		
	A	B	C
Hours required to produce each unit...................	2	1/2	1/2
Materials cost, per unit..	$12	$ 8	$ 6

The production workers are paid at a uniform rate of $7 per hour. Factory overhead rates have been determined at normal operating capacity as follows:

Variable overhead rate per hour...	$ 2
Fixed overhead rate per hour	8
Total overhead rate per hour	$10

Production times and cost for the inventory at the beginning of the year are in agreement with the times and cost for the current fiscal year.

Required:

(1) Prepare a revised income statement as requested by the president. The income before income tax on a variable costing basis will differ from the income before income tax on an absorption costing basis.

(2) Show the detail of cost of goods sold on a variable costing basis to support the revised income statement.

(3) Show why the income before income tax is more or less on the revised income statement than on the income statement given.

8-15. Comparison Variable and Absorption Costing. The president and board of directors of Kettering Frame Company are concerned about the decline in sales volume during the past three years. Various measures are being considered to revitalize sales.

Sales volume was at a normal level of 50,000 units during 1978, and the net income was reported at $360,000. In 1980, the company sold only 30,000 units and reported a net income of $84,000. The company reports net income on an absorption costing basis, and the income tax is estimated at 40% of income before income tax.

Sales and production data for the three years, 1978 to 1980, are given below. The selling price and the cost structure remained unchanged for each of the three years.

Selling price per unit	$50
Variable manufacturing cost per unit...	$15
Fixed manufacturing cost per unit based upon a normal operating capacity of 50,000 units produced per year	$20
Variable selling and administrative expense per unit sold.................	$2
Total fixed selling and administrative expense per year	$50,000

Production and sales in units for each year

	1978	1979	1980
Units produced	50,000	50,000	40,000
Units sold	50,000	40,000	30,000

There was no inventory of the finished product on hand at the beginning of 1978.

Required:

(1) Prepare a comparative income statement for the years 1978 to 1980 using the absorption costing method.

(2) Prepare a comparative income statement for the years 1978 to 1980 using the variable costing method. For this statement, estimate the amount of income tax on the basis of variable costing.

(3) If it were permissible to compute income tax on a variable costing basis, would the company have a lower tax liability under variable costing for these three years? Show amounts.

(4) Explain why there was a difference, if any, between the income before income tax for any year because of a difference in the costing method used. Show dollar amounts.

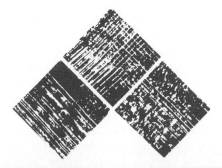

9
ACCOUNTING DATA
FOR MANAGERIAL DECISIONS

When discussing how accounting data are used in managerial decision making, consider the decision-making process as one of identifying, evaluating, and choosing among future alternative courses of action. When making decisions, managers typically have a need for various types of accounting data. As noted, decision making concerns the future; and decisions will, in part at least, rest on predictions of future events, many of which will have a quantitative dimension. Historical accounting data are almost always important as a basis for predicting the cost and revenue associated with alternative courses of future action.

In evaluating alternative courses of action, the concept of relevance is important, and it receives considerable attention in this chapter. This concept is illustrated by examining several combination decisions and the pricing problem. The latter topic provides an opportunity to consider the role of revenue predictions as well as relevant cost considerations.

RELEVANT COST DATA FOR DECISION MAKING

The costs that are relevant in making decisions are not necessarily the costs that are used in conventional accounting or in financial reporting. In fact, some of the costs to be used in decision making are not even entered in the accounting records. Opportunity costs, for example, are important in decision making but are not entered as accounting costs.

An adjustment in thinking is required in planning for the future, and this adjustment may be particularly difficult for the person who has become accustomed to conventional accounting practices. In conventional accounting, for example, the cost of a depreciable asset is assigned to the fiscal periods as depreciation. But a cost that has been incurred in the past (a sunk cost) may play no role in making plans for the future, except for the income tax effect. Tax effects are discussed in the next chapter.

In decision making, the emphasis is on the future. The past is important only as a guide in predicting the future. When a choice is to be made between alternatives, the costs that are increased or decreased as a result of a decision are the relevant costs. Thus, *relevant cost* may be defined as a future cost that will differ between alternatives. Costs that are unaffected by a decision can be ignored. These ideas are illustrated in the following sections.

Costs and Decisions — An Illustration

The problem of selecting the appropriate costs for decision making is illustrated by a short example. Lane Products, Inc., has determined the total annual cost to operate one of its manufacturing departments. Only the costs that are directly identified with this department are listed. No costs have been allocated to this operation. An outside service contractor has agreed to furnish a repair and maintenance service, and the costs that can be expected if this alternative is selected are also listed in the same way as the costs of the present operation.

	PRESENT OPERATION	ALTERNATIVE OF SERVICE CONTRACT	TYPE OF COST
Direct materials	$20,000	$20,000	Unavoidable
Direct labor	25,000	25,000	Unavoidable
Supplies	6,000	8,000	Differential by $2,000
Indirect labor	15,000	10,000	Differential by $5,000
Repairs and maintenance	4,000	—0—	Differential by $4,000; also avoidable cost
Outside services	—0—	4,000	Differential by $4,000
Depreciation	2,000	2,000	Sunk cost

Some of the costs listed are not relevant to the decision. For example, the direct materials and direct labor costs are the same in either case; therefore, with respect to this decision, these costs can be ignored. The sunk cost of $2,000 is a portion of the cost of a plant asset that is assigned to a fiscal period in financial accounting. This cost was incurred in the past and can be excluded in the decision-making process. The relevant costs are shown on the next page.

Lane Products, Inc. Service Contract Decision		
Decremental costs:		
Indirect labor..	$5,000	
Repairs and maintenance...	4,000	
Total estimated cost savings..		$9,000
Incremental costs:		
Supplies...	$2,000	
Outside services	4,000	
Total estimated cost increases		6,000
Anticipated cost advantage from service contract............................		$3,000

There is a net saving of $3,000 a year if repair and maintenance work is done by an outside contractor; everything else being equal, the company should engage the contractor.

Opportunity Cost

Opportunity costs play a vital role in decision making. As explained in Chapter 2, an *opportunity cost* is a benefit that would have been obtained from an alternative if it had not been rejected. For example, Donna Schultz, a student, may be able to earn $1,500 after taxes and other additional costs by working in the summer, but if she decides to go to summer school, she will not get the $1,500. The cost of her decision to attend summer school is not only the cost of tuition and books but is also the sacrifice of the $1,500 that she could have earned. The net proceeds from summer work are the opportunity cost of attending summer school.

Returning to the previous example, assume that another contractor presents a repair and maintenance service plan. To be acceptable, this new plan must yield cost savings each year of at least $3,000. In other words, to be acceptable, any new proposal must be at least as advantageous as the plan that is now available. The opportunity cost of not accepting the current plan is the $3,000 annual cost saving effected by it.

COMBINATION DECISIONS

Management is constantly faced with decisions as to how to make the best use of available facilities and how to combine productive resources to minimize cost. Combination decisions, several examples of which follow, have received a great deal of attention recently because of the increased availability of computers that can be programmed to solve complex problems having many variables.

Process or Sell

This is an example of the opportunity cost concept applied to a combination decision. Assume that a certain intermediate product can be produced and sold or can be processed further and sold as a completely processed product. In deciding which course of action to follow, the company compares the contribution margin from the sale of the partially processed product with the contribution margin from the sale of the completely processed product. The revenue to be derived from the sale of the partially processed product is the opportunity cost attached to the decision of further processing.

Assume, for example, that a partially processed product selling for $9 per unit is manufactured at a cost of $6. Further processing at a variable cost of $3 a unit will yield a product that can be sold at a unit price of $15. The firm can produce 10,000 units. The analysis is as follows:

DECISION ANALYSIS

Revenue from sale of final product (10,000 units @ $15)..		$150,000
Less:		
Additional processing cost (10,000 units @ $3)..	$30,000	
Revenue from sale of intermediate product (10,000 units @ $9)......................................	90,000	120,000
Net advantage in further processing..................		$ 30,000

There is a net advantage of $30,000 in further processing the product. Note that the market value of the partially processed product is considered to be the opportunity cost of further processing, and that the partial processing cost of $6 is not included in the analysis because it is incurred under either alternative. Assuming that the company continues its processing operation and realizes profit as planned, the revenue and the cost will be accounted for in the usual manner:

ACCOUNTABILITY

Revenue from sale of final product		$150,000
Less:		
Additional processing cost	$30,000	
Cost to process intermediate product	60,000	90,000
Profit		$ 60,000

Product Combinations

The product combination decision arises when several product lines are manufactured and sold. A decision must be reached as to which product combination is most profitable. Oil refineries, for example, plan refinery production to meet the varying needs of the market. During certain months, larger quantities of heating oils are produced, while in other months larger quantities of gasoline are produced. In

other industries, similar problems are encountered that involve a selection of the best combination of productive factors to meet the limitations that are imposed by internal or external conditions. An increase in the production and sale of one product line often means that
the production and sale of another line has to be curtailed. There is
only so much that can be done with a given set of productive factors.
The product lines should be manufactured and sold in the most profitable combination.

Two Products, No Constraints. Assume that a firm produces two
products, A and B, whose costs and selling prices are as follows:

	PRODUCT A	PRODUCT B
Selling price per unit..........................	$10	$8
Variable cost per unit..........................	5	6
Contribution margin per unit	$ 5	$2
Fixed cost per year.............................	$50,000	

One of the decisions faced by management is what combination of
Products A and B should be produced. The decision rule to be followed
is to choose the combination of products that maximizes contribution
margin. If fixed cost remains unaffected, net income will also be maximized. This decision rule might be implemented by choosing the
product that has the highest contribution margin per unit. If there are
no constraints with respect to either production capacity or sales capacity, this method could give the desired result. However, this is a
very unlikely situation. In most cases, the firm has a given plant facility; and it may not be possible to shift all production from Product B
to Product A. Also, it is not unusual to find various market constraints
that arise because the market will absorb only a limited number of
units of a particular product. In these cases, the break-even or cost-
volume-profit information given above is useful but insufficient to arrive at a product-combination decision. In addition, management
must have information on the amount of scarce resources used up in
producing each product.

Two Products, One Constraint. Assume that the market for each
product is unlimited and that the firm can therefore sell all units that
it produces. However, assume that the production facilities are limited
to 200,000 labor hours. In this case the scarce production factor or
limiting factor is the firm's labor force. Further assume that the labor
requirement for each product is as follows:

	PRODUCT A	PRODUCT B
Labor hours required..........................	10 hours	2 hours

Given the production constraint of 200,000 hours, it is possible to
produce 20,000 units of Product A (200,000 hours ÷ 10 hours) or
100,000 units of Product B (200,000 hours ÷ 2 hours). Note that the

firm can produce Products A and B in any combination by giving up five units of Product B for one unit of Product A.

Given this constraint, the firm should produce all Product B because it provides the greatest contribution margin per limiting factor. The alternatives are summarized as follows:

STATEMENTS OF PROFIT

	If All A Is Produced	If All B Is Produced
Sales: (20,000 units @ $10)............................	$200,000	
(100,000 units @ $8)............................		$800,000
Variable cost: (20,000 units @ $5)..................	100,000	
(100,000 units @ $6)................		600,000
Contribution margin..	$100,000	$200,000
Fixed cost...	50,000	$ 50,000
Profit...	$ 50,000	$150,000

As can be seen, with one production constraint and two products, the solution to the product-combination problem is fairly simple. An alternate solution is to calculate a contribution margin per hour of production time and to choose the product with the highest rate. The calculation is as follows:

	PRODUCT A	PRODUCT B
Selling price............................	$10	$8
Variable cost..........................	5	6
Contribution margin.............	$ 5	$2
Hour requirement..................	10 hours	2 hours
Contribution margin per hour.....................................	$5 ÷ 10 hrs. = $.50 per hr.	$2 ÷ 2 hrs. = $1 per hr.

Since Product B returns $1 per hour in contrast with 50 cents per hour for Product A, Product B is the preferred product. As a matter of fact, the firm will continue to be a one-product firm producing all B and no A as long as there is no market limitation on Product B. It is the market limitation which creates a product combination. If the firm can sell its most profitable product (in this case, Product B) in an unlimited market, there is no reason to produce any of Product A. However, as will be shown later, some of Product A will be produced if the market for Product B is limited to fewer units than can be produced.

This example forms the basis for a linear programming problem. The firm is maximizing contribution margin subject to a single production constraint. The solution is simple since there are only two products and one constraint. In such a simple case, the concept of *a rate of return per the scarce factor* is a useful and effective concept. However, as the number of products and the number of constraints increase, linear programming becomes necessary for the more complex cases.

Two Products, Many Constraints. In the previous example, it was assumed that there were no market constraints. Assume that market conditions are of such a nature that only 80,000 units of Product B can be sold but that the market for Product A is unlimited. It would be possible to solve the problem by trial and error, but a more systematic solution and one that will generalize for the many-constraints case is a graphic linear programming solution.

The previous example, involving only one production constraint, the limitation of production facilities to 200,000 labor hours, has been plotted on the following graph:

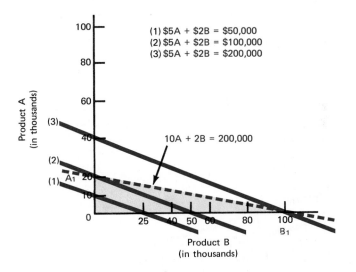

The production constraint can be given by the line **10A + 2B = 200,000**. The set of possible solutions is given by the area **0, A₁, B₁**; that is, only 200,000 hours are available, so all possible solutions must use some number of hours less than or equal to 200,000. In symbols:

(1) **10A + 2B ≤ 200,000**

This inequality states in symbol form the production constraint. If only Product B is produced, 100,000 units are possible; and if only Product A is produced, 20,000 units are possible. Other combinations that use all of the capacity (for example, 10,000 A and 50,000 B) fall on the line 10A + 2B = 200,000. The other possible solutions fall somewhere in the area 0, A₁, B₁, but these solutions do not use 100 percent of the hour capacity. These solutions are feasible or possible but not optimal. An optimal solution is somewhere on the boundary of the area 0, A₁, B₁.

The problem is to maximize contribution margin subject to a single production constraint. In equation form:

(2) **CM = $5A + $2B, where CM = contribution margin**

That is, for every unit of Product A that is sold, CM increases by $5, and for every unit of Product B, CM increases by $2. In the diagram on page 251, three lines have been plotted showing contribution margins at three different levels, $50,000, $100,000, and $200,000. These lines are "equal contribution" lines in that they show different combinations of Products A and B that give the same contribution margin. Since the objective is to maximize contribution margin, the CM lines should be moved upward and to the right until the CM line is at the boundary given by the production constraint equation. This occurs at the point **A = 0 and B = 100,000**   Higher levels of contribution margin are not feasible because of the hour constraint. This solution agrees with the one given earlier in the chapter.

The same example with the addition of the market constraint that only 80,000 units of Product B can be sold has been plotted on the diagram below.

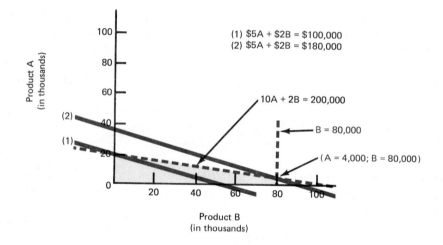

Product B
(in thousands)

In this diagram, the previous production constraint of 200,000 labor hours has been plotted. In addition, the line **B = 80,000** establishes the constraint that the market will absorb a maximum of only 80,000 units of Product B. In inequality form, this constraint is:

(2) **B ≤ 80,000**

The set of possible or feasible solutions is therefore given by the shaded area. The objective function or contribution margin equation can be moved upward and to the right until the point **A = 4,000, B = 80,000** is reached. At this point, the contribution margin is maximized at $180,000.

As can be seen in the graphic linear programming solution, the various production and marketing constraints can be plotted and, taken together, define the set of possible or feasible solutions. The objective function or contribution margin line is then determined, and a solution giving the maximum contribution margin can be found by moving the contribution margin line to higher and higher levels until the boundary formed by the constraint equations is reached. Note that this graphic technique handles almost any number of constraints but only two products. If many products are involved, the graph becomes multidimensional and impossible to work with.

Computer methods of solving linear programming problems are readily available. Solution routines for more complex problems are beyond the scope of this text but are dealt with at length in most texts on mathematical programming. For our purposes, it is sufficient to point out that the concepts discussed are directly relevant to more complex problems; what is needed (and supplied through computer methods) is a more powerful solution technique than the graphic method.

Make or Buy

Another important type of combination decision is whether to make or buy component parts. For example, assume that a company can make a part that it has been purchasing at a unit cost of $3. The company can buy materials at a cost of $1.25 per part, direct labor cost has been estimated at 80 cents for each part, and variable factory overhead has been estimated at 50 cents for each part. The company has been operating at 75 percent of normal capacity, and in the foreseeable future no use for the excess capacity is contemplated except for the possible production of the part. Production of this part will enable the company to operate at its normal capacity and will provide all parts needed for subsequent manufacturing operations. Fixed factory overhead cost amounts to $170,000 a year, whether the plant operates at 75 or 100 percent of capacity.

The incremental cost to manufacture 50,000 units of the needed part and the make or buy decision are determined as follows:

	UNIT COST	TOTAL COST
Direct materials	$1.25	$ 62,500
Direct labor	.80	40,000
Variable factory overhead	.50	25,000
Total incremental cost	$2.55	$127,500
Cost to purchase part	3.00	150,000
Net advantage in parts production	$ .45	$ 22,500

If there is no better alternative for the use of the idle facilities, the part should be manufactured and not purchased.

Note that an incorrect decision would have been made if a ratable portion of the fixed overhead cost had been included in the cost to manufacture the 50,000 parts. The allocated fixed cost would have been $42,500 (25% of $170,000) or $.85 per unit, resulting in a total unit cost of $3.40 ($2.55 + $.85). This unit cost exceeds the purchase price of $3 per part and would cause the decision-maker to reject the proposal to manufacture. Total fixed overhead cost is obviously not affected by the production of the 50,000 parts, thus the preceding analysis is incorrect. Only the costs that are increased or decreased as a result of making the part are relevant to the decision.

The Elimination of a Product Line

Choosing the proper combination of products may also involve the elimination of a product line. The income statement for Harris Department Store has been prepared for a typical year, and the data have been rearranged to show which product lines should be retained or discontinued:

Harris Department Store
Income Statement
Average Year

	Product Line				
	1	2	3	4	Total
Net sales	$86,200	$93,700	$81,200	$87,400	$348,500
Direct costs:					
Variable costs:					
Cost of goods sold............	$51,800	$55,100	$68,700	$57,900	$233,500
Supplies.............................	3,300	2,800	3,900	3,800	13,800
Transportation	1,100	1,400	1,900	2,100	6,500
Total variable cost	$56,200	$59,300	$74,500	$63,800	$253,800
Contribution margin............	$30,000	$34,400	$ 6,700	$23,600	$ 94,700
Fixed costs for the product line:					
Salaries..............................	$ 6,000	$11,000	$10,000	$ 8,000	$ 35,000
Advertising	3,000	4,500	4,500	4,200	16,200
Total fixed cost for product line	$ 9,000	$15,500	$14,500	$12,200	$ 51,200
Margin over direct costs..........	$21,000	$18,900	$ (7,800)	$11,400	$ 43,500
Fixed costs of the total operation:					
Salaries					$ 16,000
Rent....................................					5,000
Taxes..................................					2,700
Insurance............................					1,600
Heat and light.....................					1,700
Total fixed cost of operation					$ 27,000
Income before income tax					$ 16,500

The variable cost identified with each product line and the fixed costs that are specifically incurred for each product line are subtracted from sales to determine whether or not the product line can cover its own costs. Note that the analysis in this case does not depend entirely upon the variable costs. It is not a question of profit planning by planning selling prices, variable costs, or sales volume. Instead, the problem is extended further. The sales volume, the unit selling price, and the variable cost per unit are assumed. The direct costs include the variable costs and the fixed costs that are incurred for each particular product line. These costs are the *avoidable costs*. They can be avoided if a product line is discontinued. The fixed costs for the total store should not be allocated. They are the *unavoidable costs*, the costs that are incurred in any event.

Product 3 should be eliminated, unless it can be proved that the line helps to increase the sales of the profitable lines. It cannot cover its own costs. Without Product 3, the income before income tax would amount to $24,300:

PROFIT EFFECT OF ELIMINATION OF PRODUCT 3

Costs avoided by the elimination of Product 3:		
Variable cost	$74,500	
Fixed cost for the product line which can be eliminated..	14,500	
Total cost eliminated		$89,000
Less revenue contributed by Product 3................		81,200
Net advantage of elimination of Product 3..........		$ 7,800
Income before income tax, including Product 3..		16,500
Income before income tax, without Product 3		$24,300

In this example, certain costs were identified with the product lines; but it cannot be assumed that these particular costs are avoidable or unavoidable in all cases. Each situation should be evaluated on its own. The important point is that a distinction should be made between the costs that can be avoided and the costs that cannot be avoided by the decision. In this example, if the $14,500 fixed cost cannot be eliminated with Product 3, then Product 3 should be retained.

THE PRICING DECISION

One of the most difficult decisions faced by the manager is the pricing decision. In some situations, there is no pricing decision. For example, a prevailing market condition may be such that a higher price is not acceptable and there may be no incentive for charging a lower price. For example, the major decision with agricultural products is determining what quantity to produce. However, in situations where the decision-maker does have some control over the price to be charged, there is a need for information on the demand for the product. The cost side of the pricing decision is emphasized in this discussion; demand is considered, but there is no systematic discussion of the determination of product demand at various prices.

Price Based on Full Cost

The *markup pricing method* is widely used in business. To arrive at the price, a cost per unit is computed and then a markup, stated as a percentage of cost, is added. The purpose of the markup is to provide for a profit. The term "cost" as used in this method is ambiguous until carefully defined. Two definitions are possible: (1) variable cost or, (2) full cost. Full cost pricing will be discussed first.

The most widely used form of markup pricing is to base the markup on full cost; that is, the *full cost* of the unit is considered to be made up of the variable cost plus some allocated share of the fixed cost. The full cost is then used as the basis for setting price, usually by adding a percentage markup.

The Fixed Cost Problem. The proper treatment of fixed cost presents a problem in full cost pricing. Assume that a firm produces only one product and that the cost structure is as follows:

Variable materials cost	$5
Variable direct labor cost	3
Total variable cost	$8
Fixed annual overhead and other expenses	$100,000

In order to determine the full cost of a unit, it is necessary to select a specific number of units over which to allocate the fixed cost. The relationship between unit fixed cost and volume is plotted below:

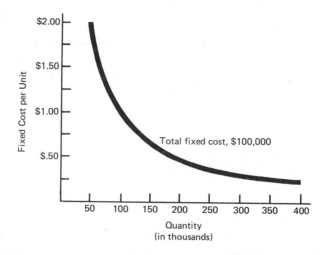

As can be seen, the fixed cost per unit decreases as the number of units increases. In an earlier discussion of job order and process cost accounting, it was indicated that the number of units at normal volume is typically used as a basis for allocating the fixed cost. If the firm has a price policy of marking up 10 percent based on full cost, the prices shown on the next page are possible, depending on the decision as to volume.

	NUMBER OF UNITS (IN THOUSANDS)					
	50	*100*	*150*	*200*	*250*	*300*
Variable cost.................	$ 8.00	$8.00	$8.00	$8.00	$8.00	$8.00
Fixed cost per unit	2.00	1.00	.67	.50	.40	.33
Total full cost	$10.00	$9.00	$8.67	$8.50	$8.40	$8.33
10% markup	1.00	.90	.87	.85	.84	.83
Selling price	$11.00	$9.90	$9.54	$9.35	$9.24	$9.16

If 200,000 units are selected as the number of units over which to spread the fixed cost, the profit (markup) per unit is stated to be 85 cents. However, the profit will not be 85 cents per unit and it will not be $170,000 for the year (200,000 units × 85 cents) if some number of units other than 200,000 units is actually sold. For example, if only 100,000 units are sold, the profit will be only $35,000, as follows:

Revenue (100,000 units × $9.35).......................		$935,000
Variable cost (100,000 units × $8)...................	$800,000	
Fixed cost	100,000	900,000
Profit...		$ 35,000

The difference in the profit per unit between 85 cents and 35 cents ($35,000 ÷ 100,000 units) is due to the fact that the fixed cost per unit based on 100,000 units is $1 and not 50 cents as stated for 200,000 units.

It may be argued that the demand situation can be considered in choosing the number of units over which to spread the fixed cost. Although a possibility, such a policy may be in conflict with the selection of normal volume as it is used in job order and process cost accounting. Note that normal volume and expected volume for next year are not necessarily the same. *Normal volume* is usually considered an average volume based on several years. If normal volume is used, the result should be a very stable price almost without regard for changes in the business cycle. Perhaps this is desirable, but there is less chance that the price will be adapted to changes in business conditions.

Another difficulty with trying to use either expected volume or normal volume for spreading fixed cost is that the number of units to be sold depends on the price, and it is the price that is being determined. Hence, any attempt to consider the demand situation in establishing the full cost of the product is likely to involve circular reasoning. The demand situation must be considered in setting the price, but the fact remains that full cost pricing does not offer a good means for considering this variable. In any particular situation, however, it may be that no other pricing method gives any better result than full cost pricing. It is usually easier to criticize a pricing method than to recommend a better one.

The Allocation Problem. When two or more products are produced, the problem of how to allocate the common cost is encountered in full cost pricing. Although the allocation problem has been discussed in previous chapters, it is reviewed here with respect to full cost pricing. The earlier discussions were primarily concerned with the cost allocation problem as it affects cost accounting systems where the data are used primarily for inventory valuation and income determination. However, the problem is much the same as that encountered in pricing. The reason for this is that the full cost data developed in cost accounting are generally the same data used in full cost pricing. At the very least, the cost accounting data provide a starting point in calculating a full cost figure for pricing purposes.

Assume that the firm produces two products, A and B, and that the cost structure is as follows:

	PRODUCT A	PRODUCT B
Variable labor cost.............................	$7	$3
Variable materials cost	2	3
Overhead and other indirect annual expenses	$200,000	

The $200,000 common cost consists of several different individual types of costs such as machine depreciation, indirect labor, insurance, and various selling and administrative expenses. In allocating these costs to the two products, the first step should be to separate and regroup those costs that are fairly homogeneous. For example, all indirect costs related to machine operations, such as machine depreciation and repairs, should be totaled. However, even after this type of regrouping, the individual cost items in any particular group are still not entirely homogeneous and hence any method of allocation chosen is likely to be a compromise and open to criticism. Assume, for example, that the $200,000 indirect cost in the example is the cost incurred to operate the factory manager's office. Should this cost be allocated on the basis of direct labor hours, direct labor cost, materials cost, or some other base that might be chosen from a long list of allocation methods? The full cost and, therefore, the price are affected by the allocation base chosen. For simplicity, assume that the volume of each product is equal. If labor cost is chosen, $140,000 (7/10 × $200,000) of the indirect cost will be assigned to Product A; whereas if materials cost is to be the base, only $80,000 (2/5 × $200,000) will be assigned to Product A. In addition to the problem of how to allocate the indirect costs, note that the allocation process itself can involve a high clerical cost in instances where the cost and product structure is a complicated one.

The Basis of Allocation. In choosing the basis of allocation for inventory costing and income determination, it is possible to use the criterion of "benefit" received by the product; that is, the problem of allocating overhead cost to products is essentially the same as allocating depreciation or any long-term asset cost to time periods. In general, accountants try to allocate these common costs according to the benefit received by the unit of costing (in this case the products) from the incurrence of the cost. The argument is frequently made that a machine-related overhead cost should be assigned to the product on the basis of machine time but that labor-related overhead should be assigned on the basis of labor hours. The justification is that the basis of allocation chosen in this manner provides a fairly good means of allocating cost according to the benefit received by the various products. A product that uses more labor hours bears a greater portion of the labor-related overhead, while a product that uses more machine time bears a greater portion of the machine-related overhead.

The question arises, however, as to whether or not the benefit criterion provides a good basis of allocation if the cost data are to be used in setting prices. This is not an easy question to answer. It is sometimes argued that full cost pricing should give a fair price that assures the firm of social approval of the pricing scheme. If this argument is valid, perhaps the allocation of common costs according to the benefit criterion is an acceptable basis for determining full cost and thus price. It would seem that the manager could publicly defend such a price, if required. However, in seeking a price that provides the greatest positive difference between revenue and cost, it is difficult to see how the dual problems of cost allocation and choosing the volume over which to spread the fixed cost can be satisfactorily solved.

Variable Cost Pricing

Another approach to cost-plus-a-markup pricing is to use the variable cost rather than the full cost as the cost base. One major advantage of this approach is that some of the difficult problems of indirect cost allocation and the spreading of fixed cost can be avoided. In order to exploit the advantages of the variable cost approach, however, it is necessary to have a reasonably accurate estimate of product demand. If such an estimate is available and if the variable cost approach is used, it may be possible to arrive at a price that approaches a maximum profit position. At the very least, such a procedure may consider more of the pertinent factors of a price decision than does the full cost approach.

Distress and Special-Order Pricing. The argument has frequently been made that variable cost pricing should be used only in pricing a special order at a special price or in a distress situation. For example, assume that a firm has excess capacity and has the opportunity to sell additional units of product in a foreign market or in an isolated sector of a domestic market. Any price above the variable cost of these additional units yields a contribution to fixed cost and hence increases total profit.

The special-order or *dumping* situation can be illustrated as follows. Assume that the company, whose capacity is 100,000 units, is currently producing and selling only 90,000 units of product each year in the regular market at a price of $1 per unit. If the variable cost per unit is 50 cents and the annual fixed cost is $30,000, the profit calculation is as follows:

Sales (90,000 units @ $1)..		$90,000
Cost: Variable cost (90,000 units @ 50¢).............	$45,000	
Fixed cost	30,000	75,000
Profit..		$15,000

The full cost of the units is 83.3 cents each ($75,000 ÷ 90,000 units). A foreign buyer approaches the company with an order for 10,000 units at 60 cents each. If sales in the foreign market will not affect the regular market, the company can add to total profit by accepting the special order even though the price is 23.3 cents below the full cost (83.3 cents − 60 cents). At a price of 60 cents, the order will contribute 10 cents per unit toward fixed cost, and profit will increase by $1,000 (10,000 units × 10 cents). In such a case, the variable cost of 50 cents may provide a better guide to action than the full cost. This same result can be seen through the comparative profit calculations shown below.

	PROFIT CALCULATION BASED ON 90,000 UNITS	PROFIT CALCULATION BASED ON 100,000 UNITS
Sales: (90,000 units @ $1)...........	$90,000	$90,000
(10,000 units @ 60¢)........		6,000
	$90,000	$96,000
Cost:		
Variable cost @ 50¢ per unit...	$45,000	$50,000
Fixed cost	30,000	30,000
	$75,000	$80,000
Profit	$15,000	$16,000

This example illustrates why some firms make price concessions in periods of excess capacity. However, the policy of accepting special orders at special prices is generally a good policy only when the special market can be kept separate from the regular market, and this is a marketing, not a cost, problem. For example, in the preceding illustration, assume that the foreign (special) market begins to affect the domestic market to the extent that the price in the domestic market drops from $1 per unit to 60 cents per unit. In this case, the firm's profit calculation for the next period would appear as follows:

Sales (100,000 units @ 60¢)		$60,000
Cost: Variable cost (100,000 units @ 50¢)	$50,000	
Fixed cost	30,000	80,000
Loss		$(20,000)

As can be seen, if the special market price takes over the domestic market, the profit decreases from $15,000 to a loss of $20,000 rather than increasing to $16,000. If the line of demarcation between the foreign and the domestic market cannot be maintained, then the lower price is bound to dominate; and the special order pricing policy would be a poor policy for the firm to follow. This type of example has served as a criticism of the use of variable costing as a basis for establishing prices. Of course, any pricing policy can lead to poor results if the decision maker fails to properly assess the market considerations. The problem lies not in the fact that variable costing instead of full cost was used, but that the market conditions were not properly assessed.

Sometimes variable cost pricing is felt to be more appropriate when sales are beyond the break-even point than when sales are below the break-even point. For example, assume, as in the previous illustration, that the selling price of the product is $1 per unit, the variable cost is 50 cents, the fixed cost is $30,000, and the capacity is 100,000 units. The break-even point is 60,000 units. It might be fallaciously contended that it is appropriate to use special order or variable cost pricing only after a sales volume of 60,000 units has been reached. Special-order pricing is not wise unless there is unused capacity, because there is no reason to lower the price while operating at full capacity. Assuming excess capacity does exist, the firm is $1,000 better off by accepting 10,000 units of additional business at 60 cents per unit if current sales are 50,000 units (below the break-even point) just as it is if current sales are 90,000 units (above the break-even point). In the former case, the loss is reduced from $5,000 to $4,000, while in the latter case profit is increased from $15,000 to $16,000. Of course, if the special market price takes over the regular market, the firm suffers a decrease in profit (or an increase in loss) regardless of what current volume is in relation to the break-even point. The appropriateness of variable cost pricing depends not so much on the volume position with respect to the break-even point, but rather on whether the regular market and the special market can be kept separate.

Even if the special market can be isolated from the regular market, and even if the special order is the most profitable use of the firm's excess capacity, there is an important legal consideration to be taken into account. From a legal standpoint, the company must be careful not to violate the Robinson-Patman Act, a federal antitrust law that relates to price discrimination between customers. This law makes it essential that the firm be able to justify a discriminatory price between customers if the effect is to lessen competition. If these above-mentioned legal and economic conditions can be satisfied, then variable cost pricing is probably appropriate in a special-order or dumping situation.

Regular Products. It is possible to build a pricing procedure for regular products using variable cost as a base. It is usually argued that variable cost is not appropriate in this situation. The use of variable cost pricing is frequently associated with a crisis situation. The presumed crisis in most cases is chronic overcapacity. Such an association is unfortunate, because a careful study of variable cost pricing gives additional insights into the pricing problem. The variable cost method is not a cure-all; but although not widely accepted in business circles, it has many features that should be considered in setting prices.

If variable cost is used, the markup that is added must be large enough to cover all fixed cost and to provide for a profit. There is always danger that the variable cost may, in time, come to be looked upon as the full cost; and in such instances the results would be disastrous. This fear is probably the main reason for the low acceptance of variable cost pricing in modern-day business. The problem, however, should not arise if operating management properly understands the kind of data it is working with. The misuse of cost data that stems from a lack of understanding is a problem throughout accounting and is not unique with variable cost pricing. Education in the proper use of cost data can do much to overcome such a defect.

Another reason why variable cost pricing is not widely accepted has to do with the inability of many conventional accounting systems to measure variable cost properly. Most systems are not geared for this type of measurement, and a careful review of job order and process costing provides convincing evidence of this. The historical reason for this situation is the overwhelming influence that inventory costing and income determination have had on cost systems. Full cost has been considered the most acceptable base for income determination due to the accounting postulate that requires revenue to be recognized only when it is realized. The realization postulate implies inventory valuation at cost. The benefit principle also reinforces the valuation of inventory at full cost. In past decades, perhaps it was clerically impossible to measure both full cost and variable cost; the measurement of variable or incremental cost presented some real difficulties. However, sophisticated computers now make it possible to measure almost any incremental quantity that is of use to management; thus, variable cost pricing is now more operational.

One of the important advantages to be gained from a detailed investigation of variable cost pricing (for regular products) is a deeper knowledge of the relationship between the markup percentage and the market demand function. In pricing policy, even if cost (whether it be a full or variable cost) can be determined, it is still necessary to add the markup in order to establish a price. If the markup is too high, the price is too high and the firm may price itself out of the market. If the markup is too low, the firm charges too low a price and foregoes profit. Hence, the proper markup is related to the market situation.

Outside Influences on Price

Throughout this discussion, the general assumption was made that the company had some control over its prices and that the object was to maximize profit. Frequently a company is virtually forced to accept prices already established by its competitors or finds it necessary to adjust its prices because of the action of others. In some cases the price is not set so that short-run profit is maximized. It may be better strategy in the long run to accept more modest profit and not attract attention that may result in the entry of others into the field. Such a strategy is an attempt to maximize long-run rather than short-run profit. Additionally, social considerations, such as environmental protection and affirmative action employment policies, may take precedence over short-run profit maximization.

By making a study of its costs and the factors that influence the demand for its products, a company can establish prices more intelligently than if either of these factors is ignored. Outside forces may make it difficult to set prices that tend to result in maximum profit; but with a knowledge of its price objectives, a company should be better prepared to take advantage of changing conditions.

QUESTIONS

1. Why is so much emphasis placed on the future in decision making? Does the past have any significance in decision making?

2. What are the relevant costs in decision making?

3. How can opportunity costs be used in deciding whether a product should be sold in a partially completed state or finished and sold as a completed product?

4. How can a manager determine whether or not a product line is making a contribution to the total operation?

5. Should fixed costs be considered in deciding whether a product line should be discontinued?

6. Distinguish between an avoidable and an unavoidable cost.

7. The proper treatment of fixed costs presents a problem in full cost pricing. Briefly explain this statement.

8. Describe the allocation problem encountered in full cost pricing.

9. What are the major considerations in deciding whether variable cost pricing is a good pricing procedure to use for special orders?

10. Assuming the decision-maker had a good measure of cost (both fixed and variable), would pricing still be a difficult problem? Explain.

EXERCISES

1. New Product Decision. The Range company plans to introduce a new product and must decide whether it is to be A or B. The selling price and cost data are as follows:

	Product A	Product B
Selling price per unit	$8	$10
Variable cost per unit	5	2

If Product A is introduced, the manager is certain that 150,000 units can be sold; and this product will use all of the available capacity. However, the manager is uncertain about the demand for Product B. This product is similar to several products now on the market which sell for slightly more than $10; hence the manager wants to set the price at $10 for Product B.

Required: Assuming that there will be no costs incurred other than those given and that the available capacity can be used to produce either Product A or Product B, calculate how many units of Product B would have to be sold to equal the contribution margin that could be earned by selling Product A.

2. Process or Sell Decision. The Hyde Meat Company produces a meat product which can be sold after slaughtering without additional processing, or it can be processed (smoked) and then sold. For the next month the company has scheduled production of 20,000 units of the product which, if sold unprocessed, would bring a selling price of $10 per unit. The variable cost associated with producing the unprocessed product is $6 per unit, and the fixed cost of the facilities used for producing the unprocessed product is $50,000 for the month. If 20,000 units of the unprocessed product are produced, the entire capacity of that part of the plant will be used. However, there will be unused capacity in the part of the plant used for the smoking process. If the 20,000 units are smoked, this capacity, which would otherwise be idle, will be entirely used.

The additional variable cost, mainly for heat and smoking ingredients, is estimated to be $3 per unit; and the selling price of the processed product is $13.50 per unit. The monthly fixed cost depreciation on the portion of the facility used for additional processing amounts to $10,000. This cost is fixed regardless of whether or not the product is processed further.

Required: Prepare an analysis to help the manager decide whether the 20,000 units should be sold processed or unprocessed.

3. Product Combination Decision. Data concerning four product lines are given below:

	Product Line			
	A	B	C	D
Selling price per unit..	$8	$25	$7	$30
Variable cost per unit..	2	10	4	25
Hours required for each unit..........................	3 hrs.	10 hrs.	1 hr.	5 hrs.
Market limit..	None	None	8,000 units	4,000 units

Total fixed cost... $80,000
Total hours available.. 98,000 hrs.

Required:

(1) Based on the above data, choose the best product combination.
(2) How would the answer change if there were no market limitations on any of the products? How much greater is the profit from this combination of products than the profit associated with the combination chosen in (1) above?

4. Opportunity Cost. The Woodburn Golf Club has been asked to host a golf tournament for the Bacon Company. The tournament would require the club to be closed to normal business for one day. This would be feasible since the tournament day would be a Monday and the course is not heavily used on Mondays. The Bacon Company has offered a flat fee of $5,000. Additional expenses for the day are estimated by the club manager to be $200, the cost of hiring some additional casual labor to help clean up after the post-tournament picnic. The manager has estimated that the loss of fees due to closing the club to normal business would be about $2,000. There would be some cost savings (estimated at $500) because several hourly-paid employees would not work that day. The manager feels that there would be no loss of future business as a result of closing for one Monday.

Required:

(1) What is the opportunity cost of closing the club to normal business?

(2) Calculate the additional profit or loss from hosting the tournament.

5. Make or Buy Decision — Graphic Solution. A firm needs two component parts, A and B, which can be manufactured or purchased. The economic information on each part is given below:

	Parts	
	A	B
Number of units required	1,000	3,000
Variable cost per unit	$15	$30
Outside price	$21	$38
Hours required per unit	1 hr.	3 hrs.
Total fixed cost	$100,000	
Total hours available	3,000 hrs.	

Any portion of the requirement can be manufactured or purchased. Define the contribution margin as the difference between the outside purchase price and the variable cost.

Required:

(1) Prepare a graph with Part A on one axis and Part B on the other. Plot the constraints.

(2) Calculate the contribution margin and the number of units of A and B associated with each corner point on the graph.

(3) Choose the best solution.

6. Elimination of a Product Line. The Community Store currently operates three departments. Over the past several months, sales and profit have declined, although the situation is now considered stable. As a result of the sales and profit decline, Department 2 has begun to show a loss and the vice-president has recommended that it be discontinued. The space could be rented to a grocery chain store which would pay a flat fee of $5,000 a month to Community Stores.

An income statement for last month, considered to be typical, is given at the top of the following page. All costs are variable except the fixed administrative costs (allocated equally to all departments) which would not change in total if the department were eliminated.

Required: Prepare an analysis and advise the vice-president whether the department should be discontinued and the space rented.

| | Department | | | |
	1	2	3	Total
Sales..	$150,000	$ 50,000	$100,000	$300,000
Costs:				
Cost of goods sold..	$ 90,000	$ 40,000	$ 50,000	$180,000
Sales salaries	5,000	1,000	4,000	10,000
Fixed administrative cost.............................	20,000	20,000	20,000	60,000
Total cost	$115,000	$ 61,000	$ 74,000	$250,000
Income before income tax.............................	$ 35,000	$(11,000)	$ 26,000	$ 50,000

7. Full Cost Pricing. The Dot Company follows the policy of calculating a selling price by adding a 10% markup to full cost. The variable cost is $40 per unit, and the total fixed cost is $1,200,000.

Required: Calculate the selling price per unit for 40,000 units, 50,000 units, and 60,000 units, assuming that fixed cost is allocated to units based on the number produced.

8. Full and Variable Cost Pricing. The Castle Company produces two products, A and B. Data on cost and production are given below:

	Product A	Product B
Materials cost per unit — variable............................	$20	$10
Labor hours required per unit....................................	4 hrs.	2 hrs.
Hourly labor rate	$10	$6
Planned production	30,000 units	20,000 units
Annual overhead — fixed...	$800,000	

Required:

(1) Assuming the manager wants to set a price with a 10% markup based on full cost, prepare an analysis showing what the selling price for each product would be if the overhead cost were allocated on the basis of labor hours.
(2) Assuming that labor cost is variable, show the manager what the markup, stated as a percentage of unit variable cost, would have to be to give prices equal to those calculated in (1).

9. Special Order Pricing. The Crane Company is selling 90,000 units of a product at $10 per unit. The variable cost is $7 per unit, and the annual fixed cost is $150,000. A discount house has offered to buy 10,000 additional units of the product which would be slightly modified, but the modifications would not affect production cost. The discount house will pay $9 per unit.

Required: If the two markets can be distinguished, should the order be accepted (assuming capacity exists and has no other use)? Would your decision be affected if the manager felt that the two markets could not be distinguished and that the lower price would likely take over the main market as well as the special market?

10. Explaining Profit Differences. The Starret Company sells for $30 per unit a product which has a variable cost of $15 per unit. The planned sales for the coming year are 100,000 units. With annual fixed cost of $550,000, the controller estimates the following profit per unit:

Selling price per unit		$30.00
Variable cost per unit	$15.00	
Fixed cost per unit ($550,000 ÷ 100,000 units)	5.50	20.50
Profit per unit		$ 9.50

During the year, the company actually sold 110,000 units; and the president, based on the controller's calculations, estimated the profit to be $1,045,000. When the statements were prepared, the profit was $1,100,000 even though all of the actual costs were as estimated.

Required: Prepare an analysis to show why the profit was $55,000 greater than had been estimated.

PROBLEMS

9-1. Product Combination Decision. The Brown Company sells two products which can be sold in any combination so long as no more than 180,000 machine hours are used. All costs are variable (labor and materials) except for the rental cost of the production facility, which is $400,000 per year. The economic data for each product are as follows:

	Product A	Product B
Selling price per unit	$15	$10
Variable cost	$ 6	$ 5
Machine hours per unit	3 hrs.	2 hrs.

Required:
(1) In the absence of any market constraints, what is the most profitable combination of products and what is the profit?
(2) If the market for Product A is limited to 50,000 units with no market limit on Product B, how does this change the best product combination and the profit?
(3) What is the best product combination (and the profit) if a shortage of materials for Product B limits the production of that product to 10,000 units and there is a market limit of 50,000 units of A?

9-2. Product Combination Decision. The Bond Company produces two products using a single production process in which the main constraint is machine hours. The economic data are given below.

	Product X	Product Y
Selling price per unit	$20	$8
Variable cost per unit	$14	$4
Machine hours per unit	1 hr.	2 hrs.
Market limitation	100,000 units	33,000 units
Total machine hours available	150,000 hrs.	
Total fixed cost	$150,000	

Required:
(1) Find the best combination of products.
(2) If demand will hold up, should the company rent additional machines for $5,000 per year which will provide 5,000 additional capacity hours per machine? How many machines should be ordered?

9-3. Determining Least-Cost Alternative. Ajax Construction, Inc., plans to erect a new building. It will use part of the space for its own offices and lease the balance of the space to tenants. The company has two alternatives: (1) do its own construction work, or (2) use an independent contractor.

Cost estimates have been prepared showing the costs of operation for the coming year during which the new building will be constructed. The costs of constructing the building, if done by Ajax, are included in that set of estimates.

If the company does its own construction work, it will not be able to handle outside construction contracts that would contribute $500,000 to net income. The costs attributable to these outside contracts are excluded from the estimated costs of operation shown below.

	Estimated Costs to Operate — Construction by Independent Contractors	Estimated Costs to Operate (Including Construction) — Construction by Ajax Company
Materials	$6,000,000	$7,000,000
Labor	3,000,000	4,800,000
Indirect materials and supplies	315,000	400,000
Supervision	650,000	780,000
Taxes and insurance	50,000	55,000
Heat and light	47,000	47,000
Maintenance and repairs	106,000	106,000
Truck and equipment operation	91,000	91,000
Depreciation	60,000	60,000
Travel	40,000	43,000
Telephone	10,000	10,000
Other utilities	50,000	50,000
Miscellaneous	10,000	10,000

The independent company has bid $4,000,000 for the job.

Required: Which of the two alternatives should be selected to obtain the lowest construction cost? Show calculations. (Ignore income tax.)

9-4. Make or Buy Decision. The Ling Company produces a part used in the final assembly of its main product. Two manufacturing operations are required to produce the part. Typical annual production of the part is 150,000 units. The estimated current costs are as follows:

Operation 1:
Materials	$120,000
Direct labor	90,000
Variable overhead	50,000
General overhead	60,000
Total cost, Operation 1	$320,000

Operation 2:
Direct labor	$ 90,000
Variable overhead	50,000
General overhead	30,000
Total cost, Operation 2	$170,000

The general overhead is fixed. The other costs are variable.

Operation 1 can be eliminated if these parts are purchased from an outside vendor. The vendor will supply 150,000 units a year at $2 per unit. These parts would still have to be processed through Operation 2. The Ling Company would have to pay freight of $5,000 per year on the purchased parts. If Operation 1 is eliminated, the space can be rented for $10,000 per year.

Required: Prepare an analysis to help the company decide whether to purchase the parts or to continue to manufacture them in Operation 1.

9-5. Make or Buy Decision. The Saul Company produces a line of iron and steel building products. Several subassemblies and parts enter into the line of products, and many of these parts and components can be either produced by Saul or purchased from outside suppliers. Several of these parts are listed below with related cost and production data.

	Iron Frames 10	Steel Frames 11	Steel Housing 12	Assembly Unit 13
Materials cost per unit................................	$2.00	$1.00	$ 8.00	$2.00
Variable labor cost per unit........................	1.50	1.00	5.00	3.00
Overhead cost per unit (100% of labor cost)...	1.50	1.00	5.00	3.00
Total cost per unit.......................................	$5.00	$3.00	$18.00	$8.00
Hours required per unit..............................	1 hr.	4 hrs.	4 hrs.	2 hrs.

The above four parts can be produced or purchased. The plant facility is flexible in that the particular department involved can produce these parts in any combination. However, the main product in this department is a steel shaft that cannot be purchased outside. This shaft is used in most of the company's products and consequently has first priority on capacity.

The materials and the labor are considered to be variable costs, but the overhead cost in total is fixed. The overhead is assigned to products at the rate of 100% of direct labor cost. This rate is a predetermined rate established from the factory overhead budget.

The capacity of the producing department is 500,000 machine hours, and 80% of the capacity is to be used for producing shafts. The forecast requirements and outside price quotations on the parts for the coming period are as follows:

Part Number	Units Required	Outside Prices
10..	100,000	$ 4.00
11..	80,000	2.60
12..	15,000	19.00
13..	100,000	4.50

Consider the contribution margin to be the difference between the outside purchase price and the appropriate cost of manufacturing.

Required: Using contribution margin analysis, show the manager how much of each product to manufacture and how much of each to purchase. What is the dollar contribution associated with your solution? Assume that a portion of the requirement for each product can be purchased.

9-6. Elimination of Product. The Ken Company currently sells three products whose quantities, selling prices, and variable costs are given at the top of the following page.

Product	Quantity	Selling Price	Variable Cost
110.....................	5,000	$15	$14
111.....................	10,000	10	4
112.....................	15,000	20	13

The fixed cost for the operation is $120,000, and it is allocated on the basis of the total units produced. The plant is currently at capacity, and each unit requires the same production time. The cost report for Product 110 given below shows that this product is not profitable.

Selling price per unit..		$15
Variable cost per unit..	$14	
Fixed cost per unit...	4	18
Loss per unit...		$(3)

The fixed cost per unit is calculated by dividing the total fixed cost, $120,000, by the units produced, 30,000.

The above report causes the sales manager to argue that Product 110 should be dropped from the product line, stating that is is difficult to make up on volume what is lost on the individual unit.

Required:

(1) If no alternative exists for the use of capacity, should Product 110 be dropped?

(2) If more of Product 111 can be sold at $10 per unit, should Product 110 be dropped?

(3) How much would the selling price of Product 110 have to be increased to make it as desirable as Product 111?

9-7. Elimination of Product Line. Assume the same situation as in Problem 9-6. However, if Product 110 is dropped, no additional units of Product 111 or Product 112 can be sold.

The sales manager finds another product, 113, which can be sold for $20 and has a variable cost of $19.75. In addition, it takes only one third the time to produce Product 113 as it takes to produce Product 110.

The sales manager argues that Product 113 should be added and Product 110 should be dropped, saying, "It is true that the contribution margin per unit is 75 cents less on Product 113 than on Product 110 (25 cents compared with $1); but since more units of Product 113 can be produced, the fixed cost per unit will also go down. As a matter of fact, the fixed cost per unit on all units will drop by $1 — from $4 ($120,000 ÷ 30,000 units) to $3 ($120,000 ÷ 40,000 units) — if we switch to Product 113."

Required: Is the sales manager right? How much would the price on Product 113 have to be increased before it would be as profitable as Product 110? Explain the error in the sales manager's reasoning.

9-8. Pricing Decision. The Kim Company is currently producing and selling two products, X and Y. The data on costs, selling prices, and volume are given below:

	Product X	Product Y
Selling price per unit	$15	$25
Variable cost per unit — labor and materials...........	11	15
Fixed overhead cost per unit allocated to products	5	5
Units sold..	10,000	30,000

The total fixed overhead is $200,000 per year and is allocated equally since each product requires equal production time. Product Y requires a higher-priced material, which explains why the variable cost of this product is higher than for Product X.

A major company in the industry is looked on as a price leader. Most of the smaller companies follow its actions on price setting. Recently this company reduced the price on Product X to $14. The sales manager and the president of Kim Company are attempting to determine what to do in response to this action. The sales manager estimates that if the price on Product X is held at $15, sales will probably decline to 9,000 units. If the company follows the price decrease and reduces the price of Product X to $14, it is estimated that volume can be maintained at 10,000 units. However, the sales manager notes that the loss on Product X is already $1 at the selling price of $15 and suggests to the president that the product be dropped entirely. Such an action would provide unused capacity, since no more units of Y can be sold and there is no substitute product immediately available. Whatever is done, argues the sales manager, the price on Product X should not be reduced to $14, since the action will only increase the loss per unit from $1 to $2.

Required: Advise the president on the proper course to follow. Show your calculations.

9-9. Special Order Pricing. The Galvin Company produces a limited line of plastic containers that are used to store and ship certain chemical compounds. The capacity of the plant is 500,000 labor hours, and it takes an average of four hours to produce one container. For the last few years, the company has been producing about 115,000 containers per year; but the prospects for the coming year look very bright. Several new industrial plants have recently located in the area, and the company management believes that the excess capacity can now be used. The average price of the standard container is $220 per unit, and the cost structure is as follows:

	Cost per Unit
Materials...	$130
Labor..	50
Overhead..	16
Total...	$196

The materials and labor are considered to be variable costs. The total overhead is fixed and is allocated to the product on the basis of hours. The rate calculation is as follows:

$$\frac{\text{Estimated overhead}}{\text{Hours of capacity}} = \frac{\$2,000,000}{500,000} = \$4 \text{ per hour}$$

The price of $220 per standard container is now fairly well established within the industry. The company set this price by adding to the full cost a profit of $24 per unit.

The company has been approached by a contracting officer for the government to build 10,000 special containers. The materials cost has been estimated to be $25 less per unit than on standard containers, and the labor time will be about the same. The sales manager has calculated the price, as shown on the next page, for the contracting officer.

	Cost per Unit
Materials..	$105
Labor	50
Overhead..	16
	$171
Markup (4 hours @ $6)	24
Price	$195

The contracting officer, in reviewing the calculation, notices that the markup based on cost for the special container ($24 ÷ $171 = 14% approximately) is higher than for the standard container ($24 ÷ $196 = 12.2% approximately). The officer argues that the price on the special container should be reduced so as to make the special container no more profitable than the standard container.

Required: Assuming that the company wants to set the special container price to make it no more profitable than the standard container, is the $195 price appropriate? If so, explain why the contracting officer's reasoning with respect to the markup percentage is incorrect. What price should be charged?

9-10. Process or Sell Decision. The Spencer Company manufactures a type of raw sheet metal that can be sold at this stage or processed more and sold as a type of alloy used in manufacturing high-grade control systems of various types. The raw sheet metal market is such that the entire output can be sold at the market price, which at the present time is $200 per ton. The processed selling price has been about $380 per ton for several years, but recently the market has been weak and the price has dropped as low as $280 on several occasions. This has caused the sales manager to suggest that the alloy is no longer profitable and should be dropped and that the entire capacity should be used to produce the raw metal. This is feasible since the production facility is interchangeable. That is, the production facility used now to produce the alloy could be devoted to producing more raw sheet metal on a ton-for-ton basis. The sales manager's suggestion is prompted by the data shown below.

	Cost per Ton of Raw Sheet Metal	Cost per Ton of Alloy
Materials	$100	
Direct labor...	20	
Overhead...	60	
Cost per ton	$180	$180
Selling price...	200	
Profit..	$ 20	
Processing cost:		
Additional materials		40
Direct labor		20
Overhead..		60
Cost per ton of alloy......................		$300
Selling price of alloy......................		280
Loss		$ (20)

The sales manager argues that, because of a $20 loss per unit on the alloy, the product should be dropped any time the price per ton falls below $300.

In the cost calculations, materials and labor costs are variable. The overhead rate per unit is calculated by estimating the total overhead for the coming year and dividing this total by the total hours of capacity available. Since the raw metal and the alloy require the same producing time, the rate per unit is the same. The total overhead is, for the most part, a fixed cost.

Required:

(1) Should the alloy be dropped and the entire production facility be used to produce raw metal if the price per ton of alloy for the coming year is estimated to be $300? Support your conclusion with an appropriate analysis.

(2) Prepare an analysis to aid the sales manager in determining the lowest alloy price that would be acceptable to the company.

9-11. Allocation of Production Between Manufacturing Plants. The Van Company has two plants producing an equivalent grade of inexpensive alloy from a material which is a waste product in the manufacture of steel. One plant is located in Michigan and the other in Ohio. The Michigan plant has been operating at 75% of capacity producing 2,700 tons of alloy per period, and the Ohio plant also has been operating at 75% of capacity producing 3,600 tons per period. For each ton of alloy, it requires a ton of materials — the waste metal. The price of the materials is $20 per ton at either plant with no limitation on the supply.

The cost and production data for a typical period are as follows:

	Michigan Plant	Ohio Plant
Materials: (2,700 tons used)	$ 54,000	
(3,600 tons used)		$ 72,000
Fixed cost per period	60,000	170,000
Variable cost (estimated to be constant per		
ton of output)	121,500	154,800
Total cost	$235,500	$396,800
Production	2,700 tons	3,600 tons
Cost per ton	$87.22	$110.22

The production manager would like to shift production to the Michigan plant to take advantage of the lower cost per ton. This plant is the older of the two plants and the fixed cost of operation is low.

Required: Prepare an analysis to show the production manager how the production should be scheduled. Assume that the present output of 6,300 tons will be continued (disregard any marketing costs and assume that the total fixed cost will not change). As part of your analysis, show the cost savings that will result from your recommendation.

9-12. Make or Buy with Complications. The management of Swann Products, Inc., has been operating at below normal capacity, and there does not appear to be an opportunity to add a new product line that will increase profit.

The production manager suggests that a component, presently being purchased from Hart Supply Company, can be produced by the company. Normally 120,000 units of this component are needed each year. The cost to manufacture 120,000 units has been estimated as shown at the beginning of the following page.

Direct materials...	$ 840,000	560
Direct labor..	480,000	320
Variable overhead..	150,000	100
Additional fixed overhead if components are made......................	90,000	90
Allocated fixed overhead (150% of direct labor)...........................	720,000	480,000
Total cost...	$2,280,000	1,550,000

This component can be purchased from Hart Supply Company at a price of $13.50 per unit.

The sales manager objects to this plan, stating that Hart Supply Company is also a customer and that the company sells 40,000 units of a finished product to the supplier and that these units add $25,000 to profit each year. This market will be lost if purchases are not made from the supplier. Furthermore, only 80,000 units of the component will be needed if the sales are lost, inasmuch as 40,000 units of this component are used to make the product sold to Hart Supply Company.

Required: Based upon the information given, should Swann Products, Inc., make the component or purchase it from Hart Supply Company?

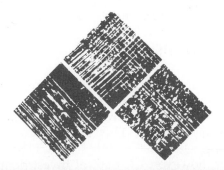

10
THE CAPITAL INVESTMENT DECISION

In the normal course of business, a company may invest in materials and process them into products that are sold. The return from this investment is received in a relatively short time after the investment is made.

In contrast, a *capital investment* is an investment that yields returns during future periods that are relatively far removed from the time of the investment. Capital investments include land and buildings, equipment, securities of other companies, and sales promotion campaigns. The common characteristic of all of these examples is that present expenditures are being made in anticipation of increased future returns.

Capital investment decisions are extremely important, and top management usually assumes direct responsibility for the authorization of substantial expenditures. Capital investment decisions deserve the attention of top management because:

1. Substantial sums of money usually are invested in capital projects.
2. The resources that are invested in a project are often committed for a long period of time.
3. It may be difficult to reverse the effects of a poor decision.
4. The success or failure of the company may depend upon a single or relatively few investment decisions.
5. Plans must be made well into an uncertain future.

THE INVESTMENT PROBLEM

Plans for capital investment are usually prepared for several years into the future. Projects are assigned priorities, costs are estimated for the various projects, and plans are made to obtain the resources required to finance the projects. This is the broad problem of capital investment planning.

In this chapter, however, the capital investment problem is examined from a more limited point of view. It is assumed that the project has received general approval and that it can be financed. The problem is to select from among competing alternatives the specific investment candidate that will produce the best returns for the company. In other words, the investment alternatives are mutually exclusive. If one alternative is accepted, the others must be rejected. For example, a new building may be needed. The company may have a choice of sites and has to decide which site to select. Advantages and disadvantages are attributed to each location. Comparisons of the quantified data are made to determine the best alternative. A similar type of problem faces the individual who needs a new home and has the means to finance it. Which home should be bought? If one is selected, the others must be rejected.

FACTORS IN THE INVESTMENT DECISION

Three important factors are involved in the evaluation of investment alternatives:

1. The net amount of the investment.
2. The expected returns from the investment.
3. The lowest acceptable rate of return on the investment.

In making an investment decision, the returns must be evaluated in relation to the investment. The return from a capital investment, however, is received in future time periods. If a comparison is to be made, the returns must be discounted to a present value. An amount such as $100 due at the end of ten years, for example, is not equivalent to $100 available today. This is because the $100 available today can be invested to produce a larger sum at the end of ten years, whereas the $100 to be received at the end of ten years cannot be invested until then. For example, if 14 percent can be earned on investment, the $100 to be received in ten years is equivalent to $27 today. Stated in another way, $27 is the present value of $100 to be received in ten years with interest compounded annually at 14 percent.

The returns that are expected from each capital investment alternative are discounted to a present value and are compared with the net amount to be invested. To be acceptable, an investment project must meet a *minimum rate-of-return* requirement. The most acceptable project is the one that shows the best return potential in relation to the amount invested and the minimum rate-of-return criterion. The minimum rate-of-return is also known as the *cut-off rate* or *hurdle rate*.

The first step in the selection process is to estimate the net investment required for each investment alternative and to estimate the returns that it should produce over its useful life. However, the definitions for net investment and net returns are somewhat different from those used in conventional accounting practice.

The Net Investment

For decision-making purposes, the net investment is not necessarily the cost that would be entered in the accounting records. Differential costs, as defined in Chapter 2, are also important to the capital investment decision. In many cases the investment is the net additional outlay of cash that is required to obtain future returns. The net investment for decision purposes is generally the net outflow of cash to support a capital investment project.

In some cases, however, the net investment is the sacrifice of an inflow of cash; that is, the opportunity cost that arises when a benefit is rejected. Assume, for example, that a building can be sold for $800,000. Should the building be sold, or should it be held for use in future operations? This is an investment decision. If the building is sold, the cost of the building and the accumulated depreciation are removed from the accounting records. The proceeds from the sale are recorded along with any gain or loss on the transaction. If management refuses the sales offer and elects to use the building in operations, it has invested $800,000 in the future operation of the building. Apparently, management has decided that the future returns justify the sacrifice of an immediate return of $800,000. Obviously, there is no cost to be recorded in the accounting records as a result of this decision. The company continues to operate as it has before. The opportunity cost is relevant only when deciding whether or not to continue operations.

The Net Returns

The returns from an investment, as defined for decision-making purposes, are not the accounting profit. Instead, the returns are the inflows of cash expected from a project reduced by the cash cost that can be directly attributed to the project. Some projects, however, are not expected to produce an inflow of cash, but they will yield returns in the form of cash savings. For example, a new type of machine may be operated at a lower labor cost; and there may be lower costs of machine maintenance and repairs. The annual cash saving, adjusted for income tax, is the annual return on the investment.

The Lowest Acceptable Rate of Return

Relative to opportunities, funds are usually scarce and can be obtained only at a cost. There is an interest charge for the use of borrowed funds. The interest cost for the use of resources is present even when the funds are furnished by the owners either as paid-in capital or as retained earnings. The owners expect to receive a return on their investment — interest, dividends, or rent, as the case may be. Normally an investment is not made unless the present value of the returns is expected to exceed the cost of the capital invested.

The *cost of capital* may be thought of as the average rate of return that a firm must pay to attract investment funds. Although an average rate of return is exceedingly difficult to measure, it must be estimated to adequately perform capital investment analysis. Funds for investment may be obtained from a number of different sources. The cost of capital associated with the issuance of long-term bonds is considered to be the after-tax interest cost. Preferred stock usually specifies a required dividend rate, and this rate may be used as the cost of capital. The cost of investment capital from common stockholders may be based on the long-term dividends which must be distributed to support the market price of the firm's common stock. This cost is the rate of discount that would equate the present value of the future dividends to the current market value of the stock. The average cost of capital to be used in determining the lowest acceptable rate of return would then be a weighted average of the various capital costs determined by the firm's capital structure.

The cost of capital may also be thought of as an opportunity cost. It is the rate of return expected in the future from the set of average investment opportunities normally available to the firm given its usual lines of business. For example, if a company can receive a 10 percent average return from certain investments, it would not accept less than 10 percent from alternative investments in the same risk category.

The determination of the cost of capital is an important and difficult part of investment analysis. A more complete discussion of cost of capital can be found in most basic finance textbooks. In the discussion that follows, it is assumed that the cost of capital has been determined.

RATING INVESTMENT ALTERNATIVES

The net returns from each investment alternative are related to the net investment, and the results are compared using the lowest acceptable rate of return as a cutoff point. One of three methods is generally employed in rating investment alternatives:

1. The payback method.
2. The discounted rate-of-return method.
3. The net present value method.

The Payback Method

Investment alternatives are sometimes evaluated by relating the returns to the cost of the investment to determine how many years it will take to recover the investment. This method is simple to apply and in many cases gives answers approximately equivalent to those given by more sophisticated methods of analysis that are described later. However, this method is reliable only if the returns are evenly distributed over the years and if the investments to be compared are equal in amount and have the same life estimates with little or no salvage values.

Assume that investment of $20,000 is expected to produce annual returns of $5,000 for ten years. No salvage recovery is expected from the investment at the end of the ten years. The investment is recovered in four years, as calculated below.

$$\frac{\$20,000 \text{ investment}}{\$5,000 \text{ annual return}} = \text{4-year payback period}$$

The ratio of the investment to the annual return is 4 to 1. Expressed in another way, the unadjusted rate of return is 25 percent, as follows:

$$\frac{\$5,000 \text{ annual return}}{\$20,000 \text{ investment}} = 25\% \text{ rate of return}$$

The alternative with the shortest payback period or the highest unadjusted rate of return is the most acceptable, provided it meets the minimum standard that has been established. If a payback period of four years satisfies the minimum standard that has been established and if no other alternative in this investment category has a shorter payback period, the investment should be accepted.

The Discounted Rate-of-Return Method

If returns are to be compared with a related investment, both the returns and the investment should be stated on a present value basis. Future dollar amounts are not equivalent to dollars in the present because of the difference in time. This discrepancy is remedied by converting future dollars to present value. (The present value concept is explained in Appendix C.)

Time-related money value differences should not be confused with the problems of changes in the purchasing power of money and foreign exchange conversions. Such differences in monetary amounts must be considered even in an economic environment where the purchasing power of money and foreign exchange rates remain constant. However, in times when inflation and unfavorable exchange rates are expected, the minimum acceptable rate of return will probably be higher in an attempt to compensate for the risk of loss of purchasing power of the returns.

A rate of return can be computed on an investment by discounting the estimated future returns at an interest (discount) rate that equates the present value of the returns with the investment. This rate of return is the discounted rate of return on the investment. To be acceptable, the discounted rate of return on an investment alternative must be at least equal to the minimum rate-of-return requirement. Ordinarily, the most acceptable investment alternative is the one that is expected to produce the highest discounted rate of return.

The discounted rate of return can be calculated by trial and error. If the annual inflows are an equal amount for each year, the ratio of the investment to the annual return is calculated just as it is in the payback method. This ratio is then compared with the present values of annuities for the same number of years given in published tables. The discount rate for the present value of an annuity that most nearly corresponds with the ratio is selected as the rate of return.

In the last example, it was assumed that a $20,000 investment would yield returns of $5,000 each year with no salvage value. The discounted rate of return is computed as follows:

(1) Determine the payback period (the ratio of the investment to the annual return).

$$\frac{\$20,000 \text{ investment}}{\$5,000 \text{ annual return}} = 4\text{-year payback period}$$

(2) Find the factor on the appropriate year line of a table of present values of $1 received annually that comes closest to the payback period.

The factor 3.923, appearing in the 22% column, is closest to 4 on the 10-year line. (See Table II on page 552.) The investment is expected to have a 10-year life in this example. Therefore, the present value factor is taken from the 10-year line of the table.

(3) Use the interest rate identified with this factor to discount the future annual returns.

$5,000 **annual** × 3.923 **present value**   = $19,615 **present value**
        return   **of $1 received**   **of returns**
                                annually for
                                10 years at 22%

If the present value of the returns is approximately equal to the present value of the investment, the discounted rate of return has been determined. In the example, the present value of the returns amounting to $19,615 is not quite equal to the investment of $20,000. The investment earns somewhat less than 22 percent. If the minimum rate-of-return requirement is 18 percent, this investment alternative would more than meet the minimum standard and would be selected provided that no competing alternative promised an even better rate of return.

The returns for each year are not always equal in amount. Returns for the early years may be relatively large when compared with returns for the later years. Conversely, a project may develop slowly with returns increasing in the later years. A discounted rate of return may have to be computed by trial and error when annual returns are unequal. An average annual return may be calculated and used to find the ratio between the investment and the annual return. This ratio is compared with the present value factors in the table for the appropriate number of years. If the returns for the early years are comparatively large, the first trial may be made by selecting a rate higher than the rate found in the table. If the returns for the early years are relatively low, a lower rate may be selected for the first trial. Using the discount rate selected, the present value for each year is computed. The present values are then added and their sum compared with the present value of the investment. An example of this procedure is given on pages 547–549.

The Net Present Value Method

Investment alternatives can be evaluated without solving for the discounted rate of return. Future dollar amounts can be discounted at the lowest acceptable rate of return and the present value of the returns compared with the present value of the investment. The alternative that produces the greatest excess of returns over the investment (on a present-value basis) is the most acceptable. If the present value of the returns is less than the present value of the investment, the investment alternative does not meet the rate-of-return requirement and should be rejected.

In the previous example, the minimum rate-of-return requirement was 18 percent. The $5,000 annual returns that are expected for ten years are discounted at 18 percent and are compared with the investment of $20,000.

$$\$5,000 \text{ annual} \times 4.494 \text{ present value of } \$1 = \$22,470$$
$$\text{return} \qquad \text{received each year}$$
$$\text{for 10 years at 18\%}$$

The excess present value or net present value of the returns is $2,470.

Present value of returns..	$22,470
Investment..	20,000
Excess present value of returns	**$ 2,470**

Assume that another investment alternative is being contemplated. The net investment is $24,000 with estimated annual returns of $6,000 to be received over a period of eight years. The returns are discounted at 18 percent and are compared with the investment of $24,000.

$$\$6,000 \text{ annual} \times 4.078 \text{ present value of } \$1 = \$24,468$$
$$\text{return} \qquad \text{received each year}$$
$$\text{for 8 years at 18\%}$$

The excess present value of the returns is $468.

Present value of returns...	$24,468
Investment...	24,000
Excess present value of returns..	$ 468

Although both alternatives exceed the minimum rate-of-return objective, the excess present value of $2,470 from the first alternative is more than the excess present value of $468 from the second alternative. Assuming that available capital limits the firm to choosing only one of the projects, the alternative with the higher excess present value should be selected.

Note that the decision is not influenced by the amount of the investment or the length of time involved. The computation in either case provides for the recovery of the investment itself plus the desired rate of return. The assumption is that returns can be reinvested at this desired rate. Hence, the alternative that produces a greater excess present value adds more to total wealth as returns are reinvested over time.

REFINING THE INVESTMENT

For decision-making purposes an *investment* is a net outflow of cash, a commitment of cash, or the sacrifice of an inflow of cash. Sometimes adjustments must be made to determine the net investment. Three typical investment adjustments are discussed at this point:

1. The avoidable costs.
2. Additional investment in current assets.
3. The net proceeds from the sale of properties to be retired as a result of the investment.

Avoidable Costs

By making an investment, a company may be able to avoid some other cost. A cost that would otherwise be incurred will not be incurred if the investment is made.

For example, a company may be considering the purchase of new equipment costing $130,000. If this equipment is not purchased, extensive repairs will have to be made to the equipment now in service. The cost of the repairs is estimated at $15,000, and this cost is deductible in computing income tax that is estimated at 40 percent of income before income tax. The tax deduction of $15,000 for repairs cost will reduce income tax by $6,000 (40 percent of $15,000). The net cost of the repairs after income tax is $9,000. The company receives a tax benefit of $6,000 from the deduction for repairs cost. Without the deduction, income tax of $6,000 would have to be paid. Hence, if an investment is made in new equipment, the company will avoid the repair cost net of income tax or will avoid a cost of $9,000 ($15,000 − $6,000). The net investment is computed at the top of the next page.

Investment in new equipment............................		$130,000
Less avoidable cost:		
Repairs cost to keep old equipment in operation...	$15,000	
Less income tax saving of 40% on repairs deduction...	6,000	
Net avoidable cost...		9,000
Net investment..		**$121,000**

The net investment of $121,000 is compared with the estimated future returns discounted at the lowest acceptable rate of return (net present value method) in making a decision. Or the estimated future returns may be discounted at a rate that equates the present value of the returns with the investment (discounted rate-of-return method) to determine if the investment meets the minimum rate of return requirement.

Additional Investment in Current Assets

Investment situations often involve the introduction of a new product line or the expansion of facilities. If the project is to be undertaken, it may have to be supported by an additional investment in current assets. For example, a new line of product may be introduced. As a result, the investment in inventory will be higher, accounts receivable will increase and the cash balance must be increased to provide for the additional operating cost. The required increment in current assets is part of the investment in the project because they must be held to support the project. When the project is eliminated, the related current assets are released.

Assume that a new project requires an investment of $500,000 in new equipment and additional current assets of $96,000 consisting of cash, accounts receivable, and inventory as shown in the following computation of the net investment.

New equipment for project................................		$500,000
Add additional current assets:		
Cash...	$18,000	
Accounts receivable	33,000	
Inventory...	45,000	
Total additional current assets		96,000
Net investment...		**$596,000**

The investment in the current assets, as well as the salvage value of the equipment, will be recovered at the termination of the project. The present value of the current assets released and of the net salvage value recovered can be included as a return from the investment in the last year of the project's life.

It is estimated that the project will yield annual returns of $120,000 after income tax for ten years and that the equipment will have a salvage value (net of income tax) of $60,000 at the end of the project. In addition, the current assets of $96,000 that were required for operations will be released. The annual returns for the first nine years are then $120,000, but the return for the tenth year is $276,000 ($120,000 return from operation of the project plus $60,000 net salvage recovery plus $96,000 release of current assets). The returns are discounted to present values and are compared with the investment according to the procedures discussed earlier in the chapter.

Net Proceeds from the Sale of Other Properties

Properties may be retired as a result of an investment decision. If new equipment is obtained, for example, the equipment currently in operation may be sold. The proceeds from the sale of the old equipment as adjusted for the income tax on any recognized gain or loss are deducted from the cost of the new equipment to arrive at the net investment. To illustrate, assume that equipment costing $100,000 is to be acquired. If this equipment is acquired, equipment having a net book value of $20,000 will be sold for $5,000. The loss of $15,000 on the sale is deductible in computing income tax estimated at 40 percent of income before tax. The company can reduce its income tax by $6,000 (40% of $15,000 loss) by selling the equipment. The total benefit to be derived from selling this equipment amounts to $11,000 — the $5,000 proceeds from the sale plus the income tax reduction of $6,000. The net investment is computed as follows:

Investment in new equipment		$100,000
Less benefit from the sale of old equipment:		
Gross proceeds...	$5,000	
Add reduction of income tax (40% of $15,000		
loss deduction)	6,000	
Total benefit		11,000
Net investment		**$ 89,000**

If a taxable gain results from the sale of property, income tax is increased. The total amount received from the sale of property is reduced by the tax on the gain to determine the net amount retained by the taxpayer.

Assume, in the last example, that the equipment having a net book value of $20,000 can be sold for $35,000 and that the gain of $15,000 will be taxed at a rate of 30 percent.[1] The net proceeds from the sale of equipment will amount to $30,500 after subtracting the tax of $4,500 (30 percent of $15,000) from the $35,000 received from the sale of the equipment.

---

[1] The federal tax rate on the ordinary income of a corporation above $100,000 is 46 percent. (In most instances throughout this text, a 40 percent rate is used to simplify illustrations.) The gain on the sale of depreciable property may be treated as a capital gain with a lower rate of tax on the actual gain as a result of the capital gains exclusion. Specific circumstances will govern whether or not the rate will be limited to 30 percent. (A 30 percent rate is used to simplify illustrations.)

The net investment in the new equipment is computed as follows:

Investment in new equipment............................		$100,000
Less net benefit from the sale of old equipment:		
Gross proceeds...	$35,000	
Less income tax on gain of $15,000 (30% of $15,000)	4,500	
Net benefit..		30,500
Net investment..		**$ 69,500**

Often the old equipment will be traded in when new equipment is acquired. There is no income tax on a gain from a trade-in transaction, nor is any loss deduction allowed. Therefore, the net investment is equal to the cost of new equipment minus the trade-in allowance.

DEPRECIATION AND INCOME TAX

In many investment projects, the firm may acquire assets which are depreciable for income tax purposes. *Depreciation* is the process of allocating an asset's cost to the accounting periods over which the asset is used. The possible tax effect of depreciation must be considered in evaluating investment proposals. Depreciation is normally thought of as an annual cost of operations to be deducted from revenue in calculating net income, but this annual cost does not constitute a cash outflow. The cash outflow normally takes place at the time the asset is purchased. However, depreciation cost is an allowable deduction in the computation of income tax, and because income tax is an out-of-pocket cost and involves a cash outflow, depreciation must be considered in investment analysis.

To illustrate, assume that Davis Supply Company can obtain for $330,000 a new machine that will have a useful life of ten years and no salvage value. This machine is expected to yield an annual cash operating saving of $90,000 without deducting depreciation and before income tax. Assuming that the income tax rate is 40 percent, the estimated net annual saving after income tax is $54,000 as computed below:

Estimated annual saving before income tax	$90,000
Less income tax at 40% of the saving.....................................	36,000
Net annual saving	$54,000

In the above computation, depreciation on the new machine has not been considered. A plant asset is in effect a collection of potential services that will benefit future years. When depreciation is based on physical units of service, the depreciation method is referred to as the *production-unit method*. When the cost of plant assets is charged equally to each year, the depreciation method is called the *straight-line method*. The formula for the straight-line method is expressed as shown at the top of the next page.

$$\frac{\text{Cost} - \text{residual value}}{\text{Estimated life in years}} = \text{Annual depreciation}$$

Using the straight-line method, depreciation of $33,000 will be deducted each year on the new machine.

$$\frac{\$330,000 \text{ cost} - \text{zero (salvage value)}}{10 \text{ years of useful life}} = \$33,000 \text{ annual depreciation}$$

The depreciation will reduce income tax by $13,200 (40% of $33,000). The income tax saving from the depreciation deduction enhances the annual cash saving. The net annual saving is actually $67,200 as computed below:

Estimated annual saving in out-of-pocket cost before income tax		$90,000
Less: Income tax on out-of-pocket cost saving (40% of $90,000)	$36,000	
Income tax saving from depreciation deduction (40% of $33,000)	$13,200	
Net income tax effect		22,800
Estimated annual saving in out-of-pocket cost after income tax		$67,200

When plant assets are replaced, depreciation on the new assets may be more or less than the depreciation on the old assets that are traded or sold. The difference in depreciation will cause the income tax to be higher or lower. For example, the new machine in the example above is expected to yield annual cash savings of $90,000 before income tax. The depreciation on the new machine is estimated each year at $33,000. If the old machine is to be traded in to acquire the new machine, the annual depreciation that could be obtained by retaining the old machine must be considered. Assume that depreciation of $15,000 could have been deducted each year for three years on the old machine. In this case, the depreciation advantage from the new machine for the first three years is only $18,000 per year. The tax saving from the depreciation advantage is $7,200 per year (40% of $18,000). The difference in depreciation can only be considered for the years in which depreciation could be deducted on the old machine. In later years, when depreciation could only be deducted on the new machine, the income tax effect would be computed by deducting the depreciation that is still available on the new machine.

Federal tax provisions may be designed to encourage or discourage capital investment. The Revenue Act of 1962 provided for an investment credit. Subject to limitations prescribed by law, the taxpayer is permitted to deduct a percentage of the cost of a property from income tax payable. The investment credit is a direct reduction against the tax and not a deduction to be used in computing tax. Furthermore, the investment credit does not reduce the depreciable base of the property. The investment credit reduces income tax for the year in which the property is acquired. Since income tax is reduced, the after-tax return on investments is increased. Historically, the investment credit has been temporarily suspended and reinstated according to the prevailing fiscal policy. When it is in force, it must be considered. In the example given previously, with a 10 percent investment credit, the amount of the investment credit would be $33,000 (10% of $330,000). The after-tax cost of the machine investment would be $330,000 less the investment tax credit of $33,000, or $297,000, and this investment cost would be compared with the after-tax cost saving of $67,200 per year.

ACCELERATED DEPRECIATION

Frequently, depreciation charges are substantial, and the selection of a depreciation method and the estimates that are made will have a material effect on the net income or net loss to be reported. In practice, an accelerated depreciation method generally results in greater tax savings. Relatively large depreciation deductions are taken in the early years of an asset's life resulting in larger net returns that can be reinvested to earn even greater returns in later years.

Two accelerated (fast write-off) methods of depreciation, the *sum-of-the-years digits method* and the *double-declining-balance method* are often used. The sum-of-the-years-digits (SYD) method is illustrated by assuming that a unit of equipment costing $60,000 has a useful life of ten years with an estimated salvage value of $5,000 at the end of that time. The digits for each of the ten years, that is $1 + 2 + 3 + 4 + \ldots + 10$ are added to produce a denominator of 55 for an allocating fraction.[2] Then, the numerator for that fraction will be 10 in the first year, 9 in the second year, 8 in the third year, etc. Depreciation for each year would be computed as shown below:

YEAR	COST SUBJECT TO DEPRECIATION		ALLOCATING FRACTION		DEPRECIATION
1	$55,000	×	10/55	=	$10,000
2	55,000	×	9/55	=	9,000
3	55,000	×	8/55	=	8,000
4	55,000	×	7/55	=	7,000
5	55,000	×	6/55	=	6,000
6	55,000	×	5/55	=	5,000
7	55,000	×	4/55	=	4,000
8	55,000	×	3/55	=	3,000
9	55,000	×	2/55	=	2,000
10	55,000	×	1/55	=	1,000

---

[2]The denominator can also be determined from the following formula:
S = sum of the digits
N = number of years of estimated useful life
$$S = N\left(\frac{N + 1}{2}\right)$$

The *double-declining-balance method* uses a rate that is twice the straight-line rate. This "double rate" is applied to the remaining undepreciated cost each year. No allowance is made for residual value in making the calculation. The total cost will never be written off, inasmuch as the rate is calculated on a balance remaining after deducting depreciation for previous years. The total cost, however, should not be reduced to an amount lower than the estimated salvage value of the asset.

If the equipment in the previous example were depreciated by the double-declining-balance method, the rate would be 20 percent, that is, twice the 10 percent rate used in writing off the cost over ten years by the straight-line method. The depreciation for the first year would be $12,000 (20% of $60,000). In the second year the 20 percent rate would be applied to the undepreciated cost of $48,000 ($60,000 minus $12,000) in arriving at a depreciation charge of $9,600.

Assume once again that Davis Supply Company can obtain for $330,000 a new machine that has a useful life of ten years with no estimated salvage value. Annual out-of-pocket cost saving is estimated at $90,000 before income tax. Depreciation will be deducted by the sum-of-the-years-digits (SYD) method. The depreciation deduction for the first year by the SYD method is $60,000 (10/55 × $330,000 cost subject to depreciation). With a 40 percent tax rate, depreciation of $60,000 reduces income tax by $24,000, as illustrated below:

Income tax on $90,000 savings in out-of-pocket cost (40%
   of $90,000)... $36,000
Less depreciation effect: 40% of depreciation of $60,000....   24,000
Income tax effect — increase in first year............................ $12,000

The net return after income tax for the first year is $78,000 and not $67,200, as it would have been using straight-line depreciation.

Savings in out-of-pocket cost before income tax.................. $90,000
Deduct increase in income tax after the effect of SYD depreciation   12,000
Savings in out-of-pocket cost after income tax $78,000

The savings after income tax will not be as large in later years. However, the company's relatively large returns in early years can be reinvested; and, as already mentioned, a dollar in the present is worth more than a dollar in the future. Furthermore, the risk that the investment will not be recovered is reduced.

The effect of SYD depreciation on investment returns may be compared with the effect of straight-line depreciation. Assume that the minimum acceptable rate of return is 15 percent. The present value of ten annual returns of $67,200 when straight-line depreciation is deducted for tax purposes is $337,277 ($67,200 × 5.019, from Table II). The net present value, excess of returns in this case, is $7,277.

Present value of returns	$337,277
Investment	330,000
Excess present value of returns	$ 7,277

With accelerated depreciation, however, the excess present value of the returns is higher. Income tax is lower in the early years using accelerated depreciation. As a result, the net returns after income tax, as shown in the first table below, are higher in the early years than they are when straight-line depreciation is deducted. Returns in the more immediate future have a higher present value than later returns, and the present value of the total returns, as shown in the second table below, is higher because of the shift of larger returns to the earlier years.

SYD DEPRECIATION

Year	*(1)* *Savings* *Before* *Income Tax*	*(2)* *Less* *Depreciation*	*(3)* *Taxable* *Savings* *(1) − (2)*	*(4)* *40% Income* *Tax* *40% × (3)*	*(5)* *Savings After* *Income Tax* *(1) − (4)*
1	$90,000	$60,000	$30,000	$12,000	$78,000
2	90,000	54,000	36,000	14,400	75,600
3	90,000	48,000	42,000	16,800	73,200
4	90,000	42,000	48,000	19,200	70,800
5	90,000	36,000	54,000	21,600	68,400
6	90,000	30,000	60,000	24,000	66,000
7	90,000	24,000	66,000	26,400	63,600
8	90,000	18,000	72,000	28,800	61,200
9	90,000	12,000	78,000	31,200	58,800
10	90,000	6,000	84,000	33,600	56,400

ACCELERATED DEPRECIATION

Year	*Savings After* *Income Tax*	*Present Value* *Factor, 15%*	*Present Value* *of Savings* *(Returns), 15%*
1	$78,000	.870	$ 67,860
2	75,600	.756	57,154
3	73,200	.658	48,166
4	70,800	.572	40,498
5	68,400	.497	33,995
6	66,000	.432	28,512
7	63,600	.376	23,914
8	61,200	.327	20,012
9	58,800	.284	16,699
10	56,400	.247	13,931
	Present value of returns at 15%		$350,741

The excess present value of the returns is $20,741 with accelerated depreciation in contrast to only $7,277 with straight-line depreciation.

Present value of returns	$350,741
Investment	330,000
Excess present value of returns	**$ 20,741**

INCREMENTAL RETURNS

The investment producing the highest discounted rate of return is not always the most desirable alternative. For example, the investments to be compared may be different in amounts. The dollar amount of the return from a larger investment in many cases will exceed the dollar return from a smaller investment having a better rate of discounted return.

Assume that Globe Transit Company has an opportunity to invest in one of two projects. Each project has an estimated life of five years with annual returns as shown below:

	Project I	Project II
Net investment	$75,000	$100,000
Annual return for each of 5 years	30,000	38,000

Investments are expected to yield a discounted rate of return of at least 15 percent.

The discounted rate of return is computed on each alternative:

	Project I	Project II	Incremental
Net investment	$75,000	$100,000	$25,000
Annual return	$30,000	$ 38,000	$ 8,000
Ratio of net investment to annual return	2.5	2.632	3.125
Present value factor from 5-year line of Table II that most nearly corresponds with ratio of net investment to annual return	2.532	2.635	3.127
Rate of return from Table II	**28%**	**26%**	**18%**

It appears that Project I should be selected because the discounted rate of return is higher. However, the key to the problem is the incremental investment and the incremental returns. If the rate of return on the incremental investment is greater than the cutoff rate of return, the additional investment should be made. In this example, an additional $8,000 a year is returned on an additional investment of $25,000. The rate of return on the incremental investment is 18 percent, and the cutoff rate is 15 percent.

A solution by the net present value method follows:

	Project I	Project II
Present value of returns at 15%:		
$30,000 × 3.352	$100,560	
$38,000 × 3.352		$127,376
Investment	75,000	100,000
Excess present value of returns	**$ 25,560**	**$ 27,376**

Project II should be selected. It yields greater excess returns on a present value basis.

The concept of incremental investment applies even though the initial investments are the same. The returns are reinvested and may be viewed as potential investments in the future. If one alternative produces larger returns than another in the early years, while the other alternative produces better returns in later years, the problem of incremental investment arises. Should the company forego the more immediate returns for even larger returns in the future? The answer will depend upon the rate at which future returns can be invested and the amount of the future returns as compared with the sacrifice of immediate returns. A solution to the problem is to discount at the lowest acceptable rate of return.

A GRAPHIC SOLUTION

Sometimes the investment problem can be understood better when the returns are depicted on a graph. The returns from each alternative are discounted at various discount rates. The investment is subtracted from the discounted returns, and the excess or negative discounted returns are plotted on a graph.

Conceptually, the graph shown below is not unlike the P/V graph used in break-even analysis. Positive discounted returns are given on a vertical scale above a zero line, and negative discounted returns are shown below the line.

Data from the previous illustration are depicted on the graph below.

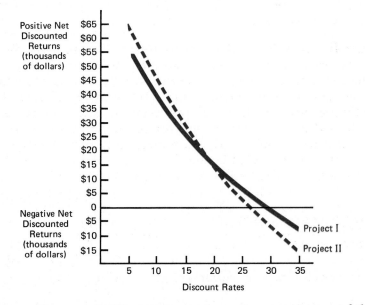

Computations at the 10 percent rate are given at the top of the next page to illustrate the procedure employed:

	PROJECT I	PROJECT II
Present value of returns	$113,730	$144,058
Less present value of investment	75,000	100,000
Net positive discounted returns	$ 38,730	$ 44,058

Note that Project II is a better investment candidate when the lowest acceptable rate of return is less than 18 percent. If the company can reinvest returns at more than 18 percent, Project I is better. The discounted rate of return for each alternative is at the point where the present value line crosses the zero axis on the chart. The cost of the investment is balanced by the discounted returns at the rate indicated at the point of crossover.

THE EVALUATION PROCESS

The task of ranking investment alternatives is usually not as difficult as the task of collecting reliable data that can be used in making the evaluation. Even with experience, it is not easy to make estimates of future returns and the rates that should be used in discounting.

Generally, certain policies and procedures are followed in the acquisition of investments of various types. For example, requests for new equipment or for special projects are reviewed by the engineering department or may even be initiated by that department as a result of studies made. The technological aspects are evaluated, and competing pieces of equipment are compared as to performance. Revenue, cost, and saving are identified with each alternative through the combined efforts of the engineers and the accountants.

Ordinarily, special forms are used to record data with respect to the cost of the investment and the anticipated returns. When the evaluation reports have been completed, they are submitted to a screening committee for critical review. Some of the investment expenditures are approved by this committee and recommended to the project or equipment planning committee of the board of directors who gives final approval or disapproval.

Sometimes the discounted return approach is rejected as an analytical tool because of the difficulty in making estimates. But the problem of estimation cannot be avoided under any method that may be used to evaluate investment alternatives. Giving recognition to time adjustments for monetary amounts does not add uncertainty. Even in a simple payback calculation, the investor must make the same estimates.

ANTICIPATION OF CHANGE

In making any decision, particularly a decision that will have a long-range effect, there is always the risk that the estimates will be rendered useless by changes in the company, the industry, or the general economic environment. While it is not possible to anticipate all changes, the problem can be approached by examining what-if-type questions.

Models may be built with a computer being used as a tool to test various assumptions. Probabilities can be assigned to various possible changes. For example, how would the investment decision be influenced if interest rates would rise or if foreign exchange rates would become unfavorable? Suppose, in the Davis Supply Company example, that conditions would be such that the lowest acceptable rate of return would increase from 15 percent to 20 percent shortly after the investment was made. If this were to happen, the present value of the returns using SYD depreciation would be $296,104; and an investment of $330,000 would be unacceptable. The probability of such a change in the minimum acceptable rate may be small, but management may wish to evaluate this possibility along with others before finalizing an investment decision.

THE POST AUDIT

After a piece of equipment has been acquired, or after a project has been started, it is watched closely. Its performance, both from a technical and an economic point of view, is audited or reviewed at the end of its "shakedown period." During this period, it may be found that certain corrections have to be made if the equipment or project is going to realize its potential. At the end of the period, an audit or review shows whether or not the investment met expectations and may indicate ways in which the operation can be improved.

The audit referred to is not an audit in the true sense of the word. It is in reality a general review and, like the original evaluation, may contain errors of estimation. The review may also be limited by the accounting information that is available. On a special project, the operating results may be shown separately in the accounting records. But on an individual piece of equipment, which is only one among many items, there may be no separate accounting. In fact, it would be difficult to identify the operating results with any one piece of equipment. Whether or not additional effort should be exerted to have separate accountability depends upon the relative importance of the investment and the cost incurred to get the additional information.

The post audit is a means by which errors of operation can be detected and corrected. The audit may also serve as a control in that employees may tend to be more careful if they realize that the equipment is under surveillance. Furthermore, project evaluations may be more thoroughly made if these evaluations are to be given a performance test at some later date. And, of course, the audit may reveal information that can be applied in future investment planning.

QUESTIONS

1. How does a capital investment differ from other investments?

2. Is a long-term investment in the capital stock of another company a capital investment?

3. Why are capital investment decisions so important?

4. What three factors are related in the evaluation of capital investment alternatives?

5. What is the net investment from a decision-making point of view?

6. Can a capital investment be made when there is no outflow of resources? Explain.

7. Are the returns from an investment the accounting profit? Explain.

8. The return from an investment is not always in the form of a net inflow of net working capital. Explain.

9. Explain the difference between the discounted rate-of-return method and the net present value method in the evaluation of investment alternatives.

10. What is the net present value of an investment alternative costing $150,000 with expected annual returns of $50,000 for a period of five years when the minimum acceptable rate of return is 20%?

11. What is an avoidable cost? Why is the avoidable cost reduced by the income tax effect?

12. In a replacement situation, how are the proceeds from the sale of old equipment used in computing the net investment?

13. In computing the net investment in a replacement situation, what is the effect of selling old equipment at a loss? At a gain?

14. Cash, accounts receivable, and inventory are classified as current assets. How can they be considered part of a capital investment in the decision-making process?

15. Why is depreciation an important factor in the computation of the annual net returns?

16. What is the advantage of accelerated depreciation in capital investment analysis?

17. The investment alternative yielding the highest discounted rate of return is the most acceptable. Will this always be true? Explain.

18. Estimates show that an advertising campaign can be expected to add $60,000 to the annual cash flow each year for three years. What is the maximum amount that you would invest in this campaign at the present time if you set a minimum rate-of-return objective of 20%?

EXERCISES

1. **Net Investment.** The management of Banks Machine Company plans to replace a sorting machine that was acquired several years ago at a cost of

$50,000. The machine has been depreciated to its salvage value of $5,000. A new sorter can be purchased for $60,000. The dealer will grant a trade-in allowance of $6,000 on the old machine. If a new machine is not purchased, Banks Machine Company will spend $20,000 to repair the old machine. Gains and losses on trade-in transactions are not subject to income tax. The cost to repair the old machine can be deducted in the first year for computing income tax. Income tax is estimated at 40% of the income subject to tax.

Required: Compute the net investment in the new machine for decision-making purposes.

2. Net Returns and Discounted Rate of Return. The Ricks Company has been considering a new production method that can reduce materials cost by an estimated $30,000 a year. The new method is also expected to result in annual savings in labor and overhead cost of $40,000. The new equipment required for this method will cost $300,000 and will be depreciated on a straight-line basis for tax purposes. There will be no residual value at the end of 10 years, the estimated life of the equipment. Income tax is estimated at 40% of income before income tax.

Required: Will the investment earn the 20% after-tax desired rate of return?

3. Sales Offer as Investment. The owner of a mini storage unit has just received an offer of $500,000 for the storage buildings. The owner is interested in another investment opportunity that can probably yield an annual discounted return of 12% after income tax. The storage unit is expected to continue to yield an annual cash flow, before income tax, of $90,000 for a period of 10 years. The book value of the storage buildings is $500,000 and straight-line depreciation is used for tax purposes. The remaining life is 10 years, so the depreciation is $50,000 per year. Zero salvage value is predicted.

Required: If income tax is 40%, should the offer for the sale of the storage unit be accepted or refused?

4. Net Investment and Discounted Rate of Return. A unit of equipment used in stamping out plastic parts can be acquired from an equipment manufacturer at a cost of $200,000. If this equipment is acquired, an old unit of equipment that is fully depreciated will be sold for $20,000.

Annual returns from the new equipment before deducting depreciation or income tax have been estimated at $70,000 for a period of 5 years. Depreciation of $40,000 is to be deducted each year, and the new equipment is expected to have no salvage value at the end of the 5 years. Income tax is at the rate of 40% on ordinary income and at the rate of 30% on any gain from the sale of equipment.

Required:
(1) Determine the net investment in the new equipment.
(2) What is the discounted rate of return on the new equipment?
(3) Will this investment be acceptable if the minimum rate of return has been established at 20%?

5. Incremental Investment and Discounted Rate of Return. A manufacturer of equipment quotes a price of $130,000 for a unit of equipment that is being considered by Tan Products, Inc. This equipment should be able to produce net returns of $41,000 each year for 5 years. Another equipment manufacturer offers a unit of equipment at a price of $180,000. This unit of equipment is expected to yield $55,000 in net returns each year for 5 years. These are mutually exclusive investment alternatives. An investment of this type is expected to yield a discounted rate of return of no less than 12%. Ignore income tax.

Required:
(1) Which investment alternative is more attractive if a discounted rate of return of 12% is expected? Show computations.
(2) What is the discounted rate of return on each investment alternative?
(3) What is the discounted rate of return on the incremental investment?

6. Net Present Value and Discounted Rate of Return. Two competing investment alternatives are being considered by the Mills Company. One alternative costs $170,000 with estimated annual returns after income tax of $50,000 each year for a period of 5 years. The other alternative costs $130,000 with estimated annual returns after income tax of $40,000 each year for a period of 5 years. An investment of this type is expected to earn a discounted rate of return of at least 15%.

Required:
(1) Determine the more desirable alternative by the net present value method. (Discount the returns at 15% and compare the discounted returns with the investment.)
(2) What is the discounted rate of return on each investment alternative?

7. Investment in Another Company. The management of Pine Enterprises, Inc., is considering the investment of $10,000,000 to acquire the assets of Radar Company, a small company that has developed a more economical means of using electrical energy. Last year Radar reported net sales of $17,000,000 and operating expenses of $14,000,000. Included in the operating expenses is depreciation of assets in the amount of $800,000. This level of earnings is expected to continue for 5 years, after which the technology will be outdated and the assets will have no value.

Required: Ignoring income tax, what approximate rate of return would be earned by the investment?

8. Investment Returns and Sales Volume. Fixtures, Inc., is considering an investment of $2,000,000 in a new product line. Depreciation of $200,000 is to be deducted in each of the next 10 years (salvage value is estimated at zero). A selling price of $40 per unit is decided upon; unit variable cost is $20. The sales division believes that a sales estimate of 50,000 units per year is realistic. The controller states that there is a solid market for only 20,000 units a year. Projects must meet a minimum rate-of-return requirement of 10%. Income tax is estimated at 40% of income before tax.

Required: Evaluate the project using each of the sales volume alternatives given. Use the net present value method.

9. Effect of Accelerated Depreciation. The molding department of Hayes, Inc., has been investigating the possibility of acquiring a new unit of equipment at a cost of $60,000. Cash savings before income tax from the use of this equipment have been estimated at $20,000 per year for a period of 5 years. At the end of 5 years, the equipment will have no salvage value. The rate to be used in evaluating investments is 10% after income tax of 40%.

Required: Calculate the net present value if straight-line depreciation is used for tax purposes and if the sum-of-the-years-digits is used as the depreciation method for tax purposes. (Round all amounts to nearest dollar.)

10. Effect of Accelerated Depreciation. At a 40% tax rate and a 20% discount rate, how much greater is the economic present value of the sum-of-the-years-digits method as compared with straight-line depreciation on a 5-year asset (no salvage value) costing $150,000? How much greater is the economic value at a 10% discount rate?

PROBLEMS

10-1. Net Investment and Returns. The management of the Creek Company has rejected an opportunity to buy new machinery costing $110,000. Although it would probably yield cash savings after income tax, including the effect of depreciation on income tax, of $30,000 each year for 5 years, it would not meet the rate-of-return objective of at least 15%.

The assistant manager believes that the investment could have met the standard if other factors had been considered. For example, if this equipment had been purchased, old equipment with a net book value of zero could have been sold for $20,000. The income tax rate for the year on the sale of equipment is 40%.

Required: Use the net present value method to determine whether or not the assistant manager is correct in the analysis.

10-2. Payback and Discounted Returns. The manager of Vieno, Inc., uses a simple payback method in selecting investment alternatives. She states that if she can recover the investment in 3 years, she is virtually in the same position as another investor who requires a discounted rate of return of 18% on a 5-year investment. In her business, the investment produces uniform returns over a 5-year period and has no residual salvage value. Three investment alternatives are outlined below:

	Alternatives		
	1	*2*	*3*
Investment...	$90,000	$24,000	$44,000
Annual return for each of 5 years........................	$30,000	$ 6,000	$10,000

Required:
(1) Which, if any, of the investment alternatives meets the 3-year payback criterion? Ignore tax effect.
(2) Evaluate the three alternatives by using the net present value method with a minimum rate of return of 18% and compare the results arrived at in (1). Ignore tax effect.

10-3. Depreciation and Rate of Return. The president of Day Company has been considering an investment of $600,000 in equipment that should have a useful life of three years with a salvage value of zero. This type of investment is expected to yield a discounted rate of return of 12%.

An estimate indicates that the cash flow before income tax from this investment will probably amount to $300,000 a year. Straight-line depreciation is normally used and income tax is 40%.

The president has been informed that depreciation may be deducted by the SYD method and that this method would make the investment more favorable than if straight-line depreciation is used. He does not understand how a "bookkeeping method," as he calls it, can help to improve the investment.

Required:

(1) Compute the net present value of the investment with straight-line depreciation.

(2) Compute the net present value of the investment with SYD depreciation.

(3) Explain to the president how a "bookkeeping method" can help to improve the investment.

10-4. Improving Investment Returns. For many years Ben Jones has been a successful manufacturer in the garment industry. Recently he has learned of an opportunity to purchase a two-story brick building for $700,000. He believes that he can operate successfully by using only one of the two floors. At the present time, he is operating in an older building where he uses both floors. This is inconvenient, he admits, but he has become accustomed to the situation.

Furthermore, he estimates that the annual returns from his business after income tax will amount to $130,000 over the next 20 years. With the prospect of more inflation and high interest rates, he would hesitate to invest unless he could obtain a discounted rate of return of at least 20%. This investment opportunity does not appear that good to him, and he is inclined to continue to operate as he has before.

His daughter, who has recently graduated from medical school, disagrees with his position:

"You forget that this area is growing. We have no professional building; and I know of several doctors, dentists, and lawyers who would be happy to have offices on the second floor if you did some remodeling. I have already obtained estimates and find that you can have the second floor remodeled for $100,000. The offices should yield annual rentals after income tax of $40,000."

Required: From the information given, does it appear that the investment can meet a minimum rate-of-return requirement of 20%? (Use the net present value method.)

10-5. Change in the Value of Money. Lauretta Donnelly, manager of the Town Company, states that she used to accept investment opportunities that yielded discounted returns (after income tax) at a rate of 12%. With an increasing cost of capital, she now expects an 18% discounted rate of return.

Two competing investment proposals are now waiting for her evaluation, and the data are presented below:

	Alternatives	
	1	2
Estimated life	5 yrs.	5 yrs.
Net investment	$160,000	$190,000
Estimated annual return before depreciation and income tax	60,000	90,000

Depreciation is to be deducted by the straight-line method, and there is no estimated salvage value at the end of the estimated life of the investment proposal.

Income tax is estimated at 40% of income before tax.

Required:

(1) Does either or both of the alternatives meet a requirement of 12%? (Use the net present value method and round all amounts to nearest dollar.)

(2) Does either or both of the alternatives meet a requirement of 18%? (Use the net present value method and round all amounts to nearest dollar.)

10-6. Sell or Use Equipment. An offer of $100,000 has been made for a unit of equipment that Milltown Products has been using to make parts for one of its divisions. The equipment is fully depreciated but can be used for 5 more years. At the end of 5 years, it is expected to have little, if any, value.

The variable cost of producing the parts is $10 per unit. A total of 10,000 units are to be manufactured each year. If the parts are not manufactured, the company must buy them from an outside supplier at a cost of $15 per unit. Also, if the parts are not produced, the space occupied by the equipment can be rented for $10,000 per year. Income tax is estimated at 40% of the income before tax. The company expects a discounted rate of return of 14% on this type of investment.

Required: Should the offer for the sale of the equipment be accepted, or should the parts be manufactured? (Use the net present value method.)

10-7. Alternative Project Requiring Additional Investment in Current Assets. An interesting project is being considered by Dandy Company. The project will require an investment of $300,000 in equipment that is expected to have a useful life of 10 years with no salvage value. Cash, accounts receivable, and inventory will be required in the amount of $100,000 and will be released at the end of 10 years. Annual cash flow returns before income tax from this project have been estimated at $100,000.

Depreciation is to be deducted by the straight-line method. Income tax is estimated at 40% of income before income tax.

A minimum rate-of-return objective has been established at 15%.

Required: Does the investment alternative meet the rate-of-return objective? (Use the net present value method.)

10-8. Incremental Investment and Returns. Peter Martin has a rate-of-return objective of 18% for acceptable capital investment projects. In the evaluation process, he prefers to use straight-line depreciation.

At the present time, he is interested in the acquisition of equipment for producing a product line which can be sold for $30 per unit with a unit variable cost of $20. His sales manager believes that there is a market for 30,000 units each year. The equipment has an installed cost of $800,000 and should have a useful life of 5 years with no salvage value.

A representative of the equipment manufacturer has gone over the cost estimates that Martin has prepared and stated that the variable cost per unit of product can be cut to $15 if an attachment for the equipment costing an additional $100,000 is acquired. This attachment will not extend the useful life of the equipment or change the salvage value.

Required: Evaluate each of the alternatives by the net present value method with straight-line depreciation. Which alternative is better? (Use a 40% income tax rate.)

10-9. Changes in Economic Environment. Four years ago National Properties, Inc., invested $10,000,000 in a venture in another country. The investment was estimated to have a 10-year life and was expected to produce a cash flow of $2,500,000 each year before income tax. It did exactly this for 4 years. Conditions are less favorable now, and the revised estimate indicates that the cash flow for each of the next 6 years will be only $1,500,000. (Because this is a foreign investment, it has a special tax status and is not subject to income tax.)

The investment can now be sold for $4,500,000. At the present time, an investment can be justified only if the discounted rate of return is expected to be no less than 18%.

Required: Should the investment be sold for $4,500,000 or continued in operation? Show computations by the net present value method and by calculating the rate of return.

10-10. Break-Even Volume and Investment. For several years, Lomax Company has used a combination of its own equipment and equipment rented from others to handle standard materials. The company has enough of its own equipment to handle routine work but sometimes must rent equipment during periods of peak activity. The cost to rent equipment from others has been estimated to average $4,000 a year.

An evaluation of the operation indicates that the company can save $.10 per unit of material by using its own equipment instead of rented equipment.

An equipment manufacturer offers the necessary additional equipment at a cost of $45,000. The equipment will probably have a useful life of 5 years with no salvage value at the end of the 5 years.

There is some uncertainty with respect to how much work will be required from the new equipment if it is purchased. Estimates of the number of units that might possibly be handled in each of the 5 years are 80,000 units, 100,000 units, and 120,000 units.

On this type of investment, a 15% discounted return is considered to be appropriate (ignore taxes).

Required:

(1) Can the investment meet the minimum rate-of-return requirement if 80,000 units are handled? If 100,000 units are handled? If 120,000 units are handled?

(2) Determine the break-even volume, that is, the number of units at which the investment can just meet the 15% return requirement. (Round all amounts to nearest dollar.)

10-11. Acquisition of Additional Units of Equipment. A new product line is being considered by the Ingram Company. A survey has been made in an attempt to estimate the potential demand for this product. A special type of equipment will be required for the manufacturing process, and one or more units of this equipment will be acquired if the project is accepted.

Data with respect to the production and sale of this product follow:

Number of Equipment Units	Product Unit Capacity
1	60,000
2	120,000
3	160,000
4	200,000

The new product line will increase out-of-pocket annual fixed cost (excluding depreciation) by $100,000. It is estimated that this increase can be expected regardless of the number of product units manufactured. The variable cost of producing a unit has been estimated at $6 and the selling price at $10. The company has the physical space to install up to 5 units of equipment. The machine sells at $300,000 per unit and the useful life is estimated at 5 years with no salvage value.

Required: Using straight-line depreciation, a 40% tax rate, a 15% discount rate, and the net present value method, determine how many machines, if any, should be purchased. Assume that the company can sell all units that can be produced under the conditions stated. Show calculations.

10-12. Timing the Investment. The capital investment committee of the board of directors of Cedric, Inc., is considering the acquisition of a unit of equipment costing $76,000. Shipping and installation costs are estimated at an additional $4,000. The equipment is expected to have a useful life of 5 years with a salvage value of $5,000 at the end of 5 years. Before considering the effect of depreciation, the annual cash flow returns after income tax from the use of this equipment are estimated at $20,000.

One member of the committee believes that the equipment now in service for this production can be used for another year. A new and improved model is expected in another year that can be acquired at a cost of $91,000. Shipping and installation costs are also estimated at $4,000, and the estimated salvage value at the end of the expected 5-year life is $5,000. Annual cash flow returns after income tax but before considering the effect of depreciation are estimated at $23,000.

The company has set a minimum rate-of-return objective of 18%. Depreciation is to be deducted by the sum-of-the-years-digits method. The income tax rate is 40%.

Required: Does it appear that the equipment should be purchased now, or should the company wait a year for the new model? Use the net present value method and show computations.

11

MANAGERIAL CONTROL
AND DECISION MAKING
IN DECENTRALIZED OPERATIONS

One of the most striking characteristics of business operation and organization during the past two decades has been the tendency toward decentralized operations. This movement has been accelerating at the same time that the number of business combinations and mergers has been increasing. Many companies are simultaneously seeking the advantages of bigness through combinations and of smallness through decentralizing the management of the combined operations.

In general, a *decentralized company* is one in which operating divisions are created. Each division is staffed with a management that has some authority for making decisions and thus becomes responsible for a segment of the company's profit. Even though the amount of decision-making authority granted to division management varies among companies, the spirit of decentralization is quite clear — to divide a company into relatively self-contained divisions and allow these divisions to operate in an autonomous fashion.

Decisions as to capital investment are sometimes centrally controlled; but decisions as to selling price and quantity and method of production are frequently delegated to the division management.

Two of the alleged advantages of decentralized organization are:

1. It provides a systematic means of delegating a portion of the decision-making responsibility to managers below top management.
2. It motivates managers in charge of certain company activities by involving them more closely with the company's profit objectives.

Top management wants to know whether the advantages mentioned above are being realized, thus necessitating the question of how best to control and evaluate division management. Division control and evaluation is usually more complex than controlling a single activity within a company. For example, in a centralized company a problem of control may exist with respect to certain production activities. A cost center may be established and reports may be generated to assure top management that the product is being produced at the lowest possible level of cost. The problem is usually one of *cost control*. In decentralized divisions, the division management may have authority over selling prices of the finished product, make or buy decisions, some investment decisions, and so forth. The problem here is mainly one of *profit control*, which is much broader and often more complex than a problem of cost control. The fact that the division manager usually has more freedom than a production supervisor in making decisions usually means that a simple cost index is not an adequate control device. Control over cost does not indicate how efficient the division manager is as a price-maker for the finished products.

THE CRITERIA NEEDED FOR A CONTROL SYSTEM

In general, in order to control anything, it is necessary to have:

1. An index (measure) of overall actual performance.
2. A standard with which to compare the actual performance.

A comparison of actual performance with standard performance produces variance information that forms a basis for corrective action.

The selection of an evaluation index is rarely an easy matter. The index chosen must encompass as many of the operating variables as possible. The operating variables that are important are those over which the supervisor or manager has control. Rarely can one single index of performance be established that encompasses all of the factors that are considered important in evaluating an operation.

In evaluating a production operation, cost is usually considered to be a good evaluation index. The cost figure that should be used is the controllable cost. However, this index, although useful, may not be sufficient for performance measurement. The cost in a certain activity may be high because the supervisor spends much time developing personnel. If this supervision helps to provide a good training ground for future managers, perhaps the supervisor is being more efficient than the cost performance indicates. From a long-run viewpoint, this situation may be quite desirable.

In a decentralized operation, the selection of the index used to evaluate division performance is usually more complex because a division manager has quite broad decision-making authority and thus has direct control over many decision factors. Consequently, a greater burden is placed on the evaluation index. Cost as an index is usually not broad enough for evaluating division operation.

Profit as a measure of division performance may also be inadequate. This index is broader than cost because it includes revenue considerations, thus reflecting the price-making authority of the division manager in the index. However, the ability of the division manager to build good customer relations, to secure employee loyalty, and to provide a good training ground for future management prospects may not be adequately reflected in the short-run profit figure. Furthermore, the ability of the division manager to produce a given level of profit with a minimum capital investment is not evident by looking at profit alone. Capital investment should be assigned to the division and a rate-of-return index should be computed by relating profit to investment. This rate-of-return index, which is broader than profit alone, may be especially useful if the division manager has some control over increases or decreases in the amount of capital invested in the division.

The problem of selecting an appropriate index is further complicated when one division furnishes goods and services to another division; hence, the divisions are not completely autonomous. In order to use division profit as an index where goods or services are transferred between divisions, it is necessary to develop a solution to the intracompany or transfer pricing problem. For example, if a warehouse division furnishes services to an operating division, a decision must be made as to the price at which the services are to be transferred for purposes of determining the warehouse division's revenue and the operating division's cost.

The overall problem is even more complex because division profit, rates of return, and transfer prices are frequently used as an aid in making decisions as well as in evaluating performance. A transfer price that is satisfactory for performance evaluation may be poorly suited for decision making.

When the index has been chosen, it is then necessary to settle on a standard against which to measure or compare the actual performance. The standard can be based on last year's results or the results of similar divisions within the company. Such standards presume that the respective operations are performing at efficiency. A better solution may be to choose independently determined standards such as a budgeted profit for the division or a budgeted rate of return. If the profit is budgeted, it is possible to consider the capital invested in the division in establishing the budget. Hence, it may be that the investment can be effectively considered without actually budgeting a rate of return.

Having described an overall system of control for division operations, the remainder of this chapter is devoted to a discussion of the following specific points:

1. The selection of a profit index.
2. The problems encountered in using division controllable profit as an evaluation index.
3. The problems encountered in determining division investment.
4. The intracompany pricing (transfer pricing) problem.

5. The possible conflicts that may arise in using transfer prices for both performance evaluation and decision making.
6. The selection of the standard against which to compare the actual performance.

THE PROFIT INDEX

The choice of the profit index is not simple. However, there really is no question of whether a performance index is needed. It is rather a question of how to construct the best one, and several different profit concepts can be used. These concepts can best be illustrated by an example. It is possible for a division to be assigned the following profit and loss data:

Revenue from division sales	$1,000
Direct division costs:	
Variable cost of goods sold and other operating costs	700
Fixed division overhead that is controllable at the division level, such as the cost of certain indirect labor and operating supplies	100
Fixed division overhead that is noncontrollable at the division level, such as the division manager's salary	50
Indirect division costs:	
Allocated (fixed) general office overhead, such as the division's share of the cost of the president's office	60

The above data make it possible to select several different profit calculations. The summary calculation below presents some of the commonly suggested alternatives.

	DIVISION CONTRIBUTION MARGIN	DIVISION CONTROLLABLE PROFIT	DIVISION DIRECT PROFIT	DIVISION NET PROFIT
Revenue	$1,000	$1,000	$1,000	$1,000
Direct cost:				
Variable cost	$ 700	$ 700	$ 700	$ 700
	$ 300			
Fixed controllable cost		100	100	100
		$ 200		
Fixed noncontrollable cost			50	50
			$ 150	
Indirect cost: Allocated home office overhead				60
				$ 90

The four profit calculations are not the only possible ones, but they are the most reasonable. The names or titles assigned to each are descriptive of each calculation, but the terminology in this area has not been standardized. The important point is to recognize what is included and excluded in each calculation.

Division Net Profit

It may appear that the best profit calculation to use in measuring division performance is the division net profit. However, net profit is usually calculated by deducting some pro rata share of the home office overhead. An example of this cost would be the cost of operating the president's office. Although each division benefits from the incurrence of such a cost, it is not controllable at the division level. Although benefit received is the main criterion used to allocate cost for income reporting to outside investors, there is a real question as to whether this criterion is the proper one for performance evaluation purposes. If controllability is accepted as the main criterion in assigning cost for evaluation purposes, then net profit is a poor measure of performance.

The main argument for using net profit, which implies an allocation of home office costs, is that it makes the division manager aware of the full cost of operating the division. Even though part of this full cost is not controllable at the division level, by reporting the full cost the division manager may work harder to control the costs which are controllable. This argument rests largely on how the division manager is motivated. Perhaps a better approach would be to assign only controllable costs to the division and then to establish a rigorous standard in hopes that the manager will be highly motivated to meet the standard. As a result, the manager will be concentrating on those costs that can be controlled at the division level.

The other difficulty in using division net profit is that some method of allocation must be found for assigning the home office cost to divisions. Whatever method is chosen is likely to be arbitrary and open to question by the division managers. In order for the allocation procedure to have the desired motivational results, it is necessary to find an allocation procedure for the home office cost that is acceptable to the division managers. If this is not done, a division manager may spend much time attempting to reduce cost by getting top management to change the allocation procedure.

Division Direct Profit

This profit calculation is defined as the total division revenue less the direct cost of the division. This concept avoids the main difficulty of division net profit in that the home office cost is not allocated. However, as can be noted from the calculation summary given on page 305, there may still be some direct costs included in the calculation that are not controllable at the division level; that is, some costs that can be traced directly to the division may not be controllable. Costs such as the division manager's salary are controllable only at the top management level. Also, some division overhead, such as insurance, taxes, and depreciation on fixed assets, is due to past investment decisions that were made by top management. If costs are to be assigned to the division on the basis of controllability, then these above-mentioned costs should be excluded from the profit calculation. If this is not done, the division profit used for performance evaluation may be increased or decreased by actions of someone outside the division.

Division Controllable Profit

This profit calculation is defined as the total division revenue less all costs that are directly traceable to the division and that are controllable by the division management. It appears that this calculation is best for performance measurement, because it reflects the results of the division manager's ability to carry out the assigned responsibility. Changes in the profit figure from year to year should be a reflection of how management responsibility is being carried out at the division level. Provided the standard used for the comparison is valid, any variances between actual and standard can be explained in terms of factors over which the division manager has control. Some of these factors may be difficult for the division manager to influence; for example, the prices of materials may be increasing. If the standard (budget) is not revised each year, unfavorable price variances will result. Even though the price cannot be influenced, perhaps alternate materials can be used or alternate sources of supply can be found. Problems of this nature may be difficult to solve, but they are part of the division management's responsibility. Failure to solve such problems is different from being unable to take action because of a lack of authority.

In calculating controllable profit, some fixed costs are included. A cost may be controllable even though it is fixed. "Fixed" does not mean fixed in amount, but rather fixed with respect to changes in volume. The division manager may be able to reduce the level of supervisory salaries by reorganizing division operations. The new cost level achieved is still fixed with respect to volume changes, but profit will increase because the total dollar amount of supervisory salaries has decreased. If the fixed controllable cost is not included, important spending variances may be overlooked.

Division Contribution Margin

The contribution margin or marginal income of the division is calculated by deducting variable costs from total revenue. Although contribution margin is useful in decision making, for performance evaluation its defect is obvious; namely, there are some controllable items of fixed cost that are excluded from the calculation. As a performance evaluation index, therefore, division contribution margin is incomplete.

The fact that controllable profit is used in overall performance evaluation should not be taken as an indication that contribution margin has to be abandoned as a decision-making technique. The report at the top of page 308 indicates both the contribution margin and the controllable profit.

Division A
Profit Report

Revenue	$1,000
Variable cost	700
Contribution margin	$ 300
Fixed controllable cost	100
Controllable profit	$ 200

In this report, both the contribution margin and the controllable profit are available as a management tool, and there is no need to choose one or the other. Furthermore, the controllable profit may be the best guide for some decisions. If a particular decision will change the level of fixed cost, then this cost should be considered. For example, if the division manager decides to eliminate a department, it may be possible to reduce supervisory salaries that are included in fixed controllable cost; thus, the entire profit statement should be used as a basis for the decision.

SOME PROBLEMS IN USING DIVISION CONTROLLABLE PROFIT AS AN EVALUATION INDEX

There are several accounting problems that must be solved in order for controllable division profit to be a good index for evaluating performance. The most important of these problems are discussed in the following paragraphs.

There are several ways in which the division manager can increase the short-run profit of the division to the detriment of the company as a whole. For example, it may be possible to delay the maintenance cost. Such an action will inflate profit, but the long-run profitability of the division and the company may be affected adversely. Expenditures that engender employee loyalty such as division social gatherings may be eliminated. By reducing supervision cost, the division manager may not develop long-run top management personnel. In short, a solution must be found to the problem of the division manager's potential to create division profit that may cause a long-run decline in company profit.

Other accounting problems may arise if profit comparisons are made between similar operating divisions. For such comparisons to be valid, all profit calculations should rest on the same inventory and depreciation procedures. A problem also arises with respect to cost items that sometimes are inventoried (and written off as used) and other times are expensed directly. For example, the purchase of indirect operating supplies may create a problem in interpreting profit differences between divisions as well as profit differences between accounting periods for the same division. If potential inventory items such as indirect production supplies are expensed when purchased, it may be that an increase in a division's profit for a period was due merely to a large purchase of supplies in the previous period. Likewise, differences in profit between divisions during a given period may be caused by a difference in the timing of purchases and the failure to reflect inventories. If these differences are significant, the profit figure will be distorted and may be difficult to interpret correctly.

Problems of revenue recognition may require attention before the division profit can be used effectively in evaluating performance. When the sale is only a matter of delivery, as can be the case for some precious metals and agricultural products that have an unlimited market at a predetermined price, for example, the ability of the division manager to influence the amount of profit and the profit pattern by choosing the time of sale may destroy comparisons between years and between divisions.

If controllable profit is to be used as an evaluation index, it is necessary to be able to define and measure controllable cost. Whether a cost is controllable depends on the level of management under consideration. The cost of owning a building may only be controllable at the top management level; the division manager may have little influence over such cost.

Controllability also has a time dimension. If the time horizon is very long, some costs may be controllable which would not be controllable in the short run. For example, the cost of owning a machine may be controllable by a department manager if the time horizon is at least as long as the life of the machine. Conversely, if the time horizon for the profit calculation is one year, perhaps only the cost of operating the machine is controllable. All costs are controllable at some level in the organization if the time horizon is sufficiently long. However, this does not resolve the problem since profit reporting periods may be as short as one month or one quarter of a year. In distinguishing controllable from noncontrollable costs, it is necessary to consider the time period as well as the level of management for whom the profit report is prepared. This applies not only to cost and revenue items but to investment items as well.

DETERMINING DIVISION INVESTMENT

If divisions are to be evaluated on the basis of rate of return on investment, it is necessary to determine the investment base to be used. There are many problems associated with this determination.

The first problem is to decide which assets to assign to the division. Many assets can be traced directly to the division. For example, a division may handle its own receivables and inventory and may even have jurisdiction over its own cash balance. Also, much of the physical property used may be traceable to a particular division. Sometimes traceable assets such as receivables, inventories, and cash are centrally administered and controlled. However, by proper account coding it is usually possible to trace receivables and inventories to the division operation even though these assets are administered centrally. If cash is centrally administered, it is usually very difficult to trace to division operations.

There is usually some investment that is common to several divisions. In such a case, no amount of coding, sorting, or classifying will provide a basis for directly tracing this investment to a division. If this type of investment is to be assigned to the division, a basis of allocation must be found. An example of common investment would be the investment in building, furniture and fixtures, and so forth, used by the central corporate administration. Any basis of allocation used to assign this type of investment must be an arbitrary one. If such an assignment is made, the division investment is no longer the traceable investment but is the traceable investment plus some allocated share of common investment.

The relevant investment base for division evaluation might be thought of as the amount of investment uniquely devoted to the support of the particular division operation. If this criterion is applied to common investment, the amount of the common investment allocated to a divison would be that part of the total common investment which could be avoided if the division did not exist. This is a difficult concept to apply, but its application can be approached by seeking relationships between the level of common investment and the level of certain division activities. For example, perhaps a relationship can be established between the level of common investment in a personnel department and the number of employees in each division.

If the above procedure cannot be applied, it is difficult to justify the allocation of common investment. At best, the procedure used is likely to be quite arbitrary. If divisions are compared with one another, this comparison will probably be affected by the basis of allocation chosen. In fact, the basis of allocation could well determine the ranking of each division. In an earlier section of the chapter, it was stated that the best profit calculation for performance evaluation is the one based only on factors under the control of the division management. If this same criterion is used in determining investment, the common investment should not be allocated. Traceable investment is a better measure of controllable investment than traceable investment plus some allocated share of common investment.

Once the method of assigning investment to divisions has been determined, it is necessary to decide the amount at which the plant assets will be stated. One might argue that replacement cost or perhaps original cost adjusted for changes in the price level should be used. It may seem that, if rate of return is to be used as a measure of division efficiency, the investment should be stated on some current value basis rather than on a historical cost basis. The obvious difficulty is the measurement problem. How would replacement costs be approximated? What happens when the specific plant or equipment asset is not replaced? If a common-dollar base is desirable, which price-level index should be used? It is easier to raise questions than to give answers in this problem area.

Up to this point, return on investment has been discussed in terms of the calculation being made in ratio form, that is, the division profit divided by the division investment. Return on investment may create problems simply because of the ratio nature of the calculation. For example, suppose that one division of a company is currently earning 30 percent on investment. The division manager may be reluctant to make additional investments at, perhaps, 20 percent because the average return of the division would be lowered. However, if investment offerings in other divisions of the company yield only 15 percent, company management may prefer that the additional investment with a yield of 20 percent be accepted. The division manager may still be reluctant to lower the past average return on investment from 30 percent even though the company management has set a standard for comparison of 15 percent. That is, the manager may choose to maximize the favorable variance between the standard and the actual; and this cannot be done if the past average return is lowered by selecting additional investments with returns of 20 percent. Thus, the use of return on investment as a ratio might restrict additional investment at the expense of company-wide profitability.

The use of residual income has been proposed as an alternative to the ratio form of determining return on investment. Residual income focuses the attention of the division manager on a dollar amount instead of a ratio. The maximization of the dollar amount will tend to be in the best interest of both the division manager and the company as a whole, thus the incongruence of goals experienced when return on investment is viewed as a ratio can be eliminated. The discussion which follows illustrates the residual income method.

In general, the *residual income* is defined as the operating profit of a division less an imputed charge for the operating capital used by the division. The problems involved in selecting the profit index and the investment base still apply to the residual income alternative. That is, a decision must still be made to determine what concept of profit and investment is to be used. For purposes of illustration, assume that division controllable profit is to be used and that a similar choice has been made for the determination of the investment base. Assume further that the current controllable profit (before any imputed capital charge) is $300,000 and the relevant investment is $1,000,000. The return on investment, then, is 30 percent; that is, $300,000 ÷ $1,000,000. Suppose top management wants the division management to accept incremental investments so long as the return is greater than 15 percent.

This percentage is then used as the imputed charge for division investment, and the residual income would be calculated as shown at the top of the following page.

Division controllable profit (before imputed capital charge)	$300,000
Less imputed capital charge (15% × $1,000,000)....................	150,000
Division residual income...	$150,000

The advantage of this evaluation index is that the division manager is concerned with increasing a dollar amount (in this case, the $150,000) and is more likely to accept incremental investments which have a yield of over 15 percent (in this example). Even if a budget standard for judging residual income is used and the division manager focuses on the variance between the budget and the actual, there would still be a tendency to select additional investments with a yield in excess of 15 percent since such investments maximize the dollar residual income and reduce an unfavorable variance or increase a favorable variance. Division management behavior under a residual income concept, then, should be more congruous with company-wide objectives.

THE INTRACOMPANY OR TRANSFER PRICING PROBLEM

In calculating division profit, problems arise when the divisions are not completely independent. If one division furnishes goods or services to another division, a transfer price must be established in order to determine the buying division's cost and the selling division's revenue. Both revenue and cost are necessary to calculate profit. There is a possible conflict in establishing transfer prices because the data may be used in making decisions as well as in calculating a profit index for performance evaluation. In this section of the chapter, the use of transfer prices for performance evaluation is emphasized. In the next section, the use of transfer prices for decision making will be discussed, and some of the possible conflicts that can arise will be explored.

The most common transfer prices are as follows:

1. Market price.
2. Negotiated or bargained market price.
3. Transfer price based on a cost calculation such as full cost or marginal (variable) cost.
4. Dual transfer prices.

Market Price

There may be real difficulty in determining a market price. The use of a market price assumes that a market exists at the transfer point. Even if this is the case, the appropriate market price may be difficult to establish. Frequently, the list or catalog price is only vaguely related to the effective market price. Often the market price is a fluctuating one. The selling division may incur less cost in selling to the buying division than would be incurred if the product were sold to outsiders. This occurs when the buying division is a captive market. In such an instance, if the market price is not adjusted downward, the selling division will get the entire benefit of the savings in shipping and marketing costs.

A more difficult problem exists where there is no real market at the transfer point. If the selling division furnishes repair, research, or storage services to the buying division, for example, it is difficult to establish a satisfactory market price for such services.

Despite the problem of arriving at market price, there is general agreement that if a market price can be determined, it is probably the best price for use in performance evaluation because the use of a decentralized organization structure is largely motivated by a desire to create smaller, autonomous operating divisions that conduct their business as separate entities. The use of a market transfer price, where possible, creates the actual market conditions under which these divisions would operate if they were separate companies rather than divisions of one organization. To the extent that market prices can be established on the basis of outside forces, they form an excellent performance indicator, because they cannot be manipulated by the individuals who have an interest in the resulting profit calculation.

For purposes of illustrating the above comments, assume that a company has two divisions, a producing division and a marketing division. The operation might be a corporate farm. The producing division is to produce a bushel of grain, which can be sold as soon as it is produced or transferred to the marketing division where the decision will be made as to the future date of sale. This situation is diagrammed below:

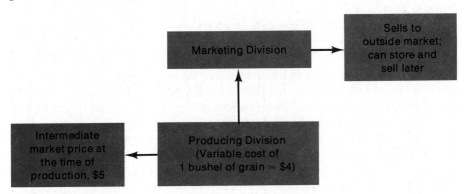

If mangement desires to evaluate each division manager, the $5 market price should be used as a transfer price. This price compared with the $4 variable production cost results in a $1 profit. This profit is dependent on the efficiency of the production operation. It also depends on the ability to produce the proper grain crop (wheat, corn, etc.) at the right time. These decisions are within the jurisdiction of the producing division manager. The marketing division should buy from the producing division only if it is felt that the grain can be stored and sold at some later date at a profit. These decisions are the responsibility of the marketing division. If the marketing division buys the bushel of grain and sells it six months later at $5.50, having incurred interest and storage costs of 30 cents, the profit resulting from this operation is 20 cents. A summary calculation is as follows:

	PRODUCING DIVISION	MARKETING DIVISION
Sales............................	$5	$5.50
Cost	4	($5 + 30¢) 5.30
Profit	$1	$ .20

The total profit for the company is $1.20; but by using a market transfer price, the total profit is divided into a producing and a marketing profit. These individual profit figures serve as the basis for evaluating each division's operation.

Negotiated or Bargained Market Price

The use of negotiated or bargained prices has often been suggested as a refinement of market-based transfer pricing. There may be real advantages in allowing the two division managers, who must have complete freedom to buy and sell outside, to arrive at the transfer price through arms-length bargaining. The selfish interest of the division managers in the division profit and related bonuses serves the company objectives as long as:

1. All transfer prices are determined by negotiation between the buyer and the seller.
2. Negotiators have all the data on alternative sources, markets, and market prices.
3. Both the buyer and seller are free to buy and sell outside the company.

A negotiated market price may solve some of the problems encountered in trying to base the market transfer price on a list price, which may have no meaning, or on a market price, which is really not applicable because the cost of selling to the division is much less than that of selling outside the firm. Furthermore, much of the friction and bad feeling that may arise from a centrally controlled market transfer price may be eliminated without incurring any misallocation of resources. Much of the division managers' time may be consumed in negotiating the transfer prices. If this is undesirable, a possible remedy is to negotiate these prices for a certain time period instead of for each transfer that takes place.

Many of the problems that arise in transfer pricing are created because the buying division is a captive customer and is unable to bargain effectively with the selling division. Real competition can be injected into the situation by encouraging the division managers to buy and sell outside and by praising them when their results are favorable.

Bargained or negotiated price may solve some of the problems encountered in transfer pricing, but such a method will probably not eliminate all of them. If the buying division can obtain a lower price by purchasing outside, it is true that the buying division's profit will be increased. However, the selling division's decrease in profit because of a loss in volume may more than offset this profit increase. In such an instance, the total company may suffer. In the long run, the selling division manager would probably lower the price so as not to create large losses because of unused capacity. If this happens, the freedom to negotiate market price is certainly superior to a centrally administered market price from which the division managers cannot depart.

Transfer Price Based on Cost

For performance evaluation, it is difficult to justify transfer prices based on either full cost or variable cost. A transfer price based on variable cost is useful in decision making; but for performance evaluation, such a figure may well result in no profit or even a loss for the selling division. In such an instance, there is little or no motivation for the selling division to supply the goods or services. Where no intermediate market exists or where there are significant imperfections in the intermediate market, there may be little choice on transfer prices and some cost measure may be the only real possibility. It is possible, of course, for management to centralize by combining the buying and selling divisions where no intermediate market exists for some of the major products or product lines; but that would undermine the decentralized nature of the organization.

The use of full cost or full cost plus a profit percentage can also create problems. If either of these measures is higher than the price from an outside vendor, the buying division would be motivated to buy outside the company and thus create excess capacity in the internal selling division. That is, the variable cost of the selling division plus some of the allocated fixed cost (full cost) might be higher than the price from an outside vendor; but if the outside price is higher than the variable cost alone, the company (overall) would be better off to have the selling division produce the good or service in question, especially if there is excess capacity in that division. This problem is discussed in more depth in the next section of the chapter.

Another difficulty in using full cost (or full cost plus a profit percentage) is that it may give rise to arguments over how full cost should be determined — essentially cost-allocation arguments. Such arguments may consume managerial time that could be better spent on other matters. On the positive side, however, using full cost or full cost plus a profit percentage can motivate the internal supplying division to accommodate the order of the buying division. Even the use of full cost as a transfer price would increase the selling division's profit so long as the full cost is greater than the variable cost and there is excess capacity. That is, the difference between the selling division's full cost and variable cost is a contribution to fixed cost (contribution margin) which increases profit.

Dual Transfer Prices

The use of dual transfer prices has been suggested as a means of creating a profit, and thus a positive motivation, in the selling division while transferring the goods or service to the buying division at variable cost. Variable cost is probably the best figure to guide the decisions of the buying division manager. If the transfer price is higher than variable cost, there is always the risk that the buying division manager will buy outside the company (because the internal price to be paid may be higher than the outside market price) and by so doing create more excess capacity in the selling division. If there is already excess capacity in the selling division, the buying division should buy from the inside division so long as the variable cost is less than the outside price.

Using variable cost as the single transfer price creates no motivation for the selling division manager to sell, since there would be no increase in the profit of the selling division. A dual system allows the selling division to "sell" at what might be considered a synthetic market price (such as variable cost plus a profit percentage or full cost plus a profit percentage), yet the transfer price to the buying division is the variable cost. Thus, the selling division manager is motivated to sell because profit will be increased and the buying division manager will buy internally unless the outside price is less than variable cost. Hence, the main purpose of the dual system is to motivate both the buying and selling division managers to make decisions that are consistent with the interests of the company as a whole.

Such a system, however, does create a problem which may or may not be important. If a dual system is used, it is not possible to add the division profits to arrive at the total company profit. That is, since both the buying and selling divisions are recognizing some of the same profits, eliminations have to be made before the total company profit can be determined. Such a problem does not seem to be especially serious, but it is sometimes cited as an argument against the dual pricing system. The example which follows illustrates the dual transfer price system and the nature of the double counting problem.

Assume that Division X (the buying division) has an order from a customer for 1,000 units of Product A at a price of $20 per unit. To fill the order, Division X must buy 1,000 units of a particular part or subassembly which can be purchased from Division Y (the selling division) or can be purchased outside the company. In addition, Division X must incur a variable cost of $10 per unit to assemble Product A. The variable cost of producing the part or subassembly in Division Y is $4 per unit, and there is capacity to produce 1,000 units of the part. Instead of using a single transfer price of $4, the company allows the buying division to buy at the variable cost of $4 and allows the selling division to sell at variable cost plus a profit percentage of 50 percent of variable cost — in this case, $2 per unit. If the intracompany transaction is completed, the partial income statements for the divisions will appear as follows:

Division X
Partial Income Statement

Sales (1,000 units @ $20)..	$20,000
Variable cost:	
Cost of parts from Division Y (1,000 units @ $4)	$ 4,000
Cost incurred in Division X (1,000 units @ $10)..	10,000
Total variable cost..	$14,000
Contribution margin...	$ 6,000

Division Y
Partial Income Statement

Sales (1,000 units @ $6)...	$6,000
Variable cost (1,000 units @ $4)..	4,000
Contribution margin...	$2,000

Although the total contribution margin for the company as a whole appears to be $8,000 ($6,000 + $2,000), it is actually only $6,000 ($20 unit selling price of the final product − $14 total unit variable cost incurred in both Divisions X and Y = $6 unit contribution margin; $6 unit contribution margin × 1,000 units = $6,000 total contribution margin). In this example, the full contribution is reflected in the statement of Division X. The additional contribution of $2,000 reflected in Division Y's income statement occurred because Division Y was allowed to "sell" at a profit percentage of variable cost. However, this transaction was not a source of outside income.

The advantages of the dual transfer price system are illustrated by the above example. On the one hand, it is desirable for Division X to use Division Y's variable cost in deciding whether to buy internally or externally. Since there is unused capacity in Division Y, the part should be purchased from that division so long as the outside price is higher than the variable cost of $4 per unit. On the other hand, motivation is provided by allowing Division Y to "sell" at variable cost plus a 50 percent profit percentage. Thus, the dual system is a way of providing the buying division with the proper information while at the same time allowing the selling division the possibility of a profit. Such a system maximizes the congruence of divisional goals with the company-wide goals.

TRANSFER PRICES FOR DECISION MAKING — A SYSTEM OF INFORMATION AND COMMUNICATION

As was indicated earlier, one of the basic reasons for decentralization is that it makes possible the delegation of decision-making authority throughout the firm. If one person or a small group can efficiently make all decisions for the firm, then much, if not all, of the impetus for decentralization will disappear. Hence, one of the basic assumptions in decentralization is that the firm-wide decision process is too complex for a few persons to effectively control.

If delegation of decision-making authority is to be effective, a communication system must be established throughout the firm. The need for a system of communication on which decisions can be based usually varies directly with the degree of decentralization involved. If all decisions are made centrally, the only need for communication is so that the subordinate managers can implement the decisions. Conversely, if the subordinate managers make and implement decisions, the need for a system of communication is enhanced.

In a decentralized operation, if the divisions are interdependent, a system of transfer prices can provide a communication system or a set of signals which the submanagers can use as a basis for their decisions. In such a setting, the system of internal prices serves the same purpose in facilitating internal transactions as the external price system does in facilitating transactions between the firm and outsiders.

To develop this point, consider the role of the external price system in providing information and communication for facilitating transactions between firms. If a make or buy decision is to be made by Firm A, the first step in the decision is to compare the inside prices of labor and materials (and other factors of production) with the outside price of the part. The decision depends primarily on how these costs compare with each other. Note that the external price system furnishes the information which guides the actions of the decision maker. Note also how much more difficult it would be to make a decision if the information on cost was not available in the form of external prices. It is in this sense that a system of prices is a powerfully efficient information system.

In a decentralized operation where divisions are interdependent, the manager of a division needs information to decide when to deal with another division and when to deal with an outside firm. For example, assume that Division B can buy a component part from Division S or from an outside firm. This problem is just another version of the make or buy situation discussed in the preceding paragraph. The decision depends primarily on a comparison of the internal transfer price (Division S's price) and the external price (the outside firm's price). If the internal transfer price is higher than the external price, the manager of Division B has a *signal* to buy outside the firm, and vice versa. It is, therefore, important that the transfer prices give the right signals; otherwise the decision process will not be carried out efficiently.

The following discussion of the problems and difficulties in using transfer prices is offered with the hope that a clear understanding of these problems will lead to better internal price systems and practices. It is difficult to anticipate all potential problems, but it is possible to describe some of the general problems of which management should be aware. Two distinct cases are distinguished: they are (1) a situation where a market exists at the transfer point and (2) a situation where a market does not exist at the transfer point.

The Intermediate Market Case

In the case of division operation, two general types of decisions may be called for: (1) how to produce and (2) how much to produce, including the decision as to both price and quantity. Assume that Division A is the selling division and Division B is the buying division. One decision B must make is whether or not to buy from A. B is encouraged to buy from A as long as the price quoted by A compares favorably with the outside market price.

In a perfectly competitive market, it makes little difference in the overall profit picture whether B buys inside or outside. A should be able to sell all of its output on the outside market; hence, B's decision to buy outside should not cause A to have any idle capacity. Furthermore, if the market is perfectly competitive, the selling costs of selling outside are likely to be about the same as the cost of selling to B.

When the market is not perfectly competitive, the situation changes somewhat. If market price is used as the transfer price, it would be undesirable for the price to be so inflexible that B might go outside to find a lower price and not buy from A without A's being allowed to lower its price. Such an action might cause A to have idle capacity, and the overall company profit would be lower than if A reduced the price to encourage B to buy internally. Actually, B should buy inside so long as A's variable cost is below the outside market price. In such a situation, a possible conflict arises. As discussed earlier, it is possible to use a dual price system; that is, the transfer price to A could be the market price and the transfer price to B could be A's variable cost. However, such a practice may destroy some of the advantages of decentralization. By using a dual standard, the competitive atmosphere may be destroyed. A negotiated market price may be preferable. A would probably not allow idle capacity to persist in the long run. Rather, the market price to B would probably be negotiated at a low enough price so that B would not continue buying outside.

For most decisions of how to produce, even where there is capital investment involved, the proper calculation is the variable cost. This is so because, from the viewpoint of the entire company, the how-to-produce decision should be made so as to achieve the minimum cost possible. Cost that changes with volume is the relevant cost, and this cost is the variable cost. Any time a market transfer price is used, there is a potential conflict that may arise in connection with how-to-produce problems. In some cases a negotiated market price may accommodate the situation, as in the example; but, in any case, the safest transfer price for the decision is the variable cost. Such a transfer price, however, is generally a poor one for performance evaluation.

In pricing and output decisions for the end product, again it is the variable cost that is relevant. This is particularly true when the intermediate market is not perfectly competitive. If the intermediate market is perfectly competitive, the market price will suffice. For example, assume that Division A produces unprocessed meat and that Division B can buy from Division A and sell the meat processed. In order to justify processing, the variable cost of processing in Division B plus the opportunity market price as determined by the intermediate (unprocessed) market must be less than the selling price of processed meat. Hence, market price will accommodate a sell-or-process-more decision in a competitive market.[1]

In the case of an imperfect intermediate market, the following decisions must be made with respect to output:

1. What price should be charged for the final product?
2. What price should be charged for the intermediate product?
3. How much of the intermediate product should be produced for sale on the outside market and how much for sale to Division B?

All of these decisions must be made on the basis of a marginal cost and a marginal revenue schedule for the several products involved. Neither market price nor a transfer price based on full cost will suffice in making these decisions. Therefore, a conflict is bound to arise between choosing a transfer price for performance evaluation and one for decision making.

The following example illustrates the imperfect market situation. Assume that Division A sells to Division B. The output of Division A is Product X_1, which can be sold at the intermediate market stage or can be transferred to Division B and processed and sold as Product X_2. The marginal revenue and variable cost information is as shown at the top of the following page.

This example is simplified by using a constant variable cost as a measure of marginal cost. In comparing the marginal costs and revenues, it can be seen that six units of X_2 can be sold in the final market before the net marginal revenue equals the variable cost of X_1 of $1.50;

---

[1] In terms of economic theory, the market price and the marginal cost in a perfectly competitive market should be equal; that is, to maximize profit, the division manager should produce and sell until marginal cost and marginal revenue are equal. In a perfectly competitive market, the demand curve is horizontal because the division can sell any output at the market price. Hence, marginal revenue and market price are equal. If production is expanded until marginal cost and marginal revenue are equated, marginal cost will equal the market price.

	DIVISION A		DIVISION B		
Number of Units	X_1 Marginal Revenue	X_1 Variable Cost	X_2 Marginal Revenue	X_2 Variable Cost	X_2 Marginal Revenue Less X_2 Variable Cost
11	$ .25	$1.50	$ .50	$1.00	$—.50
10	.25	1.50	.50	1.00	—.50
9	.50	1.50	1.00	1.00	—0—
8	.75	1.50	1.50	1.00	.50
7	1.00	1.50	2.00	1.00	1.00
6	1.25	1.50	2.50	1.00	1.50
5	1.50	1.50	3.00	1.00	2.00
4	1.75	1.50	3.50	1.00	2.50
3	2.00	1.50	4.00	1.00	3.00
2	2.25	1.50	4.50	1.00	3.50
1	2.50	1.50	5.00	1.00	4.00

therefore six units of X_1 should be sold to Division B for processing into X_2 and sale in the final market. But five units of X_1 can also be sold in the intermediate market before the marginal revenue equals the variable cost of $1.50. Hence, 11 units of X_1 should be produced.

Note that this output decision has been made by using the marginal revenue of Product X_1 and the net marginal revenue of Product X_2. A unit of X_1 has a marginal production cost of $1.50, and it should be sold in that market where the profit is the highest. In the case of the intermediate market, no further processing is necessary. The production cost of $1.50 represents the total additional cost to be incurred in selling Product X_1 in the intermediate market. However, if X_1 is processed and sold as X_2, the additonal processing cost is $1 per unit; and this amount should be deducted from the marginal revenue of X_2 to arrive at the net amount of additional revenue that will eventually accrue to the company.

In the above example, the total production schedule calls for 11 units of X_1 to be produced by Division A. It is assumed that the capacity of Division A is such that at least 11 units of X_1 can be produced. This may or may not be the case. Suppose, for example, that the capacity of Division A is limited to less than 11 units. A priority schedule must be developed to decide which units of X_1 should be sold to the intermediate market and which units should be sold to Division B for further processing and sale in the final market.

This priority schedule can be determined by comparing the marginal revenue schedules of the two divisions. For example, the first three units of X_1 should be transferred to Division B, since the net marginal revenue of this division is greater than the marginal revenue of Division A. On the 4th and 5th units, the marginal revenue of X_1 in either the final or the intermediate market is $2.50; so there is a point of indifference. The 6th unit should be allocated to the intermediate market, the 7th and 8th units have equal value in either market, the 9th unit should stay in Division A, and the 10th and 11th units have equal value in either market. The 12th unit should not be produced, since the marginal revenue in either market is lower than the marginal cost of \$1.50. The schedule which appears below, where the unit numbers are in parentheses, summarizes the priority for each unit. If for some reason the productive capacity of Division A is restricted to less than 11 units, this priority schedule should be used.

UNITS OF PRODUCT 1	MARGINAL REVENUE IF X_1 IS SOLD IN THE INTERMEDIATE MARKET	NET MARGINAL REVENUE IF X_1 IS SOLD TO DIVISION B FOR SALE IN THE FINAL MARKET
1	\$2.50 (4 or 5)	\$4.00 (1)
2	2.25 (6)	3.50 (2)
3	2.00 (7 or 8)	3.00 (3)
4	1.75 (9)	2.50 (4 or 5)
5	1.50 (10 or 11)	2.00 (7 or 8)
6	1.25	1.50 (10 or 11)
7	1.00	1.00
8	.75	.50
9	.50	—0—
10	.25	—.50
11	.25	—.50

As can be seen from the example, the allocation problem in an imperfect market situation requires variable cost transfer prices. A market transfer price may cause Division B to restrict production. This restriction could cause Division A to stop short of the most profitable level of production. Yet a variable cost transfer price is inadequate for performance evaluation. In the imperfect market situation, therefore, a conflict will undoubtedly arise where the data must also be used for pricing and output decisions.

The No Intermediate Market Case

If no intermediate market exists for the product of Division A, then Division A is really not a profit center. Such a division may still be set up as a decentralized independent operating unit, but it is more like a cost center within a centralized firm. To treat such a division as a profit center requires the determination of a transfer price that may be quite arbitrary. Furthermore, there is no real possibility for negotiation between Divisions A and B since Division A has no outside market alternative.

For decision problems, the proper transfer price for Product X_1 would be its marginal or variable cost. Since no market price exists, the main alternative is likely to be the full cost. The full cost may be an acceptable transfer price for performance evaluation; but such a figure will undoubtedly lead to poor decisions, because the buying division will be more likely to buy outside and in doing so may create excess capacity in the selling division. It is probably better to recognize Division A as a cost center and to evaluate it on the basis of a controllable cost budget or standard. The variable or marginal cost should be used as the transfer price to Division B. This figure can be used for evaluating Division B on a profit basis and it also is useful to Division B in making output and production decisions.

THE EVALUATION CRITERION OR STANDARD

The main indexes of division performance discussed earlier in this chapter were (1) division profit and (2) division return on investment with residual income as an alterative to using return on investment as a ratio. Where no intermediate market exists, it may be difficult to calculate profit, and cost may be the best performance index. Standards for cost control have been discussed in earlier chapters and will not be reviewed here.

If profit alone is used as an evaluation of division performance, the standard for measurement will probably be a profit budget for the division. This budget can be constructed by referring to other similar division operations within or outside the company. If this is done, the factors that are unique to the operations of a particular division should be considered. If the market is temporarily depressed and if this factor is not controllable by the division manager, it should receive proper consideration in establishing the budget. A detailed division profit budget should show, after a comparison with the actual performance, the parts of the division operation that are the weakest and on which a concentrated managerial effort is justified. Only the factors that are controllable by the division manager should be included in the profit budget.

The use of a profit index has been criticized on the grounds that a charge for investment controllable at the division level may not be included in the profit calculation. This criticism has probably been the main reason for the use of return on investment or its variation, residual income, as a performance index. A return on investment calculation relates profit to investment, and the resulting ratio becomes the performance index. In the residual income method, the performance index is an absolute dollar amount (rather than a ratio) calculated by deducting a capital charge from the operating profit. In either case, management must decide on an appropriate return on investment rate to use in the evaluation of a division. This return on investment rate becomes the standard for comparison if a return on investment (ratio) method is used; it becomes the capital charge if residual income is used as the performance index.

The choice of the appropriate return on investment standard is not without its problems. It is probably a mistake to compare a division's rate of return with the overall average rate desired by the top management. It may be that the division can never measure up to the desired overall average rate of return. Just because management desires 20 percent rate of return, there is no guarantee that a particular division can ever hope to earn this rate. Also, a division that earns 15 percent should not necessarily be liquidated. Even if other parts of the company can earn 20 percent on additional investment, the 15 percent division should not be liquidated unless the division investment is based on liquidation value and unless the 15 percent division can be liquidated without affecting the other operating divisions of the company. To the extent that the 15 percent return is based on historical investment, it is probably a poor guide for capital budgeting decisions; and depending on the standard used, it may be a poor index of performance.

Another problem in using a return on investment standard for judging performance can arise when the division manager does not have control over investment decisions. If the capital budget is administered centrally, it is more effective to control division investment by making the division manager's new projects compete for funds by using as a standard the best projects that exist elsewhere within the company. In this respect, the division rate of return budgeted for performance evaluation may be an extremely poor guide for additional investment because the money may find a better use elsewhere.

Even though the division manager may not have complete control over division investment in fixed assets, a good deal of control may be exercised over the working capital requirements of the division. The performance index should allow for this aspect of division operation. However, instead of calculating a rate of return on working capital investment, it is probably easier and more effective to include a charge for this investment in establishing the profit budget. This charge may be based on the rate that could be earned on working capital investment elsewhere in the company. If such a procedure is followed, the division manager will be reluctant to demand excess working capital. Furthermore, top management can also tell whether a particular division's use of working capital is as profitable as that of other divisions.

The problem of controlling and evaluating division operations in a decentralized company is exceedingly complex. Yet, top management really has no choice as to whether or not control is needed; it is rather a question of finding the most effective control device. Every manager must have some means of answering the question, "Where are the problems and the weak spots in the overall operation?" In a decentralized operation, the contact with the various parts of the operation is likely to be quite impersonal. Usually some reporting system must be used. Accounting concepts are useful because they can facilitate management by exception. If a good standard is established and if a good index of actual performance is calculated, the two can be compared and the exceptional case demanding management's attention can be found. However, since the control problem is a difficult but an important one, it behooves the manager to be very familiar with the strong features of a particular system as well as the troublesome problems that will undoubtedly be encountered in using accounting information.

QUESTIONS

1. What are the advantages of decentralization?

2. Why is cost not a good control index in evaluating a division manager who has decision power on prices and combination of products?

3. What are some of the disadvantages of using division profit as an evaluation index?

4. Briefly state the difference between division controllable profit and division direct profit.

5. Should investment which is common to several divisions be allocated to those divisions for the purpose of calculating a rate of return?

6. How is residual income defined?

7. Under what conditions are transfer prices necessary?

8. If a market transfer price can be determined, why is such a price usually considered the best one to use?

9. Briefly describe a dual transfer pricing system.

10. If the intermediate market is perfectly competitive, will a market-based transfer price ever lead to excess capacity in a producing division?

11. What is the disadvantage of using negotiated transfer prices where there is no intermediate market in which the producing division can sell its products?

EXERCISES

1. Profit Indexes. The following data are given for a division of a company:

Revenue from sales...	$16,000
Division variable cost...	7,500
Allocated home office overhead...	1,200
Fixed overhead traceable to division ($2,000 is controllable, and $4,000 is not controllable)	6,000

Required: Calculate division contribution margin, division controllable profit, division direct profit, and division net profit.

2. Transfer Price Based on Full Cost. The Lance Company has a division which produces a single product that sells for $20 per unit in the external market. The full cost of the product is $14, calculated as follows:

Variable materials and labor cost per unit...	$11
Fixed cost per unit	3*
	$14

*Total fixed cost of $300,000 divided by current production and sales of 100,000 units.

Another division has offered to buy 20,000 units at the full cost of $14. The producing division has excess capacity, and the 20,000 units can be produced without interfering with the current external sales volume of 100,000 units. The total fixed cost of the producing division will not change as a result of the order. However, the division manager of the producing division is inclined to reject the order, feeling that the division's profit position will not be improved.

Required: Explain to the division manager (by means of a calculation) why transferring 20,000 units at the full cost of $14 per unit will result in an increase in the profit of the producing division.

3. Transfer Pricing Problem. The Mack Company has a producing division which is currently producing 100,000 units but has a capacity of 150,000 units. The variable cost of the product is $20 per unit, and the total fixed cost is $600,000 or $6 per unit based on current production.

A selling division of the Mack Company offers to buy 50,000 units from the producing division at $19 per unit. The producing division manager refuses the order because the price is below variable cost. The selling division manager argues that the order should be accepted since by taking the order the producing division manager can lower the fixed cost per unit from $6 to $4 (output will increase to 150,000 units). This decrease of $2 in fixed cost per unit will more than offset the $1 difference between the variable cost and the transfer price.

Required:

(1) If you were the producing division manager, would you accept the selling division manager's argument? Why or why not? (Assume that the 100,000 units currently being produced sell for $30 per unit in the external market.)

(2) From the viewpoint of the overall company, should the order be accepted if the manager of the selling division intends to sell each unit in the outside market for $22 after incurring an additional processing cost of $2.25 per unit?

4. Comparison of Return on Investment and Residual Income. A division of the Bond Company has been reporting operating income of $1,800,000 per year based on an investment of $8,000,000. The company is considering the use of return on investment (ratio form) or residual income as an evaluation measure. At the present time, the division manager is faced with a decision on an incremental investment of $4,000,000 which will increase annual operating income by $700,000 per year.

Required: Provide a calculation which shows the difference between the two performance measures and explain the possible advantage of using residual income assuming that a 15% return on investment standard is considered acceptable.

5. Dual Transfer Price System. The Turn Company has two divisions, A and B. Division B produces a product at a variable cost of $6 per unit and sells 50,000 units to the external market at $10 per unit and 40,000 units to Division A at variable cost plus 50%. However, under the dual transfer price system in use, Division A pays only the variable cost per unit. The fixed cost of Division B is $150,000 per year.

Division A sells 40,000 units of its finished product in the external market at $20 per unit and has a variable cost of $5 per unit in addition to the cost of the subassembly purchased from Division B at variable cost. The annual fixed cost of Division A is $110,000.

Required: Show the income statements for the two divisions and the income statement for the company as a whole (assuming the company consists of only the two divisions). Explain why, under the dual transfer price system, the income for the company is less than the sum of the profit figures shown on the income statements for the two divisions.

6. Market Value Transfer Price. Company X has two divisions, M and S. Division M manufactures a product and Division S sells it. The intermediate market is perfectly competitive, but the product can be stored and sold later or processed and sold in the final processed market. Once the product is manufactured, some of it is sold by Division M and some is transferred to Division S which decides whether to hold or process and sell the product. The following information pertains to the current year.

Manufacturing cost incurred by Division M in producing 1,000,000 units..........	$6,000,000
Of the 1,000,000 units produced:	
400,000 sold by M in intermediate market..................	4,000,000
200,000 held by S for sale later (no additional processing work done on these units in Division S).................	2,000,000
400,000 processed by S and sold	5,800,000
Sales value of 600,000 units at the time they were transfered to S..................	6,000,000
Total additional processing cost of S	1,500,000

There were no beginning inventories.

Required:

(1) Prepare an income statement for the whole firm.
(2) Prepare a separate income statement for each division using a market value transfer price.

7. Decision Making in Decentralized Operation. The Quinn Company is going to build an office building for itself. The company has a construction division which builds all buildings and equipment for the entire company. The construction division has requested bids on the elevators for the building from two companies. The O Company gives a bid of $5,000,000, and the U Company bids $4,000,000. However, the O Company would buy materials for the elevators from a fabricating division of the Quinn Company. This order would result in the fabricating division earning $1,500,000 after covering all costs. Since the Quinn Company is decentralized, the construction division is not aware of this possiblity.

Required: Which bid would you expect the construction division to take? Which bid would the Quinn Company prefer to have the construction division accept?

8. Transfer Pricing Problem. The tailor shop in a men's clothing store is set up as an autonomous unit. The transfer price for tailoring services is based on the variable cost which is estimated at $8 per hour. The store manager feels that the suit and sport coat department is currently using too much tailor time and that this department could cut down on hours used by taking more care in fitting the garments. The manager has decided to double the hourly tailor rate even though this new rate will be no reflection of the real variable cost. The idea is simply to provide an incentive to the suit and sport coat department to conserve on tailor time.

Required: What possible disadvantages do you see in the store manager's action? Do you agree or disagree with this means of stressing the need to conserve tailor time? Would it make any difference if the various selling departments were required to use the tailor shop and were not allowed to take their tailor work to some outside tailor shop?

9. Allocation of Central Corporate Office Cost. The Warren Company has several operating divisions which are largely autonomous as far as decision making is concerned. The central corporate office consists mainly of the president and immediate staff. The annual cost is $6,000,000, and this cost is fixed. In calculating division profit, this cost is allocated to divisions on the basis of sales. The current allocation rate is $.30 per sales dollar based on the company-wide normal sales volume of $20,000,000 per year. The company controller does not consider this to be a transfer price but feels that the divisions are not really buying anything. In the controller's view, the charge is a method of allocating cost which should be absorbed by the divisions when they calculate their annual net income.

Required: Do you agree with the controller? In what sense is the charge a transfer price? Could the charge affect the decision of a division manager considering the introduction of a new product with a variable cost of $5 and a selling price of $7? Explain.

10. Transfer Pricing Problem. Division 1 produces 100,000 units of a product with a variable cost of $5 per unit and a fixed cost of $3 (based on $300,000 fixed cost allocated to 100,000 units of production). These units can be sold in an intermediate market for $1,000,000 ($10 per unit) or transferred to Division 2 for additional processing and sold in a processed market. The selling price processed is $14 per unit and the additional processing cost in Division 2 is $1.50 per unit. The fixed cost in the Division 2 processing unit is $100,000. At this time, there will be excess capacity in the Division 2 processing unit if the units are not transferred.

Required: Should the 100,000 units be sold by Division 1 or by Division 2? Would a transfer price based on either market price or variable cost be likely to lead to the right decision? Which price would you favor if Division 1 can always sell at least 100,000 units at $10 per unit in the intermediate market and Division 2 could buy under similar conditions?

PROBLEMS

11-1. Transfer Price Based on Full Cost. Division P of the Pond Company produces a large metal frame which is sold to Division S of the company. Division S uses these frames in constructing metal lathes which are sold to machine tool manufacturers. In Division P, the frames are produced in a stamping process and are then run through a finishing process in which they are trimmed and polished before being shipped to Division S.

The current estimate of the variable cost of materials and labor to produce a frame in the stamping process is $100 per frame. The fixed overhead associated with this process in Division P is $600,000 per year. Current production is 40,000 frames, and this is full capacity for both' the stamping and the trimming-polishing processes.

The variable cost of labor in the trimming-polishing process (no additional materials are required) is $10 per frame since labor in this process is paid on a piece-rate basis. The fixed overhead in this process is $200,000 per year, and this amount is largely due to equipment depreciation and related costs. The machines have no salvage value to speak of since they are fairly specialized equipment.

The transfer price to Division S is a full-cost transfer price, and the fixed cost per unit is calculated by prorating the current fixed cost in each process over the 40,000 frames being produced. The price is quoted for each process, and the calculation presented to the manager of Division S by the manager of Division P is as follows:

Stamping process:	
Materials and labor cost per unit..	$100
Fixed overhead cost per unit ($600,000 ÷ 40,000 units)	15
	$115
Trimming-polishing process:	
Labor cost per unit	$ 10
Fixed overhead cost per unit ($200,000 ÷ 40,000 units)	5
	$ 15
Total cost per unit..	$130

An outside company has offered to rent to Division S machinery which would perform the trimming and polishing part of the frame manufacturing. The rental cost of the machinery is $180,000 per year. With the new machinery, the labor cost per frame would remain at $10. The Division S manager sees the possibility of obtaining the frames from Division P for $115 by eliminating the $15 cost of trimming and polishing and performing these processes in Division S. An analysis is given below:

New Process:	
Machine rental cost per year..	$180,000
Labor cost ($10 × 40,000 units)	400,000
	$580,000
Current process (40,000 units @ $15 per unit, portion of Division P transfer price attributable to trimming-polishing process)....................	$600,000

The manager of Division S has approached the company vice-president of operations for approval to acquire the new machinery.

Required:

(1) As the vice-president, how would you advise the manager of Division S?

(2) Could the transfer pricing system be modified; and, if so, how?

11-2. Allocation of Central Office Overhead. The Look Company has several departments which operate quite autonomously as far as decision making is concerned. The company allocates central office overhead to all these operating departments based on the total labor dollars incurred by each division. The central office overhead budget and the allocation rate are shown at the top of the following page.

Executive offices..	$170,000
Legal...	50,000
Advertising..	40,000
Personnel..	80,000
Accounting..	60,000
Total..	$400,000

Total estimated payroll in all operating departments $500,000

Allocation rate — $400,000 ÷ $500,000 = $.80 per labor dollar

The central office overhead of $400,000 is considered to be a fixed cost. Also, once the rate is established, it is not changed for one year.

The engineering research department conducts research on certain engineering problems related to the company's products and issues reports to clients who request this service. The manager of this department is faced with a need to hire two more technical assistants because of an increased work load. If the manager works through the company's personnel department, these positions can be filled at a cost of $1,000 per month for each employee. However, the usual $.80 per dollar of payroll will also be charged against the research department's budget for central office overhead. The manager discovers that it is possible to hire the technical services of an outside engineering firm which will furnish two technical assistants for as long as they are required, and the cost will be considered a consulting cost and not part of the division's payroll. The cost will be $1,500 per month for each assistant.

Required:

(1) Is the central office overhead charge a transfer price? Explain.

(2) What is the manager of the engineering research department likely to do? Show your calculations.

(3) If the Look Company wants to continue to allocate central office overhead, advise the president how this might be done so as not to affect the hiring decisions of the various department managers.

11-3. Decision Making in Decentralized Operation. The Main Company has several divisions. Division S produces (among other products) a metal container which is sold to customers who use it for shipping liquid chemicals. The main material used in manufacturing these containers is a metal which can be purchased from Division M, one of the other divisions of the company, or from several outside sources. Division S has received a customer order for 100 containers at $300 each. It will require two tons of materials to produce the 100 containers. The manager of Division S requests bids for the materials required to produce the containers from Division M and from two outside companies. Division M, bidding a transfer price based on full cost, bids a price of $7,000 per ton on the materials order. Division M's variable cost is only $4,000 per ton, and there is excess capacity. However, Division M regularly bases price bids on full cost whether the order is from another division or from an outside customer.

The two outside companies bid $5,500 and $6,000 per ton. However, Company A, which bid $6,000, would buy the manufacturing supplies necessary to produce the materials from Division P, another division of the Main Company. The supplies would amount to $1,200 per ton of materials required, and the profit to Division P would be about 60% of the selling price.

Required:

(1) What would you expect Division S to do?

(2) Will Division S accept the right outside bid?

(3) Should Division M's transfer pricing policy be changed? If so, how?

11-4. Transfer Pricing Problem. The Cook Company has a central computer facility which is used by several operating departments for data processing and problem-solving purposes. This center's budget for the current year is given below:

Rentals	$1,000,000
Payroll, operators	200,000
Payroll, programmers	100,000
Payroll, supervision and secretarial	80,000
Miscellaneous supplies	120,000
Utilities	200,000
Total	$1,700,000

It is estimated that 10,000 computer time units will be available.

All of the costs shown in the budget are considered to be fixed, except for utilities and miscellaneous supplies, which are variable.

During the past 5 years, the computer facility has not been operated at full capacity. The percentage of capacity has increased from 40% in the first year of operation to about 70% of capacity estimated for the current year.

A transfer price policy has been established which calls for the use of a full cost per unit of time. Thus, an operating department that needs one half of a time unit would be charged at the rate of $85 [½ × ($1,700,000 ÷ 10,000 time units)]. All operating departments do most of their own programming. The central staff has four programmers who are used to solve special problems as they arise in the center.

The associate director of the center has approached the director to revise the transfer price policy to include only the variable costs. His argument is that the operating departments would thereby be encouraged to make greater use of the facility. The director's response is that she sees no reason why this should be so.

"After all," she points out, "the operating departments need only so much time anyway; and besides, the various managers cannot buy computer time outside the company. So how could the transfer price affect their behavior?"

The associate director's response is that he knows of several instances where the operating departments have secured additional outside-the-company programming services so that the program submitted would require less running time.

"In fact," he says, "I know of one case where the operating manager spent $300 on additional programming to save an estimated 2 time units of running time."

The director's response is, "He should have — after all, it cost us $170 per time unit to run the program!"

Required:

(1) Do you agree with the associate director or the director? Explain.

(2) Was the behavior of the operating manager (as described by the associate director) optimal as far as the whole company is concerned?

(continued)

(3) Assuming that the additional programming effort could not have been done inside the company, what is the maximum price that the operating manager should have paid?

11-5. Preparation of Divisional Income Statements. The Shaft Packing Company has two divisions. Division 1 is responsible for slaughtering and cutting the unprocessed meat. Division 2 processes meat such as hams, bacon, etc. Division 2 can buy meat from Division 1 or from outside suppliers. Division 1 can sell at the market price all the unprocessed meat that it can produce. The current year's income statement for the company appears below.

The Shaft Packing Company
Income Statement
For the Current Year

Sales			$2,400,000
Cost of goods sold:			
Beginning inventory		—0—	
Manufacturing costs:			
Materials, Division 1		$ 600,000	
Labor, Division 1		400,000	
Overhead, Division 1		500,000	
Processing Supplies, Division 2		200,000	
Labor, Division 2		300,000	
Overhead, Division 2		100,000	
Cost of goods available for sale		$2,100,000	
Less ending inventory cost:			
Division 1	—0—		
Division 2	$150,000	150,000	1,950,000
Gross margin			$ 450,000
Operating expenses:			
Sales and administrative, Division 1		$ 120,000	
Sales and administrative, Division 2		100,000	
Central office overhead		100,000	320,000
Income before income tax			$ 130,000

The ending inventory of $150,000 is at the cost of production incurred in Division 1. This inventory is as yet unprocessed. The market value unprocessed is $200,000. The sales for the year can be broken down as follows:

Division 1	$ 500,000
Division 2	1,900,000
	$2,400,000

The market value of the unprocessed meat actually transferred from Division 1 to Division 2 (exclusive of the ending inventory) was $1,600,000.

Required:

(1) Prepare division income statements that might be used to evaluate the performance of the two division managers.

(2) Explain the transfer pricing policy you have used in preparing the statements.

(3) Can you see any conflict in the policy you have used if this same transfer price is to be used for decision making?

11-6. Preparation of Divisional Income Statements. A large farming company has two divisions; one produces grain, and the other sells the grain. As soon as the grain is produced, it is transferred to the selling division where it is stored in anticipation of future sales at a higher price.

During the year, three grain crops of 1,500,000 bushels each were produced. All three have now been sold although some were held in inventory for various periods of time. The market price at production time was $5 per bushel for the first crop, $6 per bushel for the second, and $3 per bushel for the third. There were no beginning inventories.

The annual income statement for the entire company appears as follows:

Revenue:	
Sales (4,500,000)	$22,000,000
Cost:	
Producing division labor and materials	$10,000,000
Selling division labor	1,000,000
Producing division overhead	8,000,000
Selling division overhead	500,000
	$19,500,000
Net income	$ 2,500,000

Required: The company president is very pleased with the total profit but wants to determine whether the price speculation activities of the selling division are earning a profit. You are requested to prepare divisional income statements for the producing division and the selling division. Decide what type of transfer price, market or cost, to use. Explain which transfer price is better. Are the division income statements useful? Explain.

11-7. Evaluation of a Division Using Return on Investment. A company has a division which manufactures and sells furniture. The income statement of this division is given below:

Furniture Division
Income Statement
For the Current Year

Sales		$15,000,000
Division costs:		
Variable cost	$10,000,000	
Fixed cost	4,000,000	14,000,000
		$ 1,000,000
Allocated central office overhead		500,000
Net income		$ 500,000

Investment allocated to division — $5,000,000
Return on investment — 10%

The management is disturbed at the low return on investment. The corporate treasurer indicates that the company can earn at least 20% on additional investment in any number of other projects. Furthermore, the treasurer points out that the investment is actually understated because the plant and facility carried at cost of $5,000,000 could be disposed of for twice that amount.

An investigation reveals that the division fixed cost of $4,000,000 cannot be eliminated even if the division is sold. The allocated central office overhead is a pro rata share of operating the corporate offices, and sale of the division would not affect this cost either.

Required:

(1) Assuming that an expenditure of $1,000,000 annually would maintain the facility in good operating condition for at least 10 years, should the division be sold?

(2) If not, is there a better way of reporting the return on investment that would alert the management to consider selling if volume begins to decline?

11-8. Internal or External Sales. Citadel Company has the capacity to manufacture 700 units of a part used in machine tool production. This part is manufactured in batch lots of 100 units each. Division A makes this part at a uniform variable cost of $5 per unit. The manufactured batches can be sold either to outside customers or to Division B where the parts are used in machine tool assembly.

Data with respect to prices per batch from outside sales are given along with prices charged to outsiders after further processing in Division B.

Batch No.	Division A Price to Outside Customers	Division B Price to Outside Customers After Additional Processing
1	$15	$35
2	14	32
3	12	30
4	9	25
5	9	22
6	9	20
7	8	20

The additional processing cost of Division B for each unit of the first three batches is $10. The next three batches cost $12 per unit to process. The seventh batch costs $13 per unit to process.

Required: Decide which batches should be sold after production in Division A and which batches should be transferred to Division B for further processing. Show computations.

11-9. Transfer Pricing Problem. The Prince Company has a producing division (Division 1) that supplies several parts to another producing division (Division 2) which produces the main product. These component parts are listed below with relevant cost information:

Component No.	Variable Cost per Unit	Quantity Produced
1	$ 8	20,000
2	12	20,000
3	4	30,000
4	2	10,000

The out-of-pocket fixed cost of Division 1 amounts to $240,000. This cost consists of the salary of the division management, indirect labor, payroll, and the like. In addition, the fixed cost which is not out-of-pocket (consisting mainly of depreciation on machinery) amounts to $80,000 per period.

In calculating unit cost, the total fixed cost of $320,000 is allocated to units to arrive at a full cost. This calculation is shown below:

Component No.	Variable Cost per Unit	Fixed Cost per Unit	Full Cost per Unit
1	$ 8	$4	$12
2	12	4	16
3	4	4	8
4	2	4	6

In establishing transfer prices, the full cost is used. In Division 2, which uses the four components, the manager has authority to buy inside the company or to buy from an outside supplier. The outside prices vary somewhat throughout the year. At the present time, the outside prices are as follows:

Component No.	Outside Price
1	$12.50
2	16.20
3	8.20
4	5.80

The manager of Division 2 notices that the outside purchase price of Component 4 is $.20 lower than the transfer price and places an order with an outside supplier. Division 1 stops producing Component 4, reallocates the fixed cost to the remaining units, and adjusts the full cost transfer prices.

Required:

(1) Reallocate the fixed cost and determine the adjusted transfer prices based on full cost. If there is no communication between the two divisions, what action will the manager of Division 2 be likely to take?
(2) Comment on the deficiencies of the full cost transfer price system.
(3) Devise a method of assigning the fixed cost of Division 1 to Division 2 that will not cause Division 2 to buy outside when the components should be produced by Division 1. Consider the possibility of charging Division 2 a flat rate, regardless of the volume purchased, plus a charge per unit for the number of units purchased.

11-10. Evaluation of Alternative Transfer Pricing Systems. The Farley company has a division that manufactures shafts, some of which are used by other divisions and some of which are sold in the outside market. This division is organized in two sections which are described below:

Section 1 — Machining and Grinding. This highly mechanized section has much heavy equipment that is used to give shape to the shafts and to perform grinding operations on shafts with special requirements.

Section 2 — Cleaning and Packing. This section consists primarily of workers who clean and pack all shafts.

The costing system used by the company charges materials, direct labor, and overhead to each unit of product. The labor and the materials are considered to be variable costs, but the overhead is fixed. The overhead is allocated on the basis of the labor cost required to produce each product. Furthermore, the rate is a division rate and not a section overhead rate. This rate is developed from the information which appears on the next page.

	Direct Labor Payroll	Overhead
Section 1	$200,000	$ 800,000
Section 2	600,000	240,000
Total	$800,000	$1,040,000

Overhead rate: $\dfrac{\$1,040,000}{\$800,000} = \$1.30$ per dollar of labor cost

The average wage for Section 1 is $6 per hour; for Section 2, $3 per hour.

A full cost transfer price is used for selling shafts to other producing divisions. If an order is placed by another producing division that calls for $40 of materials and 2 hours of labor time in each section, the price that is quoted would be arrived at as follows:

	Hours	Total
Labor:		
Section 1	2	$12.00
Section 2	2	6.00
		$18.00
Overhead ($1.30 × $18)		23.40
Materials		40.00
Transfer price		$81.40

The assistant to the controller has been considering a change in the costing system whereby an overhead rate would be developed for each section. It is believed that such a system would give a more equitable price for the work done for other divisions and would be a better basis for determining the profit from sales to outsiders. Since the shaft sold on the outside market is standardized, the price is determined by the customs of the industry; and the primary decision that must be made is whether to accept or reject orders at a given price. At times the division is near enough to capacity that outside work must be stopped if inside work is to be done.

At the moment two outside orders are being considered. These orders are from another division that can buy either inside or outside the company. The details on the two orders are given below:

	Order 1	Order 2
Materials	$50	$20
Labor:		
Section 1	3 hrs.	6 hrs.
Section 2	3 hrs.	1 hr.

Required:
(1) Calculate the transfer prices for the two orders under the present system.
(2) Calculate the transfer prices under the proposed system.
(3) Explain the differences in the prices.
(4) Recalculate the transfer prices for the two orders based on variable cost only.
(5) Which of the three systems do you prefer? Why?

11-11. Transfer Price Decision. The Elkton Division of Nordic Instruments, Inc., manufactures small printed circuit boards and has the capacity to make

100,000 units of a given model each year. At the present time, only 75,000 units are being made each year and sold to an outside customer for $6.50 a unit.

Fixed manufacturing costs are applied on the basis of an annual production of 100,000 units each year. Total fixed cost for the year is $150,000. The total unit cost of each circuit board is $5.80.

The Reeves Division of Nordic Instruments, Inc., has been purchasing this type of circuit board from an outside supplier at a price of $6.50 per unit. The president of the company requests that the Elkton Division deliver 25,000 circuit boards to the Reeves Division at a price equal to the variable cost.

The superintendent of Elkton states that the division gains no advantage by selling at variable cost. No contribution is made to the recovery of the fixed cost. Furthermore, the superintendent states that the company gains nothing. The fixed cost of Elkton must be recovered and Reeves should pay the full price of $6.50 as it would by buying outside.

Required:
(1) Is the argument of the superintendent valid? Explain.
(2) What is the variable cost of manufacturing each circuit board?
(3) Describe a pricing system that should benefit the company and be acceptable to each division.

11-12. Internal Pricing Decision. Mark Dolan is the manager of the Burling Division of Ace Machine Company. This division manufactures spring assemblies that are sold to various outside customers at a price of $25 per unit.

Recently the division has been operating below normal capacity at 500,000 direct labor hours. Normal capacity has been defined at 600,000 direct labor hours and is approximately equal to the practical capacity.

Each assembly requires 15 minutes of direct labor time. The direct materials and direct labor cost per assembly is $16.20, and overhead varies at the rate of $8.40 per direct labor hour. The total fixed overhead for the year is $3,120,000.

Dolan's division has just been awarded a contract for the sale of 400,000 units in another country at a unit price of $20. This contract will not interfere with the regular sales at a price of $25, and it is anticipated that this contract can be renewed in future years.

The Judd Division of the company has started production of a product line that will require 400,000 units of the type of assembly made by the Burling Division. The president of the company states that the assemblies should be transferred between the divisions at the variable cost to the Burling Division. If Burling Division does not furnish the units, the Judd Division will be forced to purchase the assemblies on the outside market at $25 apiece. With higher costs, Judd will have lower profits on the sale of the end products.

Required:
(1) Determine the variable cost to produce each spring assembly.
(2) Under the circumstances, should the Burling Division supply the Judd Division?
(3) What price should be used for the internal transfer, assuming a transfer should be made?

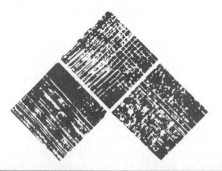

12
THE PRICE-LEVEL PROBLEM

Monetary units such as the dollar, the franc, and the pound are standards of measurement in finance and accounting and measure a given amount of purchasing power at any particular time. However, this purchasing power does not remain constant over the years. In contrast, the physical units of measurement such as the meter, kilometer, and kilogram do remain constant as standards of measurement. This peculiarity of monetary units makes it difficult to evaluate financial data. In the physical sciences, it would be similar to having a meter that measured one distance in 1979 and a different distance in 1981. When historical financial data are combined with current data, the result is a measurement in monetary units of mixed value.

The problem of rising prices has persisted for many years and in recent years has received increased attention. Three general approaches have been recommended for dealing with the problem of these changes in the purchasing power of the dollar.

1. Matching current cost against revenue.
2. Using replacement cost.
3. Adjusting historical data by published index numbers.[1]

---

[1]The Financial Accounting Standards Board has proposed that companies report the effect of price-level differences by using either current cost data or price-index-adjusted dollars or both. An income statement supplement would show net holding gains or losses on inventories, plant, property, and equipment and a purchasing power gain or loss on monetary items (cash, accounts receivable, accounts payable, etc.). In addition, the annual foreign exchange gain or loss net of tax should be shown.

All three methods will be discussed, but attention is focused primarily on adjustment by index numbers, because this method is comprehensive and does not deal merely with isolated parts of the problem.

Before discussing the price-level problem, it may be helpful to consider frequently used terms and to understand the differences in meaning between one concept and another.

Cost, sometimes called *historical* or *original cost*, is the cost that was incurred at the time the asset was acquired. A building, for example, may have been acquired in 19X1 at a cost of $250,000. The $250,000 is the cost, that is, the original cost.

The *replacement cost* is the cost to replace the asset with a similar asset under current market conditions in the normal quantities purchased. For example, the current cost to purchase a building to replace the existing building is $400,000.

It may not be possible to replace certain assets exactly. If this is the case, an estimate must be made to determine the *reproduction cost* or how much it would cost to duplicate the asset under present market conditions. Assume that the building with an original cost of $250,000 could be constructed now at a cost of $750,000; therefore, the reproduction cost is $750,000.

In the case of depreciable assets, depreciation should be deducted from the reproduction cost to reflect the accumulated deterioration of reproduction cost to date. Assume that the building costing $250,000 had a net book value of $150,000 after the deduction of accumulated depreciation of $100,000. The accumulated depreciation of $100,000 is equal to 40 percent of the cost. Using this same rate on the reproduction cost, the accumulated depreciation on the reproduction cost is $300,000 (40% × $750,000). The reproduction cost net of accumulated depreciation to date is $450,000 ($750,000 − $300,000).

If replacement cost is used instead of reproduction cost, the valuation basis already takes into account past depreciation. However, depreciation estimates must be deducted for future years.

The *current value* is the present market value of an asset. The current value does not necessarily correspond with the replacement cost or the reproduction cost net of accumulated depreciation. Assume that the building, in this example, could be sold for $500,000. The building has a current value of $500,000.

GENERAL AND SPECIFIC PRICES

A price level may be explained as:

1. The price level for a specific type of asset. The price of a specific asset may change independently of the movement of prices of other goods and services because of market characteristics peculiar to the asset in question.
2. The price level for a mixture of goods and services throughout the economy, or general price level. Since the prices of all goods and services do

not fluctuate simultaneously, technically there is no such thing as a general price level. However, the term is a convenient way to refer to the weighted average prices of selected goods and services in the economy.

It is extremely difficult to measure the effect of price-level changes on each individual or business entity. Each person or entity purchases different goods or services in various quantities at various times and is affected in different ways. About the best that can be done is to measure the impact of price-level changes by means of an average of prices for goods or services that are most commonly used.

Approximate measurements of general price-level changes may be made by using published indexes. Two widely recognized index series are the Consumer Price Index published by the Bureau of Labor Statistics, Department of Labor, and the Gross National Product Implicit Price Deflator used by the Department of Commerce to measure changes in the gross national product. The Gross National Product Implicit Price Deflator is more comprehensive and for that reason may be a better indicator of general price movement.

When prices in general go up, there is *inflation*. Conversely, when prices go down, there is *deflation*. However, all goods and services are not affected in the same way. The prices of some goods and services may be relatively stable over the years while the prices of others fluctuate greatly.

In recent years, the problems of inflation have been particularly evident not only in the United States but in other countries as well. Individuals are quite aware of increasing prices of gasoline, food, automobiles, and various other goods and services purchased. During a period of inflation, earnings from the past that are held in the form of cash lose their purchasing power. The holder of cash does not retain the purchasing power that was earned. For example, a worker may have earned $2,500 at a time when $2,500 would have purchased a new medium-sized automobile. But if the $2,500 were saved in cash and spent at a later date when $2,500 would not even purchase a new compact automobile, a loss would be suffered because of the decrease in the purchasing power of dollars.

A borrower, on the other hand, may gain by inflation. A loan taken at a lower price level provides the borrower with resources that have relatively higher purchasing power than the resources that will be used later to repay the loan at a higher price level. This gain in purchasing power goes to the borrower. Conversely, the lender loses purchasing power by lending relatively valuable dollars in comparison to those received in repayment. The effect is the opposite in a period of deflation.

MATCHING CURRENT COST AGAINST REVENUE

This approach to the price-level problem does not address the problem itself. Instead, it is an attempt to circumvent the problem.

Sometimes the effect of price-level changes is minimized during a period of rising prices by matching the most recent cost against revenue. The argument for this procedure is that net income is more accurately determined if both the revenue and the cost are on the same dollar basis. Furthermore, there can be no objection that the historical cost principle has been violated because actual cost is accounted for.

Lifo vs Fifo

The matching of the most current cost against revenue is implicit in the lifo inventory method. When *lifo* is used, the cost of the most recent purchases is matched against revenue as cost of goods sold, and the older cost remains on the balance sheet as inventory. In some circumstances, the lifo inventory method may not result in matching current cost against revenue. If the quantity sold, for example, is in excess of the current quantity purchased, the older cost will be mixed with current cost in the cost of goods sold.

The *fifo* inventory method operates in the opposite way and matches older cost against current revenue and thus may be less desirable from the income statement point of view when prices are rising. On the other hand, the current cost is shown as inventory on the balance sheet. Under the lifo method, the opposite situation prevails. The balance sheet showing the older cost is inadequate, but income measurement is improved by matching current cost against revenue.

The fifo inventory method is compared with the lifo method in the following example. Assume that 500 units of merchandise were first purchased at a cost of $3 per unit. At a later date, another 500 units were purchased at a cost of $4 per unit. The price increased again, so that by the end of the year this merchandise cost $5 per unit. During the year, 500 units were sold at a unit price of $7.

FIFO INVENTORY METHOD

Income Statement (Partial)

Sales (500 units @ $7)	$3,500
Cost of goods sold (500 units @ $3)	1,500
Gross margin	$2,000

LIFO INVENTORY METHOD

Income Statement (Partial)

Sales (500 units @ $7)	$3,500
Cost of goods sold (500 units @ $4)	2,000
Gross margin	$1,500

Both statements are acceptable in the sense that the actual cost of goods sold is matched against revenue to determine income. With the older cost matched against revenue, the fifo method maximizes the differences in income measurement due to price-level changes. With lifo, the more recent cost is deducted against revenue, thus minimizing the effect of price-level changes.

Neither method gives an entirely accurate picture. If the company is to continue with another cycle of operation and be in the same position as it was before, it must purchase 500 more units at a unit cost of $5. Hence, out of the total revenue of $3,500, only $1,000 can be viewed as a profit available for distribution to shareholders (assuming no other costs). The additional $1,000 of reported profit under fifo and the extra $500 of reported profit under lifo are know as *illusory profit* or *inventory profit*. Out of the revenue of $3,500, a total of $2,500 must be reinvested to enter another cycle of operation. A partial income statement using current replacement cost is given below. The replacement cost concept is discussed more completely later in this chapter.

REPLACEMENT COST METHOD

Income Statement (Partial)

Sales (500 units @ $7)	$3,500
Cost of goods sold (500 units @ $5)	2,500
Gross margin	$1,000

Accelerated Depreciation

Accelerated depreciation methods are usually favored because of the income tax advantage, but they may also be favored as a means of matching current cost against revenue. If a large part of the cost of a plant asset can be written off as depreciation during a few years, it is hoped that the bulk of the cost can be matched against revenue before the price level has changed to any appreciable extent. Whether or not this works in practice depends upon the movement of the price level.

The income tax advantage from accelerated depreciation methods arises because depreciation deductions in the early years of a plant asset are larger than they are under the straight-line method. During these years, the net income and income tax for each year are lower than they would be under the straight-line method of depreciation. With a lower income, the company is able to use more resources for a longer period because the tax payment is delayed. Furthermore, if the net income is used as a guide in dividend policy, the dividends are likely to be lower. However, the advantage may be only temporary. In the long run, of course, the company can only recover the cost of its investment. In later years, the depreciation deductions are smaller and the net income and the income tax each year are larger under accelerated depreciation. But, in the meantime, the company has additional resources available that can be reinvested to earn a return. Perhaps losses due to changes in the price level can be avoided or held to a minimum.

The advantage of accelerated depreciation is illustrated by assuming that Company A and Company B each earned $250,000 before deducting depreciation and income tax. Company A used accelerated depreciation and deducted $100,000 in depreciation on equipment that it had purchased at the beginning of the year. Company B, during the same period, purchased equipment having the same cost but took depreciation on a straight-line basis.

Company A paid $25,000 less in income tax than Company B as a result of deducting $50,000 more in depreciation. The depreciation deduction operates as a tax shield. Company A, with a smaller income tax, thus has $25,000 more cash with which to work.

Assume further that each company distributed all of its net income to the shareholders as dividends. Company A reported a net income of only $75,000 and paid that amount in dividends, while Company B reported a net income of $100,000 and paid that amount in dividends. Company A had a smaller income tax by $25,000 and paid $25,000 less in dividends than Company B. As a result, Company A retained $50,000 more in resources. It may be that Company A will eventually pay more income tax in future years than Company B. However, in the meantime Company A has more resources to use.

	COMPANY A (ACCELERATED DEPRECIATION)	COMPANY B (STRAIGHT-LINE DEPRECIATION)
Income before depreciation and income tax	$250,000	$250,000
Less depreciation	100,000	50,000
Income before income tax	$150,000	$200,000
Income tax (50%)	75,000	100,000
Net income	$ 75,000	$100,000
Add depreciation	100,000	50,000
Net inflow of current resources from operations	$175,000	$150,000

It should not be presumed from the foregoing discussion that accelerated depreciation is to be preferred to straight-line depreciation for financial reporting purposes. If plant assets yield services over the years at a uniform rate, then each year should bear an equal amount of the cost. On the other hand, if the services are received irregularly, a case could be made for charging off the cost of the plant assets accordingly. Accelerated depreciation methods in common use are not flexible and in many cases cannot be looked upon as a means of matching expense against revenue according to the flow of benefits received from the use of the assets. Nevertheless, accelerated depreciation can yield short-term benefits in tax accounting and can be used as an aid in managerial planning.

REPLACEMENT COSTS

The replacement cost method goes beyond the historical cost concept. Assets such as inventories and plant assets are ordinarily held for a relatively long period of time. The costs that were incurred to obtain these assets in the past — the historical costs — may be out of date when compared with current costs. On a balance sheet the costs from past periods are combined with current costs, and the total is not very meaningful. Advocates of the replacement cost method claim that the assets should be restated at current *replacement costs*, which, as the term implies, are the costs to replace the assets presently in use.

The SEC in Accounting Series Release No. 190 stated that certain registrants must include with financial statements replacement cost data with respect to inventories and plant assets for fiscal years ending after December 25, 1976. This rule governs financial reporting but in no way limits the ways in which management may adjust or use data for internal purposes.

The SEC has defined *replacement cost* as the lowest amount that would have to be paid to obtain new assets of equivalent operating or productive capability. *Depreciated replacement cost* is the replacement cost adjusted for the already expired service potential of such assets.

There has been relatively little experience in working with this rule; and in practical cases the determination of a replacement value may be quite difficult. In some cases, quoted prices are not available, and it may be necessary to use a combination of quoted prices and index adjustments to arrive at approproximate replacement valuations.

As a basic example, assume that Boyd Company has machinery with an original cost of $100,000 that was used to manufacture 5,000 units of product in 1980. Straight-line depreciation is being deducted on the basis of a 10-year life or at a rate of $10,000 per year. Other costs to manufacture the product totaled $6 per unit. The company had no inventory at the beginning of the year and sold 4,000 units of the product during the year at a price of $15 per unit. The machinery has been used for three years and could be replaced new at a cost of $150,000 at the end of the third year. The other costs to reproduce the products have been estimated at $8 per unit at the end of the year.

The gross margin is computed at the top of the next page for 1980 both by the conventional method using historical costs and by the replacement cost method.

Conventionally, profit is measured as the difference between sales revenue and the actual cost of the services and products sold. However, this profit concept makes no provision for a continuation of business operations on the same scale as before. Perhaps profit should be looked upon as a difference between revenue and actual cost with a provision being made for reentry into the market for another selling cycle. In short, the profit would be the difference between sales revenue and the cost to replace the goods and services sold.

In the example given, the gross margin computed with the historical cost was $28,000. However, the company can no longer obtain the necessary machinery for manufacturing at a cost of $100,000 nor can it obtain the other elements of product cost at a cost of $6 per unit. In

	HISTORICAL COST (CURRENT REVENUE MINUS ORIGINAL COST)	REPLACEMENT COST (CURRENT REVENUE MINUS REPLACEMENT COST)
Sales (4,000 × $15).............	$60,000	$60,000
Cost of goods sold:		
(4,000 × $8)*	32,000	
(4,000 × $11)**		44,000
Gross margin	$28,000	$16,000

*Original cost:

Depreciation $\left(\dfrac{\$100,000}{10 \text{ years}} \div 5,000 \text{ units} \right)$ .... $ 2

Other costs 6

Total unit cost .... $ 8

**Replacement cost:

Depreciation $\left(\dfrac{\$150,000}{10 \text{ years}} \div 5,000 \text{ units} \right)$ .... $ 3

Other costs 8

Total unit cost $11

order to continue, the company must provide for a cost of $150,000 to replace the machinery and must incur other costs of $8 per unit. The profit of $16,000 computed by the replacement cost method is the profit after allowing for the cost of entering a new cycle of operations.

Balance sheet data on a replacement cost basis are compared with original cost below.

	HISTORICAL COST	REPLACEMENT COST
Inventory:		
(1,000 units × $8).................................	$ 8,000	
(1,000 units × $11)..............................		$11,000
Machinery...	$100,000	$150,000
Less accumulated depreciation:		
(10% of $100,000 × 3)	30,000	
(10% of $150,000 × 3)		45,000
Net book value...	$ 70,000	$105,000

The replacement cost method has the advantage of being tailored to meet the peculiarities of a particular company and to the specific assets on an individual basis. As a practical matter, it may be quite difficult to determine the cost of replacing one unit among many related units; and under normal conditions it is not likely that an entire facility will be replaced at one time. By considering either individual components or the aggregate of all components, a certain amount of unreality is introduced. Hence, the replacement cost determined under varying circumstances is highly subjective.

The replacement cost approach is incomplete. For example, purchasing power gains or losses from holding assets such as cash or from having outstanding debt are not included in financial statements prepared using this method.

PRICE LEVEL — INDEX ADJUSTMENTS

Management is not only interested in the current values or replacement costs of certain assets but also must compare these values with price-index-adjusted costs. What portion of a gain, for example, is a true gain and what portion is merely an increase that keeps pace with the increase in general prices? To illustrate, assume that a building was acquired a number of years ago and that the cost minus accumulated depreciation is now $80,000. The company has an opportunity to sell the building for $190,000. The gain from the sale would be $110,000. However, if the general price index has increased from 100 to 220 during the period of time that the building was held, the true gain would be much less. The price-index-adjusted basis of the building is $176,000 ($80,000 × 2.20). The real gain in terms of a dollar with constant purchasing power is only $14,000 ($190,000 − $176,000).

The price-level problem may be approached by converting the dollars having mixed purchasing power to dollars having current purchasing power. This method, unlike the replacement cost method, does not introduce a new basis of accountability. Historical cost is still accounted for in the conventional way, but the historical cost is brought up to date by means of an index adjustment. All dollars are restated on a common basis; that is, they are uniform dollars of purchasing power. Published price indexes can be used in converting dollars to a common denominator of value. The conversion operation itself is simple. The difficulty lies in the selection of an index series that accomplishes the desired results without adding further distortions.

The price-level adjustments restate financial data in terms of the current dollar of purchasing power.[2] Past dollar amounts are brought up to date by the application of an index number multiplier. For example, inventory costing $6,000 when the price index was 120 would be restated in current dollars at an index of 150 as shown below.

$$\$6,000 \times 150/120 = \$7,500 \text{ cost of inventory in dollars}$$
$$\text{of the 150 price index}$$

The current index number is the numerator of the multiplier fraction, and the index number at the time of the transaction is the denominator.

The adjustment procedure makes it possible to:

1. Compute the gains and losses caused by changes in the purchasing power of the dollar.
2. Compare financial statements that have been restated in uniform current dollars of purchasing power.

___
[2]See *Accounting Research Study No. 6,* "Reporting the Financial Effects of Price-Level Changes" (New York: American Institute of Certified Public Accountants, 1963).

THE CHARACTER OF ASSETS AND EQUITIES

Not all assets and equities respond to changes in the price level in the same way. Some assets tend to adjust themselves automatically to changes in the price level. Tangible goods will usually go up or down in price in rough correspondence to the general price pattern. But cash and claims to cash remain at fixed dollar amounts without regard to shifts in the price level.

Monetary Items

Cash and claims to cash, as well as liabilities, stated in a fixed number of dollars are referred to as *monetary items*. The monetary items at any given time are always stated in current dollars of purchasing power without adjustment.

The individual who has $100 today possesses $100 of purchasing power measured in today's dollars. This is not changed by the fact that the $100 may have been received when prices were lower and when $110 worth of goods or services as measured by the current dollar could have been purchased. A comparative balance sheet expressed in current dollars of purchasing power will show $110 in cash on the balance sheet at the point of time at which the cash was received. Remember that the original $100 was then worth $110 in terms of today's dollar. On the current balance sheet the $100 is shown as $100. It has a purchasing power of $100 at the present time. The individual lost $10 in purchasing power by holding cash.

Accounts receivable and investments in bonds are similar to cash. The monetary amount is fixed. Liabilities such as accounts payable, wages payable, taxes payable, mortgage payable, and bonds payable are also expressed in fixed dollar amounts as a general rule. If an individual incurs a debt of $5,000 when the price index is 100 and repays it when the index is 110, there is a purchasing power gain of $500. At the time of repayment, the debt amounted to $5,000 in current dollars of purchasing power. But the original debt of $5,000 had a purchasing power of $5,500 when it was incurred as measured in the dollars used to repay the debt, that is, the current dollars of purchasing power.

Nonmonetary Items

Assets and equities that cannot be stated in fixed monetary amounts are referred to as *nonmonetary items*. Tangible items such as buildings, machinery, and inventories of materials or products awaiting resale tend to sell at higher or lower dollar amounts at different times. For example, a residence costing $15,000 in 1965 may sell for $35,000 at the present time, although it has been used and is no longer modern. The $15,000 in 1965 is not equivalent to $15,000 today, nor is it necessarily equivalent to $35,000 either. Probably there are other reasons explaining the increase in price. The neighborhood may be attractive, the house may have been well kept, or some addition may have been made that justifies the higher price. However, in price-level adjustment procedure the $15,000 cost would be converted to a current basis by application of the current index number in relation to the index number in 1965 to arrive at an amount that may be more or less than $35,000. The technological change in the house or other factors do not enter into the adjustment.

Investments in stocks or bonds may have the characteristics of fixed monetary claims or they may be similar to tangible properties. Bonds usually are a claim to a fixed quantity of dollars and would, therefore, be similar to cash. An investment in common stock, however, is not a stated claim to any given quantity of dollars but is an ownership claim to the assets of a business and would be somewhat similar to an investment in tangible property.

The stockholders' equity, with the exception of preferred stock that may be callable in a fixed number of dollars, is a nonmonetary item. The common stock and the retained earnings are not fixed in dollar amounts but vary as a result of many factors, including price-level changes.

FINANCIAL STATEMENTS AND INDEX CONVERSIONS

To illustrate the price-level conversion procedure, it is assumed that Delmar Company began business at the beginning of 19A and that it has conducted operations during 19A and 19B. Price index data follow:

Price index at the beginning of 19A	100
Average price index during 19A	120
Price index at the end of 19A	150
Average price index during 19B	180
Price index at the end of 19B	200

At the beginning of 19A, the stockholders of Delmar Company invested $42,000. Plant equipment costing $120,000 was purchased, a down payment of $20,000 was made, and the $100,000 balance was financed by bonds payable. An inventory of merchandise was purchased at a cost of $24,000. Assume that all sales and purchases were made on account.

Unadjusted comparative financial statements are given in summary form for 19A and 19B. The assets and equities are classified as monetary or nonmonetary items on the balance sheet rather than in the conventional current and noncurrent categories to emphasize the important distinctions in price-level accounting. Of course, the balance sheet can be presented in the conventional manner and probably would be for financial reporting purposes.

Delmar Company
Summary Comparative Balance Sheet
December 31, 19B and 19A

Assets	19B	19A
Monetary assets:		
Cash and accounts receivable	$ 87,000	$ 46,000
Nonmonetary assets:		
Inventory (fifo method)	27,000	16,000
Plant assets, net of accumulated depreciation	96,000	108,000
Total assets	$210,000	$170,000

Equities	19B	19A
Monetary equities:		
Accounts payable and other current claims payable	$ 18,000	$ 8,000
Bonds payable	100,000	100,000
Nonmonetary equities:		
Capital stock	42,000	42,000
Retained earnings	50,000	20,000
Total equities	$210,000	$170,000

Delmar Company
Summary Comparative Income Statement
For the Years Ended December 31, 19B and 19A

	19B	19A
Sales	$180,000	$120,000
Cost of goods sold	$ 90,000	$ 60,000
Other expenses, excluding depreciation	36,000	28,000
Depreciation	12,000	12,000
Total expenses	$138,000	$100,000
Net income	$ 42,000	$ 20,000

The gains and losses resulting from changes in the purchasing power of the dollar are to be computed for the two years, and the financial statements are to be restated in terms of the dollar at the end of 19B. A gain or loss in purchasing power arises from holding monetary assets and equities while the general purchasing power of the dollar increases or decreases.

Delmar Company, for example, began operations in 19A with $42,000 and ended the year with $38,000 in net current monetary assets (cash and accounts receivable of $46,000 minus accounts payable and other current claims payable of $8,000). Transactions affecting the net current monetary assets during the year are converted, as shown in the table on page 350, to uniform dollars of purchasing power at the end of 19A. The uniform dollars of purchasing power of the net current monetary assets at the end of 19A are compared with the unadjusted amount. If the unadjusted amount is less than the adjusted amount, there has been a loss in purchasing power. Conversely, if the unadjusted amount is greater than the adjusted amount, there has been a gain in purchasing power. In this case, the difference between the adjusted amount of $47,000 and the unadjusted amount of $38,000 expressed in mixed dollars of purchasing power is the loss in purchasing power on net current monetary assets for 19A stated in dollars of purchasing power at the end of 19A. All measurements, however, are to be made in terms of the most recent dollar, that is, the dollar at the end of 19B. Hence, the loss of purchasing power in 19A measured in end-of-19A dollars must be restated in terms of purchasing power at the end of 19B, and this computation is shown below the transactional analysis.

PURCHASING POWER LOSS — 19A
NET CURRENT MONETARY ASSETS

	Unadjusted Data, 19A	Multiplier	Adjusted Data 19A Dollars (End of Year)
Net current monetary assets, beginning of 19A (cash investment)	$ 42,000	150/100	$ 63,000
Add sales (increase the accounts receivable)	120,000	150/120	150,000
	$162,000		$213,000
Less:			
Initial inventory investment ...	$ 24,000	150/100	$ 36,000
Purchases (cost of goods sold plus ending inventory minus initial inventory)	52,000	150/120	65,000
Other expenses (excluding depreciation)	28,000	150/120	35,000
Down payment for plant equipment	20,000	150/100	30,000
	$124,000		$166,000
Net current monetary assets, end of 19A (cash and accounts receivable minus accounts payable and other current claims payable):			
Adjusted			$ 47,000
Unadjusted	$ 38,000		38,000
Purchasing power loss on net current monetary assets, 19A dollars (end of year).			$ 9,000

RESTATEMENT OF THE PURCHASING POWER
LOSS IN 19B DOLLARS (END OF YEAR)

$9,000 \times \dfrac{200}{150} = \$12,000$ purchasing power loss measured in 19B dollars (end of year)

A similar computation of the purchasing power gains or losses on net current monetary assets for 19B is given on the next page.

PURCHASING POWER LOSS — 19B
NET CURRENT MONETARY ASSETS

	Unadjusted Data, 19B	Multiplier	Adjusted Data 19B Dollars (End of Year)
Net current monetary assets, beginning of 19B (cash and accounts receivable minus accounts payable and other current claims payable)	$ 38,000	200/150	$ 50,667*
Add sales (increase the accounts receivable).................................	180,000	200/180	200,000
	$218,000		$250,667
Less:			
Purchases (cost of goods sold plus ending inventory minus beginning inventory)	$101,000	200/180	$112,223*
Other expenses (excluding depreciation)............................	36,000	200/180	40,000
Dividends (paid in cash at end of year)..................................	12,000	200/200	12,000
	$149,000		$164,223
Net current monetary assets, end of 19B (cash and accounts receivable minus accounts payable and other current claims payable):			
Adjusted..................................			$ 86,444
Unadjusted..........................	$ 69,000		69,000
Purchasing power loss on net current monetary assets, 19B dollars (end of year)			$ 17,444

*Rounded

The net loss in purchasing power from current monetary transactions for the two years was $29,444 ($12,000 loss for 19A + $17,444 loss for 19B). Offsetting this net loss are the gains in purchasing power from the bonds payable obligation. The computation follows:

	UNADJUSTED BONDS PAYABLE, 19A DOLLARS (BEGINNING OF YEAR)	MULTIPLIER	ADJUSTED BONDS PAYABLE, 19A DOLLARS (END OF YEAR)
19A:			
Bonds payable	$100,000	150/100	$150,000
Less unadjusted bonds payable			100,000
Gain in purchasing power 19A (end of 19A dollars)			$ 50,000

Gain in the purchasing power expressed in 19B dollars (end of year) is shown at the top of page 352.

$$\$50,000 \times \frac{200}{150} = \$66,667$$

	UADJUSTED BONDS PAYABLE, 19A DOLLARS (BEGINNING OF YEAR)	MULTIPLIER	ADJUSTED BONDS PAYABLE, 19B DOLLARS (END OF YEAR)
19B:			
Bonds payable	$100,000	200/100	$200,000
Less unadjusted bonds payable			100,000
Accumulated gain in purchasing power by the end of 19B			$100,000
Less purchasing power gain in 19A (19B dollars)			66,667
Purchasing power gain in 19B.........................			$ 33,333

The purchasing power gains and losses for the two years as measured in 19B dollars are summarized below:

	19A	19B
Purchasing power gain (loss) net current monetary assets...	$(12,000)	$(17,444)
Purchasing power gain, bonds payable.................	66,667	33,333
Net purchasing power gain	$ 54,667	$ 15,889

These net gains are shown separately on the adjusted income statement for each year and are accumulated in a separate section of retained earnings on the adjusted balance sheet.

The income statement for 19A is restated in current purchasing power dollars, that is, in the dollars at the end of 19B.

Delmar Company
Income Statement
For the Year Ended December 31, 19A

	Unadjusted	Multiplier	Adjusted
Sales...	$120,000	200/120	$200,000
Cost of goods sold:			
Initial inventory	$ 24,000	200/100	$ 48,000
Purchases made in 19A less inventory at the end of the year..	36,000	200/120	60,000
Cost of goods sold.................................	$ 60,000		$108,000
Other expenses, excluding depreciation	28,000	200/120	46,667
Depreciation	12,000	200/100	24,000
Total expenses..	$100,000		$178,667
Income from operations	$ 20,000		$ 21,333
Net gain in purchasing power			54,667
Income and purchasing power gain			$ 76,000

The income statement for 19B is given below with adjustments to the purchasing power of the dollar at the end of 19B.

Delmar Company
Income Statement
For the Year Ended December 31, 19B

	Unadjusted	Multiplier	Adjusted
Sales	$180,000	200/180	$200,000
Cost of goods sold:			
Inventory, beginning of the year	$ 16,000	200/120	$ 26,667
Purchases in 19B (cost of goods sold plus ending inventory minus beginning inventory)	101,000	200/180	112,223
	$117,000		$138,890
Less inventory, end of year	27,000	200/180	30,000
Cost of goods sold	$ 90,000		$108,890
Other expenses	36,000	200/180	40,000
Depreciation	12,000	200/100	24,000
	$138,000		$172,890
Income from operations	$ 42,000		$ 27,110
Net gain in purchasing power			15,889
Income and purchasing power gain			$ 42,999

The income statement for the two years as restated in 19B dollars (end of year) is as follows:

Delmar Company
Summary Income Statement
(Uniform Dollars of Purchasing Power
As of December 31, 19B)
For the Years Ended December 31, 19B and 19A

	19B	19A
Sales	$200,000	$200,000
Cost of goods sold	$108,890	$108,000
Other expenses, excluding depreciation	40,000	46,667
Depreciation	24,000	24,000
Total expenses	$172,890	$178,667
Income from operations	$ 27,110	$ 21,333
Net gain in purchasing power	15,889	54,667
Income and purchasing power gain	$ 42,999	$ 76,000

The unadjusted income statement indicates that the company had a much higher net income in 19B. When the income statement is restated in uniform dollars of purchasing power, however, the increase in income from operations is much smaller. The gain in purchasing power from having debt outstanding in the form of bonds payable, while a protection against the erosion in purchasing power of the dollar, cannot serve as a basis for dividend distributions. In fact, one of the objections of business managers to complete price-index-adjusted statements is that uninformed stockholders will clamor for more dividends on the basis of purchasing power gains from having debt outstanding. During periods of inflation, resources must be handled most carefully. More consideration may be given to increased investment in tangible assets that will tend to increase in value as the price level increases.

The balance sheets appearing below and at the top of the next page are restated in current dollars (dollars at the end of 19B).

Delmar Company
Summary Balance Sheet
(Uniform Dollars of Purchasing Power as of December 31, 19B)
December 31, 19A

Assets	Unadjusted	Multiplier	Adjusted
Monetary assets:			
Cash and accounts receivable............................	$ 46,000	200/150	$ 61,333
Nonmonetary assets:			
Inventory (fifo method)...	16,000	200/120	26,667
Plant assets net of accumulated depreciation ...	108,000	200/100	216,000
Total assets...	$170,000		$304,000

Equities			
Monetary equities:			
Accounts payable and other current claims payable...	$ 8,000	200/150	$ 10,667
Bonds payable	100,000	200/150	133,333
Nonmonetary equities:			
Capital stock	42,000	200/100	84,000
Retained earnings from operations	20,000		21,333
Accumulated purchasing power gain on net monetary items..			54,667
Total equities	$170,000		$304,000

Note that all items on the 19A balance sheet are on an older dollar basis and must be restated. It was stated earlier that monetary assets and equities are automatically stated in dollars of current purchasing power. This is true for any given time. The monetary assets and equities on the 19A balance sheet are in 19A dollars, but these dollars must be adjusted if the statement is to be expressed in 19B dollars. The nonmonetary items are stated in the dollars of purchasing power that were current when they were initially recorded. The index at that time is the denominator of the multiplier to be used in restating the dollar amounts.

The adjusted balance sheets, as well as the income statements, reveal that the company did not do quite as well as the unadjusted statements indicate. Some of the differences do not represent real increases or decreases but, instead, are differences that are partially attributable to a change in the level of prices. For example, cash and receivables

Delmar Company
Summary Balance Sheet
(Uniform Dollars of Purchasing Power as of December 31, 19B)
December 31, 19B

Assets	Unadjusted	Multiplier	Adjusted
Monetary assets:			
Cash and accounts receivable	$ 87,000	200/200	$ 87,000
Nonmonetary assets:			
Inventory (fifo method)	27,000	200/180	30,000
Plant assets net of accumulated depreciation	96,000	200/100	192,000
Total assets	$210,000		$309,000

Equities			
Monetary equities:			
Accounts payable and other current claims payable	$ 18,000	200/200	$ 18,000
Bonds payable	100,000	200/200	100,000
Nonmonetary equities:			
Capital stock	42,000	200/100	84,000
Retained earnings from operations	50,000		36,444*
Accumulated purchasing power gain on net monetary items			70,556
Total equities	$210,000		$309,000

*Adjusted amounts taken from adjusted income statements for the two years. The adjusted retained earnings from operations at December 31, 19B, are computed below:

Balance, January 1, 19B	$21,333
Adjusted income from operations, 19B	27,110
	$48,443
Less dividends, 19B	12,000
Balance, December 31, 19B	$36,443*

*Rounded to $36,444 on balance sheet.

increased from $46,000 at the end of 19A to $87,000 at the end of 19B. In terms of purchasing power, however, the $46,000 in cash and receivables at the end of 19A was equivalent to $61,333 measured in 19B dollars. Although there was an increase in cash and receivables from $46,000 to $87,000 as measured in absolute dollars, there was a loss of purchasing power during 19B. A comparison of other amounts on financial statements will also be more meaningful if the statements are converted to uniform dollars of purchasing power.

CURRENT VALUE AND THE PRICE INDEX

In the interpretation and use of accounting data, there are different types of questions to be answered, and the data must be selected and applied to fit the particular application. When dealing with the price-level problem, for example, comparative statements may be wanted that show all amounts converted to common dollars of purchasing power as measured by a recognized index series. Financial statements prepared on this basis reveal gains or losses in purchasing power as a result of holding monetary items and show price-level-adjusted dollar amounts instead of mixed dollars of purchasing power. A question may also be raised with respect to how current market values of the nonmonetary assets compare with the price-level-adjusted amounts. Have these assets increased enough in value to keep up with changes in general purchasing power? In order to answer this question, the balance sheet at the beginning of the fiscal period may be shown in current price-index-adjusted amounts and compared with a balance sheet at the end of the fiscal period that shows current market values.

The situation can be illustrated by assuming that Ellen Rubenstein with cash of $100,000 acquired a tract of land on July 1, 19X1, at a cost of $70,000. When the purchase was made, the price index was 100. Both the remaining cash of $30,000 and the land are still being held on December 31, 19X1, when the price index is at 120. Rubenstein recognizes that with inflation the original $100,000 in capital does not have the same purchasing power as it once had. She would like to see comparative statements on a uniform dollar basis. Comparative balance sheet information is given below in dollars of purchasing power with the index at 120.

	JULY 1	DECEMBER 31
Assets:		
Cash ($30,000 × 120/100)	$ 36,000	$ 30,000
Land ($70,000 × 120/100)	84,000	84,000
Total assets	$120,000	$114,000
Equities:		
Invested capital	$120,000	$120,000
Retained earings	—0—	(6,000)
Total equities	$120,000	$114,000

She can be informed that she lost $6,000 in purchasing power by holding cash and that the land would have to be worth at least $84,000 in order for her to keep up with the price level.

Rubenstein says that she has had an offer of $95,000 for the land and would like to know how a current value statement would compare with the original statement expressed in dollars of equal purchasing power at an index of 120.[3] Comparative balance sheet information is given at the top of the next page.

It may be explained that without considering income tax she would have a net holding gain of $5,000. The land has appreciated by $25,000 ($95,000 − $70,000), but $14,000 of the appreciation was required merely to keep abreast of the increasing price level ($84,000 −

---

[3] See Robert R. Sterling, "Relevant Financial Reporting in an Age of Price Changes," *Journal of Accountancy*, Vol. 139, No. 2 (February, 1975), pp. 42–51.

	JULY 1 (INDEX ADJUSTED)	DECEMBER 31 (CURRENT VALUES)
Assets:		
Cash ($30,000 × 1.2)............................	$ 36,000	$ 30,000
Land ($70,000 × 1.2)...........................	84,000	95,000
Total assets...	$120,000	$125,000
Equities:		
Invested capital	$120,000	$120,000
Retained earnings	—0—	5,000
Total equities	$120,000	$125,000

$70,000). Hence, there has been a real holding gain of $11,000 on the land ($95,000 − $84,000) and a loss of $6,000 by holding cash. The result is a $5,000 net real holding gain. She should also be advised that if she sells the land, the gain will be $25,000 for income tax purposes and that there will probably be no real gain for her at all after the tax is considered.

DIVIDEND POLICY

The net income reported for the year is only one element, although an important one, in the formation of dividend policy. A company may have sufficient net income to permit a legal declaration of dividends, but the assets may not be in a form suitable for distribution to the stockholders. Or the board of directors may wish to hold assets so that the company can expand without issuing additional stock or debt.

Aside from the factors just mentioned, there is some doubt as to whether or not the reported net income can be accepted as net income available to the stockholders. During a period of rising prices, the older cost may have been matched against revenue, with the result that net income is higher than it would be otherwise. On the income statement illustrated below, no adjustments were made for increased cost of replacements or for increases in the price level.

Net sales...	$9,500,000
Cost of goods sold..	5,700,000
Gross margin	$3,800,000
Operating expenses including depreciation of $200,000	2,000,000
Income before income tax	$1,800,000
Income tax	900,000
Net income...	$ 900,000

The board of directors declared a dividend of $500,000, intending to retain a portion of the earnings for the year. To continue operations, however, the company will have to replenish its inventory at a cost that is 10 percent higher. Also, depreciation restated on a current dol-

lar basis should be recorded at $300,000 in total. The income state-
ment adjusted to a current dollar basis appears below:

Net sales	$9,500,000
Cost of goods sold	6,270,000
Gross margin	$3,230,000
Operating expenses including depreciation of $300,000	2,100,000
Income before income tax	$1,130,000
Income tax	900,000
Net income	$ 230,000

According to the adjusted statement, the board of directors not
only distributed current earnings but also unintentionally distributed
earnings from past years. Note also that the income tax is higher in
relation to the income before tax.

The changes in the price level tend to distort the results. With an
increasing price level, the company may appear to be more prosperous
than it really is. Conversely, during a general decline in prices, the
situation may appear to be worse than it is. In the formation of its
dividend policy, the directors should consider the effect of changes in
the price level and should not rely entirely upon profit reported in the
conventional manner.

THE PRICE LEVEL AND MANAGEMENT POLICY

One of the most difficult problems facing business management is
the task of planning in the light of uncertainty with respect to changes
in the purchasing power of the monetary unit. In some cases, costs
may increase more rapidly than selling prices with the result that the
business can no longer be continued. In order to survive, management
must be imaginative and flexible enough to be able to shift resources
to other product lines and services that have a potential for increased
demand.

As a matter of policy, a company may attempt to maintain the
original purchasing power invested in plant assets by reinvesting an
amount equal to the price-level-adjusted depreciation each year. While
there is no assurance that a company will not suffer price-level losses
by following this policy, it is generally true that the prices of plant
assets will tend to move in the direction of the price level. However, it
must be remembered that the price of any specific asset will not necessarily increase or decrease by the amount of the change in the general
price index.

There is also the possiblity that prices and costs in the economy
may be adjusted for changes in a selected index series. This approach
has been tried in some areas. For example, there are labor contracts
that specify wage adjustments for changes in the price index. Also,
some electric utilities have been permitted to adjust rates on an index

basis as fuel and other costs increase. To illustrate, it is assumed that revenue was billed at $250,000 and that cost of $150,000 was incurred at a price index of 100. With an index of 120, assume that the cost amounts to $180,000. In order to maintain a profit margin of 40 percent on revenue [($250,000 − $150,000) ÷ $250,000], the revenue must be adjusted upward by 20 percent.

$$\$250,000 \times 120/100 = \$300,000 \text{ adjusted revenue}$$

In this way the desired relationship can be maintained.

	REVISED
Operating revenue ($250,000 × 120/100).........................	$300,000
Operating expenses	180,000
Gross margin	$120,000
Rate of gross margin ($120,000/$300,000).......................	40%

Companies engaging in international trade may try to hold cash and cash claims in a relatively strong currency (one that tends to retain purchasing power) and to have liabilities in a weak currency (one that tends to lose purchasing power). If cash claims must be held in a weak currency, a company may attempt to compensate for the potential decline in the value of that currency. Such an effort is referred to as a *hedging operation*. A hedging operation may be employed by purchasing a futures contract in a strong currency. A *futures contract* is an agreement for future delivery at a price established by the market when the contract is made. Futures contracts can be bought and sold until they become due. Futures markets are available for dealing with various farm commodities, metals, and currencies.

Assume that a sale is recorded in 10,000 units of a weak currency designated as W when four units of Currency W are worth one unit of Currency Y.

Accounts Receivable...	10,000	
Sales		10,000
To record sales in Currency W when four units of W equal one unit of Y.		

Thus, at the date of sale the value of 10,000 units of W is 2,500 units of Y. However, the seller is concerned that Currency W will deteriorate relative to Currency Y before collection can be made. To guard against this, the seller buys a futures contract for the delivery of 2,500 units of Y at a price of 10,000 units of W. With this contract, the seller is assured of receiving 2,500 units of Y for 10,000 units of W and does not have to be concerned with price fluctuations.

Assume that the seller finally collects 10,000 units of W on the sale, and at this time 10,000 units of W are worth only 2,000 units of Y. Without the futures contract, the seller would have lost 500 units of Y in the exchange of W for Y (2,500 original units at time of sale minus 2,000 units at time of collection). With the contract, however, the seller pays for the contract with the 10,000 units of W collected from the customer and receives 2,500 units of Y as agreed. Thus, in a hedging operation the buyer of the futures contract hopes to cancel out the effect of gains or losses from price fluctuations on regular operating transactions.

QUESTIONS

1. Explain what is meant by a change in the general level of prices.

2. What approaches have been recommended for dealing with the problem of changes in the purchasing power of the dollar?

3. Name two index series that are used to measure changes in the general price level.

4. During a period when prices are increasing, does an individual or business benefit by holding cash? Explain.

5. How does a borrower benefit during a period of increasing prices?

6. As a general rule, is older cost or more recent cost shown on the balance sheet when the lifo inventory method is used?

7. Is current cost matched against revenue when the fifo inventory method is used? Explain.

8. How can accelerated depreciation methods reduce the impact of price-level changes?

9. What is replacement cost? Is the replacement cost the same as the price-level-adjusted cost? Explain.

10. Dollar amounts from the past are brought up to date by the application of an index number multiplier. What index number is used as the numerator of the multiplier fraction? The denominator of the multiplier?

11. If you were a lender, would you prefer to have the debt paid in a fixed number of dollars or in dollars adjusted for changes in the price level as measured by a selected index?

12. Distinguish between monetary items and nonmonetary items.

13. Assume that you own a tract of land or other nonmonetary asset. How might you distinguish between a reported gain or loss from sale and a real gain or loss as measured in dollars of uniform purchasing power?

14. Explain how a board of directors can unintentionally distribute more than the amount of current earnings as dividends.

15. How can a futures contract in foreign currency protect a company against variations in the value of the currency relative to the domestic currency?

EXERCISES

1. **Debt and Price Levels.** Standard Company incurred a debt of $32,000 when the price index was at 160. One year later the debt was still outstanding, and the price index was at 180.

Required: Compute the gain or loss in purchasing power during the year.

2. Income and Monetary Assets. Benner Appliance Company held cash and accounts receivable amounting to $70,000 at the beginning of the year when the price index was at 100. During the year, revenue of $120,000 was realized at a price index of 120. Expenses of operation amounting to $90,000 were paid at a price index of 150. At the end of the year, the price index was 200.

Required: Compute the gain or loss in purchasing power for the year.

3. Price Index and Assets. At the end of the year, Suncrest Company had cash of $28,000 and inventory of $36,000. Both the cash and the inventory were obtained when the price index was at 120. The price index at the end of the year was 150.

Required: Show how the cash and the inventory would appear on a balance sheet stated in current dollars of purchasing power at the end of the year.

4. Lifo and Fifo Inventory. The president of Frederick Processing Company would like to see how the income statement would appear for the year if it were prepared on a lifo inventory basis. Inventory has been maintained on a fifo basis. Sales for the year were $3,400,000. Inventory at the beginning of the year consisted of 8,000 units each with a cost of $15. During the year the company purchased 60,000 units at a price of $20 each. Another 30,000 units were purchased at a price of $25 each. The inventory at the end of the year consisted of 12,000 units.

Required:
(1) Prepare a partial income statement with inventory maintained on a fifo basis.
(2) Prepare a partial income statement with inventory on a lifo basis. A perpetual flow of the cost of merchandise sold is not kept during the year. For beginning inventory, use the data given by the fifo method.

5. Accelerated Depreciation. Radwell Fixtures, Inc., has been deducting depreciation by the straight-line method. The president of the company plans to use the SYD method on future acquisitions of equipment. With straight-line depreciation, the president believes that the company does not recover enough depreciation to replace equipment retired. For example, experience shows that a unit of equipment that cost $60,000 5 years ago would cost $80,000 at present prices. The selling price of second-hand equipment that is 5 years old is $30,000. In another 5 years, the equipment would have no resale value and new equipment is expected to cost $100,000. This equipment is being depreciated over 10 years by the straight-line method with no allowance for salvage value at the end of 10 years. The president plans to take depreciation on new equipment of this type by the SYD method over 5 years with no provision for salvage value at the end of 5 years.

Required:
(1) How much of the cost was recovered by depreciation over 5 years by the straight-line method? Including the proceeds from the sale of the old equipment, how much has been retained for replacement at the end of 5 years?
(2) How much would be available for replacement at the end of 5 years by the SYD method according to the president's plan? (Assume no complications because of income tax. Use cost of $60,000 for the illustration.)

6. Replacement Cost and Current Value. Boggs Melting Company has a stone building that was built a number of years ago at a cost of $320,000. Accumulated depreciation on the building at the present time is $225,000. Appraisal estimates show that the building has a sales value of $1,200,000 at present. Reproduction cost estimates are difficult to obtain inasmuch as buildings of this quality are no longer being constructed. However, one appraiser estimates that a new building of this type would cost at least $2,800,000 to construct. Accumulated depreciation on the reproduction cost would be $700,000.

Required: Show how the building would appear on a balance sheet prepared by the conventional cost method. As supplemental information, give reproduction cost data.

7. Inventory Costing Methods. During the past year, Apple and Shelton, Inc., has increased its inventory in anticipation of increased sales in the next year. Perpetual inventory records are not maintained. In the past year, 140,000 units of product were sold at a unit price of $30. Inventory and purchase data follow:

	Number of Units	Unit Cost	Total Cost
Inventory balance at the beginning of the year	20,000	$12	$240,000
Purchases:			
January	30,000	14	420,000
March	60,000	15	900,000
June	20,000	20	400,000
September	25,000	21	525,000
December	10,000	22	220,000

Required:

(1) Compute the gross margin using the fifo method of accounting for inventory cost. Determine the cost of the inventory at the end of the year.

(2) Compute the gross margin using the lifo method of accounting for inventory cost. Determine the cost of the inventory at the end of the year.

8. Dividend Policy. Littleton Brothers, Inc., reported a net income of $335,000 in 1980. Cost of goods sold included cost incurred in past years and amounted to $421,000. Analysis reveals that at the present time it would cost $517,000 to replace these goods. Depreciation on the original cost of the plant assets amounted to $83,000. Based on replacement cost the depreciation should have been shown at $106,000.

Required: How much of the net income for 1980 could be distributed as dividends with provision for the retention of resources necessary for continuance of the business on the same scale as before? (Do not consider the income tax effect.)

9. Current Value and Index Value. Suzanne Forbes purchased 200 acres of land several years ago at a price of $400 an acre. She has received an offer of $130,000 for this tract of land and wants to know if the value of her land has kept pace with the increase in general prices. The price index when she purchased the land was 80. The price index is now 120.

Required: Did the increase in the value of the land keep up with the increase in general prices as measured by the index? Can she realize a true gain from sale of the land, or is the gain merely a reflection of general price increases?

10. Current Value and Index Value. Russell Marioni has a savings account amounting to $19,670. Ten years ago he deposited $10,000 in the account, and the interest was compounded on this amount at a rate of 7% per year. Ten years ago the price index was 100. At present, the price index is at 180.

> **Required:**
> (1) Did Marioni's savings account keep up with the increase in the price level? Show computations.
> (2) If the price index is 220 at the present time, would Marioni be ahead or behind? Show computations.

11. Investments and the Price Index. Ten years ago Noreen Hamilton had savings accumulated in the amount of $40,000. She was concerned about the deteriorating purchasing power of the dollar and considered investments that would perhaps tend to follow the changes in general prices. At the same time, she considered that other investments might be better under conditions of relative stability. The price index ten years ago was 100. Today the index is at 180.

She purchased $10,000 in common stocks that were recommended to her as growth stocks that would serve as a hedge against inflation. She also purchased $10,000 worth of gold coins. As a steady and conservative investment, she purchased high grade bonds for $20,000.

The shares of stock are now worth $4,000, the gold coins are worth $32,000, and the bonds are still worth $20,000.

> **Required:** Compare the price-adjusted cost of her assets with the original cost and with the current market values.

12. Fixed Income and Retirement. Benson Taylor retired 10 years ago on an annual pension of $15,000. At that time the price index was 120. At the present time the index is at 180. Taylor is finding it more difficult to live on his pension than he did at the time he retired.

> **Required:**
> (1) Show Taylor how his pension shrank in purchasing power. Convert the present pension of $15,000 to dollars of purchasing power ten years ago.
> (2) How many dollars should Taylor now receive to maintain the purchasing power of $15,000 that he received 10 years ago?

13. Foreign Currency Variations. Dorsett Valley Farms sells in both domestic and foreign markets. The president of the company, Diane Siemenski, is pleased at the acceptance of the product in another country. At the same time, she is concerned about the stability of the currency in that country. The currency unit is now worth 60 cents. It appears quite likely that the value may decline to 40 cents in the near future. The company has a large order for export at an agreed price of 75,000 units of this country's currency.

> **Required:**
> (1) Determine the value of this order in dollars at present exchange rates. How many dollars would be collected if the value of the currency declines to 40 cents per unit?
> (2) How can Siemenski protect the company against exchange fluctuations? Explain.

14. Dividends and the Price Level. An income statement for Schuller Products Company in summary form for the year 1980 is given on page 364.

Sales	$567,000
Cost of goods sold	$312,000
Operating expenses	75,000
Total cost	$387,000
Income before income tax	$180,000
Income tax	72,000
Net income	$108,000

The board of directors plans to distribute $50,000 of the net income in dividends.

It would now cost $147,000 to replace the inventory sold, and depreciation based on the replacement cost of plant assets would result in operating expenses that would be $15,000 higher than the expenses listed.

Required:

(1) Prepare the income statement on the basis of the replacement cost data given.
(2) Can the board distribute dividends of $50,000 and still maintain the resources possessed at the beginning of the year? Explain.

15. Debt and the Price Level. The Anamat Company issued bonds in the amount of $3,600,000 to finance growth. The bonds were issued when the price index was 80. The bond agreement states that half the bond issue is to be retired in 10 years, and the other half is to be retired after another 10 years. When the bonds were issued, the company management was concerned about having the resources available to meet the $1,800,000 payment due at the end of 10 years. At that time, the total net inflow of cash to the firm was only $150,000 per year.

At the end of 10 years, the price index was at 180, and the annual net cash inflow for the past 4 years has been no lower than $500,000.

Required:

(1) Compute the purchasing power of the debt repaid at the end of the first 10 years. (State in terms of dollars 10 years ago.)
(2) Based on a net cash inflow of $150,000 each year, how long would it take to repay a loan of $1,800,000? (Assume that the entire $150,000 is set aside for that purpose with no interest return.)
(3) Based on a net cash inflow of $500,000 each year, how long would it take to repay a loan of $1,800,000? (Assume that the entire $500,000 is set aside for that purpose with no interest return.)
(4) Restate the balance of the debt after the first installment has been paid. Restate the debt in terms of current purchasing power dollars and determine the gain in purchasing power over the 10 years on the debt still remaining.

PROBLEMS

12-1. Index-Adjusted Billing. The Van Pelt Metals Company manufactures a product that includes 100 grams of a metal that moves up and down in price over relatively short intervals. When the metal cost $150 for 100 grams the customers were billed as shown on the next page.

Cost of metal..	$150
Labor and overhead	50
	$200
Profit of 20%...	40
Selling price of product	$240

In light of the volatility of metal prices, the company has announced that prices will be adjusted up or down as the price of the metal changes. The $40 markup for profit will not be adjusted for price changes in the metal.

Prices for the metal are given over a period of two years in 100-gram units.

Months	Cost of 100 Grams of Metal
19X1	
January to June...	$180
July to December...	270
19X2	
January to June...	324
July to December...	540

Required: Determine prices for the product during each of the 6-month periods given. Assume no change in labor and overhead costs or in the dollar amount of the markup for profit.

12-2. Index-Adjusted Loan. West Finance Company, in an attempt to reduce potential losses in purchasing power while loans are outstanding, has decided to maintain an interest rate of 7% but to adjust the amount of the loan to be repaid by using an index series. Assume that a loan of $540,000 was made when the index was 120. The loan with interest on the unadjusted loan balance was to be repaid a year later when the index was 160.

Required:

(1) How much should West Finance Company receive at the end of the year? Identify interest as a separate item.
(2) As a customer under the conditions outlined, would you rather repay the loan as adjusted with interest at 7% for the year on the unadjusted balance, or would you rather have a straight loan with the annual interest rate at 12%?

12-3. Original Cost and Reproduction Cost. For over 20 years, Ogilvie Products, Inc., has operated with a building that was acquired at a cost of $860,000. Depreciation has been deducted by the straight-line method with an estimated useful life of 50 years and a salvage value of $60,000 at the end of 50 years. Accumulated depreciation at the present time amounts to $368,000.

According to reliable estimates, it would now cost $2,600,000 to construct a comparable building. The new building would be expected to have a useful life of 50 years and a salvage value of $200,000 at the end of the 50 years. A real estate firm has estimated that $1,700,000 could be realized from the sale of the building.

Required:

(1) Compute the reproduction cost and the net amount after deducting accumulated depreciation based on reproduction cost.
(2) Is the current value as indicated by the potential sales value relevant in this situation?

12-4. Balance Sheet in Uniform Dollars. A summary balance sheet for Leiby Machine Company appears below in abbreviated form as of June 30, 19X2.

Cash and accounts receivable	$ 72,000
Plant and equipment, net of depreciation	176,000
Total assets	$248,000
Current debt	$ 30,000
Long-term debt	150,000
Owners' equity	68,000
Total equities	$248,000

The price index is 160. The plant and equipment and the long-term debt were acquired when the price index was at 80.

Required: Revise the summary balance sheet to restate all assets and equities in dollars at the 160 price index.

12-5. Balance Sheet in Uniform Dollars. Dawn Cleaver does not believe that the balance sheet of Anderson Supply Company gives a proper statement of the financial position inasmuch as the data are in dollars of mixed purchasing power. As a member of the board of directors, she requests that the statement be given in uniform dollars of purchasing power with the Consumer Price Index being used for the conversions.

Balance sheet data are given below as of October 31, 19X2:

Assets

Cash	$ 130,000
Accounts receivable	270,000
Inventory	420,000
Investment in Magna Industries	250,000
Plant and equipment, net of accumulated depreciation	280,000
Total assets	$1,350,000

Equities

Accounts payable and other current claims payable	$ 330,000
Long-term notes payable	200,000
Capital stock	540,000
Retained earnings	280,000
Total equities	$1,350,000

The assets and equities were acquired at the following price index levels:

	Index
Cash, accounts receivable, and accounts payable and other current claims payable	160 (average)
Inventory	120
Investment in Magna Industries	100
Plant and equipment	80
Long-term notes payable	80
Capital stock	60

The index at October 31, 19X2, was 200.

Required: Prepare a balance sheet in uniform dollars of purchasing power at an index of 200.

12-6. Purchasing Power and Monetary Assets and Equities. The Joplin Company had cash and accounts receivable of $135,000 at January 1, 19X1. The inventory at that date cost $105,000, and accounts payable were $45,000. The inventory was acquired at an index of 80. The price index on January 1, 19X1, was 100.

Transactions for the year 19X1 are summarized below:

	Unadjusted Amount	Index
(1) Sales..	$480,000	120 (average)
(2) Purchases:		
January to June.....................................	165,000	110 (average)
July to December...................................	80,000	120 (average)
(3) Expenses paid....................................	70,000	140
(4) Dividends paid....................................	90,000	180

At the end of the year, the company had cash and accounts receivable of $220,000 and accounts payable of $55,000. The price index at December 31, 19X1, was 180.

Required: Compute the gain or loss in purchasing power for the year by holding net monetary assets.

12-7. Purchasing Power, Monetary Assets and Income Statement. On July 1, 19X1, James Company had cash and accounts receivable of $117,000 and an inventory costing $135,000. These assets were acquired at the beginning of the fiscal year when the price index was 90. There were no accounts payable at the beginning of the year.

During the year, the company purchased merchandise at $528,000 when the index was 120. Sales were made at an index of 150 in the amount of $870,000. Operating expenses were incurred in the amount of $45,000 at an index of 180. Dividends of $100,000 were paid at an index of 200. There were no accounts payable at the end of the fiscal year. The inventory at June 30, 19X2, was $110,000 and was acquired near June 30 when the index was 220.

Required:

(1) Compute the purchasing power gain or loss from holding cash and accounts receivable.
(2) Prepare a summary income statement by the conventional method. Income tax is at the rate of 40% of income before tax and was paid at an index of 220.
(3) Prepare a summary income statement on a uniform dollar basis with the index at 220. _-75,800_

12-8. Income Statement in Uniform Dollars. An income statement for Barnet Fixtures, Inc., for the year ended June 30, 19X2, is given on page 368.

Sales of $650,000 were made when the price index was at 130. The balance of the sales were made when the price index was at 180. Cost of goods sold of $600,000 was at the price index of 120, and the balance of the cost of goods sold was at the price index of 180.

Operating expenses of $80,000 were incurred at a price index of 160, and $10,000 was incurred at a price index of 200.

Depreciation was deducted on plant assets that were acquired at a price index of 60.

Barnet Fixtures, Inc.
Income Statement
For the Year Ended June 30, 19X2

Net sales...	$1,190,000
Cost of goods sold	$ 870,000
Operating expenses, excluding depreciation...	90,000
Depreciation	60,000
Total expenses..	$1,020,000
Net income..	$ 170,000

The president of the company believes that the company would have earned a much lower net income if measurements had been made in uniform dollars of purchasing power. Before recommending dividends, he would like to see what the results would have been if all dollars were restated at an index of 220, the index at June 30, 19X2.

Required:

(1) Prepare an income statement on a uniform dollar basis at an index of 220.

(2) Is there a basis for the president's concern? Explain.

12-9. Gains and Losses on Investments. Malcolm Zimmer has invested in various assets over the past few years as follows:

Total Amount Invested	Common Stock	Bonds	Coins	Land	Price Index at Time of Investment
$ 8,000	$8,000				80
15,000	8,000		$7,000		100
21,000	6,000	$3,000		$12,000	120
18,000		9,000		9,000	150

At the present time the price index is at 200. Costs and present market values are given below.

Price Index at Time of Investment	Type of Investment	Cost	Present Market Value
80	Common stock	$ 8,000	$ 5,000
100	Common stock	8,000	7,000
	Coins	7,000	21,000
120	Common stock	6,000	5,000
	Bonds	3,000	3,000
	Land	12,000	15,000
150	Bonds	9,000	9,000
	Land	9,000	12,000

Required:

(1) Compute the conventional gain or loss on the holdings by comparing cost and market value. Show gains or losses by investment classification.

(2) Restate all investments in dollars at the price index of 200.

(3) Compare by investment category classifications the present market values of the investments with the costs stated in dollars having a purchasing power of 200.

12-10. Investment Policy and Price Level. Raymond Clayton, the president of Clayton Fixtures, Inc., has been concerned about the effects of inflation for several years. As a result, he has advocated a policy of operating with a minimum of monetary assets and has reinvested profits in modern equipment that is not only more efficient but also tends to follow the price level even as second-hand equipment. To a large extent, he has financed acquisitions by long-term loans.

A balance sheet at June 30, 19X2 is given below.

Clayton Fixtures, Inc.
Balance Sheet
June 30, 19X2

Assets

Cash..	$ 38,000
Accounts receivable..	30,000
Inventory	72,000
Land..	170,000
Buildings, net of accumulated depreciation....................................	680,000
Equipment, net of accumulated depreciation	840,000
Total assets...	$1,830,000

Equities

Accounts payable..	$ 60,000
Short-term loans..	20,000
Long-term loans	1,000,000
Capital stock..	100,000
Retained earnings...	650,000
Total equities..	$1,830,000

The price index at June 30, 19X2, was 200. Inventory was acquired at a price index of 180. Land costing $60,000 was acquired at an index of 120, and land costing $110,000 was acquired at an index of 100. The buildings were purchased at an index of 100. Equipment with a net book value of $300,000 was acquired at an index of 100, and equipment with a net book value of $540,000 was acquired at an index of 180. Capital stock was issued at an index of 100.

Required:

(1) Prepare a balance sheet on a uniform dollar basis at an index of 200.
(2) Assume that the price level decreased to 100. Prepare a balance sheet at an index of 100.

12-11. Replacement Cost and Lifo Inventory. An income statement for the year ended September 30, 19X2, is given at the top of page 370.

The company has used the fifo method to compute the cost of goods sold.

At the end of the year, the cost to replace the merchandise sold would amount to $12 per unit.

Required:

(1) Prepare an income statement with cost of goods sold computed by the lifo method.
(2) Prepare an income statement using current replacement cost.

Agro Company
Income Statement
For the Year Ended September 30, 19X2

Sales (150,000 units @ $20)...	$3,000,000
Cost of goods sold:	
Inventory, October 1, 19X1 (20,000 units @ $6)..	$ 120,000
Purchases (160,000 units @ $7)	1,120,000
	$1,240,000
Less inventory, September 30, 19X1 (30,000 units @ $7).............................	210,000
Cost of goods sold..	$1,030,000
Gross margin...	$1,970,000
Operating expenses...	1,460,000
Income before income tax...	$ 510,000

(3) Which of the two income statements would be more useful to management in future planning?

(4) Would a statement on a price-index-adjusted basis be more useful to management? Explain.

12-12. Land Investment. Lakeview Company has future plans to locate plants in various parts of the country and has saved funds for that purpose. The president of the company believes that it is more appropriate to invest in various land sites now rather than to hold funds in the form of securities or to take chances on the conditions of a future capital market for later borrowing or capital stock issues. Some later financing will be necessary, but management would like to keep the amount as low as possible.

The president states, "Land will always go up in value. They aren't making any more of it." If the land is not needed, the plan is to sell unused portions at a gain.

Investments in land were made as follows:

	Cost	Price Index
Tract #1	$ 80,000	100
Tract #2	180,000	120
Tract #3	250,000	125
Tract #4	280,000	140

Five years later, the price index was at 180. The tracts of land were appraised as follows:

	Current Value
Tract #1..	$165,000
Tract #2..	190,000
Tract #3..	240,000
Tract #4..	400,000

Required:

(1) Prepare a report to show the original cost, the index-adjusted costs, and the current values of the tracts.

(2) Point out possible fallacies in the position taken by the president.

12-13. Billings in Foreign Currency. Coulter and Fulmer, Inc., sells merchandise in a country where the price level has been increasing rapidly in a very short period of time. As a result, the company is reluctant to extend credit in this country's currency.

Two different credit plans have been established. One plan extends credit with a limit of 60 days with a 30% charge added to all sales paid more than 15 days after date of sale. The other plan extends credit for as long as 6 months after sale with the provision that payment be made in units of purchasing power at time of the sale as determined by an index series.

Credit sales were made on August 1 under the 60-day plan in the amount of 370,000 currency units. The price index on August 1 was 185. Credit sales were made on the same date under the 6-month plan in the amount of 740,000 currency units. On October 1, the price index was 230, and on February 1 of the following year, it was 320.

Required:
(1) How much will be collected under the 60-day plan on October 1, assuming that all sales will be collected? How does this amount correspond with the price-index-adjusted amount?
(2) How much will be collected under the 6-month plan on the following February 1?

12-14. Protection on Currency Conversions. Baden and Page, Inc., has a large order for the sale of merchandise in another country. The merchandise is to be billed and collected in the currency of the other country. Management believes that this currency is relatively unstable and wishes to protect the company from fluctuations in foreign exchange. At the present time, 20 units of this currency are equal to one dollar. The billing for the export sale is 1,400,000 units of currency, and the company plans to convert this sale to $70,000 when collection is made.

Required:
(1) Explain how the company can plan for the realization of $70,000 when the sale is collected.
(2) At the time of collection, explain what will happen under the plan. Assume that 50 units of currency will be needed at that time to equal one dollar.

12-15. Comprehensive Price Index Problem. The balance sheet given on page 372 for Steuben Patterns, Inc., has been adjusted to a uniform dollar basis at an index of 100.

Transactions for the year, 19X2, are summarized as follows:

(1) Sales:
    At index of 120.. $240,000
    At index of 150.. 150,000
(2) Purchases:
    At index of 100.. 110,000
    At index of 120.. 84,000
(3) Cost of goods sold was $243,000.

The inventory of $36,000 at the end of the year was all acquired at the index of 120.

Steuben Patterns, Inc.
Balance Sheet
(Uniform dollars at index of 100)
December 31, 19X1

Assets

Cash	$140,000
Accounts receivable	145,000
Inventory	85,000
Plant assets, net of accumulated depreciation	180,000
Total assets	$550,000

Equities

Accounts payable and other current claims payable	$ 30,000
Bonds payable	100,000
Capital stock	50,000
Retained earnings:	
Operations	310,000
Accumulated purchasing power gains	60,000
Total equities	$550,000

    (4) Operating expenses for the year, excluding depreciation, were $45,000. They were incurred at an average index for the year of 150.

    (5) Accounts payable at the end of the year amounted to $40,000.

    (6) Accounts receivable at the end of the year amounted to $125,000.

    (7) Depreciation for the year was on assets acquired at an index of 100 and amounted to $15,000.

    (8) Income tax of $35,000 was computed and paid at an index of 200.

    (9) The index at December 31, 19X2, was 200.

  (10) The cash balance at December 31, 19X2, was $286,000.

Required:

    (1) Compute the purchasing power gain or loss for the year from holding net monetary assets.

    (2) Prepare an income statement for the year in mixed dollars and convert the statement to uniform dollars of purchasing power at an index of 200.

    (3) Prepare a balance sheet in mixed dollars of purchasing power at December 31, 19X2.

    (4) Prepare a comparative balance sheet in uniform dollars of purchasing power at an index of 200. (Balance sheet at December 31, 19X2 and 19X1 adjusted to an index of 200.)

13
ANALYSIS OF
FINANCIAL STATEMENTS

Stockholders, creditors, employees, prospective investors, and the public at large judge a company, in part at least, by financial measurements that are revealed through statement analysis. Business management, recognizing that the statements are a report on the company and on managerial skill, see statement analysis as a means for self-evaluation. Knowledge derived from analysis can be combined with other information in planning and controlling various aspects of the business. Also, statement analysis reveals how closely financial data are interlocked. No one piece of financial information is isolated; and financial statement analysis is important, if for no other reason, because it can give the reader a better understanding of business operations and the related financial effects.

Statement analysis furnishes general answers to the following questions:

1. Does the company earn adequate profit?
2. Can the company pay its bills promptly? In other words, does it have sufficient liquidity?
3. Is an investment in the company a safe investment?

Exact answers cannot be given to these questions; the answers depend upon what will happen in an uncertain future. But statement analysis can reveal what has taken place in the past and give some indication of what can be expected.

RATE-OF-RETURN CONCEPT

The rate-of-return concept is employed to evaluate the earning power of a company. The percentage of net income to sales is the rate of return on sales, the percentage of net income to assets is the rate of return on assets, and the percentage of net income to owners' equity is the rate of return on the owners' equity. These respective percentages, or rates of return, reveal the relationships between the net earnings and the sales revenue, the net earnings and the assets employed, and the net earnings and the owners' interest in the business.

Rate of Return — Assets

The rate of return on assets is one of the most important measurements obtained from an analysis of financial statements. This rate of return is computed as follows:

$$\frac{\text{Net income}}{\text{Assets}} = \text{Rate of return on assets}$$

Both the net income and the assets must be defined carefully in order to obtain a rate of return that is appropriate for a given purpose.

Net Income

For purposes of financial statement analysis, the income statement should be adjusted to remove items that are of an unusual nature and that are not expected to recur with regularity. For example, a loss from a fire should not be included in the computation of net income. If the loss is not removed, the rate of return may be distorted. Furthermore, if unusual items are allowed to remain in the income statement, comparisons cannot be made with other years. In effect, "net income" becomes synonymous with "income from continuing operation," thus excluding extraordinary items, disposals of segments of a business, and the cumulative effect of changes in accounting principle.

The dividends and the interest earned on investments are included in net income if the investments are also included in the asset base, but the dividends and the interest should be excluded if the investments have been removed from the assets category.

The income before the deduction of interest expense and income tax is used if the intention is to measure operational performance. A manager may be responsible for how an asset is used but may have had nothing to do with the acquisition of the asset. Resources are often borrowed to finance the purchase of assets; and interest expense, the cost of borrowing resources, should not be charged to personnel who have had no part in making these financial arrangements. Furthermore, comparisons between companies may be distorted by differences in financing. To test the effectiveness of operation as opposed to financing, interest expense should not be deducted from income.

Top management, on the other hand, is responsible not only for how the assets are used but also for how they are acquired. Therefore, it is proper to use the income after the deduction of interest to evaluate the total managerial effort. The rate of return is then a rate of return to the owners on the total asset investment since the income has already been reduced for amounts due to other equity holders. In other words, income has already been reduced by the interest on the debt.

Likewise, income tax may or may not be deducted depending upon circumstances. Management at the operating level has no control over the computation of income tax or the tax planning activities; consequently, income before the income tax deduction would be a more appropriate measurement of its efficiency. From the owners' viewpoint, however, there can be no return until all expenses, including income tax, have been deducted. The income tax is as much an expense of doing business as any other expense and should be considered as such in rating the total business performance.

The Asset Base

Assets as shown on the balance sheet may also have to be adjusted in making rate-of-return computations. The nature of the adjustments depends upon the definition of the rate of return. Since assets increase or decrease during the year, a rate-of-return measurement may be more meaningful if the assets are averaged. When reference is made in this chapter to total assets or to total owners' equity, it is assumed that the data have been properly averaged or are representative data for rate-of-return computations.

Assets that are not available for productive use should be excluded from the asset base in the calculation of a rate of return on assets that are actively employed in profit-making activity. The cost of idle facilities, for example, and the cost of construction in process produce nothing in the way of current profit. Presumably these assets are expected to yield profit at a later date. At the present time, however, there is no profit yield, and the cost should be subtracted from the asset base so that the return will be related to the assets that produced it. An additional rate of return calculation may be made with the cost of standby and idle facilities included in the asset base. This rate of return can be compared with the rate of return on the productive assets and may reveal that management is retaining more nonproductive assets than is warranted.

If management at the operating level is to be evaluated, investments in the securities of other companies should also be eliminated. Operating management cannot take credit for the dividends or interest earned on investments, nor can it be held responsible for the cost of the investments.

Asset Turnover and Rate of Return

In seeking a given rate of return, management recognizes that various factors interlock. These factors are:

1. The rate of profit on the sales dollar.
2. The volume of sales.
3. The investment in assets.
4. The ratio of sales to the asset investment (asset turnover).

The rate of return on total assets depends upon the ratio of net income to sales and the ratio of sales to total assets. Often these relationships are expressed in equation form as follows:

$$\frac{\text{Net income}}{\text{Total assets}} = \frac{\text{Net income}}{\text{Sales}} \times \frac{\text{Sales}}{\text{Total assets}}$$

or

$$\begin{array}{c}\text{Rate of return} \\ \text{on total assets}\end{array} = \begin{array}{c}\text{Rate of return} \\ \text{on sales}\end{array} \times \text{Asset turnover}$$

Assume that two companies each with assets of $500,000 earn a 20 percent return on assets, or $100,000 in net income. Company A is a manufacturer and turns its assets over only once but earns a 20 percent return on sales. Company B is a retailer and turns its assets over ten times but earns only 2 percent on the sales dollar.

RATE OF RETURN ON ASSETS

	Company A	*Company B*
Net sales	$500,000	$5,000,000
Total assets	$500,000	$500,000
Net income	$100,000	$100,000
Percentage of net income to net sales (rate of return on sales)	20%	2%
Asset turnover	1	10
Rate of return on total assets	20%	20%

Company A relies upon its profit margin to obtain a 20 percent return on assets, while Company B depends upon turnover. By doubling asset turnover, Company A can double the rate of return on assets with the same volume of sales and profit percentage. If Company B can increase its profit margin to 4 percent of net sales, it can also double the rate of return on assets with the same sales volume and turnover.

Various combinations of turnovers and profit percentages can be computed to arrive at a combination that most likely will be realized in seeking a certain rate of return. By examining these relationships, management can in certain industries, however, impose limitations. For example, a company that manufactures heavy equipment generally requires a large asset investment. It may be difficult to improve asset turnover to any extent, and an improved rate of return on assets may depend largely upon an increased rate of return on sales.

THE MANAGEMENT OF ASSETS

Different types of assets or resources must be available and be employed in balanced proportions to achieve an optimum rate of return. Cash, accounts receivable, inventory, various plant assets, and a supply of labor are all necessary in the production of goods and services for sale to customers.

With a surplus of assets, the company is in a good position to meet emergency situations and does not have to plan operating activity with much precision. But there is a price for this luxury. The rate of return on assets tends to be depressed with a large asset base; and the cost to hold large inventories or reserve plant facilities, for example, may be beyond reason. Creditors and stockholders furnish resources at a cost, and efforts must be made to minimize that cost. Conversely, if the investment in assets is too small, the company may not be able to meet production schedules promptly and may lose sales and customers.

A balanced asset structure is essential. It is possible to have an excess investment in one asset category with a shortage in another. For example, more plant and equipment may be available than is necessary for the production of one line of product while there is a shortage of facilities in another area. Inventories may be stockpiled beyond reasonable need when there is a shortage of cash to meet obligations to creditors, or collection policy may be lax, resulting in large accounts receivable balances that should be realized in cash.

The Combination of Assets

In conducting operations, resources may be combined in various ways. To some extent, one factor of production may be substituted for another. For example, it may be possible to use more automated equipment and less labor. A shift of this sort has both advantages and disadvantages that must be evaluated. Some of the cost and problems associated with labor are avoided, but cost and problems associated with the maintenance and operation of sophisticated equipment are added.

In a manufacturing operation, three cost elements are combined to form the finished product:

1. Direct materials.
2. Direct labor.
3. Factory overhead.

Direct Materials

Within limits it may be possible to substitute one type of material for another or to reduce the quantity of materials used. A shift to a less expensive material or a saving in quantity may reduce cost of production and reduce the investment in inventory. As a result, the rate of return on assets is improved.

Direct Labor

As stated earlier, there may be an opportunity to substitute equipment for labor or vice versa. Before making any changes, management should evaluate the effect on the rate of return. With labor or equipment management, there is the question of how much time is needed for production. In evaluating alternative combinations of labor and equipment, cost and time must be considered together. As pointed out in Chapter 6, overhead cost that varies with labor or machine hours is influenced by labor time or machine time and must also be recognized in any evaluation of alternatives.

Factory Overhead

With the different types of overhead, the rate of return can be improved by paying attention to the need for certain costs. Both the variable and fixed overhead should be examined for possible savings. There is often a tendency to authorize additions to fixed overhead without adequately evaluating potential needs. Fixed overhead thus becomes institutionalized as an established "necessity." For example, does an annual training program at a national training center produce results that justify travel and lodging costs? Could the same or even better results be obtained via training programs at local offices?

Rate of Return by Segment

In examining the various aspects of rate of return such as revenue, cost, and supporting assets, it is important to determine not only the rate of return for the company as a unit but also the rates of return for segments of the company such as divisions or product lines. Attempts to compute rates of return by segments are complicated when assets are shared by two or more segments. How much of the asset base should be assigned to one segment as compared with another? Attempts to allocate the supporting assets can become quite arbitrary.

Perhaps the best approach is to consider only the assets that can be directly identified with a segment. It may be recognized that each segment receives benefits from assets shared in common with other segments. However, in determining the profitability of a segment, it may be better not to make allocations that are questionable.

Assume that Heiser and Wolf, Inc., operates with three product line divisions. Data with respect to operations for 1981 are given at the top of the next page.

Note that the rates of return for the segments are computed by excluding expenses that are not directly identified with the segments. It is true that these rates do not reflect the support furnished at the top corporate level. However, the rates are useful in that they indicate which divisions are more profitable in relation to the assets that they employ. In still another way, they reveal whether or not top corporate management is operating efficiently. In the example given, the cost

Heiser and Wolf, Inc.
Operating Data
For the year 1981

| | Product Line Divisions | | | |
	1	2	3	Total
Sales..	$250,000	$320,000	$400,000	$ 970,000
Direct cost of division	180,000	230,000	300,000	710,000
(1) Margin over direct cost of division...	$ 70,000	$ 90,000	$100,000	$ 260,000
Cost common to total operation.............				140,000
(2) Net income..				$ 120,000
(3) Assets identified directly with division...	$350,000	$540,000	$250,000	$1,140,000
Assets common to total operation.........				360,000
(4) Total assets				$1,500,000
Rate of return on segment assets [(1) ÷ (3)]..	20%	16.7%	40%	
Rate of return, overall [(2) ÷ (4)].............				8%

common to the overall operation is relatively high. This depresses the total net income substantially and, when considered along with the addition of the assets used in common, significantly reduces the rate of return. Perhaps the cost of top administration should be examined more closely.

Depreciable Assets

In working with rates of return in total or by segments, the question arises as to how depreciable assets should be handled. Should depreciable assets be shown at the gross amount or at the net amount after the deduction for accumulated depreciation?

Assume that a net income of $50,000 has been earned for the year and that most of the assets employed were depreciable assets. Total assets with no reduction for accumulated depreciation had a cost of $500,000. A rate of return on assets is computed below.

$$\frac{\$50,000 \text{ net income}}{\$500,000 \text{ total assets}} = 10\% \text{ rate of return on assets}$$

Suppose that the accumulated depreciation was $200,000. Then the asset base would be $300,000 ($500,000 − $200,000) if assets are to be included net of accumulated depreciation.

$$\frac{\$50,000 \text{ net income}}{\$300,000 \text{ total assets}} = 16.7\% \text{ rate of return on assets}$$

The rate of return, of course, is higher when computed on a lower asset base. Furthermore, assuming no other changes, the rate of return tends to increase in the future as the asset base is reduced even more by depreciation.

Instead of being concerned about the effect of depreciation on the asset base, it may be more to the point to determine if the net income and the asset base are stated in comparable dollars of purchasing power. In Chapter 12, it was pointed out that comparisons cannot be made properly with mixed dollars of purchasing power.

A more realistic rate of return may be measured on a current value basis. For example, assume that the net income would be $40,000 rather than $50,000 if the income statement is on a current value basis. The depreciable assets and other assets have a combined current value of $600,000. The rate of return on assets should then be recomputed as follows:

$$\frac{\$40,000 \text{ net income}}{\$600,000 \text{ total assets}} = 6.7\% \text{ return on assets}$$

The result is significantly different. The rate of return is much lower when both the net income and the assets are stated on a comparable current dollar basis.

In management situations, one can be deceived by an artificially high rate of return and retain an unsatisfactory investment. The high rate of return may result from the use of an outdated asset base. For example, one may boast of an investment that has been yielding a 30 percent return. A number of years ago the investment cost $60,000 and now earns $18,000 a year with a present market value of $300,000. It is incorrectly reasoned that the current rate of return is 30 percent:

$$\frac{\$18,000 \text{ net income}}{\$60,000 \text{ original cost of investment}} = 30\% \text{ rate of return on investment}$$

The current rate of return is only 6 percent:

$$\frac{\$ \ 18,000 \text{ net income}}{\$300,000 \text{ value of investment}} = 6\% \text{ rate of return on investment}$$

The investment should be evaluated on the basis of current value, not historical cost. There is an opportunity cost of $300,000 attached to the decision to hold the investment; that is, the real question is whether or not $300,000 could be employed elsewhere to earn more than a 6 percent return.

LEVERAGE

The rate of return on assets is important, but it is also important to go a step further and determine the rate of return on the owners' equity. This rate of return depends upon decisions made with respect to the financial structure and also upon profit that in turn depends upon the effective employment of available resources.

Resources or capital may be furnished directly by the owners through the sale of capital stock if the business is incorporated or may be furnished indirectly by the owners through the reinvestment of profit that has been retained. Capital may also be furnished by outsiders either in the form of short-term credit or long-term credit. Ordinarily a business employs resources that have been furnished by both owners and outsiders in a ratio relative to management's philosophy toward risk taking.

The equity of the common stockholders is the residual equity, i.e., the equity remaining after provision has been made for the claims of all other equity holders. The stockholders' equity, for example, is reduced by the liquidation value of preferred stock. Similarly, net income must be reduced by the dividend claims of preferred stockholders.

The rate of return on the common stockholders' equity is computed as follows:

$$\frac{\text{Net income less dividend requirements on preferred stock}}{\text{Average common stockholders' equity}} = \frac{\text{Rate of return on common stockholders' equity}}{}$$

If there is only one class of stock outstanding, the rate of return is net income as a percentage of the average stockholders' equity, with the average being computed as a simple average of the balances at the beginning and at the end of the year or, if desired, an average of monthly balances.

Management sometimes tries to increase the rate of return on the owners' equity by using resources furnished by outsiders. If borrowed assets can be put to work to earn a return in excess of the interest cost, the owners will benefit. Suppose that $100,000 can be borrowed at 9 percent and put to work to earn 20 percent. The owners receive a net return after interest cost of $11,000 without any investment on their part. Using borrowed assets to enhance the return to the owners is called *leverage* or *trading on the equity*.

Leverage is frequently employed by finance companies, savings and loan institutions, and public utilities. The finance company, for example, many lend money at 9 percent interest. Without a fresh source of funds, a finance company would have to wait until payments were made on the loans before it could make additional loans. Instead of doing this, the company borrows money at, perhaps, 7 percent interest and pledges loans as security. The money obtained at 7 percent interest cost is loaned at 9 percent with the owners of the finance company receiving the advantage of the interest differential.

The effect of leverage is illustrated by the following example. Company A and Company B each possesses assets in the total amount of

$1,000,000. Each company has current liabilities of $100,000. Company A has no long-term debt and has a stockholders' equity of $900,000. Company B, on the other hand, has $500,000 of 8 percent bonds payable and a stockholders' equity of $400,000. Summary balance sheet data as of December 31, 1981, are given below.

	COMPANY A	COMPANY B
Total assets	$1,000,000	$1,000,000
Equities:		
Current liabilities	$ 100,000	$ 100,000
Bonds payable, 8%	—0—	500,000
Stockholders' equity..............................	900,000	400,000
Total equities..	$1,000,000	$1,000,000

Each company earns income before interest and income tax of $200,000, or, in other words, earns a 20 percent return on the assets before interest and income tax.

Summary income statement data for the two companies for 1981 are given below:

	COMPANY A	COMPANY B
Income before interest and income tax....	$ 200,000	$ 200,000
Interest (8% of $500,000)	—0—	40,000
Income before income tax	$ 200,000	$ 160,000
Income tax (40%).......................................	80,000	64,000
Net income..	$ 120,000	$ 96,000
Total assets	$1,000,000	$1,000,000
Stockholders' equity	$ 900,000	$ 400,000
Rate of return on total assets....................	**12%**	**9.6%**
Rate of return on stockholders' equity	**13.33%**	**24%**

The rates of return on total assets and on stockholders' equity have been computed for each company after deducting both interest and income tax from income. The rate of return of 13.33 percent on the stockholders' equity of Company A is only slightly higher than the rate of return of 12 percent on the total assets. The leverage from the current liabilities accounts for this differential.

Company B earns a lower rate of return on total assets than Company A because of the interest on the bonds. But the rate of return on the stockholders' equity is much higher. The stockholders' investment in Company B is $500,000 less than in Company A; and the resources obtained from the bond issue earn more than the interest cost, as shown at the top of the next page.

Earnings on $500,000 furnished by the bond-
holders:
Income before interest and income tax (20%
of $500,000) $100,000
Less income tax (40%) 40,000

Income before interest, after income tax........... $ 60,000
Cost of $500,000 furnished by the bondhold-
ers:
Interest (8% of $500,000) $40,000
Less income taxes (40%)................................... 16,000

Interest after income tax 24,000
Net return for the stockholders .... $ 36,000

The rate of return on the stockholders' equity is, of course, higher. The investment base is lower, and the bonds earn $36,000 for the owners net of interest and income tax.

WITHOUT BOND LEVERAGE — COMPANY A

$$\frac{\$120,000 \text{ net income}}{\$900,000 \text{ stockholders' equity}} = 13.33\% \text{ rate of return on stockholders' equity}$$

WITH BOND LEVERAGE — COMPANY B

$$\frac{\$\ 96,000 \text{ net income}}{\$400,000 \text{ stockholders' equity}} = 24\% \text{ rate of return on stockholders' equity}$$

Although there are advantages to leverage, there are also disadvantages. With leverage there is greater risk. Possibly the borrowed assets will not even earn the interest cost or may earn so little that the additional expected return is not worth the risk. When conditions are unfavorable, the owners of the leveraged company do not benefit from debt and in extreme cases may even have to relinquish control to the creditors.

EARNINGS AND MARKET VALUE OF STOCK

The rate of return on stockholders' equity depends upon the earnings in relation to the total investment and the ways in which the total investment is financed. This rate of return as computed from data appearing on past financial statements may not necessarily be in agreement with the rate of return used by investors to determine the market price of the stock.

The market price of a stock depends upon many factors; one of the most important is anticipated future earnings. The market price of a stock should be approximately equal to the present value of the expected future earnings per share. The rate used to discount the future earnings is the rate desired by investors as determined by market conditions and conditions within the industry and within the company itself. Past earnings may serve as a guide as to what may be expected in the future, but the value of a stock depends upon future earnings rather than earnings in the past.

The net income for any one year may be stated on a unit basis as the *earnings per share* of outstanding stock. For example, a company with 1,000,000 shares of common stock outstanding may report a net income for the year of $2,500,000. Assuming that there is no dividend requirement on preferred stock, the earnings per common share are $2.50 ($2,500,000 net income ÷ 1,000,000 shares outstanding).

The price of a stock is sensitive to the prospects for future earnings, and investors establish the price on the basis of their estimates of the future and the rate of return that they expect on investments. The rate of return in the market may be considerably different than the rate of return computed from data appearing on the financial statements. This difference can be readily understood when it is recognized that the stockholders' equity on the balance sheet has resulted from past investments by the stockholders and reinvested earnings. The market rate of return, on the other hand, is not determined as a relationship between the net earnings of the past year and the stockholders' equity as it appears in the accounting records. Rather, it is a relationship between expected future earnings and the market value of the stock.

Sometimes a book value per share of stock is computed. The *book value per share* of stock is equal to the stockholders' equity identified with that class of stock divided by the number of shares outstanding. Assume that a company with one class of stock outstanding has a stockholders' equity of $35,000,000 with 1,000,000 shares of stock outstanding. The book value per share is then $35.

$$\frac{\text{Stockholders' equity}}{\substack{\text{Number of shares} \\ \text{outstanding}}} = \frac{\$35,000,000}{1,000,000} = \$35 \text{ book value per share}$$

The book value per share and the market price per share may differ widely, as would be expected, considering that the market price is determined by future anticipations while book value is determined by amounts recorded in the past. Normally the stock of a company with prospects for growth sells for a price that is considerably higher than book value. On the other hand, a company in a declining industry may sell for a price that is even less than book value.

COMPREHENSIVE ANALYSIS

The analysis of financial statements extends beyond the concept of earning power and encompasses both the income statement and the balance sheet. Data from both the income statement and the balance sheet may be brought together in the form of ratios to reveal important relationships. In short, statement analysis calls attention to the significant relationships that would otherwise be buried in a maze of detail.

Furthermore, the ratios pertaining to any given year cannot stand alone. There should be a basis for comparison between years and between companies. Ordinarily the statements and the ratios for the current year are presented along with the statements and the ratios for one or two preceding years so that improvements or deteriorations can be detected. Comparisons are made not only with the company's own past performance but also with the average performance of the industry.

SOME HAZARDS OF ANALYSIS

There are many pitfalls to be avoided in analysis; and, at best, statement analysis can be used as a rough approximation. However, it serves as a general guide, pointing to areas that need further management study and investigation.

A Mixture of Valuations

One of the most serious defects of analysis results from a mixture of dollar valuations on the financial statements. In Chapter 12 it was pointed out that dollars do not have the same purchasing power at all times and that, as a result, financial statements may include a mixture of dollar valuations. Relationships can be distorted if dollars of current purchasing power are compared with dollars having some other purchasing power. Data should be adjusted to a common purchasing power basis if relationships are to be meaningful.

Differences Between Companies

In comparing companies, inherent differences must be considered. A relationship that may indicate great risk for one company may be quite reasonable for another. For example, a company in a cyclical industry has a less certain profit and should have a smaller proportion of debt in its equity structure than an electric power company. The electric power company has a relatively stable market and can safely operate with a high proportion of debt. Therefore, there is little basis for comparison between two such companies.

Variations in Accounting Methods and Estimates

A comparison between companies is even more difficult when differences in methods of accounting are considered. Significant variations between companies are often caused by the methods of matching cost against revenue. One company, for example, may capitalize a cost and write it off against revenue in future years while another company elects to write off a similar cost in the year that it is incurred. Estimation also varies. One company may depreciate a unit of equipment over 10 years while another company depreciates a similar unit over 12 years. Both companies may be justified by differences in how the equipment is used in operations.

An Average Concept

There is always the risk that the data do not truly represent what has taken place throughout the year. To overcome this problem, data may be averaged either by taking an average of the beginning and ending balances or by obtaining monthly averages. For example, a relationship between outstanding balances due from customers and credit sales may show how rapidly collections are being made from customers. The amount shown for accounts receivable at the end of the year, however, may be abnormally high or low because of seasonality. A better measurement can be made by selecting an average balance that would be more typical of the situation throughout the year.

ILLUSTRATION OF ANALYSIS

Financial statements are given in thousands of dollars for Durban Products, Inc., below.

Durban Products, Inc.
Balance Sheet
December 31, 1981, 1980, and 1979
(In thousands of dollars)

	1981	1980	1979
Assets			
Current assets:			
Cash	$ 488	$ 523	$ 384
Accounts receivable, net of uncollectibles	2,130	1,145	520
Inventories:			
Finished goods	1,033	617	426
Materials	1,157	738	282
Prepaid expenses	14	37	23
Total current assets	$ 4,822	$3,060	$1,635
Plant assets, net of accumulated depreciation	8,418	6,748	3,427
Total assets	$13,240	$9,808	$5,062
Equities			
Current liabilities:			
Accounts payable	$ 1,951	$ 637	$ 215
Notes payable	100	80	50
Other current liabilities	1,044	523	158
Total current liabilities	$ 3,095	$1,240	$ 423
Long-term notes payable	4,000	3,500	—0—
Stockholders' equity:			
Capital stock, $1 par value	300	300	300
Paid-in capital in excess of par value	1,250	1,250	1,250
Retained earnings	4,595	3,518	3,089
Total equities	$13,240	$9,808	$5,062

In the income statement below, the percentage of increase or decrease of each item over the base year 1979 is given beside the dollar amounts. The trend percentages are helpful in that they call attention to large proportionate changes, but they can be misleading if used improperly. The percentages of increase computed on a small base may be large, but the dollar amount involved may be relatively insignificant. For example, an increase from $20 to $60 is an increase of 200 percent; but the absolute amount of increase is only $40. On the other hand an increase of $100,000 measured from a base of $400,000 is stated as an increase of only 25%. Thus, one must consider the dollar amount of increase or decrease as well as the percentage.

Durban Products, Inc.
Income Statement
For the Years Ended December 31, 1981, 1980, and 1979
(In thousands of dollars)

				Percentages — Increase or (Decrease)	
	1981	*1980*	*1979*	*1981 over 1979*	*1980 over 1979*
Net sales	$15,240	$5,811	$3,140	385.4%	85.1%
Cost of goods sold	11,787	3,933	1,632	622.2%	141.0%
Gross margin	$ 3,453	$1,878	$1,508	129.0%	24.5%
Operating expenses	1,127	915	739	52.5%	23.8%
Operating income	$ 2,326	$ 963	$ 769	202.5%	25.2%
Interest expense	430	148	5	8500.0%	2860.0%
Income before income tax	$ 1,896	$ 815	$ 764	148.2%	6.7%
Provision for income tax	759	326	306	148.0%	6.5%
Net income	$ 1,137	$ 489	$ 458	148.3%	6.8%
Depreciation included in cost of goods sold and operating expenses	$ 486	$ 317	$ 184	164.1%	72.3%

A common base year should be used consistently in making the computations. Comparison is more difficult if base years are changed. For Durban Products, Inc., 1979 was used as the base year, and the results for 1980 and 1981 were both related to that year. Normally the earliest year in a series is used as a base. A percentage of change can be computed only if there is a positive amount for the base year.

A REVIEW OF EARNING POWER

For purposes of illustration, it is assumed that the average amounts of the assets and the equities for the year are equivalent to the balances at the end of the year. It is also assumed that the dollar amounts are on the same price-level basis and that they can be compared in other respects. Dividends of 20 cents a share, a total amount of $60,000, were declared and paid in each of the three years.

In absolute terms, net sales and net income have increased; yet, as shown below, the percentage of net income to net sales has decreased, indicating that cost in total has increased at a faster rate than revenue. Operating expenses, however, have decreased as a percentage of net sales while the cost of goods sold has increased relative to sales as shown by the much lower gross margin rate. The substantial reduction in gross margin percentage indicates that perhaps the mix of products sold may have changed, with a greater proportion of less profitable lines being sold. The cost of the merchandise also may have increased relative to selling prices. Various factors may account for changes in the rate of gross margin, and investigation may reveal possibilities for corrections.

EARNING POWER RELATIONSHIPS

Percentages, Net Income, and Dividends per Share	1981	1980	1979
(1) Net income to net sales* ...	7.5%	8.4%	14.6%
(2) Gross margin rate..............	22.7%	32.3%	48.0%
(3) Percentage of operating expense to net sales	7.4%	15.7%	23.5%
(4) Net income to total assets*............................	8.6%	5.0%	9.0%
(5) Net income to stockholders' equity*	18.5%	9.6%	9.9%
(6) Net income per share........	$3.79	$1.63	$1.53
(7) Dividends per share	$.20	$.20	$.20
(8) Net income........................	$1,137,000	$489,000	$458,000
(9) Total assets	$13,240,000	$9,808,000	$5,062,000
(10) Total stockholders' equity	$6,145,000	$5,068,000	$4,639,000
(11) Number of shares of stock outstanding	300,000	300,000	300,000

*Also referred to as rate of return on sales (1), total assets (4), or stockholders' equity (5).

The rate of return on total assets decreased in 1980 but returned to almost the 1979 level in 1981. This percentage in 1981 was somewhat higher than the percentage of net income to net sales, indicating that the assets turned over more than once during the year.

$$\frac{\text{Net sales}}{\text{Total assets}} = \frac{\$15,240,000}{\$13,240,000} = 1.15 \text{ asset turnover}$$

The rate of return on total assets is then equal to 1.15 times the rate of return on net sales. The calculation is made as follows:

7.5% return on net sales × 1.15 turnover = 8.6% return on total assets

The rate of return on the stockholders' equity each year is greater than the rate of return on the total assets, and the difference in 1981 is much greater than it was in 1979. This means that the company is making more use of leverage. On the basis of the information given, no judgment can be made as to whether or not leverage is justified. If the company is in a cyclical industry, debt can be a handicap. If business declines, it may become difficult to pay the interest and to retire the debt according to schedule. It appears, however, that Durban Products, Inc., may have sacrificed some safety for potentially greater growth. The net income per share has increased from year to year, and the dividends are well covered. Management has tried to finance a part of the growth by a retention of earnings. The expansion in plant assets, however, has been financed to a large extent by long-term debt. Further evaluation depends upon a more complete analysis of the company as viewed against the backdrop of the industry.

THE MANAGEMENT OF WORKING CAPITAL

The current assets of a business are put to active use in conducting operations and are sometimes called *working capital*. The term "working capital" is also applied to the excess of the current assets over the current liabilities. To avoid any misunderstanding, the excess of current assets over current liabilities will be referred to in this text as *net working capital*.

There is a very close relationship between the income statement and the current assets and current liabilities on the balance sheet. For example, materials and services may be purchased on credit terms with the liability being shown as a current liability. Costs identified with the products appear under the inventories caption in the current asset classification. When the inventories are sold to customers, the accounts receivable is increased by the amounts billed, and the inventory cost is reduced by the cost of the goods delivered. Ultimately, cash is realized from the accounts receivable and applied to the reduction of the current liabilities arising out of operating transactions. If the business is successful, it should generate more cash than it uses in operations. This cash may be used to acquire plant assets or investments, to retire long-term debt, to increase net working capital, or to make payments of dividends to the stockholders.

Within certain limits, the operating cycle should be repeated as frequently as possible. The inventories should be converted rapidly into accounts receivable and cash, current obligations should be paid, and the cycle should be started again. Limitations are imposed, however, by the nature of the business and by the investment required to support business volume. In some lines of business, rapid turnover cannot be expected. In the shipbuilding industry, for example, materials cannot be converted quickly into a finished product. The nature of the product, the time required for its production, and the demand for the product according to the season have an effect upon the rapidity of the conversion of current assets.

A company that earns a relatively low return on sales may be able to maintain a satisfactory rate of return on its investment by a rapid turnover of that investment. On the other hand, if the return on sales is fairly high, the rate earned on the investment can be maintained with a lower turnover.

Current Asset Turnover

Sometimes the ratio of cost of goods sold and expenses to current assets (the current asset turnover) is computed. In computing current asset turnover, depreciation should be eliminated from the cost of goods sold and expenses because the depreciation charge for the year is not dependent upon current assets.

A rapid turnover of current assets generally indicates that the current assets are more liquid. Inventories are probably not being built up needlessly if the ratio of cost of goods sold and expenses to current assets is fairly high, considering the nature of the industry. Other things being equal, increased turnover should result in a better rate of return on current assets and on total assets. This is true, however, only if the profit per turnover can be maintained.

Turnover in itself does not give the complete answer. Turnover may increase, but if the rate of return per turnover decreases, there may be a smaller rate of return on total assets. In fact, an increase in the current asset turnover may indicate that the company is trying to support too large a volume of business on its current investment.

The current asset turnover analysis for Durban Products, Inc., follows:

CURRENT ASSET TURNOVER AND RATE OF RETURN

	1981	1980	1979
Cost of goods sold and operating expenses, less depreciation	$12,428,000	$4,531,000	$2,187,000
Current assets	$4,822,000	$3,060,000	$1,635,000
Net income	$1,137,000	$489,000	$458,000
Current asset turnover	2.58 times	1.48 times	1.34 times
Rate of return on current assets	23.6%	16.0%	28.0%
Rate of return per turnover (Rate of return ÷ Number of turnovers)	9.1%	10.8%	20.9%

The turnover has increased since 1979. Both rate of return on current assets and the rate of return per turnover were lower in 1981 than in 1979. This indicates that the current assets are being worked harder but that they are earning less.

Current and Acid-Test Ratios

The general ability of a company to meet its short-term indebtedness is measured by the current ratio. The *current ratio* is the ratio of current assets to current liabilities. Although a ratio of 2 to 1 has often been singled out as desirable, this rule of thumb is not necessarily valid. Ratios will vary in different industries. In fact, some companies may operate quite satisfactorily with ratios of only slightly more than 1 to 1.

The current ratio for Durban Products, Inc., was more than 3 to 1 at the end of 1979 but has decreased to less than 2 to 1 at the end of 1981. The current assets have increased, but the current liabilities have increased by an even greater rate.

CURRENT RATIO

	1981	1980	1979
Current assets............................	$4,822,000	$3,060,000	$1,635,000
Current liabilities.....................	$3,095,000	$1,240,000	$423,000
Current ratio	**1.56**	**2.47**	**3.87**

A more rigorous measurement of the company's ability to service short-term debt is made by excluding inventories and prepaid expenses from current assets in computing the ratio. The so-called *quick assets* consisting of cash, marketable securities, and accounts receivable are divided by the current liabilities in the computation of the *acid-test ratio*. It is generally considered that a dollar in quick assets should lie behind each dollar of current debt.

ACID-TEST RATIO

	1981	1980	1979
Quick assets.............................	$2,618,000	$1,668,000	$904,000
Current liabilities.....................	$3,095,000	$1,240,000	$423,000
Acid-test ratio........................	**.85**	**1.35**	**2.14**

The substantial decrease of the acid-test ratio since 1979 indicates that the company is much less liquid at the end of 1981 than it was at the end of 1979.

Accounts Receivable Turnover

Analysis of the working capital can be extended further to determine how long it takes for inventories and accounts receivable to be converted into cash.

When the customers accounts are collected promptly with little loss or collection expense, it is much easier to meet obligations when they become due. But if there is a severe time lag in the collection of accounts receivable, this may have an adverse effect upon a company's ability to pay its debts. Conversely, higher turnovers may offset a lower current ratio. An approximation of the average time required to collect accounts receivable can be calculated by dividing the net credit sales by the average balances of accounts receivable that are outstanding. The turnover, referred to as the *accounts receivable turnover*, can be converted into the number of days that sales are in accounts receivable by dividing the turnover into 360 (or 365) days.

It is assumed that Durban Products, Inc., made all of its sales on credit and that the ending accounts receivable can be considered to be typical of the balances throughout the year. The accounts receivable turnover computations given below show that Durban Products, Inc., has increased turnover, thereby reducing the collection period.

ACCOUNTS RECEIVABLE TURNOVER

	1981	1980	1979
Net credit sales......................	$15,240,000	$5,811,000	$3,140,000
Accounts receivable	$2,130,000	$1,145,000	$520,000
Accounts receivable turnover....................................	7.15 times	5.08 times	6.04 times
Number of days sales in accounts receivable (360 days ÷ Number of turnovers)..........................	50 days	71 days	60 days

Inventory Turnovers

Turnovers can also be computed for the inventory investments. A turnover of the average investment in materials is calculated by dividing the cost of materials used during the year by the average investment in materials. Too high a ratio may indicate that the inventory balance is too low. Orders then have to be placed more frequently, and there is a risk of production slowdowns because of insufficient materials. Conversely, a low ratio may call attention to an investment that is too high in relation to the production requirements. Funds may be needlessly tied up in materials inventory.

A turnover of finished goods is calculated by dividing the cost of goods sold by the average finished goods inventory. The average number of days that sales are in inventory can also be calculated. In addition, the gross margin per inventory turnover may be computed as an indication of profitability in relation to inventory movement. These computations for Durban Products, Inc., are shown below:

FINISHED GOODS TURNOVER

	1981	1980	1979
Cost of goods sold..................	$11,787,000	$3,933,000	$1,632,000
Average inventory of finished goods........................	$1,033,000	$617,000	$426,000
Inventory turnover	11.4 times	6.4 times	3.8 times
Number of days' sales in inventory (360 days ÷ Number of turnovers)	32 days	56 days	95 days
Gross margin..........................	$3,453,000	$1,878,000	$1,508,000
Gross margin per turnover (Gross margin ÷ Number of turnovers).......................	$302,895	$293,438	$396,842

The ratios show that Durban has not increased its investment in finished goods in relation to sales. Inventory turnover has improved.

The inventory turnover is significant, but it is also important to find out how much is being earned per turnover. A company may be moving its inventories more rapidly and be more liquid, but the amount earned for each turnover or even the total earned may be less. Durban Products, Inc., increased its turnover of inventory but earned less per turnover in 1981 than in 1979. The company earned a larger total gross margin in 1981 by more rapid inventory turnover. However, the company earned less in proportion to inventory investment.

THE EQUITY RELATIONSHIPS

Ordinarily, as a company progresses, the owners' proportionate share in the total equity should increase or at least should be maintained at some established level. When the relative interest of outsiders is increased, there is an advantage to the owners in that they get the benefit of a return on assets furnished by others; yet in gaining this advantage there is increased risk. The relative interests of the various equity holders in Durban Products, Inc., are given at the end of each of the three years:

	1981	1980	1979
Current liabilities	23.4%	12.6%	8.4%
Long-term liabilities	30.2	35.7	—0—
Stockholders' equity	46.4	51.7	91.6
	100.0%	100.0%	100.0%

The proportionate interest of the owners has declined substantially since 1979. However, in 1979 the company had very little debt in its equity structure and was not getting much benefit from leverage. On the other hand, there may be too much debt in the equity structure at the end of 1981. Justification of greater risk depends on the level and stability of future earnings.

NET INCOME AND FIXED CHARGES

Risk has many aspects, but one important aspect concerns the fixed charges imposed against earnings. Resources obtained from outsiders can be used to produce increased profit for the stockholders. However, a fixed charge is imposed for the use of these resources. For example, rental payments must be made for leased equipment, interest must be paid on debt, and dividends must be paid on preferred stock. If the level of revenue drops enough, the company may not be able to meet its fixed charge obligations; thus both the outsiders who have furnished resources and the stockholders may suffer losses.

A computation may be made of the number of times that fixed charges are covered by earnings. This computation is made by dividing the income before the charges are deducted by the fixed charges.

Durban Products, Inc., had no fixed charges aside from interest, and the computations for the company are given below.

TIMES INTEREST EARNED

	1981	1980	1979
Operating income	$2,326,000	$963,000	$769,000
Interest	$430,000	$148,000	$5,000
Times interest earned	5.4 times	6.5 times	153.8 times

The interest charges are well covered, but the trend indicates increasing risk.

AN EVALUATION OF THE COMPANY

One particular percentage or relationship may not be too significant in itself. Taken together, however, the results of analysis help to point out areas that require attention.

Durban Products, Inc., has grown considerably since 1979, and there are many favorable points. Sales volume has increased; and even with a reduced gross margin rate, the rate of return on assets in 1981 is about equal to the rate of return in 1979. Operating expenses appear to be under control and are not increasing proportionately. Inventories appear to be turning over well, and collections on accounts receivable are proceeding at a faster rate.

However, there are also some weak spots. It appears that the company may have been too conservative in 1979 but has gone to the other extreme in 1981. With an increased proportion of debt in the equity structure in 1981, the company is under more strain financially. Obligations will be more difficult to meet, and the question may be raised as to whether or not there is sufficient net working capital to support the larger scale of operation.

The equity structure should be balanced by the issuance of more capital stock. This gives the stockholders a larger proportionate interest in the firm, thereby reducing the risk and providing net working capital to support the expanded scale of operation.

QUESTIONS

1. What three basic questions can be answered by statement analysis?

2. How is rate of return on sales computed? On assets? On owners' equity?

3. What is asset turnover? What effect does a higher asset turnover tend to have on the rate of return on assets? Give a logical explanation for this effect on the rate of return on assets.

4. If management is unable to increase asset turnover, what other alternatives may be used to improve the rate of return on assets?

5. If rate of return is to be used to evaluate management at the operating level, what adjustments should be made to net income and to the assets?

6. How can there be a disadvantage in having more assets than are needed?

7. Is it possible to substitute one factor of production for another? Explain.

8. Explain how the asset base is determined in computing the rate of return for a segment of a business.

9. Explain how the rate of return for the total business may be considerably lower than the rate of return for any of the segments.

10. The rate of return will tend to increase as the asset base is reduced by depreciation. Explain how this effect can be avoided through a more accurate computation of the rate of return.

11. What is leverage? Explain how it works.

12. Explain the difference between the market value of a share of stock and its book value.

13. List some of the pitfalls to be avoided in the analysis of financial statements.

14. What is indicated by an increased current asset turnover with a lower rate of return per turnover?

15. In general, what is being measured by the current ratio and by the acid-test ratio? What is the difference between the two ratios?

16. If net credit sales for the year are $15,000,000 and the average accounts receivable are $3,000,000, how many days does it take to collect accounts receivable on the average?

17. If the cost of goods sold is $7,200,000 and the average inventory of merchandise is $600,000, how many days does it take to convert inventory to sales on the average?

18. If it has been determined that accounts receivable should be collected in 40 days and that inventory turns over every 30 days, how long is the operating cycle?

19. Why is a computation made to determine how many times fixed charges are earned?

20. What may be indicated by an evaluation that shows a sharp increase in the current ratio and a rate of return on stockholders' equity that is approaching the rate of return on assets?

EXERCISES

1. **Rate of Return Relationships.** Medford Milling Company earned $250,000 on net sales of $1,250,000 during 1981. The average investment in assets during the year was $2,000,000.

Required:

(1) Compute the rate of return on net sales.
(2) Compute the rate of return on the average asset investment.
(3) Compute the asset turnover

2. Changing Rate of Return Relationships. For several years Tabor Supply Company has earned 10% on net sales with an asset turnover of 1.5 each year. With new product lines, net sales are estimated at $5,000,000 next year with the rate of return on sales increasing to 15%. The average investment in assets is estimated at $4,000,000 for next year.

Required:

(1) Compute the former rate of return on assets.
(2) Compute the new asset turnover.
(3) What is the new expected rate of return on assets?

3. Asset Base and Rate of Return. The management of Fenway Products Company has decided to reduce an excessive investment in assets by disposing of machinery that is no longer needed and by reducing the balances carried in inventories. In the past the company earned 10% on an average asset investment of $3,000,000. With the reduction in assets, the average investment in assets should be down to $2,400,000.

Required: Compute the expected rate of return on assets after reductions have been made.

4. Turnover and Rate-of-Return Relationships. In the situations outlined below, compute the rate of return on net sales, the rate of return on assets, the asset turnover, or the net sales as requested.

(1) Assets are turned over 2.5 times in earning 8% on net sales. What is the rate of return on the assets?
(2) With an asset turnover of 4.2, what must the rate of return be on net sales if the rate of return on the assets is to be 21%?
(3) Net income is equal to 10% of net sales, and the net sales are equal to 160% of the assets. What is the rate of return on assets?
(4) The return on total assets has been computed at 12½%. The net income was $400,000, and the asset turnover was 2.4. You do not have the net sales figure but have been asked to give the amount of net sales and the rate of return on the sales dollar.
(5) If the rate of return on the net sales decreases from 10% to 5%, what must the asset turnover be to maintain a rate of return of 20% on the assets?
(6) If the total cost of operation excluding income tax amounts to $1,690,000 for the year, what must net sales be if the net income is 8% of net sales? Income tax has been computed at $150,000.
(7) The rate of return on assets decreased from 24% to 18%, although net income remained at 6% percent of net sales. Compute the decrease in the asset turnover.
(8) Net sales for the year were $4,500,000. Assets turned over twice during the year. Cost of goods sold and operating expenses including income tax amounted to $4,275,000. Compute the rate of return on net sales and on total assets.

5. Rate-of-Return Relationships. Plans are being made for the next year by the management of Beth Home Products Company. The average assets to be employed for the year are estimated at $2,000,000 with 40% of this amount borrowed at no interest cost. Materials and labor cost for the year is estimated at $3,000,000. Operating cost is to be $700,000. Customers are to be billed at 150% of materials and labor cost. The income tax is estimated at 50% of income before tax.

Required:

(1) Compute the estimated rate of return on sales.
(2) Compute the estimated rate of return on average total assets. (Total management effort is to be evaluated.)
(3) Compute the expected asset turnover.
(4) Compute the rate of return on the stockholders' equity.

6. Asset Base and Rate of Return. The management of Pelham Equipment Company has tried to handle a large volume of sales on a small asset base. For example, last year the company earned 5% on net sales of $5,000,000. The average asset base for the year was $1,000,000. This year the company planned to increase sales volume even more but through inability to meet delivery schedules to customers promptly had net sales of only $3,000,000. The rate of return on net sales was the same, and the asset base still averaged at $1,000,000.

Required:

(1) Compute the asset turnover and the rate of return on assets for last year.
(2) Compute the asset turnover and the rate of return on assets for the current year.
(3) Explain why the company may have been in a poor position to sustain sales volume.

7. Segment Rate of Return. The Colby Company produces and sells three major product lines, each line being produced at a separate division. The president of the company wants to know what the rate of return is for each division and for the company in total.

Data pertaining to the operation for last year are given below.

	Net Income	Average Assets
Division #1	$ 20,000	$ 500,000
Division #2	120,000	1,000,000
Division #3	110,000	900,000

The average assets are the assets directly identifiable with the divisions. In addition, there are corporate assets (averaged) of $800,000 that are not directly identifiable with any division. Expenses after deducting the effect of income tax that are common to the total operation have been allocated to the three divisions in computation of net income. These corporate expenses were $200,000 in total and were allocated 40: 40: 20.

Required: Compute the rate of return on average assets for each division and for the company in total. (Carry to three decimal places.)

8. Segment Rate of Return. A rate of return on assets has been computed for Allison Company, as shown on the next page. Allison Company has a chemical division and a paint division.

Required: Compute a revised rate of return for each of the two divisions.

	Chemical Division	Paint Division	Total
Sales	$400,000	$800,000	$1,200,000
Cost of goods sold	$200,000	$300,000	$ 500,000
Direct expenses of division	100,000	200,000	300,000
Indirect expenses of division	50,000	100,000	150,000
Total	$350,000	$600,000	$ 950,000
Income from operations	$ 50,000	$200,000	$ 250,000
Average assets directly identified with division	$300,000	$500,000	$ 800,000
Average assets allocated to divisions	100,000	300,000	400,000
Total assets	$400,000	$800,000	$1,200,000
Rate of return on assets	12.5%	25%	20.8%

9. Depreciation and Rate of Return. Ward Hudson, Inc., has a plant and equipment in operation on June 30, 1981, that have a cost of $800,000. Accumulated depreciation of $500,000 has been deducted. If the plant and equipment were replaced at June 30, 1981, the cost of replacement would be $1,500,000. Estimated accumulated depreciation on replacement cost is $800,000. During the year ended June 30, 1981, the company reported a net income of $100,000 after deducting depreciation of $50,000 on the cost of plant and equipment. Based on replacement cost, the depreciation for the fiscal year would amount to $100,000.

Required:

(1) Compute the rate of return on the plant and equipment, using the cost net of accumulated depreciation.
(2) Compute the rate of return using replacement cost net of accumulated depreciation on the replacement cost.

10. Depreciation and Rate of Return. The management of McLean and Elder, Inc., is concerned that the rate of return is inflated by computing the return with net income computed in mixed dollars of purchasing power and plant assets at original cost net of accumulated depreciation. For example, the rate of return on assets last year was 40%, computed with a net income of $60,000 and net plant assets of $150,000. The current value of the plant assets in their present condition has been estimated at $400,000, and net income revised to show current dollar revenue and expenses has been recomputed at $25,000.

Required: Compute the revised rate of return on the plant assets.

11. Leverage and Rate of Return. Wilda Kaier has inherited cash and properties through her grandfather's estate. Her interests and educational background have prepared her for a career in chemistry and biology. An opportunity has come to her attention for establishing a business in medical supplies. She estimates that sales each year at a conservative figure should amount to $600,000. A gross margin of 40% can be earned with annual costs of operation of $120,000. At the very least, sales should be no less than $500,000 with the same rate of gross margin and the same amount of operating expenses. Income tax is estimated at 40% of income before tax. The business will require assets of $700,000, and she plans to invest $400,000 of her own money and finance the balance by a bank loan with interest at 10% a year. Because she can earn an 8% return on her money through other investments, she wants a business investment that will yield at least 10% to compensate her for the additional risk.

Required:

(1) Does it appear that Kaier's investment will yield the required return objective on sales of $600,000? On sales of $500,000? Show computations.

(2) Compute the estimated rate of return on total assets under both sales estimates.

12. Current Asset Turnover. Video Displays, Inc., has enjoyed rapid growth with net income increasing from $125,000 in 1980 to $310,000 in 1981. Cost of goods sold and operating expenses excluding depreciation amounted to $920,000 in 1980 and to $4,250,000 in 1981. The average investment in current assets was $460,000 in 1980 and $1,080,000 in 1981. The company had some difficulties in meeting delivery schedules in 1981 and in making payments to creditors.

Required:

(1) Compute the rate of return on current assets for each year.
(2) Compute the current asset turnover for each year.
(3) What was the rate of return per turnover each year?
(4) Can you explain why the company may be having trouble in meeting delivery schedules and in making payments to creditors?

13. Measures of Liquidity. The management of Brookshire Mills, Inc., is concerned about the relatively low current ratio and the volume of low margin sales in relation to the current assets.

A summary of data from the financial report of 1980 and estimates for 1981 are given below.

	1980 Data	1981 Estimates
Cost of goods sold and operating expenses less depreciation...	$6,480,000	$5,150,000
Current assets..	3,240,000	2,480,000
Current liabilities...	1,850,000	1,220,000
Net income..	380,000	350,000

In 1981 the company plans to reduce sales volume and concentrate on relatively high profit margin items.

Required:

(1) Compute the current ratio, the current asset turnover, and the rate of return per turnover of current assets for 1980.
(2) Make the same computations for the 1981 estimates.
(3) Comment on changes observed in the current ratio, the current asset turnover, and the rate of return per turnover.

14. Turnovers and the Operating Cycle. In planning a short-term loan policy, the president of Littleton Company would like to have an approximate idea of how long it takes to convert inventories to cash.

Data taken from the records indicate that the average cost of materials used during the year amounted to $6,900,000 and that an average materials inventory was $230,000. Finished goods in stock averaged $1,600,000, and the cost of goods sold was $16,000,000.

Credit sales for the year were $24,000,000, and the average accounts receivable balance was $1,200,000.

Required:

(1) Compute both of the inventory turnovers and the turnover of accounts receivable.
(2) How many days should it take on the average to convert materials into cash? (Use a 360-day year.)

15. Net Income and Fixed Charges. Margate Chemical Company must make substantial payments each year on equipment it leases from others. In addition, there is interest to be paid on debt each year. Both the company and its creditors are concerned about whether or not the company can meet these obligations each year inasmuch as sales volume has been decreasing.

A condensed income statement is given for the past three years:

	1981	1980	1979
Net sales	$620,000	$870,000	$960,000
Cost of goods sold	$330,000	$480,000	$520,000
Operating expenses excluding rent	130,000	145,000	175,000
Rent expense	50,000	50,000	50,000
Interest expense	80,000	80,000	80,000
Income tax	12,000	46,000	54,000
Total expenses	$602,000	$801,000	$879,000
Net income	$ 18,000	$ 69,000	$ 81,000

Required: Determine how many times the fixed charges were earned for each of the three years.

PROBLEMS

13-1. Changes and Rate of Return. The board of directors of Symonds Company plans to substitute a new product line for one of the present lines. By doing this and by making use of more leverage, the directors believe that the rate of return on stockholders' equity can be improved.

Data from the past year are given along with estimated data for the current year with changes made:

	Past Year	Estimated, Current Year
Net income	$ 322,000	$ 352,000
Net sales	4,600,000	4,400,000
Average total assets	6,900,000	5,280,000
Average stockholders' equity	4,300,000	3,500,000

Required:

(1) Compute the rate of return on sales, the asset turnover, the rate of return on assets, and the rate of return on stockholders' equity for both years. (Round to third decimal place.)
(2) Does it appear that the objective of the board of directors will be realized? Point out any negative factors that should be considered.

13-2. Rate of Return and Equity Relationships. A consultant for Squiers Machine Company states that an investment in the company would be relatively

safe, but it would yield little more than government bonds. Financial summaries from the last annual report are given to prove the point:

Net income	$ 190,000
Net sales	3,800,000
Average total assets	2,800,000
Average stockholders' equity	2,100,000

The consultant proposes that excessive inventory investments be cut drasti-
cally. With proper planning, deliveries can be made promptly without carrying
large stocks of merchandise. Furthermore, prices should be increased selectively with low margin lines being discontinued. Also, the dividend policy
should be more liberal. With a large accumulation of earnings, there is a risk of
an additional income tax on excessive accumulated earnings. Finally, the consultant recommends that more debt be added to the equity structure and
states that this can be done without incurring too much risk.

A plan is proposed that should yield the following results by next year:

Net income	$ 340,000
Net sales	4,000,000
Average total assets	2,200,000
Average stockholders' equity	1,000,000

Required:

(1) Compute the rate of return on net sales, on average total assets, and
on average stockholders' equity for the past year.
(2) What was the stockholders' proportionate interest in total equity last
year?
(3) Compute the estimated rate of return on net sales, on average total
assets, and on average stockholders' equity as contemplated by the
consultant.
(4) If the consultant's proposal is accepted, what will be the stockholders'
proportionate interest in total equity?

13-3. Rate-of-Return Relationships and Net Income per Share. Summarized
financial data for Mauriello Finishing Company as of June 30, 1980, follow:

Total assets	$4,800,000
Total liabilities	$2,400,000
Net income for the fiscal year ended June 30, 1980	$ 240,000
Number of shares of common stock outstanding	100,000
Net sales	$6,000,000

At the beginning of July 1980, a product line that proved to be unprofitable
was dropped. Assets used to support this line have been sold.

A new product line has been added to replace the old line. It is estimated
that the average asset investment to support this line wil amount to $1,500,000.
Part of the cost will be financed by the issuance of 20,000 shares of common
stock at a price of $50 per share. The balance will be financed by notes pay-
able. The new product line is expected to add $200,000 to net income during
the fiscal year ending June 30, 1981. Sales of the new product line are estimated at $2,000,000.

During the fiscal year ended June 30, 1981, the company estimates that the
net income without including the new product line will amount to $300,000 on
net sales of $3,000,000. Total assets at June 30, 1981, have been estimated at
$6,800,000. No dividends are to be distributed to the stockholders.

Required:

(1) Compute the rate of return on sales, the asset turnover, the rate of return on the assets, and the rate of return on the stockholders' equity for the fiscal year ended June 30, 1980. (Use assets and stockholders' equity at the end of the fiscal year and round computations to the third decimal place.)

(2) Compute the estimated rate of return on sales, the asset turnover, the rate of return on the asset investment, and the rate of return on the stockholders' equity for the fiscal year ended June 30, 1981. (Use assets and stockholders' equity at the end of the fiscal year and round computations to the third decimal place.)

(3) Compare the net income per share for the year ended June 30, 1980, with the estimated net income per share for the year ended June 30, 1981.

(4) On the basis of your analysis, would you accept the new product line?

13-4. Rates of Return by Segments. Three product lines are produced by Gavin Instruments Company in separate operating divisions. The president of the company is concerned that Division 3 is not earning a sufficient rate of return. Data to support this belief are given below.

	Product Divisions		
	1	2	3
Sales..	$620,000	$760,000	$530,000
Cost of goods sold...............................	$280,000	$515,000	$290,000
Operating expenses..............................	135,000	165,000	180,000
Total expenses.................................	$415,000	$680,000	$470,000
Net income...	$205,000	$ 80,000	$ 60,000
Supporting asset investment..................	$820,000	$400,000	$600,000
Rate of return on assets........................	25%	20%	10%

Closer examination reveals that included in the operating expenses are corporate expenses of $250,000 common to the total operation. Of this amount, $100,000 was allocated to Division 3 with the balance divided equally between Divisions 1 and 2. The supporting asset investment includes assets that are not directly attributable to the operation of any particular division. Assets in the amount of $150,000 that are common to the total operation have been allocated to Division 3 with $200,000 in common assets equally divided between the other two divisions.

Required: From the information furnished, recompute the rate of return for each division and for the total operation. Why was the rate of return for Division 3, as originally computed, relatively low?

13-5. Evaluating the Asset Base. When Lois Demery joined Ziegler Products, Inc., as a member of the board of directors, she was informed that the company earned an exceptionally good rate of return on assets and stockholders' equity. Data taken from last year's annual report were presented to support this statement and are shown at the top of the next page.

Demery noted that the plant assets were obtained many years ago and that no replacements had been made in recent years.

She requests information with respect to how the assets, stockholders' equity, and net income would appear if all items were shown on a current-

Current assets..	$230,000
Plant assets, net of accumulated depreciation.............................	540,000
Total assets...	$770,000
Stockholders' equity..	$500,000
Net income..	$160,000

dollar basis. A report of this type has been prepared, and the results are given below.

Current assets..	$ 340,000
Plant assets, net of accumulated depreciation......................	1,360,000
Total assets	$1,700,000
Stockholders' equity	$1,200,000
Net income..	$ 90,000

Required:

(1) Compute the rate of return on total assets and on stockholders' equity from the original data.

(2) Compute the rate of return on total assets and on stockholders' equity after making adjustments.

(3) Comment on any reasons for differences in the rates of return.

13-6. Comparison of Rates of Return. Plain Products, Inc., sells essential products at a relatively low profit margin on sales while Luxury Company handles much less sales volume but earns a much better return on the sales dollar.

Summarized financial statements for the two companies are given for 1980:

Income Statement
For the Year Ended June 30, 1980

	Plain Products, Inc.	Luxury Company
Net sales...	$5,600,000	$1,760,000
Cost of goods sold and expenses.........................	5,152,000	1,232,000
Net income...	$ 448,000	$ 528,000

Balance Sheet
June 30, 1980

	Plain Products, Inc.	Luxury Company
Assets		
Current assets...	$2,060,000	$3,180,000
Plant assets	1,680,000	3,120,000
Total assets	$3,740,000	$6,300,000
Equities		
Current liabilities	$ 810,000	$1,200,000
Long-term debt...	500,000	3,000,000
Stockholders' equity..	2,430,000	2,100,000
Total equities..	$3,740,000	$6,300,000

Required:

(1) Compare the two companies by computing the following percentages and ratios:
   (a) Rate of return on sales.
   (b) Rate of return on assets.
   (c) Rate of return on stockholders' equity.
   (d) Asset turnover.

(2) Which company earns a better rate of return for the stockholders? Point out factors that help to enhance the rate of return for the stockholders.

13-7. Measures of Liquidity. A financial analyst expresses concern that Opelika Products, Inc., is attempting to handle a large volume of business without a proportionate increase in a supporting investment of current assets. With insufficient working capital, the company may be forced to borrow more to support the increased scale of operation and may overextend itself.

Financial data for the past three years are summarized below:

	1981	1980	1979
Current assets:			
Cash	$ 610,000	$ 680,000	$ 750,000
Accounts receivable	580,000	570,000	340,000
Inventories	1,070,000	1,230,000	1,240,000
Total current assets	$2,260,000	$2,480,000	$2,330,000
Total current liabilities	$1,020,000	$1,350,000	$1,240,000
Cost of goods sold and operating expenses excluding depreciation	$4,560,000	$2,600,000	$2,500,000
Net income	$ 650,000	$ 480,000	$ 370,000

Required: Compute relationships that will give an indication of the trend in liquidity and point out various factors that should be considered. (Do not average data.)

13-8. Inventory and Accounts Receivable Turnovers. On July 1, the creditors of Spiral Products, Inc., extended until November 1 the terms for payment of amounts due them and requested that cash of $800,000 be raised by that time.

The company had an inventory of materials on hand at July 1 costing $200,000 and an inventory of finished goods costing $162,000. There was no work in process on that date.

Data from past operations indicate that it takes 60 days to convert materials into finished products. Combined labor and overhead required for conversion are equal to 80% of the materials cost, and cash is available for the required labor and overhead payments. The manufacturing cost of the product is equal to 60% of the selling price.

Last year the company reported net credit sales of $6,200,000 and had an average accounts receivable balance of $775,000. After the product is manufactured, it takes about 15 days to deliver the product to customers.

There were no accounts receivable outstanding on July 1, and all cash had been paid over to creditors to reduce past indebtedness with the exception of the cash needed to pay labor and overhead costs for processing inventory and the cash needed for operating expenses until November 1.

Required: From the information given, does it appear that the creditors' terms can be met by November 1? Show computations and comment on the situation as you see it. (Use a 360-day year.)

13-9. Evaluation of Company Progress. A new management group assumed control of Morgan and Gardner, Inc., late in 1980. The former management was criticized for being too venturesome and putting the company in a position where it could be forced into bankruptcy. The new management is trying to obtain more balance in the asset and equity structure with reasonable profitability.

Summarized financial statements for 1980 and 1981 are given below:

Morgan and Gardner, Inc.
Income Statement
For the Years Ended December 31, 1981 and 1980
(In thousands of dollars)

	1981	1980
Net sales..	$6,380	$7,840
Cost of goods sold......................................	$3,450	$5,230
Operating expenses....................................	960	1,040
	$4,410	$6,270
Income from operations.............................	$1,970	$1,570
Interest expense...	130	210
Income before income tax...........................	$1,840	$1,360
Income tax	730	540
Net income..	$1,110	$ 820

Morgan and Gardner, Inc.
Balance Sheet
December 31, 1981 and 1980
(In thousands of dollars)

	1981	1980
Assets		
Current assets:		
Cash..	$1,740	$ 460
Marketable securities................................	1,000	100
Accounts receivable..................................	470	330
Inventories..	1,290	1,470
Total current assets	$4,500	$2,360
Plant and machinery, net of accumulated depreciation	2,370	1,660
Total assets	$6,870	$4,020
Equities		
Current liabilities:		
Accounts payable......................................	$ 950	$ 970
Other amounts currently due.....................	810	950
Total current liabilities	$1,760	$1,920
Notes payable, 10%, due June 30, 1990..........................	400	700
Capital stock, $10 par value.......................	1,000	200
Paid-in capital in excess of par	1,700	300
Retained earnings......................................	2,010	900
Total equities..	$6,870	$4,020

Required:

(1) Evaluate the changes made in 1981 by computing the following amounts, ratios, and percentages for both years. Assume all sales are on credit. (Use asset and equity amounts without averaging.)
   (a) Operating rate of return on net sales.
   (b) Net income as a percentage of total assets.
   (c) Net income as a percentage of stockholders' equity.
   (d) Current ratio and acid-test ratio.
   (e) Turnover of accounts receivable and inventory.
   (f) Earnings per share.
   (g) Book value per share.
(2) From your analysis, does it appear that the management has taken steps to bring the company into a more secure position?

13-10. Comprehensive Analysis. George Kalmbach, the president and principal stockholder of Sky-Vue Products, Inc., has had phenomenal success in the sale of a line of quality china that is distinctively designed. The company has been in business for only two years, and Kalmbach has been amazed at the tremendous market acceptance. At the same time, he needs more capital to expand the operation to meet customer demand. He has approached you as vice-president of Benefit Finance Company to extend a line of short-term credit.

Summarized financial statements for the past two years are given below and on the next page.

Sky-Vue Products, Inc.
Income Statement
For the Years Ended June 30, 1981 and 1980
(In thousands of dollars)

	1981	1980
Net sales	$8,322	$1,260
Cost of sales	$5,825	$ 756
*Operating expenses and interest	1,587	189
Income tax	455	158
	$7,867	$1,103
Net income	$ 455	$ 157

*Includes depreciation expense of $76,000 in 1980 and $163,000 in 1981.

Required:

(1) From the information given, compute for each year the relationships that will reveal earning power:
   (a) Rate of return on net sales.
   (b) Rate of return on total assets at the end of each year.
   (c) Rate of return on stockholders' equity at the end of each year.
   (d) Asset turnover.
(2) From the information given, compute for each year the relationships that will reveal relative liquidity and safety of investment:
   (a) Current ratio.
   (b) Accounts receivable turnover.

Sky-Vue Products, Inc.
Balance Sheet
June 30, 1981 and 1980
(In thousands of dollars)

Assets	1981	1980
Cash...	$ 153	$ 93
Accounts receivable, net	1,387	126
Inventory	485	63
*Buildings and furnishings, net of accumulated depreciation.....	1,901	1,704
Total assets	$3,926	$1,986

Equities		
Accounts payable..	$ 657	$ 143
Short-term bank loans...	486	67
Accrued expenses...	171	19
Mortgage loan	1,500	1,100
Capital stock...	500	500
Retained earnings	612	157
Total equities..	$3,926	$1,986

*Accumulated depreciation of $76,000 at June 30, 1980, and $239,000 at June 30, 1981.

    (c) Inventory turnover.
    (d) Percentage of stockholders' equity to total equities.
(3) As a loan officer of Benefit Finance Company, comment on the relationships and make a comparison between years. What advice might you give to Kalmbach?

(For purposes of the problem, use year-end amounts. Do not attempt to average.)

13-11. Comprehensive Analysis. Financial statements are given below and on the next page for Sikorski Fastener Company.

Sikorski Fastener Company
Income Statement
For the Year Ended December 31, 1981

Net sales..	$5,800,000
Cost of goods sold...	$4,640,000
Operating expenses..	540,000
Interest expense...	128,500
Income tax..	245,750
	$5,554,250
Net Income...	$ 245,750

    The president of the company is concerned about the low rate of return and the increasing difficulty of meeting obligations as they become due. Customarily, the company has been paying dividends each year of $1 per share of stock; and this practice has been continued even though cash is badly needed to support business operations.
    Plans have already been made to introduce new product lines that will yield higher profit margins. In the meantime, plans for next year indicate that

Sikorski Fastener Company
Balance Sheet
December 31, 1981

Assets

Cash	$ 185,000
Accounts receivable	550,000
Inventories:	
Finished goods	775,000
Materials	250,000
Plant and equipment, net of accumulated depreciation	2,820,000
Total assets	$4,580,000

Equities

Current liabilities	$1,765,000
Long-term debt	1,450,000
Capital stock, $1 par value	200,000
Paid-in capital in excess of par	400,000
Retained earnings	765,000
Total equities	$4,580,000

net sales revenue can be increased by 5% as a result of a slight increase in sales volume. Furthermore, operating economies are expected to result in a decrease of $480,000 in the cost of goods sold. The other costs are expected to remain the same with income tax being equal to 50% of income before income tax.

Depreciation of $250,000 is included in cost of goods sold and operating expenses and is expected to be the same in the next year. Dividends of $1 per share are to be paid next year, and current liabilities are to be reduced by $200,000 if possible. Accounts receivable will remain at the same level, materials inventory is to be $760,000, and finished goods inventory is to be $700,000 at the end of next year. No additions or retirements of plant and equipment are to be made during the next year.

Required:

(1) Prepare an estimated income statement for the next year and a balance sheet at the end of the year.

(2) Determine the following relationships from the financial statements given for 1981:

(a) Rate of return on sales.
(b) Asset turnover.
(c) Rate of return on assets.
(d) Rate of return on stockholders' equity.
(e) Percentage of stockholders' equity to total equity.
(f) Current ratio.
(g) Number of times that interest is earned.

(3) Determine the relationships required in (2) from the estimated financial statements for the next year. (Do not average data.)

(4) Does it appear that some improvement can be made in earning power and safety as a result of the relatively small increase in sales volume coupled with cost savings? Discuss.

13-12. Comprehensive Analysis. The president of Sedgwick Tools, Inc., had hoped for a better profit in 1981 than in 1980 as a result of a combination of increased sales volume and a reduction in production costs. Financial statements reveal that the profit did not increase very much, and the president would like to receive a report that would provide a summary of some basic financial relationships. These relationships, hopefully, will reveal certain areas that should receive more attention in planning.

Income statements for 1980 and 1981 are given in summary form below.

Sedgwick Tools, Inc.
Income Statement
For the Years Ended September 30, 1981 and 1980
(In thousands of dollars)

	1981	1980
Net sales	$1,930	$1,750
Cost of sales	$1,254	$1,225
Operating expenses and interest	390	262
Income tax	143	132
	$1,787	$1,619
Net income	$ 143	$ 131

The balance sheet at the end of each fiscal year has been restated on an average basis to provide a basis for analysis. The revised balance sheet is given below.

Sedgwick Tools, Inc.
Balance Sheet (as revised)
September 30, 1981 and 1980
(In thousands of dollars)

Assets	1981	1980
Current assets:		
Cash	$ 231	$ 212
Accounts receivable, net of uncollectibles	320	290
Inventories	251	306
Total current assets	$ 802	$ 808
Plant and equipment, net of accumulated depreciation	950	980
Total assets	$1,752	$1,788

Equities		
Current liabilities:		
Accounts payable and accrued expenses	$ 637	$ 702
Long term notes payable	300	300
Stockholders' equity:		
Capital stock	500	500
Retained earnings	315	286
Total equities	$1,752	$1,788

Required:

(1) Compute the percentage of each classification on the income statements to net sales. Comment on changes in the relationships between the two years.

(2) Compute the rate of return on assets and on stockholders' equity for each year. Determine the asset turnover for each year.

(3) Determine the accounts receivable turnover for each year. Does it appear that accounts receivable are being collected more promptly?

(4) Determine the inventory turnover for each year. Does it appear that inventory investment is being reduced relative to sales activity?

(5) Determine the current ratio for each year from the data given. Comment.

(6) Determine the percentages of current assets and plant and equipment to total assets for each year. Also determine the percentage of stockholders' equity to total equity for each year. Comment.

14

TRACING THE FLOW
OF NET WORKING CAPITAL
AND CASH

In Chapter 13 a great deal of attention was paid to the profitability of the firm as measured by the relationship between net income and assets and between net income and stockholders' equity. It was also indicated that in order to remain profitable a firm must have sufficient current resources to maintain the volume of operations and to discharge debt when it becomes due. In this chapter attention is directed to two important flow statements that can help management to plan and control the inflow and outflow of the current resources that are vital to company operation. These statements are:

1. *The Statement of Sources and Uses of Net Working Capital* — Measures the inflows and outflows of net working capital that result from any type of activity.
2. *The Statement of Cash Receipts and Disbursements* — Measures the inflows and outflows of cash that result from any type of activity.

DESCRIPTION AND EVALUATION OF THE STATEMENTS

The two statements are very similar, differing only with respect to the detail provided. The statement of sources and uses of net working capital gives a broad perspective, showing how the total current assets minus the total current liabilities have flowed in and out of the business during the fiscal period. This statement is more useful for longer-term planning, periods of six months to a year or more, when broad approximations are acceptable. In contrast, the statement of cash receipts and disbursements deals specifically with the inflow and outflow of cash and is more appropriate for short-term planning from month to month.

For long-range planning, the information furnished by a statement of sources and uses of net working capital is sufficient. For example, management may want to know if enough net working capital will be available two years from now to make a payment on long-term debt. It may not be possible or even necessary to make an exact projection of the cash flow for two years. Current resources can generally be converted into cash for repayment in a relatively short time, and an estimate of net working capital will serve the purpose for a longer range forecast.

In contrast, a statement of cash receipts and disbursements tends to be more useful in short-run analysis. Reliable projections of cash receipts and disbursements can generally be made for the immediate future but not for years in advance. The treasurer of a company, for example, may project cash collections expected from accounts receivable over the month. During periods when the cash outflow for purchases and operating expenses is expected to exceed the cash inflow, arrangements may be made to borrow on short-term notes. In periods when the cash receipts are substantially larger than cash disbursements, plans may be made to liquidate the short-term notes and to invest any excess cash in temporary investments.

Sometimes the statement of sources and uses of net working capital is extended to include shifts within the noncurrent balance sheet categories. For example, capital stock may be issued in exchange for plant and equipment. Net working capital is not affected by this type of transaction, but there is a significant change in the financial structure. This extended statement is called a *statement of changes in financial position*. The American Institute of Certified Public Accountants recommends that a statement of changes in financial position be presented as a basic financial statement for each period in which an income statement is presented.[1] This recommendation governs financial reporting but does not bind management in the preparation of reports and other data that are to be used exclusively for internal purposes.

THE SIGNIFICANCE OF NET WORKING CAPITAL FLOWS

An analysis of how net working capital is provided and used can be applied in many ways. Some of the more important applications are listed as follows:

---

[1] *Opinions of the Accounting Principles Board, No. 19,* "Reporting Changes in Financial Position" (New York: American Institute of Certified Public Accountants, 1971), par. 7.

1. It may suggest ways in which the net working capital position can be improved.
2. It focuses attention on what resources are available for the acquisition of plant assets or other investments.
3. It can help in the selection of the best investment alternative.
4. It can be used in deciding how to finance the acquisition of plant assets and other long-term investments.
5. It can be used in planning for the retirement of long-term debt.
6. It can also serve in the planning of a sound dividend policy.

A statement of the sources and uses of net working capital tells management where net working capital was obtained in the past and how it was put to use. With this background, management can then make plans for the future. Estimates can be made of future net working capital flows that can be applied to the retirement of long-term debt, to the expansion or replacement of plant facilities, or to the payment of dividends.

Profit is very important, but there are other elements to be considered in a successful business operation. For example, a company may earn an adequate return on investment, but at the same time the net working capital position may deteriorate, resulting in serious liquidity problems. With a large proportion of the resources frozen in the form of plant assets or other long-term investments, the company may have to increase its debt excessively to obtain liquid resources.

Often a company that is growing rapidly is faced with a shortage of net working capital. Profit may be increasing, but the company may not have the liquid resources that are required to expand plant facilities to meet increased sales demand. To obtain liquid resources, the company may borrow heavily. As a result, the interest of the owners is proportionately smaller with increased risk in the event of business reverses.

NET WORKING CAPITAL FLOWS

A statement of sources and uses of net working capital indicates how net working capital is acquired and used. A company in the normal course of events has transactions that change net working capital and others that have no effect on net working capital. The transactions may be classified in the following manner:

1. Transactions that result in an increase or decrease in the net current balance sheet accounts:
   (a) Certain income statement transactions.
   (b) Transactions that affect both current and noncurrent balance sheet accounts.
2. Transactions that do not increase or decrease the net current balance sheet accounts:
   (a) Shifts within the current balance sheet structure that have no effect on the net balance.
   (b) Transactions that affect only the noncurrent balance sheet accounts.

The transactions classified under (1), on the previous page, change net working capital and are explained in a statement of sources and uses of net working capital. For example, sales normally increase cash or accounts receivable while expenses such as salaries, rent, insurance, and taxes either decrease cash or increase accounts payable. Hence, such income statement transactions either increase or reduce net working capital.

Transactions affecting both current and noncurrent balance sheet accounts also change net working capital. Cash (part of net working capital) is increased by borrowing on a long-term note (noncurrent balance sheet account). Conversely, net working capital is reduced by the retirement of long-term debt or by the acquisition of the company's own stock (treasury stock).

The transactions in classification (2) do not affect net working capital. For example, cash may be collected on accounts receivable, or accounts payable may be converted to short-term notes payable. Transactions such as these cause shifts within the net working capital structure but do not increase or decrease the net balance.

There are transactions that affect only the noncurrent balance sheet accounts. Depreciation expense, for example, reduces plant assets. Net working capital is neither increased nor decreased. Hence, in determining the net inflow of net working capital from operations, depreciation expense is added to net income to reverse the effect of the depreciation deduction.

Shifts may also occur in the noncurrent area. Long-term notes payable may be exchanged for capital stock, or a long-term investment may be acquired by issuing capital stock. These transactions do not increase or decrease net working capital. As stated earlier, the effect of these transactions must be reported on a statement of changes in financial position, but not on a statement of sources and uses of net working captial.

Sources of Net Working Capital

Some of the most common sources of net working capital are:

1. Operations.
2. Investment by the owners.
3. Issuance of long-term debt.
4. Sale of long-term investments.
5. Sale of plant assets.

Changes in all noncurrent balance sheet accounts are analyzed to determine their effect on the net working capital balance. Net working capital is normally increased as a result of transactions that (1) decrease noncurrent assets or (2) increase noncurrent equities. For example, long-term investments or plant assets can be sold to provide additional net working capital. Net working capital can also be increased by long-term borrowing or by issuing additional shares of stock in return for cash, other current assets, or in return for cancellation of short-term debt. In any given fiscal period, a company obtains its net working capital from many different sources.

Ordinarily, profitable operation is expected to be the main source of net working capital. In the long run a successful business acquires plant assets and investments, pays long-term debt, and distributes dividends to the stockholders from the net working capital generated as a result of rendering goods and services to customers.

The following summary shows the effect of certain income statement items on net working capital.

INCOME STATEMENT ITEM	CHANGES IN ASSETS AND LIABILITIES	EFFECT ON NET WORKING CAPITAL
Sales	Increases accounts receivable or cash	Increases net working capital
Gain on sale of plant assets	Part of increase of net working capital arising from sale of plant assets	Excluded from net working capital received from operations. (The *total* amount received from the sale is reported separately.)
Cost of goods sold	Decreases inventory	Decreases net working capital
Wages, rent, repairs, and other operating expenses that are currently paid	Decreases cash or prepayments or increases current liabilities	Decreases net working capital
Depreciation, depletion, and amortization	Decreases plant assets or intangibles	Does not affect net working capital

As shown below, the net income is restated to reflect a flow of net working capital from operations by adding or deducting items that do not affect the net working capital flow from operations.

Net income	$XXX
Add depreciation	XXX
	$XXX
Less gain on sale of plant assets	XXX
Net working capital flow from operations	$XXX

Depreciation, for example, is offset against revenue in the determination of net income or loss but is in no way related to net working capital. Net income is closed to the owners' equity at the end of the fiscal period and is lower than it would have been if depreciation had not been deducted. Therefore, depreciation has reduced a noncurrent equity (the owners' equity) and has reduced a noncurrent asset (the plant asset) with no effect on net working capital.

Sometimes it is said that depreciation provides net working capital that may be used for expansion or for the replacement of plant assets. This is not true. The net working capital is provided by the revenue from sales, not from depreciation. Depreciation, unlike many operating expenses, does not require the use of net working capital. The net increase or decrease in net working capital from operations is generally computed by adding depreciation and other expenses not requiring the use of net working capital to the net income or subtracting them from the net loss.

Uses of Net Working Capital.

Some of the more common ways in which net working capital is put to use are:

1. Acquisition of investments, plant assets, or other noncurrent assets.
2. The retirement of long-term debt or the redemption of an issue of capital stock.
3. The acquisition of treasury stock.
4. The payment of dividends.
5. Involuntary losses on operations.

Net working capital is normally decreased as a result of transactions that (1) increase noncurrent assets or (2) decrease noncurrent equities. For example, if cash is used to purchase plant assets, the noncurrent asset is increased and net working capital is decreased. If long-term debt is retired by using available cash, net working capital is also reduced.

Operations are not always profitable. In fact, an operating loss may be of such magnitude that there may even be a decrease in net working capital from operating activity after the depreciation and other items that have no effect on net working capital have been applied in computing the net working capital flow from operations. A short example is given below:

Net loss on operations	$(115,000)
Add depreciation	21,000
Net working capital reduction from operations	$(94,000)

In still other circumstances a net loss may be reported; yet when depreciation or other charges not requiring net working capital are considered, there may be a net inflow of net working capital from operations as shown below:

Net loss on operations	$(8,000)
Add depreciation	21,000
Net working capital provided by operations	$ 13,000

A COMPREHENSIVE ILLUSTRATION — SOURCES AND USES OF NET WORKING CAPITAL

A statement of sources and uses of net working capital can often be prepared quite easily from comparative balance sheets, income statement data for the period, and supplementary data. The sources and uses of net working capital analysis can be made in a three-step procedure as follows:

1. Compute the increase or decrease in net working capital.
2. Determine the net working capital provided by operations.
3. Analyze the changes in the noncurrent assets and equities for the effect of the changes on net working capital.

Step 1 computes the increase or decrease in net working capital, and Steps 2 and 3 explain how this increase or decrease is obtained.

A comparative balance sheet as of December 31, 1980 and 1981, and an income statement for 1981 are given for Myron Products, Inc., below and at the top of page 418.

Myron Products, Inc.
Comparative Balance Sheet
December 31, 1981 and 1980

	1981	1980	Changes Debit	Changes Credit
Current assets:				
Cash	$ 22,100	$ 18,300		
Marketable securities	14,000	15,000		
Accounts receivable	43,200	44,900		
Inventories	76,200	67,100		
Total current assets	$155,500	$145,300		
Current liabilities:				
Accounts payable	$ 10,300	$ 11,500		
Wages payable	8,500	8,100		
Estimated income tax payable	56,100	52,400		
Dividends payable	6,000	5,000		
Total current liabilities	$ 80,900	$ 77,000		
Net working capital	$ 74,600	$ 68,300	$ 6,300	
Investment in Haven, Inc.	26,000	—0—	26,000	
Plant assets, net of depreciation	82,000	64,000	18,000	
	$182,600	$132,300		
Less: Long-term notes	$ 25,000	$ 15,000		$10,000
Bonds payable	—0—	35,000	35,000	
	$ 25,000	$ 50,000		
Stockholders' equity	$157,600	$ 82,300		
Detail of stockholders' equity:				
Capital received from stockholders	$ 60,000	$ 15,000		45,000
Retained earnings	97,600	67,300		30,300
Total stockholders' equity	$157,600	$ 82,300	$85,300	$85,300

Myron Products, Inc.
Income Statement
For the Year Ended December 31, 1981

Sales and other income:	
Net sales	$326,400
Gain on sale of equipment	3,200
	$329,600
Costs and expenses:	
Cost of goods sold	$149,800
Operating expenses, including depreciation of $7,000	57,800
Interest expense	4,000
Income tax	56,100
	$267,700
Net income	$ 61,900

Additional data are given below.

(1) Myron Products, Inc., paid $26,000 in 1981 for an investment in the stock of Haven, Inc.
(2) Details on the plant assets follow:

	1981	1980
Plant assets	$96,000	$76,000
Accumulated depreciation	14,000	12,000
Plant assets, net of accumulated depreciation	$82,000	$64,000

During the year equipment costing $12,000 with accumulated depreciation of $5,000 was sold.

(3) No payments were made on the long-term notes in 1981.
(4) The bonds payable were converted to capital stock.
(5) Additional shares of stock were issued to the shareholders in 1981 as a dividend. The stock dividend amounted to $10,000. Cash dividends amounting to $21,600 were also declared.
(6) A statement of changes in retained earnings is summarized below:

Balance of retained earnings, beginning of 1981	$ 67,300
Net income, 1981	61,900
	$129,200
Less: Stock dividends	$ 10,000
Cash dividends	21,600
	$ 31,600
Balance of retained earnings, end of 1981	$ 97,600

SCHEDULE OF CHANGES IN NET WORKING CAPITAL

The first step in preparing a statment of sources and uses of net working capital is to determine the increase or decrease in net working capital. If detail with respect to the specific account changes within the net working capital category is desired, a schedule of changes in net working capital can be prepared as follows:

Myron Products, Inc.
Schedule of Changes in Net Working Capital
For the Year Ended December 31, 1981

| | December 31 | | Net Working Capital | |
	1981	1980	Increase	Decrease
Current assets:				
Cash	$ 22,100	$ 18,300	$ 3,800	
Marketable securities	14,000	15,000		$ 1,000
Accounts receivable	43,200	44,900		1,700
Inventories	76,200	67,100	9,100	
Total current assets	$155,500	$145,300		
Current liabilities:				
Accounts payable	$ 10,300	$ 11,500	1,200	
Wages payable	8,500	8,100		400
Estimated income tax payable	56,100	52,400		3,700
Dividends payable	6,000	5,000		1,000
Total current liabilities	$ 80,900	$ 77,000		
Net working capital	$ 74,600	$ 68,300		
Increase in net working capital				6,300
Total			$14,100	$14,100

Net working capital is increased by increases in the current assets and is decreased by decreases in the current assets. The opposite is true for changes in current liabilities. The current liabilities are a negative factor in the computation of net working capital. Therefore, an increase in a current liability decreases net working capital, and a decrease in a current liability increases net working capital. In this illustration, net working capital has increased by $6,300. The next two steps of the analysis explain how net working capital was provided and used to bring about the net increase of $6,300.

Net Working Capital from Operations

Net income and net working capital from operations normally are not the same figure. As explained earlier, there are transactions that affect net income that do not affect net working capital. The net income for 1981 of $61,900 includes the effect of a depreciation deduction of $7,000. Since depreciation does not reduce net working capital, the effect of the deduction is removed by adding it back to net income.

The gain on the sale of equipment does represent an inflow of net working capital, but it is deducted from net income in the computation of the net inflow of net working capital from operations. The total amount received from the sale of the equipment (the recovery of the net book value of the asset and the gain) is reported as one item on the sources and uses of net working capital statement. If the gain were included in both the net working capital flow from operations and the net working capital received from the sale of the asset, double-counting would occur. The double-counting is avoided by deducting the gain in computing the flow of net working capital from operations.

Net income..	$61,900
Add depreciation..	7,000
	$68,900
Less gain on sale of equipment...	3,200
Net working capital flow from operations............................	$65,700

If there is a loss on the sale of a noncurrent asset, the loss is added to net income in calculating the flow of the net working capital from operations. Although the loss is a deduction in computing net income, it does not reduce net working capital. The total amount received from the sale of the asset is reported as one item on the statement of sources and uses of net working capital.

Analysis of Noncurrent Items

The final step in the analysis is to explain the effect of the changes in the noncurrent balance sheet items.

(1) Investment in Haven, Inc., +**$26,000**.

The investment was increased by $26,000; and, with no information to the contrary, it can be assumed that net working capital of $26,000 was used to acquire this investment.

(2) Plant assets (gross), +$20,000.

The detail on the plant assets shows that the plant assets before deducting accumulated depreciation increased by $20,000 ($96,000 − $76,000). It is stated that equipment costing $12,000 was sold. This decreased plant assets, yet the assets increased by a net amount of $20,000. Apparently plant assets costing $32,000 were acquired.

Cost of assets acquired...	**$32,000**
Less cost of assets sold...	12,000
Net increase in assets..	$20,000

In short, add the $12,000 deduction resulting from the sale to the net increase to obtain the cost of acquisition, $32,000. The net book value of the equipment sold was $7,000 ($12,000 cost − $5,000 accumulated depreciation). The equipment was sold at a gain of **$3,200**. Hence, **$10,200** was the net amount received from the sale of equipment.

Assume that the detail on plant assets is not given. The increase in net plant assets of $18,000 ($82,000 − $64,000) can be converted to a gross increase of $20,000 by analysis of the changes in accumulated depreciation. Then analysis for the net working capital effect can proceed as usual. Changes in accumulated depreciation can be accounted for as follows:

Depreciation expense (increases accumulated depreciation)...	**$7,000**
Less accumulated depreciation removed by sale of equipment	5,000
Net increase in accumulated depreciation	$2,000

With a net increase of $2,000 in accumulated depreciation, the net plant asset increase of $18,000 is $2,000 less than the gross increase of $20,000.

(3) Long-term notes, **+$10,000**.

No payments were made during the year, and the increase of $10,000 indicates that this amount was provided by long-term borrowing.

(4) Bonds payable, −$35,000.

The bonds payable were converted to capital stock with no effect on net working capital. There has been a change in the financial structure, and this will be revealed on a statement of changes in financial position.

(5) Capital stock, +$45,000.

The conversion of bonds payable in the amount of $35,000 and the stock dividend of $10,000 account for the increase of $45,000. There is no effect on net working capital. The stock dividend is not viewed as a substantive change in financial structure and does not have to be reported on a statement of changes in financial position. However, the conversion of bonds to stock should be reported on such a statement.

(6) Retained earnings, +$30,300.

The statement of changes in retained earnings shows that cash dividends of **$21,600** were declared. These dividends reduced net working capital.

Statement of Sources and Uses of Net Working Capital

The results of the analysis are incorporated in the following statement:

Myron Products, Inc.
Statement of Sources and Uses of Net Working Capital
For the Year Ended December 31, 1981

Sources of net working capital:		
Operating activity:		
Net income	$61,900	
Add depreciation	7,000	
	$68,900	
Less gain on sale of equipment	3,200	
Net working capital from operations		$65,700
Sale of equipment		10,200
Issuance of long-term notes		10,000
Total sources		$85,900
Uses of net working capital:		
Acquisition of investment in Haven, Inc.		$26,000
Acquisition of plant assets		32,000
Dividends payable in cash		21,600
Total uses		$79,600
Net increase in net working capital		$ 6,300

Statement of Changes in Financial Position

The statement of sources and uses of net working capital can be expanded to a statement of changes in financial position, as shown below, by including the changes in noncurrent assets and equities that do not pass through net working capital. In this illustration bonds payable of $35,000 were converted to capital stock. Net working capital was not affected, but there was an overall change in the financial structure. For the sake of convenience this transaction can be described and labeled both as a source and a use since it balances out with no effect on net working capital. It is treated as if two separate transactions occured; that is, net working capital was increased by the issuance of stock, the funds from which were used to redeem the bonds payable.

Myron Products, Inc.
Statement of Changes in Financial Position
For the Year Ended December 31, 1981

Sources of funds:		
Operating activity:		
Net income...	$61,900	
Add depreciation...	7,000	
	$68,900	
Less gain on sale of equipment....................................	3,200	
Net working capital from operations		$ 65,700
Sale of equipment..		10,200
Issuance of long-term notes		10,000
Capital stock issued (direct issue in exchange for bonds payable retired)		35,000
Total sources		$120,900
Uses of funds:		
Acquisition of investment in Haven, Inc.		$ 26,000
Acquisition of plant assets..		32,000
Dividends payable in cash		21,600
Bonds payable redeemed (by issue of capital stock)		35,000
Total uses...		$114,600
Net increase in funds		$ 6,300

THE DEMAND FOR NET WORKING CAPITAL

The techniques of net working capital analysis can also be applied in the preparation of estimates of future sources and uses of net working capital. Planning net working capital flow is an important part of budgeting and is applied in making decisions as to whether or not certain investments should be made. A statement of estimated flow of net working capital can be prepared for future years and rearranged to show how much net working capital should be available after all required commitments have been met.

Assume, for example, that The Webb Company has estimated a net income of $1,350,000 for the year ending June 30, 1981. Depreciation and other charges not requiring the use of net working capital are estimated at $240,000 and are added back to obtain the expected flow of net working capital from operations of $1,590,000. Plans for dividends, the proceeds from the sale of plant assets, payment on debt, and a planned increase in net working capital are added or deducted to yield net working capital of $1,210,000 which is available for approved projects, projects under consideration, or projects still to be considered. The planned increase of net working capital for the year of $200,000 is treated as if it were a use on the estimated statement and is deducted to arrive at the net working capital of $1,210,000 that may be applied for other purposes. An estimated statement is shown below.

The Webb Company
Statement of Estimated Sources and Uses of
Net Working Capital
For the Year Ending June 30, 1981

Net income	$1,350,000
Add depreciation and other charges not requiring the use of net working capital	240,000
	$1,590,000
Less dividends	160,000
Estimated net working capital to be provided from operations after dividends	$1,430,000
Add proceeds from sale of plant assets	80,000
	$1,510,000
Less payment on debt	100,000
	$1,410,000
Planned increase (decrease) in net working capital	200,000
Net working capital available	$1,210,000
Demand for net working capital:	
Approved projects	$ 800,000
Unapproved projects	300,000
Amount still available	110,000
Total demand for net working captial	$1,210,000

CASH FLOW

In making plans for the more immediate future, management wants to know how much cash will be available to meet obligations to trade creditors, to pay bank loans, to pay dividends to stockholders, and to make payments on the currently maturing portion of long-term debt. With careful planning, there should be enough cash available for the payment of obligations on schedule; but the cash balance should not be excessive. Cash in itself is not productive and, if not immediately needed, should be employed to earn a return. Ordinarily excess cash will be invested in short-term securities that can be easily liquidated.

A statement of the flow of cash, known as a statement of cash receipts and disbursements, can be prepared by extending the steps used in the analysis of sources and uses of net working capital. Recall that changes in noncurrent assets and equities are analyzed for the effect on net working capital. These relationships are summarized in T-account form:

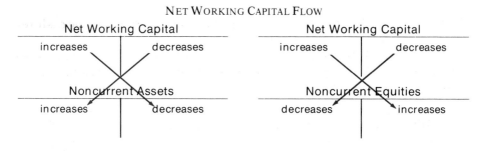

NET WORKING CAPITAL FLOW

To determine cash changes, the noncurrent assets and noncurrent equities are analyzed as before, and changes in current assets other than cash and changes in current liabilities are also analyzed. The following T-account summary illustrates how the changes in cash can be related to the changes in other balance sheet classifications.

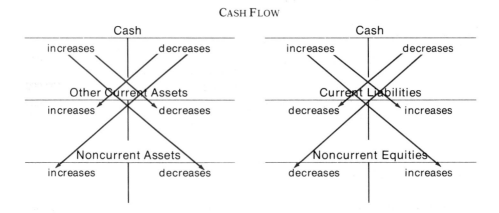

CASH FLOW

Cash and Operations

There is a close relationship between the revenues and expenses and the current assets and liabilities. The relationships are summarized on the next page.

CURRENT ASSETS	RELATED TO
Cash	Sales
Accounts receivable	
Inventory	Cost of goods sold
Prepaid expenses	Operating and other expenses, excluding depreciation and the amortization of other noncurrent items

CURRENT LIABILITIES	
Accounts payable	Cost of goods sold
Operating costs payable	Operating and other expenses, excluding depreciation and the amortization of other noncurrent items

In analysis, an income statement can be restated in terms of cash received and disbursed for each item:

(1) In the illustration given for Myron Products, Inc., accounts receivable decreased by $1,700. This indicates that collections on account were greater than sales revenue.

Sales	$326,400
Add decrease in accounts receivable	1,700
Collections from sales activity	$328,100

If accounts receivable had increased, the increase would be deducted from the current period sales to obtain the cash inflow.

In more complicated situations, increases or decreases in accounts receivable may arise not only from cash collection activity but also as a result of the write-off of uncollectible accounts. Assume that an accounts receivable account appears as follows:

Accounts Receivable

Beginning balance	50,000	Write-off of uncollectible	
Sales	1,000,000	accounts	20,000
		Cash collections (a)	**930,000**
		Ending balance	100,000
	1,050,000		1,050,000

Cash

Cash collections (a)	**930,000**	

Superficial analysis would indicate that the $50,000 increase in accounts receivable should be deducted from sales of $1,000,000 to obtain cash collections of $950,000. However, the write-off of uncollectible accounts reduced accounts receivable with no corresponding cash flow. The analysis should be made as shown at the top of page 426.

If there is estimated uncollectible accounts expense, it is recorded with a credit being made to the allowance for doubtful accounts. The

Accounts receivable, beginning balance........		$ 50,000
Sales..		1,000,000
Potential cash collections..............................		$1,050,000
Less:		
Write-off of uncollectible accounts............	$ 20,000	
Ending balance of accounts receivable (to be collected)	100,000	120,000
Current collections...		$ 930,000

net accounts receivable is reduced as a result of this entry, but there is no effect on the flow of cash. The estimated uncollectible accounts expense, like depreciation, is not deducted in computing the net inflow of cash from operations.

(2) The cash paid for merchandise is computed from cost of goods sold in two steps:

1. Purchases during the year are computed by relating cost of goods sold to the change in the inventory.
2. Cash payments for merchandise are computed by relating purchases to the change in the accounts payable.

In the illustration given for Myron Products, Inc., inventory has increased by $9,100. This means that purchases were in excess of the cost of goods sold.

Cost of goods sold..	$149,800
Add inventory increase..	9,100
Cost of purchases..	$158,900

If inventory had decreased, purchases would be less than cost of goods sold by the amount of the decrease.

In the next step, cash payments are calculated by relating the purchases to the changes in the accounts payable. The accounts payable decreased by $1,200 because payments were greater than purchases.

Cost of purchases..	$158,900
Add accounts payable decrease	1,200
Cash payments for merchandise...	$160,100

The analysis is repeated in T-account form:

Cash

	Cash payments (c).........................	**160,100**

Accounts Payable

Cash payments (c).........................	**160,100**		Beginning balance	11,500
Ending balance............................	10,300		Purchases (b)................................	**158,900**
	170,400			170,400

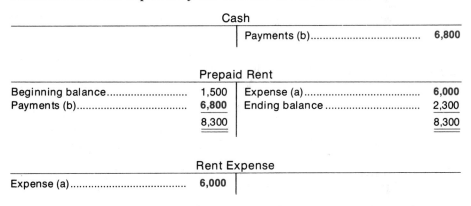

Inventory

Beginning balance.........................	67,100	Cost of goods sold (a)....................	**149,800**
Purchases (b)................................	**158,900**	Ending balance.............................	76,200
	226,000		226,000

Cost of Goods Sold

Cost of goods sold (a)....................	**149,800**

(3) Cash was also disbursed to pay operating and other expenses. These payments can be computed by relating the expenses to prepayment accounts and accrued liabilities. Prepayment accounts are similar to inventory accounts. Assume, for example, that there was prepaid rent of $1,500 at the beginning of the year, rent expense of $6,000, and $2,300 of prepaid rent at the end of the year. The "inventory" of prepaid rent increased because cash payments for insurance premiums exceeded the rent expense by the amount of the increase.

Cash

	Payments (b)......................................	**6,800**

Prepaid Rent

Beginning balance...........................	1,500	Expense (a).......................................	**6,000**
Payments (b)...................................	**6,800**	Ending balance	2,300
	8,300		8,300

Rent Expense

Expense (a).......................................	**6,000**

Conversely, a decrease in the prepayment would mean that cash payments were less than the expense by the amount of the decrease.

(4) Accured liabilities are like accounts payable. If the liability is decreased, payments are more than expenses. When debts are reduced, more goods and services are being paid for than are being used. Conversely, when debts increase, expenses are greater than payments.

In the example for Myron Products, Inc., wages payable increased from $8,100 to $8,500. Payments for wages were less than the expense by the amount of the increase of $400. Also, the income tax liability increased by $3,700. Income tax expense of $56,100, when reduced by the $3,700 liability increase, yields the payments of $52,400. In this particular case, the company paid the entire amount that was owed at the beginning of the year and at the end of the year owed the current tax expense.

Cash

	Payments (b)	**52,400**

Estimated Income Tax Payable

Payments (b)	**52,400**	Beginning balance	52,400
Ending balance	56,100	Expense (a)	**56,100**
	108,500		108,500

Income Tax Expense

Expense (a)	**56,100**

(5) Depreciation and uncollectible accounts expense are operating expenses not requiring a cash disbursement and are subtracted to compute the cash disbursed for operating and other expenses.

(6) Receipts from the sale of plant assets are added in their entirety on the statement of cash receipts and disbursements. To avoid double-counting, the gains or losses on such sales are deducted or added back in determining cash flows from operations.

A schedule of the cash flow from operations for Myron Products, Inc., is given below. Explanations of the amounts appearing in the cash effect columns immediately follow the schedule.

	Income Statement	Cash Effect Increase	Cash Effect Decrease	Cash Flow
Net sales	$326,400	(a) $1,700		$328,100
Gain on sale of equipment	3,200		(g) $3,200	—0—
	$329,600			$328,100
Cost of goods sold	$149,800	(b) 9,100		$160,100
		(c) 1,200		
Operating expenses	57,800		(d) 7,000	50,400
			(e) 400	
Interest expense	4,000			4,000
Income tax	56,100		(f) 3,700	52,400
	$267,700			$266,900
Net income	$ 61,900			
Net cash flow from operations				$ 61,200

(a) Add decrease in accounts receivable.
(b) Add increase in inventory.
(c) Add decrease in accounts payable.
(d) Eliminate depreciation.
(e) Subtract increase in wages payable.
(f) Subtract increase in estimated income tax payable.
(g) Eliminate gain on sale of equipment.

Analysis of Other Current Items

Certain current assets and liabilities are not related to income statement classifications. Changes in these categories are analyzed separately. In the illustration, marketable securities decreased by $1,000; with no information to the contrary, this indicates that cash was increased by a corresponding amount. The increase of $1,000 in dividends payable is subtracted from the cash dividends of $21,600 to obtain cash payment of dividends in the amount of $20,600.

A Statement of Cash Flow

The remainder of the analysis for cash flow is the same as it was for sources and uses of net working capital — an analysis of changes in noncurrent balance sheet items. Cash flow analysis extends net working capital analysis by examining the cash effect of changes in the accounts that comprise net working capital. Most of these accounts are related to the income statement items and are so related in the analysis. A statement of cash receipts and disbursements for Myron Products, Inc., is given below.

Myron Products, Inc.
Statement of Cash Receipts and Disbursements
For the Year Ended December 31, 1981

Cash balance, January 1, 1981		$ 18,300
Add:		
Net cash flow from operations	$61,200	
Receipts from sale of marketable securities	1,000	
Receipts from sale of equipment	10,200	
Receipts from long-term notes	10,000	82,400
		$100,700
Less:		
Disbursements for dividends	$20,600	
Disbursements for investment in Haven, Inc.	26,000	
Disbursements for plant assets	32,000	78,600
Cash balance, December 31, 1981		$ 22,100

Simplified Cash Flow from Operations

The cash flow from operating activity can be computed more simply if detail with respect to the income statement classifications is not desired. The effect of cash flow increases or decreases in current asset or current liability items can be added or deducted from net income. In the example just given for Myron Products, Inc., the cash flow from operating activity could have been computed as follows:

Net income		$61,900
Add:		
Decrease in accounts receivable		1,700
Depreciation		7,000
Increase in wages payable		400
Increase in income tax payable		3,700
		$74,700
Deduct:		
Increase in inventory		$ 9,100
Decrease in accounts payable		1,200
Gain on sale of equipment		3,200
		$13,500
Net cash flow from operations		$61,200

QUESTIONS

1. Identify two important flow statements that are helpful in the measurement of liquidity.

2. What is the net working capital?

3. How can a statement of sources and uses of net working capital be used by management?

4. When can a statement of cash receipts and disbursements be more helpful in planning?

5. There are many transactions that result in an increase or a decrease in the net current balance sheet accounts. Give two general types of transactions that fit in this category.

6. Explain in general how net working capital is increased or decreased by income statement transactions.

7. Is net working capital increased or decreased by transactions that affect only the noncurrent balance sheet accounts? Explain.

8. Name some major sources of net working capital.

9. Does depreciation provide net working capital for a business? Explain.

10. List some ways in which net working capital may be used.

11. Is it possible for a business to have net losses from operations and yet increase its net working capital? Explain.

12. Give the three steps that must be taken to prepare a statement of sources and uses of net working capital.

13. What additional information is provided to convert a statement of sources and uses of net working capital into a statement of changes in financial position?

14. What additional analysis is required in the preparation of a statement of cash receipts and disbursements?

15. Explain the logic of why a decrease in a liability account indicates that the cash disbursement was larger than the amount of the related expense on the income statement.

16. If prepaid rent has increased during the year, does this indicate that more or less cash was disbursed than the amount shown as rent expense?

17. Company W reported a net loss of $61,000 for 1980. Depreciation of $126,000 was deducted in computing the net loss. Compute the increase or decrease in net working capital from operations.

18. The manager of Channel Fixtures, Inc., states that cash dividends in the amount of $115,000 were declared but were not paid during the year. Inasmuch as the dividends were not paid, the manager insists that there was no effect on net working capital. Explain.

EXERCISES

1. Collections on Accounts Receivable. The accounts receivable balance on the records of Dahlgard Stores, Inc., was $127,000 on July 1, 1980. Credit sales were recorded at $530,000 during the quarter ended September 30, 1980. The accounts receivable balance at September 30, 1980, was $119,000. In going over the records, you found that accounts receivable of $19,000 were written off during the quarter as being uncollectible.

Required: How much cash was collected on credit sales during the quarter?

2. Payments for Merchandise. The manager of Green Value Stores, Inc., is planning for the quarter ending June 30, 1980, and wants to know how much cash must be paid for merchandise purchases. The inventory of merchandise is to be increased by $23,000 during the quarter. Sales have been estimated at $180,000. The cost of goods sold is equal to 70% of sales. Accounts payable is expected to increase by $7,000 during the quarter.

Required: How much cash will be disbursed during the quarter for merchandise?

3. Sale of Equipment. During the year, Wedon Supply Company sold a machine that had an original cost of $168,000. At the date of sale, accumulated depreciation on the machine amounted to $114,000. A loss of $16,000 was reported from the sale of the machine.

Required: How much was received from the sale of the machine?

4. Schedule of Changes in Net Working Capital. David Bradburn knows that net working capital has increased by a substantial amount during 1980, and he wants to know how the increases or decreases were distributed in the individual accounts. Balance sheet data as of December 31, 1979 and 1980, are given below in mixed order.

	1980	1979
Plant and equipment, net of depreciation	$134,000	$146,000
Inventory	73,000	37,000
Investment in Tower Company	80,000	80,000
Cash	41,000	38,000
Prepaid rent	3,000	5,000
Accounts receivable	68,000	56,000
Total assets	$399,000	$362,000
Wages payable	$ 17,000	$ 19,000
Loans payable, March 1, 1986	50,000	50,000
Short-term bank loans	20,000	26,000
Accrued payroll taxes	2,000	5,000
Estimated income tax payable	26,000	29,000
Capital stock	120,000	120,000
Accounts payable	45,000	41,000
Retained earnings	119,000	72,000
Total equities	$399,000	$362,000

Required: Prepare a schedule of changes in net working capital for the year.

5. Estimated Cash Flow. The Department of Parks and Recreation of Riverton is planning the expected cash flow from operation of the municipal golf course. During the spring, the outlays are relatively large because of the damages caused by winter snows. On April 1, the department has a cash balance for the golf course operation in the amount of $26,500. Season tickets are sold for $250 each with a discount of $25 given if the purchaser pays the entire amount by April 30. In April, the department estimates disbursements of $17,200 to reseed and renovate the course. Other operational costs including salaries for personnel have been estimated at $10,600 for April. Past experience indicates that 40 of the seasonal tickets will be purchased and paid for during April. Collections from day-to-day greens fees are estimated at $3,700 for April.

Required: From the information given, does it appear that the golf course can operate during April without getting additional funds from the department? Prepare a statement of estimated cash receipts and disbursements for the month of April.

6. Net Working Capital from Operations. North Country Mines, Inc., prepared an income statement for 1980 as follows:

North Country Mines, Inc.
Income Statement
For the Year Ended December 31, 1980

Net sales	$1,321,000
Revenue from participation rights	268,000
Total revenue	$1,589,000
Cost of materials, labor, and overhead	$ 976,000
Property tax and insurance	34,000
Administrative expenses	123,000
Amortization of goodwill	46,000
Depletion of mining properties	214,000
Depreciation	117,000
Loss on sale of conveyor system	153,000
Total expenses	$1,663,000
Net loss	$(74,000)

Required: Compute the increase or decrease in net working capital from operations for the year by preparing a statement of sources and uses of net working capital from operations.

7. Estimated Net Working Capital Flow. The president of Fredonia Patterns, Inc., wants an estimate of the net working capital that should be available on April 30, 1980. In addition, a statement is to be furnished showing the sources and uses of net working capital for the quarter ending April 30, 1980. Summarized balance sheet data are given as of February 1, 1980.

Net working capital	$ 49,000
Plant and equipment, net of accumulated depreciation	161,000
Notes payable, due on June 30, 1990	50,000
Capital stock	50,000
Retained earnings	110,000

Sales for the quarter are estimated at $640,000. Cost of goods sold and operating expenses including depreciation of $16,000 are estimated at 70% of sales. A loss of $12,000 is expected on the sale of equipment with a net book value of $40,000, and income tax is estimated at $70,000. The net book value of equipment on the balance sheet at April 30 is estimated at $120,000.

Required: Prepare a statement of estimated sources and uses of net working capital for the quarter ending April 30, 1980.

8. Incomplete Data and Net Working Capital. You have been given incomplete data with respect to Stipka Products Company. You know that dividends of $25,000 have been paid during the year and that depreciation expense of $14,000 was deducted on the income statement. No plant assets were sold during the year. Noncurrent balance sheet accounts are given below.

	1980	1979
Plant assets, net of depreciation..................................	$176,000	$150,000
Long-term debt...	55,000	25,000
Capital stock	30,000	20,000
Retained earnings..	177,000	142,000

Required: Prepare a statement of sources and uses of net working capital for the year 1980.

9. Analysis of Changes in Equipment. From partial information, you are trying to determine how much Haver and Gregg, Inc., received from the sale of equipment in 1980. Accumulated depreciation on the equipment has increased by $28,000 during the year, and depreciation expense for the year was $41,000. Equipment, net of accumulated depreciation, was shown as follows on the annual report:

	December 31	
	1980	1979
Equipment, net of depreciation....................................	$119,600	$143,600

New equipment was acquired during the year at a cost of $52,000. A loss of $4,300 was reported on the sale of equipment.

Required: How much was received from the sale of equipment? Show computations.

10. Net Working Capital and Cash Flow. Data from the financial statements of Prince Fuel Company are given for 1980.

	Balances	
	December 31, 1980	January 1, 1980
Cash	$ 73,000	$ 44,900
Accounts receivable	93,600	63,500
Inventory...	89,400	78,600
Current assets...	$256,000	$187,000
Accounts payable..	$ 33,000	$ 38,000

The income statement for the year shows net sales of $430,000, cost of goods sold of $268,000, and operating expenses of $86,000. Included in operating expenses is depreciation of $4,000. A gain of $2,000 is reported from the sale of equipment.

No equipment was acquired, and the equipment sold had a net book value of $22,000 at date of sale. A long-term note in the amount of $30,000 was paid.

Required:
(1) From the information given, prepare a statement of sources and uses of net working capital.
(2) Also prepare a statement of cash receipts and disbursements for the year.

11. Estimated Cash Flow. Sharon Ruhf has budgeted operations for the next year as follows:

(1) Gross margin is estimated at 40%.
(2) Inventory will be decreased during the year by $9,200 and by the end of the year should amount to $15,000. The inventory at the end of the year should be equal to 10% of the cost of goods sold.
(3) Accounts receivable are to be decreased by $5,000.
(4) Accounts payable are expected to increase by $3,300.
(5) Operating expenses are estimated at 20% of sales.
(6) Accrued operating expenses will be decreased by $1,700.
(7) Depreciation of $15,000 has been included in the operating expense estimate described in (5).

Ruhf plans to pay $10,000 for new equipment and hopes to be able to withdraw $5,000 each month for personal living expenses.

Required: Can Ruhf withdraw $5,000 each month for personal living expenses without reducing the cash balance on hand at the beginning of the year? Support your position with a schedule of estimated cash receipts and disbursements.

12. Cash Flow Effect of Sales and Cost of Goods Sold. Maple Planing Company reported net sales of $370,000 for the fiscal year. More stringent collection terms were followed during the year, and the accounts receivable balance was decreased by $28,600.

The inventory of merchandise at the beginning of the year was $18,700 and at the end of the year was $23,300. The cost of goods sold was recorded at $216,900, but it was subsequently discovered that both the inventory and cost of goods sold were incorrectly stated because of a return of merchandise by a customer who had not ordered the items delivered. The merchandise cost $2,700, and the cost of the return to inventory was not recorded. The sales returns and allowances had been properly recorded.

The accounts payable increased by $7,700 during the fiscal year.

Required: Determine the cash inflow from sales activity and the cash outflow resulting from merchandise acquisitions.

13. Planning Debt Retirement. The president of Warfel and Sandler, Inc., is concerned about the prospect of paying off long-term notes of $300,000 that become due for payment in three years. You have been asked to assemble data to indicate whether or not the debt can be retired without issuing new notes or capital stock.

(1) The net income next year has been estimated at $90,000 and is expected to increase at an annually compounded rate of 10% over the next two years.
(2) Goodwill is to be amortized in the amount of $16,000 for each of the three years and has been included in making the net income estimates.
(3) Depreciation of $23,000 is to be deducted each year and has been included in making the net income estimates.
(4) During the second year, the company plans to retire old equipment and estimates that $18,000 should be realized from the retirement. No gain or loss is expected from the transaction.
(5) Dividends of $25,000 are to be paid to the stockholders for each of the three years.

Required: Prepare a statement of estimated sources and uses of net working capital for the three years to show whether or not the long-term notes can be paid as planned. (Combine the three years.)

14. Estimated Cash Flow from Operations. An estimated income statement for Kidder Machine Company for November, 1980, is given below in summary form.

Net sales	$147,300
Cost of goods sold	76,100
Gross margin	$ 71,200
Supplies used	$ 8,600
Wages and payroll taxes	17,100
Taxes and insurance	4,200
Advertising	7,500
Amortization of patents	1,200
Depreciation expense	9,800
Total expenses	$ 48,400
Net income	$ 22,800

Changes in current assets and liabilites have been estimated as follows:

Increases:	
Accounts payable	$3,800
Inventory	5,400
Supplies	800
Decreases:	
Accounts receivable	4,600
Prepaid advertising	900
Prepaid taxes and insurance	500
Accrued wages and payroll taxes	1,300

Required: Convert each item on the income statement to a cash flow basis by relating it to the increases or decreases in corresponding current assets or liabilities.

15. Estimated Cash Flow. Warren Boyd is the owner and manager of Arlington Company. He is in the process of preparing a budget for the last six months of 1980. Income statement estimates for each month are given below in thousands of dollars:

	July	Aug.	Sept.	Oct.	Nov.	Dec.
Net sales	$46	$41	$51	$73	$86	$94
Cost of goods sold	$25	$23	$28	$34	$44	$48
Operating expenses, excluding depreciation	8	7	8	11	12	14
Depreciation	4	4	4	4	5	5
Total expenses	$37	$34	$40	$49	$61	$67
Net income	$ 9	$ 7	$11	$24	$25	$27

During the six-month period, Boyd anticipates the following changes in certain balance sheet accounts during each month. The increases (decreases) are given in thousands of dollars:

	July	Aug.	Sept.	Oct.	Nov.	Dec.
Accounts receivable	$3	$2	$6	$(2)	$(3)	$(4)
Inventory	4	4	7	-0-	(5)	(8)
Accounts payable	-0-	1	3	1	(2)	(2)

The cash balance on July 1 is $23,000. New equipment costing $43,000 is to be purchased for cash in October. An investment in the bonds of Hogan Blenders, Inc., in the amount of $25,000 is to be made in August. Each month Boyd plans to withdraw $2,000 for his personal use.

Required: Boyd hopes to have a cash balance of no less than $20,000 at all times. Can this be accomplished without securing a bank loan or obtaining cash from other sources? (To answer this question, prepare a cash budget with a column for each month and a total column. Start with the beginning cash balance and add receipts and deduct disbursements to solve for the ending cash balance.)

PROBLEMS

14-1. Explanation of Decrease in Net Working Capital. Rosa Marino finds it hard to understand why net working capital decreased by $18,000 during the last fiscal quarter when the net income for the quarter was $23,000. She had expected that the net working capital would increase by the amount of the net income. Depreciation of $3,000 was deducted on the income statement.

Noncurrent balance sheet items from the statements at the beginning and at the end of the quarter are given below.

	Beginning of Quarter	End of Quarter
Investment in Hyde Company	$15,000	$27,000
Plant and equipment, net of accumulated depreciation	61,000	80,000
Retained earnings	78,000	91,000

Required: Prepare a statement of sources and uses of net working capital that will show why Marino's expectations were not realized.

14-2. Statement of Sources and Uses of Net Working Capital from Incomplete Data. The noncurrent assets and equities of Sabine Company are given at the beginning and at the end of the year.

	Beginning of Year	End of Year
Plant assets, net of depreciation	$133,000	$312,000
Investment in the stock of Lester Company	125,000	250,000
Bonds payable	-0-	200,000
Capital stock	100,000	200,000
Retained earnings	217,000	263,000

You are unable to obtain complete balance sheet data or an income statement for the year, but you have obtained the following information:

Dividends of $35,000 were paid. The gross plant assets increased by $188,000 even though equipment costing $45,000 with a net book value of $38,000 was sold. A loss of $3,000 was recorded on the sale.

Required: Prepare a statement of sources and uses of net working capital from the limited information available.

14-3. Net Loss and Net Working Capital Increase. Donald Calkins, the president of Oxford Treads, Inc., was surprised to find that the net working capital increased during the year in spite of a substantial net loss. During the year, the company did not borrow on a long-term basis nor did it issue capital stock. The president is quite puzzled about how net working capital could have increased when nothing took place that could account for it.

You have been given summary financial statements as follows:

Oxford Treads, Inc.
Income Statement
For the Year Ended December 31, 1980

Sales...	$875,000
Cost of goods sold and operating expenses including depreciation of $118,000..	$692,000
Loss on retirement of equipment..	230,000
Total expenses	$922,000
Net loss...	$(47,000)

Oxford Treads, Inc.
Comparative Balance Sheet
December 31, 1980 and 1979

	1980	1979
Assets		
Current assets	$1,607,000	$ 936,000
Plant and equipment, net of accumulated depreciation............	878,000	1,376,000
Total assets..	$2,485,000	$2,312,000
Equities		
Current liabilities..	$ 722,000	$ 502,000
Capital stock...	1,600,000	1,600,000
Retained earnings...	163,000	210,000
Total equities..	$2,485,000	$2,312,000

Required:

(1) Prepare a statement of sources and uses of net working capital for the year.
(2) Explain to Calkins how the net working capital increased in spite of the net loss for the year.

14-4. Net Working Capital and Acquisitions. The executive vice-president of Tollinger Mills, Inc., is reviewing plans for the expansion of company operations. In making the expansion, it is recognized that adequate net working capital must be on hand to support the increased level of operation. Estimates indicate that net working capital should be no less than $850,000. At the beginning of 1980, the company had net working capital of $1,830,000.

Planned acquisitions for 1980 are listed below:

Land...	$ 132,000
Building..	2,500,000
Equipment..	3,200,000
Total	$5,832,000

An estimated income statement for 1980 follows:

Tollinger Mills, Inc.
Estimated Income Statement
For the Year Ending December 31, 1980

Net sales	$2,870,000
Cost of goods sold, including depreciation of $246,000	$1,290,000
Operating expenses, including depreciation of $81,000	724,000
Interest expense	68,000
Income tax	315,000
Gain on sale of equipment	(170,000)
Total	$2,227,000
Net income	$ 643,000

The equipment to be sold during the year is to have a net book value of $980,000 at date of sale.

The company has accumulated net working capital in anticipation of the acquisitions, and the amount in excess of the required minimum is to be used to finance any additions.

As part of the planning, the executive vice-president wants to know how much will be required through additional long-term debt or issuance of capital stock to finance the acquisitions.

Required: Prepare a statement of estimated sources and uses of net working capital that will show how much capital must be obtained through the issue of long-term debt or capital stock.

14-5. Net Working Capital Flow and Acquisitions. The president of Atkinson Motors, Inc., has been looking at the financial statements of a competitor, Hedges Motor Company. The president observes that the company invested $7,000,000 in new plant and equipment in 1980 and did not finance it by the issuance of debt or capital stock. Furthermore, dividend payments to stockholders were not reduced. The president asks you to determine how the competitor was able to finance these additions without borrowing or issuing stock.

In 1979 equipment having a net book value of $1,280,000 was sold at a gain of $460,000 net of income tax. No other plant assets were sold.

Financial data for the three-year period follow:

	Year Ended December 31 (In thousands of dollars)		
	1980	1979	1978
*Net income	$1,063	$1,026	$974
Depreciation deducted for the year	618	612	605
Dividends declared and paid	300	300	300

*Excludes effect of gain on sale of equipment.

A comparative balance sheet for Hedges Motor Company is given on the following page.

Required:

(1) Explain to the president how net working capital was acquired for the plant additions made by Hedges Motor Company.
(2) Prepare statements for 1979 and 1980 that will show how net working capital was obtained and put to use.

Hedges Motor Company
Comparative Balance Sheet
December 31, 1980, 1979, and 1978
(In thousands of dollars)

	1980	1979	1978
Assets			
Cash	$ 724	$ 612	$ 735
Marketable securites	800	6,500	4,000
Accounts receivable	932	987	812
Inventory	2,040	1,645	1,033
Plant and equipment, net of depreciation	11,430	5,048	6,940
Total assets	$15,926	$14,792	$13,520
Equities			
Accounts payable	$ 872	$ 617	$ 562
Other current payables	618	502	471
Capital stock	1,500	1,500	1,500
Paid-in capital in excess of par	1,200	1,200	1,200
Retained earnings	11,736	10,973	9,787
Total equities	$15,926	$14,792	$13,520

14-6. Operational Flow of Net Working Capital and Cash. Arthur Wilhelmi operates a health food store and gift shop. Next year he plans a cash increase for the business of about $25,000. Net income for the year has been estimated at $65,000, and Wilhelmi plans to withdraw $40,000 for his personal use. In his opinion, he states that depreciation will provide cash to buy new equipment.

An estimated income statement is given below:

Arthur Wilhelmi
Estimated Income Statement
For the Year Ending December 31, 1980

Net Sales	$685,000
Cost of goods sold	$420,000
Operating expenses, including depreciation of $45,000	200,000
Total expenses	$620,000
Net income	$ 65,000

The business has been growing; and from information available, you estimate that current assets and liabilities at the end of the year will be as indicated in the table on the following page. Your estimates include the plan for the acquisition of fixtures costing $55,000 and the personal withdrawals of $40,000.

Required: From the data given, prepare a statement of estimated sources and uses of net working capital and a statement of estimated cash receipts and disbursements. Explain to Wilhelmi why the cash balance will not increase as he anticipates even though net working capital is expected to increase by a modest amount.

	Estimated Balances December 31, 1980	Actual Balances January 1, 1980
Current assets:		
Cash	$ 12,000	$ 22,400
Accounts receivable	52,000	48,200
Inventories	97,000	73,100
Prepaid expenses	8,900	8,600
Total current assets	$169,900	$152,300
Current liabilities:		
Accounts payable	$ 22,500	$ 32,500
Bank loans	40,000	30,000
Accrued operating expenses	8,500	5,900
Total current liabilities	$ 71,000	$ 68,400
Net working capital	$ 98,900	$ 83,900

14-7. Estimated Sources and Uses of Net Working Capital. Hobart City Transit Authority has made plans as follows for the next fiscal year:

(1) Payments of $250,000 are to be made to reduce bonded debt.
(2) A grant of $200,000 is to be received from the city for capital expenditures.
(3) New buses costing $760,000 and a terminal costing $520,000 are to be acquired.
(4) Transit Authority bonds in the amount of $1,000,000 are to be issued.
(5) The board hopes to have a net working capital balance at the end of the year of no less than $130,000.

An estimated income statement on an accrual basis is given for the total operation of the transit authority.

Hobart City Transit Authority
Estimated Income Statement
For the Year Ending June 30, 1980

Revenue:	
Intracity fares	$ 620,000
Charters	155,000
City grant	300,000
Total revenue	$1,075,000
Expenses:	
Operating cost	$ 815,000
Depreciation	136,000
Total expenses	$ 951,000
Net income	$ 124,000

A balance sheet at June 30, 1979, is given on the next page.

The Transit Authority was established by the city several years ago for the purpose of providing cheap mass transit within the city area. While the Authority may earn a profit, the main purpose is to provide a useful service to the public.

Required: Prepare a statement that will show whether or not it appears likely that net working capital will be at least $130,000 by June 30, 1980.

Hobart City Transit Authority
Balance Sheet
June 30, 1979

Assets

Cash	$ 212,000
Accounts receivable, charters	34,000
Inventory of fuel and parts	67,000
Transit equipment, net of accumulated depreciation	1,080,000
Total assets	$1,393,000

Equities

Accounts payable	$ 123,000
Bonds payable, due February 1, 1990	800,000
Transit Authority equity	470,000
Total equities	$1,393,000

14-8. Cash Flow and Net Loss. During the year ended June 30, 1980, Anacosta Specialties, Inc., sustained a net loss that is primarily attributable to cost increases that could not be passed along to customers by increasing selling prices. Clyde Spengler, the president of the company, is surprised to find that the cash balance has increased during the year in spite of the net loss. The cash increase is even more puzzling in light of increases in inventory and slower cash collections on customer accounts.

The income statement for the year ended June 30, 1980, follows below and a comparative balance sheet as of June 30, 1979 and 1980, is shown on the next page.

Anacosta Specialties, Inc.
Income Statement
For the Year Ended June 30, 1980
(In thousands of dollars)

Net sales	$1,294
Cost of goods sold	$ 816
Wages and payroll taxes	132
Rent	54
Insurance	16
Utilities	41
Other operating expenses	21
Depreciation	238
Amortization of goodwill	20
Total expenses	$1,338
Operating loss	$(44)
Interest expense	28
Net loss	$(72)

Required:

(1) Prepare a schedule to show the cash flow result of operations for the fiscal year. Adjust each item on the income statement to a cash flow basis.

(2) Prepare a statement of cash receipts and disbursements that will explain how the cash balance increased during the fiscal year.

(continued)

Anacosta Specialities, Inc.
Comparative Balance Sheet
June 30, 1980 and 1979
(In thousands of dollars)

	1980	1979
Assets		
Cash	$ 578	$ 371
Accounts receivable	198	173
Inventory	136	114
Prepaid rent	17	42
Prepaid insurance	3	9
Land	46	46
Building and equipment, net of depreciation	1,699	1,937
Goodwill	240	260
Total assets	$2,917	$2,952
Equities		
Liabilities:		
Accounts payable	$ 136	$ 139
Notes payable (bank loans)	150	120
Interest payable	8	6
Accrued wages and payroll taxes	35	29
Other accrued operating expenses	5	3
Total liabilities	$ 334	$ 297
Stockholders' equity:		
Capital stock	$ 300	$ 300
Paid-in capital in excess of par	1,700	1,700
Retained earnings	583	655
Total stockholders' equity	$2,583	$2,655
Total equities	$2,917	$2,952

(3) Explain to Spengler how the cash balance increased in spite of unfavorable factors.

14-9. Cash Flow and Dividends. Business for Pride Products Company is expected to be slow during the next quarter but should pick up later in the year. If possible, the board of directors would like to continue the policy of paying a 40 cent dividend per share of stock each quarter. There are 600,000 shares of common stock outstanding, and the board will not vote for the dividend if it will reduce the cash balance at the beginning of the quarter by more than $50,000.

An estimated income statement for the next quarter is given below:

Pride Products Company
Estimated Income Statement
For the Next Quarter

Net sales	$1,487,000
Cost of goods sold, including depreciation of $86,000	$1,072,000
Selling and administrative expenses	215,000
Income tax	80,000
Total expenses	$1,367,000
Net income	$ 120,000

Estimates indicate that accounts receivable should be reduced during the quarter by $25,000 as a result of a stricter policy on collections. However, inventories must be increased by $75,000 in anticipation of future sales. Payments on the accounts payable will be delayed, with the result being that accounts payable will increase by $45,000. The liability for selling and administrative expenses is to be increased by $10,000. An income tax payment for the quarter will be made in the amount of $60,000. New equipment will be acquired and paid for during the quarter in the amount of $32,000.

Required: From the information given, does it appear that the regular dividend of 40 cents a share can be paid under the terms given? Support your conclusion with a statement of estimated cash flow for the quarter. (Show estimated receipts and subtract estimated disbursements to solve for expected increase or decrease in cash.)

14-10. Net Working Capital and Cash Flow. One of the affiliated companies of Ulser Brands, Inc., Lubitz Brothers, Inc., has been able to increase net working capital and the cash balance during the year ended December 31, 1980. These increases were made in spite of the fact that the company made substantial investments in new property and plant. As a vice-president of Ulser Brands, Inc., you would like to know how the company was able to increase net working capital and cash while adding to the investment in plant.

An income statement for the year is available, but balance sheet data are incomplete. You do know that long-term notes payable are outstanding and that the company borrows cash from time to time on short-term bank loans. Also, during the year the company received $315,000 from the sale of machinery and equipment. The company estimated bad debt losses for the year in the amount of $36,000. This amount is included in the income statement with other operating expenses.

An income statement and available balance sheet data are given below and on the next page.

Lubitz Brothers, Inc.
Income Statement
For the Year Ended December 31, 1980
(In thousands of dollars)

Net sales		$18,783
Cost of goods sold		14,848
Gross margin		$ 3,935
Operating expenses:		
Wages expense	$ 832	
Insurance expense	42	
Property tax	32	
Depreciation	478	
Other operating expenses	146	1,530
Operating income		$ 2,405
Other deductions:		
Interest expense	$ 700	
Loss on sale of marketable securities	33	
Loss on sale of plant equipment	65	798
Income before income tax		$ 1,607
Income tax		642
Net income		$ 965

BALANCE SHEET DATA

	December 31	
	1980	1979
Current assets:		
Cash	$ 2,032	$1,161
Marketable securities	2,120	2,480
Accounts receivable, net of estimated uncollectibles	3,750	3,246
Inventories	3,125	2,838
Prepaid insurance and property tax	83	76
Total current assets	$11,110	$9,801
Current liabilities:		
Accounts payable	$ 2,236	$2,642
Bank loans payable	600	800
Wages payable	92	87
Other accured operating expenses	108	73
Dividends payable	0	245
Income tax payable	584	426
Total current liabilities	$ 3,620	$4,273
Net working capital	$ 7,490	$5,528
Increase in net working capital		1,962
Total	$ 7,490	$7,490
Property, plant and equipment, net of accumulated depreciation	$ 8,237	$4,682
Stockholders' equity:		
Capital stock, $10 par value	$ 3,675	$2,450
Paid-in capital in excess of par	2,205	980
Retained earnings	1,215	740
Total stockholders' equity	$ 7,095	$4,170

Required:

(1) Prepare a statement of sources and uses of net working capital for the year ended December 31, 1980.

(2) Prepare a statement of cash receipts and disbursements. (Show the detail of cash receipts and disbursements from operations.)

14-11. Net Working Capital Flow. Financial statements are given below and on the next page for Swift and Hendricks, Inc.

Swift and Hendricks, Inc.
Income Statement
For the Year Ended June 30, 1981

Net sales	$3,850,000
Cost of goods sold	$1,135,800*
Operating expenses	846,100*
Interest expense	73,000
Loss on sale of equipment	18,000
Income tax	878,400
Total expenses	$2,951,300
Net income	$ 898,700

*Included in cost of goods sold and operating expenses is depreciation expense of $31,000 on the buildings and $65,000 on the equipment.

Swift and Hendricks, Inc.
Comparative Balance Sheet
June 30, 1981 and 1980

	1981	1980
Assets		
Current assets:		
Cash	$ 432,000	$ 378,000
Accounts receivable	264,300	271,200
Inventories	308,800	306,400
Total current assets	$1,005,100	$ 955,600
Investment in Cable Products, Inc.	$ 850,000	$ 280,000
Plant and equipment:		
Land	$ 143,000	$ 86,000
Buildings, net of accumulated depreciation	625,000	608,000
Equipment, net of accumulated depreciation	343,000	481,000
Total plant and equipment	$1,111,000	$1,175,000
Total assets	$2,966,100	$2,410,600
Equities		
Current liabilities:		
Accounts payable	$ 86,700	$ 73,400
Wages and payroll taxes payable	16,900	14,300
Other accrued liabilities	146,300	84,600
Total current liabilities	$ 249,900	$ 172,300
Notes payable, due July 1, 1988	$ 350,000	$ 800,000
Stockholders' equity:		
Capital stock, $10 par value	$ 800,000	$ 500,000
Premium on capital stock	280,000	120,000
Retained earnings	1,286,200	818,300
Total stockholders' equity	$2,366,200	$1,438,300
Total equities	$2,966,100	$2,410,600

Additional data:

(1) Equipment having a net book value of $249,000 was sold during the fiscal year.

(2) There were no building retirements during the fiscal year.

(3) There were no shifts between items within the noncurrent asset or noncurrent equity structure.

Required: From the information given, prepare a statement of sources and uses of net working capital for the fiscal year.

14-12. Statement of Changes in Financial Position. The management of Consolidated Metals, Inc., has been searching for acquisition candidates, and you have been asked to make a preliminary investigation of Roberts and Thorpe, Inc. Financial statements for the fiscal year ended September 30, 1980, are given on the following page.

Roberts and Thorpe, Inc.
Income Statement
For the Year Ended September 30, 1980
(In thousands of dollars)

Sales	$5,684
Cost of goods sold including depreciation of $280	$2,740
Operating expenses including depreciation of $310	1,030
Interest expense	80
Loss on sale of equipment	76
Loss from June 16 fire	220
Income tax	615
Total expenses	$4,761
Net income	$ 923

Roberts and Thorpe, Inc.
Comparative Balance Sheet
September 30, 1980 and 1979
(In thousands of dollars)

	1980	1979
Assets		
Current assets:		
Cash	$ 2,820	$ 2,567
Temporary investments	150	65
Accounts receivable	2,641	2,840
Inventories	3,872	2,960
Prepaid expenses	46	35
Total current assets	$ 9,529	$ 8,467
Investment in Pendleton Crafts, Inc.	3,800	—0—
Plant, property, and equipment:		
Land	2,630	1,520
Buildings, net of accumulated depreciation	4,360	3,810
Equipment, net of accumulated depreciation	4,784	4,400
Total assets	$25,103	$18,197
Equities		
Current liabilities:		
Accounts payable	$ 1,094	$ 963
Bank loans payable	1,230	850
Accrued operating expenses	167	152
Income tax payable	370	210
Total current liabilities	$ 2,861	$ 2,175
Bonds payable, net of unamortized discount	3,765	3,750
Stockholders' equity:		
Capital stock, $10 par value	9,600	6,800
Paid-in capital in excess of par	6,400	3,600
Retained earnings	2,477	1,872
Total equities	$25,103	$18,197

During the course of your investigation, you have developed the following information which appears on the next page.

(1) The investment in Pendleton Crafts, Inc., was acquired upon the issuance of 190,000 shares of capital stock having a market value of $20 per share at the time of the acquisition.

(2) A fire during the fiscal year destroyed the wing of a building that had a net book value of $260,000 at the time of the loss. Equipment having a net book value of $380,000 was also destroyed in the fire. The insurance recovery amounted to $420,000.

(3) The net book value of equipment sold during the fiscal year was $238,000.

(4) Included in the total depreciation charges for the year is depreciation of $160,000 on the buildings.

(5) No bonds were issued during the fiscal year.

(6) The only entries to Retained Earnings were those to close out the net income for the year and to record dividends declared.

Required: Prepare a statement of changes in financial position from the information furnished.

14-13. Statement of Changes in Financial Position. During the fiscal year ended June 30, 1980, West Bank Company made substantial investments in new product lines and in a modernization program. Significant changes made during the fiscal year are listed below:

(1) Equipment with a net book value of $128,000 was sold during the year.

(2) All of the capital stock of Braden Products, Inc., was acquired upon payment of $500,000 in cash and the issuance of 10,000 shares of stock of West Bank Company. The stock of West Bank Company was selling for $40 a share at the time.

(3) Bonds having a face value of $2,000,000 were issued on June 30, 1980, at 98.

(4) Marketable securities that cost $400,000 were sold for $430,000.

(5) New equipment was purchased during the year, but there were no building retirements.

(6) A new building was purchased at a cost of $1,700,000.

(7) Cash dividends of $300,000 were paid.

Financial statements for the fiscal year ended June 30, 1980, are given below and on the next page.

West Bank Company
Income Statement
For the Year Ended June 30, 1980
(In thousands of dollars)

Net sales	$4,861
Cost of goods sold and operating expenses, including depreciation of $383,000	3,146
Operating income	$1,715
Interest expense	$(15)
Gain on sale of equipment	52
Gain on sale of marketable securities	30
Total	$ 67
Income before income tax	$1,782
Income tax	712
Net income	$1,070

West Bank Company
Comparative Balance Sheet
June 30, 1980 and 1979
(In thousands of dollars)

	1980	1979
Assets		
Cash..	$1,064	$ 884
Marketable securities......................................	550	650
Accounts receivable..	283	161
Inventories...	337	172
Investment in Braden Products, Inc.	900	—0—
Land..	86	86
Buildings, net of depreciation........................	2,190	643
Equipment, net of depreciation.......................	704	485
Total assets..	$6,114	$3,081
Equities		
Accounts payable..	$ 187	$ 215
Short-term bank loans	100	100
Accrued operating expenses...........................	41	83
Income tax payable	286	313
Bonds payable, net of discount......................	1,960	—0—
Capital stock, $10 par value...........................	1,100	1,000
Paid-in capital in excess of par......................	800	500
Retained earnings	1,640	870
Total equities	$6,114	$3,081

Required: Prepare a statement of changes in financial position for West Bank Company for the year ended June 30, 1980.

14-14. Statement of Changes in Financial Position. During the fiscal year ended June 30, 1981, Trotter Company, Inc., made substantial changes, eliminating an investment in Coburn Fixtures, Inc., and making preparations for growth of sales in other product lines.

Diane McMahon, the president of Trotter Company, Inc., expressed surprise at the increase in the net working capital during the fiscal year. She noted that the cash balance decreased and wondered how net working capital could increase when the cash balance decreased.

An income statement for the fiscal year ended June 30, 1981, is given below and a comparative balance sheet at June 30, 1980 and 1981 on page 449.

Trotter Company, Inc.
Income Statement
For the Year Ended June 30, 1981
(In thousands of dollars)

Net sales..	$14,348
Cost of goods sold...	$ 8,058
Operating expenses...	2,157
Interest expense..	736
Loss on sale of Coburn Fixtures, Inc.	157
Gain on sale of equipment...............................	(384)
Income tax	1,750
Total net deductions	$12,474
Net income...	$ 1,874

Trotter Company, Inc.
Comparative Balance Sheet
June 30, 1981 and 1980
(In thousands of dollars)

	1981	1980
Assets		
Current assets:		
Cash and marketable securities	$ 2,792	$ 3,561
Accounts receivable	2,775	1,946
Inventory	3,836	3,071
Prepaid expenses	218	186
Total current assets	$ 9,621	$ 8,764
Investment in Coburn Fixtures, Inc.	—0—	$ 1,280
Land, plant, and equipment:		
Land	$ 1,816	$ 652
Buildings, net of accumulated depreciation	2,580	2,830
Machinery and equipment, net of accumulated depreciation	3,119	3,183
Total land, plant, and equipment	$ 7,515	$ 6,665
Total assets	$17,136	$16,709
Equities		
Current liabilities:		
Accounts payable	$ 1,261	$ 1,148
Short-term bank loans	2,300	2,000
Accrued expenses payable	422	386
Total current liabilities	$ 3,983	$ 3,534
Long-term notes payable	$ 4,200	$ 8,500
Stockholders' equity:		
Capital stock, $10 par value	$ 2,998	$ 1,340
Premium on capital stock	2,386	480
Retained earnings	3,569	2,855
Total stockholders' equity	$ 8,953	$ 4,675
Total equities	$17,136	$16,709

Additional information:

(1) Depreciation of $512,000 is included in the income statement as a part of cost of goods sold and operating expenses.

(2) No additions were made to the buildings during the fiscal year, and no buildings were retired.

(3) Stock dividends in the amount of $520,000 were transferred from retained earnings to capital stock and premium on capital stock.

(4) Land was acquired by issue of stock valued at $744,000.

(5) Long-term notes of $2,300,000 were converted to capital stock at the book value of the notes.

(6) The equipment sold had a net book value of $742,000.

(7) The only entries to Retained Earnings were those to close out the net income and to record dividends for the fiscal year.

Required:

(1) Prepare a statement of changes in financial position for the year ended June 30, 1981.

(2) Explain how the cash balance could decrease while the net working capital increased. (A statement of cash receipts and disbursements is not required.)

14-15. Estimated Cash Receipts and Disbursements. Walsh and Hoerner, Inc., has expanded operations without sufficient net working capital to support the expanded scope of operations. At the end of 1980, the company is faced with an acute cash shortage.

Short-term bank loans have been increased in order to pay for current operating costs. The bank refuses to extend more credit until the company shows that it has taken steps to improve its cash and net working capital position.

The current assets and current liabilities as of December 31, 1980, are set forth below.

Current assets:	
Cash	$ 647,300
Accounts receivable, net of uncollectibles	1,174,000
Inventories	1,843,800
Supplies inventory	138,100
Unexpired insurance	4,500
Total current assets	$3,807,700
Current liabilities:	
Accounts payable	$2,346,700
Bank loans payable	1,650,000
Rent payable	15,000
Wages and payroll taxes payable	47,000
Estimated income tax payable	137,200
Total current liabilities	$4,195,900

The loan officer at the bank recommends that the accounts payable be reduced to $1,500,000 and that the bank loans payable be reduced to $500,000 by March 31, 1981.

The president of the company recognizes that some drastic measures must be taken to meet the stipulations of the loan officer and he plans to reduce the inventory to $1,400,000 by March 31, 1981, by selling many of the slow-moving items at lower prices. A more rigorous collection policy will be undertaken to reduce accounts receivable, net of allowance for uncollectibles, to $860,000 by March 31.

Other current asset and current liability balances (with the exception of cash) have been estimated as follows:

Unexpired insurance	$ 2,000
Supplies inventory	120,000
Rent payable	12,000
Wages and payroll taxes payable	56,000
Estimated income tax payable	153,000

An estimated income statement for the first quarter of 1981 is on page 451.

During the quarter, the company plans to sell long-term investments that have been recorded in the accounts at $847,000.

Required:

(1) On the basis of the estimates, prepare a statement of cash receipts and disbursements for the quarter ending March 31, 1981. Show the detail of cash flow from operating activity.

Walsh and Hoerner, Inc.
Estimated Income Statement
For the Quarter Ending March 31, 1981

Net sales	$6,342,800
Cost of goods sold	4,435,200
Gross margin	$1,907,600
Operating expenses:	
Wages and payroll taxes	$ 635,700
Supplies used	384,200
Depreciation	216,400
Estimated uncollectible accounts expense	72,000
Rent expense	52,000
Amortization of goodwill	48,000
Insurance expense	14,600
Total operating expenses	$1,422,900
Operating income	$ 484,700
Interest expense	$ 126,500
Loss on sale of investments, net of income tax effect	55,000
Total	$ 181,500
Income before income tax	$ 303,200
Estimated income tax	120,000
Net income	$ 183,200

(2) Can the objectives be accomplished without reducing the cash balance below the amount at December 31, 1980?

15
A MASTER BUDGET PLAN

In Chapter 1, the importance of business planning was stressed. Budgeting concepts were introduced and a budget for a merchandising operation was illustrated. Subsequent chapters explored topics that included cost behavior, cost control, and cost allocation. Cost was also used in making decisions and profit was measured for business segments. In addition, accounting for inflation and for the sources and uses of net working capital and cash was explained.

At this point you are in a better position to appreciate how various factors interlock to form a budget. A general plan is established for the company, and from this plan separate budgets are prepared for the various divisions and departments. The many separate budgets are interrelated and are brought together to form a master budget plan or a comprehensive and coordinated budget for the year. In this chapter, the overall budgeting operation will be examined primarily from the point of view of a manufacturing enterprise.

BUDGET LIMITATIONS

The budgeting process begins with an estimate of the limiting factor. Ordinarily, a commercial or industrial firm is limited by the amount of service or volume of products that can be sold to the customers. The company estimates how much can be sold and then prepares budgets accordingly. In some circumstances, however, a company may have no trouble in selling all that can be produced. In this case, the limiting factor is production. If materials are scarce, the availability of materials may impose the limit, and plans are restricted by the quantity of materials that can be obtained. In other situations, labor shortages or the lack of equipment may impose limitations.

A not-for-profit entity must also begin the budgeting process with a concept of the amount of service that can be provided. A university, for example, may be restricted by the number of students that can be admitted. Generally, a not-for-profit entity such as a governmental unit begins the budgeting process by considering the amount of service to be provided. After a budget of expenditures has been established, the tax revenue required to meet the expenditures is estimated. If it appears that tax revenue will be insufficient, then cuts have to be made in the services or increases have to made in the taxes. The commercial or industrial entity approaches the budgeting process in the opposite way. First, revenue is planned. Then, all other budgets including the various expense budgets are prepared for the anticipated level of sales activity.

Budget Relationships

The business firm attempts to design a sales budget that is realistic in view of its knowledge of all important variables. This budget then serves as a keystone for the master budget. All other budgets are related to the sales budget either directly or indirectly. The individual budgets and their relationship to one another are set forth at the top of the next page.

Since the activities and the budgets for all phases of the business operation are influenced by sales, plant production is geared to the expected demands of customers as set forth in a sales budget; and the cost of selling the product and administering the business is also planned in relation to sales activity. Selling expenses such as advertising, travel, and entertainment are not only dependent upon sales activity but also help to create it. There is a certain degree of interdependence. Capital expenditures, on the other hand, are only indirectly related to the sales of any one year. Ordinarily, long-range plans for asset acquisitions are not curtailed because of estimates of reduced sales in any given year. The plans, however, may be postponed or revised if there is little prospect for sales recovery over the long run.

The detailed budgets underlying the budgets of production, selling expenses, administrative expenses, and capital expenditures are prepared from the summary budgets to which they are related. Finally, the various budgets are drawn together in the cash budget. For example, a budget of materials to be used can be prepared only after a decision has been reached as to what types and quantities of products are to be made. The budget of products to be made is, of course, derived in turn from the sales budget. The materials consumption budget is then

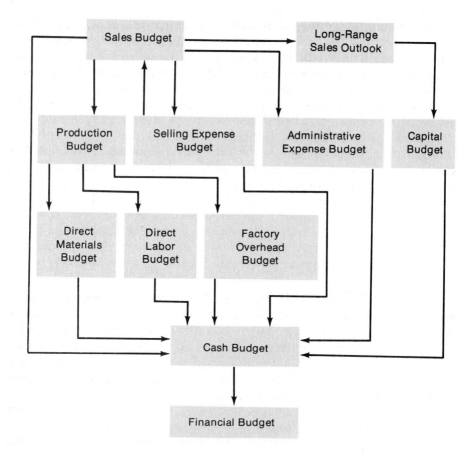

translated into a purchases budget by estimating materials inventory levels and relating them to budgeted consumption. The purchases budget is then converted to dollars. Plans are made to pay for the materials purchased, and these plans are a part of the cash budget for the year. Thus, the budgeting process that begins with sales is tied in eventually with the cash budget.

The cash receipts and disbursements from all sources are estimated according to time period, and these estimates constitute the cash budget. There will be times when cash receipts exceed disbursements, or times when disbursements exceed receipts. In a given month, for example, an insurance policy may come up for renewal or an extraordinarily large tax payment may fall due. During this month, cash outflows may exceed cash inflows.

Variations in the flow of cash during the year can be evened out by making use of short-term credit. A line of credit is drawn upon during the months in which cash outflows are heavy. Loans are then repaid with interest at a later date when the cash inflow exceeds the outflow. Planning short-term credit is a part of the financial budgeting operation.

The financial budget is based upon estimates of the cash flow, which in turn depend upon anticipated revenue and expected cost. Long-term debt is planned in the same manner, with projections being extended further into the future. In the final analysis, this budget, like all the others, is based upon sales in the immediate or distant future.

After a sales estimate has been drawn up and coordinated with plans for production, individual cost budgets can be prepared. Cost is usually accounted for along functional lines; that is, according to whether it pertains to manufacturing, selling, or administration. This same manner of classification is usually followed in budgeting, with the cost being subdivided by activity and department. The following discussion focuses on cost budgets and the ways in which they are prepared and interlocked to form the master budget plan for a company.

SALES FORECASTING AND THE SALES BUDGET

The sales estimate is the basis for the various other budgets that in aggregate constitute the overall budget. The quantity of products to be produced depends upon the sales budget. The production budget with all of the details for required materials, labor, and overhead is governed by sales. The selling and administrative expense budgets are also related to the sales budget. Hence, the budgeting process begins with a determination of anticipated sales volume.

Sales are ordinarily restricted only by the limitations imposed by productive capacity and the demand for the products or services. However, there may be other limitations that must be considered. For example, if a company cannot obtain sufficient fuel to meet production requirements, available fuel will impose a further limitation on sales. Or if a critical material for which there is no substitute is limited in supply, then the availability of such material is the limiting factor. The sales budget that forms the basis for other budgets in turn is dependent upon sales demand or some scarcity factor such as fuel, materials, or labor.

Before a sales budget in units of product or in dollars can be developed, there must be a sales forecast. The forecast is based upon a variety of interacting factors such as price policy, the general economic outlook, conditions within the industry, governmental policies, and the position of the company in the economy. In relatively large companies, an economic forecasting department or a division of the controller's department devotes its full time to economic forecasting with forecasts prepared not only for the immediate future but for 10 to 20 years hence.

Methods used in forecasting sales vary widely. Each industry and company has distinctive characteristics which tend to create differences in outlook. In general, the sales forecast is based upon an analysis of past sales and an estimate of future economic prospects.

Sales from past years can be broken down by product lines, regions, and salespeople to provide a basis for estimating possible future sales. The regional sales managers and salespeople prepare sales estimates for the coming year in light of their knowledge of the past and their expectations for the future. Higher echelons of management who are better informed with respect to the total economic picture review these estimates and fit them into a composite forecast for the company, making adjustments wherever necessary.

A sales forecast is sometimes made on a more scientific basis by fitting the business activity of the company to published indexes and reports on the economy at large. A given company may find that its activity tends to follow the Federal Reserve Board's Index, statistics on bank deposits, national income, population trends, and so forth. It is possible to predict future sales trends from established relationships.

Many factors operate to complicate sales forecasting. A company may appear to fit into a particular industry grouping, yet upon closer examination it may be found that the company handles many different lines of products and in reality has the attributes of several industries. In addition, products may be sold through various channels in different territories or even in different countries. Some products, such as food staples and clothing, are produced for sale to the consumer, while other products are indirectly related to consumer demand. For example, basic products such as glass, steel, and aluminum are not sold to the consumer directly but are used in the manufacture of other products. The demand for basic products that are used in making other products is said to be a *derived demand*. Sales forecasts for these products depend upon forecasts and data prepared for other industries. The demand for paint and lumber, for example, is influenced to a large extent by the number of new housing starts planned. If products are sold to automobile manufacturers, then the demand is derived from forecasts of new car sales.

Sometimes a computer is used in forecasting. The computer is a means by which diverse information can be brought together in various combinations and tested for validity. A watch manufacturer, for example, knows that watches are often purchased as graduation gifts and that sales bear a relationship to the number of graduates in a given year. But the manufacturer may not know how high a correlation there is between watch sales and the number of students graduating. Various factors that have a bearing on watch sales can be brought together in weighted formulas and can be tested on the computer. Experimentation and testing reveal whether or not the weights used in any of the formulas are valid. If a reasonable degree of correlation is found to exist in any formula tested, the formula may be used in estimating the sales potential.

A forecast of sales on an industry-wide basis must be broken down so that it applies to a particular company. Each company looks at its position relative to the total market and calculates its share of the market. In some areas and in certain product lines, one company may dominate; while in other areas and in other product lines, the sales may be divided in different proportions. Market studies show customer preference by locality and may reveal why one brand sells better than another. Market surveys are not made so that they can be used in budgeting, but data taken from surveys can often be applied in budget preparation.

The general approach to budgeting is illustrated by assembling a master budget plan for Ward and Company. To keep the illustration manageable, budgets for departments and smaller units of the business are omitted and the annual budget is broken down into six-month periods instead of calendar quarters or individual months.

Ward and Company sells one product line which is manufactured in a single plant. A sales forecast for the industry has been used as a guide in preparing a sales forecast for the company. Various adjustments to the forecast have been made so that it conforms with the realistic prospects for the company. A sales budget stated in units of product and dollars is given below.

	FIRST SIX MONTHS	SECOND SIX MONTHS	ANNUAL
Units of product	10,000	15,000	25,000
Unit selling price	× $25	× $25	× $25
Sales revenue	$250,000	$375,000	$625,000

The gross sales as budgeted will not be realized even if the actual sales are made according to plan. Some customers return products or expect allowances for damaged goods or incorrectly processed orders. Still others fail to pay what they owe, and their accounts have to be written off as uncollectible. Management is reluctant to admit that accounts cannot be collected or that allowances of any consequence will be granted. Nevertheless, if the budget is to be realistic, provision must be made for deductions from gross sales revenue.

A study of past experience shows that Ward and Company has not realized 5 percent of its billed revenue each year because of returns, allowances, and uncollectible accounts. The returns and allowances have averaged about 3 percent of gross sales, while uncollectible accounts have averaged about 2 percent. From all indications, future revenue will be reduced in approximately the same proportions; and the budget that appears at the top of the next page has been prepared on that basis.

SALES AND PRODUCTION

The sales budget serves as the basis for the production budget. From an estimate of sales, it is possible to plan the manufacture of the

Ward and Company
Sales Revenue Budget
Net of Returns, Allowances, and Uncollectibles
For the Year Ending December 31, 1981

	First Six Months	Second Six Months	Annual
Gross sales revenue	$250,000	$375,000	$625,000
Returns and allowances	$ 7,500	$ 11,250	$ 18,750
Uncollectible accounts	5,000	7,500	12,500
Total deductions	$ 12,500	$ 18,750	$ 31,250
Net sales	$237,500	$356,250	$593,750

requisite quantities of products. In making its plans, the manufacturing division schedules production so that deliveries can be made to customers promptly. Therefore, the plans for production have to be synchronized with the sales budget.

Also, the sales division is limited in its planning by the capabilities and the capacity of the manufacturing division. The demand may be present for a particular product, but perhaps it cannot be manufactured at an acceptable cost. The company then has to abandon prospects for the sale of the product or find a way to cut the cost. When products are required to meet exacting standards and specifications, the sales division and the manufacturing division together have to work closely with the customers. The sales potential exists, for example, but the company will not get the order if the manufacturing division cannot meet the stringent standards imposed. Sales estimates must also be tied in with manufacturing capacity. It is possible, of course, to sell more than the factory can normally produce by depleting inventories, by subletting the work, or by producing at overcapacity. However, at some point a limit is reached, and the company is forced to add to its productive capacity if it expects to increase its sales volume.

Sales and production must be closely coordinated. Neither function can be planned in isolation. The sales division depends upon the plant for its products, and the manufacturing division is guided by sales estimates.

INVENTORIES AND PRODUCTION

Assuming that a workable sales budget has been agreed upon, plans can be drawn to produce the quantities of products specified. If the products are relatively perishable or if they cannot be stored, they have to be manufactured at about the time they are to be sold. On the other hand, if the products can be stored, the production schedule can be more flexible.

Given a choice, a company may choose to operate at a fairly uniform level of production throughout the year; or, it may prefer to manufacture products as they are needed. With variations in sales volume throughout the year, inventories increase or decrease if production is held at a constant level. When production is tied closely to sales, inventories do not vary to any extent, but production fluctuates with sales. Each approach to the production problem has its cost advantages and disadvantages, and the decision generally is made on a least cost basis.

When production is stabilized at a certain level, the manufacturing cost tends to be more uniformly distributed throughout the year. In all likelihood, the manufacturing cost is also lower. Plant facilities are not overworked in some months, only to remain idle at some later time. By employing workers steadily throughout the year, the company can retain skilled employees and avoid the cost of hiring, training, and paying increased unemployment insurance rates.

However, other problems arise when production is stabilized. Inventories of finished product are built up when sales volume is low and are liquidated during the busy sales season. The variations in inventory create a storage problem and add to carrying cost. Funds may be invested in inventories when they could be used elsewhere to better advantage. The interest cost of this nonproductive investment must be taken into account. Furthermore, there is a risk that the inventories will deteriorate in storage, will become obsolete, or will not sell in the quantities anticipated. This general type of problem is also encountered in planning materials inventories.

Some compromise should be made. If sales volume is irregular, it is not possible to schedule production evenly throughout the year and to maintain a constant level of inventory at the same time. A middle position can be reached at which cost and inconveniences are at a minimum. The plant should be operated at a fairly even rate throughout the year without allowing the inventories to pile up beyond reason. Peaks and valleys in the operating cycle can be leveled out to some extent by selecting product lines that sell heavily in different seasons.

If at all possible, a flexible position should be taken. Moderate inventory reserves may be held so that unexpected increases in demand can be met. In planning the use of plant facilities and other productive factors, some leeway should be allowed so that production can be increased or decreased within limits while using the existing labor and facilities. In order to have flexibility, the flow of work must be carefully planned by cost centers. A bottleneck in one department can stall production for the entire plant, thereby creating rigidity.

THE PRODUCTION BUDGET ILLUSTRATED

The production budget stems from the sales budget; but, as explained in the preceding paragraphs, there is some degree of latitude.

Inventories may be built up or liquidated depending upon the policy adopted by management and the outlook for future sales. The sales budget, on a unit basis related to the desired inventory level, can be converted into a budget of units to be manufactured.

In the budget given for Ward and Company, sales are to exceed production by 1,000 units. According to the plan, 15,000 units are to be manufactured in the first half of the year, and 9,000 units are to be manufactured in the last half of the year. Inventories are being built up during the first six months in anticipation of the increased sales volume for the last half of the year. Apparently, sales volume is expected to be lower in the early part of the following year since the production for the last half of the year is reduced.

Ward and Company
Production Budget — Units of Product
For the Year Ending December 31, 1981

	First Six Months	Second Six Months	Annual
Units to be sold	10,000	15,000	25,000
Less estimated inventory at beginning of six-month period	2,000	7,000	2,000
Total	8,000	8,000	23,000
Add desired inventory at end of six-month period	7,000	1,000	1,000
Units to be produced	15,000	9,000	24,000

THE MANUFACTURING COST BUDGET

The production budget is the key to the manufacturing cost budget. After decisions have been reached as to what quantities of products are to be manufactured, the manufacturing cost can be estimated. Manufacturing cost is budgeted in the same way that it is accounted for, by cost element. The manufacturing cost budget is nothing more than the summary of the direct materials budget, the direct labor budget, and the factory overhead budget.

The Direct Materials Budget

The quantities of materials that are required for manufacturing the products are estimated, with the estimate being translated into a budget of purchases for the year. Purchases, like production, are planned in relation to the inventories. If materials can be stored, the purchasing department has a certain amount of leeway and is not forced to follow the fluctuations of the production cycle. Perhaps materials can be purchased in advance at a particularly favorable price, or savings may be obtained by purchasing in large quantity lots. The purchasing department, however, cannot be permitted to operate without restraint. Savings that are obtained by purchasing under favorable conditions can be more than offset by the cost of carrying excessive quantities in inventory. Ordinarily a company tries to seek a compromise position, one in which neither the cost of purchasing nor the cost of storing an inventory is excessive.

The materials inventories are balanced so that there is not an excess of one item and a lack of another. If inventory control is inadequate, quantities of one type of material may be built up beyond any reasonable need while some other material may be in short supply. The investment in aggregate inventory may be large, yet production may have to be curtailed because some essential part is not available.

Inventories should be planned so that they vary only within maximum and minimum limits. These limits are set for each item of material by estimating how much is needed during a procurement period. There is no point in carrying a supply that is greatly in excess of current need. Conversely, inventory balances can be trimmed to a point where there is a real risk that shipments will not be received in time for factory use.

Careful estimates must be made of how many units of different types of materials are needed to make the various products. If standards have been established, they can be used and adjusted as necessary in reaching a reasonable estimate of how much material will probably be used. The materials requirements are then translated into a budget of materials to be purchased by subtracting the estimated beginning inventory and by adding the desired ending inventory.

The Purchases Budget

In the Ward and Company illustration, two materials are used to manufacture the product. Two units of Material A and one unit of Material B are used for each unit of product. A purchases budget for these two materials expressed in physical units is given at the top of page 462.

Unit costs are estimated and used in converting the purchases budget to a dollar basis. The budget expressed in dollar amounts aids the treasurer in the planning of future cash disbursements and also is a step in the collection of the manufacturing costs that eventually appear on the estimated income statement and balance sheet. The purchasing department is in the best position to furnish data with respect to estimated cost. It maintains contact with suppliers and knows what prices are offered by competing firms. Even so, the task of estimating future prices is difficult. To a certain extent, past records of materials consumption can be used in planning a materials requirement budget; but historical prices will not necessarily hold in the future. Published price schedules and announcements of effective dates for price changes help in immediate planning, but beyond this point estimates have to be based upon a forecast of market conditions.

In addition to the cost of the material itself, there are other costs that should be included as a part of the materials cost. In Chapter 6 it

Ward and Company
Purchases Budget
For the Year Ending December 31, 1981
(In units)

	First Six Months	Second Six Months	Annual
Material A:			
Production requirement	30,000	18,000	48,000
Less estimated inventory at beginning of period	5,000	3,000	5,000
Total	25,000	15,000	43,000
Add desired inventory at end of period	3,000	2,000	2,000
Units to be purchased	28,000	17,000	45,000
Material B:			
Production requirement	15,000	9,000	24,000
Less estimated inventory at beginning of period	3,000	2,000	3,000
Total	12,000	7,000	21,000
Add desired inventory at end of period	2,000	1,000	1,000
Units to be purchased	14,000	8,000	22,000

was stated that freight on incoming materials and the cost of purchasing, receiving, handling, and storing materials are a part of materials cost. Usually it is difficult to relate these costs to any specific item of material purchased; as a matter of expediency, they are often budgeted as a part of factory overhead.

The purchases budget in dollars for Ward and Company is given below. It is assumed that costs such as freight, handling, and other costs related to materials have been estimated and are included as a part of the materials cost.

Ward and Company
Purchases Budget
For the Year Ending December 31, 1981

	First Six Months	Second Six Months	Annual
Estimated cost of materials to be used	$75,000	$45,000	$120,000
Less estimated inventory at beginning of period	13,000	8,000	13,000
Total	$62,000	$37,000	$107,000
Add desired inventory at end of period	8,000	5,000	5,000
Estimated cost of materials to be purchased	$70,000	$42,000	$112,000

The Direct Labor Budget

Direct labor is also estimated first on a physical quantity basis. Production quotas are translated into labor requirements. There is no inventory planning problem as such, but there are many other similar problems. Workers meeting the qualifications set by the production division are hired by the personnel department. The new employees may have to be trained, in which case they must be hired in advance of the time when they begin work on the production line. Hiring plans should be coordinated closely with production plans. An ill-conceived employment policy can be costly. With improper timing, there is a risk that trained workers will not be available when needed or, conversely, that they will be ready before they can be utilized. If too many employees are hired or if anticipated increases in production are not permanent, some workers may have to be terminated. This represents the loss of an investment in training cost and may help to boost unemployment tax rates, not to mention the damage to reputation that a company suffers in the labor market by hiring and laying off workers repeatedly.

The labor time required to manufacture the products can be estimated from standards or from records of past performance. In either event, adjustments most likely have to be made. New production methods may bring about savings in labor time, thus making past records of performance obsolete. Some allowance also has to be made for idle time, setup time, and other expected variations from the standards in setting up a budget of total labor hours.

Labor hours are broken down by pay classifications, with estimated rates being applied in the calculation of a labor cost budget. Rates are often specified by jobs in labor contracts, with provisions being made for adjustment in pay under given circumstances. Estimates are more difficult to make if a contract change is anticipated during the year or if cost-of-living increases and other indefinite factors play a part in the determination of wage rates. Various fringe benefits, such as pensions, group insurance, and vacations, add to labor cost and may create uncertainties in budgeting. Labor cost is sometimes projected from average standard rates used in product costing, with the rates being adjusted as necessary.

A direct labor budget in hours has been assembled for Ward and Company and has been converted to direct labor dollars on the assumption that labor is paid at a uniform rate of $8 an hour. The direct labor budget is reproduced below:

Ward and Company
Direct Labor Budget
For the Year Ending December 31, 1981

	First Six Months	Second Six Months	Annual
Budget of hours	7,500	4,500	12,000
Labor rate per hour	× $8	× $8	× $8
Estimated labor cost	$60,000	$36,000	$96,000

The Factory Overhead Budget

Ordinarily, factory overhead cost is given considerable attention. Individual cost classifications are examined closely to see how the cost reacts to changes in volume or in relation to other factors. Past records may show that a cost generally follows a certain pattern of increase or decrease in response to a change in some other cost or activity. One company may find that certain overhead costs are influenced by indirect labor hours, while another company bases estimates of overhead on direct labor hours or even on materials cost or machine hours.

For many companies, the best opportunity for cost savings lies in the factory overhead area. Direct materials cost and direct labor cost are often determined by factors that are beyond the control of management. For example, materials of a specified quality may be required and may be obtainable only at set prices, or labor contracts may prescribe what rates have to be paid for various types of work. Whenever possible, of course, management searches for ways to save materials, to substitute cheaper materials, or to reduce labor cost by improving methods of production. In addition, there probably will be opportunities to trim overhead cost. An apparently insigificant saving on a unit basis can be surprisingly large when the total effect is appraised. A small waste in the use of some lubricant, for example, is unimportant if only one machine is considered, but when this waste is multiplied by all machines in the plant, the loss may be substantial. By paying attention to details, management can control overhead cost and thereby increase profit.

The forecast budget of factory overhead, unlike the budget used to cost products or to control cost in the plant departments, is an estimate of the cost that can be expected during the next year. Products, however, are usually costed with overhead budget at the normal capacity level even if it is reasonably certain that the plant will not operate at that level in the coming year. Relatively tight budgets that can be used for controlling plant costs should be adhered to in practice if the company is to achieve its aims. Yet, if it appears that variances will develop in spite of all efforts, the variances should be included in a forecast budget so that all costs can be anticipated before they arise. A falsely optimistic budget can create difficulties in other areas of planning. For instance, the cash disbursements budget and the financial budget for the year are incorrect to the extent that cash requirements have been understated.

The forecast budget of factory overhead for Ward and Company for the next year appears on the next page in summary form:

The overhead cost anticipated for the year has been distributed to the six-month periods on an accrual basis. At this point, no relationship between the costs and the cash disbursements has been established. For example, taxes and insurance cost of $3,000 has been spread over the year with $1,500 being apportioned to each six

Ward and Company
Factory Overhead Budget
For the Year Ending December 31, 1981

	First Six Months	Second Six Months	Annual
Variable:			
Supplies	$22,500	$13,500	$ 36,000
Heat, light, and power..	15,000	9,000	24,000
Repairs and maintenance...	7,500	4,500	12,000
Total variable overhead...	$45,000	$27,000	$ 72,000
Fixed:			
Supervision...	$25,000	$25,000	$ 50,000
Indirect labor	6,000	6,000	12,000
Taxes and insurance...	1,500	1,500	3,000
Heat, light, and power...	2,500	2,500	5,000
Repairs and maintenance...	4,000	4,000	8,000
Depreciation	6,000	6,000	12,000
Total fixed overhead...	$45,000	$45,000	$ 90,000
Total factory overhead	$90,000	$72,000	$162,000

months. Probably payments for insurance protection will not follow this pattern. The entire cost may be prepaid at one time, or payments in varying amounts may be made throughout the life of the policies. The budget only reveals that the taxes and insurance expense for the year will probably amount to $3,000. There is no indication as to whether the cost has been paid or whether it is a reasonable cost.

THE SELLING EXPENSE BUDGET

The cost of promoting, selling, and distributing the products is budgeted in much the same way as the manufacturing cost. Although the selling cost is not included as a part of product cost, it is frequently broken down by product lines, sales regions, customers, salespersons, or some other significant unit basis. Analysis may reveal that it costs too much to sell a certain product or that the company would do better by concentrating on a particular customer group. Perhaps the cost of operating a retail unit is not justified by the return, in which case it may be better to close the unit or to seek more profitable sales outlets. Cost analysis can be applied in planning sales activity, revealing what it probably costs to sell different quantities and combinations of products. Furthermore, if cost is budgeted and accumulated on a unit of responsibility basis, it is possible to detect differences by sales region, salesperson, customer group, and so forth. Thus the selling cost, like the manufacturing cost, can be identified by area of responsibility and can be used as a means for control.

It is not as easy to budget selling expenses for the year as it might appear. Some of the expenses, of course, can be estimated with little or no difficulty. For example, the relatively fixed cost of operating a sales office, such as rent, sales salaries, heat and light, and depreciation of equipment, presents little or no problem. Similarly, sales commissions based upon a stipulated percentage of net sales can be calculated directly from a budget of net sales. Many of the selling expenses, however, bear no direct relationship to sales and may be arbitrarily determined by managerial policy.

Promotional expenses and shipping expenses, for example, are dependent upon sales, but they are also influenced by other factors. Promotional expenses such as advertising, travel, and entertainment not only are governed by sales but also help to determine sales. Shipping expenses vary according to the destination of the products and agreements reached with customers.

Budgets for sales promotion and advertising are often made on an appropriation basis, with the amount to be spent left to the general discretion of management. The amount to be spent depends upon the sales objectives, studies of past results, and estimates of how much must be spent to attain the objectives. Sometimes promotional expenses are budgeted at a certain percentage of sales, but this policy is not generally recommended. With a decline in sales, there would be a reduction in sales promotion. This could lead to further decreases in sales, aggravating a condition that is already unsatisfactory. Perhaps even greater expenditures for promotion can be justified when sales are declining.

Selling expenses for Ward and Company have been estimated and summarized in the budget given at the top of the next page.

THE GENERAL AND ADMINISTRATIVE EXPENSE BUDGET

The cost of administration and the cost of maintaining a corporate form of business are frequently looked upon as fixed costs. While these costs are less directly related to sales, they are nevertheless dependent upon sales volume in the long run. With minor variations in business activity, the cost of operating the administrative offices remains relatively fixed. However, during prolonged periods of inactivity, this cost is reduced. Office personnel are laid off, officers' salaries are cut, and various economy measures are instituted during a business slump. In relatively prosperous times, costs tend to creep upward and excesses may be overlooked. The result is that changes in administrative costs tend to lag behind changes in business conditions.

Administrative cost, like manufacturing and selling costs, is broken down for use in control. Budgets of costs chargeable to individual administrative supervisors provide controls against which actual costs

Ward and Company
Selling Expense Budget
For the Year Ending December 31, 1981

	First Six Months	Second Six Months	Annual
Variable:			
Sales supplies...	$ 1,500	$ 2,250	$ 3,750
Telephone...	1,000	1,500	2,500
Shipping expense	3,000	4,500	7,500
Delivery expense	2,500	3,750	6,250
Total variable cost	$ 8,000	$12,000	$20,000
Fixed:			
Sales salaries...	$15,000	$15,000	$30,000
Advertising...	4,000	4,000	8,000
Travel and entertainment	4,000	4,000	8,000
Sales office rent	3,000	3,000	6,000
Utilities	1,500	1,500	3,000
Depreciation	1,000	1,000	2,000
Total fixed cost	$28,500	$28,500	$57,000
Total selling expense.......................................	$36,500	$40,500	$77,000

can be compared. By following the general principles of cost accounting, it is also possible to set standards of work performance for various activities and to establish cost standards. For example, the cost to process specific accounting data or the cost to assemble data for reports can be calculated by using techniques similar to those employed in job order manufacturing operations. The cost is either directly or indirectly identified with the activity, and the actual cost is then compared with a predetermined budget. If variations are unfavorable and material in amount, the necessary remedial steps should be taken.

A budget of estimated general and administrative expenses for Ward and Company is given at the top of page 468. This budget, along with the budget of manufacturing cost and the budget of selling expenses, is used in planning cash disbursements and in the preparation of an estimated income statement.

THE CAPITAL BUDGET

A plan for the acquisition of various properties such as buildings, machinery, equipment, and other long-term investment is sometimes referred to as a *capital budget* or as a *capital expenditure budget*. For purposes of this discussion, assume that plans for the acquisition of capital assets have been approved by top management, and that these plans are ready to be interlocked with the budget plans for the year. Each year a provision must be made in the current annual budget for the portion of the plan to be carried out that year. Expenditures for

Ward and Company
General and Administrative Expense Budget
For the Year Ending December 31, 1981

	First Six Months	Second Six Months	Total
Variable:			
Supplies used	$ 2,800	$ 4,200	$ 7,000
Heat and light	1,000	1,500	2,500
Telephone	1,200	1,800	3,000
Total variable expense	$ 5,000	$ 7,500	$12,500
Fixed:			
Officers' salaries	$20,000	$20,000	$40,000
Office salaries	7,000	7,000	14,000
Professional services	500	500	1,000
Corporate taxes	500	500	1,000
Donations	250	250	500
Rent	1,250	1,250	2,500
Heat and light	1,750	1,750	3,500
Telephone	1,000	1,000	2,000
Depreciation	250	250	500
Total fixed expense	$32,500	$32,500	$65,000
Total general and administrative expense	$37,500	$40,000	$77,500

minor additions and replacements are not planned far in advance nor do they require the approval of top management. Ordinarily, supervisors at the lower levels are granted appropriations that can be used in acquiring properties whose costs lie within prescribed limits.

Although properties that are used in operations for long periods of time are not acquired on the basis of current sales estimates, the prospects for immediate sales have some influence. If the outlook for sales is not promising, projects that have been planned for the current year may be postponed or cut back, or the original schedule may be followed so that the company is ready to capture opportunities when conditions are favorable. Replacements and minor additions are more likely to be influenced by the current sales picture.

During the coming year, Ward and Company expects to proceed with plans for modernization; and late in the year, they plan to spend $800,000 for new machinery. Part of the cost is to be financed by the issue of $600,000 in equipment notes.

The capital budget is set forth at the top of the next page.

THE CASH RECEIPTS BUDGET

Normally, sales activity is expected to produce the bulk of the cash receipts. If sales are made on a credit basis, accounts receivable are

Ward and Company
Capital Budget
For the Year Ending December 31, 1981

	First Six Months	Second Six Months	Annual
New machinery	—0—	$800,000	$800,000
Less cost to be financed by notes	—0—	600,000	600,000
Current cash expenditures	—0—	$200,000	$200,000

eventually translated into cash as customers pay their accounts. The time required to collect outstanding accounts has to be estimated, and provision must be made for discounts, returns, allowance granted, and uncollectible accounts. From a study of past records and recent experience in the rate of collections, it should be possible to predict approximate receipts on account. The collection pattern for Ward and Company is given below:

> 70% of the net sales for the six months is collected during the six months.
> 20% of the net sales for the six months is collected during the following six months.
> 10% of the net sales for the six months is collected during the second six months following.

Returns and allowances and uncollectible accounts cannot be determined exactly in the six months in which the goods are sold; but, as discussed earlier, Ward and Company estimates that about 3 percent of gross sales for any six months are returned or reduced by allowances granted and that 2 percent of gross sales will be uncollectible. Net sales for the first six months of the previous year, 1980, amounted to $180,000. It is anticipated that net sales will amount to $330,000 in the last six months of 1980, the period in which the budgeting operation for the next year is being completed.

A partial budget of cash receipts is prepared by applying the collection percentages to the appropriate net sales for each six-month period. Additionally, accounts receivable balances are estimated as they will probably appear at the end of each six-month period net of returns, allowances, and uncollectibles. The accounts receivable collection schedule for Ward and Company is given at the top of the following page.

In the last six months of the coming year, Ward and Company expects to receive $200,000 from the redemption of marketable securities. Included in this amount is interest of $20,000. Bank loans are to be made as needed, but cash receipts from this source are planned after both receipts and disbursements have been budgeted. The cash receipts budget for Ward and Company appears on the next page immediately under the accounts receivable collection schedule.

Ward and Company
Schedule of Estimated Collections on Accounts Receivable
and Computation of Net Receivables Balances
For the Year Ending December 31, 1981

	First Six Months	Second Six Months	Annual
Net accounts receivable, beginning of period	$ 84,000	$ 71,250	$ 84,000
Net sales	237,500	356,250	593,750
Total	$321,500	$427,500	$677,750
Collections:			
70% of net sales for the six months........................	$166,250	$249,375	$415,625
20% of net sales of the preceding six months.........	66,000	47,500	113,500
10% of net sales of the second preceding six months..	18,000	33,000	51,000
Total collections and reduction of receivables...........	$250,250	$329,875	$580,125
Net accounts receivable, end of period	$ 71,250	$ 97,625	$ 97,625

Ward and Company
Summary of Cash Receipts
For the Year Ending December 31, 1981

	First Six Months	Second Six Months	Annual
Collections on accounts receivable............................	$250,250	$329,875	$580,125
Redemption of marketable securities.........................	—0—	180,000	180,000
Interest received	—0—	20,000	20,000
Total cash receipts	$250,250	$529,875	$780,125

THE CASH PAYMENTS BUDGET

The various cost budgets for capital acquisitions, commitments for the discharge of debt, and plans for dividend payments are brought together in a *cash payments budget*. If at all possible, payments are scheduled at convenient times, that is, when cash balances are expected to be sufficiently high. Frequently the demand for cash is not spread evenly throughout the year. Several large payments may become due in one particular month, in which case the company must either plan to retain cash for these payments or to borrow if cash receipts in that month are not expected to be sufficient.

Disbursements are not always made at the same time that cost is incurred or materials and services are used. Advertising, insurance, and rent, for example, are often paid in advance with the cost being absorbed against future operations. Payments for materials, labor, supplies, and other costs of operation frequently follow acquisition and use. A budget of cash disbursements is made by scheduling payments that must be made for materials, labor, other operating costs, dividends, debt service, and so forth.

Freedom in planning is restricted somewhat by customary practice and by commitments that have already been made. Ordinarily, employees have to be paid at periodic intervals, and rents usually are paid on a monthly or on an annual basis. Some payments, however, may be prepaid or deferred as desired. If discounts are allowed on certain purchases, however, payments should be made within the discount period.

The cash payment schedule for Ward and Company is given below.

Ward and Company
Schedule of Cash Payments
For the Year Ending December 31, 1981

	First Six Months	Second Six Months	Annual
Materials purchases	$ 36,000	$ 78,000	$114,000
Direct labor	62,000	35,000	97,000
Factory overhead	61,000	87,000	148,000
Selling expense	32,500	38,500	71,000
General and administrative expense	26,000	48,500	74,500
Plant asset acquisitions	—0—	200,000	200,000
Income tax payments	16,000	—0—	16,000
Dividends	10,000	10,000	20,000
Total payments scheduled	$243,500	$497,000	$740,500

The schedule indicates that disbursements are unusually large during the last half of the year, primarily due to the payment for the new machinery. Anticipating this situation, management has, wherever possible, reduced cash disbursements during the first six months. This makes it possible for the company to obtain one large bank loan under more favorable terms than it could get with a series of small loans. Also, the debt will not be outstanding for a longer period than necessary.

FINANCIAL PLANNING

Budgeted cash receipts and disbursements are brought together to form a total cash budget. From this summary of estimated cash flows, it is possible to anticipate future cash balances. In some months, receipts may not be large enough to cover disbursements, in which case the cash balance is reduced. If the outflow of cash is too great, plans have to be made to borrow funds. In other months when receipts are greater than disbursements, loans can be repaid, investments can be made in marketable securities, and cash balances can be built up.

Financial plans are made so that a minimum balance of cash is available at all times. The amount to be held depends upon estimated future cash flows and the financial policy adopted. In general, the cash balance should be large enough to enable the company to meet its payrolls and to pay its operating cost for the next month with some allowance being made for contingencies and miscalculations in planning. By holding adequate cash balances, management is able to cope with small adversities and is not forced to borrow under unfavorable conditions. While cash reserves are being used, management can make alternate plans and can secure additional cash from other sources to meet future needs.

Opinions differ as to what amount of cash should be held. Some companies maintain fairly substantial cash balances and have a secondary reserve consisting of marketable securities that can easily be converted into cash. Many other companies, however, prefer to operate with smaller cash reserves, relying upon bank credit when cash is needed. Often a line of credit is established at a bank. Cash up to a certain limit can be borrowed when needed, with arrangement made for repayment.

The management of Ward and Company believes that it can compete more successfully and can obtain larger orders with the increased volume of output expected from the new machinery. With a larger volume of business, the company needs more cash. Anticipating the need for a larger cash balance, management plans to build the minimum balance to $100,000 by the end of the year. During the year, the cash balance is to be no less than $60,000. Bank loans are not needed during the first half of the year, but a short-term loan of $100,000 is to be taken at the beginning of the last six months.

Compare the summary cash budget given below with the estimated income statement on page 475. Note that the net income for each six-month period does not correspond with the increase or decrease in the cash balance, because the accrual concept used for mea-

Ward and Company
Summary Cash Budget
For the Year Ending December 31, 1981

	First Six Months	Second Six Months	Annual
Cash balance, beginning	$ 68,000	$ 74,750	$ 68,000
Budgeted receipts	$250,250	$529,875	$780,125
Budgeted disbursements	243,500	497,000	740,500
Excess of receipts over disbursements	$ 6,750	$ 32,875	$ 39,625
Bank loans		100,000	100,000
Interest on bank loans (deduct)		(5,000)	(5,000)
Cash balance, ending	$ 74,750	$202,625	$202,625

suring net income ignores the timing of the cash receipts and disbursements.

The summary cash budget for Ward and Company has been designed so that the financial plans stand out separately. The bank loan and the interest on the loan are shown beneath the planned increases or decreases in the cash balance. If loans were repaid, they would be shown in this section also. The resulting cash balances as they should appear at the end of each six months are shown on the last line of the budget.

A plan showing how cash flows in or out of the business is dependent upon the other budgets and is in itself important enough to justify much of the effort expended in budget preparation. Preliminary estimates may reveal that disbursements are lumped together and that, with more careful planning, payments can be spread out more evenly throughout the year. As a result, less bank credit is needed and interest cost is lower. Banks and other credit-granting institutions are more inclined to grant loans with favorable terms if the loan request is supported by a methodical cash plan which provides reasonable assurance that the loans can be repaid on schedule.

THE ESTIMATED INCOME STATEMENT

An estimated income statement can be prepared from the budget data for the year. The *estimated* or *pro forma income statement* is a summary of the expected results and shows whether or not profit plans as reflected in the budgets can be realized. It brings together the various revenue and expense budgets, making it easier to evaluate the overall operation. Management can compare its actual income statement with the estimated statement both during the year and at the end of the year. If budgeted profit is to be realized, adjustments may have to be made as operations progress. Perhaps the budget itself requires revision. At the end of the year, a comparison of actual results with the budget may indicate areas of operation that deserve more attention in the future; or a comparison may reveal ways to prepare more realistic budgets.

In practice, an estimated income statement is broken down by quarters and by months. In addition, it is subdivided according to product lines, sales regions, and customer groupings. From an analysis of the statements, management can determine which products, regions, or customers groups are likely to be the most profitable. Plans for the year may be revised if it appears that better alternatives are available, and actual operations may be conducted so that profits are maximized.

The estimated income statement for Ward and Company has been prepared from the revenue and cost budgets. The products were costed at standard costs by the absorption costing method. The standard costs per unit of product are given on the next page.

Direct materials:		
Material A (2 units @ $2)		$ 4
Material B (1 unit @ $1)		1
Standard materials cost		$ 5
Direct labor (½ hour @ $8)		4
Factory overhead:		
Variable (½ direct labor hour @ $6)	$3	
Fixed (½ direct labor hour @ $6)	3	
Standard overhead cost		6
Total standard cost per product unit		$15

The total fixed factory overhead has been budgeted at $90,000 for the year. Operating at normal capacity, the company should produce 30,000 units of a product per year or 15,000 units each six months. Hence, the $90,000 budgeted for fixed overhead is costed to the products at the rate of $3 per unit of product ($90,000 ÷ 30,000). The overhead is costed on a direct labor hour basis. The company normally operates at 15,000 direct labor hours per year with a fixed overhead rate of $6 per hour ($90,000 ÷ 15,000). Using either direct labor hours or product units, the rate is $3 per unit of product. The variable rate of $3 per unit is obtained by dividing the budgeted variable cost of $72,000, which is anticipated at an activity level of 12,000 direct labor hours, by the expected production of 24,000 units.

An estimated income statement for Ward and Company is given on the next page.

The company expects to operate close to the standard cost during the year and anticipates no significant variances aside from the capacity or volume variance. During the first six months, the company plans to operate at normal capacity and produce 15,000 units. However, in the last six months only 9,000 units will be produced. As a result, the company will be producing 24,000 units for the year or 80 percent of normal capacity. Hence, 20 percent of the fixed overhead will not be absorbed by the products. The unfavorable capacity variance is then 20 percent of the total fixed overhead of $90,000 or $18,000.

Note the effect on profit between the two six-month periods by building up inventory during the first six months and selling it off during the second six months. The result comes about by shifting fixed cost from one fiscal period to another as a part of inventory cost. If the budget had been prepared by the variable costing method, the results would have been as follows:

Unit contribution margin:	
Selling price	$25.00
Less 5% allowance for returns and uncollectibles	1.25
Net selling price	$23.75
Variable manufacturing cost ($15 − $3 fixed cost)	12.00
Unit contribution margin	$11.75

	First Six Months	Second Six Months
Beginning inventory (units)	2,000	7,000
Ending inventory (units)	7,000	1,000
Total contribution margin (units sold × $11.75)	$117,500	$176,250
Less fixed factory overhead	45,000	45,000
Gross margin	$ 72,500	$131,250

Ward and Company
Estimated Income Statement
For the Year Ending December 31, 1981

	First Six Months	Second Six Months	Total
Net sales	$237,500	$356,250	$593,750
Cost of goods sold:			
Beginning inventory	$ 30,000	$105,000	$ 30,000
Current production	225,000	135,000	360,000
Total	$255,000	$240,000	$390,000
Less ending inventory	105,000	15,000	15,000
Total cost of goods sold at standard	$150,000	$225,000	$375,000
Capacity variance	—0—	18,000	18,000
Total cost of goods sold	$150,000	$243,000	$393,000
Gross margin	$ 87,500	$113,250	$200,750
Selling expense	$ 36,500	$ 40,500	$ 77,000
General and administrative expense	37,500	40,000	77,500
Total operating expenses	$ 74,000	$ 80,500	$154,500
Operating income	$ 13,500	$ 32,750	$ 46,250
Interest earned		$(20,000)	$(20,000)
Interest expense		5,000	5,000
Income tax	$ 5,400	19,100	24,500
Total net deductions	$ 5,400	$ 4,100	$ 9,500
Net income	$ 8,100	$ 28,650	$ 36,750

The gross margin for the first six months by absorption costing was $87,500 or $15,000 more than the $72,500 reported under variable costing. This resulted from taking $15,000 of fixed cost out of the first six months as a part of the inventory at the end of the period. Inventory increased by 5,000 units during the six months. With a fixed cost of $3 per unit, $15,000 was carried over to the next six months.

In the last six months, the gross margin was less under absorption costing:

Gross margin:	
Variable costing	$131,250
Absorption costing	113,250
Gross margin difference	$ 18,000

During the last six months, inventory was decreased by 6,000 units. The fixed cost in the inventory of $18,000 (6,000 units × $3 per unit) was charged against the period and reduced profit.

The selling expenses and the administrative expenses shown on the budgeted income statement have been taken directly from the expense budgets. Details with respect to interest earned and interest expense have been gathered from the cash budget. Income tax is estimated at approximately 40 percent of the income before tax.

THE ESTIMATED BALANCE SHEET

The *estimated* or *pro forma balance sheet* indicates budgeted financial position for some later date. Like the estimated income statement, it is a summary budget statement that depends upon the various individual budgets which have been prepared. It can be compared with historical statements to show how the assets and the equities are affected by operations during the budget year. Balance sheets from past years may reveal unfavorable trends. Perhaps debt has been increasing beyond a safe limit. These trends should have been recognized in the preparation of the budget for the year, and any remedial action taken should be reflected in the estimated balance sheet for the end of the budget year.

The estimated balance sheet also serves as a point of reference during the year. Interim statements prepared at various dates can be compared with corresponding budget statements. It may be possible to detect some unfavorable variation that should be corrected during the year, or the budget itself may require revision.

A comparison of the budget statements with the actual statements can be utilized in the preparation of future budgets. Knowledge gained by experience can be applied in making better estimates and in controlling operations more effectively so that they tend to conform to the budget.

The differences noted in a comparison between budget and actual statements reveal that the company cannot earn the profit it hopes to or have the financial position it wants without paying close attention to the budget throughout the year. These statements clearly indicate that the desired profit and financial position can be achieved only by making careful plans that are implemented by all members of the organization.

The estimated balance sheet for Ward and Company is given at the top of the following page.

WORK SHEET

Financial statements for the following year can be prepared directly from the budgets, but it may be easier to gather all of the data on a work sheet before attempting to prepare the statements. A work

Ward and Company
Estimated Balance Sheet
January 1, June 30, and December 31, 1981

	January 1, 1981	June 30, 1981	December 31, 1981
Assets			
Current assets:			
Cash..	$ 68,000	$ 74,750	$ 202,625
Marketable securities....................................	230,000	230,000	50,000
Accounts receivable, net	84,000	71,250	97,625
Inventories:			
Finished goods	30,000	105,000	15,000
Materials..	13,000	8,000	5,000
Total current assets	$425,000	$489,000	$ 370,250
Plant and equipment, net of depreciation	170,000	162,750	955,500
Total assets..	$595,000	$651,750	$1,325,750
Equities			
Current liabilities:			
Accounts payable...	$ 56,000	$125,250	$ 61,500
Notes payable, bank.....................................	—0—	—0—	100,000
Estimated income tax payable	16,000	5,400	24,500
Total current liabilities....................................	$ 72,000	$130,650	$ 186,000
Notes payable, equipment...............................	—0—	—0—	600,000
Stockholders' equity:			
Capital stock, $1 par value	20,000	20,000	20,000
Retained earnings	503,000	501,100	519,750
Total equities..	$595,000	$651,750	$1,325,750

sheet that summarizes the transactions for the budget year for Ward and Company is given on page 478. By following the same general methods of summarization, interim statements can be prepared for a six-month period or for a calendar quarter.

The transactions for the year are taken from the budgets indicated below and are shown on the work sheet opposite the numbers given in parentheses:

(1) Accounts Receivable.. 593,750
       Sales...   593,750
           Composite entry for net sales.

(2) Cost of Goods Sold 393,000
       Accounts Payable   358,000
       Accumulated Depreciation..   12,000
       Materials...   8,000
       Finished Goods   15,000
           Composite entry for cost of goods sold. Combine direct materials used, direct labor, and factory overhead for charge to cost of goods sold. Credit inventories for planned inventory reductions.

Ward and Company
Budget Work Sheet
For the Year Ending December 31, 1981

Accounts	Balance Sheet January 1, 1981		Budgeted Transactions		Estimated Results December 31, 1981	
	Dr.	Cr.	Dr.	Cr.	Dr.	Cr.
Cash	68,000		(4) 875,125	(5) 740,500	202,625	
Marketable Securities	230,000			(4) 180,000	50,000	
Accounts Receivable, net	84,000		(1) 593,750	(4) 580,125	97,625	
Inventories:						
Finished Goods	30,000			(2) 15,000	15,000	
Materials	13,000			(2) 8,000	5,000	
Plant and Equipment, net	170,000		(5) 200,000 (6) 600,000	(2) 12,000 (3) 2,500	955,500	
Accounts Payable		56,000	(5) 504,500	(2) 358,000 (3) 152,000		61,500
Notes Payable, Bank				(4) 100,000		100,000
Estimated Income Tax Payable		16,000	(5) 16,000	(7) 24,500		24,500
Notes Payable, Equipment				(6) 600,000		600,000
Capital Stock		20,000				20,000
Retained Earnings		503,000	(5) 20,000	(8) 36,750		519,750
Sales				(1) 593,750		
Cost of goods Sold			(2) 393,000			
Selling Expense			(3) 77,000			
General and Administrative Expense			(3) 77,500			
Interest Earned				(4) 20,000		
Interest Expense			(4) 5,000			
Income Tax			(7) 24,500			
Net Income			(8) 36,750			
	595,000	595,000	3,423,125	3,423,125	1,325,750	1,325,750

(3) Selling Expense... 77,000
    General and Administrative Expense................................. 77,500
      Accounts Payable 152,000
      Accumulated Depreciation... 2,500
        Composite entry for selling and administrative expenses.

(4) Cash... 875,125
    Interest Expense.. 5,000
      Accounts Receivable... 580,125
      Marketable Securities.. 180,000
      Interest Earned.. 20,000
      Notes Payable, Bank.. 100,000
        Composite entry from cash receipts and summary cash budget.

(5) Accounts Payable... 504,500
    Plant and Equipment.. 200,000
    Estimated Income Tax Payable... 16,000
    Retained Earnings... 20,000
      Cash... 740,500
        Composite entry from cash payments budget. Combine purchases and cost and expense items for charge to accounts payable. Direct charge to retained earnings for dividends.

(6) Plant and Equipment... 600,000
    Notes Payable, Equipment.. 600,000
        Portion of machinery financed, taken from capital budget.

(7) Income Tax.. 24,500
    Estimated Income Tax Payable....................................... 24,500
        Computed from income statement data in previous entries at rate of 40%.

(8) Net Income.. 36,750
    Retained Earnings 36,750
        Closing computed net income to retained earnings.

THE USE OF BUDGETS

It may appear from the illustrations given that budgets can be drawn up quite accurately and brought together into financial statements. Unfortunately, this is not always so. The mechanical process of bringing the data together on work sheets can be carried out exactly, but all of the data used has been taken from estimates that may or may not prove to be correct. Thus, the budget summaries and the statements are only as good as the estimates upon which they rest.

By preparing a budget, management learns more about its operations and with experience can improve the accuracy of its estimates. Management learns how cost varies with the volume of sales and production and observes how certain peculiarities in some aspect of the operation influence cost. With continued practice, it is possible to avoid errors and to arrive at better budget estimates.

Budgets are used as a guide in conducting operations, and when actual operations are compared with the budget, discrepancies reveal the need for further attention in the areas where material discrepancies occur. Usually reports are prepared showing actual data in one column and budget data in an adjoining column. Differences are then computed and shown in still another column. Often the variations are also expressed as percentages. If variations are material, they are traced to determine underlying causes. Attention to only those items that exhibit significant variation from budgeted amounts is known as *management by exception*.

Sometimes outside factors beyond the control of the company are responsible for budget variations, in which case the budget may have to be revised. Conversely, it may be found that the budget is in error due to poor estimation under existing circumstances, or it may be that budgeted operations were not properly implemented.

QUESTIONS

1. What is the usual limiting factor in the preparation of a budget for a commercial or industrial firm?

2. What limiting factor may be imposed on a not-for-profit entity in budget preparation?

3. Why is the sales budget considered to be the keystone for the total budget?

4. What steps can be taken to even out the effect of differences in the flow of cash over the year?

5. Is it possible to have an excessive inventory investment while running the risk of inventory shortages? Explain.

6. Name three major budgets that are combined to form the manufacturing cost budget.

7. How is a direct materials budget translated into a purchases budget?

8. In labor planning, what problems are similar to inventory planning for materials?

9. What are labor fringe benefits?

10. Why are relatively small cost savings on a unit basis important?

11. Is the factory overhead budget equivalent to a budget of cash disbursements for factory overhead? Explain.

12. Which of the costs normally included in a factory overhead budget would require no cash disbursement?

13. Why may selling cost be broken down by product lines, sales regions, customers, salespeople, and so forth?

14. Why is it a poor policy to budget promotional expenses at a certain percentage of sales?

15. General and administrative expenses are usually considered to be fixed in amount and to be influenced very little by changes in sales activity. Explain.

16. What is a capital budget?

17. How are long-range plans for the acquisition of plant assets included in current budgets?

18. Explain why cash receipts from customers may not fall in the same fiscal period as sales revenue.

19. What budgets are combined in planning a cash disbursements budget?

20. What are the advantages and disadvantages in holding large cash reserves?

21. How is a cash budget used in planning short-term bank loans?

22. What type of costing method is used when fixed factory overhead is included as a part of product cost?

23. Why would profit tend to be higher under absorption costing when inventories are being increased?

24. How can management benefit from the experience gained in the preparation of a budget?

EXERCISES

1. Budget Limits. The administration of Centerville Campus of Big State University is planning a budget for the next fiscal year. There is classroom space available for 1,500 students, and it is anticipated that many students who apply for admission will have to be assigned to other campus locations. There is university housing available for only 900 students. The food plan can accommodate 1,200 students. Students will be accepted if there is classroom space but may have to seek their own room and board facilities. Students from within the state are charged $1,000 tuition for the year and students from other states are charged $2,000 tuition for the year. Quotas have been established so that one third of the students are from out of state. The annual bill for a room is $600 and for board, $700.

   Required: Prepare a tentative revenue budget for the amounts to be billed to the students.

2. Budget Limits. A sales forecast shows that Strauss and Company can sell 150,000 units of a product next year at a price of $40 per unit. The company has enough equipment and other facilities for a maximum production of 130,000 units a year. However, a shortage of materials needed to manufacture the product may reduce production to 120,000 units.

   Required: Determine the sales revenue that can be anticipated next year from the information given.

3. Production Limitations. The vice-president of sales of Kraible, Inc., estimates that 200,000 units of a fabricated part can be sold next year at a price of $28 per unit. Labor and materials are in short supply. Only 42,000 labor hours will be available for this production, and only 724,000 units of materials can be purchased on the market. The inventory of materials at the beginning of the year consists of 8,000 units, and there are 6,000 units of finished goods at the beginning of the year. Production data are given below:

Materials — 4 units, each costing $.50, required for each unit of product.
Labor — 15 minutes for each unit of product. Rate per hour, $8.
Variable overhead — rate of $4 per hour.
Fixed overhead — $200,000 applied at a normal production level of 50,000 labor hours per year.

Required:

(1) How many units can be sold next year with constraints taken into consideration?

(2) Prepare a summary statement of revenue, manufacturing cost, and expected manufacturing profit for the next year.

(3) How much manufacturing profit could have been earned by producing and selling 200,000 units?

4. A Production Budget. The budget for Samuels Company shows that sales volume of a certain product line should be distributed over the year as follows:

First quarter   — 88,000 units
Second quarter — 124,000
Third quarter   — 156,000
Fourth quarter — 92,000

At the end of each quarter, an inventory of finished products equal to 25% of the sales for the next quarter is to be on hand. This requirement was met at the beginning of the year. Sales volume for the first quarter of the year following the budget year has been estimated at 96,000 units.

The estimated cost to manufacture each unit is $15.

Required:

(1) Prepare a production budget in units of product for each quarter.

(2) Estimate the total production cost for each quarter.

5. Materials Cost. Sales estimates show that Nesbitt Windings, Inc., should sell a certain product line next year as follows:

First quarter   — 45,000 units
Second quarter — 72,000
Third quarter   — 96,000
Fourth quarter — 120,000

There were 15,000 units of finished product in the inventory at the beginning of the year, and plans are being made to have an inventory of finished product equal to one third of the sales for the next quarter. Sales are estimated at 123,000 units for the first quarter of the year following the budget year and at 132,000 for the second quarter of that year.

Three units of materials are required for each unit produced. Each unit of materials costs $5. Inventory levels for materials are to follow the same pattern as for finished product, that is, to be equal to one third of the needs for the following quarter. This requirement was met at the beginning of the year.

Required:

(1) Prepare a purchases budget for materials for the year by quarters.

(2) Determine the estimated cost of purchases by quarters.

6. Purchases and Cash Payments. A production budget by fiscal quarter for Quigly Plains, Inc., is given on the next page.

First quarter — 35,000 units
Second quarter — 28,000
Third quarter — 43,000
Fourth quarter — 47,000

Five units of materials are used in producing each unit of product; each unit costs $.40. The materials inventory is to be equal to 20% of production requirements for the next quarter. This requirement was met at the beginning of the year. Production for the first quarter following the budget year has been estimated at 50,000 units.

Accounts payable for materials purchased are estimated at $15,600 at the beginning of the current budget year. It is estimated that accounts payable at the end of the quarter for materials purchased will be equal to 30% of the purchases during the quarter.

Required:

(1) Determine the number of units of materials to be purchased each quarter.
(2) Determine the cost of materials to be purchased by quarters.
(3) Estimate the payments to be made each quarter for materials.

7. Labor Cost Budget. A labor cost budget is being prepared by Wolfe Building Supply Company for the third quarter of 1981. Each employee is paid a regular rate of $9.20 per hour and receives an overtime rate equal to 1½ times the regular rate. The company has estimated that vacation pay is equal to $.80 for each regular hour of work and that other fringe benefits, such as medical plans and pensions, are equal to 20% of regular hourly wages with regular pay for overtime hours excluded. (Overtime hours are excluded in the computation of vacation pay and other fringe benefit costs.) The labor hour budget is given below:

	Regular	Overtime	Total
July	6,800	700	7,500
August	7,200	600	7,800
September	5,400	200	5,600

Required: Compute the total labor cost per month including all fringe benefit costs. Then, classify the total labor cost for regular hours, overtime, vacation pay, and other fringe benefits.

8. Labor Cost Budget. Budget plans of Amsterdam Fittings, Inc., are being revised for the last two quarters of 1981. Two product lines are manufactured. Under the revised plan, production in units of product has been estimated as follows:

	Product Lines	
	1	2
Third quarter	15,000	18,000
Fourth quarter	20,000	21,000

The labor rate per hour is to be $8.50 during the third quarter and $9.20 during the fourth quarter. Standards indicate that 30 minutes are required to produce each unit of Product #1 and that 15 minutes are required to produce each unit of Product #2. There are some uncertainties with respect to the production time needed to manufacture Product #2, and it has been decided to budget 10% more time than the standard for this line of product.

In preparation of the budget, provision is to be made for the fringe benefit cost such as pensions and medical health insurance. The fringe benefit cost is to be estimated at 20% of the total labor cost.

Required:

(1) Prepare a budget of labor cost for each product line for each quarter.
(2) Prepare a budget of fringe benefit cost in total for each quarter.

9. Factory Overhead Budget. The Hooper Company is planning an overhead cost budget for the next year. Past cost studies indicate that costs have followed behavior patterns as given below:

	Variable Rate for Direct Labor Hour
Indirect materials and supplies..	$ .90
Heat, light, and power	1.20
Repairs and maintenance	4.60
Lubrication..	.50

In addition, management has estimated fixed factory overhead costs as follows:

Supervision	$ 44,000
Indirect labor..	36,000
Heat, light, and power..	14,500
Repairs and maintenance...	17,200
Taxes and Insurance	8,300
Depreciation...	9,000
Total	$129,000

A fixed overhead rate of $4.30 per direct labor hour has been established for costing the fixed overhead to the products.

During the next year, the company plans to manufacture 150,000 units of product. Products are produced at the rate of 6 units per hour.

Required:

(1) Prepare a factory overhead budget showing variable and fixed costs separately.
(2) Compute the variable and fixed overhead costs per unit of product.
(3) Determine the capacity variance, if any.

10. Factory Overhead and Cash Payments. A factory overhead budget for Gaines Manufacturing Company is given below for the third quarter of the next year:

Materials and supplies used	$51,700
Indirect labor..	23,200
Insurance..	1,700
Property tax...	2,000
Heat and light...	3,250
Lubrication	1,540
Repairs and maintenance...	2,780
Depreciation...	3,000
Total	$89,170

Payments of $3,700 are to be made on supplies used during the preceding quarter, and $4,300 of supplies are to be prepaid by the end of the quarter. The liability for unpaid indirect labor was $8,300 at the end of the second quarter and is to be $6,100 by the end of the third quarter. Prepaid insurance was $1,700 at the beginning of the third quarter and is to be zero at the end of the third quarter. Property tax for the year in the amount of $8,000 is to be paid in the third quarter. Heat and light cost is not budgeted for payment until the fourth quarter. Lubrication and repairs and maintenance costs are to be paid during the quarter.

Required: Prepare a budget of cash payments for factory overhead in the third quarter.

11. Estimated Balance Sheet. Balance sheet data for Petrie Plastics Company at the beginning of 1981 are given below:

Assets

Cash...	$112,000
Accounts receivable..	46,000
Inventories:	
Finished goods	20,000
Materials...	17,000
Plant and equipment, net of depreciation...........................	120,000
Total assets	$315,000

Equities

Accounts payable..	$ 18,000
Capital stock..	150,000
Retained earnings	147,000
Total equities..	$315,000

Budget data for the first six months of 1981 are given below:

(1) Sales are estimated at $1,200,000 with collections on sales estimated at $1,140,000.
(2) Equipment having a net book value of $20,000 is to be sold for $23,000.
(3) The standard manufactured cost of the finished product is $5 per unit. Finished goods is to be increased by 1,000 units during the first six months.
(4) Materials are to be purchased at a cost of $158,000. Materials used in production are to cost $151,000, and payments of $155,000 are to be made for materials purchased.
(5) Labor and overhead cost estimated at $604,000 is to be paid during the six months with the exception of depreciation included at $20,000.
(6) Selling and administrative expense of $130,000 is to be paid during the six months.
(7) Each unit of product is to be sold for $8.
(8) Income tax is to be estimated at 50% of income before tax. No payments for income tax are planned.

Required: Prepare an estimated balance sheet at June 30, 1981.

12. Manufacturing Cost Budget. Bidwell Manufacturing Company is in the process of preparing a manufacturing cost budget for the next year. The standard cost to make one unit of product is given on the next page.

The company plans to manufacture 60,000 units of product during the year. There are 5,000 units of product in the finished goods inventory at the beginning of the year. It is estimated that 50,000 units will be sold during the year.

Direct materials:
Material A (3 units each at $2) .... $ 6
Material B (2 units each at $5) 10
Direct labor (3 hours each at $9) 27
Variable overhead ($4 per labor hour) 12
Fixed overhead (computed at normal capacity of 80,000 units) .... _18_
    Total unit cost $73

Required:

(1) Compute the cost of goods manufactured during the year including any capacity variance.
(2) Determine the standard cost of goods sold.
(3) What would the cost of goods sold be if the variable costing method were used?
(4) Why is the cost of goods sold less by the absorption costing method than by the variable costing method after adding the total fixed cost to the variable cost?

13. Manufacturing Cost Budget. A production budget for the first six months of 1981, divided into two quarters, is given for Haven Supply Company.

	First Quarter	Second Quarter	Total
Units to be manufactured	90,000	80,000	170,000

Direct materials costing $523,000 are to be purchased. Materials costing $270,000 are to be used for production during the first quarter, and materials costing $240,000 are to be used during the second quarter. Labor is paid at the rate of $8 per hour, and two hours are needed for the production of each unit of product. Variable factory overhead varies at the rate of $3 per direct labor hour. The fixed factory overhead is applied to the products at a rate of $4 per unit of product on the basis of a standard production of 100,000 units of product each quarter.

Required:

(1) Compute the estimated manufacturing cost for each cost element for each quarter.
(2) Determine the amount of the overhead capacity variance, if any, for each quarter.

14. Cash Flow and Income Statement. Cox Minerals, Inc., plans to sell 280,000 units of product at a unit price of $6 during the fiscal quarter ended March 31, 1981. An inventory of 50,000 units with a standard unit cost of $3 is to be on hand at the beginning of the fiscal quarter. The company plans to make 250,000 units during the quarter with materials cost of $125,000, direct labor cost of $125,000, and variable factory overhead cost of $75,000. All costs incurred were in agreement with the standard cost. The fixed factory overhead cost was also in agreement with the standard cost at $510,000. Fixed overhead is applied to the products at the rate of $1.70 per unit. Depreciation of $80,000 is included in factory overhead cost. Payments of $132,000 are to be made for materials purchased. Direct labor in the amount of $123,000 is to be paid. The payments for factory overhead are budgeted at $487,000. Collections on sales activity have been estimated at $1,732,000.

The cash balance on January 1, 1981, is to be $178,000.

Required:

(1) Prepare an estimated income statement for manufacturing for the quarter ending March 31, 1981.
(2) From the information furnished, prepare an estimated statement of cash receipts and disbursements for the quarter.

15. Financial Statements and Cash Budget. A balance sheet in summary form is given for McFarland Stores, Inc., as of August 31, 1980.

Cash	$ 26,842
Accounts receivable	34,265
Inventory	41,680
Prepaid expenses	1,735
Total assets	$104,522
Accounts payable	$ 21,643
Accrued expenses payable	2,345
Capital stock	50,000
Retained earnings	30,534
Total equities	$104,522

Summary budget data for the fiscal year ending August 31, 1981, are as follows:

(1) Merchandise purchases, $233,100.
(2) Payments for merchandise purchased, $229,700.
(3) Various operating expenses, $51,300.
(4) Included in the operating expenses are expired prepayments of $426; and prepayments of expenses as of August 31, 1981, are estimated to total $1,655.
(5) Accrued expenses payable are estimated at $2,140 as of August 31, 1981. These expenses are included in item (3).
(6) Estimated collections on accounts receivable, $412,820.
(7) Estimated sales, $405,600, and estimated cost of goods sold, $251,800. (All sales are on credit terms.)
(8) Income tax is to be estimated at 50% of income before tax; and for purposes of the problem, assume that they are all paid within the fiscal year.

Required:

(1) Prepare an estimated income statement for the year ending August 31, 1981.
(2) Prepare an estimated statement of cash receipts and disbursements for the year ending August 31, 1981.
(3) Prepare an estimated balance sheet as of August 31, 1981.

PROBLEMS

15-1. Sales Budget from Incomplete Data. You have information with respect to direct materials to be purchased and the inventories of materials and finished goods planned for each of the quarters of 1981. However, you cannot locate the budget of units to be sold each quarter, and you need the information to answer a question at a budget meeting to be held within the next hour.

Three units of direct material are needed for each unit of product manufactured. An inventory of 60,000 units of materials is on hand to begin the year. This inventory level is to be maintained until the end of the fourth quarter when it will be reduced to 30,000 units.

Purchases for the year have been planned as follows:

	Units of Material
First quarter..	150,000
Second quarter...	210,000
Third quarter..	210,000
Fourth quarter..	210,000

The inventory of finished goods is 15,000 units at the beginning of the year. During the first quarter, it will be reduced to 5,000 units and will remain at that level until the last quarter when it will be increased to 10,000 units.

Required: Prepare a budget of sales in units of product for each quarter.

15-2. Purchases Budget. Pamela Patterns, Inc., manufactures various products for the Christmas trade and delivers to retail outlets during the fall. A sales budget for one of the product lines is given below:

	Number of Units
September...	18,500
October..	37,300
November..	46,800
December..	41,300

There is no inventory of product on hand at September 1, and no inventory is to be carried over to the next season. During the season, however, the company produces enough in any given month to provide for 10% of the sales of the following month.

About 60 days are required in production. Hence, if production is started in September, the product will be ready for delivery in November.

This particular product line requires direct materials as follows:

	Units of Material per Unit of Product
Part A...	3
Part B...	2
Part C...	4

The parts must be purchased one month before they are needed in production. No inventory of parts, however, is carried over to another month.

Required: Determine the number of units of each part that must be purchased according to the month of purchase.

15-3. Purchases Budget. Production estimates have been made by Yoder Plate Company for the last six months of 1980 and for the first month of 1981. Two product lines are to be manufactured in the following quantities:

	Product A	Product B
July..	3,300	6,500
August..	3,700	7,100
September	4,800	12,600
October..	5,100	15,200
November...	5,700	12,700
December...	5,900	7,300
January..	6,300	7,100

The purchasing department buys materials in the month before they are required in production. Materials requirements per unit of product and prices are given below:

Materials Code	Product Line	Requirements per Unit of Product	Unit Materials Price
430	A	10 units	$.70
518	B	4	.60

The purchasing department has found a new supplier for Material 430 and can terminate its contract with the present supplier after September 30. The new supplier can furnish the quantity and quality of material desired at a price of $.60 per unit of material.

Required:

(1) Prepare a purchases budget in units of material and in dollars for each month from July to December, inclusive.

(2) Compute the total savings in the cost of materials purchased that can be expected by dealing with the new supplier.

15-4. Sales and Cash Requirements. Small kits of tools for sale to householders are manufactured by Dixon and Mayberry Company. These kits or units are sold to distributors for $20 each.

The president of the company, James Dixon, is concerned about various loans that must be repaid during the year. In planning a sales budget for the year, he would like to know how many units must be sold in January in order to obtain enough cash to pay $1,025,000 on loans and interest that become due on March 31.

The pattern of collections on sales has been estimated as follows:

70% of the sales are collected during the month of sale.

15% of the sales are collected during the month following the sale.

10% of the sales are collected during the second month following the sale.

 5% of the sales consist of returns and uncollectibles.

Cash payments equal to 40% of the sales are required for out-of-pocket costs to manufacture and sell the product. Assume that the payments are made during the month of sale.

Fixed cost that must be paid each month is estimated at $900,000.

Dixon recognizes that collections from sales made during February and March may be applied to payments on the loan due on March 31, but he also knows that other obligations must be paid during April and May. Hence, he hopes that proceeds from the January sales will be sufficient for repayment of the loan due on March 31.

Required: How many units of the product must be sold in January to meet the payment requirements for January and the loan repayment in March? Show computations.

15-5. Direct Labor Cost Budget. Gossett and Williams, Inc., manufactures three lines of modern office furniture. At the present time, there are 20 qualified employees available for this work, and new personnel are to be hired and trained for the busy spring and summer production schedule. Each employee works approximately 150 hours a month and is paid at the rate of $9 per hour.

Production plans, based on anticipated sales demand, are given on the next page in units for each of the three lines of product.

		Product Lines	
	Desk	File Cabinet	Book Shelf
April	360	150	100
May	370	120	120
June	410	160	140
July	530	180	150
August	520	200	130
September	520	170	120

The direct labor time required for one person to produce each unit of product has been estimated as follows:

Desk	6 hours
File cabinet	3
Book shelf	3

Required:

(1) Prepare a budget of direct labor hours for each month and convert it into a budget of direct labor cost.

(2) How many employees will be needed for production for each month?

15-6. Estimated Contribution Margin by Product Line. Lester and Dugan, Inc., manufactures two types of sleeping bags for campers.

Budget plans are being prepared for the next fiscal year. Market studies indicate that the total demand in the United States for one type known as Arctic Pal will amount to 3,000,000 units. The company estimates that it will have 20% of this market. Export trade has been developed, and it is believed that the company can sell 200,000 units in this market.

The other product line, designated as Hiker, is sold only in the United States. The total market is estimated at 2,000,000 units, and the company should be able to retain its market share at 30%.

The cost of materials per unit of product has been estimated as follows:

	Arctic Pal	Hiker
Cover	$12	$7
Lining	6	3
Fasteners and straps	2	2

Direct labor time and cost have also been estimated:

	Arctic Pal	Hiker
Direct labor time (per product)	1 hour	½ hour
Direct labor cost (per hour)	$7	$6

Variable overhead costs have been estimated as follows:

	Arctic Pal	Hiker
Indirect materials per unit	$ .80	$ .50
Machine operation cost per unit	2.00	2.00
Other variable cost per unit	.50	.20

Shipping and delivery cost for Arctic Pal is estimated at $1 a unit in the domestic market and at $1.50 per unit in the export market.

Arctic Pal sells for $46 per unit in the domestic market and for $43 per unit in the export market. Hiker sells for $28 per unit with shipping and delivery cost estimated at $1 a unit.

Required: Prepare a budget showing both the unit contribution margin and the total contribution margin for each product line in each market. Show cost detail.

15-7. Factory Overhead Budget and Cash Payments Budget. Data which follow pertain to the factory overhead cost budgeted by Kitlinger Appliances, Inc., for 1981.

(1) Indirect materials and factory supplies are to be purchased during the year at a cost of $286,000. The inventory of these materials and supplies is to be increased by $11,680 by the end of the year.

(2) The accounts payable consist of obligations arising out of the purchase of direct and indirect materials used in manufacturing operations. Approximately 20% of both the beginning and the ending balances of accounts payable represents amounts due for indirect materials purchased. The accounts payable were $84,500 as of January 1, 1981, and are expected to be $94,000 as of December 31, 1981.

(3) Payments for indirect labor are planned at $77,800. The liability for indirect labor is expected to increase by $6,300 during the year.

(4) The payroll taxes on the indirect labor for the year are estimated at $7,150. The liability for payroll taxes will probably be $400 higher at the end of the year than at the beginning.

(5) Property tax was $8,200 for the fiscal year of the city ending June 30, 1981. It is anticipated that tax for the fiscal year ending June 30, 1982, will be $9,300. The company pays its property tax for the next fiscal year of the city during June of each year.

(6) Prepaid factory insurance of $3,000 as of January 1, 1981, provides insurance coverage up to and including July 31, 1981. Another policy costing $1,800 is to be taken on May 1, 1981. Payment of the total premium on this policy will be made in April, 1981, and the insurance coverage extends from May 1, 1981 to April 30, 1984.

(7) Electric service cost $630 per month in December 1980, and is to be at the rate of $630 each month for the first three months of 1981 and $690 per month for the last nine months of the year. Electric bills are paid in the month following the month that the cost is incurred.

(8) The company owed $580 at the beginning of the year for fuel oil purchased. Nothing is to be owed at the end of the year, and the inventory of oil is to be increased by $170 by the end of the year. During the year, purchases of oil are estimated at $6,840.

(9) The inventory of repairs and maintenance materials will be increased by $2,700 during the year. Payments for repairs and maintenance are estimated at $27,500. Included in the payment estimate is a provision for reduction of the liability for repairs and maintenance in the amount of $380.

(10) Rent for the factory building in the amount of $8,300 is to be paid during the year. Rent of $850 was owed at the beginning of the year. Prepaid rent of $250 is planned for the end of the year.

(11) Depreciation on factory equipment has been budgeted at $37,000.

Required:

(1) Prepare a factory overhead cost budget for the year ending December 31, 1981.

(2) Prepare a budget of cash payments for factory overhead for the year ending December 31, 1981.

15-8. Production Budget and Cash Payments Budget. Oliver Clifton is responsible for the operation of one of the manufacturing divisions of Rollins and Brenner, Inc. A budget is prepared for the direct materials, direct labor, and factory overhead cost. The budget for the second quarter (April, May, and June) is being revised in accordance with the revised sales forecast. The sales forecast in number of units of product is given below:

	Number of Units (Sales)
February	2,300
March	2,600
April	3,100
May	3,500
June	3,300
July	2,800
August	2,700

All units are manufactured in the month preceding the month of sale. Direct materials are all purchased in the month preceding the month of production and are paid for during the following month (month of production).

Direct labor cost is paid during the month of production.

A factory overhead budget is given below.

	March	April	May	June
Indirect materials ($4 per unit produced, paid during month of production)				
Supplies	$ 170	$ 200	$ 180	$ 220
Indirect labor	2,600	2,600	2,600	2,600
Travel	130	220	280	210
Telephone and postage	230	230	230	230
Repairs and maintenance	1,740	1,230	1,170	1,020
Taxes	150	150	150	150
Insurance	400	400	400	400
Depreciation	500	500	500	500

The out-of-pocket factory overhead costs are paid during the month incurred with the following exceptions:

Repairs and maintenance, paid the following month.

Taxes, paid for the year, $1,800, in May.

Insurance, paid for the year, $4,800, in April.

Direct materials costs are incurred as follows:

	Unit Cost of Materials per Product
6 units of Material A	$ 5
2 units of Material B	20
1 unit of Material C	35

Direct labor hours and costs are:

1½ hours of labor at $8 per hour for each unit of product.
2 hours of labor at $7 per hour for each unit of product.

Required:

(1) Prepare a manufacturing cost budget for each month of the second quarter (April, May, and June). Budget direct materials for the month of purchase.

(2) Prepare a cash payments budget for the manufacturing costs for each month of the second quarter (April, May, and June).

15-9. Cash Budget. The Eshbaugh Supply Company is preparing for the heavy sales season that is anticipated for the fourth quarter of 1981. The treasurer, Helen Delaney, expresses concern with respect to the cash position. Relatively large cash disbursements must be made during this quarter, and receipts from sales are not expected until after the first of the year.

The cash balance at the beginning of the fourth quarter is estimated to be $213,000 and should not fall below $100,000 by the end of the year.

Collections from sales activity should amount to $916,000 during the quarter, and payments to suppliers of merchandise have been budgeted at $842,000.

Operating and other expenses for the quarter are listed below:

Supplies used	$ 54,300
Wages and salaries	137,100
Payroll taxes	12,800
Medical insurance premiums	8,200
Property tax	6,700
Insurance expense	4,300
Heat and light	3,600
Water and sewer	1,400
Repairs	3,200
Maintenance	5,700
Depreciation — building	4,600
Depreciation — furniture and fixtures	12,400
Interest expense	11,300
Total expenses	$265,600

In addition to the expenses listed, payments on income tax during the quarter are estimated at $62,000.

Payments relating to the various expenses have been budgeted as follows:

(1) Interest of $4,000 is to be paid, plus a $40,000 payment of debt principal.
(2) Property tax of $26,800 is to be paid during the quarter.
(3) Accrued wages and salaries payable are expected to increase by $14,200. The liability for payroll taxes is to increase by $2,300.
(4) The unexpired insurance account is to decrease by $4,300.
(5) The medical insurance premiums for the year in the amount of $26,000 are to be paid during the quarter.
(6) The liability for heat and light is to be reduced by $2,000.
(7) All other expenses listed that require cash settlement are approximately equal to the planned disbursements.

Required:

(1) Prepare a cash receipts and disbursements budget for the quarter from the information given.
(2) Will Delaney be required to borrow cash on a short-term basis? If so, how much cash must be borrowed?

15-10. Cash Budget. The board of directors of Durham Parts, Inc., has authorized an expansion program to be launched during 1981. In January 1981, a loan of $20,000,000 is to be obtained by means of debenture notes with interest at the rate of 8% per year. The interest is to be paid quarterly with the interest for the first quarter to be paid in April.

Actual and estimated sales data are given below for the one product line that is produced and sold.

	Units Sold	Unit Selling Price	Unit Variable Cost
1980 Actual data:			
November	28,000	$40	$30
December	30,000	40	30
1981 Estimated data:			
January	30,000	40	30
February	32,000	40	30
March	33,000	40	30
April	33,000	40	30
May	35,000	40	30
June	35,000	40	30

All variable costs are out-of-pocket costs. Eighty percent of these costs are to be paid during the month of sale, and the remaining 20% are to be paid in the following month. (Round payments to the nearest $1,000.)

Collections on sales are estimated as follows:

30% collected in month of sale.
50% collected in first month after sale.
15% collected in second month after sale.

Each month the company must pay $150,000 for fixed operating cost.

In additon to the regularly scheduled sources and requirements for cash, there are other payments that must be made in certain months:

January	— Income tax	$ 150,000
	Construction payments	19,300,000
February	— Construction payments	1,500,000
March	— Income tax	150,000
April	— New equipment	300,000

The receipt of the loan in January and the interest on the loan due in April are not included in the above receipts and disbursements.

A cash balance of $600,000 is to be maintained for the first four months of the year, and the minimum balance is to be approximately $800,000 by May 31 and during June. Cash in excess of this amount is to be invested in short-term securities, and cash deficiencies are to be taken care of by short-term loans.

On January 1, the company had a cash balance of $600,000 and no short-term bank loans. For the purposes of this problem, ignore interest collected on short-term investments and interest paid on short-term loans. Also disregard the effect of the timing and cash receipts and payments within a month. If there is a deficiency of cash and if there are short-term securities available, redeem the short-term securities before obtaining short-term loans.

Required: Prepare a cash budget for the first six months of the year. (Show in thousands of dollars.)

15-11. Estimated Financial Statements. A summary balance sheet at December 31, 1980, for Barnes Equipment Company is given at the top of the following page.

Barnes Equipment Company
Balance Sheet
December 31, 1980

Assets

Cash..	$283,000
Accounts receivable...	171,000
Inventory (variable cost)	194,000
Plant and equipment, net of depreciation.......................................	336,000
Total assets...	$984,000

Equities

Accounts payable...	$107,000
Accrued expenses payable...	11,000
Income tax payable..	43,000
Capital stock..	500,000
Retained earnings...	323,000
Total equities..	$984,000

Plans for the year 1981 are outlined below.

(1) Sales for the two product lines have been estimated as follows:

	Units	Selling Price
Product 1	15,000	$50
Product 2	22,000	30

(2) The cost of materials to be purchased and used in production has been estimated at $372,000.

(3) Direct labor cost to be incurred and paid, $194,000.

(4) Variable manufacturing cost has been estimated at $236,000. Payments have been estimated at $228,000.

(5) Fixed factory overhead including depreciation of $17,000 is estimated at $143,000. Payments are estimated at $132,000.

(6) Accounts receivable are estimated at $148,000 by the end of the year.

(7) The inventory, consisting solely of finished goods, is planned at $187,000 at the end of the year.

(8) The only cost flowing through accounts payable is the cost of materials purchased. Payments for materials are estimated at $386,000.

(9) Selling and administrative expenses have been estimated as follows:

Variable..	$118,000
Fixed	80,000

These expenses are all to be paid within the year.

(10) Income tax is estimated at 40% of income before tax. The income tax liability is to be reduced by $6,000 by the end of the year.

Required: Prepare an estimated income statement for the year and an estimated balance sheet at December 31, 1981. The variable costing method is to be used in the preparation of the income statement. Use a work sheet to prepare the statements. Round amounts to the nearest thousand dollars.

The American Institute of Certified Public Accountants has defined accounting as follows:

> Accounting is the art of recording, classifying, and summarizing in a significant manner and in terms of money, transactions and events which are, in part at least, of a financial character, and interpreting the results thereof.[1]

THE ACCOUNTING CYCLE

In this appendix the recording, classifying, and summarizing aspects of accounting — that is, the accounting cycle — will be described and illustrated.

Duality

The properties of an entity and the rights in those properties are accounted for as they enter or leave the business, as they circulate within the business, or as they stand at any point in time. The properties are called *assets*, and the rights in the properties are called *equities*. The rights or equities of outsiders are called *liabilities*, and the

---

[1]*Accounting Research and Terminology Bulletins — Final Edition*, "Accounting Terminology Bulletins, No. 1, Review and Résumé" (New York: American Institute of Certified Public Accountants, 1961), par. 9.

rights of the owners are called the *owners' equity*. Some typical assets are described below:

> Cash — cash on hand or on deposit in banks.
> Accounts receivable — amounts owed by customers of the business.
> Inventory — materials to be used in manufacturing products and finished or partly finished products and merchandise to be sold to customers.
> Land — real estate owned and used by the business.
> Building — building owned and used in conducting business activities.
> Equipment — equipment owned and used in conducting business activities.

Some typical equities are described below:

> Accounts payable — amounts owed to trade creditors of the business.
> Notes payable — promissory notes owed to the bank or to other outsiders.
> Mortgage payable — debt owed and secured by a mortgage on business property.
> John Adams, capital — designation of the interest in a business of an owner named John Adams.

Both the assets and the equities are accounted for simultaneously. A business transaction does not affect just one item alone. There are at least two items to be considered in each transaction. It would not be possible, for example, for a business to have a transaction that resulted only in the increase of the asset cash. There must be some explanation as to why cash increased. Cash may have been received in exchange for some other asset that left the business, or the cash may have entered the business as a result of a loan made by some outsider or as a result of investment by the owner.

The dual aspect of each transaction forms the basis underlying what is called *double-entry accounting*. In double-entry accounting, it is recognized that no asset can exist without someone having a claim or a right to it. Therefore, both the specific assets and the equities are accounted for at the time that transactions are recorded. The assets of a business can be increased by:

1. Donations.
2. Investments by the owners.
3. The service performed by the business.
4. Loans or credit furnished by outsiders.

Assets obtained through loans or credit result in an increase in liabilities. In all the other situations listed above, the owners' equity is increased. Both the increase in the assets and the increase in the rights to the assets are recorded. The total assets of a business can be decreased by:

1. Losses such as fire or theft.
2. Withdrawal of assets by owners, such as dividend payments.
3. The use of assets, such as inventory, to conduct operations.
4. Donations to others.
5. The settlement of the claims (liabilities) of outsiders.

The use of assets to settle the claims of outsiders results in a reduction in liabilities. In all the other situations listed, the owners' equity is decreased. The decrease in the asset and the decrease in the equity are both recorded.

One asset may be exchanged for another, or one type of equity may be converted to another form. For example, an account receivable from a customer in the amount of $2,000 may be collected. Total assets remain unchanged in amount. There has only been a change in the composition of the assets: cash has increased by $2,000, and the account receivable from the customer has been reduced by $2,000. The holder of a note against the company may be issued stock in exchange for rights as a creditor; that is, the liability for the the note payable is eliminated and is replaced with an addition to the owners' equity. The total equity in the firm is the same in amount as it was before, but the form of the equity has changed.

The Accounting Equation and Transactions

The relationship between the properties called *assets* and the rights in the properties called *equities* can be expressed in the form of an equation, as follows:

Assets = Equities

The rights of outsiders called *liabilities* and the rights of the owners called *owners' equity* or *capital* are recognized and expressed as a relationship, which is known as the *accounting equation*:

Assets = Liabilities + Capital

A *business transaction* is an event or condition that requires an entry in the accounting records. Business transactions can be expressed in terms of their effect on the accounting equation. The effect of changes on the three basic elements can be illustrated by examining the accounting equation and some typical transactions. The amounts are numbered so that they can be identified with the transactions.

(1) Karen Weaver begins business on October 1 by investing $75,000 in cash. After this transaction, the business has cash as an asset in the amount of $75,000; and the owner's equity, that is the claim of Weaver on the assets, is $75,000.

(2) Weaver pays $900 for the rental of a store for three months. The asset cash is traded for the asset prepaid rent, representing the right to occupy the store for three months.

(3) New equipment costing $30,000 is purchased for the store on account. An asset is increased in exchange for an increase in a liability.

(4) Payments of $28,000 are made to the creditors from whom equipment was purchased. The asset cash is reduced by $28,000, and the liability accounts payable is reduced by $28,000.

Assets			=	Liabilities	+	Capital
Cash	+	Prepaid Rent	+ Equipment =	Accounts Payable	+	Karen Weaver Capital
(1) +75,000						+75,000
(2) −900		+900				
(3)			+30,000	+30,000		
(4) −28,000				−28,000		

The Accounting Equation and Revenue and Expense

In the previous illustration, no transactions were included which required the recognition of revenue or expense. Assets are increased by revenue received for services performed by a business. *Revenue* can be defined as the consideration received by the business for rendering goods and services to its customers. Terms used for particular types of revenue, such as *sales*, indicate how the revenue was earned. Revenue is treated as an increase in capital.

Expense can be defined as a measure of the decrease in assets incurred in the process of producing revenue. Terms used for particular types of expenses, such as *rent*, indicate how the asset was used. Expense is treated as a reduction in capital.

The relationship between assets, liabilities, capital, revenue, and expense can be expressed with the accounting equation as shown below.

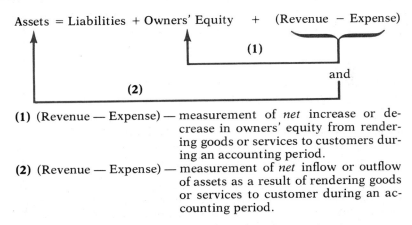

(1) (Revenue — Expense) — measurement of *net* increase or decrease in owners' equity from rendering goods or services to customers during an accounting period.

(2) (Revenue — Expense) — measurement of *net* inflow or outflow of assets as a result of rendering goods or services to customer during an accounting period.

The equation as presented above is somewhat oversimplified, but it is essentially true. Revenue and expense accounts measure aggregate increases or decreases in assets, but no specific assets are identified. More precisely, it may be stated that *net* assets (assets − liabilities) are increased or decreased when revenue and expense are recognized. Sometimes assets are received with a corresponding liability being recorded until goods or services are delivered. When the goods or services are delivered, the liability is reduced and revenue is recorded.

For example, a cash deposit may be received from a customer with a liability being recorded for the obligation to deliver goods or services in the future. Eventually, when the goods or services are delivered, the liability is removed and revenue is recognized.

Often the relationship between the assets and the revenue and expenses is direct. For example, assets such as cash or accounts receivable are usually increased when sales revenue is recorded. At the same time, cost of goods sold is recorded as an expense and the inventory (asset) is reduced.

Source Documents

A business transaction is ordinarily supported by some form or *source document* which serves as evidence or proof of the transaction and gives information about what has happened. It may be received from an outsider, or it may originate within the business unit. A bill or an invoice received from a supplier of materials supports an entry to record an increase in the materials inventory asset and the accounts payable liability. Sometimes materials are transferred within the company. A document is usually prepared to support the transfer and to give the essential facts of the transaction. The materials inventory of one division is increased, while the materials inventory of the other division is decreased. Forms originating within the enterprise are also sent to outsiders. Bills or invoices are mailed to customers when sales are made, and checks are sent to creditors in payment of amounts owed.

Accounts

The method of accumulating data should be designed so that information can be collected easily.

Data can be collected by classification in *accounts*. In essence, accounts are pages or cards divided into two halves by a vertical line and may appear somewhat as shown at the right.

debit side	credit side

There is an account for each asset, liability, owner's equity, revenue, and expense. The left side of the account is called the *debit* side of the account, and the right side of the account is called the *credit* side. Debit and credit are the terms used for left and right in accounting. A book of accounts or a file of account cards is referred to as a ledger.

Increases in accounts are recorded on one side of the account, and decreases are recorded on the other side. The balance of the account is the difference between the sum of the items on each side of the account. There is a debit balance if the amounts on the left side are greater, and there is a credit balance if the amounts on the right side are greater.

Increases and Decreases in Accounts. Special rules for recording increases and decreases are employed for each basic type of account: asset, liability, owners' equity, revenue, and expense. The accounting equation is given once more to show the rules of increase and decrease:

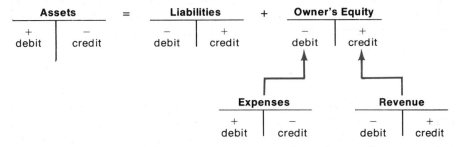

The increases and decreases are arranged so that each transaction can be recorded and classified properly while maintaining an equality of debits and credits. If the recording process is carried out properly in the mechanical sense, the sum of the accounts with debit balances will equal the sum of the accounts with credit balances.

Note that the equation itself can be stated as follows:

Assets = Liabilities + Owners' Equity + (Revenue − Expenses)

This merely says that assets are equal to the claims that individuals or other entities have in those assets. Revenue and expenses measure how assets enter or leave the business in performing services for customers, and the net result is eventually added to the owners' equity.

The rules to be followed for debiting and crediting accounts are arbitrarily defined but are logically consistent. For example, a debit means an *increase* in any asset, but a debit will also *decrease* any liability or owners' equity account. The rules of debit and credit have been set up so that the accounting equation will hold true and so that debits will always be equaled by credits. Therefore, assets will always equal equities; and the sum of the amounts shown as debits will always agree with the sum of the amounts shown as credits. Note that a revenue account is credited to increase it. This is logical inasmuch as an increase in revenue is an increase in the owners' equity; and, therefore, an increase in revenue is handled in the same way as a direct increase in owners' equity. Similarly, increases in expenses reduce owners' equity and, like direct reductions in owners' equity, are recorded by debits.

Use of Accounts. The transactions previously given for Weaver have been expanded and are listed and numbered below:

(1) Karen Weaver invested $75,000 in cash to begin business operations.
(2) A $900 prepayment was made for rent of a store for three months.
(3) Equipment was purchased on account at a cost of $30,000.
(4) Cash of $28,000 was paid to the creditors from whom equipment was purchased.

(5) Merchandise costing $50,000 was purchased on credit terms.
(6) Merchandise was sold to customers on account for $48,000.
(7) Paid wages of $800 in cash for two weeks.
(8) Received a promissory note for $8,000 from a customer on account.
(9) Paid cash of $200 for heat and light for one month.

The ledger accounts with the transactions analyzed and entered according to the rules of increase and decrease shown by the accounting equation are given below. The entries are numbered so that they can be identified with the transactions.

Assets		=	Liabilities		+	Owner's Equity	
Dr.	Cr.		Dr.	Cr.		Dr.	Cr.
+	–		–	+		–	+

Cash			Accounts Payable			Karen Weaver, Capital	
(1) 75,000	(2) 900	(4) 28,000	(3) 30,000			(1) 75,000
	(4) 28,000		(5) 50,000			
	(7) 800					
	(9) 200					

Plus
Revenue

	Accounts Receivable				Dr.	Cr.
(6) 48,000	(8) 8,000				–	+

Notes Receivable
(8) 8,000

Sales
(6) 48,000

Minus
Expenses

Prepaid Rent
(2) 900

Dr. + | Cr. –

Equipment
(3) 30,000

Purchases
(5) 50,000

Wages Expense
(7) 800

Heat and Light Expense
(9) 200

The Journal

The direct recording of transactions in the ledger accounts is inconvenient and errors are difficult to find. It takes time to leaf through the ledger pages or cards; and if there are many transactions, there is no time to enter each transaction in the ledger cards as it takes place. Furthermore, there should be some chronological record of the transactions with the entire transaction being shown in one place. Errors can then be located with less difficulty by tracing transactions from the chronological record to the ledger accounts.

A preliminary analysis of transactions is made in a book of original entry called a *journal*. In its simplest form, the journal consists of a book with a column for dates at the left, a wide Description column for account titles and explanations, and two columns for entering monetary amounts. The first of the two monetary columns is called the Debit column, and the second is called the Credit column. A simple journal of this type is usually called a *general journal*. The preliminary record entered in the journal is called a *journal entry*.

Each transaction is analyzed to identify the accounts that are to be debited and credited. The transaction is then recorded as follows:

1. The date is entered in the Date column.
2. The name of the account to be debited is entered in the Description column, and the dollar amount is entered in the Debit money column.
3. The name of the account to be credited is entered in the Description column on the next line in an indented position, and the dollar amount is entered in the Credit money column.
4. A brief explanation of the transaction is written beneath the account titles.

The general journal entries for Weaver's transactions would appear as shown below:

General Journal   Page 1

Date		Description	Post. Ref.	Debit	Credit
19--					
Oct.	1	Cash		75,000.00	
		Karen Weaver, Capital			75,000.00
		Investment of $75,000 by Karen Weaver.			
	1	Prepaid Rent		900.00	
		Cash			900.00
		Rent paid in advance for 3 months.			
	2	Equipment		30,000.00	
		Accounts Payable			30,000.00
		Equipment bought on account.			
	6	Accounts Payable		28,000.00	
		Cash			28,000.00
		Creditors paid on account.			
	9	Purchases		50,000.00	
		Accounts Payable			50,000.00
		Merchandise purchased on account.			
	12	Accounts Receivable		48,000.00	
		Sales			48,000.00
		Merchandise sold on account.			
	15	Wages Expense		800.00	
		Cash			800.00
		Wages paid for two weeks.			
	15	Notes Receivable		8,000.00	
		Accounts Receivable			8,000.00
		Note received from customer on account.			
	30	Heat and Light Expense		200.00	
		Cash			200.00
		Utilities paid for October.			

Posting

The number and the kind of accounts kept in the ledger depend upon the information desired or required. It is advisable to keep separate accounts for each type of asset, liability, revenue, and expense. An owner's equity or capital account should be kept for information relative to the owners' equity in the business. Generally, a list of accounts, called a *chart of accounts*, is prepared and each account is assigned a number. After the transactions have been recorded in the journal, the information is transferred to the ledger accounts through a process called *posting*. When information is posted from the journal to the ledger, the date and amount of each transaction and the page number of the journal are entered in the account. The narrow column headed "Post. Ref." in the journal is a cross-reference column called the *posting reference column*. The number of the ledger account is entered in the "Post. Ref." column so that a transaction can be easily traced to the ledger accounts if that should become necessary at a later date. Space is also provided in the ledger accounts for page numbers of the journal where the transactions were first entered. Thus a transaction can easily be traced from the journal to the ledger or from the ledger back to the journal.

Posting is a process of organizing data according to account classifications from the chronological record contained in the journal. After the data have been classified in the accounts and summarized, they can be used in the preparation of financial statements and reports.

While the two-column journal does provide a chronological record of transactions with both parts of the transaction in one place, it is not very helpful as a labor-saving device. In fact, there is more accounting work because the transaction must be entered first in the journal and then it must be posted to the ledger accounts. Weaver would have to make a journal entry for each transaction, then post the information from the journal to the ledger accounts before the ledger would contain the debits and the credits shown on page 502.

Special Journals

Often business transactions of a certain type are repeated time and again. There are likely to be many purchases of merchandise, sales to customers, cash receipts, and cash disbursements. To record each transaction separately in a two-column journal as an increase or as a decrease to a given account is unduly burdensome. Transactions of a similar type should be classified together, summarized for a period such as a month, and posted as one aggregate transaction for the month.

There are several types of journals, each type being designed to serve a special purpose. For example, all sales transactions could be entered in a sales journal. Similarly, purchases, cash receipts, and cash disbursements are entered respectively in a purchases journal, a cash receipts journal, and a cash disbursements journal. Other specialized journals can be used if transactions occur frequently enough to warrant their use. A manufacturing company, for example, may use a special journal to record materials withdrawn and transferred to production. Miscellaneous transactions that do not occur often enough to merit the use of a special journal are entered in the two-column general journal referred to earlier.

The special journals have columns so that similar transactions can be conveniently added together and posted as one transaction. For example, sales for the month may be shown in a sales journal designed as follows:

Sales Journal   Page 4

DATE		ACCOUNT DEBITED	POST. REF.	CASH DR.	ACCOUNTS RECEIVABLE DR.	SALES CR.
1980 Oct.	4	Customer A		500		500
	11	Customer B			2,300	2,300
	18	Customer A		800		800
	25	Customer E			1,500	1,500
				1,300	3,800	5,100

This design indicates that sales are often made on both cash and credit terms, since the sales journal has a column for cash debits, a column for accounts receivable debits, and a column for sales credits. At the end of the month, the sum of the two debit columns should be equal to the sum of the credit column.

It should not be inferred from the example given that all sales journals are designed with three columns. Journals are designed to fit the needs of the user, and special columns are provided for frequently used accounts.

Trial Balance

After posting from the journal to the ledger accounts, the balances of the accounts are determined and are listed on a *trial balance*. This listing shows whether or not the debit balances are equal to the credit balances. Mechanical accuracy is verified if the total of the debit balances and the credit balances is equal. However, this does not prove that all amounts have been recorded in the proper accounts.

A balance for the cash account, for example, is computed by subtracting the sum of the credit entries of $29,900 from the sum of the debit entries of $75,000 to obtain a debit balance of $45,100. Other account balances are similarly computed, and all balances are listed to form the trial balance given below:

Karen Weaver
Trial Balance
October 31, 19--

	Dr.	Cr.
Cash	45,100	
Accounts Receivable	40,000	
Notes Receivable	8,000	
Prepaid Rent	900	
Equipment	30,000	
Accounts Payable		52,000
Karen Weaver, Capital		75,000
Sales		48,000
Purchases	50,000	
Wages Expense	800	
Heat and Light Expense	200	
	175,000	175,000

ADJUSTING PROCESS

Business transactions are accumulated over an interval of time designated as an *accounting period* or a *fiscal period*. The period of time may be a month, a quarter of a year, a year, or any other significant time interval. Ordinarily, financial measurements are made over a period of a year, with the year being divided into months or quarters. During the course of a fiscal period, a company records purchases, sales, cash receipts, cash disbursements, returns of merchandise from customers, payrolls, transfers of materials and labor into production, and other events that arise in the normal course of its operations. Other important information may not be recorded at all, or the information may be recorded but with the passage of time may require adjustment. The adjustments are made after the transactions for the fiscal period have been recorded and after a trial balance has been prepared. To illustrate the adjusting procedure, adjustment data are given along with ledger accounts.
Adjustment data:

(1) Wages in the amount of $700 have been earned by the employees at October 31 but have not been paid or recorded.
(2) The note receivable has been outstanding for half of the month and yields interest at 12%. The total interest earned is $40 [($8,000 × 12%) ÷ (12 × ½)].
(3) Rent of $900 was prepaid for three months beginning October 1.
(4) The equipment was acquired at a cost of $30,000. Depreciation of the equipment has been estimated at $250.
(5) The inventory of merchandise on hand was counted and assigned a cost of $10,000.

(6) It has been estimated that sales in the amount of $1,500 are not collectible.

Usually, the adjustments for a company can be classified under the following three general headings:

1. The accrual adjustment
2. The prepayment adjustment
3. The valuation adjustment

Accrual Adjustments

Often wages, rent, interest, and the various costs of business operations are recorded only at the time they are paid. However, some costs grow or *accrue* with the passage of time. For example, wages are earned by the employees each working day even though they are paid at designated times.

Since the last payroll, wages of $700 have been earned. The additional expense and the liability are computed and the effect of the adjusting entry is illustrated in the T accounts below:

Wages Expense		Wages Payable	
800			700
700			

Looking at accruals in another way, assets and revenue also grow or accrue. Weaver has earned a total of $40 on the note receivable. The ledger accounts after posting the adjusting entry would appear as follows:

Interest Receivable		Interest Earned	
40			40

The need for accrual adjustments arises when all of the data pertaining to the fiscal period have not been recorded. Expenses that increase with the passage of time must be recorded, whether paid or not; and the liability for unpaid expenses must also be recognized. Similarly, revenue that increases with the passage of time must be recorded, whether collected or not; and the asset representing the amount due must be recognized.

In the following accounting period, when the $40 interest receivable is collected in cash, the collection is viewed as a conversion of assets; that is, the asset cash is increased and the asset interest receivable is decreased. The revenue was recognized in the prior accounting period even though the cash was not received until the subsequent period. Revenue is viewed as being the result of the earning process. The cash collection may or may not take place at the same time that the revenue is actually recognized (recorded).

Prepayment Adjustments

Business events should be properly analyzed and recorded as they occur. For example, an asset may be recorded at the time it is acquired for cash, or a liability may be recorded when an advance collection is received from a customer. By the end of the fiscal period, however, the situation may have changed. An adjustment may be required to show the part of the asset that was used in profit-making activity. The expense will be recorded, and the asset previously entered will be reduced. Likewise, deliveries of products may have been made against advance collections received from customers. The liability initially entered in the records will be reduced, and the portion earned will be recorded as revenue. Adjustments made to separate expenses from assets and revenue from liabilities are referred to as *prepayment adjustments*.

Karen Weaver, for example, has prepaid rent of $900 at the beginning of October. At the end of the month, one third of the prepaid rent has expired. The adjusting entry to record the rent expense and the reduction of the asset will bring the accounts up to date as follows:

Prepaid Rent		Rent Expense	
900	300	300	

The Depreciation Adjustment

To conduct business operations, a company normally requires the use of buildings, fixtures, machinery, and equipment. Assets of this type have a relatively long useful life and are classified under the general heading of *plant assets* or *fixed assets*. The expense resulting from the use of these assets is designated as *depreciation expense*. *Depreciation* represents an estimate of the physical wear and tear as well as any obsolescence relative to the use of the asset.

Plant assets are somewhat like prepaid expenses. The cost of a plant asset, like the cost of an insurance policy, for example, is allocated over its useful life. Ordinarily the plant asset has a longer life than the prepaid expense, but the adjustment procedure is somewhat similar. Unlike the prepayment, however, the plant asset may not be paid for at the time it is acquired. Debt may have been incurred to finance the cost of the asset. But the way in which it is financed has no effect upon the allocation of its cost to operations. The cost is allocated or assigned to time periods according to the flow of benefits received from the use of the asset over its useful life.

An asset such as a building or a piece of equipment has a limited useful life; it does not yield benefits indefinitely. It eventually wears out, becomes outmoded with the passage of time and changes in technology, or becomes inadequate as the company grows and requires the use of larger assets or assets with greater productive capacity. Over the total period of time the asset is in use, its cost is allocated to the various fiscal periods as depreciation expense.

Generally the cost of a plant asset is substantial, and the asset may be in service for a number of years. Often detailed underlying records are maintained to show the original cost of the asset, the name of the company from which the asset was purchased, the history of maintenance and repair service, the depreciation that has been recorded each year, and other pertinent details with respect to the asset and its operation. Ordinarily the plant asset account itself is not credited directly when depreciation adjustments are made. Instead, a special asset reduction account called "Accumulated Depreciation" or "Allowance for Depreciation" is credited. The original cost is then preserved in the plant asset account, and the reductions because of depreciation are shown in a separate offsetting account. The remaining cost to be charged against future operations, or the *net book value* of the asset, as it is called, is equal to the balance shown in the plant asset account minus the balance shown in the accumulated depreciation account. The accumulated depreciation account has a credit balance and is frequently referred to as a *contra asset account*.

Assume that Weaver has estimated the useful life of the equipment at 10 years with no provision for salvage value. Each month depreciation of $250 [($30,000 ÷ 10) ÷ 12] is to be deducted. When an equal amount of cost is assigned to each accounting period, the company is said to be recording depreciation according to the *straight-line method*.

After the adjusting entry is posted, the ledger accounts appear as:

Equipment		Accumulated Depreciation — Equipment		Depreciation Expense — Equipment	
30,000			250	250	

There is no necessary connection between the net book value of a plant asset and its market value. At the end of the first accounting period Weaver might be able to sell the equipment for more or less than the net book value of $29,750. Depreciation policy is not intended as a device for the valuation of plant assets. It is merely a means of allocating the cost to the fiscal periods during which the assets are in service. The allocation of cost is made to facilitate the determination of net income for the period.

The depreciation procedure in accounting is an estimating process and is filled with uncertainty. An estimate of the useful life and the salvage value is required, and a judgment on how to assign the cost must be made. As a result, accounting data are not as precise as they may appear. Estimates and human judgments enter into the processing operation, depreciation policy being a good example. The user of accounting information must be aware of these underlying judgments and estimates. The student of accounting should be constantly on the alert for other areas in the accounting process where estimates and judgments are filled with uncertainty.

The Inventory Adjustment

Some companies maintain *perpetual* inventory records, recording purchases as additions to inventory and withdrawals or sales as deductions from inventory and as increases in cost of goods sold. The inventory records should then show the proper balances on hand at all times. At the end of the fiscal year, a physical count may reveal errors in the book record that should be corrected. However, if the accounting system is operating properly and if there is proper control over the physical inventories, the corrections should not be substantial in amount.

Many companies do not keep a perpetual record of inventories. The purchases are recorded, but there is no record of the cost of items withdrawn or sold. As a general rule, it is impractical to record the cost of items sold if merchandise is sold to customers over the counter in relatively small lots. At the end of the fiscal year, the physical quantity remaining in inventory can be determined by count. Cost is then identified with the inventory according to the particular costing method that is employed. The cost of goods sold during the year is then computed indirectly as the sum of the beginning inventory and purchases minus the inventory at the end of the year. This method of arriving at inventory cost and the cost of goods sold is called the *periodic* inventory method.

A variety of practices may be employed in making the periodic inventory adjustment. The essential point is that the cost of goods sold should be determined as accurately as possible and that the inventory at the end of the year should be valued properly.

The inventory adjustment may be made by setting up a new account entitled "Cost of Goods Sold." The balance of inventory at the beginning of the year and the purchases for the year are closed out by credits, with the debit being entered in the cost of goods sold account. At this point, the cost of goods sold account has a balance representing the cost of goods available for sale. It is converted to cost of goods sold by removing the cost attached to the inventory remaining at the end of the year. This is accomplished by a debit to the merchandise inventory account in an amount equal to the cost of the inventory at the end of the year and by a credit to the cost of goods sold account.

To illustrate: (a) The inventory at the beginning of the month (no inventory existed at the beginning of the month) and the purchases of $50,000 are transferred (closed) to Cost of Goods Sold. (b) At the end of the month, a count of the inventory reveals that the merchandise on hand cost $10,000. After the adjustments are recorded, the affected ledger accounts are shown below:

Merchandise Inventory		Purchases		Cost of Goods Sold	
(b) **10,000**		50,000 | (a) **50,000**		(a) **50,000** | (b) **10,000**	

Valuation Adjustments

There is another type of adjustment that may be looked upon as being a valuation adjustment. Certain assets, such as marketable securities, accounts receivable from customers, and inventories are to be realized in cash in the normal course of events. But the assets may not be realized at the amounts shown in the ledger accounts.

Accounts receivable, for example, show the amounts due from the customers; but not all of the customers will pay their accounts. There will be uncollectible accounts. At the end of the year, there is no way of knowing which customers will default. Yet, sales should be charged with the estimated uncollectible accounts arising out of sales operations for the year. An adjusting entry is made to record the estimated uncollectible accounts chargeable to the year, and the credit is made not to accounts receivable but to an account that may be entitled "Allowance for Doubtful Accounts."

Of the total accounts receivable of $40,000, Weaver estimates that $1,500 will not be collected. When the estimate is made, no specific accounts receivable have been identified as uncollectible. Therefore, the credit is made to an allowance account. The affected ledger accounts after posting the adjusting entry are given below.

Accounts Receivable		Allowance for Doubtful Accounts		Uncollectible Accounts Expense	
40,000			1,500	1,500	

In the next accounting period, as specific accounts are identified as being uncollectible, they will be written off against the allowance for doubtful accounts. Assume that one of the customers defaults during the next accounting period in the amount of $400. After recording the default, the affected ledger accounts would appear as follows:

Accounts Receivable		Allowance for Doubtful Accounts	
40,000	400	400	1,500

The estimating procedure previously illustrated is subject to errors in judgment but nevertheless tends to produce more useful data than would be the case if the estimate were not made. There is no logical reason why losses on customers' accounts should be matched against revenue of the fiscal period in which the losses are detected. The losses should be matched against the revenue recorded when the initial transaction took place. Unfortunately, no exact determination of the losses can be made at that point. It should be possible, however, to make reasonable estimates based on past experience. Hence, this device is a method for recognizing the uncollectible accounts expense in the period in which the sale was made and not in a subsequent period when the account receivable is actually judged to be uncollectible.

Marketable securities and inventories are also subject to valuation adjustments. It is customary to value marketable securities and inventories at the lower of cost or market. If market values are lower than cost, an adjustment may be made to charge a loss to the year in which the market decline occurred. The offsetting credit may be made directly to the asset account or to an adjunct allowance account similar in concept to the allowance account used with accounts receivable.

Adjusted Trial Balance

After the adjusting entries are posted, an adjusted trial balance is prepared. An adjusted trial balance for Karen Weaver is given below.

Karen Weaver
Adjusted Trial Balance
October 31, 19--

	Dr.	Cr.
Cash	45,100	
Accounts Receivable	40,000	
Allowance for Doubtful Accounts		1,500
Notes Receivable	8,000	
Interest Receivable	40	
Merchandise Inventory, October 31	10,000	
Prepaid Rent	600	
Equipment	30,000	
Accumulated Depreciation — Equipment		250
Accounts Payable		52,000
Wages Payable		700
Karen Weaver, Capital		75,000
Sales		48,000
Cost of Goods Sold	40,000	
Wages Expense	1,500	
Uncollectible Accounts Expense	1,500	
Rent Expense	300	
Depreciation Expense — Equipment	250	
Heat and Light Expense	200	
Interest Earned		40
	177,490	177,490

Financial Statements

From an adjusted trial balance, the financial statements can be prepared. A statement of revenue and expenses is called an *income statement*. Expenses are deducted from revenue. If revenue exceeds expenses, the difference is called *net income*. If expenses exceed revenue, the difference is called *net loss*. The income statement shows the net changes in owners' equity that result from operating at a profit or at a loss. The income statement is used to measure revenue and expenses for a given accounting period or a fiscal period. An income statement for Karen Weaver is given on the next page.

Karen Weaver
Income Statement
For Month Ended October 30, 19—-

Sales		$48,000
Cost of goods sold		40,000
Gross margin		$ 8,000
Operating expenses:		
Wages	$1,500	
Uncollectible accounts	1,500	
Rent	300	
Depreciation	250	
Heat and light	200	3,750
Operating income		$ 4,250
Add interest earned		40
Net income		$ 4,290

A *balance sheet* is essentially a formal classified listing of assets and equities at one particular time. As time passes and as other transactions take place, the balance sheet becomes out of date; but as of the balance sheet date, it is a statement of the financial position of the enterprise. A balance sheet for Karen Weaver on October 31 is given below:

Karen Weaver
Balance Sheet
October 31, 19—-

Assets

Cash		$ 45,100
Accounts receivable	$40,000	
Less allowance for doubtful accounts	1,500	38,500
Notes receivable		8,000
Interest receivable		40
Merchandise inventory		10,000
Prepaid rent		600
Equipment	$30,000	
Less accumulated depreciation	250	29,750
Total assets		$131,990

Equities

Liabilities:		
Accounts payable		$ 52,000
Wages payable		700
Total liabilities		$ 52,700
Owner's equity:		
Karen Weaver, capital		79,290
Total equities		$131,990

Note that the owner's equity is $4,290 more than the owner's equity shown on the adjusted trial balance. The net income of $4,290 has been added to the $75,000 on the adjusted trial balance to yield an owner's equity of $79,290 at the end of the month.

THE CLOSING PROCEDURE

At the end of the accounting period, the revenue, expense, and cost of goods sold accounts have served their purpose. Measurements of the extent of the net increase or decrease in net assets resulting from profit-making activity during the accounting period have been taken. Now the income statement accounts can be closed; that is, the balances can be reduced to zero so that new measurements can be made in the following year. Revenue and expense classifications are like meters that measure the flow of liquids or gases for an interval of time. When the time interval has lapsed, the dials on the meters are set back to zero so that new measurements can be made for the next period of time. The closing entry for Karen Weaver on October 31 would be made as follows:

Sales	48,000	
Interest Earned	40	
Cost of Goods Sold		40,000
Wages Expense		1,500
Uncollectible Accounts Expense		1,500
Rent Expense		300
Depreciation Expense — Equipment		250
Heat and Light Expense		200
Karen Weaver, Capital		4,290

    Entry to close revenue and expense accounts for the year and to close net income to Karen Weaver's capital account.

After the revenue and expense accounts are closed, only the asset, liability, and owner's equity accounts have balances to be carried forward to the next accounting period and to serve as a cumulative record. The balances after closing are listed on a post-closing trial balance. The purpose of this final trial balance is to prove that the general ledger is in balance before transactions are entered for the new year. The ledger is now ready to receive entries for the next fiscal year, and the cycle of processing accounting data is repeated again.

The post-closing trial balance for Karen Weaver on October 31, 19--, is given at the top of the next page.

FORMS OF BUSINESS OWNERSHIP

Up to this point in the discussion of the accounting cycle, it has been assumed that one person owned the business, that is, the business was a *proprietorship*. With a proprietorship, the owner's equity is simply shown in one account and designated by the name of the owner, for example, Karen Weaver, Capital or Karen Weaver, Proprietorship.

Karen Weaver
Post-Closing Trial Balance
October 31, 19--

	Dr.	Cr.
Cash	45,100	
Accounts Receivable	40,000	
Allowance for Doubtful Accounts		1,500
Notes Receivable	8,000	
Interest Receivable	40	
Merchandise Inventory, December 31	10,000	
Prepaid Rent	600	
Equipment	30,000	
Accumulated Depreciation — Equipment		250
Accounts Payable		52,000
Wages Payable		700
Karen Weaver, Capital		79,290
	133,740	133,740

Actually, there are various legal forms of business ownership. The most important forms are:

1. The proprietorship.
2. The partnership.
3. The corporation.

A business that is owned jointly by two or more individuals or entities who share ownership is designated as a *partnership*. Each partner's interest is identified by his or her name and is designated as his or her capital.

A business may also be *incorporated*; that is, the business is given an existence apart from its owners through a charter issued by a state. The *corporation* is like a person at law, being able to transact business in its own right and having the legal rights and responsibilities of individuals in the commercial field.

The owners' equity in a corporation is not identified according to the persons who have ownership rights; that is, the stockholders. Instead, the owners' equity is shown under two broad general classifications:

1. The investment of the owners, which under ordinary circumstances will remain as a permanent investment.
2. The accumulated retained earnings of the business. In general, the accumulated retained earnings will be the total of all profits reduced by losses and by cash dividend payments.

In the formation of a corporation, the organizers agree that a certain stated amount shall be invested for each share issued. This original investment constitutes a permanent investment, assuming, of course, that there is no reorganization or other drastic change in the corporate structure. The amount of this stipulated investment is designated as *capital stock* if only one class of stock is issued. If more than one class of stock is issued, the stated amount for each class is shown separately and is appropriately designated as *preferred stock* or as *common stock*, as the case may be.

Often a corporation will receive more than the legal minimum investment per share. For example, it may be agreed that for each share issued there will be $1 invested and credited to capital stock. The shares are issued, however, for $5 each. The amount of the investment in excess of the stated value, in this case $4 per share, is credited to Paid-In Capital in Excess of Stated Value. Ordinarily, the amount credited to this account cannot be withdrawn and is looked upon as a part of the permanent investment.

The accumulated net earnings of the corporation as reduced by net losses, distributions to the owners, or transfers to paid-in capital are called *retained earnings*. Barring restrictions that may be imposed by law or by contractual agreement, the retained earnings establish the amounts that may be withdrawn by the owners as dividends.

SOME BASIC CONCEPTS

The mechanical features of processing accounting data have been discussed, but there is much more involved in the preparation of data for presentation in the financial statements. Certain fundamental concepts are observed, some of which are discussed at this point.

The Going Concern

In accounting, the assumption is made that a business will continue to operate in the future and that it will not cease doing business, sell its assets, and make final payments to creditors and owners. Therefore, it is said that accounting is carried out on a *going concern* basis. The plant assets, for example, are not normally adjusted to liquidation values. Presumably the plant assets will not be sold but will be used in future business operations. On the balance sheet given for Tobinton Products, Inc., on page 524, the building and equipment, for example, are shown at a net amount of $254,500. This does not mean that they can be sold for that amount. The valuation of $254,500 is the undepreciated cost to be carried forward to future years. As the building and equipment are used in conducting operations, a cost of using them will be recognized in the determination of net income or net loss.

There are, of course, circumstances in which the going concern assumption would not apply. If a business is to be discontinued, a different type of statement could be prepared and assets could be revalued at amounts that would possibly be realized upon their sale. However, this would be a special case, and the business would not be a going concern but would be a "quit concern."

Cost

Cost is conventionally used as the basis for accountability. Assets when acquired under normal circumstances are recorded at the price arrived at by negotiation between two independent parties dealing at arm's length. Simply stated, the *cost* of an asset to the purchaser is the price that must be paid now or later to obtain it. The fair value of the asset is not relevant in recording the transaction. A purchaser may acquire an asset at a cost that is greater or less than the fair value determined in the marketplace. If so, the asset is accounted for at the purchaser's cost, value notwithstanding.

Accounting for cost is an extremely complex process. In conducting business operations, some assets lose their original identity, that is, they are converted into some other form. For example, materials used in a chemical process often cannot be identified as such in the end product. Costs are traced through operations, wherever possible, as the assets are transferred or converted in the course of operations.

One of the principal objectives in accounting for cost is the measurement of profit and loss. The cost attached to the products or services sold is matched against the consideration received from the customers in the determination of profit or loss. This is not always easy to do. For example, several product lines may be produced together, with one particular cost common to all lines. The assignment of the cost to any one line is difficult at best, with further complexities being introduced when attempts are made to apportion the cost attached to any one line between the cost of the goods or services sold and the cost remaining on hand as inventory.

The Realization Concept

The profit and loss of a business is measured as the difference between the consideration received from customers and the cost attached to the products or services given in exchange. In conventional accounting, profit is not recognized unless it is realized. For the most part, realization depends upon an agreement with a customer to pay a stipulated amount for the product.

The point at which the revenue is realized will vary depending upon circumstances. The amount of the consideration received from the customer is frequently looked upon as being realized when title to the items sold is vested in the customer. At that point there is an enforceable claim against the customer. It is not necessary that the consideration be in the form of cash; the promise of the customer to make eventual payment is sufficient. In some cases, profit realization and cash realization go together. For example, a barber will realize the amount to be received from the customer when the service is given the customer, and the consideration will be realized in cash immediately after the service has been given. For all practical purposes, it can be said that the barber would be entitled to measure profit as cash is realized. On the other hand, when merchandise is delivered to customers on installment sales, there may be considerable doubt as to whether or not the promise of the customer to make eventual payment will be fulfilled. Profit on installment sales may be looked upon as realized when cash is collected.

In some cases, profit is realized before delivery is made to the customer and before cash is collected. For example, a shipbuilder may build a vessel on government contract. As the work progresses, profit may be realized by matching cost for the percentage of work completed against a corresponding percentage of the amount of the consideration to be received. This method of accounting for profit, known as the *percentage-of-completion* method, is sometimes used by contractors who build highways, buildings, bridges, and other structures and properties that are completed over a relatively long period of time.

Periodicity

The income statement has already been described as a statement pertaining to a given period of time only. Ideally, no measurement of net income or net loss should be made while a business is still actively conducting operations. A more accurate measurement of the net income or the net loss could be made after a company had ceased doing business and had sold all of its assets and had paid off all of its liabilities. The net income or loss would then be the difference between the amount ultimately realized by the owners and their initial investment. As a practical matter, however, measurements must be made while the business is in progress and the results must be reported periodically.

Ordinarily revenue and expense are measured over a period of one year. This year does not necessarily correspond with the calendar year but instead may correspond with the natural cycle of business activity. Logically, a fiscal year should end with the close of a cycle of business activity, that is, when inventories and accounts receivable are at a minimum but before new inventory is acquired for another cycle of sales and subsequent collections. For example, a department store may choose a year extending from March 1 of one year to February 28 (or 29) of the next calendar year. The Christmas sales and the January sales for the same season will then fall within the same year, and the inventories and the amounts receivable will generally be low just before merchandise is purchased for spring and summer sales. The year chosen for financial measurements is called the *fiscal year* or *fiscal period*.

Although a year is generally the longest period of time used in making measurements, it is possible to take measurements over shorter time intervals, such as a quarter of a year or a month. During the year, an income statement may be prepared for both a given month and for the year to date, or for a quarter of a year and the year to date. Sometimes the data for a corresponding period in the previous year is presented along with the current data, thus making comparison possible.

Matching

A reasonably accurate measurement of the net income or the net loss for a fiscal period depends upon the matching of expenses against related revenue. The matching of revenue and expense is difficult. With a going concern there is always the possibility that a revenue or an expense should have been recognized in a previous fiscal period or that it should have been deferred until some future period. If expenses have not been properly offset against revenue, the resulting net income or net loss for the fiscal period will be reported incorrectly.

The revenue and the expense pertaining to a fiscal period may have to be estimated. A company might sell a product under an agreement to guarantee against defects and furnish future maintenance and repair services. Not only must the estimated liability to the customer be recognized, but the expense of giving this service should be estimated and offset against the revenue resulting from the initial sales transaction. The cost of giving this service to the customer is related to the sales transaction; therefore, the estimated expense and liability should be recorded during the period in which the sale was made.

When a company purchases a piece of equipment, the cost of the equipment should be matched against the revenue of the future fiscal periods that will benefit from its use. The portion of the cost which should be deferred and matched against the revenue of any given year depends upon the estimation of the useful life and salvage value of the equipment. There are many similar situations in which matching must be done on an estimated basis. Estimates have to be made on a judgmental basis using information available.

Consistency

Not only are the results of an accounting system dependent in many cases upon estimates, but also they are influenced by the choice of an accounting method and the consistency with which it is applied. For example, inventories may be accounted for on a first-in, first-out basis, a last-in, first-out basis, or by some other means.

The *first-in, first-out (fifo)* method of costing inventories occurs when the older cost is traced through to the cost of goods sold while the more recent cost is identified with the inventories at the end of the period. On the other hand, the more recent cost may be traced through to the cost of goods sold, with the older cost being held as inventories at the end of the period. This method of costing is called the *last-in, first-out (lifo)* method. Inventory cost may also be averaged, with the cost of goods sold and the inventories at the end of the period stated on an average cost basis according to the particular averaging technique employed. The distinction between the cost to be matched against revenue as cost of goods sold and the cost to be held as inventories is highly important in the income determination process. One method of accounting for the flow of cost cannot be labeled as the correct method to the exclusion of all others. Yet, the choice of a particular method and the way in which it is carried out over the years has an influence on the profit reported as well as on the inventory cost for the balance sheet.

Assume, for example, that a company keeping its inventory records on a fifo basis computed its cost of goods sold for a year as shown below:

Inventory, January 1 (50,000 units @ $2)	$ 100,000
Purchases:	
January to June (150,000 units @ $3)	450,000
July to December (200,000 units @ $4)	800,000
Cost of goods available	$1,350,000
Less inventory, December 31 (40,000 units @ $4)	160,000
Cost of goods sold	**$1,190,000**

If the company had decided for some valid reason to change its method of accounting for inventories to the lifo method at the beginning of the year, it would compute a different cost of goods sold and a different inventory cost at the end of the year. The results might have appeared as follows:

Inventory, January 1 (50,000 units @ $2)	$ 100,000
Purchases:	
January to June (150,000 units @ $3)	450,000
July to December (200,000 units @ $4)	800,000
Cost of goods available	$1,350,000
Less inventory, December 31 (40,000 units @ $2)	80,000
Cost of goods sold	**$1,270,000**

The cost of goods sold is higher by $80,000 than it would have been without the change. Unless this is pointed out, the reader of the financial statements in making a comparison with the previous years might reach an inaccurate conclusion as to why the cost of goods sold had increased.

An accounting method or procedure once chosen should be followed consistently from year to year. Consistency in accounting is not advocated just for the sake of consistency, but rather to avoid the confusion that would result if profit or loss were to be calculated on a different basis each year. Desirable changes should be made, of course; but when changes are made, the effect of such changes upon the financial statements should be fully disclosed.

The Accrual Principle

Revenue and expense are accounted for on the accrual basis. *Revenue* is defined as the consideration (measured in monetary terms) received for rendering goods and services. Revenue is usually recognized when the following conditions are satisfied:

1. The amount of revenue must be capable of objective measurement.
2. The earning process must be reasonably complete or complete enough so that the cost of completion can be determined.
3. The revenue must be realized.

Revenue is not necessarily recognized at the time cash is collected. For example, goods and services are often sold on credit terms. At some later date collections will be made from the customers, but collections of cash are not a realization of revenue. Instead, the collections are a realization in cash of the asset, accounts receivable, which was increased at the time revenue was recorded, that is, at the date when goods or services were delivered and billed.

Occasionally customers will pay in advance for goods and services that will be delivered later. The advance payments have not been earned and cannot be recorded as revenue. The company, in accepting these advance payments, is obligated to the customers until it makes delivery. As deliveries are made, the liability is reduced and revenue is earned. If the accounting records have not been kept up to date during the fiscal period, adjusting entries will be made at the end of the period so that the portion of the advance earned is shown as revenue with the portion still owed to the customers being shown as a liability.

When merchandise is sold on the installment plan, there may be some question as to whether or not revenue should be recognized when deliveries are made to the customers. The collections may not be made according to plan, and the merchandise may have to be repossessed. Under the circumstances, there may be a justification for the recognition of revenue as collections are made. At that time there is no question about the realization of the revenue.

Reductions in revenue should be offset against the corresponding revenue recorded. Cash discounts and allowances granted to customers should be estimated and deducted from the related revenue. The loss is related to the revenue and not to the period of time in which the discount or the allowance is finally granted.

Similarly, expenses are carefully matched against related revenue and are not necessarily recognized when cash payments are made for goods and services. An expense occurs when the asset leaves the business as a result of revenue-producing activity and not when cash payments are made to creditors. The cost of the asset becomes expense in the fiscal period that benefits from the use of the asset. For example, supplies may be purchased on credit terms. At the time of purchase the supplies are recorded as an asset, and a liability to the creditor is recorded. When payment is made for the supplies, the liability to the creditor is reduced. But the payment is not related to the use of the supplies. As the supplies are used in earning revenue, the cost of the portion used should be recorded as expense with the supplies asset account being reduced by a corresponding amount.

Often expenses will have to be estimated. Goods and services may be delivered with an agreement that defects will be corrected or that future services will be given without charge. The costs to correct the defects and to furnish the additional services should be estimated and deducted as expenses in the same period in which the related revenue is recorded.

The problem of matching expenses against revenue in the income determination process is a challenging problem. The identification of revenue with a given interval of time is not an exact process, nor is it a simple matter to identify expenses with the resulting revenue. Judgments and estimates will have to be made in many cases, using the best information that is available to management.

Conservatism

Usually the accountant takes a conservative position. Revenue is generally not recognized by recording value increases that may take place on unsold products or merchandise, even if it can be demonstrated that the items in question can be sold at the current market prices in excess of their cost. The principles of valuing assets at cost and recognizing revenue only when the sale is made go hand in hand. If market increments were recorded, assets would be reflected at market value and not at cost.

On the other hand, losses may be recorded when the market price declines below cost. This inconsistency in the application of accounting principles has been justified on the basis of conservatism. As a rule the accountant is skeptical of claims that assets are worth more than cost but will be more inclined to accept evidence that assets may be realized at even less than cost. Conservatism can be carried too far, however. It has merit in that the readers of the balance sheet are not led to expect that marketable securities, for example, can be realized at cost when in reality the current market prices are below cost. But excessive undervaluation can make the business appear to be in poor financial condition when such is not the case. Investment may be discouraged if a business appears to be less valuable than it is. The accountant must recognize that persons can be injured by understatements as well as by overstatement.

Valuation

The reader of the balance sheet should be acquainted with the principles of valuation that are commonly applied in arriving at the dollar amounts shown for the various assets and equities. Sometimes the basis of valuation is indicated in the body of the statement or in accompanying footnotes. In many cases, however, the basis of valuation is not given, it being assumed that the reader is familiar with conventional practices. Recently the conventional practices of valuation have been criticized. Questions have been raised as to whether or not assets should be valued at cost on the balance sheet when there is evidence that the assets are worth considerably more or less than cost.[1] Or is the profit for a fiscal period properly measured when historical cost is matched against revenue as expense in the period of sale? The valuation problem cannot be separated from the problem of income determination. With rapid inflation in the past few years, the problem of financial measurement has been receiving increasing attention not only from accountants but from various business groups and the average consumer.

BALANCE SHEET CLASSIFICATIONS

A classified balance sheet for Tobinton Products, Inc., as of April 30, 1980, is illustrated on page 524.

Both the assets and the equities are usually listed separately and are not reduced by offsetting one against the other. This holds true even though specific assets may be pledged to secure the payment of a debt such as notes payable or bonds payable. Ordinarily the debt holder will receive payment in cash and will lay claim to the assets pledged only if the debtor defaults. The equity holders are said to have an *undivided interest* in the total assets. Thus, the equities are looked upon as a measurement of the extent of the rights of any individual or entity to the total assets but not to any particular asset. In the statement given for Tobinton Products, Inc., the holders of the long-term notes payable do not have a $75,000 interest in cash, accounts receivable, inventories, or any other specific asset. They do, however, have a $75,000 claim against the assets in total.

On the balance sheet the assets and the equities are listed under classifications according to their general characteristics. Similar assets or similar equities are listed together, so that it is a relatively simple matter to make a comparison of one classification with another or to make comparisons within a classification. Some of the most commonly used classifications are listed below:

ASSETS	EQUITIES
Current assets	Current liabilities
Investments	Long-term liabilities
Plant assets	Deferred revenue
Intangible assets	Other liabilities
Other assets	Owners' equity

Current Assets

The *current assets* include cash and other assets that in the normal course of events are converted into cash within the operating cycle. A

---

[1]See Robert T. Sprouse and Maurice Moonitz, *A Tentative Set of Broad Accounting Principles for Business Enterprises*, Accounting Research Study No. 3 (New York: American Institute of Certified Public Accountants, 1962).

Tobinton Products, Inc.
Balance Sheet
April 30, 1980

Assets

Current assets:

Cash			$ 41,370
Marketable securities at cost (market value, $38,250)			36,430
Notes receivable			3,000
Accounts receivable		$ 68,490	
Less allowance for discounts, returns, allowances, and doubtful accounts		2,640	65,850
Inventories			86,420
Prepaid insurance			1,770	$234,840
Investment in stock of Rabold Mills, Inc.				165,000

Plant assets:

Land			$ 14,600	
Building and equipment		$292,700	
Less accumulated depreciation		38,200	254,500	269,100

Intangible assets:

Organization expense			$ 4,900	
Goodwill			28,000	32,900

Other assets:

Advances to company officers		8,500
Total assets		$710,340

Equities

Current liabilities:

Bank loans		$ 18,000
Accounts payable		41,350
Accrued payroll and other expenses		19,540
Estimated income tax payable		28,400	$107,290
Long-term notes, due August 31, 1985		75,000
Deferred rental revenue		2,700

Stockholders' equity:

Capital stock, $10 par value, 5,000 shares issued and outstanding		$ 50,000
Premium on stock		82,500
Retained earnings		392,850	525,350
Total equities		$710,340

manufacturing enterprise, for example, will use cash to acquire inventories of materials that are converted into finished products and sold to customers. Cash is collected from the customers, and the circle from cash back to cash is called an *operating cycle*. In a merchandising business, one part of the cycle is eliminated. Materials are not purchased for conversion into finished products. Instead, the finished products are purchased and are sold directly to the customers.

Several operating cycles may be completed in a year, or it may take more than a year to complete one operating cycle. The time required to complete an operating cycle depends upon the nature of the business.

It is conceivable that virtually all of the assets of a business can be converted into cash within the time required to complete an operating cycle. But a current asset is an asset that is converted into cash within an operating cycle *in the normal course of events*. Assets such as buildings, machinery, and equipment that are used in conducting the business are not converted into cash in the normal course of operations. They are held because they provide useful services for the business; they are excluded from the current asset classification.

On the other hand, a manufacturer or a dealer who holds assets such as buildings, machinery, and equipment for resale to customers in the regular course of the business includes these items in the inventory under the classification of current assets. The manufacturer or dealer does not hold these assets for use in the business but holds them as an inventory of product in the expectation that the assets will be converted into cash in the normal course of operations. An automobile dealer, for example, has company cars that are not to be sold but are to be used in operating the business. These cars are not included in the inventory. But the cars that are held for resale to customers are an inventory of product that should be listed under the current assets.

In many cases, the operating cycle does not extend beyond a year. However, there are exceptions. An inventory of liquor in the distilling industry must be aged, for example, and may be shown as a current asset even though it will not be converted into cash within the next year. It qualifies as a current asset inasmuch as it is converted into cash in the normal course of events within the operating cycle of the business.

Investments

Investments are funds in cash or security form held for a designated purpose or for an indefinite period of time. This classification includes investment in the stocks or bonds of another company, real estate or mortgages held for income-producing purposes, and investments held for a pension or other special fund.

Plant Assets

The assets such as land, buildings, machinery, and equipment that are to be used in business operations over a relatively long period of time are often classified as *fixed assets* or more specifically as *plant assets* or as plant and equipment. It is not expected that these assets will be sold and converted into cash as are inventories. Plant assets produce income indirectly through their use in operations.

On the balance sheet for Tobinton Products, Inc., the land is shown separately at $14,600; the building and the equipment are shown at both the gross amount and at the net amount after deducting accumulated depreciation. Land does not have a limited useful life and is not reduced by depreciation. However, the cost of buildings, equipment, and other plant assets having a limited useful life is matched against revenue during the fiscal periods in which they are used.

Adjustments are usually not made in conventional accounting practice to restate plant assets at current replacement cost or at net realizable value. Plant assets, unlike the inventories, are not to be sold in the normal course of operations. Instead, they are used in performing the work of the business enterprise. The investment in plant assets should be recovered gradually as the assets are used in producing profit, but it is not expected that the investment will be recovered by direct sale as is the case with inventory.

In accounting for profit, the replacement cost of a plant asset and its net realizable value are not generally considered; yet in special decision-making situations these valuations can be applied. When equipment is to be replaced, for example, management considers the current replacement cost and the amount that should be realized upon the sale or trade-in of the present equipment. During the course of operations, recognition may also be given to the possibility that new equipment may cost more in the future. Profit that would otherwise be distributed to the stockholders as dividends may be retained to the extent of the anticipated increase in replacement cost. By following this policy, the company hopes to be able to retain the purchasing power of its initial investment.

Intangible Assets

Other fixed assets that lack physical substance are often referred to as *intangible assets*. The intangible assets consist of valuable rights, privileges, or advantages. Although the intangibles lack physical substance, they have value. Sometimes the rights, privileges, and advantages of a business are worth more than all of the other assets combined.

Typical items included as intangible assets are patents, franchises, organization expense, and goodwill. *Patents* give the business an exclusive privilege of using a certain process in manufacturing. *Franchises* permit a company to handle a given product or to operate within a given territory or along a certain route. To become incorporated, a company must incur certain costs, such as the initial incorporation fee to the state and the cost of legal services in connection with the formation of the corporation. These costs are the costs of the privilege of having a corporation and are designated as *organization expense*. A company is said to possess *goodwill* if it can earn a higher-than-normal rate of return upon invested resources. The higher rate of return may be caused by various factors such as managerial skill, popular acceptance of the products, or some other favorable circumstance. In setting a selling price for a prosperous business, it is recognized that the business as such may be worth more than the fair market value of the properties listed on the balance sheet as reduced by the liabilities. In other words, a value is placed on the anticipated earnings above an established normal level.

Goodwill is recorded only when it is purchased or sold. Frequently goodwill is recorded when a profitable business is acquired or when there is a change in the form of ownership. In the balance sheet given for Tobinton Products, Inc., goodwill is shown at $28,000. Perhaps the business was at one time a sole proprietorship and developed goodwill. When the business was incorporated, stockholders purchased ownership interests and in doing so recognized and paid for goodwill. Or Tobinton Products, Inc., may have purchased some other business, paying in excess of the values of the listed properties transferred less the liabilities assumed. This additional payment was made for anticipated future earnings above a normal level or, in short, was a payment for goodwill.

The cost of an intangible asset should be written off on the income statements over the fiscal periods during which it is estimated that the asset will yield benefits. For example, a franchise may enable a company to operate over a given route for only a stipulated period of time. The cost of the franchise should then be written off during the estimated fiscal periods that will benefit.

Other Assets

There are other assets that cannot be classified as current assets, investments, plant assets, or intangible assets. These assets are listed as other assets. Frequently the other assets consist of advances made to company officers, cost of buildings in the process of construction, and miscellaneous funds held for special purposes.

Current Liabilities

On the equity side of the balance sheet, as on the asset side, a distinction is made between current and long-term items. The *current liabilities* are obligations that are to be discharged within the normal operating cycle of the business and in most circumstances are liabilities that are to be paid within the next year by using the assets now classified as current. The amounts owed under current liabilities often arise as a result of acquiring current assets, such as inventory, or acquiring services that will be used in current operations. The amounts owed to trade creditors arising out of the purchase of materials or merchandise are shown as accounts payable. If the company is obligated under promissory notes that support bank loans or other amounts owed, the liability is shown as notes payable. Other current liabilities may include the estimated amount payable for income tax and the various amounts owed for wages and salaries of employees, utility bills, payroll taxes, local property tax, and other services.

Long-Term Liabilities

Debts not falling due until more than a year from the balance sheet date are generally classified as *long-term liabilities*. Notes, bonds, and mortgages are often listed under this heading. If a portion of the long-term debt is to become due within the next year and is to be paid, it should be removed from the long-term debt classification and shown under current liabilities with a caption such as "current installment of long-term debt payable." This reclassification will not be necessary, however, if the debt is to be refunded. Tobinton Products, Inc., has a long-term debt of $75,000 evidenced by notes that will not become due until August 31, 1985. No portion of this debt is to be paid during the next fiscal year; therefore, the entire amount is shown separately and is excluded from the current liability classification.

Other Liabilities

Liabilities, like assets, cannot always be classified as being either current or long-term. In some cases the creditors will not expect to receive payment either in the near or the distant future.

Deferred Revenue

Customers may make advance payments for merchandise or services. The obligation to the customers will, as a general rule, be settled by delivery of the products or services and not by cash payment. Advance collections received from customers are usually classified as *deferred revenue*, pending delivery of the products or services. On the balance sheet given for Tobinton Products, Inc., rent has been collected in advance from the tenants who have leased space in the building. When Tobinton Products, Inc., gives rental service to the tenants, the obligation will be removed from the balance sheet. The rentals will then be realized and shown on the income statement.

Owners' Equity

The *owners' equity* in a corporation, often called *stockholders' equity*, is subdivided:

1. One portion represents the amount invested by the owners directly, plus any portion of retained earnings converted into paid-in capital.
2. The other portion represents the retention of net earnings in the business.

This rigid distinction is necessary because of the nature of a corporation. Ordinarily the owners of a corporation, that is, the stockholders, are not personally liable for the debts contracted by the company. A stockholder may lose the amount invested, but creditors usually cannot look to the stockholder's personal assets for satisfaction of their claims. Under normal circumstances, the owners may withdraw as cash dividends an amount measured by the corporate earnings. This rule gives the creditors some assurance that a certain portion of the assets equivalent to the stockholders' investment cannot be arbitrarily withdrawn. Of course, this portion could be depleted because of operating losses.

The investment by the stockholders or the paid-in capital may also be divided into two portions. One portion of the investment is the legal minimum that must be invested according to the corporate charter as approved by the state. Each share of stock may be assigned a par value such as $1, $5, or $10 per share. For each share issued, the stipulated value is to be received by the corporation. This minimum investment is generally labeled as *capital stock*. Any amount invested in the corporation that is in excess of par value is shown separately and is labeled as *premium on stock* or as *paid-in capital in excess of par value*.

Sometimes shares are not assigned a par value. The state may require that the entire amount received from the sale of no-par stock be held as the legal minimum investment, in which case the total amount received would be credited to capital stock. In some states, however, no-par shares are virtually equivalent to par-value shares for accounting purposes in that they are assigned a stated value per share. Any amount received in excess of the stated value can be classified as *paid-in capital in excess of stated value*.

Ordinarily, the premium on stock or the paid-in capital in excess of stated value is not reduced as a result of dividend distributions. Many states, however, allow dividends to be charged against this portion of the stockholders' investment, but some states require that the source of such dividends be revealed to the stockholders.

If stock is issued at less than its par value or its stated value, it is issued at a discount. Some states do not permit the issuance of stock at a discount, while other states hold the stockholders liable to creditors to the extent of the stock discount if the corporation cannot meet the claims of its creditors.

The accumulated net earnings of a corporation are shown under a separate heading such as *retained earnings* or *reinvested earnings*. As a general rule, this portion of the stockholders' equity may be voluntarily reduced by the distribution of dividends to the stockholders and, of course, involuntarily by losses. Net losses in excess of retained earnings are shown as a deduction in the stockholders' equity section and are labeled as a *deficit*.

The owners' equity in an unincorporated business is shown more simply. The interest of each owner is given in total, usually with no distinction being made between the portion invested and the accumulated net earnings. The creditors are not concerned about the amount invested because, if necessary, they can attach the personal assets of the owners. The owners' equity in a partnership may appear as follows:

Owners' equity:
Craig Bergman, Capital	$161,000
Lucy Sutton, Capital	53,000
Total owners' equity	$214,000

INCOME STATEMENT CLASSIFICATIONS

The income statement, like the balance sheet, is a classified statement. An income statement for Tobinton Products, Inc., for the fiscal year ended April 30, 1981, is illustrated below.

Tobinton Products, Inc.
Income Statement
For the Year Ended April 30, 1981

Net sales			$1,283,480
Cost of goods sold			756,560
Gross margin			$ 526,920
Selling expenses:			
Sales salaries		$79,940	
Advertising		31,870	
Travel and entertainment		6,460	
Freight and delivery		4,850	
Depreciation		6,140	$ 129,260
General and administrative expenses:			
Officers' salaries		$53,180	
Office salaries		38,870	
Taxes		7,610	
Insurance		1,740	
Utilities		6,480	
Uncollectible accounts expense		6,760	
Amortization of organization expense		2,450	
Amortization of goodwill		4,000	
Depreciation		1,050	122,140
Total operating expenses			$ 251,400
Operating income			$ 275,520
Other revenue and expense:			
Interest and dividends earned		$ 5,320	
Rent revenue		8,600	
		$13,920	
Less interest expense		9,340	4,580
Income before income tax			$ 280,100
Estimated income tax			139,600
Income before extraordinary loss			$ 140,500
Loss on fire at Woodward plant (net of tax saving of $19,000)			21,000
Net income			$ 119,500
Earnings per share of stock			$23.90

Operating Revenue

The revenue resulting from the predominant activities of the business is listed first and is called the *operating revenue*. The gross operating revenue is often reduced by customer returns and allowances and cash discounts in arriving at net operating revenue. Tobinton Products, Inc., earns gross operating revenue by making sales to customers; and this revenue has been reduced by returns and allowances and cash discounts in arriving at the net sales of $1,283,480.

Cost of Goods Sold

If a company is engaged in selling goods, the cost of goods sold is computed and is deducted from the net sales to obtain the gross margin. The cost of goods sold can be computed quite easily in two steps as follows:

(1) Finished goods available at the beginning of the fiscal period $+$ Cost of goods manufactured or purchased during the fiscal period $=$ Cost of goods available for sale during the fiscal period

(2) Cost of goods available for sale during the fiscal period $-$ Finished goods available at the end of the fiscal period $=$ Cost of goods sold

Gross Margin

The gross margin of $526,920 is equal to the net sales of $1,283,480 reduced by the cost of goods sold of $756,560. *Gross margin* measures the difference between the net revenue realized from the sale of goods and their cost. No final profit has been earned at this point, of course, because there are operating expenses and other revenue and expenses that must be considered. However, the gross margin is significant. The relationship between the gross margin and net sales may be expressed as a percentage. A comparison of gross margin percentages between years may reveal that selling prices are increasing or decreasing relative to the cost of goods sold. Or it may reveal a change in a mix of products sold. Under certain conditions, gross margin percentages can also be used to estimate the amount of inventory that should be available.

If an inventory has been destroyed or stolen, an insurance claim can be established by using the typical gross margin percentage to estimate the amount of the inventory loss. The cost of the goods sold up to the time of the loss is estimated to be equal to the complement of the gross margin percentage multiplied by net sales. The estimated cost of goods sold is then subtracted from the cost of the goods that were available for sale to arrive at an estimated cost of the inventory at the time of the loss. The cost of the goods available for sale is equal to the cost of the inventory at the beginning of the fiscal period plus the cost of purchases or goods manufactured to the point of the loss.

Operating Expenses

The expenses of operating the business are then classified according to functional purpose and are deducted from the gross margin to arrive at the operating income. Expenses of promoting, selling, and distributing products are classified as *selling expenses* and include such items as advertising, sales commissions, delivery expense, sales supplies used, travel and entertainment, and sales office rent. The general expenses of business administration are classified as *general and administrative expenses* and include such items as officers' salaries, office salaries, office supplies used, taxes, insurance and uncollectible accounts expense.

Other Revenue and Expense

Various incidental or miscellaneous revenue and expenses not related to the main operating purpose of the business are combined with the operating income in the computation of income before income tax. In this example, interest, dividends, and rents were earned, and interest expense was incurred.

Income Tax

Corporate federal income tax is as much an expense for an incorporated business as any other operating expense. Yet it is usually shown separately near the bottom of the statement because (1) it is based upon the taxable income or loss for the period, and (2) it is usually a significant amount.

Extraordinary Gains and Losses

Unusual gains and losses that are not expected to recur are shown as *extraordinary gains and losses*. The Accounting Principles Board has defined extraordinary items strictly.[2] In order to qualify as an extraordinary item, a transaction or event must be both unusual in nature and infrequent in occurrence; and the amount must be material. The definition of "unusual" depends upon the nature of the business and the environment in which it operates. For example, the gain or loss from the retirement of plant assets would not be considered unusual in most circumstances and, hence, should not be reported as an extraor-

---

[2]See *Opinions of the Accounting Principles Board, No. 30*, "Reporting the Results of Operations" (New York: American Institute of Certified Public Accountants, 1973), pars. 19–24.

dinary gain or loss. On the other hand, a fire loss or a loss from some type of natural disaster, if material in amount and both unusual in nature and infrequent in occurrence, would be classified as extraordinary on the income statement. Extraordinary items are shown on the income statement net of the related income tax. Note, for example, that the fire loss on page 530 would have been $40,000 before tax.

Net Income

The final result on the income statement is labeled net income if the revenue and gains exceed the expenses and losses. Otherwise, the net result is labeled a net loss.

Earnings per Share

Those who read financial reports look for the earnings per share of stock. If there is only one class of stock outstanding with no complexities in the equity structure, the computation can be made quite easily by dividing the number of shares of outstanding stock into the net income. In the illustration given for Tobinton Products, Inc., the earnings per share were computed at $23.90 ($119,500 net income ÷ 5,000 outstanding shares). With two or more classes of stock outstanding or with senior securities (bonds or preferred stock) that may be converted to common stock, the computation becomes more complicated. The rights to earnings by security holders other than the common stockholders must be considered before computing the earnings per share of common stock.

BALANCE SHEET, END OF FISCAL YEAR

A balance sheet for Tobinton Products, Inc., at the end of the fiscal year April 30, 1981, is given on the next page.

A STATEMENT OF CHANGES IN RETAINED EARNINGS

The *statement of changes in retained earnings* connects the stockholders' equity in retained earnings as shown on the balance sheet with the results as shown on the income statement. Other additions or deductions are also shown in the computation of retained earnings at the end of the fiscal period.

A statement of changes in retained earnings for Tobinton Products, Inc. is given at the bottom of page 534. The dividends are a distribution of earnings to the stockholders and are not an expense of doing business. Hence, they are deducted on the statement of changes in retained earnings.

Tobinton Products, Inc.
Balance Sheet
April 30, 1981

Assets

Current assets:

Cash		$ 40,680	
Marketable securities at cost (market value, $74,200)		71,740	
Notes receivable		14,000	
Accounts receivable	$ 94,380		
Less allowances for discounts, returns, allowances, and doubtful accounts	2,870	91,510	
Inventories		96,400	
Prepaid insurance		2,080	$316,410
Investment in bonds of Konrad, Inc.			50,000

Plant assets:

Land		$ 14,600	
Building and equipment	$381,150		
Less accumulated depreciation	45,390	335,760	350,360

Intangible assets:

Organization expense		$ 2,450	
Goodwill		24,000	26,450

Other assets:

Advances to company officers			8,500
Total assets			$751,720

Equities

Current liabilities:

Bank loans		$ 10,000	
Accounts payable		31,250	
Accrued payroll and other expenses		25,420	
Estimated income tax payable		46,500	$113,170
Long-term notes, due August 31, 1985			75,000
Deferred rental revenue			2,700

Stockholders' equity:

Capital stock, $10 par value, 5,000 shares issued and outstanding		$ 50,000	
Premium on stock		82,500	
Retained earnings		428,350	560,850
Total equities			$751,720

Tobinton Products, Inc.
Statement of Changes in Retained Earnings
For the Year Ended April 30, 1981

Balance of retained earnings, April 30, 1980	$392,850
Add net income for the year	119,500
	$512,350
Less dividends	84,000
Balance of retained earnings, April 30, 1981	$428,350

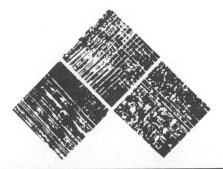

B-1. Recording Directly to Ledger Accounts. Frank Mussio began business on September 1, 19--, at a store on College Avenue. He sells jackets, shirts, and various novelties that are embossed with the university or fraternity insignia. Mussio deposited $4,600 in a separate bank account for store operations. A check for $1,700 was written for store fixtures and counters. Rent of $250 was paid by check for use of the store in September. Merchandise costing $3,300 was purchased on credit terms. During the month, cash sales of $5,900 were recorded on the cash register and deposited in the bank account for the store. A check in the amount of $280 was issued for supplies that were used during the month, and a check for $320 was for wages paid to a student who worked in the store during the evenings. A check for $2,100 was mailed to the supplier from whom the merchandise was purchased. At the end of the month, merchandise costing $800 was on hand. Depreciation on the counters and fixtures for the month has been estimated at $20.

Required:

(1) Record the transactions for the month of September directly in the ledger accounts. Use the ledger account titles given below:

Cash	Sales
Merchandise Inventory	Purchases
Store Fixtures	Cost of Goods Sold
Accumulated Depreciation — Store Fixtures	Wages Expense
	Rent Expense
Accounts Payable	Supplies Expense
Frank Mussio, Capital	Depreciation Expense — Store Fixtures

(2) Prepare an adjusted trial balance as of September 30, 19--.
(3) Prepare an income statement for month of September.
(4) Prepare a balance sheet as of September 30, 19--.

B-2. Journal Entries, Ledger, and Trial Balance. Eleanor Keefer owns and operates Western Record Store. A post-closing trial balance at June 30, 19--, is given below.

Western Record Store
Post-Closing Trial Balance
June 30, 19--

	Dr.	Cr.
Cash	3,450	
Accounts Receivable	1,730	
Merchandise Inventory	2,340	
Accounts Payable		2,170
Eleanor Keefer, Capital		5,350
	7,520	7,520

Transactions for the month of July are summarized below. (Add ledger accounts as needed.)

(a) Merchandise costing $6,180 was purchased on credit terms.
(b) Rent for the store and equipment in the amount of $250 was paid for the month of July.
(c) Merchandise was sold to customers on credit terms in the amount of $8,740.
(d) Payment of wages for the month was made in the amount of $980.
(e) A payment of $90 was made for electric service in July.
(f) Cash of $9,300 was collected on accounts receivable.
(g) Keefer withdrew $1,500 during the month for personal use.

Required:

(1) Prepare journal entries to record the transactions.
(2) Record the balances at June 30 in ledger accounts. Post the journal entries to the ledger accounts.
(3) Prepare a trial balance at July 31.

B-3 Adjusting Entries and Adjusted Trial Balance. Transactions for the month of August 19--, have been recorded by journal entry and posted to the ledger accounts of Magill Furnishings. A trial balance at August 31, 19--, is given on the next page.

Data to be used for making adjustments are given below:

(a) Advertising used for the month amounted to $760, but only $680 of this amount was paid and recorded.
(b) Some of the equipment was rented to another store during the month at an agreed rental of $200 for the month. Magill did not collect any of the rent during the month.
(c) Customers paid $800 in advance for merchandise to be delivered at a later date. The collection was recorded as a credit to Advances from Customers. During August, deliveries of $650 were made against the advances.

Magill Furnishings
Trial Balance
August 31, 19--

	Dr.	Cr.
Cash	4,370	
Accounts Receivable	8,260	
Allowance for Doubtful Accounts		320
Merchandise Inventory, August 1	4,190	
Prepaid Insurance	330	
Equipment	11,400	
Accumulated Depreciation — Equipment		1,500
Accounts Payable		3,270
Advances from Customers		800
Thomas Magill, Capital		12,920
Sales		43,700
Purchases	31,200	
Wages Expense	1,750	
Advertising Expense	680	
Utilities Expense	330	
	62,510	62,510

(d) The prepaid insurance of $330 provides insurance coverage for 11 months.
(e) Depreciation for the month of August has been estimated at $50.
(f) It has been estimated that sales during August in the amount of $600 will not be collectible.
(g) Inventory at the end of August has been counted and assigned a cost of $3,840.

Required: Prepare a form with six columns and label the column headings as follows:

Accounts	Trial Balance		Adjustments		Adjusted Trial Balance	
	Dr.	Cr.	Dr.	Cr.	Dr.	Cr.

Copy the trial balance in the first pair of columns. Enter adjustment information as debits and credits in the second pair of columns opposite the appropriate accounts. Add account titles as necessary. Combine the data in the trial balance and adjustment columns and extend final amounts to the adjusted trial balance columns.

B-4. Adjusting Entries by Type. Information with respect to adjustment situations is given below for Castor Company:

(a) A building costing $850,000 was acquired on July 1, 19--. Estimates indicate that the building should have a useful life of 20 years with a salvage value of $50,000 at the end of the 20 years. The difference between the cost of the building and the salvage value is to be written off over the 20 years in equal annual amounts.
(b) Utility bills were paid in advance in the amount of $4,000 on January 1, 19--. During the year, the company used $3,720 of the utility service.
(c) Wages amounting to $47,800 were paid during the year. The employees earned an additional $630 that was not recorded or paid by December 31.

(d) A portion of a warehouse has been rented to Herd Company at an agreed monthly rental of $700. On October 1, Castor Company collected rent for the period extending from October 1 to February 28 of the following year and recorded the collection as a credit to Rent Collected in Advance.

(e) The inventory at January 1 was $15,800. Purchases during the year amounted to $106,000. At the end of the year, inventory was counted and given a cost of $14,900.

(f) Castor Company estimates that 2% of the credit sales of $195,000 will prove to be uncollectible.

Required: Prepare adjusting journal entries for each situation given. Identify each situation by type as a prepaid, accrual, valuation, or inventory adjustment.

B-5. Adjusting Entries and Statements. A trial balance is given for Selden Company at March 31, 19--. Financial statements and closing entries were last made on December 31 of the previous year.

Selden Company
Trial Balance
March 31, 19--

	Dr.	Cr.
Cash	14,300	
Accounts Receivable	17,600	
Merchandise Inventory	19,400	
Prepaid Rent	4,800	
Equipment	47,000	
Accumulated Depreciation — Equipment		8,000
Accounts Payable		15,300
Capital Stock		20,000
Retained Earnings		34,100
Sales		135,000
Purchases	84,600	
Wages Expense	16,700	
Taxes and Insurance	4,300	
Heat and Light	3,700	
	212,400	212,400

Adjustment data are given below.

(a) Rent has been prepaid for the entire year, beginning January 1.

(b) Total wages earned by employees amounted to $18,600 in the first quarter. A large portion of this amount has been paid and recorded.

(c) Depreciation of equipment for the quarter has been estimated at $500.

(d) The inventory at the end of March has been counted and assigned a cost of $20,800.

Required:

(1) Set up ledger accounts from the trial balance and enter balances at March 31.

(2) Enter adjustment data directly in the ledger accounts. Open up new ledger accounts as needed.

(3) Prepare an adjusted trial balance, an income statement for the first quarter of the year, and a balance sheet at March 31, 19--.

(4) Enter closing entries directly in the ledger accounts.
(5) Prepare a post-closing trial balance at March 31, 19--.

B-6. Financial Statements. An adjusted trial balance is given below for Van Kirk Company with the accounts in random sequence.

Van Kirk Company
Adjusted Trial Balance
September 30, 19--

	Dr.	Cr.
Cost of Goods Sold	146,300	
Wages Expense	18,400	
Wages Payable		1,200
Accounts Payable		32,500
Notes Payable (long-term)		50,000
Land	6,000	
Accounts Receivable	19,200	
Cash	31,800	
Building and Equipment	145,000	
Sales		220,000
Advertising Expense	1,600	
Prepaid Rent	3,000	
Capital Stock, $1 par value		40,000
Rent Expense	1,200	
Depreciation Expense — Building and Equipment	3,000	
Merchandise Inventory, September 30	24,300	
Estimated Income Tax Payable		7,000
Accumulated Depreciation — Building and Equipment		18,000
Heat and Light Expense	2,600	
Taxes and Insurance Expense	3,400	
Income Tax Expense	17,000	
Dividends	10,000	
Retained Earnings		65,100
Interest Expense	1,000	
	433,800	433,800

Required: Prepare an income statement for the fiscal quarter ended September 30, and prepare a classified balance sheet for September 30.

B-7. Ledger-Adjusting and Closing. At the top of the next page, ledger accounts for Tri-City Appliance, Inc., are given after all transactions for the quarter ended June 30, 19--, have been recorded.

Adjustment data are given below.

(a) The insurance recorded as prepaid insurance provides protection from April 1 to December 31, 19--.
(b) Wages of $600 were earned by the employees at June 20 but were not paid or recorded by that date.
(c) Estimates indicate that 1% of the sales for the quarter will probably be uncollectible.
(d) Depreciation is recorded on the equipment at the rate of $300 per month.
(e) The inventory at June 30 has been counted and has been given a cost of $18,400.

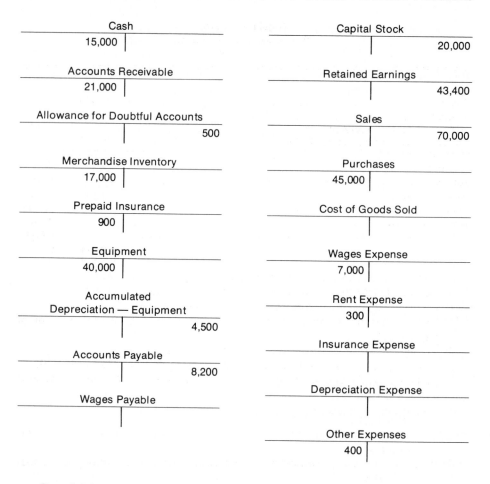

Cash		Capital Stock	
15,000			20,000

Accounts Receivable		Retained Earnings	
21,000			43,400

Allowance for Doubtful Accounts		Sales	
	500		70,000

Merchandise Inventory		Purchases	
17,000		45,000	

Prepaid Insurance		Cost of Goods Sold	
900			

Equipment		Wages Expense	
40,000		7,000	

Accumulated Depreciation — Equipment		Rent Expense	
	4,500	300	

Accounts Payable		Insurance Expense	
	8,200		

Wages Payable		Depreciation Expense	

		Other Expenses	
		400	

Required:

(1) Copy the ledger accounts with the balances at June 30. Record adjusting entries directly in the ledger accounts. Add any additional accounts needed.

(2) Prepare an income statement for the quarter ended June 30, 19--, and a balance sheet at June 30, 19--.

(3) Record closing entries directly in the ledger accounts.

(4) Prepare a post-closing trial balance.

B-8. The Accounting Cycle. A post-closing trial balance for Angela Burns, Inc., at June 30, 19--. is given at the top of the next page.

Transactions for the following quarter ended September 30 are summarized below:

(1) Sales to customers on credit terms amounted to $104,000.

(2) An accounts receivable in the amount of $200 was written off as uncollectible.

(3) Merchandise costing $58,000 was purchased on account.

(4) Wages of $8,100 were paid during the quarter for wages earned by employees.

Angela Burns, Inc.
Post-Closing Trial Balance
June 30, 19--

	Dr.	Cr.
Cash	14,100	
Accounts Receivable	36,500	
Allowance for Doubtful Accounts...		600
Merchandise Inventory, June 30, 19--.......................................	14,800	
Prepaid Rent...	2,400	
Equipment	56,000	
Accumulated Depreciation — Equipment....................................		12,000
Accounts Payable..		6,500
Notes Payable...		30,000
Capital Stock..		25,000
Retained Earnings..		49,700
	123,800	123,800

(5) Cash of $93,700 was collected on the accounts receivable.
(6) Cash of $12,000 was paid to acquire new equipment.
(7) Advertising was used and paid for in the amount of $3,800.
(8) Heat and light expense for the quarter was paid for in the amount of $4,700.
(9) Income tax for the quarter has been estimated at $10,000.
(10) Payments on accounts payable during the quarter amounted to $61,000.
(11) Dividends of $4,000 were paid during the quarter. Record in an account entitled Dividends.

Adjustment data are given below.

(a) It has been estimated that sales in the amount of $1,000 will be uncollectible.
(b) The inventory at September 30 has been counted and assigned a cost of $15,600.
(c) Prepaid rent at June 30 consisted of rent for the last six months of the year.
(d) Depreciation on the equipment has been estimated at $1,400 for the quarter.
(e) Interest on the notes payable is at the annual rate of 8%.

Required:
(1) Prepare journal entries to record the transactions for the quarter ended September 30.
(2) Post the journal entries to ledger accounts. Set up ledger accounts as needed with beginning balances when appropriate.
(3) Prepare journal entries to record the adjustments for the quarter ended September 30.
(4) Post the journal entries to ledger accounts.
(5) Prepare an adjusted trial balance.
(6) Prepare an income statement for the quarter and a balance sheet at September 30, 19--.
(7) Prepare closing journal entries and post the entries to the ledger accounts.
(8) Prepare a post-closing trial balance at September 30, 19--.

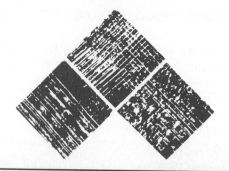

APPENDIX C

THE PRESENT VALUE CONCEPT

An amount of money to be received in the future is not equivalent to the same amount of money held at the present time. When confronted with a choice, anyone would rather have $100 today, for example, than the prospect of receiving $100 two years from now. The $100 that is available today can be invested to return more than $100 two years from now.

The time value of money can be compared with the visual perspective of distance, as shown below:

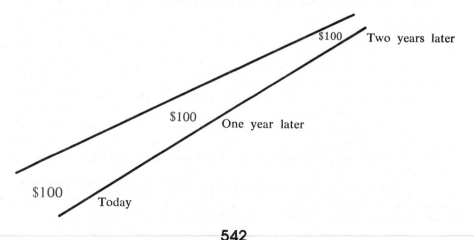

With physical objects at a distance, the objects appear to be smaller but are in reality as large as similar objects that are close at hand. In the case of money, however, it is no illusion.

A future sum of money is of less magnitude than the same amount of money today. This is because money today can grow to a larger sum through investment. For example, $100 invested at 10 percent compound interest per year will be worth $121 at the end of two years.

$100 initial investment × 1.10 = $110 value of the investment at the end of Year 1

$110 value of the investment × 1.10 = $121 value of the investment at the end of Year 1 at the end of Year 2

The $100 received today grows to $121 by the end of two years and thus is larger than $100 to be received at the end of two years.

The investment plus compound interest is called the *compound amount*. The compound amount of $100 in two years with interest compounded at the rate of 10 percent annually is $121. The formula for the compound amount of $1 follows:

$$\text{Compound amount} = (1 + i)^n$$

i = interest rate
n = number of years

In the example given, the compound amount could have been computed as follows:

Compound amount of $1 = $(1.10)^2$
Compound amount of $1 = (1.10) × (1.10)
Compound amount of $1 = $1.21
Compound amount of $100 = 100 × $1.21 or $121

A person who can earn 10 percent compound interest looks upon the receipt of $121 in two years as being equivalent to $100 today. Such a person is indifferent as to whether he or she has $100 today or $121 in two years.

Obviously, many business decisions involve the investment of dollars with the expectation that more dollars will be received at some future time. The returns are compared with the investment in making the investment decision. The returns and the investment, however, are not on the same time basis. Before a comparison can be made, the present and future dollars must be stated on an equivalent time basis.[1] Present dollars may be placed on a future dollar basis; that is, the compound amount of a present investment may be computed. If a business person has $100 available for investment and believes that a 10 percent return with interest compounded annually can be earned, he or she will expect to receive $121 at the end of two years from a present investment of $100. Hence, an investment opportunity that is

---

[1]The adjustments to place monetary amounts on an equivalent time basis should not be confused with price-level adjustments. The adjustments are made for different purposes. Adjustments for differences in time are required even if the price level remains the same.

expected to yield $115 in two years from a present investment of $100 is unacceptable if $121 can normally be expected from a $100 investment. In short, the potential investor does not believe that $115 in two years is equivalent to $100 today if he or she can expect to receive $121 from other investment opportunities that are available.

The Present Value of a Future Amount

It is also possible to move in the other direction and to compute the present value of an amount of money that is to be received in the future. Expressed in another way, how much money must be invested today in order to receive a certain amount of money in the future? Or a debtor may look at the situation from a different point of view. How much money must be paid now to settle a debt that will become due in the future? In business, a choice must often be made between having a given amount of money now or the prospect of receiving a monetary return in the future. Does the expected future return justify the investment? This can be determined by computing the present value of the future return and comparing it with the amount invested.

The present value of a future amount of money can be computed by mutliplying the future amount by the present value of $1. The formula for the present value of $1 follows:

$$\text{Present value of \$1} = \frac{1}{(1 + i)^n}$$

i = interest rate
n = number of years

Assume, for example, that $121 is to be received two year later with interest compounded annually at 10 percent. How much money must be invested today to get $121 at the end of two years?

Solve for the present value of $1 in two years with interest compounded annually at 10 percent.

Present value of $1, 2 years, 10% interest	$= \dfrac{1}{(1.10)^2}$
Present value of $1, 2 years, 10% interest	= $.826446
Present value of $121, 2 years, 10% interest	$= \dfrac{\$121 \times \$.826446}{\text{or } \$100}$

The computation may also be made as follows:

	Year 1	Year 2
Present value, $100	$110	$121

$121 = 110% of the amount invested by the end of Year 1
$121 ÷ 1.10 = $110 amount at the end of Year 1
$110 = 110% of the amount invested at the beginning of Year 1 (present value)
$110 ÷ 1.10 = $100 amount invested at the beginning of Year 1, or the present value

This is summarized below:

$$\frac{\$121/1.10}{1.10} \text{ is equivalent to } \frac{\$121}{(1.10)^2}$$

or

$$\frac{1}{(1.10)^2} \times \$121 = \$100 \text{ present value}$$

In the computation of a present value, the interest is removed from a future amount to arrive at the initial amount invested. The process of reducing future values to present values is called *discounting*. The present value is sometimes called the *discounted value*. The interest to be subtracted is called the *discount*, and the rate of interest is called the *discount rate*.

It is seldom necessary to compute either the compound amount or the present value of $1. The compound amounts of $1 at various interest rates for various years and the present values of $1 at various interest rates for various years are listed in published tables. A table for the present values of $1 is given on page 551 as Table I. The table gives the decimal equivalent for $\frac{1}{(1 + i)^n}$. For example, the value of $\frac{1}{(1.10)^2}$ is .826. Thus, the present value of $121 received two years hence at 10 percent is $100 ($121 × .826 [slight difference due to rounding decimal equivalent]). By using the tables, it is possible to determine the present value of any amount of money to be received in the future by multiplying the future value by the figure given in the table.

The Present Value of a Series of Future Amounts

Often it is necessary to compute the present value of a series of amounts that will be received at periodic intervals in the future. For example, managment may be considering the acquisition of new equipment or the addition of a new product line. Do the expected future returns from the investment in the equipment or the new product line justify the investment? The future returns can be discounted at the rate of return expected from similar investments, and the result can be compared with the amount to be invested. In other words, the future returns are converted to present value equivalents so that they can be compared with the investment.

It would be possible, of course, to compute the compound (future) amount of the investment by adding compound interest to the investment and to compare this amount with the compound (future) amount of the returns. The comparison would then be based on future values. The normal practice, however, is to make comparisons in the present. Hence, future dollar amounts are usually discounted to a present value.

The present value of a series of returns to be received at periodic intervals in the future is nothing more than the sum of the present values of the individual returns. Assume that $1,000 is to be received at the end of each year for five years with interest compounded annually at 10 percent. What is the present value of these five annual receipts of $1,000? The present value of five annual returns of $1,000 received at the end of each year with interest compounded at 10 percent can be computed as shown below:

END OF YEAR	RETURNS	COMPUTATION		
1	$1,000	$1,000 \times \dfrac{1}{1.10}$ =	$ 909	present value of $1,000 received at end of Year 1
2	1,000	$1,000 \times \dfrac{1}{(1.10)^2}$ =	826	present value of $1,000 received at end of Year 2
3	1,000	$1,000 \times \dfrac{1}{(1.10)^3}$ =	751	present value of $1,000 received at end of Year 3
4	1,000	$1,000 \times \dfrac{1}{(1.10)^4}$ =	683	present value of $1,000 received at end of Year 4
5	1,000	$1,000 \times \dfrac{1}{(1.10)^5}$ =	621	present value of $1,000 received at end of Year 5

Present value of $1,000 received at the end of each year for 5 years $3,790

The same result can also be computed as shown below:

$$\$1,000 \left(\frac{1}{1.10} + \frac{1}{(1.10)^2} + \frac{1}{(1.10)^3} + \frac{1}{(1.10)^4} + \frac{1}{(1.10)^5} \right) = \$3,790$$

The decimal equivalents of the fractions in the equation can be found in the table of present values of $1 (Table I):

$$(.909 + .826 + .751 + .683 + .621)$$

The sum of the present values is 3.79, and the present value of $1,000 received each year for five years at 10 percent interest compounded annually is $3,790:

$$\$1,000 \ (3.79) = \$3,790$$

Note that the factor, 3.79, can be read from Table II on page 552. The difference between this amount and the amount appearing in the table is due to rounding. The values in Table II are the sums of those given in Table I.

The Present Value Concept Applied

The concept of present value is applied whenever future dollar amounts are to be compared with present dollar amounts. A dollar to be received at some future date is not equivalent to the dollar received today because of the time difference. The dollars to be received in the future are discounted at an appropriate discount rate so that they can be compared with the dollars in the present.

For example, a company may be planning to invest $50,000 in a project that will probably yield $10,000 after income tax each year for ten years. If the company has other investment opportunities that will yield a 12 percent return after tax, should it make the $50,000 investment in this project? The solution to this problem can be obtained by discounting the annual returns of $10,000 at the 12 percent rate and comparing the result with the $50,000 to be invested. In other words, the anticipated annual returns of $10,000 are reduced to a present value, and the present value of the returns is compared with the amount to be invested. If the present value of the returns is greater than the amount of the investment, the investment will earn more than the 12 percent minimum rate-of-return requirement and is desirable. On the other hand, if the present value of the returns is less than $50,000, the investment in the project should be rejected. It will not earn as much as other investment opportunities. The method briefly described above is applied in making investment decisions and is referred to as *the net present value method*. This method is discussed more completely in Chapter 10.

The $10,000 annual returns are discounted at 12 percent as follows:

$10,000 annual return × $5.65 present value of $1 received each year for 10 years with interest compounded annually at 12% (See Table II on page 552.)

= $56,500 present value of annual returns of $10,000 for 10 years at 12% interest compounded annually

The project should be accepted. Returns on a present value basis are greater than the amount invested, indicating that the project is earning more than the minimum rate of return established at 12 percent.[2]

Another approach may be taken in making investment decisions. The discounted rate of return on the investment project may be determined and compared with the minimum rate of return. The discounted rate of return approach is also discussed in Chapter 10. The rate-of-return calculation is illustrated by using the data from the pre-

---

[2]The returns from business investments are not necessarily received at the end of each year. Usually they are received throughout the year while operations are being conducted. A more accurate calculation can be made by using a continuous discount rate. However, this not necessary. In making business decisions, management must compare alternatives and select the best alternative from among those that are available. For this purpose, annual discounting is acceptable, it being assumed that the pattern of the returns within the year will be the same for all of the alternatives.

vious illustration. What is the discounted rate of return when $10,000 is received each year for ten years on an investment of $50,000? Stated in another way, what discount rate will equate the $50,000 investment with the $10,000 annual returns?

$$\$50,000 = \$10,000 \times \text{discount rate}$$

To calculate the discounted rate of return, divide the investment by the annual return; that is, find the ratio of the investment to the annual return:

$$\frac{\$50,000 \text{ investment}}{\$10,000 \text{ annual return}} = 5 \text{ ratio of investment to annual return}$$

This ratio is compared with the values appearing in the table of the present values of $1 received annually for the number of years involved, in this case ten years. Select the value in the table that most closely corresponds with the ratio. The value in the table for ten years that most closely corresponds with the ratio is 5.019 in the 15 percent column.

The discounted rate of return on the investment is a little more than 15 percent. Multiply the annual return of $10,000 by the value in the table for 15 percent for ten years.

$10,000 annual return × $5.019 present value of $1 received annually for 10 years with interest compounded annually at 15%

= $50,190 present value of annual returns of $10,000 with interest compounded annually at 15%

The present value of the annual returns amounting to $50,190 is somewhat greater than the investment of $50,000 when the annual returns are discounted at 15 percent. This indicates that the discounted rate of return is somewhat more than 15 percent.

Sometimes the discounted rate of return cannot be computed so easily. The returns for each year may not be equal. For example, an investment of $90,000 is expected to produce returns for five years as follows:

YEARS	RETURNS
1	$ 40,000
2	40,000
3	30,000
4	20,000
5	20,000
Total................	$150,000

The average return is $30,000 and may be used in computing a ratio of the investment to the annual return.

Total returns of $150,000 ÷ 5 years = $30,000 average annual return

$$\frac{\$90,000 \text{ investment}}{\$30,000 \text{ average annual return}} = 3 \text{ ratio of investment to average annual return}$$

This ratio is compared with the values in Table II, page 552, and is closest to 2.991 on the five-year line for 20 percent.

In this illustration, the returns for the earlier years are larger than the returns for the later years. Therefore, the discounted rate of return will be higher than 20 percent. More immediate returns have a greater present value than returns that will be realized in later years. This would be expected considering that these relatively large returns will be available for investment at an earlier date. A trial rate of 24 percent may be used. The present values for each year are then computed at 24 percent from the table showing the present values of $1.

YEARS	RETURNS		PRESENT VALUES OF $1 AT 24%		PRESENT VALUE OF RETURNS
1	$40,000	×	$.806	=	$32,240
2	40,000	×	.650	=	26,000
3	30,000	×	.524	=	15,720
4	20,000	×	.423	=	8,460
5	20,000	×	.341	=	6,820
	Present value of the annual returns				$89,240

The discounted rate of return is slightly less than 24 percent. Ordinarily, the approximate discounted rate of return can be calculated with no more than three trials. If the discounted returns are less than the present value of the investment, use a lower rate for the next trial. If the discounted returns are greater than the present value of the investment, use a higher rate.

When the returns for the later years are large in relation to the returns for the earlier years, the same general procedure can be followed. However, the first trial should be made with a rate that is somewhat lower than the rate computed by using the average annual return. Later returns have less power than earlier returns because they cannot be reinvested as soon. The discounted rate of return, therefore, will be somewhat lower.

An Investment Illustration

The Wilcox Mining Company plans to invest $1,650,000 in further mine development. This investment should produce $500,000 after income tax each year for five years, after which the mine will be worthless. Should this investment be made if alternative investment situations can be expected to yield a discounted rate of return after income tax of 18 percent? What is the discounted rate of return on the mine development alternative?

The first question can be answered by discounting the annual returns at the lowest rate of return that will be accepted, that is, at 18 percent.

$500,000 annual return × $3.127 present value of $1 received annually
for 5 years, interest compounded at
18%

= $1,563,500 present value of annual returns, 5 years, 18% compound interest

The mine development plan should be rejected. It will not yield the desired rate of return. The discounted returns are only $1,563,500, and the investment is $1,650,000.

The second question can be answered by solving for the discount rate that will equate the annual returns with the investment. Find the ratio of the investment to the annual return.

$$\frac{\$1,650,000 \text{ investment}}{\$500,000 \text{ annual return}} = 3.3 \text{ ratio of investment to annual return}$$

The table of present values of $1 received annually shows that 3.352 is closest to the ratio of 3.3. This value is on the five-year line for 15 percent.

$500,000 annual return × $3.352 present value of $1 received annually
for 5 years, interest compounded at
15%

= $1,676,000 present value of annual returns, 15% compound interest

The discounted rate of return is more than 15 percent, but it is less than 16 percent.

$500,000 annual return × $3.274 present value of $1 received annually
for 5 years, interest compounded at
16%

= $1,637,000 present value of annual returns, 16% compound interest

TABLE I
Present Value of $1

Years Hence	4%	5%	6%	8%	10%	12%	14%	15%	16%	18%	20%	22%	24%	25%	26%	28%	30%	35%	40%
1	0.962	0.952	0.943	0.926	0.909	0.893	0.877	0.870	0.862	0.847	0.833	0.820	0.806	0.800	0.794	0.781	0.769	0.741	0.714
2	0.925	0.907	0.890	0.857	0.826	0.797	0.769	0.756	0.743	0.718	0.694	0.672	0.650	0.640	0.630	0.610	0.592	0.549	0.510
3	0.889	0.864	0.840	0.794	0.751	0.712	0.675	0.658	0.641	0.609	0.579	0.551	0.524	0.512	0.500	0.477	0.455	0.406	0.364
4	0.855	0.823	0.792	0.735	0.683	0.636	0.592	0.572	0.552	0.516	0.482	0.451	0.423	0.410	0.397	0.373	0.350	0.301	0.260
5	0.822	0.784	0.747	0.681	0.621	0.567	0.519	0.497	0.476	0.437	0.402	0.370	0.341	0.328	0.315	0.291	0.269	0.223	0.186
6	0.790	0.746	0.705	0.630	0.564	0.507	0.456	0.432	0.410	0.370	0.335	0.303	0.275	0.262	0.250	0.227	0.207	0.165	0.133
7	0.760	0.711	0.665	0.583	0.513	0.452	0.400	0.376	0.354	0.314	0.279	0.249	0.222	0.210	0.198	0.178	0.159	0.122	0.095
8	0.731	0.677	0.627	0.540	0.467	0.404	0.351	0.327	0.305	0.266	0.233	0.204	0.179	0.168	0.157	0.139	0.123	0.091	0.068
9	0.703	0.645	0.592	0.500	0.424	0.361	0.308	0.284	0.263	0.225	0.194	0.167	0.144	0.134	0.125	0.108	0.094	0.067	0.048
10	0.676	0.614	0.558	0.463	0.386	0.322	0.270	0.247	0.227	0.191	0.162	0.137	0.116	0.107	0.099	0.085	0.073	0.050	0.035
11	0.650	0.585	0.527	0.429	0.350	0.287	0.237	0.215	0.195	0.162	0.135	0.112	0.094	0.086	0.079	0.066	0.056	0.037	0.025
12	0.625	0.557	0.497	0.397	0.319	0.257	0.208	0.187	0.168	0.137	0.112	0.092	0.076	0.069	0.062	0.052	0.043	0.027	0.018
13	0.601	0.530	0.469	0.368	0.290	0.229	0.182	0.163	0.145	0.116	0.093	0.075	0.061	0.055	0.050	0.040	0.033	0.020	0.013
14	0.577	0.505	0.442	0.340	0.263	0.205	0.160	0.141	0.125	0.099	0.078	0.062	0.049	0.044	0.039	0.032	0.025	0.015	0.009
15	0.555	0.481	0.417	0.315	0.239	0.183	0.140	0.123	0.108	0.084	0.065	0.051	0.040	0.035	0.031	0.025	0.020	0.011	0.006
16	0.534	0.458	0.394	0.292	0.218	0.163	0.123	0.107	0.093	0.071	0.054	0.042	0.032	0.028	0.025	0.019	0.015	0.008	0.005
17	0.513	0.436	0.371	0.270	0.198	0.146	0.108	0.093	0.080	0.060	0.045	0.034	0.026	0.023	0.020	0.015	0.012	0.006	0.003
18	0.494	0.416	0.350	0.250	0.180	0.130	0.095	0.081	0.069	0.051	0.038	0.028	0.021	0.018	0.016	0.012	0.009	0.005	0.002
19	0.475	0.396	0.331	0.232	0.164	0.116	0.083	0.070	0.060	0.043	0.031	0.023	0.017	0.014	0.012	0.009	0.007	0.003	0.002
20	0.456	0.377	0.312	0.215	0.149	0.104	0.073	0.061	0.051	0.037	0.026	0.019	0.014	0.012	0.010	0.007	0.005	0.002	0.001
21	0.439	0.359	0.294	0.199	0.135	0.093	0.064	0.053	0.044	0.031	0.022	0.015	0.011	0.009	0.008	0.006	0.004	0.002	0.001
22	0.422	0.342	0.278	0.184	0.123	0.083	0.056	0.046	0.038	0.026	0.018	0.013	0.009	0.007	0.006	0.004	0.003	0.001	0.001
23	0.406	0.326	0.262	0.170	0.112	0.074	0.049	0.040	0.033	0.022	0.015	0.010	0.007	0.006	0.005	0.003	0.002	0.001	—
24	0.390	0.310	0.247	0.158	0.102	0.066	0.043	0.035	0.028	0.019	0.013	0.008	0.006	0.005	0.004	0.003	0.002	0.001	—
25	0.375	0.295	0.233	0.146	0.092	0.059	0.038	0.030	0.024	0.016	0.010	0.007	0.005	0.004	0.003	0.002	0.001	0.001	—
26	0.361	0.281	0.220	0.135	0.084	0.053	0.033	0.026	0.021	0.014	0.009	0.006	0.004	0.003	0.002	0.002	0.001	—	—
27	0.347	0.268	0.207	0.125	0.076	0.047	0.029	0.023	0.018	0.011	0.007	0.005	0.003	0.002	0.002	0.001	0.001	—	—
28	0.333	0.255	0.196	0.116	0.069	0.042	0.026	0.020	0.016	0.010	0.006	0.004	0.002	0.002	0.002	0.001	0.001	—	—
29	0.321	0.243	0.185	0.107	0.063	0.037	0.022	0.017	0.014	0.008	0.005	0.003	0.002	0.002	0.001	0.001	—	—	—
30	0.308	0.231	0.174	0.099	0.057	0.033	0.020	0.015	0.012	0.007	0.004	0.003	0.002	0.001	0.001	—	—	—	—
35	0.253	0.181	0.130	0.068	0.036	0.019	0.010	0.008	0.006	0.003	0.002	0.001	0.001	—	—	—	—	—	—
40	0.208	0.142	0.097	0.046	0.022	0.011	0.005	0.004	0.003	0.001	0.001	—	—	—	—	—	—	—	—
45	0.171	0.111	0.073	0.031	0.014	0.006	0.003	0.002	0.001	0.001	—	—	—	—	—	—	—	—	—
50	0.141	0.087	0.054	0.021	0.009	0.003	0.001	0.001	0.001	—	—	—	—	—	—	—	—	—	—

TABLE II
Present Value of $1 Received Annually for N Years

Years (N)	4%	5%	6%	8%	10%	12%	14%	15%	16%	18%	20%	22%	24%	25%	26%	28%	30%	35%	40%
1	0.962	0.952	0.943	0.926	0.909	0.893	0.877	0.870	0.862	0.847	0.833	0.820	0.806	0.800	0.794	0.781	0.769	0.741	0.714
2	1.886	1.859	1.833	1.783	1.736	1.690	1.647	1.626	1.605	1.566	1.528	1.492	1.457	1.440	1.424	1.392	1.361	1.289	1.224
3	2.775	2.723	2.673	2.577	2.487	2.402	2.322	2.283	2.246	2.174	2.106	2.042	1.981	1.952	1.923	1.868	1.816	1.696	1.589
4	3.630	3.546	3.465	3.312	3.170	3.037	2.914	2.855	2.798	2.690	2.589	2.494	2.404	2.362	2.320	2.241	2.166	1.997	1.849
5	4.452	4.330	4.212	3.993	3.791	3.605	3.433	3.352	3.274	3.127	2.991	2.864	2.745	2.689	2.635	2.532	2.436	2.220	2.035
6	5.242	5.076	4.917	4.623	4.355	4.111	3.889	3.784	3.685	3.498	3.326	3.167	3.020	2.951	2.885	2.759	2.643	2.385	2.168
7	6.002	5.786	5.582	5.206	4.868	4.564	4.288	4.160	4.039	3.812	3.605	3.416	3.242	3.161	3.083	2.937	2.802	2.508	2.263
8	6.733	6.463	6.210	5.747	5.335	4.968	4.639	4.487	4.344	4.078	3.837	3.619	3.421	3.329	3.241	3.076	2.925	2.598	2.331
9	7.435	7.108	6.802	6.247	5.759	5.328	4.946	4.772	4.607	4.303	4.031	3.786	3.566	3.463	3.366	3.184	3.019	2.665	2.379
10	8.111	7.722	7.360	6.710	6.145	5.650	5.216	5.019	4.833	4.494	4.192	3.923	3.682	3.571	3.465	3.269	3.092	2.715	2.414
11	8.760	8.306	7.887	7.139	6.495	5.938	5.453	5.234	5.029	4.656	4.327	4.035	3.776	3.656	3.544	3.335	3.147	2.752	2.438
12	9.385	8.863	8.384	7.536	6.814	6.194	5.660	5.421	5.197	4.793	4.439	4.127	3.851	3.725	3.606	3.387	3.190	2.779	2.456
13	9.986	9.394	8.853	7.904	7.103	6.424	5.842	5.583	5.342	4.910	4.533	4.203	3.912	3.780	3.656	3.427	3.223	2.799	2.468
14	10.563	9.899	9.295	8.244	7.367	6.628	6.002	5.724	5.468	5.008	4.611	4.265	3.962	3.824	3.695	3.459	3.249	2.814	2.477
15	11.118	10.380	9.712	8.559	7.606	6.811	6.142	5.847	5.575	5.092	4.675	4.315	4.001	3.859	3.726	3.483	3.268	2.825	2.484
16	11.652	10.838	10.106	8.851	7.824	6.974	6.265	5.954	5.669	5.162	4.730	4.357	4.033	3.887	3.751	3.503	3.283	2.834	2.489
17	12.166	11.274	10.477	9.122	8.022	7.120	6.373	6.047	5.749	5.222	4.775	4.391	4.059	3.910	3.771	3.518	3.295	2.840	2.492
18	12.659	11.690	10.828	9.372	8.201	7.250	6.467	6.128	5.818	5.273	4.812	4.419	4.080	3.928	3.786	3.529	3.304	2.844	2.494
19	13.134	12.085	11.158	9.604	8.365	7.366	6.550	6.198	5.877	5.316	4.844	4.442	4.097	3.942	3.799	3.539	3.311	2.848	2.496
20	13.590	12.462	11.470	9.818	8.514	7.469	6.623	6.259	5.929	5.353	4.870	4.460	4.110	3.954	3.808	3.546	3.316	2.850	2.497
21	14.029	12.821	11.764	10.017	8.649	7.562	6.687	6.312	5.973	5.384	4.891	4.476	4.121	3.963	3.816	3.551	3.320	2.852	2.498
22	14.451	13.163	12.042	10.201	8.772	7.645	6.743	6.359	6.011	5.410	4.909	4.488	4.130	3.970	3.822	3.556	3.323	2.853	2.498
23	14.857	13.489	12.303	10.371	8.883	7.718	6.792	6.399	6.044	5.432	4.925	4.499	4.137	3.976	3.827	3.559	3.325	2.854	2.499
24	15.247	13.799	12.550	10.529	8.985	7.784	6.835	6.434	6.073	5.451	4.937	4.507	4.143	3.981	3.831	3.562	3.327	2.855	2.499
25	15.622	14.094	12.783	10.675	9.077	7.843	6.873	6.464	6.097	5.467	4.948	4.514	4.147	3.985	3.834	3.564	3.329	2.856	2.499
26	15.983	14.375	13.003	10.810	9.161	7.896	6.906	6.491	6.118	5.480	4.956	4.520	4.151	3.988	3.837	3.566	3.330	2.856	2.500
27	16.330	14.643	13.211	10.935	9.237	7.943	6.935	6.514	6.136	5.492	4.964	4.524	4.154	3.990	3.839	3.567	3.331	2.856	2.500
28	16.663	14.898	13.406	11.051	9.307	7.984	6.961	6.534	6.152	5.502	4.970	4.528	4.157	3.992	3.840	3.568	3.331	2.857	2.500
29	16.984	15.141	13.591	11.158	9.370	8.022	6.983	6.551	6.166	5.510	4.975	4.531	4.159	3.994	3.841	3.569	3.332	2.857	2.500
30	17.292	15.373	13.765	11.258	9.427	8.055	7.003	6.566	6.177	5.517	4.979	4.534	4.160	3.995	3.842	3.569	3.332	2.857	2.500
35	18.665	16.374	14.498	11.655	9.644	8.176	7.070	6.617	6.215	5.539	4.992	4.541	4.164	3.998	3.845	3.571	3.333	2.857	2.500
40	19.793	17.159	15.046	11.925	9.779	8.244	7.105	6.642	6.234	5.548	4.997	4.544	4.166	3.999	3.846	3.571	3.333	2.857	2.500
45	20.720	17.774	15.456	12.108	9.863	8.283	7.123	6.654	6.242	5.552	4.999	4.545	4.166	3.999	3.846	3.571	3.333	2.857	2.500
50	21.482	18.256	15.762	12.234	9.915	8.304	7.133	6.661	6.246	5.554	4.999	4.545	4.167	4.000	3.846	3.571	3.333	2.857	2.500

INDEX

A

Absorption costing, 216; and variable costing compared, 218; income statement, 231
Accelerated depreciation, 287, 342
Accountant, contribution of, 5
Accounting, defined, 496; double-entry, 496; responsibility, 38; variations in methods and estimates, 385
Accounting cycle, 496
Accounting data, use of, 9
Accounting equation, 499; and transactions, 498
Accounting period, 506
Accounts, 500; chart of, 503; increases and decreases in, 501; use of, 501
Accounts receivable turnover, 391
Accrual adjustments, 507
Accrual principle, 520
Accrue, defined, 507
Acid-test ratio, 390
Adjusted trial balance, 511
Adjusting process, 506

Adjustments, accrual, 507; depreciation, 508; inventory, 510; prepayment, 508; valuation, 511
Administrative and general expense budget, 466
Administrative expenses, 532
Allocation, cost, 35, 257; *illus.*, 36
Analysis, break even, 88, 92; comprehensive, 384; cost-volume-profit, 88; of financial statements, 386; of noncurrent items, 420; some hazards of, 385
Asset, current, turnover, 390
Asset base, 375
Assets, 496, 498; combination of, 377; current, 523; depreciable, 379; fixed, 508, 525; intangible, 526; management of, 377; other, 527; plant, 508, 525; turnover and rate of return on, 376
Assets and equities, character of, 347
Asset valuation, 523
Attainable standards, 158
Audit, post, 293
Authority, 3
Average concept, 386
Avoidable costs, 255, 282

B

Balance of sales and production, 220

Balance sheet, 513; classified, *illus.*, 524; comparative, *illus.*, 417; end of fiscal year, 533; estimated, *illus.*, 21, 476; *illus.*, 18, 513; pro forma, 476

Balance sheet analysis, illustrated, 386

Balancing order and storage costs, 165

Bargained market price, 314

Base year, 387

Basic concepts, 516

Book value, net, 509; per share, 384

Break-even analysis, 88; an alternative form of, 92; defined, 88

Break-even chart, 89; cost detail on the, 90, *illus.*, 91; *illus.*, 89

Break-even point, 88, 228

Budget, 3, 6, 30, 43; capital expenditure, 467; capital investment, defined, 13; cash, 20; cash payments, 19, 470; cash receipts, 19, 468; control, defined, 13; defined, 10; direct labor, 462; direct materials, 460; factory overhead, 464; general and administrative expense, 466; illustration of, 17; long-range, 13; product, 12; production, 459; progressive, 15; project, 12; purchases, 461; responsibility, defined, 13; rolling, 15; self-imposed, 16; selling expense, 465; sensitivity to changes in, 21

Budget, flexible, 12, 123; and variances, 189; defined, 12; summarized, *illus.*, 190

Budgetary control, defined, 10

Budget coordination, 16

Budget estimation, 16

Budgeting, scope of, 11

Budgeting by computer, 14

Budgeting process, *illus.*, 11

Budget limitations, 452

Budget period, 15

Budget rate, 124

Budget relationships, 453

Budgets, advantages of, 10; preparation of, 16; use of, 479

Budget slack, 14

Budget variances and variable costing, 229

Budget work sheet, *illus.*, 478

Business transaction, 498

By-products, 137

C

Capacity, normal, 127, 195; practical plant, defined, 195

Capacity and control, plant, 194

Capacity variance, 36, 126, 193; defined, 33

Capital, 498; working, management of, 389; working and net working, defined, 389

Capital budget, 467; *illus.*, 469

Capital expenditure budget, 467

Capital investment, 275; defined, 13

Capital investment budget, 13; defined, 13

Capital stock, 516, 529

Cash and operations, 424

Cash budget, *illus.*, 20, 22

Cash flow, 423; from operations, 429; statement of, 429

Cash payments budget, 470; *illus.*, 19

Cash receipts and disbursements statement, *illus.*, 429

Cash receipts budget, 468; *illus.*, 19, 22

Change, anticipation of, 292

Chart of accounts, 503

Classification of decisions by function and time element, 5

Closing procedure, 514

Coefficient of determination, 72

Combination decisions, 247

Commercial enterprise, 2

Committed costs, defined, 31

Common stock, 516

Communication and information system, transfer prices, 318

Companies, differences between, 385

Company, decentralized, 302

Company evaluation, 394

Compound amount, 543

Comprehensive analysis, 384

Computer budgeting, 14

Conservatism, 522

Consistency, 519

Contra asset account, 509

Contribution margin, 87, 220; division, 307; weighted, 101

Control, 8; cost, 303; costs and, 33; profit, 303

Control and capacity, plant, 194

Control and planning decisions, 3

Control budget, defined, 13

Control features, responsibility accounting, 42

Controllable costs, defined, 37

Controllable profit, division, 307; division, as evaluation index, 308
Controllable variance, 191, 192
Control limits, 66
Control of factory overhead, 125
Control system, criteria needed for, 303
Coproducts, 136
Corporation, 515
Cost, 339, 517; classification by function, 118; decremental, *illus.*, 46; defined, 30; departmental, 34; depreciated replacement, defined, 344; differential, *illus.*, 46; direct, 37, defined, 35; direct labor, 119; direct materials, 119; factory overhead, 119; full, defined, 7; historical, 339, defined, 128; indirect, defined, 35; irrelevant, defined, 45; job order, 120, 128; labor, additions to, 171; natural classification, 118; nonmanufacturing, 200; opportunity, 139, 247; defined, 47; original, 339; period, 117; process, 131, 136; product, 32, 118; replacement, 339, 343, defined, 344; reproduction, 339; standard, 128, *illus.*, 197; sunk, defined, *illus.*, 46; transfer price based on, 315; unit, 131; variable, 259; *see also* Costs
Cost accounting beyond manufacturing area, 118
Cost allocation, 35, 41; *illus.*, 36
Cost alternatives, 47
Cost and revenue lines, curvature of, 90, *illus.*, 91
Cost budget, manufacturing, 460
Cost control, 8, 303
Cost data for decision making, 245
Cost detail on the break-even chart, 90; *illus.*, 91
Cost elements, 119, 135
Cost estimation, 61; significance of, 62
Cost flow, *illus.*, 133; process, 132
Cost incurred, 138
Costing, absorption, 216; direct, 120, 218; full, 217; product, 32; variable, 218
Costing factory overhead, 122
Costing procedure, 120
Cost of goods sold, 120, 531
Cost overun, 122
Cost report, *illus.*, 39, 40
Costs, 30, 116; avoidable, 255, 282; committed, defined, 31; controllable, defined, 37; decision making,

illus., 47; differential, 44, defined, 7; direct, .34; discretionary, 31; fixed, 31, 99, defined, 31; indirect, 34; managed, 31; noncontrollable, 37; programmed, defined, 31; semivariable, defined, 32; unavoidable, 255; uncontrollable, defined, 37; variable, 31, 95, defined, 32; *see also* Cost
Costs and, control, 33; decisions, 246; planning, 43
Cost segregation, 62
Cost standard, 34
Cost transitions, 117
Cost-volume-profit analysis, 88
Credit, 500
Criterion, evaluation, 323
Current asset, 523
Current assets, additional investment in, 283
Current asset turnover, 390
Current cost, matched against revenue, 340
Current items, analysis of other, 428
Current liabilities, 527
Current ratio, 390
Current value, 339; and price index, 355
Curvature of revenue and cost lines, 90; *illus.*, 91

D

Debit, 500
Decentralized company, 302
Decision, investment, 276; pricing, 255
Decision making, relevant cost data for, 245; transfer prices for, 318; variable costing in planning and, 228
Decision-making costs, 47; *illus.*, 48
Decisions, combination, 247; make or buy, 253; managerial, 4, 5; process or sell, 248
Decisions and costs, 246
Decisions classified by function and time element, 5
Decreases in accounts, 501
Decremental cost, *illus.*, 46
Deferred revenue, 528
Deficit, 529
Deflation, 340
Demand, derived, 456
Departmental cost, 34

Departmental production report, 131, 132
Depreciable assets, 379
Depreciated replacement cost, defined, 344
Depreciation, 508; accelerated, 287, 342; defined, 285; double-declining-balance, 287; production unit method of, 285; straight line, 285; sum-of-the-years digits, 287
Depreciation adjustment, 508
Depreciation and income tax, 285
Depreciation expense, 508
Derived demand, 456
Differences between companies, 385
Differential costs, 44; defined, 7; *illus.*, 46
Differential revenue, defined, 7
Direct cost, 34, 37; defined, 35
Direct costing, 218
Direct labor, 119, 120, 378
Direct labor budget, 462; *illus.*, 463
Direct materials, 119, 120, 377
Direct materials budget, 460
Direct profit, division, 306
Discount, 545
Discounted rate-of-return method, 279; *illus.*, 291
Discounted value, 545
Discounting, 545
Discount rate, 545
Discretionary costs, 31
Dividend policy, 357
Division contribution margin, 307
Division controllable profit, 307; as an evaluation index, 308
Division direct profit, 306
Division investment, determining, 309
Division net profit, 306
Double-declining-balance depreciation, 287
Double-entry accounting, 496
Duality, 496
Dual transfer prices, 316
Dumping, 259

E

Earning power, 387
Earnings, reinvested, 529; retained, 516, 529
Earnings and market value of stock, 383
Earnings per share, 384, 533

Efficiency variance, defined, 192; labor, 170
Elimination of product line, 254
Employee motivation by standards, 157
Equation, accounting, 498, 499
Equities, 496, 498
Equities and assets, character of, 347
Equity, owner's, 497, 528; trading on the, 381
Equity relationships, 393
Equivalent units, defined, 134
Estimated balance sheet, 476; *illus.*, 21
Estimated conditional standard deviation, 67; *illus.*, 69, 70
Estimated income statement, 472; *illus.*, 18
Estimation, cost, 61; significance of, 62
Evaluation and description of statement, 411
Evaluation criterion or standard, 323
Evaluation index, division controllable profit, 308
Evaluation of company, 394
Evaluation process, 292
Expenses, defined, 499; depreciation, 508; general and administrative, 532; operating, 532; other, 532; selling, 532
Extraordinary gains and losses, 532

F

Factor for overhead allocation, 123
Factory overhead, 119, 378; budget, 464; control of, 125
Factory overhead costing, 122
Favorable variance, 159
Fifo, 341, 519
Financial planning, 471
Financial statements, 512; and index conversions, 348
Finished goods, 120
First-in, first-out (fifo), 341, 519
Fiscal, period, 506; 518; year, 10, 518
Fixed assets, 508, 525
Fixed charges and net income, 393
Fixed cost effect on profit, 100
Fixed costs, 99; defined, 31; troublesome, 32

Flexible budget, 123; defined, 12
Flexible budget and variances, 189
Franchises, 526
Fringe benefits, 171
Full cost, defined, 7; price based on, 256
Full costing method, 217
Function, classification of decisions by, 5
Future, planning for, 3
Futures contract, 359

G

Gains and losses, extraordinary, 532
General and administrative expense budget, 466; *illus.*, 468
General expenses, 532
General journal, 503
Going concern, 516
Goodwill, 526
Governmental unit, 2
Gross margin, 531

H

Hedging operation, 359
High-low point, 64
Historical cost, 339; defined, 128
Hours of operation, 12

I

Illusory profit, 342
Incentives, 172
Income, net, 512, 533; residual, 311
Income statement, 512; absorption costing, 231; budget and actual variable costing, *illus.*, 230, 231; comparative, *illus.*, 173; comparative, absorption and variable costing, *illus.*, 219, 222; comparative, absorption costing, *illus.*, 223; comparative, *illus.*, 173; comparative, variable costing, *illus.*, 224; estimated 473, *illus.*, 18, 475; partial, dual transfer price, *illus.*, 317; partial, manufacturing, *illus.*, 221; product combination, *illus.*, 254; pro forma, 473; purchasing power, adjustments, *illus.*, 352; variable costing, 230

Income statement analysis, *illus.*, 387
Income statement classifications, 530
Income tax, 532
Income tax and depreciation, 285
Incorporated, 515
Increases in accounts, 501
Incremental returns, 290
Incurred cost, 138
Index, price, and current value, 355
Index adjustments, price level, 346
Index conversions and financial statements, 348
Index numbers, 159
Indirect cost, 34; defined, 35
Individual responsibility, 13
Inflation, 340
Information and communication system, transfer prices, 318
Intangible assets, 526
Interest, undivided, 523
Intermediate market, 319
Internal control, 164
Intracompany or transfer pricing, 312
Inventories and production, 458
Inventory, periodic, 510; perpetual, 510; profits and, 225
Inventory adjustment, 510
Inventory level, 164
Inventory profit, 342
Inventory turnovers, 392
Investment, 525; capital, 276, defined, 275; determining division, 309; net, 277; refining the, 282
Investment alternatives, rating of, 278
Investment decision, 276
Investment evaluation, 292
Investment illustration, 549
Investment in additional current assets, 283
Investment problem, graphic solution, *illus.*, 291
Irrelevant cost, defined, 45

J

Job order cost, 120; 128
Joint cost, defined, 136
Joint product costing, 136
Joint products, defined, 136
Journal, 502; general 503
Journal entry, 502
Journals, special, 504

L

Labor, direct, 378
Labor cost, additions to, 171
Labor efficiency variance, 170
Labor productivity, 172
Labor rate variance, defined, 169
Labor standards and control, 169
Last-in, first-out (lifo), 341, 519
Learning curve, 173; *illus.*, 174
Learning phase, 174
Leverage, 380; or trading on the equity, 381
Liabilities, 496, 498; long-term, 528; other, 528
Lifo, 341, 519
Linear programming, 140
Line of regression, 64; *illus.*, 63, 66, 70
Long-range budget, 13
Long-term liabilities, 528
Long-term plans, 104
Loose standards, 158
Loss, net, 512
Losses and gains, extraordinary, 532
Lowest acceptable rate of return, 278

M

Managed costs, 31
Management, method of, 3; objective of, 2; of assets, 377; of working capital, 389
Management accounting, defined, 1
Management by exception, 156, 480
Management policy and price level, 358
Management system, *illus.*, 11
Managerial, accounting, defined, 1; decisions, 4, 5
Manufacturing cost budget, 460
Manufacturing margin, 220
Margin, contribution, 87, 220; manufacturing, 220
Market, intermediate, 319
Market price, 312; determination of, *illus.*, 313; negotiated or bargained, 314
Market value of stock and earnings, 383
Markup pricing method, 256
Master budget plan, 14
Matching, 519
Materials, direct, 377

Materials acquisition, 163
Materials price variance, 160
Materials quantity variance, 161
Materials standards control, 159
Materials usage variance, 161
Methods of operation, 4
Monetary items, 347
Motivation by standards, 157
Multiple regression, 75

N

Negotiated market price, 314
Net book value, 509
Net income, 374, 512, 533; and fixed charges, 393
Net investment, 277
Net loss, 512
Net present value method, 281, 547
Net proceeds from the sale of other properties, 284
Net profit, division, 306
Net returns, 277
Net working capital, defined, 389; demand for, 422; schedule of changes in, 418; *illus.*, 419; sources and uses of, 417; sources of 414; uses of, 416
Net working capital flows, 413; significance of, 412
Net working capital from operations, 419
Noncontrollable costs, 37
Noncurrent items, analysis of, 420
Nonmanufacturing costs, 200
Nonmonetary items, 347
Normal capacity, 127, 195
Normal distribution, defined, 67
Normal volume, 257
Null hypothesis, 74

O

On-line, real-time system, defined, 156
Operating cycle, 524
Operating data, *illus.*, 379
Operating expenses, 532
Operating revenue, 531
Operation, method of, size of, products or services in, 4
Operations, cash and, 424; cash flow from, 429; net working capital from, 419

Operations report, *illus.*, 8
Opportunity cost, 139, 247; defined, 47; *illus.*, 47
Order and storage costs, balancing of, 165
Organization expense, 526
Original cost, 339
Other assets, 527
Other current items, analysis of, 428
Other liabilities, 528
Other revenue and expense, 532
Overhead, factory, 378; variable, 125
Overhead rate, 123
Overhead variance, 191; disposition of, 126
Overhead variances, summary of, 196
Owner's equity, 497, 498, 528
Ownership, forms of business, 514

P

Partnership, 515
Par value, paid-in capital in excess of, 529
Patents, 526
Payback method, 279
Percentage-of-completion, 518
Period cost, 117
Periodic inventory, 510
Periodicity, 518
Perpetual inventory, 510
Personal attitudes towards budgeting, 13
Planning, 6; financial, 471; profit, 87; variable costing in decision making and, 228
Planning and control decisions, 3
Planning and costs, 43
Plant assets, 508, 525
Plant capacity, practical, defined, 195
Plant capacity and control, 194
Post audit, 293
Posting, 503
Posting reference column, 503
Practical plant capacity, defined, 195
Preferred stock, 516
Premium on stock, 529
Preparation of budgets, 16

Prepayment adjustments, 508
Present value, net, 281
Present value concept applied, 547
Present value, of a future amount, 544; of a series of future amounts, 545
Price, based on full cost, 256; general and specific, 339; market, 312; market, negotiated or bargained, 314; outside influences on, 262; transfer, based on cost, 315
Price index and current value, 355
Price level, 339; and management policy, 358; index adjustments, 346
Price policy, 97
Prices, dual transfer, 316
Price variance, 159; materials, 160
Pricing, intracompany or transfer, 312; markup method, 256; variable cost, 259
Pricing decision, 255
Process cost accounting problems, 136
Process cost flow, 132
Process cost system, 131
Process or sell, 248
Procurement period, defined, 164
Product budget, 12
Product combinations, 248
Product cost, 32, 118
Product costing, 32
Production and inventories, 458
Production and sales, 226, 457; balance of, 220; out of balance, 222
Production budget, 459
Production order, *illus.*, 129
Production report, departmental, 131; *illus.*, 132
Production unit method of depreciation, 285
Product line, elimination of, 254
Product mix decision, 137
Profit, division controllable, 307; division direct, 306; division net, 306; illusory, 342; inventory, 342
Profit affected by price and volume 97
Profit and inventory, 225
Profit control, 303
Profit goal, 92
Profit index, 305

Profit objective, 2

Profit planning, 87

Profit-volume graph, 93; *illus.*, 94, 96, 99, 100, 103, 104

Pro forma, balance sheet, 476; income statement, 473

Programmed costs, defined, 31

Programming, linear, 140

Progressive budget, 15

Project budget, 12

Proprietorship, 514

Purchases budget, *illus.*, 19, 461, 462

Q

Quality of standards, 157

Quantity variance, 159; materials, 161

Quick assets, 391

R

r² test, 72

Rate of return, 374; asset turnover and, 376; by segment, 378; discounted method, 279; lowest acceptable, 278; per scarce factor, 250

Rate variance, labor, defined, 169

Realization concept, 517

Refining the investment, 282

Regression, line of, 63, 64; *illus.*, 63, 66; multiple, 75

Reinvested earnings, 529

Replacement cost, 339, 343; defined, 344; depreciated, defined, 344

Reproduction cost, 339

Residual income, 311

Responsibility accounting, 38; control features, 42; defined, 8; difficulties with, 41

Responsibility budget, defined, 13

Retained earnings, 516, 529; statement of changes in, 533

Return, lowest acceptable rate of, 278

Returns, net, 277

Revenue, deferred, 528; defined, 499, 520; differential, defined, 7; operating, 531; other, 532

Revenue and cost lines, curvature of, 90; *illus.*, 91

Revenue matched against current cost, 340

Rolling budget, 15

S

Sale of other properties, net proceeds from, 284

Sales and production, 226, 457; balance of, 220; out of balance, 222

Sales budget and sales forecasting, 455

Sales mix, changes in, 101

Sales revenue budget, *illus.*, 458

Sales volume, 94

Scarce factor, 104; rate of return per, 250

Schedule of cash payments, *illus.*, 471

Securities and Exchange Commission, replacement cost, 344

Segregation, cost, 62

Self-imposed budget, 16

Selling expense budget, 465; *illus.*, 467

Selling expenses, 532

Sell or process, 248

Semivariable costs, defined, 32

Service contract decision, *illus.*, 247

Share, book value per, 384; earnings per, 384

Shipping routes, 167

Short-term plans, 104

Size of operation, 4

Slack, budget, 14

Source document, 500

Special journals, 504

Spending variance, defined, 191

Spurious correlation, 75

Standard, evaluation, 323

Standard cost, 34, 128; *illus.*, 197

Standard cost accounting, advantages, 155

Standard deviation, 165; estimated conditional, 67, *illus.*, 69, 70

Standards, attainable, 158; bulletin, basic, or bogies, 159; loose, 158; motivation by, 157; quality of, 157; revising the, 159; strict, 157; use of, 154

Stated value, paid-in capital in excess of, 529

Statement, description and evaluation, 411; estimated income, 472; income, 512

Statement of cash flow, 429

Statement of cash receipts and disbursements, 411

Statement of changes in financial position, 412, 422

Statement of changes in retained earnings, 533

Statement of sources and uses of net working capital, 411, 421
Statements, financial, 512; and index conversions, 348
Stock, capital, 516
Stock, common, 516
Stock, earnings and market value of, 383
Stock, preferred, 516
Stockholders' equity, 528
Storage and order costs, balancing of, 165
Straight line depreciation, 285, 509
Strict standards, 157
Summary cash budget, *illus.*, 472
Summary of cash receipts, *illus.*, 470
Summary of overhead variances, 196
Sum-of-the-years digits depreciation, 287
Sunk cost, defined, 46; *illus.*, 46

T

Time constraints, 139
Time element, classification of decisions by, 5
Timing concept, 15
Trading on the equity or leverage, 381
Transaction, accounting, 498; business, 498
Transfer or intracompany pricing, 312
Transfer price, market, division operation, *illus.*, 313
Transfer prices, based on cost, 315; dual 316; for decision making, 318; intermediate market case, 319; no intermediate market case, 322
Transportation model, 169
Trial balance, 505; adjusted, 511
Turnover, accounts receivable, 391; current asset, 390; inventory, 392
t-value, 73

U

Unavoidable costs, 254
Uncontrollable costs, defined, 37

Undivided interest, 523
Unfavorable variance, 159
Unit cost, 131
Usage variance, materials, 161
Use of accounts, 501

V

Valuation, 522
Valuation adjustment, 511
Valuations, mixture of, 385
Value, current, and the price index, 355
Variable and absorption costing compared, 218
Variable cost, pricing, 259
Variable costing, 218; advantages of, 226; and budget variances, 229; disadvantages of, 227; income statement, 230; in planning and decision making, 228
Variable costs, 31, 95; defined, 32
Variable overhead, 125
Variance, capacity, 36, 126; capacity or volume, 193; controllable, 191; efficiency, defined, 192; favorable, 127, 159; labor efficiency, 170; labor rate, defined, 169; materials price, 160; materials quantity, 161; materials usage, 161; overabsorbed, 127; overapplied, 127; overhead, 191; price, 159; quantity, 159; spending, defined, 191; unabsorbed, 127; underapplied, 127; unfavorable, 127, 159; volume, 126
Variances, overhead, summary of, 196; summary of, 175
Variances and flexible budget, 189
Visual fit, 63
Volume, normal, 257
Volume variance, 126, 193

W

Working capital, defined, 389
Working capital, management of, 389
Working capital, net, defined, 389
Work in process, 120, 121, 133
Work sheet, budget, 477; *illus.*, 478

Weeks and Dates	Readings and Topics	Problems and Tests
Apr. 23-27	Chapter 12	
Apr. 27	Price Level Problem	12-5 and 12-7
Apr. 30-May 4	Chapter 14	
May 2	Flow of Net Working Capital and Cash	Test #3 (Chaps. 8,9,10, and 12)
May 7 and 8	Review	